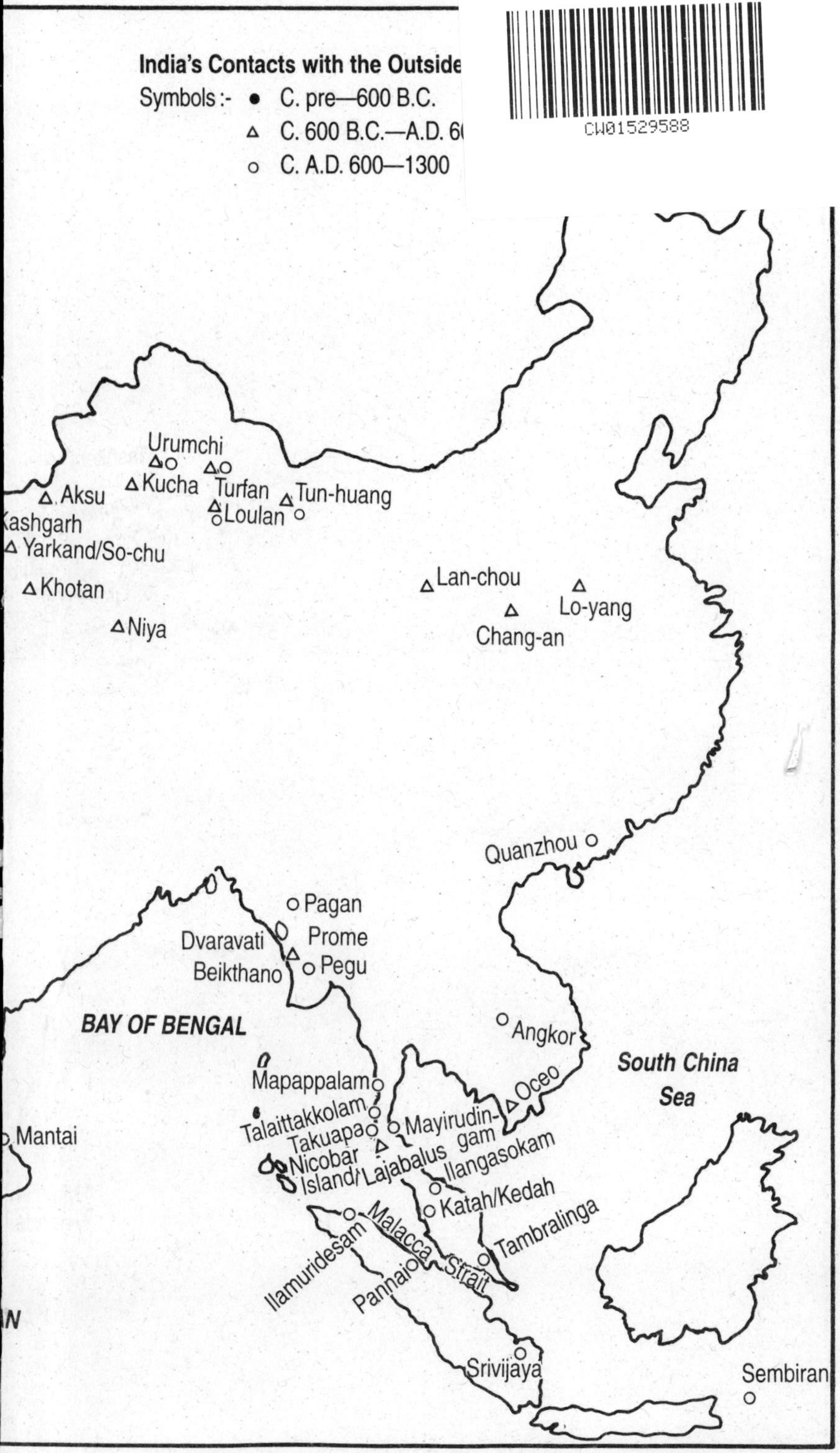
India's Contacts with the Outside
Symbols :- • C. pre—600 B.C.
△ C. 600 B.C.—A.D. 6
○ C. A.D. 600—1300
Urumchi
Aksu
Kucha
Turfan
Tun-huang
Loulan
ashgarh
Yarkand/So-chu
Khotan
Niya
Lan-chou
Lo-yang
Chang-an
Quanzhou
Pagan
Dvaravati
Prome
Beikthano
Pegu
BAY OF BENGAL
Angkor
South China Sea
Oceo
Mapappalam
Talaittakkolam
Takuapa
Mayirudin-gam
Nicobar Island
Lajabalus
Ilangasokam
Katah/Kedah
Mantai
Malacca Strait
Ilamuridesam
Tambralinga
Pannai
Srivijaya
Sembiran
AN

TRADE IN EARLY INDIA

OXFORD IN INDIA READINGS
Themes in Indian History

General Editors

- Basudev Chatterji
- Neeladri Bhattacharya
- C.A. Bayly
- Muzaffar Alam
- Romila Thapar

TRADE IN EARLY INDIA

Edited by
RANABIR CHAKRAVARTI

OXFORD
UNIVERSITY PRESS

OXFORD
UNIVERSITY PRESS

YMCA Library Building, Jai Singh Road, New Delhi 110001

Oxford University Press is a department of the University of Oxford. It furthers the University's objective of excellence in research, scholarship, and education by publishing worldwide in

Oxford New York
Athens Auckland Bangkok Bogota Buenos Aires Cape Town
Chennai Dar es Salaam Delhi Florence Hong Kong Istanbul
Karachi Kolkata Kuala Lumpur Madrid Melbourne Mexico City Mumbai
Nairobi Paris Sao Paolo Singapore Taipei Tokyo Toronto Warsaw

with associated companies in

Berlin Ibadan

Published in India
By Oxford University Press, New Delhi

ISBN 0 19 564795 5

Typeset by Comprint, New Delhi 110029
Printed in India by Roopak Printer, Noida
and published by Manzar Khan, Oxford University Press
YMCA Library Building, Jai Singh Road, New Delhi 110001

To

the everlasting memory of
Professor Ashin Das Gupta
who opened my eyes to the
history of Indian trade

CONTENTS

General Editors' Preface *ix*
Author's Preface *xi*
Acknowledgements *xiii*
Abbreviations *xv*

1 Introduction
RANABIR CHAKRAVARTI 1

2 Harappan Trade in Its 'World' Context
SHEREEN RATNAGAR 102

3 The Harappan Civilization Beyond the Indian Subcontinent
MAURIZIO TOSI 128

4 Dāna and Dakṣiṇā as Forms of Exchange
ROMILA THAPAR 152

5 The Problem of the *Seṭṭhi* in Buddhist Jātakas
IVO FISER 166

6 Coastal and Overseas Trade in Pre-Gupta Vaṅga and Kalinga
B.N. MUKHERJEE 199

7 New Light on Maritime Loans: P. Vindob G 40822
LIONEL CASSON 228

8 Indian Feudal Trade Charters
D.D. KOSAMBI 244

9 Monarchs, Merchants and a Maṭha in Northern Konkan (*c.* AD 900–1053)
RANABIR CHAKRAVARTI 257

10 Markets and Merchants in Early Medieval Rajasthan
BRAJADULAL CHATTOPADHYAYA 282

11 Geographical Considerations in the Localization of Ancient Sea-Ports of India
JEAN DELOCHE 312

12 The Medieval South Indian Guilds: Their Role in Trade and Urbanization
R. CHAMPAKALAKSHMI 326

13 Trading Community and Merchant Corporations
V.K. JAIN 344

14 Usury in Early Mediaeval Times
R.S. SHARMA 370

15 The Gurjara-Pratiharas
JOHN S. DEYELL 396

16 From Aden to India
S.D. GOITEIN 416

Annotated Bibliography 435

The Reading List 463

GENERAL EDITORS' PREFACE

This series focuses on important themes in Indian history, which have long been the subject of interest and debate, or which have acquired importance more recently.

Each volume in the series consists of, first, a detailed introduction; second, a careful selection of the essays and book-extracts vital to a proper understanding of the theme; and finally, an annotated bibliography.

Using this consistent format, each volume seeks as a whole to critically assess the state of the art on its theme, chart the historiographical shifts that have occurred since the theme emerged, rethink old problems, address questions which were considered closed, locate the theme within wider historiographical debates, and post new issues of inquiry by which further research may be made possible.

The economic history of the Indian subcontinent was initially dominated by the study of agrarian relations and questions relating to land ownership and revenue. The recognition of the significance of trade to many parts of the subcontinent, and in fact the priority of exchange and trade over other economic activities in some areas is of relatively recent origin. A number of features contributed to this: the realization from Greek sources that there was both overland and maritime trade with different parts of India, sources which have since been backed by archaeological discoveries which are changing the understanding of the nature of this trade; and references to merchants and exchange in texts and inscriptions from India, some limited to local exchange and others referring to overland ventures to distant places in Central Asia, or the use of maritime routes to South-East Asia and southern China.

Archaeology has been an important source of evidence of the trading activities of the Harappans, as also indicating exchange and the distribution of products within the subcontinent, such as the Northern Black Polished pottery and punch-marked coins.

The essays in this volume present the evidence for varieties of exchange and patterns of trade and, in some cases, raise questions regarding these patterns. The patterns changed both from the early period to the later and from region to region. Although it may be difficult to speak of a uniform situation throughout the subcontinent, there are, nevertheless, certain trends which become significant at particular times.

The introduction seeks to explain how the focus on exchange and commerce became an important part of the study of Indian history. It points to and analyses what might be called embedded economies, where exchange is part of another system of relationships; it considers the role of commerce in the functioning of major states and their revenues; it comments on documents considered significant in the history of commerce in early India; and it attempts to assess the economic importance of this activity during various periods.

AUTHOR'S PREFACE

As *Trade in Early India* takes it final shape in print, it is my pleasant duty to record here the generous help and encouragement I received from various persons and institutions in the preparation of this volume. I should begin by thanking Oxford University Press for kindly asking me to edit this volume in their well-established 'Themes in Indian History' series. I am thankful to the editors at OUP for their constant cooperation in bringing out this volume.

I would like to place on record my grateful thanks to the General Editors of this Series for commenting on my plan for the volume and for reading the draft of my Introduction and the Annotated Bibliography. I shall be failing in my duty if I do not acknowledge here the time and energy which Professor Romila Thapar ungrudgingly spent over my Introduction and the Bibliography in spite of her many commitments and pre-occupations. Needless to say, I was the beneficiary of the discussions with her which spanned several hours. At the initial stage of planning the contents and thrusts of this volume, I received valuable suggestions from Professor Chris Bayly, one of the General Editors and Professor, St. Catherine's College, Cambridge and also from Dr Gordon Johnson, President, Wolfson College, Cambridge. Interaction with them indeed enriched me.

Considerable help was rendered for preparing the Bibliography by Mr Krishnendu Ray, Lecturer, Department of History, Gobardanga College and Ms Sudarsana Chowdhury, Lecturer, Department of History, Dinabandhu Andrews College, both under the University of Calcutta. It would have been difficult for me to prepare the three maps in this volume without the valuable and sustained assistance of Ms Suchandra Ghosh, Lecturer, Department of Ancient Indian History and Culture, University of Calcutta. It must be pointed out here that these three maps were prepared neither on the basis of any cartographic principle nor to any scale; my main intention in incorporating the maps is to give the reader an idea of the location of the places frequently mentioned in the text. My most sincere thanks go to all three, although the final responsibility of any shortcoming in the preparation of the Bibliography and the maps entirely lies with me.

I would also like to record here my sincere thanks to the Museum of the Directorate of Archaeology, Government of West Bengal, for kindly granting me the permission to publish the photograph of an inscribed terracotta seal showing a ship (from Chandraketugarh, West Bengal), now in their collection.

Finally, I would like to pay here my homage to the late lamented Professor Ashin Das Gupta who kindled in me a sustained interest in and penchant for the study of trade history and especially the maritime trade in the Indian Ocean. His untimely demise has created a void in this field, which has become all the poorer for his absence. I was immensely fortunate to have engaged with him in many lively discussions on Indian trade and traders, even when his health was failing; it was a pure delight and joy to receive from him his insights and imaginative analyses of early Indian trade. His premature passing away does not give me an opportunity to present him with the published version of this volume. I would, therefore, like to humbly dedicate this book to the memory of Ashin Das Gupta as a mark of my indebtedness and gratitude to him.

RANBIR CHAKRAVARTI
Department of Ancient Indian History and Culture
University of Calcutta
20th January 2001

ACKNOWLEDGEMENTS

The editor and the publisher would like to thank the following for permission to include the present articles in this volume.

Shereen Ratnagar, 'Harappan Trade in Its "World" Context', from *Man and Environment*, vol. XIX (1–2): pp. 115–27, 1994. Published by the Indian Society for Prehistoric and Quaternary Studies, Deccan College, Pune.

Maurizio Tosi, 'The Harappan Civilization Beyond the Indian Subcontinent', from *The Harappan Civilization: A Recent Perspective* edited by G.L. Possehl, second edition, pp. 365–78, 1991. Published by Oxford & IBH, New Delhi.

Romila Thapar, 'Dāna and Dakṣiṇa as Forms of Exchange', from *Indica*, vol. XIII, pp. 37–48, 1976. Published by the Heras Institute of Indian History and Culture, St Xavier's College, Bombay.

Ivo Fiser, 'The Problem of the *Seṭṭhi* in Buddhist Jātakas', from *Archiv Orientalni*, vol. XXII, pp. 238–66, 1954.

B.N. Mukherjee, 'Coastal and Overseas Trade in Pre-Gupta Vaṅga and Kalinga', from *Vinayatoshini,* Benoytosh Centenary Volume, edited by Shyamalkanti Chakravarti, pp. 181–92, 1996, Calcutta. Published by the Benoytosh Centenary Committee.

Lionel Casson, 'New Light on Maritime Loans: P. Vindob G 40822', from *Zeitschrift fur Papyrologie und Epigraphik*, Band 84, pp. 195–206, 1990. Published by the University of Michigan, Ann Arbor, Michigan.

D.D. Kosambi, 'Indian Feudal Trade Charters', from *Journal of the Economic and Social History of the Orient*, II, pp. 281–93, 1958.

Ranabir Chakravarti, 'Monarchs, Merchants, and a Maṭha in Northern Konkan (*c.* AD 900–1053)', from *Indian Economic and Social History Review*, XXVII, 2, pp. 189–208, 1990. Published by Sage Publications India Pvt. Ltd.

Brajadulal Chattopadhyaya, 'Markets and Merchants in Early Medieval Rajasthan', from *The Making of Early Medieval India*, pp. 89–119, 1994. Published by Oxford University Press, Delhi.

Jean Deloche, 'Geographical Considerations in the Localization of

Ancient Sea-Ports in India', from *Indian Economic and Social History Review*, xx, 4, pp. 439–48, 1983.

R. Champakalakshmi, 'The Medieval South Indian Guilds: Their Role in Trade and Urbanization', from *Society and Ideology in India, Essays in Honour of Professor R.S. Sharma*, edited by D.N. Jha, pp. 81–93, 1996. Published by Munshiram Manoharlal, Delhi.

V.K. Jain, 'Trading Community and Merchant Corporations', from *Trade and Traders in Western India 1000–1300*, Delhi, 1989, pp. 209–232.

R.S. Sharma, 'Usury in Early Medieval Times', from *Perspectives in the Social and Economic History of Early India*, pp. 193–227, 1983. Published by Munshiram Manoharlal Publishers Pvt. Ltd, Delhi.

John S. Deyell, 'The Gurjara-Pratiharas', from *Living Without Silver: A Monetary History of Early Medieval North India*, 1990. Published by Oxford University Press, Delhi.

S.D. Goitein, 'From Aden to India: Specimens of the Correspondence of Indian Traders of the Twelfth Century', from *Journal of the Economic and Social History of the Orient*, XXIII, pp. 43–66, 1980. Published by E.J. Brill, Leiden, The Netherlands.

ABBREVIATIONS

AA: *American Journal of Archaeology*, Norwood, Mass.

ABORI: *Annals of the Bhandarkar Oriental Research Institute*, Pune.

ARE: *Annual Report of Indian Epigraphy,* Delhi.

BASOR: *Bulletin of the American Society of Oriental Research,* Chicago.

BEFEO: *Bulletin de l'Ecole Francaine d'Extreme Orient*, Hanoi and Paris.

BSOAS: *Bulletin of the School of Oriental and African Studies*, London.

EI: *Epigraphia Indica*, Ootacamond.

EW: *East and West*, Rome.

FIC: *Frontiers of the Indus Civilization*, ed. by S.P. Gupta and B.B. Lal, Delhi, 1984.

HC: *Harappan Civilization, a Contemporary Perspective*, Delhi, 1992 (second edition).

IESHR: *The Indian Economic and Social History Review*, Delhi.

IHQ: *Indian Historical Quarterly*, Calcutta.

IHR: *Indian Historical Review*, Delhi.

IMB: *Indian Museum Bulletin*, Calcutta.

JAIH: *Journal of Ancient Indian History*, Calcutta.

JAOS: *Journal of the American Society of Oriental Studies*, Chicago.

JAS: *Journal of the Asiatic Society*, Calcutta.

JASB: *Journal of the Asiatic Society of Bengal*, Calcutta.

JBBRAS: *Journal of the Bombay Branch of the Royal Asiatic Society*, Bombay.

JBORS: *Journal of the Bihar and Orissa Research Society*, Patna.

JBRS: *Journal of the Bihar Research Society*, Patna.

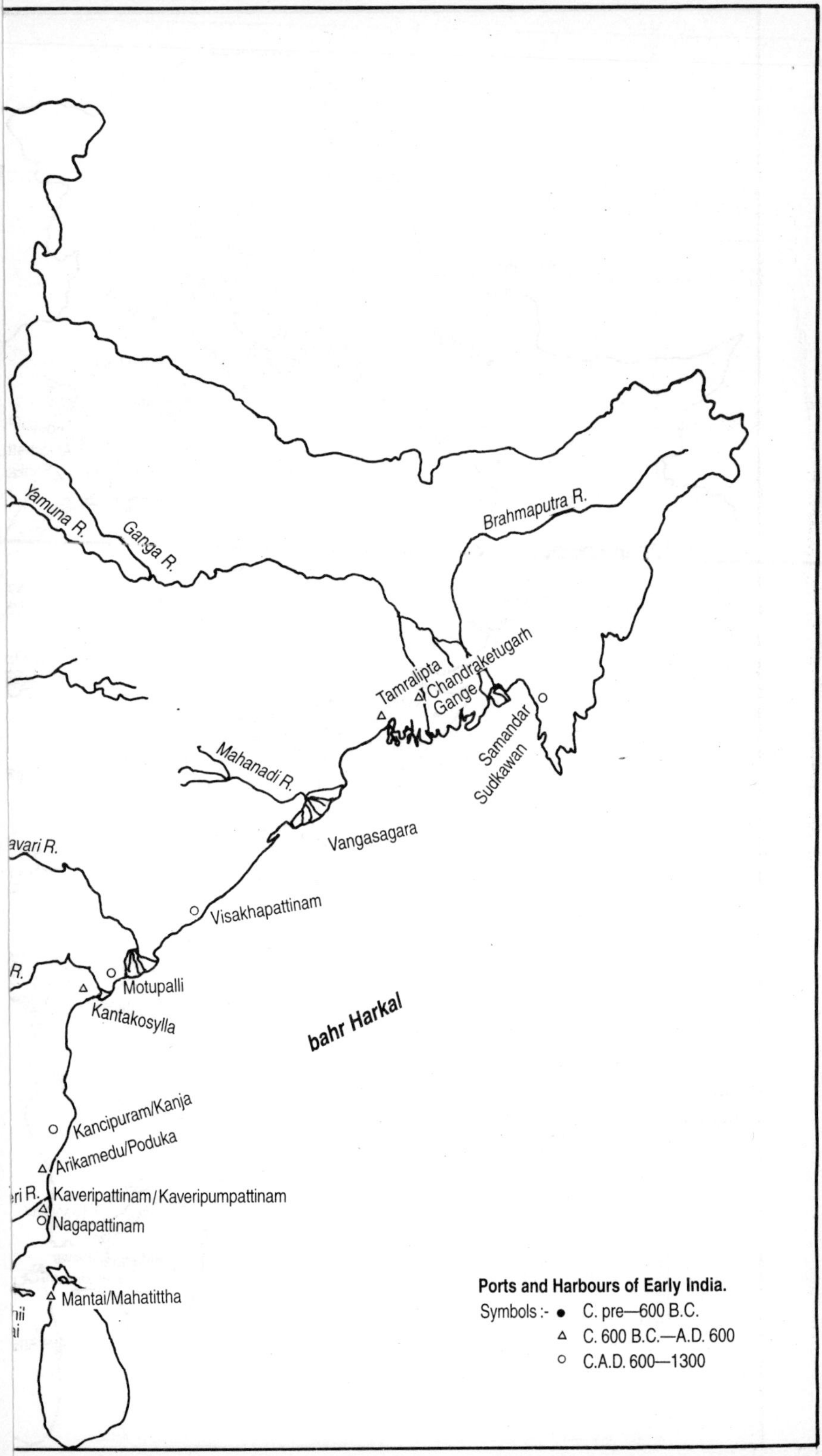

Yamuna R.
Ganga R.
Brahmaputra R.
Tamralipta
Chandraketugarh
Gange
Samandar
Sudkawan
Mahanadi R.
Vangasagara
avari R.
Visakhapattinam
R.
Motupalli
Kantakosylla
bahr Harkal
Kancipuram/Kanja
Arikamedu/Poduka
eri R.
Kaveripattinam/Kaveripumpattinam
Nagapattinam
Mantai/Mahatittha
nii
ai
Ports and Harbours of Early India.
Symbols :- ● C. pre—600 B.C.
△ C. 600 B.C.—A.D. 600
○ C.A.D. 600—1300

Chapter One

Introduction

RANABIR CHAKRAVARTI

I

The present volume of essays and extracts titled *Trade in Early India* underlines the importance of trade as one of the themes in understanding India's past up to AD 1300. Discussions on, and related to, trade, crafts and urban centres essentially pertain to the inquiries into the non-agrarian sector of the economy and society in a given area. The historiography of the subcontinent presents a general and overall image that different facets of traditional Indian culture—society, economy, polity, belief systems, creative and performing arts—were steeped in a rural ethos, largely on account of the millennial continuity of agriculture as the very backbone of the Indian economy from the past down to recent times. In the studies of the material milieu of the subcontinent one cannot but note the relegation of the inquiries into the non-agrarian sector of the economy almost as an appendage to the voluminous works on Indian agriculture and its related aspects.[1]

[1] See for example Tapan Raychaudhuri and Irfan Habib (eds.), *The Cambridge Economic History of India, Vol. I (1200–1750)*, Cambridge, 1982, (Indian rpt., Delhi, 1984). This has a distinct thrust on the discussions on the agrarian material milieu, though the non-agrarian economy has been represented therein. It is significant to note that Irfan Habib opines that India prior to the Mughal times was a 'pure' peasant economy, a self contained community. It was pushed into trade and commodity production virtually as a consequence of the Mughal revenue system. See his 'Potentialities of Capitalistic Development in the Economy of Mughal India', *Journal of Economic History*, XXIX, 1969, pp. 32–78. Simon Digby, 'Economic Conditions before 1200', in Tapan Raychaudhuri and Irfan Habib (eds.), *op. cit.*, pp. 45–47 (Indian rpt.) reduces the accounts of early Indian trade virtually to *marginalia*.

On the other hand, the very basis of Europe's vigorous contacts with India from the late fifteenth century onwards was its prime interest to reach India and the 'Indies' for trade. Europe perceived India and the East as an area yielding exotic, exciting and mysterious products which were seen as luxuries in the European markets. India was seen as a land of riches, and trade with such a land offered prospects, both real and imaginary, of fabulous gains. The lure of trade in Africa and Asia, and especially India, pushed the Portuguese into the southern Atlantic and the Indian Ocean, paving the way for the creation of the *Estado da India Portuguesa.* This was followed by the arrival in the same zone—with varying degrees of success—of the Dutch, the French, and the English East India Companies, culminating in the establishment of the overall supremacy of the English East India Company, and the final carving out of the British Empire. With the increasing political and commercial control of the English East India Company (and later the British Empire) over the subcontinent there was a consequent urge to grasp what the British in particular and Westerners in general assumed as the salient features of an alien area and its diverse peoples. With a view to ensuring the domination over a subject people in a colonial empire, the image of a vastly different Orient—often typified by India—was constructed. The image was that of an eternal, immutable, static and stagnant India (and by extension the Orient), stuck to its rural agrarian milieu, in stark contrast to the vibrant, innovative, adventurous, progressive and, therefore, dominant West (especially the British Empire). The notion that Indian society remained substantially unchanged was asserted by James Mill as early as 1817 and this was soon accepted as the standardized perception of pre-modern India.[2] The imagination of a timeless and invariant East was further strengthened by Karl Marx's formulation of the Asiatic Mode of Production. The formulation was made to sharpen the difference between the dynamic West, acquainted with the passages from antiquity through feudalism to capitalism of modern times, and the immutable Orient. At the root of this changelessness, in the opinion of Marx, was the age-old village community in India. The traditional Indian village is generally viewed as self-sufficient and enclosed; therefore, there would be little urge to produce the exchangeable surplus which could be taken to the market. The point is that the absence of commercial towns discourages a historical

[2] James Mill, *History of British India*, London, 1817.

dialectic and precludes the rise of industrialization and capitalism. Seen from this point of view, trade and exchange would be treated only as marginal factors in the social formation in a pre-capitalist society like India. This, in turn, would leave little scope for any interaction with the outside world for rural Indians. Consequently, any innovative spirit, any possibility of social transformation through acculturation and any inclination for substantial change in the Indian scenario of the pre-colonial age has to be ruled out. The self-sufficient and enclosed village communities became nearly synonymous with a repetitive, stagnant and vegetative life.[3] The discovery of masterly creations in the Sanskrit language by the West (especially the outstanding contributions of Friedrich Max Muller) convinced the colonial masters that traditional Indian culture was not only steeped in ruralism, but also was virtually synonymous with spiritual searches and the quest for other-worldliness.[4] Europe and especially the British Empire were projected as the harbingers of the spirit of scientific inquiry, technological advancements, trade and commerce, as well as a civilizing and modernizing force to a traditional land tied to the plough. Capitalism and the colonial empire were seen as catalysts that integrated India with the world economy.

II

The impact of colonial rule paved the way for, among other things, the study of the subcontinent's past, following the principles of the Occidental academic discipline called 'history', 'gechischte'.[5] As the constructed image of India in antiquity was rooted in its spirituality, studies of its political and socio-economic institutions were treated as trivialities. The main thrust of the historian was to present a dynastic

[3] Brendan O'Leary, *The Asiatic Mode of Production: Oriental Despotism, Historical Materialism and Indian History*, Oxford, 1989.

[4] That such a notion is deeply entrenched in the more or less recent scholarly perceptions of Indian culture can be demonstrated by William Theodore de Bary (ed.), *Sources of Indian Tradition*, New York, 1958. A.L. Basham (ed.), *A Cultural History of India*, Oxford, 1975 provides a more balanced approach and deals with material culture, spiritual traditions, and creative urges in India in a historical outline.

[5] Though the Sanskrit term *itihāsa* (*iti ha āsa*; i.e. so verily it was in the past) is commonly held to be synonymous with 'history', the two are not identical.

narrative of pre-modern India, faithfully following the West's predilection for the perusal of political events. It was also emphatically claimed that as ancient Indians had little sense of linear progression of time, they also had little sense of chronicling political events which was the primary concern of Western scholars. But, sometimes, works devoted to dynastic history contained at least some glimpses of socio-economic life, almost in the form of marginal notes. One may find such a trend in the four-volume monumental survey of Indian history up to the fall of the Vijayanagara empire by Christian Lassen.[6] The interest of scholars in early Indian religious ideas and practices provided a great fillip to what is designated as Indology. The principal focus of Indological scholarship was on the sacerdotal Vedic literature which offered immense information on beliefs, rituals and philosophical speculations. However, only marginal efforts were made to explore whether the Vedic texts would throw light on economic life in general and exchange-oriented activities in particular. With only little interest in economic and social history, sustained academic pursuits to delve into a perusal of ancient trade on the basis of Vedic literature can seldom be noted. A significant turn can be discerned with the growing recognition of Pali canonical texts as sources of early Indian history. These texts were, of course, principally taken up for understanding Buddhism by celebrated scholars whose primary expertise lay not in socio-economic history, but in languages. But, nevertheless, the Pali texts and especially the *Jātaka* stories were found to have been familiar with a milieu which was in sharp contrast to the Vedic way of life championing the cult of animal sacrifices (*yajñas*). The Pali literature throws much more light on the material conditions prevailing in the middle Ganga valley around the sixth and fifth centuries BC. So the utilization of the Pali texts, though primarily for the reconstruction of the history of early Buddhism, led to an improved understanding of the socio-economic situation in north India. The two foremost examples of such pioneering studies are seen in the contributions of Richard Fick at the very end of the nineteenth century and Mrs T.W. Rhys Davids in the early decades of the twentieth century. While the Vedic texts clearly highlight rural life with agriculture and cattle-rearing as the foremost occupations, the Pali texts, in contrast, show a distinct preference for urban settings. Gleanings from Pali texts, therefore, offered

[6] Christian Lassen, *Indische Alterthumskunde*, in four volumes, 1847–61.

significant impressions of the non-agrarian sectors of the economy, including data on transactions of commodities, types of merchants, and use of metallic currency.[7] *Seṭṭhis* (rich merchants) and *sātthavāhas* (caravan traders) acquired considerable prominence in these works, which may be considered as trend-setters in the economic historiography of ancient India for several decades.

An event of enormous importance in this context was the discovery and subsequent editing and translation of the famous *Arthaśāstra* by Shama Sastri in the first two decades of the twentieth century.[8] There were few texts in economic historiography which did not touch upon this new source material. The *Arthaśāstra* devotes considerable attention to trade and traders. But more than showering economic and political data, the text is celebrated for demonstrating the capability of the early Indian mind to formulate concepts of material life and political economy. The *Arthaśāstra* is also considered an exceptional treatise as it strongly recommended the state's participation in and control over economic activities, including trade. The ancient theoretician is also widely known for recognizing the revenue-yielding potential of commerce. The *Arthaśāstra* has undoubtedly loomed large in the economic historiography of ancient India since the second decade of the twentieth century. Recent scholarship on early Indian polity and economy, however, views the text more as an ideal than as reflecting actualities.

Though the importance of commerce in the history of early India could no longer be brushed aside, writing the dynastic narratives was certainly the primary concern of historians. V.A. Smith's pronouncement that the Macedonian invasion was the sheet anchor of Indian history clearly implied that Indian political history emerged as the outcome of the impact of the West.[9] The Macedonian invasion was

[7] Richard Fick, *Die Sociale Gliederung im Nordostlichen im Indien zu Buddhas Zeit*, Kiel, 1897; tr. into English by S.K. Maitra, *The Social Organization in North-east India in Buddha's Time*, Calcutta, 1920 (rpt. Varanasi, 1972); Mrs T.W. Rhys Davids, 'Notes on Early Economic Conditions in North India', *JRAS*, 1901; Mrs T.W. Rhys Davids, 'Economic Conditions in Early Buddhist Literature', in E.J. Rapson (ed.), *Cambridge History of India*, I, (Indian rpt.), Delhi, 1977, pp. 176–95.

[8] The discovery of the text was made in 1905, the edited text was published in 1909, and the first English translation appeared in 1915.

[9] V.A. Smith, *Early History of India*, Oxford, 1903. The work was widely read as a text book by students of Indian history and also by the aspiring examinees of the ICS examination.

perceived as a major external stimulus to open up the insularity of India. It was expected that brisk contacts, commercial and cultural, between the subcontinent and the West would follow the breaking up of the isolation of India. The message was to establish the benign long-term effects of Macedonian and other conquests by the West on Indian history and culture. That external conquest and commerce were closely tied to each other and were beneficial to India was clear. Such logic of colonial historiography undoubtedly sought to validate and justify colonial rule, which was based largely on the twin planks of commerce and conquest.

Notices of India in the Classical texts began to attract the attention of historians as early as the first half of the nineteenth century. These texts testified to the existence of trade relations between India and the Graeco-Roman world. Western scholarship eulogized the Classical world for not merely initiating commercial linkages with the East, but also for bringing the fruits of a Classical culture to a backward area.[10] The theme was taken up systematically, with far more competent handling of the ancient textual materials by Western scholars in the first half of the twentieth century. The paucity of indigenous sources, presumed by them, led to a greater reliance on the Classical texts. This, of course, resulted in a more thorough understanding of India's external trade. The great demand for Indian merchandise (often luxury and exotic items) in the marketplaces of the Hellenistic world, figuring prominently in the Classical accounts of Strabo, Diodorus, Arrian, the *Periplus of the Erythraean Sea*, Pliny and Ptolemy could not be dismissed. India's position in ancient international trade had to be recognized. The famous statement of Pliny that the love of gain brought the Roman Empire nearer India, his lamentation for the drainage of huge wealth to India to meet the affluent Romans' demand for luxuries, the descriptive geography of the voyages and the Indian coasts in the *Periplus of the Erythraean Sea* and the mention of a Temple of Augustus at Muziris (Cranganore, Kerala) in the *Tabula Peutangariana* spoke for themselves. The result was a spurt of publications on Indo-Roman trade (late first century BC to the middle

[10] The works of M. Elphinstone, *The History of India*, originally published in 1839 (rpt., Allahabad, 1966) and J. Forbes, *Oriental Memoirs*, in two volumes, London, 1834 belong to this genre.

of the third century AD) by Western scholars.[11] There was a change in the Western perception of early Indian material culture, but it was still very much rooted to the concepts of enclosed rural life and the insularity of ancient Indians. To illustrate this attitude, a quotation from a leading authority on Indo-Roman commerce is cited.

The moving force from first to last came from the West; the little-changing people of the East allowed the West to find them out. We have then as now, a disjointed aggregate of countries but *without the uniting force of British rule* which she now has and *while open to commerce, content generally* to remain with her borders and *to engage in agriculture* (italics mine).[12]

Ancient India is thus recognized in colonial historiography as an important trading zone, but it became so only because of an external stimulant, namely the commercial initiatives of the Westerners. This, in other words, implied a justification of the entry into, and later control of, India's trade by colonial forces from the West. The story of the subject, so far unfolded, tells us that by the early part of the twentieth century research on ancient trade had become a well-established ingredient of early Indian historiography. Western Indologists and historians are to be given due credit for introducing trade as a specialized subject within Indian historical studies. But the pronounced bias of colonial historiography that claimed that Indians rarely took an initiative in commerce did not go unchallenged for

[11] An elaborate survey of the literature on Roman trade with India is separately given in the Annotated Bibliography. Mention is made here only of the pioneering works. H.G. Rawlinson, *Intercourse Between India and the Western World*, Cambridge, 1916; M.P. Charlesworth, *Routes and Commerce of the Roman Empire*, 1924; E.H. Warmington, *The Commerce Between the Roman Empire and India,* London, 1928 (rpt., Delhi, 1974). The discovery of the archaeological site of Arikamedu (near Pondicherry) furnished visible and material proof of India's overseas trade with the West, so far largely known from literary accounts. See R.E.M. Wheeler and Krishna Deva, 'Arikamedu: An Indo-Roman Trading Station on the East Coast of India', *Ancient India,* 2, 1946, pp. 17–124. That the Greek presence in the north-western borderland of India was conducive to India's overland trade with different parts of Central Asia, West Asia, and Eurasia becomes evident in W.W. Tarn, *The Greeks in Bactria and India,* Cambridge, 1951.

[12] E.H. Warmington, *op. cit.*, pp. 1–2.

long. The search for an alternative approach was prompted by the strong Swadeshi movement which followed the partition of Bengal (1905) and the nationalist movements in the 1920s..There was a genuine urge to study the economic conditions (including the history of trade) of pre-modern India to examine whether pre-colonial India had been better off than it was under British rule. Nationalist historians, enthused by the discovery of the *Arthaśāstra*, painstakingly gleaned data from diverse literary texts to present a counterpoint to the colonial perceptions of early Indian commerce. Motichandra's study of ancient Indian texts was directed at proving that the movements of men and merchandise within the subcontinent and sometimes beyond it took place without non-Indian initiatives.[13] The much cherished notion that ancient Indians were not seafarers because of religious strictures was effectively refuted by R.K. Mookerji who culled textual evidence to prove that early Indian shipping and maritime trade existed.[14] The intellectual scene was ready for the search to prove the presence of ancient Indians abroad. The attention was focused on mainland and maritime South-East Asia, broadly designated as Suvarṇabhūmi and Suvarṇadvīpa in early Indian literature (cf. the corresponding terms Chryse Chora and Chryse Chersonesis in the Classical accounts). The spread of Buddhism and sectarian Brahmanical cults and Sanskrit, as well as of early Indian art and iconographic traditions in South-East Asia, were related to India's intimate commercial contacts with these regions over several centuries, beginning from the second century BC. Trade and traders were seen as purveyors of the very best facets of Indian culture in South-East Asia, which was perceived to have been an area with a relatively 'backward' material and spiritual culture. A large number of Indian nationalist scholars proudly demonstrated the role of Indian merchants and long-distance trade as civilizational forces. The vision of ancient Hindu colonies in South-East Asia, prior to the Islamization of the region, was fondly nurtured and immensely popularized. The ancient Indians were given much greater credit than the European masters, as the former had established 'colonies' much earlier than the latter. The process of Indian colonization was seen as morally more

[13] Motichandra, *Sarthavaha* (in Hindi), Patna, 1953, translated into English as *Trade and Trade Routes in Ancient India*, Delhi, 1977.

[14] R.K. Mookerji, *Indian Shipping, A History of Seaborne Trade and Maritime Activity of the Indians from the Earliest Times*, London, 1912, (second ed., Bombay, 1957).

correct, as it was achieved by peaceful and cultural conquests (leading to a number of settlements of Indian merchants) and not by the ferocity and striking power of the Europeans. The role of Indian merchants and religious missionaries in ancient South-East Asia has been glorified and validated by the concept of a Greater India, with India holding the centre stage. How, and to what extent, such a concept caught the imagination of many nationalist historians will be evident from the foundation of the Greater India Society, which had a prestigious journal.[15] The concept of a Greater India underlined the spread of Indian people and the dissemination of Indian culture from the Indian mainland to a number of neighbouring countries, mostly located in South-East Asia. The construction of the image of India at the centre of Greater India, sending merchants and preachers to distant lands, seems to have been influenced by the modern experience of the spread and domination of British culture. It was pointed out that the Classical perception viewed many areas in South-East Asia as being within India Extra Gangem (an expression coined by Ptolemy in his *Geographike Huphegesis*, AD 150); similarly, Arab and Persian texts (ninth to thirteenth centuries AD) often placed areas like Sanf (Champa) and Quimer (Khmer) within Hindustan. The main thrust of the argument was that early Indians were active merchants and seafarers and were involved in spreading Indian culture

[15] Among the Indian experts in this field R.C. Majumdar's *Ancient Indian Colonies in the Far East*, vol. I (*Champā*), Lahore, 1927, vol. II (*Suvarṇadvīpa*), Calcutta, 1938; *Hindu Colonies in the Far East*, Calcutta, 1944, loom large. In the south, K. A. Nilakanta Sastri led the way; see for example his *South India and South East Asia*, Madras, 1980; also see B. Ch. Chhabra, 'Expansion of the Indo-Aryan Culture during the Pallava Rule as Evidenced by Inscriptions', *JRASBL*, 1935, pp. 1–64. The most famous non-Indian exponent of this school was G. Coedes through his voluminous publications, notably *The Indianized States of South East Asia*, 1968. This view was subsequently severely criticized and virtually discarded in the recent historiography of early South-East Asia which relegates Indian influences to marginality. See in this context I.W. Mabbett, 'The Indianization of South-East Asia', *JSEAS*, VII, 1977, pp. 1–14, 143–61; P. Pelliot, 'Satyānṛta in Suvarṇadvīpa', in J.A. Sablov and C.C. Lamberg-Karlovsky (eds.), *Ancient Civilization and Trade*, Albuquerque, 1975, pp. 227–83; relevant essays in Hermann Kulke, *Kings and Cults*, Delhi, 1994. There are a number of scholars who would accept Indian influences on, but not the Indianization of, early South-East Asian culture.

abroad. The proponents of the model of Greater India were largely influenced by the pattern of European expansion in Asia and Africa during the eighteenth and nineteenth centuries.

The preceding pages attempt to situate the beginning of scholarly interests in early Indian trade around the second half of the nineteenth and the early part of the twentieth centuries. Though the initial steps were taken by European scholars, they were not always specialist historians. Indian scholarship soon followed suit. The nationalist historians effectively challenged many colonial standpoints on the economic and political history of pre-modern India, but their counterpoints were also heavily influenced by Western thought.

An important question thus emerged: from when did the exchange of goods become an important ingredient of Indian socio-economic life. Before the discovery of the Harappan civilization in 1922, scholars generally examined the Vedic and the Buddhist literature for the necessary data for trade in a remote period. The archaeological evidence of the widespread trade of the Harappan civilization (2600–1700 BC), both within India and beyond, pushed back the antiquity of early Indian trade to the bronze age. The recent researches on the famous pre-Harappan site at Mehrgarh (in the Bolan valley, Pakistan) strongly indicate the availability of non-local objects at Mehrgarh. It is likely that these objects were procured by the people of Mehrgarh through exchange. This would suggest the beginning of exchange-related functions in a pre-Harappan context (around the fifth millennium BC). The point will be discussed at length in a later section.[16] It is generally expected that trade would become a regular feature in a given economy when it had already experienced sedentary agriculture and some developments in crafts production. In other words, such a society is generally found to have reached the capability and capacity to generate exchangeable products which would be disposed of for profit. Anthropological and ethno-historical surveys of traditional communities, however, strongly demonstrate the possibility of the exchange of items among hunting-gathering and nomadic (non-sedentary) groups, conducted in a manner different from 'trade' which is based on supply, demand and price. This is generally termed as exchange and found in simpler societies rather

[16] For a general account of Mehrgarh, see J.F. Jarrige, fn. 68, Bridget Allchin and F.R. Allchin, *The Rise of Civilisation in India and Pakistan*, Cambridge, 1982.

than in more complex and developed agrarian communities with sharper social stratification. As an economic activity such exchanges are considered a precursor to trade and commerce, which belong to the non-agrarian sector of the economy. This is, however, not to suggest that one can postulate a linear development from exchange to trade in a uniform manner in the early history of India. A more elaborate discussion on this issue will be taken up in a subsequent section.

Historians up to the middle of the twentieth century generally aimed at presenting the narrative of items of trade (exports and imports), ports and marts, merchants and their professional organizations, trade routes and systems of credit in early India. The pioneering efforts of historians and linguists unravelled many unknown facts of early Indian trade and commerce. The conventional historiography of early Indian trade usually did not pay adequate attention to changes in the pattern of commercial activities or to the booms and slumps in trade. The description of trade routes often gave the impression that such routes existed forever, without any changes in their history. Descriptions of external commerce of early India are found to have been more attractive to the historian than accounts of trade within the subcontinent. But for the references to various types of sources datable to different periods, the conventional narrative of early Indian trade rarely gives an impression that there was a shift in commodities, location of ports and marts, conditions of travels and routes. Such a descriptive approach to early Indian trade has been considerably conditioned by the nature of early sources. Scholars depended rather heavily on literary texts (indigenous and foreign), both normative and creative literature, which are often difficult to date precisely. Besides, very little, if any at all, quantifiable information was offered by these texts; these at the most gave some impressions about economic activities, including trade. Moreover, the stereotyped nature of the literary impressions often reinforces the perception of the immutable and unvarying pattern of trading activities in early India. There, however, has been a growing concern about the limitations of literary materials for the study of early Indian material life since the middle of the twentieth century. Historians of early Indian economy and society have therefore taken recourse to studying diverse types of archaeological data—information from explored and excavated sites, inscriptions, coins and art objects—to overcome, to some extent, the limitations of literary evidence. An earlier notion that field archaeological evidence only assumed significance for the study of a period which was bereft of scripts and written records no longer holds true. As archaeology often yields visible and material remains of a way of life in bygone ages, its significance as a source is no less in the 'historic' times than in the pre-literate periods. A major advantage of archaeological evidence is its greater reliability and specificity in terms of its provenance and dating when compared to literary materials. This is, however, not to suggest the relegation of the importance of literary data. A perusal of the history of trade in early India is nowadays oriented to a judicious combination of archaeological and literary evidence. Economic historians of early India are now more aware of the importance of placing their data in the context of geographical and chronological positions of such evidence. The result of such efforts is the emergence of an image of diversities, dynamics and liveliness of socio-economic, political and cultural activities in early India; certainly a major shift from the previous preference for a pan-Indian and invariant perspective. Along with the use of diverse source materials, the historian of early Indian trade has been showing during the recent decades a keenness to use methods and perspectives from related disciplines in other human and earth sciences, e.g. anthropology, sociology, economics, geography, geology, oceanography, etc.[17] The above overview of the trends in the study of early Indian trade may now be followed by a discussion on new methodologies and perspectives on early trade in general, i.e. trade in pre-industrial society and its relevance to the study of early Indian trade.

III

The changing contours of the historiography of early trade and exchanges in India have been touched upon in the preceding section. Inquiries into different types of exchanges in the past, of which trade is a relatively advanced and complex form, have been a subject of keen interest among historians of the pre-industrial economy. The common tendency has been to examine commercial activities in terms of: (a) the wants/ requirements/ goals of human beings, (b) the system

[17] R.S. Sharma and D.N. Jha, 'The Economic History of India up to AD 1200: Trends and Prospects', *JESHO*, XVI, 1974, pp. 48–80; B.D. Chattopadhyaya, 'Trends of Research in Ancient Indian Economic History', *JAIH*, XVIII, 1988–89 (1991), pp. 109–131; Hermann Kulke, 'A Passage to India: Temples, Merchants and the Ocean', *JESHO*, XXXV, 1993, pp. 154–80.

of producing goods with a view to meeting those requirements either for use or for profit by an optimum (and not necessarily the maximum) utilization of available resources (or raw materials), and (c) the consumption and distribution of commodities by exchange at market places. If a producer has the capacity to produce more items than his immediate needs, the excess products are generally meant for transaction at the exchange centre. It is in the context of the exchangeability of certain products that the trader assumes significance in a given material milieu. This suggests that the trader functions as a vital link between the actual producer and the actual consumer/ user of a product. He is, strictly speaking, neither a direct producer nor a consumer and engages in trade for profit. The earlier approach to the study of trade history would have been to situate trade and traders in the context of supply, demand, and price-fixed markets. This is a complex process involving the interplay of various factors, including the state-based polity (distinct from the lineage polity) and an administrative structure. The state system operates in a sharply differentiated society and is more complex than the clan-based society held together by the kinship bond. The prime mover of trade in a state society is the classic law of comparative advantage.[18] Advancement in the economy is also inseparably associated with the specialization of crafts, occupations and professions and the division of labour. This in turn implies that no single person is in a position to produce everything that is required; so, everyone is, in a way, dependent on the proper procurement of certain items produced by others at different places, far and near. The urge to acquire certain items—not available locally and readily—holds a crucial clue to the economic activity called exchange and trade.

The above-mentioned concepts are related to the conditions existing mostly in the modern market-oriented societies in the developed and industrialized nations. Economists of the formalist school uphold that such conditions can be traced more or less uniformly in the development of commerce in different societies.

On the other hand, Morgan's fieldwork among the American Indians in the nineteenth century established that life in primitive and archaic communities often did not correspond to the European pattern of social, economic, and political development.[19] These communities also

[18] N.B. Harte, *The Study of Economic History*, London, 1967.

[19] Richard F. Salisbury, 'Trade and Markets', in David L. Sills, *The International Encyclopaedia of the Social Sciences*, XVI, pp. 118–22.

could not be judged solely by the yardstick of the European/Western experience of development and the growth of commerce. The conditions of primitive and tribal peoples were often seen as frozen in time and as situations of a remote antiquity surviving and continuing in the present. The so-called primitive character of these communities was seen in the backwardness of their technology, systems of production, their clan-based social organization and belief systems. The widely-held notion was to consider primitive economies as natural economies. In such economies, production for subsistence is the order of the day and there is little incentive towards production for exchange (i.e. producing the exchangeable surplus with a view to transacting them).

This takes us to the path-breaking research of Marcell Mauss. He challenged the nearly perennial standpoint that primitive economies were natural economies. He further demonstrated that many clan-based primitive communities with relatively simple social organizations had the capacity to generate surplus products which were exchanged with members of other clans. However, the surplus products were not necessarily exchanged for purely economic motives, but for gaining social pre-eminence and prestige. Such exchanges often took the shape of gifts between communities on ceremonial occasions. The items exchanged as gifts might have been valuable, exotic and prestige goods, but could also belong to the realm of ritual objects. The exchange of items through gifts in a spirit of reciprocity may also eventually lead to a spirit of competition among participating communities. Such a process in the long run might pave the way for the emergence of more prestigious lineages and ultimately to ruling groups. This is what Mauss termed as 'gift economy', which is related to his formulation of the 'modes of exchange'.[20] In other words, exchanges based on reciprocity are viewed as being capable of bringing in social and political complexities. The resultant restructuring of tribal societies can further lead to the advent of state societies, gradually replacing lineage societies. The next step was taken by Levi-Strauss who went beyond the concept of the exchange of items through gift-giving. His anthropological research demonstrated that such exchanges could also involve the exchange of human resources, i.e. the gift of women through marriage.[21] This explains the very

[20] Marcell Mauss, *The Gift*, New York, 1967.
[21] Claude Levi-Strauss, *The Elementary Structure of Kinship*, London, 1969.

ceremony of the exchange of women, i.e. the institution of marriage, is intimately associated with the giving of gifts of consumable articles.

Thus, anthropologists, particularly economic anthropologists, would try to situate trade in an overall human culture. Marxist ideas, which have immensely influenced the study of economic history, give priority to economic factors and forces as determinants of social forms. Recent understanding of many non-European and relatively simpler societies, on the other hand, underlines the importance of social and cultural forms for economic development and growth. Parsons, for example, considers social systems as having functional subsystems; economics is perceived as an adaptive subsystem.[22]

In this context, it may be useful to briefly discuss the ideas of K. Polanyi, the founder of the substantivist school, which challenged many established notions of the formalist school of economists. The substantivist position considers trade to be a relatively peaceful method of acquiring goods which are not locally available.[23] Countering the universality and uniformity of the concept of market trade of the formalists—with its foundations based on the formulations of the relative scarcity of locally available products, optimization of production, surplus production, and transaction of exchangeable surplus—Polanyi argues that market trade is to be associated only with modern industrial capitalist economies. He discounts any possibility of market trade with supply–demand and price mechanisms in pre-capitalist societies. The crucial element here is the market. The market, or more precisely the 'open market', is viewed as a price-setting institution of relatively recent origin. Market trading requires a large number of buyers and sellers, leading to the situation of perfect competition which is reached when distinct relations between price, supply, demand and transactions are worked out. Exchanges taking place at prices other than the competitive one give rise to the situation of imperfect competition in the institution of markets. To the substantivists, the market is different from the marketplace which serves as the spot for the exchange of commodities. That is why Polanyi perceives marketless trading in the ancient Near East. The substantivist position accepts the

[22] Manning Nash, 'Economic Anthropology', in David L. Sills (ed.), *op. cit.*, IV, pp. 359–65; also Helen Codere, 'Exchange and Display', in David L. Sills, *op. cit.*, V, pp. 239–45.

[23] K. Polanyi, C.M. Arensberg and H.W. Pearson (eds.), *Trade and Markets in the Early Empire*, New York, 1957.

existence of trade and traders from remote times, but asserts the absence of markets as a price-setting institution. A major ingredient in Polanyi's concept of pre-market trade is the 'port of trade'. By this he did not necessarily connote a harbour where trade took place. It was conceived as a town or a small state, not necessarily located on the sea coast, which would function as an enclave where foreign traders would meet appointed local representatives. The foreign traders were meant to be confined within that enclave. If, and when, trade takes place in the context of relatively well-organized bodies and more or less formal treaty relationships, such a situation is labelled as administered trade by the substantivists. The position of the merchant under such circumstances is one of subjection in the absence of perfect competition of market trading.[24]

An extension of the above mentioned concept of pre-modern trade is forcefully presented by Renfrew by combining his archaeological studies of ancient economies with mathematical models. Movement within a social/spatial unit(s) amounts to internal trade, according to Renfrew, who defines external trade as movements between those units and/or across cultural boundaries. In Renfrew's scheme, ancient trade is often integrally linked with the early state module. Once again, one may note that trade is seen here as an agent of change in relatively simpler societies. It recognizes that the impact of trade could lead to the transformation of a society into a relatively complex one through the mechanism of early state formation. Renfrew has brought out no less than ten forms of trading by emphasizing their spatial aspects. These are: (i) direct access, (ii) home-based reciprocity, (iii) boundary reciprocity, (iv) down-the-line trade, (v) central place distribution, (vi) central place market exchange, (vii) middleman trading, (viii) emissary trading, (ix) colonial enclave, and (x) port of trade.[25] Belshaw situates trade in a wider social context when he says that 'all

[24] K. Polanyi, *The Great Transformation*, Boston, 1957; K. Polanyi, 'The Port of Trade as an Ecological and Evolutionary Type', *Proceedings of the 1961 Annual Meeting of the American Ethnological Society,* Seattle, 1961; for a collection of Polanyi's diverse ideas, see George Dalton, *Primitive, Archaic and Modern Economics: Essays of Karl Polanyi*, New York, 1968; we have mostly used here S.C. Humphreys, 'History, Economics and Anthropology', *History and Theory*, VIII, 1969, pp. 165–212.

[25] Colin Renfrew, 'Trade as Action at Distance: Questions of Integration and Communication', in J.A. Sabloff and C.C. Lamberg-Karlovsky (eds.), *op. cit.*, pp. 3–59.

enduring social relations involve transactions which have an exchange aspect.'[26]

The spatial aspect of exchange may not be easily related to any evolutionary or linear pattern. But it is likely that the earliest kind of exchange could have originated among diverse hunting bands at the boundaries of their respective areas. Hermes, the Greek god, presides over both boundary and trade; moreover, Hermes is also known as a trickster.[27] Significantly enough, there emerges an association between exchange-oriented activities and some amount of deception and fraud. It is a fairly common experience that while the wealth of a merchant is the principal determinant of his position in the society, the general perception of wealth earned is not free from doubt. The *vaṇik* is branded as an open thief (*prakāśyataskara*) in some ancient Indian theoretical treatises, a point which will be discussed more elaborately in a subsequent section.

One of the most ancient images of such exchanges probably figures in Herodotus' account of primitive transactions somewhere on the northern and western coast of Africa. In such a description, Curtin finds an early image of 'silent trade'. According to it, people with their wares, assembled from distant and different places at an accustomed spot of exchange, usually located away from towns and villages. They deposited their goods and went away. Then local groups interested in the exchanges appeared; they too deposited their goods and went away. This was followed by the return of the first group who examined the value of the objects they found. If they considered the exchange equitable, they would take the local items and leave their own. If not, they would adjust the quantity of their wares before going away again and would await a silent response from their counterparts. Though it will be extremely difficult to furnish known historical data in support of this, it highlights the possibilities of exchange without a spoken word and without the intervention of any broker mediating between two groups of traders who did not actually meet one another.[28]

[26] Cyril Belshaw, *Traditional Exchange and Modern Market*, Delhi (Indian rpt.), 1969, p. 4.

[27] Norman O. Brown, *Hermes the Thief: The Evolution of a Myth*, New York, 1969 (second edition), pp. 38–46.

[28] Herodotus, *Histories*, IV, p. 196; P.J. Hamilton Grierson, *The Silent Trade: A Contribution to the Early History of Human Intercourse*, Edinburgh, 1903; also see Philip D. Curtin, *Cross Cultural Trade in World History*, Cambridge, 1984, pp. 12–13.

Such primitive exchanges would be conducted not at a marketplace, but at convenient points probably located at boundaries or at some familiar spots outside an urban or rural space. These would in fact involve exchanging items without too much accompanying information. In a more developed society, the exchange of items and information is expected to be simultaneous and intertwined. A major change is encountered with the emergence of the marketplace which is recognized as a fixed point of transaction and generally found in an advanced and more complex society which has experienced urbanism and state polity. Marketplaces within an early civilization are hardly encountered at the fringes or peripheral zones of the civilization, but mostly at the heart of urban centres. Such a situation is often appreciated by historians by using the central place theory and the concept of economics of location, borrowed from geographers.[29] In the non-sedentary communities of hunter-gatherers and nomads, people tend to spread out across the landscape to survive and sustain themselves, as there is little scope for specialization of occupation and division of labour in such societies. The advent of sedentary agricultural society paved the way for specialized functions and wholetime professionals. These functions seem to have been generally performed not at peripheral areas but at central places which were often non-rural areas. The appearance of such a central place would be marked by a distinctive and monumental structure, usually a temple dedicated to a divinity or divinities. A temple normally attracts large crowds which include traders and vendors. The importance of a temple as a point of convergence of peoples from diverse areas must have been understood by the ruler to realize its potential for trade.

As multifarious functions performed by specialists would tend to cluster at such a place, it would often result in the emergence of urban centres and would become the central place within the urban space. A society technically more proficient than others would also possess a greater range of multifunctionality. It, therefore, follows that some centres—usually urban in character—would be more multifunctional than others. This, in turn, paves the way for the formation of an urban hierarchy and also the graded importance of

[29] These are influential in sharpening the present ideas of the 'centre' and the 'periphery' in a world dominated by capitalism and the development of the dependency school. See the multivolume study by Immanuel Wallerstein, *The Modern World System*, New York, 1974.

marketplaces. The less multifunctional centres would be dependent on the more multifunctional ones. As human communities experience varied degrees of technological progress and complexities in the course of time, places situated lower in the gradation of settlements would tend to depend more on those placed higher. In this context, historians have borrowed from the geographical concept of the 'central place' The idea is that important places or spots of exchange may show a range of dependent relations, not only to each other, but also to the nucleus of the 'central place'. The development of exchange-oriented activities at the central places leads to the formation and imposition of some kind of order and security. This could be an authority structure at the central place responsible for maintaining discipline and order; such an authority would be sustained by a resource base created by the realization of imposts, dues and revenues. The exchange of materials and information at the central place, the presence of an authority structure ensuring security and order, and the resource-gathering functions of that authority at the central place clearly distinguish it from chiefdom societies. The new features and attendant changes should be related to the complex situation, better known as civilization. This has a further linkage with what is viewed as the 'early state module'. The increasing complexities could have hardly left the exchange-oriented activities unaltered and, as a result, the simpler exchanges were transformed into more formal trade and commerce. When several such early state modules appear on the scene, there is a distinct likelihood of exchange relations among them. As the early state modules would be involved in transactions beyond their respective territories, external and long-distance commerce would be in the offing. The fusion or amalgamation of the early state modules into an expansive and supra-regional empire could also logically encourage the rise of a higher-order central place.[30]

These anthropological and sociological ideas may be of some help to the trade historian of early India. This is not to suggest that there are easily identifiable data that can be conveniently fitted to these models. The point is that these may encourage inquiries to identify various levels of trade of early India which cannot be perceived, in our present state of understanding, as having undergone a uniform development of commerce. The Harappan civilization, noted for its far-flung trade contacts in the subcontinent and beyond, must have

[30] Colin Renfrew, 'Trade as Action at Distance', *op. cit.*, pp. 12–21.

interacted within India with societies and cultures which had not reached the very high degree of organization of economic life that is found in the Harappan urban material milieu. There is archaeological proof of the contacts between the Harappans and peoples associated with neolithic/ chalcolithic cultures in different parts of the subcontinent. These contacts were mainly for the procurement of raw materials for Harappan craftsmen. The widespread contacts of the Harappans could not have been possible but for an efficient communication and transportation system that possibly was operated by domesticated animals. Such animals must have been supplied to the urban residents of the civilization by their breeders and keepers. It would be logical to surmise that the animal breeders were semi-nomadic or nomadic communities, living beyond the sedentary society. Harappan contacts with these groups probably did not assume the character of commerce. On the other hand, the Harappan intercourse with Mesopotamia appears to have been organized, ordered and complex enough to be labelled as trade. The Harappan civilization thus experienced different types of exchange relations with various contemporary communities in the subcontinent and beyond.[31] The *Ṛgveda*, one of the earliest extant literary creations in the Indo-European languages, informs us of a society which was largely based on cattle-keeping and some agriculture. It is hardly likely that such a society participated in full-fledged commercial transactions. On the other hand, the *Ṛgveda* (IV.24.10) suggests that cattle was the medium of exchange. Attention may be drawn in this context to the Rgvedic description of *paṇis* who were looked down upon for their hostile and unintelligible speech and who were known for their distant travels and wealth.[32] Kosambi saw in this account the impressions of the non-Vedic/pre-Vedic (the Harappan?) merchants.[33] This is suggestive of the Rgvedic people's knowledge of, and possible contacts with, certain other linguistic groups or families. Linguists explain that linguistic change can occur as a result of (among other factors) contacts between languages belonging to either the same or different language families.

[31] Shereen Ratnagar, *Encounters: The Westerly Trade of the Harappans*, Delhi, 1981.

[32] A.A. McDonell and A.B. Keith, *The Vedic Index of Names and Subjects*, I, London, 1910, pp. 471–73.

[33] D.D. Kosambi, *The Culture and Civilization of Ancient India in Historical Outline*, (Indian rpt.), Delhi, 1972, p. 80; D.D. Kosambi, *An Introduction to the Study of Indian History*, Bombay, 1956, pp. 86–87.

In the evolution of the Indo-Aryan (IA) language there are known cases of structural changes in the IA and borrowing of words of non-Aryan origin.[34] 'This in turn raises the question concerning the mechanism by which linguistic convergence takes place and the social conditions which favoured it'.[35] Linguists also recognize that prolonged contacts between two communities which have a developed speech pattern result in bilingualism. 'It is commonly admitted that extensive borrowing from one language to another can occur only through the agency of the bilingual section of the society'.[36] One may only venture to infer—and by no means prove—that such bilingualism and extensive borrowing between the speakers of the Aryan and non-Aryan languages could have materialized by their regular contact at the level of peaceful exchange and also hostile wars and booty collection.

The subsequent later Vedic literature (*c.* 1000–600 BC) shows that it had a better acquaintance with sedentary agrarian society in the Indo-Ganga divide, the upper Ganga valley and the Ganga-Yamuna doab. This is evident through some developments in crafts and industries which offer more information on exchange.[37] Thus an entire hymn

[34] Suniti Kumar Chatterjee, 'Race Movements and Prehistoric Cultures', in R.C. Majumdar (ed.), *The Vedic Age*, Bombay, 1951, pp. 150–66.

[35] K. Meenakshi, 'Linguistics and the Study of Early Indian History', in Romila Thapar (ed.), *op. cit.*, p. 55.

[36] Ibid., p. 63.

[37] The development of agriculture in the later Vedic times is also associated with the growing rigours of the four-*varṇa* system. The two upper *varṇas*, the brāhmaṇa and the kṣatriya, are placed in sharp opposition to the two lower *varṇas*, the vaiśya and the śūdra. An impressive list of crafts and professions is found in the account of the Puruṣamedha sacrifice in the *Yajurveda*. Also noticeable is the increase of the power of the later Vedic ruler for whom a number of sacrifices are recommended in the *Saṁhitā* and the *Brāhmaṇa* texts. The polity of the later Vedic period is different and more complex than that seen in the Rgvedic times. In spite of sharp differentiation in the later Vedic society, a full-fledged monarchical state was yet to appear since a well-defined territory, a standing army and a regular revenue machinery did not develop during this period. The occasional and irregular demand of *bali* (an obligatory impost) by the later Vedic ruler was, according to Romila Thapar (*From Lineage to State*, Delhi, 1984), prestation. R.S. Sharma, *Material Culture and Social Formations in Ancient India*, Delhi, 1983; R.S. Sharma, *The Origin of the State in India*, Bombay, 1990, considers the later Vedic polity as being on the threshold of a state system and a proto-state. The evidence of growing exchange in the later Vedic times has to be appreciated against this background.

of the *Atharvaveda* (III.15) is devoted to charms and prayers meant for success in exchange-related activities. The interesting point here is the reference to three types of exchanges: *prapaṇa* (barter), *pratipaṇa* (exchange of merchandise) and *vikraya* (sale of objects).

As success in all these would lead to the gain of a hundred treasures (*śatadhana*), an ardent prayer is offered to Agni. That three different forms of exchange could coexist is clearly brought out by this hymn. Since the earliest known coins in the subcontinent (i.e. metallic medium of exchange) are datable to the sixth–fifth centuries BC, it would be difficult to read in the account of the gain of a hundred treasures any possibility of monetary transactions during the later Vedic times. Exchanges in the later Vedic times show greater complexities than those prevalent during the Rgvedic age. But the image is, at the most, one of incipient trade, along with barter and the exchange of merchandise.

An unusual attempt at the utilization of modern scientific techniques to understand exchange relations in remote times can be seen in the computer analysis of the Jorwe pottery. In order to study the similarities and distinctiveness of the chalcolithic potteries from Chandoli, Nevasa and Inamgaon (all in Maharashtra), a sample of twenty-five pots from Chandoli, thirty-three from Inamgaon and thirty-six from Nevasa were analysed by a computer programme. The statistical study, a rarity in research on early Indian exchange and trade, showed a similarity between, pots of Inamgaon and Chandoli; on the other hand, the pots from Inamgaon differed from those of Nevasa. The similarity led to the inference that:

> . . . in all probability the Inamgaon potter was supplying pottery to all the inhabitants of Chandoli. The latter, however, was a small settlement, almost hamlet, and could not have afforded the services of a full time potter.[38]

The application of ethnohistorical and/or ethnoarchaeological methods by Bridget Allchin has also generated significant insights into the possible manner of exchanges in simpler societies. She has studied the annual movement of the Badawal community of nomadic stock breeders from Gujarat to Central India and their return to Gujarat. They were found to have traded in various products and items on this annual circuit. According to her, this could hold crucial

[38] M.K. Dhavalikar and A.R. Marathe, 'Jorwe Pottery—A Statistical Study', *Bulletin of the Deccan College Research Institute*, XXXVIII, 1978–79, pp. 17–22; the quotation is from p. 22.

clues to the understanding of similar exchanges in the proto-historic times.[39]

Asymmetrical relations could have well existed when exchanges took place between a more complex and evolved society and a relatively simple folk/tribal/lineage society. Such contacts must have been established between the expanding Mauryan empire in the Deccan and the existing megalithic people there. It is now evident that the Mauryan empire had definite material interests in capturing and controlling the Deccan which was rich in mineral resources (this point is taken up subsequently). Despite the presence of Dravidian speakers in this area, Mauryan rule introduced the north Indian Prakrit language and Brāhmī script there. Its further impact can be easily seen in the emergence of the Tamil-Brāhmī script in the immediate post-Maurya period. The Mauryan economic interests in the Deccan, including trade, resulted in the advent of a number of traits of north Indian culture as intrusive elements in peninsular India with far-reaching consequences. The hallmark of the then material culture in the peninsular region is found in the burial culture of the megalithic people who used metals, including iron and the Black and Red Ware (BRW), but who did not experience either urbanism or state polity.[40] In southern Karnataka and northern Malabar, the river Kaveri provided the vital linkage between the coastal megalithic sites and the ones in the interior. The similarities in gold jewellery found as grave goods from megalithic sites in this area, especially in the Nilgiris, can be a pointer to the protohistoric exchange circuits. It may be also possible that some of the jewellery found in graves could have been uniform because of their ritual or social function. In this context, the Palghat gap must have provided the vital passage. At Kodumanal the megalithic phase (*c.* 250 BC–AD 100) yielded semi-precious stones and iron deposits, implying the procurement and movement of natural resources. The subsequent early historical phase (*c.* AD 100–250) shows not only agricultural activities, but also contains one hundred potsherds with inscribed personal names and informs us of the presence of *nikama*, i.e. *nigama* or a guild-like mercantile organization.

[39] Bridget Allchin, 'Ethnoarchaeology in South Asia', in J. Schotsmans and M. Taddei (eds.), *South Asian Archaeology*, in two volumes, Naples, 1985, pp. 21–33; particularly pp. 21–22.

[40] See the relevant overview of megalithic cultures and sites in A. Ghosh, (ed.), *An Encyclopaedia of Indian Archaeology*, II, Delhi, 1989.

We have underlined the importance of tracing different levels and types of exchange activities in early India which could exist side by side and also overlap. The appearance of minted metallic pieces as a medium of exchange (i.e. coins) indicates a higher form of exchange. Exchanges of the pre-currency phase are generally equated with barter, which is viewed as being more ancient and primitive than money-based commerce. Humphrey has argued against this well-entrenched notion. He did not find any instance of a pure or predominantly barter economy, nor any clear evidence of the transformation of a barter economy into an economy experiencing money and marketplaces. Barter is seen by him not as an evolutionary phase setting the stage for money-based transactions, but as something co-existing with monetary transactions. According to him, barter can be accommodated into the more sophisticated system of minted metallic currency and marketplace trade. In the event of the disintegration of the economy or a fall in the money supply, barter, in Humphrey's formulation, can assume considerable importance.[41] The point which we would like to emphasize is that in a traditional society like India with its immense regional diversities, the more primitive and the sophisticated types of exchange need not be treated as merely having evolutionary and mutually exclusive and oppositional features.

Going through the historiography of trade in early India, one cannot miss the tendency of scholars, especially of the pre-1950 days, to label all sorts of centres of exchanges as markets and trade centres. In view of the acute scarcity of data regarding the exact location of such centres and their position in the hierarchy of market centres, it is admittedly an uphill task for the historian to spell out the specific character of these marketplaces. But it also has to be considered that conscious differentiations were made in ancient literary texts to refer to different types of exchange centres. The range begins from rural-level *haṭṭas/haṭṭikas* (=modern *hats* in north India). These are closely related to *yātrās* or fairs (held periodically, especially during festivals). At the other end of the spectrum may be situated large and complex marketplaces within an urban (*nagara/pura*) space or located in or close to a *velākula* (harbour). A *puṭabhedana*, known in Indian literature probably since the fifth–fourth centuries BC, signified a centre of exchange with facilities for the storage of exchangeable

[41] C. Humphrey, 'Barter and Economic Disintegration', *Man*, XX, 1985, pp. 48–72.

commodities. It may be a place for what in modern parlance is called 'breaking the bulk'. The vital linkage between the rural-level exchange centre and the large marketplace within an urban area seems to have been provided, especially from the early medieval period onwards, by trade centres of the intermediate category such as *maṇḍapikā*, *peṇṭha* and *nagaram*. The nuances of these classificatory terms in early Indian sources are often ironed out in the conventional narratives of trade as 'markets'. The chief feature of such studies is the 'black box' type of narrative, directed to the accumulation of data, but with little urge for analysis and explanation of information. There is also a tendency to take literary descriptions of commerce at their face value and juxtapose literary accounts of widely separated periods to throw light on trade in general.[42]

In the conventional historiography of early Indian trade, there is also the tendency to treat the merchant as an undifferentiated category. The term *vaṇik* or *śreṣṭhī* is often indiscriminately used as a blanket term to denote any one engaged in trade. By this, authors seem to have ignored that early Indian literary texts used distinct terms to denote different categories and levels of merchants, e.g. *vaṇik*, *vaidehaka* (these two terms probably denote petty merchants), *banjara* (itinerant pedlar), *āpaṇika* (shopkeeper engaged in retail trade), *śreṣṭhī* (very rich merchant), *sārthavāha* (caravan trader), *nauvittaka* (ship-owning merchant), *rājaśreṣṭhī* (royal merchant), etc. Recent historiography indicates a greater awareness of these different categories and of the merchant's position in the overall social and political milieu. The limitations of the traditional scholarship cannot take away from the fact that the most significant contribution of the conventional approach to the study of early Indian trade was to prepare a strong and reliable empirical base and chronological framework which led to an analytical and problem-oriented perusal of the history of trade in early India.

[42] An instance of this may be found in the chapter on the economic conditions in A.S. Altekar, *The Rāṣṭrakūṭas and Their Times*, Bombay, 1958. Writing on the period from *c.* eighth century to the second half of the tenth century, Altekar cited information from the *Periplus of the Erythraean Sea* (*c.* late first century AD) and Arabic and Persian sources (*c.* middle of the ninth to fourteenth centuries). It gives an impression that the chronological gap of several centuries between the two types of sources was frozen and that the pattern of trade remained static and unaltered over these centuries.

A brief discussion on the commodities figuring prominently in the trade of early India can be made at this juncture. Both Occidental and indigenous perspectives on traditional trade in India have a common character: India was viewed as a land rich in exotic, prestigious and luxury items that were often endowed with magical power and were of significance in rituals. Spices like pepper and cardamom, textile products like the celebrated muslin and precious stones, and gems like diamonds and pearls loom large in the accounts of India's exportable items. That India also participated in the transit trade of Chinese silk and many South-East Asian exotic spices (e.g. clove and cinnamon) to the West did not escape the attention of historians. Looking at the situation during the early medieval period, a perusal of the accounts of Chau-ju-Kua (a Chinese officer of the Sung period supervising commerce in *c.* 1225), Marco Polo (late thirteenth century) and Ibn Battuta (first half of the fourteenth century) leaves a similar impression—the traditional trade of India consisted of luxuries. This is not projected merely in the accounts of India's exports, but also in the story of the import of war horses and precious metals like gold and silver to India. This is a perspective that is inseparably associated with the craze for Eastern luxuries and exotic objects in Roman times (cf. the accounts of Pliny and Tiberius) and in the medieval Italian city states as well, through which the image of India as a land of diverse luxuries spread to Portugal and Spain. The European urge to reach out for distant Asian markets was largely prompted by the desire to procure the much-coveted Eastern rarities. This stereotyped image of Indian trade is once again instrumental in establishing the invariant nature of traditional Asian as well as Indian trade. The general characterization of early Indian trade by scholars of different genres (including Marxist historians, who must be credited with exploding the myth of the immutable and stagnant Indian society) is that it involved transactions of high-value, small quantity, portable, luxury commodities over the centuries.[43] Even J.E. van Leur, who felt the need of freeing Asian historiography from the hegemony of European thought and who stressed the appreciation

[43] C.G.F. Simkin, *The Traditional Trade of Asia*, London, 1966. The perceptions about India and Asia during the age of European expansion are strongly embedded in the European fancy for Eastern products. See in this context, Donald F. Lach, *Asia in the Making of Europe*, in three volumes, 1965.

of the local features of Asian cultures, could not move away from the fixed idea that Asian trade, till the advent of European companies, consisted essentially of luxury commodities and, therefore, was unchanging during the pre-modern times.[44] The other implication of such a standpoint would be that the trade in luxuries was relevant to the handful of rich and powerful people and could hardly take root in the day-to-day life of the common people. In other words, early Indian trade, chiefly consisting of precious objects, was not considered to be an agent of significant changes in Indian history. To many economic historians, the accounts of early Indian trade tell spectacular tales, but it was a side show to the predominantly agrarian scenario in India.

The nearly unaltered focus of historians on the luxury trade leads to an examination of the very nature of luxury items. This can be understood by looking at the difference between luxuries and necessities. 'A necessity is a good whose consumption does not increase in proportion with income; a luxury is one whose consumption increases more than proportionately.'[45] But what is viewed as an expensive item at the point of consumption may not necessarily be the same at the time of its production, manufacture or procurement. Thus the pepper of Malabar, coveted over centuries in the West, was not a precious item in the coastal society of Malabar. The ivory of Dosarene (southern part of Orissa), for instance, is highly spoken of in the *Periplus*, but whether it was an expensive commodity in coastal Orissa cannot be ascertained. Similarly, precious Chinese ceramics did reach Indian marketplaces and urban centres during the early medieval and medieval ages, but were themselves not regarded as luxuries at their production centres.[46] Analysing the character of high-value objects, Appadurai goes beyond economic considerations. Luxuries are, according to him, 'goods whose principal use is rhetorical and social, goods are simply incarnation sign, the necessity to which they respond is fundamentally political'.[47]

He further identifies five attributes of luxuries: (a) the restriction of its use to the elite, either by price or by law; (b) the complexities of its procurement and acquisition which may or may not be related to

[44] J.E. van Leur, *Indonesian Trade and Society*, The Hague, 1955.

[45] Kenneth McPherson, *The Indian Ocean, A History of the People and the Sea*, Delhi, 1993, p. 78.

[46] Ibid., pp. 78–82.

[47] Arjun Appadurai, *The Social Life of Things*, Cambridge, 1986, p. 38.

real 'scarcity' of such objects; (c) semiotic virtuosity, i.e. the ability of the object to signal a social message, especially for its clientele; (d) these must be consumed in an appropriate manner following a well-set code of conduct; and (e) close interaction between their consumption and the body, person and the personality of their users. In a recent study of silk as a luxury item during AD 600–1200 Xin Ri Liu demonstrated, with reference to Appadurai's list of attributes, that the use of silk had earlier been restricted by law but subsequently by price. This was a change of far-reaching consequence, clearly implying that transactions in luxuries were not bereft of significant transformation. 'The shift meant that silk became a real commodity in the market.'[48]

The Ganga valley, especially the middle Ganga valley, experienced the formation of *mahājanapadas* (territorial states, mostly monarchical) and also urban centres from the sixth century BC onwards. This has been related to the process of the emergence of 'primary states'. The spread of the state and urban society to greater parts of the subcontinent, following the pattern already encountered in the Ganga valley, can be seen during the period from *c.* 200 BC to AD 300. As the beginnings of state and urban formation were felt in dispersed parts of the subcontinent during the post-Maurya period, this process is described as the formation of the secondary states and urban centres, the epicentre of which lay in the Ganga valley.[49] Prior to *c.* 200 BC vast areas of central India, the Deccan and south India were characterized by relatively simpler, lineage-based pre-state polities and an agro-pastoral subsistence economy. Such tribal societies generally favour more or less equitable access to power and resources among its members, though these are not egalitarian societies. Inter-tribal exchanges could lead the tribal chiefs and leaders to procure rare and prestigious goods, often endowed with ritual and magical significance. An outcome of this is the concentration of greater wealth, prestige and power in the hands of a select group in the tribal society. The availability of such goods through exchange can break up the autarkic situation and the resultant stratification in society encourages the

[48] Xinru Liu, *Silk and Religion, An Exploration of Material Life and the Thought of People, AD 600–1200*, Delhi, 1996, p. 3.

[49] F.R. Allchin (ed.), *Archaeology of Early Historic South Asia*, Cambridge, 1995; B.D. Chattopadhyaya, 'Urban Centres in Early Bengal', *Pratnasamiksha*, II–III, 1993–94, pp. 169–92.

formation of the state.[50] As the formation of the state is to be appreciated in terms of social change, exchange of luxuries could be an effective state-forming mechanism, especially in the case of the rise of secondary states. For costly materials may reach areas of secondary state formation as intrusive elements from the epicentric zone. A more elaborate discussion in a subsequent section will show how the pan-Indian expansion of the Mauryan power with its metropolitan area in Magadha facilitated the penetration of many traits of north Indian material culture into the peninsular part through commerce. Economic and political anthropologists have driven home the significance of the role of trade in luxuries in the emergence of secondary states and urban societies; in other words, the importance of trade in precious objects is recognized as an agent of social change.[51]

The cherished notion of the traditional Asian (including Indian) trade as consisting only of luxuries is further strengthened by Van Leur's formulation that it was carried on by pedlar merchants. The portrayal of the petty merchant hawking his wares from mart to mart or from harbour to harbour fitted well with the image of transactions in small quantity, high-value and portable merchandise. Van Leur also propounded the view that politically powerful nobles of Asia's coastal society exercised immense control over the maritime trade in Asia. They were, in his opinion, the most important element in the traditional maritime trade of Asia. Intent upon demonstrating the fundamental transformation in traditional Asian society due to the impact of European capital and colonialism, Van Leur emphasized that the pre-modern trading world of Asia was changeless and timeless. There could be, at the most, periods of highs and lows in the traditional trade of Asia, but there was little possibility of any fundamental structural change. Though Van Leur mainly spoke of conditions in Indonesia, his ideas about luxury trade and pedlars were not unrelated to Indian conditions.[52] This immensely thought-provoking thesis has

[50] M. Sahlins, 'On the Sociology of Primitive Exchange', in M. Bantom (ed.), *The Relevance of Models for Social Anthropology*, London, 1965; M. Fried, *The Evolution of Political Society*, New York, 1965.

[51] According to Arjun Appadurai, *op. cit.*, pp. 36–37, the main clue for the expansion of trade, industry and financial capital in Europe during the period from the fourteenth to the eighteenth century may be found in the increasing demand for luxury goods, including silk.

[52] J.E. van Leur, *op. cit.*

enriched the understanding of pre-modern Asian and Indian trade. But it did not remain unchallenged. Even if one concedes for the sake of argument that traditional Asian and Indian commerce revolved solely around precious commodities, one has to recognize the role of luxury trade as an agent of social change. This is particularly relevant to the emergence of secondary states and urban society in India during *c.* 200 BC and AD 300.

A major shift in the recent study of early Indian trade can be noticed in the historian's recognition of the transaction in staples along with luxuries. After all, the trade in luxuries, in spite of bringing big profits to merchants, was meant for a handful of the rich and the powerful. On the other hand, daily necessities—though definitely less costly than luxury items—could touch the daily life of the larger community and could be transacted in bulk. The Harappan civilization saw simultaneous trade in precious gems like lapis lazuli and bulk items like timber and copper. Mesopotamian cuneiform documents of the second half of the third millennium BC tell us about the availability of Meluhhan (generally identified with the Indus valley) timber. Recent archaeological evidence points to the procurement of copper from Magan (probably the Oman peninsula) by the Harappans.[53] This is clearly suggestive of long-distance trade in necessities in a remote period. Coming to the early historical times, the Buddha, on his way to Rājagṛha, is said to have met Belaṭṭha Kaccāna who was travelling with 500 wagons carrying many jars of sugar.[54] Another essential commodity must have been salt; it was certainly transacted over a wide area as salt was not produced and available at all places. The Saṅgam texts, the earliest literary creation in Tamil, leave little room for doubt about the active role of the Paratavars who were at once fishermen, sailors and salt-dealers.[55] The revenue-bearing potential of this essential commodity is fully grasped by Pliny (death AD 79).

> There are. . . mountains of natural salt, such as Oromenus in India where it is like blocks of stone from a quarry and ever replaces itself, *bringing greater revenue to the kings* than those from gold and silver. (italics mine)[56]

[53] Shereen Ratnagar, *op. cit.*

[54] *Vinaya Piṭaka*, tr. I.B. Horner, in five volumes, London, 1938–52, vol. I, p. 224.

[55] R. Champakalakshmi, *Trade, Ideology and Urbanization, South India 300 BC to AD 1300*, Delhi, 1996, pp. 106–107

[56] Pliny, *Naturalis Historia*, tr. H. Rackham, London and Cambridge, Mass.,

The Oromenus mountain is generally identified with the Salt Range in Pakistan. At the time of Pliny, the area appears to have been a part of the mighty Kuṣāṇa empire. That a dealer in salt could amass considerable wealth is amply borne out by impressive patronage and donations to temples in the early medieval town (*pattana*) of Siyadoni by a salt merchant (*nemakavaṇija*).[57] Significantly enough, the *Periplus of the Erythraean Sea*, a text routinely utilized to demonstrate the import and export of luxuries during the age of the Indo-Roman commerce, informs us of the regular supply of 'large quantities of cloth of ordinary quality' from Tagara (= Ter, Osmanabad district, Maharashtra) to Barygaza, the premier port in western India.[58] A close perusal of Arab accounts of India cannot but highlight the continuous demand for two essential items of Indian origin in Arabia, namely timber for boat building and coconut coir to stitch the wooden planks of vessels.[59] Both these commodities must have been traded in bulk. A lively maritime trade in iron, copper and other staples looms large in the Jewish business letters of 'India traders' (*c.* AD eleventh–thirteenth centuries), plying between India and the Red Sea ports.[60]

The hackneyed image of early Indian trade revolving merely around luxuries cannot be taken for granted at the present state of our knowledge. The other major stereotype, namely the overwhelming presence of petty pedlars, has also undergone serious criticism. The immense wealth of the *seṭṭhi*, the influence exerted by the *rājaśreṣṭhi* and the impressive financial gains made by the *nauvittaka* are well documented and one cannot reduce them to the position of trivial pedlars. An interesting observation by Ashin Das Gupta on medieval Indian merchants demands our attention in this context. He counters the general labeling of traditional Indian trade as peddling trade and

---

rpt., 1942; see XI.11.1. In the contemporary Deccan, the Sātavāhanas showed distinct interests in salt which was subject to a royal levy (*sa-lavaṇa*). The *Arthaśāstra* (II.12. chapter dealing with the functions of the Ākarādhyakṣa or the director of mines) strongly recommends official supervision of the production and sale of salt.

[57] F. Kielhorn, 'The Siyadoni Stone Inscription of Vikrama Samvat 960 to 1025', *EI*, I, 1891, pp. 162–79.

[58] *Periplus Maris Erythraei*, ed. and tr. by L. Casson, Princeton, 1989, p. 83, section 51.

[59] G.F. Hourani, *The Arab Seafaring*, Beirut, 1951.

[60] S.D. Goitein, *Letters of Medieval Jewish Traders*, Princeton, 1973.

clearly recognizes that the merchant millionaire of medieval India (e.g. the Jagat Seths, Baharji Bohra and Abdul Ghafur) played an active role in economic life. If the peddling trade is characterized among other things by uncertainties of the market and favouring transactions in retail, then this gives an insight into the psyche of pedlars and that of the merchant princes.

> . . . They belonged to the fringe of a vast continental society which they were unable to influence, . . . they lived in a world fragmented within itself and unable even to rise to an awareness of its own identity. . . They knew such terrible uncertainties that they were content to live from one to the next. . . They were no pedlars in the scale of their operations, but it is possible that they *remained pedlars somewhere deep in their minds*. (italics mine)[61]

IV

In view of our discussions in the preceding sections it would be difficult to dismiss trade as a sideshow in the economic historiography of early India. One may also take into consideration the futility of harping on the invariant nature of early Indian trade and commerce. Before the 1950s several works on early Indian society and economy had a chapter on ancient trade, treated mostly in a compartmentalized manner. The interrelation of trade with crafts production and urbanization, on the one hand, and the connections between trade and the agrarian sector, on the other, were rarely focused upon. Recent understandings of the early Indian material milieu, especially during the last four decades, are marked with the awareness of the possibilities of changes in social and economic life outside dynastic shifts. This has led to the marking of several stages or phases in early Indian social and economic history.[62]

Periodizing Indian history remains one of the problems of the study

[61] Ashin Das Gupta, Presidential Address, Medieval India section, *PIHC*, Jadavpur session, 1974, p. 107. The above quote is presented not to suggest that a similar mentality necessarily pervaded the functions and thinking of early Indian merchants. There would have surely been a change of mindset in the patterrn and thinking of traders between the early middle ages and the time of the Jagat Seths.

[62] R.S. Sharma, *Perspectives in the Social and Economic History of Early India*, New Delhi, 1983, especially the two chapters entitled, 'Stages in the Ancient Economy', pp. 105–45.

of Indian history. The general notion and the text-book approach very much favour the date AD 1200 or 1206 to mark the end of the ancient and the beginning of the medieval phase in Indian history. The logic, of course, lies in the establishment of the Delhi Sultanate around that time. But the demerits of assigning the watershed between historical epochs on the basis of religious affiliations of political powers are well known. Moreover, the penetration of Islam as a potent political force into the Deccan and the far south took place in the first half of the fourteenth century. All these have resulted in the modification of the traditional chronological divisions. The onset of the 'medieval' period is now placed in *c.* AD 1300 and the pre-1300 phase is designated as 'early' instead of the more popular term 'ancient'. The common notion that the phase up to the end of the thirteenth century was a single and undifferentiated chronological entity has been sharply criticized. The alternative approach to the periodization of Indian history suggests that the early period has the following distinct phases: (i) the pre-literate (more popularly called the pre- and proto-historic)—from the earliest items to *c.* 600 BC; (ii) the early historical—*c.* 600 BC to AD 300; (iii) the late ancient (generally labelled as the Gupta/Classical period—*c.* AD 300–600; and (iv) the early medieval (also known as the post-Gupta) *c.* AD 600–1300. The 'ancient' phase is taken to cover the period from the earliest times to the end of the sixth century. It is differentiated from the 'early medieval' and is considered to be accommodated within the 'early phase' (i.e. up to *c.* 1300) of Indian history.[63]

The history of early Indian trade nowadays is treated not in isolation, but takes into account the then agrarian situation and also the urban scenario. Considerable attention is also paid to the question whether and how far early Indian rulers promoted trade and were interested in the revenue-bearing potential of trade. Accounts of ancient sea voyages for trading purposes are found in both indigenous texts and Classical, Arabic, Persian, Chinese and medieval European accounts which have been utilized by various historians. Of late,

[63] This scheme of terminating the 'ancient' phase around the end of the sixth century AD is not entirely new. H.C. Raychaudhuri, *Political History of Ancient India*, Delhi, 1995 (eighth edition with Commentary by B.N. Mukherjee), closed his study with the end of the sixth century AD. The preference for the term 'early' as a chronological segment up to *c.* AD 1300 is also seen in A.L. Basham (ed.), *A Cultural History of India.*

historians tend to situate the sea-borne trade from and to India in the overall background of the Indian Ocean trade. The role of geography in India's maritime trade can hardly be overestimated. That the subcontinent along with Sri Lanka stands almost at the very centre of the Indian Ocean is an inescapable geographical reality. Prior to the advent of steam navigation, movements of vessels across the greater part of the Indian Ocean were largely guided by the more or less predictable alterations of the monsoon wind system. India, therefore, shared some of the common patterns of maritime trade with many regions of the Indian Ocean. In other words, early Indian sea-borne commerce is being treated now in the overall context of trade in the Indian Ocean which provides a major link—economic, political and cultural—among diverse communities in Asia and Africa (particularly east Africa). Looking at the contributions to the study of India's role in the early Indian Ocean trade, one cannot but note the virtual identification of sea-trade with long-distance oceanic contacts in the current historiography. The scholarly attention to the history of coastal traffic is naturally inadequate. This assumes importance as the subcontinent has two long coast lines in the west and the east, washed respectively by the Arabian Sea and the Bay of Bengal. The story of coastal trade in early India may not offer exciting anecdotes and dramatic actions typically associated with the narratives of sea-borne commerce. The risks, the uncertainties and the spirit of adventure invariably accompanying long-distance high sea voyages have a counterpoint in the relatively more sedate, less flamboyant and safer journeys along the coast. The historian of early Indian trade may not, therefore, be sufficiently attracted to the study of coastal trade and voyages. On the other hand, the strength and vitality of coastal networks lie in the ability to hold their own in the face of a boom and slump in the overseas commerce. Moreover, the coastal networks, converging often at a premier port, were indispensable for the very sustenance of long-distance trade. The pattern of navigation along the coast would also generally remain unaltered, since it was largely shaped by natural factors, e.g. the alteration of the monsoons, the sea currents and the facilities of anchorage. Changes in the patterns and structure of coastal trade are expected to have occurred at a slow pace, sometimes nearly imperceptible. The impressive distribution of Rouletted Ware (RW), datable from *c.* second century BC to the second half of the first century AD (if not even later), virtually along the entire length of the east coast (from Alaganakulam in the Pandyan country to Chandraketugarh in Bengal) certainly speaks of a littoral network. The RW has been reported only from 'urban' and/or notable religious centres, and not from village sites. In fact, the RW sites have been discovered in Sri Lanka (e.g. Kantarodai, Mantai and Anuradhapura), thereby implying linkages between the eastern coast of India and the island.[64] If one looks at the description of the convergence of monks and nuns from diverse places at a Buddhist monastery at Nagarjunakonda (eastern Deccan, Andhra Pradesh) in an inscription of *c.* third century AD, the list of countries includes, among others, the names of Vaṅga (south-eastern and eastern Bengal), Ḍāmila (Tamil-speaking area in the far south) and Tāmraparṇi (Sri Lanka).[65] The epigraphic material corroborates the field archaeological data on coastal linkages along the eastern littoral.[66] These issues will be addressed in the following section.

V

In view of our previous discussions on the periodization of early India from the earliest traceable times to AD 1300, we would like to present here an overview of early Indian trade. But before that a few words about the pieces and extracts selected in this volume. In these selections an element of chronological presentation has been maintained without, however, at all implying a linear development of trade in

[64] Vimala Begley, 'From Iron Age to Early Historical in South Indian Archaeology', in Jerome Jacobson (ed.), *Studies in the Archaeology of India and Pakistan*, Delhi, 1986, pp. 297–319. Begley considers that the Arikamedu RW was not an import, but a regional product, though the technique of decoration must have been imported from the pre-Roman Classical world. She further opines that both the RW and its technology must have been traded extensively.

[65] D.C. Sircar, *Select Inscriptions Bearing on Indian History and Civilization (SI)*, I, Calcutta, 1965, pp. 233–36 (The Nagarjunakonda Inscription of Virapurushadatta, regnal year 14).

[66] A recent attempt at examining coastal trade, with the Konkan area on the western sea-board as a case study, has been made by Ranabir Chakravarti, 'Coastal Trade and Voyages in Konkan: The Early Medieval Scenario', *IESHR*, XXXV, 2, 1998. Sanjay Subrahmanyam, *The Political Economy of Commerce: Southern India 1500–1650*, Delhi, 1990, pp. 46–90 (chapter 2 of the book), stresses the 'complementarities between coastal and overland trade on the one hand and overseas trade on the other'(p. 89).

early India. One of the criteria of selection has certainly been to ensure that they address important issues and controversies related to the study of early Indian trade. Some of the articles and extracts have been selected for the purpose of presenting new evidence of early trade. An archaeological perspective, drawing from field archaeological, epigraphic, numismatic and art historical data, has not been lost sight of in our selection. One of the main aims of this volume is to cater to the needs of graduate, postgraduate and research students for whom a thorough acquaintance with the available sources (suggesting their strengths and limitations alike) for the study of early Indian trade and the methodologies of handling these impressionistic evidences[67] is of immense importance. Attempts have been made to bring in the situations and sources of trade in the Deccan and South India. There is a marked tendency among historians of ancient India to draw broad inferences and generalizations largely on the basis of north Indian and even the Ganga valley situations. It is high time that such an imbalance in historical focus is redressed.

In the light of our recent knowledge of pre-Harappan neolithic and chalcolithic cultures, one may find some dependable evidence of exchange relations among pre-Harappan communities. Most works on early Indian material life generally begin with the far-flung and complex urban economic life in the Harappan civilization. The Harappan economic life in general and trade in particular was, in fact, an elaboration and maturation of a number of trends prevailing in the exchange-oriented activities among several pre-Harappan communities and settlements in the north-western part of the sub-continent. One may name here the highly significant pre-Harappan sites of Mehrgarh in the Bolan valley, Pakistan and Mundigak in Afghanistan. The aceramic neolithic phase at Mehrgarh (around the sixth millennium BC) has yielded, among other objects, turquoise, lapis lazuli and copper. These semi-precious gem-stones and a base metal like copper are likely to have been carried over some distance to Mehrgarh. There is a distinct possibility of their being procured from disparate areas through some exchange mechanisms, though

[67] It is tempting to label such aspects of early trade in India, virtually without any figures and statistics, as qualitative in contrast to the quantifiable data on trade of the early modern and colonial periods. The cue can be taken from L. Udovitch, 'Commercial Techniques in Early Medieval Islamic Trade', in D.S. Richards (ed.), *Islam and the Trade of Asia*, London, 1970, pp. 37–62.

definite information on the pattern and nature of this exchange system is lacking.[68] Mundigak in Afghanistan is another pre-Harappan site, known for its seals which must have been required for some kind of transactions.[69] We highlight the significance of these two sites to suggest that the history of exchanges in South Asia may be pushed back prior to the advent of the first urban society. But the meagre data on transactional activities at these two pre-Harappan sites will not be discussed. Readers may find it uncomfortable to begin the history of Indian trade by grappling with highly sophisticated methods of decoding messages in the fragmented data of preliterate archaeological cultures.

One cannot deny that a much clearer image of exchange-oriented activities is available during the period of the Harappan civilization (*c.* 2500–1750 BC). One of the three great bronze age civilizations of the Old World, the Harappan civilization is known for its flourishing agricultural economy, diversified crafts in stone and metals (no use of iron tools, however) and far-flung trade both within the subcontinent and beyond. Embracing an extensive territory (nearly half a million square miles and larger than the present size of Pakistan) and characterized by remarkable cultural uniformity and maturity, the

[68] Even in the aceramic neolithic phase, the Mehrgarh people had already acquired a distinctly sedentary character, indicated by impressions of cereals on lumps of clay, sickle elements and the remains of mud-brick structures. Mehrgarh as a settlement subsequently assumed a character more complex than a rural habitat. Just prior to *c.* 2500 BC the site becomes integrated with what is called 'early Harappan' and then Mehrgarh was abandoned. See Jean-Francois Jarrige, 'Excavations at Mehrgarh: Their Significance for Understanding the Background of the Harappan Civilization', in G.L. Possehl (ed.), *Harappan Civilization: A Contemporary Perspective*, Delhi, 1982, pp. 79–84; also see Bridget Allchin and F.R. Allchin, *The Rise of Civilization in India and Pakistan.* The discovery of cotton from Mehrgarh merits particular attention. It is commonly believed that the Harappans were the earliest producers and users of cotton. But Mehrgarh distinctly suggests the knowledge and use of cotton in pre-Harappan times.

[69] The complex material culture at pre-Harappan Mundigak may be appreciated in the light of the discovery of granaries, impressive structures with rows of columns and terracotta modelling of mother-goddess figurines. Vide, Bridget Allchin and F.R. Allchin, *The Rise of Civilisation in India and Pakistan.*

Harappan civilization is sometimes labelled an 'empire' with twin capitals, Harappa and Mohenjodaro[70]. The maintenance of uniformity in material life over such a vast area and over several centuries cannot but point to the prevalence of an efficient and impressive authority, though the nature of this authority is difficult to ascertain with present facts.[71] Trade must have been a major ingredient of the non-agrarian sector of the Harappan economy, more so because of the urban character of the material life of the Harappans.

Ever since C.J. Gadd discovered about two dozen seals, either original Harappan seals or close copies of the Harappan ones, from Mesopotamia, there has been a thrust on the study of the long-distance trade of the Harappans.[72] In-depth analyses of artefacts over several decades have led to a more mature understanding of the nature and patterns of contacts of the Harappans. There has been a general consensus among archaeologists that since Sind and the alluvial plains of the Punjab were virtually bereft of useful minerals, the Harappan people must have felt the need to establish exchange relations with diverse areas for the procurement of raw materials. Thus copper could have been brought from Rajasthan, south India, Baluchistan and the Oman peninsula. As the Harappans could have had access to the mines of copper in Rajasthan, the copper of Oman could have been procured by them to provide the metal to Elam and Mesopotamia. The area around the Kolar gold fields in present-day Karnataka was used by the local neolithic communities, it is suggested, to provide the Harappan civilization with gold. Another precious metal, silver, seems to have been

[70] Bridget Allchin and F.R. Allchin, *The Genesis of a Civilization*, Delhi, 1997; Bridget Allchin and F.R. Allchin, *Rise of Civilization in India and Pakistan*, have used this appellation. At the time of the partition of India in 1947 most of the important sites of the Harappan culture were located in Pakistan. The last half century has brought to light a large number of sites in India, thereby enlarging the geographical focus of the civilization. For a statement on this, see B.K. Thapar, *Recent Archaeological Discoveries in India*, Tokyo, 1989. To this must be added the discovery of Dholavira in Cutch; R.S. Bisht, 'Dholavira: New Horizons of the Indus Civilization', *Puratattva*, XX, 1989–90, pp. 71–82.

[71] A recent attempt in this direction has been made by Shereen Ratnagar, *Enquiries into the Political Organization of the Harappan Society*, Pune, 1991.

[72] A.L. Openheim, 'The Seafaring Merchants of Ur', *JAOS*, LXXIV, 1954, pp. 6–17.

available from Iran. The major source of diverse types of semi-precious stones (such as agate, chalcedony, jasper, carnelian, etc.), indispensable for the flourishing bead industry, has been located in western India and the central and western part of the Deccan. The likely area for the supply of jade, a prestige item meant for the craft of the jeweller, is Central Asia. There is little doubt that the Harappans acquired the precious gem lapis lazuli from the Badakshan area in Afghanistan.[73] Shortughai, the northernmost site of the Harappan civilization, lies close to the lapis lazuli mines and seems to have been a Harappan trading outpost to facilitate the procurement of this luxury item.[74] Historiographically speaking, there has been a recent shift from the study of Harappan trade in luxuries to the transactions in necessities. Shereen Ratnagar emphasizes that the procurement of vital resources was a major driving force of the Harappan civilization's far-flung commercial contacts. She highlights the significance of trade in metals of relatively lesser value, as trade in precious metals and minerals, however valuable, has to be associated with the tastes and inclinations of a numerically small (though possibly influential and powerful) group in a given society.[75]

In the very rich and voluminous historiography that exists on Harappan trade, considerable reliance is placed on the evidence of seals which are rightly viewed as trade mechanisms. To this has been added of late the artefactual evidence of the occurrence of a varied and profuse number of items. On the one hand, etched carnelian beads, ivory objects, beads with tubular perforations, barrel-shaped weights, the representation of the bull with the manger (a typically Harappan motif), the trefoil design (inseparably associated with the Harappan culture) must eloquently speak of the contacts of the Harappan civilization with the findspots of these artefacts in West Asia, Oman and Mesopotamia. On the other hand, the discovery of the button seals of the Persian Gulf variety at Lothal is an indicator of contacts between coastal Gujarat and the Gulf. There has been a preference for the study of the external trade of the Harappan civilization, especially with Mesopotamia and Elam. Its major impetus comes from the

[73] Shereen Ratnagar, *Encounters: The Westerly Trade of the Harappans.*

[74] H.P. Francfort, 'The Early Periods of Shortughai (Harappan) and the Western Bactrian Culture of Dashly', in B. Allchin (ed.), *South Asian Archaeology*, Cambridge, 1981, pp. 170–75.

[75] Shereen Ratnagar, *Encounters: The Westerly Trade of the Harappans.*

decipherment of Sumerian and Akkadian cuneiform documents which inform us about the intimate trade relations of Sargonid Akkad with Tilmun/Dilmun, Magan and Meluhha. Though there have been lively controversies about the exact location and identification of these three areas (see Annotated Bibliography), a large number of scholars tend to place Meluhha in the lower Indus valley. The representations of boats/vessels on Harappan terracotta seals, the identification of an impressive harbour with a dockyard at Lothal by S.R. Rao[76] (though his claim for the remains of a dockyard has been contested; see the Annotated Bibliography), and the discovery of Harappan outposts at Suktagendor and Sotkakoh in the Makran littorals strongly suggest the Harappans' interests in maritime trade in the Persian Gulf, the Gulf of Oman and the northern parts of the Arabian Sea. The Harappan maritime trade seems to have maintained close linkages with Bahrain and its adjacent islands of Failaka and Tarul. The occurrence of lapis lazuli objects, ivory pieces and the Indus pictograms (among other items) at the Bahraini site of Ras-al-Qala amply demonstrate such contacts. Moreover, the area is generally identified with Tilmun/Dilmuns, which area however does not appear to have been the producer of such items which, according to the Mesopotamian cuneiform documents, were sent from Tilmun/Dilmun to Mesopotamia. Field archaeological materials from Bahrain and its adjoining areas would correspond to the textual impression that the area functioned as the entrepot in the Gulf maritime trade and therefore could have acted as an intermediary between the Indus valley and Mesopotamia.[77]

There has been admittedly a conspicuous emphasis on the study of the maritime contacts of the Indus civilization, largely on account of the availability of a reasonable amount of data in the West Asian context. Attention has also been paid to the presence of etched carnelian beads—a typical Harappan product—at the Iranian sites of Hissar, Marlik,

[76] S.R. Rao, *Lothal and the Indus Civilization,* Bombay, 1973; S.R. Rao, *Lothal—A Harappan Port Town (1955–62)*, Delhi, 1979–85.

[77] G. Weisgerber, 'Makan and Meluha—Third Millennium BC Copper Production in Oman and the Evidence of Contact with the Indus Valley', in Bridget Allchin (ed.), *South Asian Archaeology*, Cambridge, 1981, pp. 196–201. Previously many archaeologists preferred to equate Makan with the Makran coast where two Harappan sites, Suktagendor and Sotkakoh were located. See Mortimer Wheeler, *The Indus Civilization*, London, 1968 (third edition).

Shahdad and Bakum and also at Mundigak in southern Afghanistan. These would portray 'contacts between the Indus civilization and neighbouring regions. It is evident that the region was an integral part of the interregional network of exchange or trade of specific items emanating from their respective production centres.'[78] Thanks to the significant studies of the materials from the Iranian site of Tepe Yahya by Lamberg-Karlovsky, the Indus valley trade with Iran, obviously overland in nature, is now an important part of the literature on Harappan trade. In fact, the location of Tepe Yahya strongly suggests that it provided a linkage between the Mesopotamian and the Indus cultures.[79]

The numbers of Indus-like objects in West Asian sites is rather poor and may not imply a sizeable scale of trade. The Mesopotamian products or the Mesopotamian-inspired items are even rarer in India. Lamberg-Karlovsky explains that the inadequacy of the material evidence of the exchangeable items was mainly due to the 'indirect contact-trade' between the Mesopotamian and the Harappan civilizations. The widespread distribution of some Harappan products, such as bangles (mainly produced at Chanhudaro) and etched carnelian beads may indicate that a significant aspect of the Harappan trade was in the transaction of manufactured or finished goods. In other words, Harappan merchants may not have been interested merely in the procurement of raw materials. It is, of course, not easy to ascertain whether and to what extent Harappan trade was geared to the distribution of essentials or was sustained by an urge for the exchange of luxuries. What is more or less certain is that the use of a standardized script (also a standardized language?), the utilization of seals and sealings and weights and measures must have largely facilitated the trading activities of the Harappans. It is difficult to assess the position of merchants in the Harappan urban society, though Kosambi strongly argued for their social pre-eminence.[80] In this context a residential structure unearthed from Banawali (Hissar district, Haryana) may be considered. It has yielded more than one seal, a few weights and a large number of jars embedded in the floor of the

[78] B.K. Thapar and M. Rafique Mughal, *op. cit.*, in *History of Humanity*, I, p. 257.

[79] C.C. Lamberg-Karlovsky, 'Trade Mechanism in Indus–Mesopotamian Inter-relations', *JAOS*, 92, 1972, pp. 222–29.

[80] D.D. Kosambi, *op. cit.*, p. 80.

house. The discovery of these objects led R.S. Bisht, the excavator, to identify the house as the dwelling of a merchant. The house, moreover, has a sitting room, paved with mud bricks, and a bathroom fitted with a wash basin, located near the drain to carry off waste water from the house to the main drain on the street. It gives the impression that the dwelling merchant was probably well off.[81]

These preliminary comments on Harappan trade would indicate why our selection of essays/extracts opens with two essays on this theme, respectively by Shereen Ratnagar and M. Tosi. Tosi enlightens us on the long-distance contacts of the Harappans with the 'west', i.e. the Akkadian and Omanese contacts. Of particular significance is his discussion on the visual representation of the interpreter of the Meluhhan language on a cuneiform tablet. Shereen Ratnagar's essay addresses many of the debates and issues related to the Harappan connection with the Euphrates and the Tigris valleys. Such debates have certainly enriched our understanding of the Harappan trade and helped fresh probes into the subject (see Annotated Biblio-graphy).

The scenario of exchange-oriented activities during the period from the second half of the second millennium BC to about the seventh century BC is sharply different from the image of the Harappan trade. Our main source of information is the vast Vedic literature which throws light on the period from *c.* 1500 to 600 BC. A perusal of the *Ṛgveda* shows that the major settlement was located in the area watered by the Indus and its western and eastern tributaries. In the conventional historiography of early Indian economic life, the *Ṛgveda* is considered to have contained some data on trade. Attention has been drawn to descriptions of wealthy *paṇis* undertaking distant journeys for substantial gains (*śatadhana*). Reading into the accounts of *paṇis* have led many historians to consider them as the forerunners of the regular *vaṇiks*. The Rgvedic term *niṣka* has been occasionally taken to mean a gold coin. But this meaning of the term *niṣka* is seen in the sources of the Gupta period (AD fourth–sixth centuries) and it is hazardous to interpret the Rgvedic term in the light of a much later connotation. On the other hand, the *Ṛgveda* leaves an unmistakable impression that *puras* (i.e. fortified or walled settlements) were nearly

[81] R.S. Bisht, 'Excavations at Banawali: 1974–77', in G.L. Possehl (ed.), *Harappan Civilization: A Contemporary Perspective*, Delhi, 1982, pp. 113–24.

an anathema to the Rgvedic people.[82] Probings into the text do underline that the material life of the *Ṛgveda* was steeped in cattle keeping and animal breeding activities. There is little doubt that cattle wealth (*godhana*) constituted the most important aspect of the social wealth of the Rgvedic days. According to one estimation, there are 176 references to the term *go* and only about thirty-three references to agriculture. It would be difficult to imagine the prevalence of regular commercial activities in such a material background. The *Ṛgveda* therefore speaks of a sharp rupture from the urban Harappan economy.[83] The text-book image that 'haggling in the market was well-known'[84] in the Rgvedic society may not stand scrutiny. Textual gleanings from the *Rgveda* have also been used to show the prevalence of seafaring in the second half of the second millennium BC. The term *samudra* occasionally figures in the text. Attention has also been drawn to the term *nau* (vessel) and *śatāritranau* (vessel fitted with a hundred oars). Such descriptions were earlier taken in their literal sense. Given the navigational technology of the time, it would be difficult to accept the existence and regular use of vessels with a hundred oars. Moreover, scholars are not unanimous if the term *samudra* really stood for the sea and whether the Rgvedic people could differentiate the sea from the vast sheet of water of the Indus at the point of its confluence with the Arabian Sea. That the *Ṛgveda* was acquainted with regular seafaring is claimed on the basis of the expression *śatāritranau* and the praise of the *samudra* by a person going through it (*Ṛgveda* IV.50). In the light of the predominantly semi-pastoral material culture of the Rgvedic people it would be, however, difficult to construct an account of their regular seaborne commercial activities.[85]

[82] For a conventional narrative on the economic activities, including exchanges, during the Rgvedic times, see N.C. Bandyopadhyay, *Economic Life and Progress in Ancient India*, Calcutta, 1945; also R.C. Majumdar (ed.), *The Vedic Age*, Bombay, 1951, pp. 398–403; a more incisive analysis is provided by W. Rau, *Staat und Gesellschaft im alten Indien,* Weisfaden, 1957.

[83] R.S. Sharma, *Material Culture and Social Formations in Ancient India,* pp. 22–55.

[84] R.C. Majumdar (ed.), *The Vedic Age*, p. 399.

[85] The controversy among scholars on the knowledge of the sea and the possibility of seafaring activities during the early Vedic age is available in A.A. McDonell and A.B. Keith, *Vedic Index of Names and Subjects*, II, London, 1912, pp. 431–33.

The later Vedic literature suggests the gradual shift of Vedic settlements from the Punjab to the east and south-east. The combined evidence of the later Vedic texts and the more or less coeval Painted Grey Ware (PGW) culture[86] indicates that the principal settlement area of this period penetrated into the fertile Ganga valley[87]. It is hardly surprising that available information speaks of agriculture as the mainstay of economic life and also indicates developments in crafts (including the use of iron tools, mainly for offensive and defensive purposes and the manufacture of pottery). There is also a corresponding increase in our data on exchange-oriented activities than that presented by the *Ṛgveda*. The wealthy *paṇi* continues to figure in the *Atharvaveda* and the *Vājasaneyī Saṁhitā*. The term *vaṇij*, generally meaning a petty dealer or trader, figures in the *Vājasaneyī Saṁhitā* and the *Taittirīya Brāhmaṇa*. The *Atharvaveda* gives an impression of some of the exchangeable items like *durśa* (garments), *pavasta* (coverlets) and *ajina* (deerskin). If the first two are finished/ manufactured items, the third one seems to have been procured from the pastoral and hunting-gathering groups. Some areas began to be associated with certain exchangeable items: Gandharan wool, and the *guggula* or incense from the lower Indus area and horses from Sindhu country. The *Atharvaveda* furnishes a prayer of a *vaṇij* to Indra for ensuring success in his ventures: Indra is invoked as his 'guide and leader, chasing ill-will, wild beasts and highway robbers'. No less interesting is the mention of the *kusīdin* or the usurer in the *Śatapatha Brāhmaṇa* and the reference to *kusīda* in the sense of borrowing in the *Taittirīya Saṁhitā*.[88] In keeping with these developments, a few references to certain terms can be seen denoting weight systems related to metallic pieces. The smallest of such units of weight standards is designated *kṛṣnala* (berry of *abrus precatorius*), equivalent

86 For a general introduction to the Painted Grey Ware, see A. Ghosh, *op. cit.*

87 This area embraced the Indo-Ganga divide, the upper Ganga valley and the Ganga-Yamuna doab, with Brahmarṣideśa (the land between the Sarasvatī and the Dṛṣadvatī, located in present-day Haryana) as the most coveted area (*śiṣṭadeśa*). Vide H.C. Raychaudhuri, *Studies in Indian Antiquity*, Calcutta, 1957 for the location of Brahmarṣideśa/Śiṣṭadeśa.

88 R.C. Majumdar (ed.), *The Vedic Age*, pp. 465–66 for a general description; also see N.C. Bandyopadhyaya, *op. cit.* An analytical study of the changing material milieu of the later Vedic period is presented by R.S. Sharma, *Material Culture and Social Formations in Ancient India*, pp. 56–88.

to 1.8 grain. This appears to have been the basic unit of weight (*māna*). The term *śatamāna*, the highest unit in the weight standard, should denote 1.8 grain x 100 = 180 grains. Later Vedic texts describe the *śatamāna* as made of either gold or silver, i.e. of precious metals. These terms have often been taken to denote metallic pieces of definite weight standard, meant for circulation. In other words, many economic historians argue in favour of the presence of a metallic medium of exchange or coins in the later Vedic period.[89] Empirically speaking, the main problem of accepting such a position is that the earliest specimen of Indian coinage cannot be placed before *c.* 600 BC. Such coins are found from hoards at Taxila and Chaman-i-Huzuri (near Kabul) along with other coins which cannot be dated prior to 600 BC. Though more information is furnished by the later Vedic literature on the exchange of products than the *Ṛgveda*, regular trade based on monetary transactions cannot be expected to have emerged. From the point of view of the study of material culture, the later Vedic texts have been mainly surveyed and analysed to explain the emergence of sedentary agricultural settlements in the Ganga valley and the advent of the *varṇa*-based social norms, providing the necessary ideology to the growing power of the ruler (the Kṣatriya)[90]. Interestingly enough, the *Gṛhyasūtra* dealing with domestic rites and rituals, prescribes the performance of the *paṇyasiddhi* rite to ensure success in trade. This shows that rituals of sacrifices were used at times for profits in trading ventures.[91] This might further suggest that though the economic significance of *paṇya* or exchange of items is recognized, trade was yet to be strongly rooted to the then economy which is characterized as 'prestation economy'. The prestation economy, however, was not bereft of the elements of exchanges promoted by ritual performances. At this juncture, it would be appropriate to place before the reader the study by Romila Thapar of *dāna* and *dakṣiṇā*,

[89] A.A. McDonell and A.B. Keith, *The Vedic Index*, I: 185 (*kṛṣṇala*), II, pp. 128–29 (*māna*).

[90] Though the later part of the Vedic period witnessed many changes in material life, the society was yet to experience a well-developed state system. R.S. Sharma, *Origin of the State in India*, Bombay, 1990, situates the later Vedic material culture on the threshold of the state system.

[91] Romila Thapar, *From Lineage to State*, Delhi, 1984. The Gṛhyasūtra belongs to the period which witnessed the emergence of urban centres in the Ganga valley (around the seventh–sixth centuries BC).

two socio-religious practices with strong ritual support, as forms of exchange. She was evidently inspired by the celebrated anthropological inquiries into gifts by Marcell Mauss which we have already discussed above. Romila Thapar's contribution shows us how interesting formulations on material life can be arrived at by using sacred texts with the help of a new methodology.

VI

The period of nearly three centuries from the sixth century BC to *c.* 325 BC is considered a landmark in Indian history on various counts. A number of new tendencies began to surface with significant consequences in the history of the subcontinent. The most apparent change can be traced in the political situation. A number of territorial states (*mahājanapadas*), both monarchical and non-monarchical (*gaṇarājyas*) are encountered for the first time. Early Buddhist texts mention sixteen such powers. There is a noticeable concentration of major *mahājanapadas* in the middle Ganga valley, covering eastern UP and Bihar. This in fact is the main theatre of the interplay of many new forces and changes. The political scene is marked by the gradual ascendancy of Magadha (in south Bihar), and by the second half of the fourth century BC Magadha was invincible in all of north India.[92] The social and cultural scene offers no less exciting changes in that it saw the emergence and rise of a number of new and heretical religious ideas that did not conform to the ritual-oriented Vedic religion and the social and ritual pre-eminence of the brāhmaṇa. Foremost among these were Buddhism, Jainism and Ajivikism. These have often been judged as protestant socio-religious movements, strongly negating the cult of *yajñas* or sacrifices. The most significant change in the material culture is clearly visible in the emergence of urban centres in the Ganga valley. Since the decline of the Harappan civilization, cities for the first time appeared in the subcontinent; that is why it is designated as the second urbanization in Indian history and also called the Ganga valley civilization. The emergence of urban centres in north India, moreover, coincides with the arrival of minted metallic pieces as the medium of exchange, i.e. coins. All these emphatically point to the burgeoning of the economy, especially its non-agrarian sector.

[92] See in this context, H.C. Raychaudhuri, *Political History of Ancient India*, eighth edition.

An understanding of trade during this period has to be situated in this context. The urban development in the Ganga valley during the time of the Buddha, however, cannot be divorced at all from the then agrarian milieu. The non-food-producing residents of the urban area (i.e. specialist and wholetime craftsmen, merchants, rulers and administrators and religious leaders) could be sustained by the secure supply of food generated in the surrounding rural area or in distant hinterlands. The availability of agrarian surplus in the Ganga valley can, therefore, be reasonably inferred. Historians are sharply divided in their explanations of the generation of this agrarian surplus, i.e. whether by technological improvements (use of iron tools), by politico-administrative institutions or by natural factors.[93]

Historians' inquiries and lively debates are facilitated by the availability of diverse sources for this period: both textual and field archaeological materials have been effectively utilized. Textual information is mostly furnished by Buddhist texts in Pali and to some extent by the Jaina texts in Prakrit. The famous grammatical treatise, the *Aṣṭādhyāyī* of Pāṇini, also belongs to the same period and has been utilized for gleaning data on material life. Though the Buddhist and the Jaina canonical literature are of course religious literature, they contain more matter-of-fact notices of the socio-economic and political situations than the voluminous Vedic literature dealing largely with the performances of *yajñas* and rituals. But one cannot ignore the fact that none of the Pali canonical texts was contemporary to the Buddha. The master always preached verbally and it was only after his *parinirvāṇa* that the principal tenets of Buddhism were reduced to writing. Thus all Buddhist canonical texts belong to a period later than the time of the Buddha himself. Only the texts of definitely pre-Maurya date (viz. *Vinayapiṭaka*, *Dighanikāya*, *Majjhimanikāya*, *Aṅguttaranikāya*, *Saṁyuttanikāya* and *Suttanipāta*) can be considered as having reliably retained some impressions of the conditions of the Ganga valley in the sixth–fifth centuries BC. Besides, recent scholar-

93 A. Ghosh, *The City in Early Historical India*, Simla, 1973; R.S. Sharma, 'Iron and Urbanization in the Ganga Valley', *IHR*, I, 1974, pp. 98–103; Ranabir Chakravarti, 'Early Historical India: A Study in Its Material Milieu', in Debiprasad Chattopadhyaya (ed.), *History of Science and Technology in Ancient India*, II, Calcutta, 1991, pp. 305–45; K.T.S. Sarao, *Urban Centres and Urbanization as Reflected in the Pali Vinaya and Sutta Piṭakas*, Delhi, 1990; D.K. Chakrabarti, *Theoretical Issues in Indian Archaeology*, Delhi, 1988.

ship seriously questions the long-standing use of the *Jātaka* stories (related to stories of the previous births of the Buddha) for understanding the material culture during the time of the Buddha.[94] The literary data are now effectively combined with the archaeological evidence to demonstrate the unmistakable growth of cities, structural activities in brick, use of iron technology, arrival of the new and advanced pottery technology—the Northern Black Polished Ware—and the emergence of coinage in north India in general and the Ganga plains in particular[95]. The appreciable change in the material milieu is evident in the distinct preference of the Buddha and also Mahāvīra for urban centres (*nagara*) to rural settlements for preaching and residence. The *Sūtra* texts, on the other hand, viewed cities with scorn and suspicion and recommended the performance of penances for visiting cities as the city signified permanent non-study (*anadhyāya*) of the Vedas.[96]

The principal wealth-producing community in the *varṇa*-divided society was the vaiśya. The later Vedic literature ascribed to the vaiśya the occupations of agriculture, cattle-keeping and trade, but systematically subjected him to numerous disabilities. There was only a thin line of demarcation between the vaiśya and the lowest *varṇa*, the śūdra.[97] That the two upper *varṇas* stood in opposition to the two lower ones is clearly evident from the later Vedic texts. The same occupations (*kasi*, *go-rakkha* and *vanijja*) are branded in Pali canons as noble ones (*ukkaṭṭhakammas*), fit to be taken up by men of high status (*ukkaṭṭhakulas*), including the khattiya, the bamhana and the gahapati.[98] The contrasts in the attitudes to trade in Vedic and Buddhist texts cannot be missed. There is also a corresponding approval of trade as a profession in the Jaina ideals. The excessive emphasis of the Jaina canons on non-violence considered that some living beings could be unintentionally killed during ploughing; but no such

[94] The point has been driven home by N. Wagle, *Society at the Time of the Buddha*, Bombay, 1966.

[95] R.S. Sharma, *Material Culture and Social Formations in Ancient India*, pp. 89–134; R.S. Sharma, *Perspectives on the Social and Economic History of Early India*, pp. 118–27.

[96] N. Wagle, *op. cit.*

[97] R.C. Majumdar (ed.), *The Vedic Age*, pp. 455–56.

[98] A recent discussion on this changing attitude to trade is available in Uma Chakravarti, *The Social Dimensions of Early Buddhism*, Delhi, 1987.

harmful effects were perceived in trade; therefore, trade was preferred to agriculture in the Jaina tenets.[99]

Among diverse types of traders the *seṭṭhi* (i.e. Sanskrit *śreṣṭhī*) figures prominently for the first time in the Pali canonical literature as the merchant par excellence and hence is so called. The description that he possessed eighty crores of wealth (*asitikoṭivibha*) is certainly an exaggerated and stereotyped one, but nevertheless it recognizes his fabulous wealth, gained obviously through trade. An interesting comparison and contrast between *kasi* and *vaṇijjā* is found in the following account. Agriculture required constant care and supervision and was full of uncertainties and problems; it would yield profuse wealth only when the cultivator was very successful. *Vaṇijjā*, on the other hand, was a less tiresome profession and despite the uncertainties there were definite possibilities of great profit within a short period.[100] In a dialogue with Sariputta, the Buddha commented that there could be four possible outcomes for a person connected to trade (*vaṇijjayutta*): it could end in failure (*chedagāminī*), it could bring less success than expected (*na yathābhippāya*), it could be as successful as anticipated (*yathābhippāya*), and it could yield much in excess than expected gain (*parābhippāya*).[101] The Buddhist texts also seem to have been aware of several other types of traders, besides the *seṭṭhi*. One encounters therein the *sātthavāha* or the caravan trader, often described to have undertaken distant journeys from the eastern (*puvvanta*) to the western limits (*aparānta*). The *Dīghanikāya* tells us about a *sātthavāha*'s journey across the desert with a thousand wagons (*gośakaṭa*) with his merchandise.[102] According to another story, the wandering Buddha met Belaṭṭha Kaccana, a dealer in an essential commodity like molasses.[103] An examination into the Pali texts shows that the *pāpanika* (shopkeeper), the *krayavikrayika* (retail dealer), *vasanika* (investor of money) and *vaṇija*

[99] J.C. Jain, *Economic Life in Ancient India as Depicted by Jaina Canonical Literature*, Varanasi, 1980.

[100] *Majjhimanikāya*, ed., V. Treckner and Lord Chalmers, London, 1838–99, II, p. 232.

[101] *Aṅguttaranikāya,* ed., R. Morris and E. Hardf, London, 1885–1900, II, pp. 81–2.

[102] *Dīghanikāya*, ed., T.W. Rhys Davids and J.E. Carpenter, London, 1890–1911, I, p. 71.

[103] *Aṅguttaranikāya*, I, p. 83.

(petty trader) were considered as distinct types of traders.[104] Another prominent type of dealer appears as the *seṭṭhi-gahapati*. The Pali texts, however, never use the three apparently similar terms, *seṭṭhi*, *gahapati* and *seṭṭhi-gahapati*, as synonymous ones. While the *seṭṭhi* was a very wealthy merchant, the *gahapati* seems to have been noted for his sizeable landholdings. The *seṭṭhi-gahapati* occasionally figures in the Pali texts as a wealthy person who invests some money with a shopkeeper or a tailor (*tunnavāya*) or a weaver (*tantuvāya*). One may reasonably infer that some prosperous *gahapatis* probably invested a part of their wealth, derived mainly from their landed estates, in small business enterprises. Their profession was not directly trade, but closely associated with it. Judged in this light, trading activities appear to have been linked in a way with the agrarian sector. But more significantly it clearly shows the social approval and encouragement of accumulation of wealth by rich landowners who could also act as investors in trade.[105] This once again speaks of the changing material and ideological milieu in the sixth-fifth centuries BC. The central importance of the cult of sacrifices (*yajñas*) in the Vedic texts would have required the utilization of the excess or surplus resources in the *yajñas*; there is little compatibility between the accumulation of wealth through trade and investment and the furtherance of the cult of Vedic *yajñas*. The negation of the ritual-oriented sacrifices must have been beneficial to wealthy people, some of whom could be in a position to give part of their wealth on loan for making further monetary gain. The rise of the *seṭṭhi-gahapati* as an investor seems to have been an outcome of this changed socio-religious attitude to *yajñas*. It is, therefore, consistent with the development of socio-economic life that loan (*iṇa* i.e. *ṛṇa*) is viewed in the Pali canons as essential for launching and maintaining an enterprise (*kammante payojeyya*). But the borrower is advised that he must be able to repay the loan and also maintain his family.[106] It is clearly stated that from any business (*yena kenāci kammaṭṭhānena*) a person may begin by earning half a *kāhāpaṇa* (a coin term), then 50 *kāhāpaṇas* daily. When his gains are 100 *kāhāpaṇas* per day he becomes well off and a rich man when his venture yields the daily return of 1000 *kāhāpaṇas*.[107] The regular

[104]Romila Thapar, *From Lineage to State*, pp. 100–101.
[105]See in this context, N. Wagle, *op. cit.* p. 154; Romila Thapar, *From Lineage to State*, p. 102.
[106]*Dīghanikāya*, I, p. 71.
[107]*Aṅguttaranikāya*, V, p. 83.

interactions and linkages between the new religious ideas and the mercantile community are clearly illustrated by the Buddhist narratives of itinerant monks and merchants sharing the same shelter during the prolonged rainy season (*vassāvāsa*).

That trade was well established in the material life of north India is also portrayed by the famous grammatical treatise, the *Aṣṭādhyāyī* of Pāṇini. The grammarian, however, is silent on *seṭṭhis* and uses the generic term *vaṇij* to denote a merchant. The area around present-day Sialkot—Pānini's native land—in the north-west probably did not experience the emergence of the millionaire merchant comparable to the *seṭṭhīs* of the middle Ganga valley. Nevertheless, Pāṇini informs us of different types of *vaṇij:* e.g. *go-vaṇija* (cattle dealer), *aśva-vaṇija* (horse trader), *Gāndhārī vaṇija* and *Madra vaṇija.*[108] Pāṇini's classification of the *vaṇij* is thus made either on the basis of the commodities they dealt in or of the areas they traded in or with both.

The Pali literature further provides us with images of routes of communications. The Buddha and his wandering *bhikkhus* must have followed well-traversed routes. Thus the Buddha on his last journey, according to the *Mahāparinivvāṇasuttanta*, started from Rājagaha in south Bihar and went through Amabalaṭhṭhika, Nālanda, Pāṭaligāma, Koṭigāma, Vaiśālī, Pāva and Kuśinārā where he attained his *parinirvāṇa*. The *Suttanipāta* account of Baveru's journey from Patiṭṭhāna (Pratiṣṭhāna or Paithan in the central Deccan) to Sāvatthi (Śrāvastī, the capital of Kośala *mahajānapada*, i.e. the present-day Lucknow-Gonda-Faizabad-Bahraich region in UP) amply demonstrates a long overland route passing through Māhissati (Mandhata, Nimar dt., MP), Ujeni (Ujjain, MP), Vedisā (near Bhopal, MP), Tumbavana (Tumain in eastern MP) and Kauśāmbī (near Allahabad, UP).[109] This has been rightly described as a north-south trunk road of great antiquity. The most famous physician of the age of the Buddha, Jīvaka is described to have undertaken a journey from Takkhasilā (Taxila near Rawalpindi, Pakistan) to Bhadraṁkara (Sialkot), Udumbara (Pathankot) and Rohitaka (Rohtak). It probably has a close correspondence to the Uttarāpatha (northern) route of Pāṇini. These

[108]V.S. Agrawala, *India as Known to Pāṇini*, Lucknow, 1953, pp. 238–41. Pāṇini is known to have been born at Śālātura which was situated close to present-day Sialkot in the Punjab.

[109]A.N. Bose, *The Social and Rural Economy of Northern India*, II, Calcutta, 1967, p. 41.

literary impressions of considerable movements, contacts and communications in the greater parts of north India are further corroborated by the distribution of the archaeological sites yielding NBPW. The NBPW does not merely betray an advanced pottery-manufacturing technology (superior to the previous PGW), but also seems to have been a luxury product, mainly encountered at urban sites. In other words, the distribution of the NBPW sites speaks of a distinct network of exchange. The early NBPW, dated from 600 BC to 300 BC, is undoubtedly a product of the middle Ganga valley. Its archaeological occurrence is noted from Charasadda (ancient Puskalavati, near Peshawar in Pakistan), Taxila (near Rawalpindi, Pakistan), Ludhiana, Hissar, Ambala, Rohtak, Kurukshetra, Amritsar, Gurudaspur (sites in the Punjab and Haryana), Mathura, Agra, Aligarh, Meerut, Bulandshahr, Etawah, Etah, Lucknow, Gorakhpur, Basti, Varanasi, Allahabad, Fatehpur, Mirzapur, Azamgarh (sites in UP), Gaya, Patna, Saran, Monghyr and Purnea (sites in Bihar).[110] The flat Gangetic plains must have been naturally conducive to commercial movements and political integration as well. The Ganga itself appears to have facilitated inland riverine communication, as is indicated by several Buddhist stories; but the role of north Indian rivers, in providing suitable communication channels has only occasionally been highlighted in the economic historiography of early India.[111]

In addition to the NBPW, another archaeological material provides solid evidence of brisk commerce in north India. This is the stratified evidence of the use of coins coming from the north-west. The earliest known coins are called punch-marked coins, mostly made of silver (occasionally of copper) and may be the same as the *kāhāpaṇa/ kārṣāpaṇa* type of coins figuring in literary sources. Of the 1,171 pieces found in the Taxila hoard of coins, datable to the last quarter of the fourth century BC, as many as 1,055 were of the punch-marked variety. Similarly, a handsome number of punch-marked coins were reported from the Chaman-i-Huzuri hoard near Kabul, also ascribed to *c.* fifth–fourth centuries BC.[112] Textual evidence would suggest that

[110] A. Ghosh (ed.), *An Encyclopaedia of Indian Archaeology*, I, Delhi, 1989.

[111] S.G. Darian, 'The Economic History of the Ganges to the End of the Gupta Times', *JESHO*, XIII, 1970, pp. 67–87.

[112] J. Marshall, *Taxila*, II, Cambridge, 1951, pp. 843–45; P. Curiel and D. Schlumberger, *Tresors monetaires d'Afghanistan*, Paris, 1953, pp. 31ff; B.N. Mukherjee, *The Techniques of Minting Coins in Ancient and Medieval India*, Delhi, 1997, pp. 4, 13–14, especially note 13.

the *kārṣāpaṇa* coin was struck on the weight standard of 32 *ratis*, i.e. 57.5 grains. These punch-marked coins are uninscribed and carry several marks as symbols. The exact issuing authority of these coins cannot be ascertained. It has been conjectured that the earliest punch-marked coins were struck by merchants or mercantile organizations like the *śreṇī*. These lengthy comments on the growing importance of trade in the economic life in north India from the sixth century BC onwards are made to highlight the changing material culture in the Ganga valley. Though there have been many in-depth studies of trade during the time of the Buddha, these are largely (barring a few exceptions) based on the *Jātaka* stories. The present genre of research on early historical times, however, is more inclined to the study of urbanization and state formation in the Ganga valley than on that of trade[113], despite the availability of better documentation. That is why no representative article on the trade of this period has been included in this volume. (For detailed comments see Annotated Biblio-graphy.)

The Mauryan period (*c.* 324–187 BC) is generally considered as a landmark in terms of the developments in state polity and changing material conditions. The Mauryas carved out an almost pan-Indian empire. Designated variously as *rājaviṣaya* (the royal domain), *vijita* (conquered territory), Jambudvīpa and Pṛthvī in Asokan edicts, the empire stretched from Afghanistan in the north to Karnataka in the south and from Kathiawad in the west to Kalinga (if not up to north Bengal) in the east.[114] It has been suggested that the empire may be viewed as consisting of three zones: (a) Magadha in Bihar as the metropolitan state, (b) the core areas incorporating the erstwhile *mahājanapadas* (territorial states), and (c) peripheral regions.[115] The previous perception of the Maurya empire as a unitary and monolithic

[113]There are several studies of the processes of state formation and urbanization in north India during this period. For a recent statement on these aspects with a distinct emphasis on archaeological evidence, see F.R. Allchin *et al.*, *The Archaeology of Early Historic South Asia, City and State Formation*. The work highlights the interrelatedness between urbanization and the rise of the territorial state, as both are held as signifiers of social change.

[114]For the political history of the Mauryas, vide H.C. Raychaudhuri, *Political History of Ancient India*, eighth edition, with Commentary; the Commentary contains extensive discussions on the recent addition to our knowledge of the Mauryan rule.

[115]Romila Thapar, *The Mauryas Revisited*, Calcutta, 1987.

state has of late been replaced by the image of a very powerful state with a distinct urge for centripetality, but not without imbalances and uneven developments in the material culture in the three zones mentioned above. It has also been recognized that the Mauryas systematically exploited the resources of the peripheral zones for the development of its metropolitan state. The vast Mauryan empire was carved out and maintained by a large army and an equally impressive administrative organization. This would have required enormous resources, which were collected by the Mauryas through a well-established revenue system. Agricultural and craft production and also trade were in part state-controlled and in part managed by parallel non-governmental enterprises which were under the supervision of the state authority. The Mauryas are duly credited for giving the state a participatory role in the production and distribution of commodities for the first time in Indian history. Mauryan studies in recent decades have focused more on the nature of the Maurya state than on the economic history of the realm. Besides, the researches of the economic historian are more preoccupied with the study of agrarian conditions in the Maurya realm. That agriculture and the revenue from the agrarian sector must have been the mainstay of their economy cannot be refuted. But that was, of course, considerably supplemented by levies on trade, if the recommendations of the *Arthaśāstra* and the observations of the Classical authors on trade are taken into consideration. The spread of the use of NBPW and punch-marked coins over the greater parts of India since *c.* 300 BC is also compatible with the literary evidence of trade during the Mauryan times. According to the Classical accounts, the *astynomoi*, a category of municipal officers at Pāṭaliputra, had the joint responsibility of looking after markets, harbours and temples. A number of them were directly entrusted with the care of foreigners, supervision of merchants' activities and collection of one-tenth of the sale proceeds from merchants. The Mauryas, therefore, appear to have appreciated the importance of urban centres such as Pāṭaliputra as centres of commerce, including long-distance external trade.[116]

The state supervision and control of trade is advocated in stronger terms in the *Kauṭilīya Arthaśāstra* . We are told that the overall super-

[116]U.N. Ghoshal, *A History of Indian Public Life,* II, London, 1966; R.S. Sharma, *Perspectives in the Social and Economic History of Early India,* pp. 128–36; G. Bongard-Levin, *Mauryan India*, Delhi, 1985.

vision and the framing of the commercial policy of the state are entrusted to the *paṇyādhyakṣa* or the Director of Trade. The *paṇyādhyakṣa* is to oversee trade both within the realm (*svaviṣaya*) and abroad (*paraviṣaya*). His thorough knowledge of diverse items of trade, their respective countries of origin, the manner and mode of their being brought to the trade centre and the fluctuations in their demand and prices is strongly recommended. The *Arthaśāstra* expects the *paṇyādhyakṣa* to choose between a wide distribution (*vikṣepa*) and a single-channel centralized distribution (*saṁkṣepa*) policy, depending upon the condition of glut or scarcity of exchangeable commodities. The *paṇyādhyakṣa* ideally should strike a balance between the economic interests of the producer and those of the consumer by directly intervening in transactions. One of his duties is also to arrange for the sale of royal items (*rājapaṇya*) produced in royal farms (*sītā*) and manufactories (*karmāntas*). In spite of his distrust of merchants, Kauṭilya seems to have promoted foreign trade. Imported goods are liberally encouraged, literally with favourable invitation (*parabhūmijaṁ paṇyamanugraheṇāvāhayet*). Moreover, sailors and caravan merchants coming from abroad are allowed certain fiscal remissions (*nāvikasārthavāhebhyaśca pariharamatikṣamaṁ dadyāt*). The same spirit is displayed when the text recommends (IV. 2.28–30) 10 per cent profit for the foreign commodities and only 5 per cent profit for the indigenous goods. Perhaps the most interesting concession granted to the foreign merchant is that he should not be sued in a court of law for disputes in money matters (*anabhiyogāścārtheṣvāgantunām*).

The *paṇyādhyakṣa* is also entrusted with the state's trading abroad (*paraviṣaya*). Kauṭilya clearly stresses that the *paṇyādhaykṣa* should explore the profit potentials from both the export and import trade. In case of there being no profit from this trade (*astyudaye*), he should assess the possibilities of economic advantages of barter. Kauṭilya the advises the *paṇyādhyakṣa* to go wherever there is profit and to avoid a situation of no profit (*yato lābhastato gacchet, alābhaṁparivarjayet*).[117]

The *Arthaśāstra* seems to have been well aware of the revenue-bearing potential of trade, including foreign trade. This would be implied by the *durga* (fortified urban centre) being considered the first head of revenue, ahead of the *rāṣṭra* or the countryside (i.e. the agrarian

[117] *Kauṭilīya Arthaśāstra*, ed. and tr. by R.P. Kangle, *op. cit.*; the functions of the *paṇyādhyakṣa* figures in II. 16.

sector).[118] In this perhaps lies the logic of creating a post of the Director of Tolls and Customs (*śulkādhyakṣa*); the *śulka* must have been imposed on long-distance trade, including foreign trade. The imported commodity is to be levied a duty of one-fifth of the value of the said item. The *śulkādhyakṣa*'s functions are oriented towards the collection of tolls and administrative control over traders as well.[119] His duties along with the assignments of the *paṇyadhyakṣa* are envisaged as ensuring overall state control over trade and also financial advantage to the state authority. It is difficult to determine whether and to what extent the Mauryas actually controlled and supervised trade. In other words, it is pertinent to ask whether the impressions we get about Mauryan supervision of trade are mainly confined to Kauṭilya's recommendations and ideals. The prescriptions of the *Arthaśāstra* to impose state control on trade may have some correspondence to what Polanyi termed as 'administered trade'.

The Mauryan attitude to the sea and maritime trade is not directly known. However, Megasthenes considered that the Mauryas had a state monopoly on shipbuilding.[120] The veracity of this statement cannot be ascertained. But the *Arthaśastra* recommends the state supervision of shipping under the officer, *nāvadhyakṣa* (Director of Shipping, *Arthaśāstra* II.28). One has to take into account the fact that the Mauryan realm included within it long stretches of coastal strip on both the sea-boards of India. Among the findspots of Aśoka's edicts are sites like Sopara in Konkan, Girnar in Kathiawad, and Dhauli and Jaugada in Orissa, which are situated on or near the coast. Sopara was actually a well-known port in Buddhist and Classical texts.[121] All these data may imply some interests of the Mauryas in sea-borne commerce, though our information is very meagre.

That the Mauryas maintained close ties with the Seleucid rulers of West Asia is clearly proved by the visit of Megasthenes to the Mauryan

[118]The recommendation is meant for the *samāharttā*, the Collector General of revenue, who is to watch over (*avekṣeta*) seven heads of revenue; *Kauṭilīya Arthaśāstra*, II. 6. *Durga* is the first head, as it yields the maximum variety of taxes (22 to be exact).

[119]For the functions of the *śulkādhyakṣas* see *Kautilīya Arthaśāstra*, II. 21–22.

[120]J.W. McCrindle, *Ancient India as Described by Megasthenes and Arrian*, Calcutta, 1921, p. 85.

[121]Romila Thapar, *Aśoka and the Decline of the Mauryas*, London, 1961, p. 169. Sopara and Girnar have each yielded a set of fourteen rock edicts of Aśoka.

capital. Greek texts speak of the continuity of this relation during the reign of Bindusāra (Amitrakhates of the Greeks). The external contacts of the Mauryas increased during the reign of Aśoka (*c.* 272–233 BC). Some areas / rulers, situated in the unconquered frontier or outlying regions in relation to the Maurya empire (*aṁta avijita* and *pratyanta*), are mentioned in the edicts in the context of Aśoka's propagating the policy of *dhamma* within his realm and outside as well. These include the five *Yonarājas* (rulers of West Asia) figuring in Aśoka's edicts.[122] The extensive external contacts of the Mauryas in West Asia and the eastern Mediterranean regions are clearly demonstrated here.

This would presuppose the existence of a regular communication network launched and maintained by the Mauryas for facilitating their contacts with Greek rulers of West Asia. Eratosthenes (275–194 BC), a junior contemporary of Aśoka, was aware of a royal road which connected West Asia with Palibothra or Pāṭaliputra. Arrian too speaks of such a road. Attention may also be given to the observation of Megasthenes that officers in charge of the countryside (*agoranomoi*) were entrusted, among other things, with the construction of roads and with the setting up of pillars after every ten *stadia* (1 *stadium* = 606¾ feet) to show the by-roads and distances.[123]

Aśoka's measures to ensure public benefits, following his concept of *dhamma*, included the construction and maintenance of roads on which sometimes planted were trees to provide shade and rest houses and wells were built.[124] The roads were not only vitally necessary for men and merchandise to travel on, but were essential for the exchange of information throughout the empire. A perusal of Aśoka's edicts shows that there was official approval for the creation of many versions of the central drafts of the edicts according to the local requirements in

[122]They are explicitly mentioned in the RE XIII of Aśoka, though their presence is also recorded in the RE II; see *SI*, I, pp. 35–37 and 17–18.

[123]Strabo (*Geographikon*, ed. and tr. by H.L. Jones, London and Cambridge, Mass, rpt., 1942), XV.I, section II quotes Eratosthenes. The account of the construction and maintenance of roads by the *agoranomoi* is in XV.I, section 50. For the *Biblithekes Historikes* of Diodorus Siculus see R.C. Majumdar, *The Classical Accounts of India*, Calcutta, 1960, pp. 232–43; there are variations and even contradictions in the accounts of Arrian, Strabo and Diodoros who summarized Megasthenes' *Indica* and /or quoted excerpts from it.

[124]These instructions are seen in his RE II and PE VII. See R.G. Basak, *Asokan Edicts*, Calcutta, 1959.

different parts of the empire. These central drafts were certainly prepared at Pāṭaliputra under the direct supervision of the emperor. This is irrefutable evidence of the effective network of an information and communication system as well, without which the chain of command from the apex political authority could not have been maintained.[125] One may also recall that the emperor himself is known to have been on the move over as long a period as 256 nights.[126] Aśoka's visits, possibly from Pāṭaliputra, to Lumbinīgrāma in the Nepalese terai, to Sambodhi or Bodhgaya, to Sarnath near Vārāṇasī and to Sanchi in eastern MP are well recorded in his edicts. That the emperor was heading for the Upunithavihāra in Manemadeśa (in eastern MP) is explicitly stated in a minor rock edict from Panguraria.[127] The introduction of Aśoka's policy of quinquennial and triennial official tours by Rājukas, Yutas and Prādeśikas (RE III and PE VII) further strengthens the impression of the Mauryan care for the routes of communication. It is true that Aśoka's edicts offer only fragmented glimpses of these routes as the edicts were not written to describe the Mauryan road system. The Brahmagiri, Jatinga-Ramesvar and Siddapur versions of the minor rock edict record the presence of a scribe named Capaḍa (*Capaḍena likhita*) whose epithet *lipikara* was written in Kharoṣṭhī.[128] Kharoṣṭhī is generally used in Aśokan edicts found in the north-west and its stray occurrence in a Brāhmī record from the Deccan is a likely indicator that the scribe came to the Deccan somewhere from the north-west.

How many of these roads were royal highways, as mentioned by the Classical authors, cannot be ascertained with our present knowledge. The impressions of a major road in the north-western borderland of India, however, are retained in two Aramaic edicts of Aśoka, found from Laghman in Afghanistan and issued in his year 16 (Aśoka is called Prydrs mlk'= King Priyadarśī). Both the edicts mention a *krpty* (= *kārapathi*). The term *kāra*, an Iranian word, stands for the lord or the military chief, while *pathi* denotes way. The word *kārapathi* then means

[125]G. Fussman, 'Central and Provincial Administration in Ancient India: The Problem of the Maurya Empire', *IHR*, XIV, 1987–88, pp. 43–72, has presented a reconstruction of the possible lines of communication in the vast Mauryan realm. The infrastructure of communication was, of course, inadequate for the needs of the expansive empire.

[126]See the MRE I of Aśoka, *SI,* I, pp. 47–50.

[127]D.C. Sircar, 'Synoptical Texts of Minor Rock Edicts I and II of Aśoka', *JAIH*, XII, 1978–79, p. 7.

[128]*SI*, I, p. 51, footnote 8.

the lord's way, i.e. the royal highway and can easily be equated with the Indian word *rājapatha*. The *kārapathi* in the two Laghman edicts seems to have been the same as the royal road figuring in the Classical literature. Significantly enough, both the Laghman edicts contain names of places and their respective distances from the findspots of the two records. The two Laghman edicts are in fact distance recorders and direction-giving signals, the like of which were reported by the Greek authors. The second Laghman edict ends with the name of one Whsu (= Vasu?), the dispenser of meritorious works (*prtbg* = *purtabhāga*) and governor (*skn*). As the officer in charge of meritorious works he could have been entrusted with providing wells and shady trees on the highway, the maintenance of the highway, etc. His functions therefore closely resemble those of the *agoranomoi* of the Classical authors.[129]

It is not easy to pinpoint the exact course of this overland route connecting the north Indian plains with West Asia through Laghman in the north-western borderland of the subcontinent. A major overland route of the time of the Arsacid ruler Mithridates I (*c.* 174–138/37 BC, i.e. not far removed from the final collapse of the Maurya empire) of Iran figures in the *Naturalis Historia* of Pliny. It will be a logical assumption to relate the Mauryan royal road, passing through Laghman, to this long-distance route.[130]

VII

The attempts of the Mauryan administration to control and supervise trade are not encountered in subsequent times. The creation of a nearly pan-Indian empire under a single paramount power was also not repeated in early Indian history after the collapse of the Maurya realm. The downfall of the Maurya empire in *c.* 187 BC did not, however, result in any catastrophe, economic and political. The period of nearly five hundred years, from *c.* 200 BC to AD 300, is marked by the development of sedentary agrarian settlements (based on regular plough cultivation), the remarkable proliferation of crafts and professions (along with the growing importance of organizations of crafts, called *śreṇī*,

[129]The two Laghman edicts were edited and translated for the first time by B.N. Mukherjee, *Studies in the Aramaic Edicts of Aśoka*, Calcutta, 1983, chapter I. It is strange that these documents have only rarely been utilized by economic historians of early India.

[130]B.N. Mukherjee, *An Agrippan Source—Studies in Indo-Parthian History*, Calcutta, 1969.

gaṇa, saṁgha, nikāya, etc. in Indian sources), the conspicuous growth of trade, including the unprecedented increase in the external trade, especially the sea-borne trade and the peak of the second phase of urbanization in India. The more or less contemporary spread of the monarchical state system cannot be divorced from the changes in the material milieu. Many areas outside the Ganga valley, especially those in the Deccan and south India, experienced the emergence of the monarchical state and urban life. As the pattern of state and urban formations, seen previously in the Ganga valley (from the sixth to the fourth centuries BC), arose in various parts of the subcontinent, the process of the emergence of secondary states and secondary urban centres can be traced during the five centuries (*c.* 200 BC to AD 300). The Ganga valley and especially the middle Ganga valley, therefore, assumes the position of an epicentre from where the impulses of urban formation and state formation spread to disparate regions of India. It is likely that the expansion of Magadha's power to nearly pan-Indian proportions resulted in the penetration of some of the principal traits of the material culture of the Ganga valley into the peninsular parts.

Politically speaking, the north Indian plains were dominated for about a century and a half by the Śuṅgas and the Kāṇvas since the fall of the Mauryan empire. The north-western parts, particularly the borderland, witnessed a series of invasions by the Greeks (Bactrians and Indo-Greeks), the Śakas, the Pahlavas and the Kuṣāṇas, the last-mentioned power being the most formidable of them all. In the Deccan and Kalinga (Orissa and the adjacent areas) rose the Sātavāhana and the Mahāmeghavāhana dynasties respectively. The far south witnessed the arrival of a number of powerful chiefships which were yet to blossom into full-fledged monarchies. Outstanding among these chiefships were the Coḷas in the lower Kaveri valley and the Kaveri delta, the Pāṇḍyas in the Tamraparni and the Vaigai valleys, and the Ceras in Kerala.[131] Theories of state formation recognize the importance of the luxury trade in the emergence of the secondary states.[132]

[131] An updated overview of the political powers of the post-Maurya period is available in H.C. Raychaudhuri, *Political History of Ancient India*, eighth edition with Commentary. Recent perspectives of political history do not consider these centuries as 'dark', as had earlier been proposed. cf. Sudhakar Chattopadhyay, *Early History of North India*, Calcutta, 1958. D.D. Kosambi, *An Introduction to the Study of Indian History*, Bombay, 1956, treated this phase as one of trade and an interlude of foreign invasions.

[132] R.S. Kipp and E.M. Schortman, 'The Political Impact of Trade in

The arrival of a number of foreign ruling houses in the northern, north-western and western parts of India did not result in any major political crisis, but led to firmer contacts of the subcontinent with the West. The process reached its zenith in India's contacts—initially overland, then maritime—with the Roman empire from *c.* late first century BC to the middle of the third century AD. South Asia, however, did not initially participate actively in the direct long-distance commerce with the Mediterranean world. The demand for the celebrated Chinese luxury item, silk, in the West was largely instrumental in the emergence and development of a far-flung overland network of routes called the Silk Road (being an English rendering of the German expression Seidenstrasse, coined in the nineteenth century). The route began from Loyang in China and reached the two Mediterranean ports at Antioch and Alexandria by traversing through Central Asia, West Asia and Eurasia. From Dunhuang in China the route bifurcated into two, the northern and the southern Silk Routes, located respectively to the north and south of the Taklamakan desert. The two branches converged at Kashgarh in Xingchiang or Chinese Turkestan and passed through Afghanistan and Iran to reach the famous marts of Seleucia and Palmyra which were connected to the two Mediterranean ports mentioned above.[133] Bactria in north-eastern Afghanistan holds an important

---

Chiefdoms', *American Anthropologist*, 91, 1989, pp. 370–85; S. Senaviratne, 'Kalinga and Andhra: The Process of Secondary State Formation in Early India', in H.J.M. Claessen and P. Skalnik (eds.), *The Study of the State*, The Hague, 1981, pp. 317–38.

[133]The published literature on the Silk Road is voluminous. L. Bulnois, *The Silk Road*, London, 1966, provides a useful overview; also see the *Cambridge History of Iran*, vol III, chapter 13. Central Asia certainly played a crucial role in this trade relation. The Central Asian situation is mainly reflected in the Chinese texts. B. Watson, *Records of the Grand Historians of China*, New York, 1961; E. Zürcher, 'The Yüeh-chih and Kaniṣka in the Chinese Literature', in A.L. Basham (ed.), *Papers on the Date of Kaniṣka*, London, 1968. The importance of Central Asia in the long range of historical studies is underlined by Andre Gunder Frank, 'The Centrality of Central Asia', *Studies in History*, VIII, 1992, pp. 43–98. A recent statement on this situation is made by Richard N. Frye and Boris A. Litvinsky, 'The Oasis States of Central Asia', in *The History of Humanity*, III, UNESCO, Paris, 1996, pp. 461–64. Also see Xinru Liu, *Silk and Religion, An Exploration of Material Life and the Thought of People*, Delhi, 1996.

position in this context because of its being at the crossroads of Asia and close to the borderland of the subcontinent. The fertility of the soil and the trading importance of its capital, Bactra (Mazar-i-Shariff), paved the way for its emergence to a powerful Greek kingdom in *c.* 230 BC.[134] The invasion of India by the Bactrian Greeks resulted in the intimate contacts between the subcontinent and Bactria. The Greeks in Bactria were overthrown in *c.* 129–30 BC by the Central Asian nomadic group, the Śakas, who in their turn were ousted around the first century BC by another Central Asian nomadic tribe, the Yüeh-chih. One of the five clans (*yabgus*) of the Yüeh-chih became immensely powerful and figured prominently in the Chinese texts as the Kuei shuang. The Kuei shuang is better known and celebrated in history as the mighty Kuṣāṇas who established a huge empire, including in it parts of north India, with its primary stronghold in Bactria.[135] During the rise of the Kuṣāṇa empire, with Bactria as its springboard, there were three other major powers: the Han empire in China, the Arsacid (Imperial Parthian) empire in Iran, and the Roman empire in the west. 'All these empires had a consistent policy towards trade and it was as a result of this exceptional state of affairs that the land silk route came into being'.[136] Of these the Arsacid empire, which occupied the significant position of being a geographical and commercial intermediary, was known for its extortionate policy. It is only natural that there was need for an alternative intermediary to facilitate the movement of merchandise along the long-distance overland route.[137] The

[134]W.W. Tarn, *The Greeks in Bactria and India*, Cambridge, 1951 is the classic study on the history of Bactria. J.C. Gardin and P. Gentelle, 'L'Exploitation Du Sol En Bactriane Antique', *BEFEO*, LXVI, 1979, pp. 1–29; Diodorus (*Bibliothekes Historikes*, tr., C.H. Oldfather, London, 1935–54) said: 'Ninus laid hands on the treasures of Bactria consisting of gold and silver' (II. 5–7).

[135]R.N. Frye, 'The Rise of the Kushan Empire', in *The History of Humanity*, III, pp. 456–60.

[136]L. Bulnois, *op. cit.*, p. 60.

[137]How and how much the economic advantages of trade prompted powers in West Asia, Central Asia and the north-western borderland of the subcontinent to launch aggressive designs is dicussed by Ranabir Chakravarti, *Warfare for Wealth: Early Indian Perspective*, Calcutta, 1986, pp. 78–85. The area of Kao-fu or Kabul is described in the Chinese text Hou Han shu thus: 'They excel in commerce and internally (privately) they are very wealthy. The (political) allegiance has never been constant; the three countries Tien-chu, Chi-pin, and An-hsi have possessed it when they are strong

advent of the mighty Kuṣāṇa empire (*c.* first century BC to AD 262) fulfilled this historical need. At the height of its power during the time of Kaniska I, the Kuṣāṇa empire included the north-western borderland of the subcontinent, the whole of present-day Pakistan and from the Punjab in the west to Campā (Bhagalpur) in the east, parts of the Malwa plateau and possibly Gujarat in India.[138] A considerable portion of the northern part of the subcontinent was intimately linked with the north-west, politically and commercially too.

This political development of immense significance coincided with the understanding of a geographical phenomenon of the utmost significance, namely, the discovery and the better utilization of the monsoon wind system by Graeco-Roman sailors. The immediate impact of this knowledge was seen in the development of maritime trade in the western sector of the Indian Ocean. Though the popular view is that the Classical authors named it the Hippalus wind after the discoverer, the reading of the very name Hippalus has recently been questioned on the basis of a revised reading of Pliny (see Annotated Bibliography). It is, however, recognized that the monsoon wind was not a European discovery and was in fact used by Asian (including Indian) sailors prior to its regular use by Graeco-Roman sailors. The Classical sources are replete with references to the regular oceanic voyages between the Red Sea ports and Indian harbours. Asian luxury items, including the most coveted Chinese silk, could reach the Roman world not merely along the overland Silk Road, but could also be diverted

and have lost it when they are weak'. E. Zürcher, *op. cit.*, pp. 367–68. The three areas denote respectively the lower Indus valley under the Kuṣāṇas, Kashmir and the Imperial Parthian (Arsacid) domain in Iran.

[138] B.N. Mukherjee, *The Rise and Fall of the Kushāṇa Empire*, Calcutta, 1988. The maximum extent of the Kuṣāṇa empire in the east was up to Śrīcampā near Bhagalpur, Bihar in the regnal year 1 of Kaniṣka I. It included Ozono (Ujjaiyinī in western MP), Kosombo (Kauśāmbī near Allahabad), Sagido (Sāketa) and Palibothro (Pāṭaliputra). This is known from the recently discovered Bactrian inscription of Kaniṣka from Rabatak in Afghanistan. See Nicholas Sims-Williams and J. Cribb, 'A New Bactrian Inscription of Kanishka the Great', *Silk Road Art and Archaeology*, 4, 1995/96, pp. 75–142; the same record has been re-edited, with significant variations in reading and interpretation, by B.N. Mukherjee, 'The Great Kuṣāṇa Testament,' *IMB*, XXX, 1995 (but actually published in 1998), pp. 1–105. There is, however, little proof that the successors of Kaniṣka were able to retain any control over the territories to the east of Mathurā; Mathurā remained till the very end an integral part of the Kuṣāṇa empire.

through the subcontinent from where these could be shipped for the Roman markets. This is the background in a nutshell of the incorporation of South Asia for the first time in an international commercial network, both overland and overseas.

The scholarly recognition of the importance of this commercial interaction between the subcontinent and the West in general resulted in the construction of what is popularly called Indo-Roman commerce. Indo-Roman trade occupies an important place in the history of Indian trade and possesses a rich and alive historiography. The history of this trade has been studied for a long time chiefly on the basis of the Classical accounts. The most cited sources are the *Periplus of the Erythraean Sea*, a text written by an anonymous Greek sailor, probably belonging to the last quarter of the first century AD. The text is a mine of information on maritime trade, items of trade, ports and marts, patterns of navigation and sailing in the northern and western parts of the Indian Ocean. The Indian littorals and products loom large in the text. Two new editions of this source in the 1980s have certainly acted as a fillip to the study of Indo-Roman commerce.[139] The other celebrated text is the *Natural History* by Pliny (died in AD 79) who mentioned a large number of Indian imports to the Roman markets.[140] The *Geographike Huphegesis* of Claudius Ptolemy has an important section on the subcontinent. The text is dated around the middle of the second century AD and mentions many Indian ports, harbours and inland cities with occasional references to certain products available there.[141] These three texts have naturally been very regularly and rather heavily used by historians. Indigenous textual materials, like the *Jātaka* texts in the north Indian context and the Saṅgam literature in south India, also show a distinct awareness of the growing volume of India's trade with areas abroad. We know about India's commercial contacts with the Roman world due to the availability of archaeological sources. An important proof of India's trade with the Roman world is seen in the large number of coin hoards, mostly in south India, yielding

[139] *The Periplus of the Erythraean Sea*, tr. by W.W. Schoff, Delhi, 1974 (rpt.); G.W.B. Huntingford, tr., London, 1980; *The Periplus Maris Erythraei*, ed. and tr. by L. Casson, Princeton, 1989.

[140] Pliny, *Naturalis Historia*, tr. by H. Rackham, London, Cambridge, Mass., rpt., 1942.

[141] Claudius Ptolemy, *Geographike Huphegesis*, tr. by E.L. Stevenson, New York, 1932; the information regarding India is mostly found in section VII of the text.

Roman coins which were used both as bullion and also as local currencies. The importance of the discovery of Italian pottery, called Arretine ware, from Arikamedu (near Pondicherry) is also duly recognized. In recent times there has been a considerable increase in the artefactual evidence of the Indo-Roman trade in the form of amphorae, glassworks and objects of art along with the use of pottery and coins.[142]

Textual and archaeological materials leave little room for doubt about the important participation of India in the long-distance trade with the West. Pliny noted that India came 'nearer' the Roman empire 'through the love for gain'.[143] When Strabo stayed with his friend Aelius Gallus, the Roman prefect of Egypt, he appreciated that 'about one hundred and twenty ships sail from Myos Hormos to India, although in the time of the Ptolemies scarcely one would venture on this voyage and commerce with the Indies'.[144] He also informs us of an embassy sent by a Pandian king (of the region around Madurai) to the Roman emperor Augustus. The commercial character and importance of this embassy have been established by Warmington.[145] Thanks to a graphic description left behind by Pliny, historians are able to trace the development of the sea-route to the west coast of

[142]The recent thrust on the utilization of archaeological evidence for the study of Indo-Roman trade is evident in Vimala Begley and Richard Daniel de Puma, (eds.), *Rome and India, the Ancient Sea Trade*, Delhi, 1992. The importance of field archaeological data for the study of this trade was for the first time effectively demonstrated by the excavations at Arikamedu, near Pondicherry. See R.E.M. Wheeler and Krishna Deva, 'Arikamedu: An Indo-Roman Trading Station on the East Coast of India', *Ancient India*, 2, 1946, pp. 17–124; J.M. Casal, *Fouilles de Virampatnam-Arikamedu*, Paris. Vimala Begley, 'Arikamedu Reconsidered', *American Journal of Archaeology*, 87, 1983, pp. 461–81, has brought to light fresh data and new assessments on the antiquity of the settlement and trade in Arikamedu. The bibliography of this trade is voluminous. E.H. Warmington, *Commerce Between the Roman Empire and India*, Delhi, 1974 (rpt.), is the classic study on the subject. The most exhaustive bibliography is presented by M.G. Raschke, 'New Studies in Roman Commerce with the East', in *Aufstieg und Niedergang der Romischer Welt*, Berlin, 1978, pp. 604–1361. The maximum concentration of find spots of Roman coins from south India clearly suggests that this area was the prime point of maritime contacts with the Roman empire.

[143]Pliny, *op. cit.*, VI.26, pp. 96–101.

[144]Strabo, *op. cit.*, II.5.12.

[145]E.H. Warmington, *op. cit.*, p. 35ff.

India in four stages. The most developed route, which was also the shortest and the safest, began from the Red Sea port of Myos Hormos and/or Berenice and reached the famous Malabar port of Muziris (Muciri of the Tamil Saṅgam texts) in forty days by following the Hippalus (i.e. the south-western monsoon) wind.[146] Pliny states that the earliest point of maritime contacts between India and the West was Patalene in the Indus delta; the subsequent point was the port of Barbaricum on the middle mouth of the Indus. The third stage made Sigerius or Jaigarh on the Konkan coast the most convenient harbour and finally, Muziris became the most important port of call. The unmistakable impression is that as knowledge and utilization of the monsoon wind grew, the sea-borne route gradually shifted more to the southern part of the west coast. Lionel Casson's in-depth probe into the *Periplus of the Erythraean Sea* and other related Classical texts have enlightened us on the sailing patterns. He has rightly suggested that the ports on the western sea-board of India would remain closed during the height of the monsoon. And Graeco-Roman sailors would therefore start their voyage for the western Indian sea-board (especially Muziris) when the fury of the monsoons would lessen around late August and early September. He has also suggested that the actual sailing time would span only twenty days instead of forty as described by Pliny who, in his opinion, probably made a miscalculation.[147] These textual studies have been further supplemented by E. Sidebotham on the basis of archaeological researches on the Red Sea ports and the area around Aden at the mouth of the Red Sea/ Gulf of Aden. One can hardly overlook the fact that the Red Sea became the principal sealane in the western Indian Ocean for the sea-borne trade between India and the Roman world.[148] Prior to the age of Indo-Roman trade the Persian Gulf had played a similar role in the western Indian Ocean. This is particularly evident from recent data on what is termed the Gulf archaeology, to which the contributions

[146]Pliny, *op. cit.*, VI.26.104.

[147]L. Casson, 'Rome's Maritime Trade in the Far East', *The American Neptune*, XLVIII, 1988, pp. 149–53; L. Casson, 'Ancient Naval Technology and the Route to India', in Vimala Begley and Richard Daniel de Puma (eds.), *op. cit.*, pp. 8–11; L. Casson, 'Rome's Trade with the East: The Sea Voyage to Africa and India', *Transactions of the American Philological Association*, 110, 1980, pp. 21–36.

[148]Steven E. Sidebotham, 'Ports of the Red Sea and the Arabia-India Trade', in Vimala Begley and Richard Daniel de Puma (eds.), *op. cit.*, pp. 12–38.

of J.F. Salles deserve special mention.[149] The historiography of the overseas Indo-Roman trade places greater emphasis on the western littorals which had premier ports like Barbaricum (at the mouth of the Indus), Barygaza (at the mouth of the Narmada) and Muziris near Cranganore in Malabar. Historians have paid great attention to these ports. But more crucial problems like the port-hinterland relationship and the factors responsible for the primacy of certain ports over others have been generally left out. A close examination of Ptolemy's *Geography* cannot but dwell upon the growing importance of the harbours on the east coast from the second half of the second century AD onwards. Ports like Colchi (Korkai near Tutikorin), Khaberos (Kāverīpaṭṭinam of the Saṅgam texts, located in the Kaveri delta), Kontakossylla and Allosygne (on the Andhra coast) and Tamalites (Tāmralipta on the Bengal coast) are given some prominence in his *Geography*. Ptolemy is, in fact, the first Western writer to have informed us of the Bay of Bengal, which he termed the Gangetic Gulf. The importance of this new situation is to be appreciated in the light of increasing cultural and commercial ties with South-East Asia, a point which will be taken up later.

The above survey of the studies on the Indo-Roman trade is not to suggest that such trade was entirely sea-borne. The north-west undoubtedly continued to be a major outlet for the overland contacts between South Asia and West and Central Asia. Begram near Kabul has yielded exotic wares of Mediterranean, Indian and Chinese origin. Wheeler considered Begram as a site where tolls and customs were levied from merchants.[150] An area not far away from this zone of active overland commerce is the Karakorum highway. A Pak-German team has discovered a large number of antiquities from sites on the present-day Karakorum highway. Kharoṣṭhī inscriptions, petroglyphs, etchings, etc. amply demonstrate the utilization of this very difficult route, but certainly a short cut, by diverse types of merchants, including Sogdian and Chinese traders. This probably corresponds to what has been described as the Chi-pin (an area including

[149]J.F. Salles, 'Hellenistic Seafaring in the Indian Ocean, a Perspective from Arabia', in Himanshu Prabha Ray and J.F. Salles (eds.), *Tradition and Archaeology, Early Maritime Contacts in the Indian Ocean*, Delhi, 1996, pp. 293–310.

[150]R.E.M. Wheeler, *Rome Beyond the Imperial Frontiers*, Harmondsworth, 1955.

Kashmir) route in ancient Chinese texts.[151] It must be clearly pointed out that the Karakorum highway was not directly connected with the overland trade with the Roman empire. The *Periplus* points to the overland movements of commodities from Kabul, Puṣkalāvatī and Taxila in the north-west to the port of Barygaza. This overland route seems to have passed through the Punjab and come up to the famous city of Mathurā, itself a well-known trade centre. Mathurā was well connected with Ujjaiyinī in Malwa which was further linked with Barygaza.[152] No less interesting is the movement of Buddhist monks of Kalyāṇa (near present-day Mumbai) to Dalverjin Tepe, being known from inscribed gold tablets.[153] The overseas maritime trade of India could have hardly flourished without a well-established network of roads linking the harbours with their respective hinterlands.

We feel that Fiser's study of the *seṭṭhi* on the basis of the Buddhist *Jātaka* tales has a distinct relevance to our recent understandings of trade in early historical India, though it was originally published four decades ago. Our next selection is an extremely significant study by Casson of a recently discovered trade document. This single document, so far a unique one in the context of Indo-Roman trade, records a loan contract between two Graeco-Roman merchants at the famous port of Muziris from where precious commodities were shipped on a vessel named Hermopollon. Six parcels of precious Indian commodities like Gangetic nard, ivory, tusk and fine fabric were shipped to a premier Red Sea port, most probably Berenice or Myos Hormos. From there the goods were to be transported across the desert on the back of camels to Koptos. Then from Koptos they were transported on the

[151] K. Jettmar, (ed.), *Antiquities from Northern Pakistan*, I, in two parts, Munich, 1989; K. Jettmar, 'Sogdians in the Indus Valley', *Histoire et Cultes de L'Asie Centrale Preisalamique*, CNRS, Paris, 1991, pp. 251–53 (with plates).

[152] *The Periplus*, tr. L. Casson, *op. cit.*, sections 48 and 64. Mathurā became conspicuous as a trade centre and also a city in north India since the late centuries BC. Mathurā, however, did not possess a rich agricultural hinterland and did not locally produce enough exchangeable commodities, except the famous textiles (śātikā). Its immense importance therefore lies in its being a nodal point in the overland communication system. See S. G. Bajpai, 'Mathura: Trade Routes, Commerce and Communication Patterns, Post Mauryan Period to the End of the Kushana Period', in D. M. Srinivasan (ed.), *Mathura—The Cultural Heritage*, Delhi, 1989, pp. 46–58.

[153] G. Bongard-Levin and A. Visagin, *The Image of India*, Moscow, 1984, p. 206.

riverine vessels on the Nile to the famous port of Alexandria at the Nile delta. The trade document clearly shows that 25 per cent customs duty was charged on these commodities at Alexandria. It is rather surprising that this document is silent on the export of pepper, the most important spice exported from India. The immense importance of pepper as an export item continues unabated from this period onwards.[154] In view of the recognition of the eastern littorals in the history of India's maritime trade[155], we would like to highlight the commercial importance of the Bengal coast in the light of B.N. Mukherjee's researches on the Kharoṣṭhī-Brāhmī documents (consisting mostly of terracotta seals, sealings, inscribed potteries and potsherds with labels), ascribed by him to the first three or four centuries of the Christian era. In this paper he also devotes considerable attention to the question of money circulation on the Bengal coast and adjacent Kalinga and combines it with inscriptional data. The paper offers a new perspective on the relatively less-known commercial activities on the Bengal coast which is the major outlet for the landlocked Ganga valley.[156]

The changing perception of the trade in the Bay of Bengal and the east coast of India has certainly encouraged the study of India's contacts with South-East Asia. India's commerce is not seen as a civilizing force in terms of socio-economic and political developments in South-East Asia nowadays. The influence of Indian culture on different societies in South-East Asia is, however, not denied. M.G. Raschke in his monumental survey of Roman trade with the 'east'

[154]Romila Thapar, 'Black Gold: South Asia and the Roman Maritime Trade', *South Asia* (n.s.), 15, 1992, pp. 1–28.

[155]cf. L. Casson, 'Rome's Trade with the Eastern Coast of India', *Cahiers d'histoire*, 1988, pp. 303–08.

[156]Earlier authorities on the history of ancient Bengal such as R.C. Majumdar (ed.), *History of Bengal*, I, Dhaka, 1943 and Niharranjan Ray, *Bangalir Itihas*, Adiparva (in Bengali), in two volumes, second edition, Calcutta, 1980, could begin a connected account of ancient Bengal hardly before *c.* fourth century AD, largely due to the lack of evidence prior to that period. Some of B.N. Mukherjee's readings of the Kharoṣṭhī-Brāhmī documents have been criticized by I. Mahadevan in the *Journal of the Epigraphic Society of India*, 1993. B.N. Mukherjee's rejoinder to Mahadevan appears in the same *Journal* in 1994. The significance of these documents as new evidence for the study of the history of trade is recognized by Himanshu Prabha Ray, 'Trade and Contacts', in Romila Thapar (ed.), *op. cit.*, p. 159.

raises doubts about the frequency of Indians' voyages to South-East Asia. He also questions the extent to which these sailings were related to regular transactions or whether they were prompted by the urge to procure prestigious goods.[157] The subject is pursued not merely on the basis of the literary images of Suvarṇadvīpa and Suvarṇabhūmi. Historians of early Indian trade nowadays attach greater importance to the more concrete archaeological evidence for the appreciation of the commercial and cultural contacts between the two areas.

India's contacts with mainland South-East Asia (i.e. Burma, Thailand, Malaysia, and Indonesia) can be pushed back to *c*. 500–400 BC on the basis of datable wares like beads of semi-precious stones, iron objects and pottery. This contact was largely coastal in character. More overseas voyages and close contact between India and South-East Asia are noted from *c*. first century AD onwards. Beiktahno in the Irrawaddy delta, Oc-eo in the Mekong delta, Khukan Lakpad in the Malay peninsula, the Isthmus of Kra, and Kuala Seiling to the south of Kedah are key sites in this network. These sites have yielded among other things Brahmi documents, Rouletted Ware and carnelian seals of definite Indian workmanship. Imports to India appear to have included tin, essential for the manufacture of bronze, and various types of spices like clove, cinnamon, etc. The spices were probably meant ultimately for the Roman market, though these were first sent westwards to Indian ports from where these were then transshipped. There is some tangible proof of the presence of Roman products from South-East Asian sites. For instance, typical Classical motifs, like Tyche and Perseus, are seen on carnelian intaglios discovered from Khukan Lukpad, Oc-eo and Nakom Pathom. The discovery of Roman lamps and bronze figurines is also reported from a number of sites. These artefacts are assigned to *c*. second/third centuries AD. These materials may bear the impressions of the Roman interests in directly reaching South-East Asia, but how far the Classical merchants were able to penetrate the indigenous trading network of South-East Asia, is difficult to ascertain.[158] The Bengal coast, the littorals of

[157] M.G. Raschke, *op. cit.*

[158] Ian C. Glover, 'Recent Archaeological Evidence for Early Maritime Contacts between India and South East Asia', in Himanshu Prabha Ray and J.F. Salles (eds.), *op. cit.*, pp. 129–58; Himanshu Prabha Ray, 'Early Maritime Contacts between South and South-east Asia', *Journal of South-East Asian Studies*, XX, 1989, pp. 42–54.

Andhra Pradesh and the Coromandel coast were the main points of overseas contacts with South-East Asia. An aphaterion or the point of departure of ships bound for Chryse Chora and Chryse Chersonesis (=Suvarṇabhūmi and Suvarṇadvīpa) is, significantly enough, placed by Ptolemy on the Andhra coast.[159]

The Ganga valley has been noted for its agrarian prosperity, urban centres and brisk trade since at least the sixth century BC. The period from *c.* 200 BC to AD 300 also witnessed the continuity of this trend in north India. But these five centuries have a special significance in the context of the growth of commerce in the Deccan and south India, particularly long-distance maritime commerce. After giving accounts of Muziris (in Caelobothras or Cera country) and ports and marts in the Pandian kingdom, Pliny says, 'But all these names of tribes and ports and towns are to be found in none of previous writers, which seem to show that local conditions of the places were changing.'[160] These changes are sought to be located in the emergence of urban and state society on a pan-India scale. The role of long-distance trade has been given some importance in the study of the formation of the secondary urban centres in the Deccan and south India. Descriptions of the presence of the *yavana* merchants in south Indian cities figure regularly and prominently in the Tamil Saṅgam literature. This has prompted many historians to attribute the emergence of urban centres in peninsular India largely to external trade. Champakalakshmi shows that the cities occurred in early historical south India largely due to non-local elements. She explains and illustrates this in terms of not only the impact of foreign trade, but also the penetration of the traits of the Ganga valley material culture as intrusive elements into the economic conditions of south India. It would logically follow that such urban centres would gradually lose their relevance with the disappearance of these extraneous elements in course of time.[161] H. Sarkar's incisive studies of urban centres in early historical Andhra also pays adequate attention to trade in this region. But he shows that most of the items of trade were agro-based or

[159]Ptolemy, *op. cit.*, VII.1.15.

[160]Pliny, *op. cit.*, VI.149.

[161]R. Champakalakshmi, *Trade, Ideology and Urbanization: South India 300 BC to AD 1300*, Delhi, 1996; see especially Chapter 2 which views urbanization in south India as the result of the an impact of the external stimulus.

animal-based products and did not belong to the category of manufactured commodities; that is why he designates urban centres in the early historical eastern Deccan as 'agro-cities'.[162]

In the virtual absence of statistical accounts, it is an uphill task to pronounce whether the Indian or the Roman empire derived more profit out of this trade, though readings in the accounts of the items of exports and imports, furnished both by Classical sources and Indian sources (literary and archaeological as well) point to the possibility of the balance of trade being more in favour of India than the Roman empire. An eloquent testimony to this is found in the famous lamentation of Pliny that there was an immense expenditure of Roman gold for procuring Indian luxuries. This has often resulted in the perception that the drainage of Roman gold into India over a couple of centuries resulted in the economic crisis during the later years of the Roman empire. This interpretation regarding the drainage of Roman wealth on the basis of Pliny's accounts has recently been questioned.[163]

VIII

North India came under the political paramountcy of the Gupta empire (*c*. AD 320–570) which fought many wars to supplant most of the contemporary powers in Āryāvartta. The most formidable power in central India and the Deccan, contemporary to the Imperial Guptas, were the Vākāṭakas. The three centuries (*c*. AD 300–600) are generally marked in text books as the Gupta or the Gupta-Vākāṭaka age. In the conventional historiography of India this phase has been eulogized as the 'golden age' or the 'Classical age', an image strongly contested by many historians especially from the 1950s onwards.[164] The most significant hallmark of the material life in this period has been alternatively identified in the creation of *agrahāras*. The term *agrahāra* stands for the donation of plot(s) of land and/village(s),

[162]H. Sarkar, 'Emergence of Urban Centres in Early Historic Andhradesa', in B.M. Pande and B.D. Chattopadhyaya (eds.), *Archaeology and History*, II, Delhi, 1987, pp. 631–42.

[163]P. Bernardi, 'The Economic Problems of the Roman Empire at the Time of Its Decline', in Carlo M. Cippola (ed.), *The Economic Decline of Empires*, London, 1970.

[164]D.N Jha, *Ancient India: An Introductory Outline*, Delhi, 1978; Romila Thapar, *Interpreting Early India*, Delhi, 1992.

which were exempted from revenue and granted generally in favour of religious persons and/or institutions, by issuing copper plate charters under the instruction of the ruler. Copper plates undoubtedly proliferated from the Vākāṭaka-Gupta age onwards, particularly during the period from *c.* AD 600 to 1200. These landgrants form the bulk of our information regarding the socio-economic, political and cultural conditions in India for the period from roughly the fourth century to the thirteenth century.[165] These charters throw a flood of light on agrarian history since these record the transfer of landed property but information on trade naturally is very little.

The preponderance of copper plate charters has been interpreted by a group of scholars as an indicator of a major shift in the material life which became rooted to the rural agrarian economy. In other words, the huge number of landgrants are seen as a pointer to the gradual receding of the non-agrarian sector of the economy to the background during the Gupta and the post-Gupta times. A number of Marxist historians have argued that the decline in the volume of trade with the Roman empire after *c.* AD 300 caused economic problems in India. According to them, the material milieu began to be increasingly oriented to a self-sufficient and enclosed village economy which replaced the vibrant urban economy of the early historical times. The formulation of Indian feudalism attempts at constructing the image of languishing trade, especially long-distance trade, in the period from the fourth to the twelfth century. The urban economy, including commercial activities, are, therefore, suggested to have gradually decreased in three stages: (a) 300–600, (b) 600–1000, and (c) 1000–1200. The changing perspectives on Indian feudalism, however, admit the possibility of the growth of trade once again from AD 1000/1100. [166]

[165]D.C. Sircar clearly demonstrated the immense importance of landgrants for the study of early Indian social, economic and cultural history by himself editing a large number of copper plates. His main interest, however, lay in the conventional narratives of the ruling dynasties. See his *Indian Epigraphy*, Delhi, 1965; also R.S. Sharma, *Perspectives in the Social and Economic History of Early India*, ch. XV, pp. 218–27 for the value of landgrant records for the reconstruction of early Indian economic life.

[166]The bibliography on Indian feudalism is extensive. Here only the representative works are cited. D.D. Kosambi, *op. cit.* D.D. Kosambi. 'On the Development of Feudalism in India', *ABORI*, XXVI, 1956, pp. 258–69; 'Origins of Feudalism in Kashmir', *JBBRAS*, The Sarddhasatabdi Commemoration Volume, 1956–57, pp.108–20; R.S. Sharma, *Indian*

The proponents of Indian feudalism would, therefore, imply that the first chronological segment (AD 300–600), more or less coinciding with the Gupta age, began to show the initial signals of declining commerce in India. In sharp contrast to the superb gold and silver coins of the Guptas, the Vākāṭaka rulers are not known to have issued any coins. This is further corroborated by a single occurrence of 'merchant' in the entire Vākāṭaka epigraphy. All these are interpreted as marks of a transformation in economic life in which trade and the money economy were becoming less and less relevant.[167]

This is not to imply that trade became non-existent during the Gupta times. On the other hand, there are plenty of literary images of brisk commercial transactions. For instance, the term *kraya-vikraya* in the sense of commercial transactions appears in the famous Sanskrit lexicon, the *Amarakośa* or the *Nāmaliṅgānuśāsana*, ascribed to the Gupta period. Kalidāsa seems to have been well aware of *vipaṇis* or shops which were sometimes arranged on both sides of the road (*apānamārga*).[168] The Gupta records from Puṇḍravardhana (north Bengal) and the Gupta seals from Vaiśālī in north Bihar regularly refer to the chief merchant of the city (*nagaraśreṣṭhī*) and the leader of the caravan traders (*sārthavāha*). What is particularly significant is the inclusion of the representatives of the mercantile community in the district board (*viṣyādhiṣṭhānādhikaraṇa*) in north Bengal during the fifth and sixth centuries AD, though they were not by any means

---

Feudalism, Delhi, 1980 (second edition); B.N.S. Yadava, *Society and Culture in North India in the Twelfth Century*, Allahabad, 1973; D.N. Jha (ed.), *Feudal Social Formation in Early India*, Delhi, 1987; K.M. Shrimali, *Agrarian Structure in Central India and the Northern Deccan—A Study in Vākāṭaka Inscriptions*, New Delhi, 1987; V.K. Thakur, *Historiography of Indian Feudalism: Towards a Model of Early Medieval Indian Economy (c. AD 600–1000)*, Patna-Delhi, 1989. Niharranjan Ray, 'The Medieval Factor in Indian History', General President's Address, *PIHC*, Patiala session, 1967, without explicitly mentioning feudalism, virtually equated and identified feudalism with medievalism in Indian history.

[167]One cannot, however, lose sight of the fact that the most flourishing phase in the history of Ajanta belongs to the Vākāṭaka period. A major cultural centre like Ajanta could not have reached its zenith during a period of economic crisis, including the decline in trade in the Deccan.

[168]For a general account of trade during the period from *c.* AD fourth to the sixth centuries, see U.N. Ghoshal, 'Economic Conditions', in R.C. Majumdar, (ed.), *The Classical Age*, Bombay, 1970, pp. 599–601; P.L. Gupta, *The Gupta Empire*, II, Varanasi, 1977, chapter on Economic Conditions.

government officials. This tendency to allow representations of local interest groups at district-level administration is one of the innovations of the Gupta provincial administrative system.[169] The active role of the merchant in the town council is also portrayed in the contemporary drama, the *Mṛcchakaṭika* of Śūdraka.[170]

Bengal has yielded a number of copper plates of the fifth–sixth centuries which occasionally mention boat-parking stations (*naudaṇḍakas/ naubandhakas*). A ship-building area (*nāvatakṣeṇī*) also figures in a sixth-century record from Faridpur (Bangladesh).[171] The regularity of riverine trade in deltaic Bengal is unmistakable as these boat-parking stations are mentioned as landmarks in rural spaces. These could have provided the facilities of inland movements in a riverine (*nadīmātṛka*) area like Bengal which is known for its connections with the Bay of Bengal. Little wonder then that the port of Tāmralipta (possibly near Tamluk, Medinipur district, West Bengal) is highly spoken of as a premier port (*velākula*) in Daṇḍī's *Daśakumāracarita* (*c.* seventh century).[172] Fa Hsien and Hsüan Tsang spoke eloquently about the importance of this premier port in the Gangetic delta. Fa Hsien (travels in India from *c.* 399–415) left India for his return journey to China from Tāmralipta. His account shows that he boarded a merchant ship at Tāmralipta and sailed directly to Sri Lanka, whence he undertook the voyage to Java to finally reach China.[173] The direct sea-borne contacts between the Bengal coast and Sri Lanka and the indications of the sea route from Bengal to China through Sri Lanka and South-East Asia are clearly illustrated. A master mariner (*mahānāvika*) named Buddhagupta figures in a sixth-century

[169]The prominent position of the *nagaraśreṣṭhī* and the *sārthavāha* is seen in the five copper plates from Damodarpur (now in Bangladesh), dated from the Gupta Era 124 to 224, i.e. AD 444 to 544. See R.G. Basak, 'The Five Damodarpur Copper Plate Inscriptions of the Gupta Period', *EI*, XV, 1919, pp. 113–45. Also B.C. Sen, *Some Historical Aspects of the Inscriptions of Bengal (pre-Muhammadan Period)*, Calcutta, 1942.

[170]*Mṛcchakaṭika* of Śūdraka, ed. M. R. Kale, Delhi, 1962, see Act IX.

[171]*SI*, I, pp. 366, 369; their economic importance is discussed by Ranabir Chakravarti, 'Maritime Trade and Voyages in Ancient Bengal', *JAIH*, XIX, 1992–93 (1996), pp. 145–71.

[172]Lallanji Gopal, *The Economic Life of Northern India c.* AD *700–1200*, Varanasi, 1965, p. 128.

[173]J. Legge (tr.), *A Record of Buddhistic Kingdoms*, (Indian rpt.), Delhi, 1971, pp. 111–13.

AD seal as a resident of Raktamṛttikāmahāvihāra (the ruins of this monastery found in Murshidabad district, West Bengal). His presence is noted significantly in the Malay peninsula from where the seal was discovered.[174] This once again underlines the importance of the Bengal coast in the network in the eastern sector of the Indian Ocean.

Further down the east coast, the Toṇḍaimaṇḍalam area in Tamil Nadu had an excellent port at Mahāvalīpuram, closely associated with the history of the Pallavas of Kāñcī. In the Coḷa area (around Tanjore in the Kaveri delta) the port of Kāverīpaṭṭiṇam was certainly in a flourishing condition, as the two famous Tamil epics, the *Śilāppādikāram* and the *Maṇimekalai*, would show. The coast in the Tamil area served as a major point of contact with Sri Lanka and South-East Asia.[175]

The sea-borne trade on the west coast of India is, of course, not as impressive as it had been during the first three centuries of the Christian era. Nevertheless, the Byzantine emperors in Constantinople and the Sasanid power in Iran show lively interest in the maritime trade in the Persian Gulf and the Arabian Sea. The *Christian Topography* of Cosmas Indicopleustes (*c.* late sixth century AD) highlights the importance of a few ports on the western sea-board and speaks very highly of Sri Lanka.[176] The distribution of the Red Ware sites in coastal Gujarat, the Indus delta, the Makran coast, and the coastal areas of Iran may suggest a trade network, the textual impressions of which are available in Cosmas's accounts.[177] This sets the stage for the presentation of D.D. Kosambi's famous study of an organization of merchants (*vaṇiggrāma*) in Kathiawad, situated in the context of the initial stage of feudal formation in India. Mercantile activities are located by him in the growing feudalization of the material culture in India.

[174] *SI*, I, p. 497. The term *mahānāvika* has been interpreted by Sircar to denote the captain or navigator of a large vessel (*mahānau*). It was S.R. Das, *Rajbadidanga 1962, Excavation Report,* Calcutta 1968, who excavated the famous monastery. It was situated, according to Hsüan Tsang, at the outskirts of Karṇasuvarṇa, the capital of Śaśāṅka.

[175] B. Ch. Chhabra, *op. cit.*, pp. 1–64.

[176] S.K. Maity, *Economic Life of Northern India in the Gupta Period* (*c.* AD 300–550), Calcutta, 1957. Also consult David Whitehouse and Andrew Williamson, 'Sasanian Maritime Trade', *Iran XI*, 1973, pp. 29–49.

[177] Nancy Pinto Orton, 'Red Polished Ware in Gujarat: A Catalogue of Twelve Sites', in Vimala Begley and Richard Daniel de Puma (eds.), *op. cit.*, pp. 46–81.

The four centuries from *c.* AD 600 to 1000 are seen as the period of the crystallization of the traits of the 'feudal economy' all over India. It is impossible to miss the proliferation of copper plate charters in an all-India context. R.S. Sharma and his followers strongly argue for a rapid decline of trade and especially long-distance trade which was virtually marginalized. The typical symptoms of the self-sufficient and enclosed village economy are found by Sharma in three areas: the Ganga-Yamuna doab and Rajasthan under the Gurjara-Pratihāras, Bengal and Bihar under the Pālas, and the Deccan under the Rāṣṭrakūṭas. The assumption of a closed village economy allows little scope for the exchange of products, as commodities produced in a given area are believed to have been consumed by the local people with little urge for exchange. This perception of a major slump in trade is coupled with the idea of a decrease in the number of minted metallic currency in the early medieval times, particularly from AD 600 to 1000. The vibrant money economy during the early centuries was replaced by cowry shells as the principal medium of exchange. The repeated references to *kapardakas* or cowry shells in copper plates and the occasional discovery of the same from a few archaeological sites substantiate this point. It has been argued that cowry shells were restrictive of long-distance transactions which must have required high-quality coinage of precious metals. The money economy was in a serious crisis and minted metallic pieces lost their relevance in the context of a slump in trade. The outstanding powers like the Rāṣṭrakūṭas, the Pālas, and the Senas are not known to have issued any coins. Coins issued in some other areas and by other dynasties are denied any economic significance, as their metallic content and purity were not beyond doubt. Such coins of dubious value and authenticity were hardly fit to be used in long-distance trade. Judged from this point of view, the shortage in the availability of coins would force the political authorities to issue landgrants to officers of the realm in lieu of cash payments—furthering the ruralization of the material milieu, but proving detrimental to commerce and urbanism.[178] Sifting through the voluminous Puranic literature and many local chronicles, scholars have presented data on the declining role of the *vaiśyas* as merchants. The Purāṇas prophesied that they would be reduced to artisan (*karmopajīvin*), grinder or thresher of paddy

[178]R.S. Sharma, *Indian Feudalism*, especially the chapter 'Feudal Economy in the Three Kingdoms'.

(*taṇḍulakārin*) and oil miller (*tailakāra*).[179] The decline of trade and the decrease in the importance of merchants in early medieval society play a role in the overall decay of the non-agrarian sector of the economy and the formation of the self-sufficient and enclosed rural society.

The image of dwindling commerce was followed up by the strong suggestion of an overall decay in urban centres. Early historical cities, which reached their zenith during the early centuries of the Christian era, experienced a downward slide as an impact of the languishing trade and the fall in the use of a metallic medium of exchange. The rise of the nomadic Huns appears to have adversely affected the security and stability of the highways of overland trade connecting northern India with the north-western borderlands of the subcontinent and Western and Central Asia. An early impression of the decay of towns in the Ganga valley has been discerned in Hsüan Tsang's account (first half of the seventh century) of their distressed and deserted conditions. Moreover, the description of towns transforming into villages (*nayarāṇī gāmabhuyāni hohinti*) in indigenous literary texts has been taken into consideration. Recent studies have coupled literary data with archaeological information on the widespread utilization of reused bricks in urban areas and signs of desertion of cities from the beginning of the seventh century. This has convinced the proponents of Indian feudalism of a definite process of de-urbanization that had set in first in the Ganga valley and then spanned across the entire subcontinent. Cities and towns are seen at the most as politico-military headquarters (*jayaskandhāvāras*) or as pilgrim centres (*tīrthas*), thereby suggesting that the importance of urban areas as centres of crafts and commerce had virtually become a thing of the past.[180] The above summary of the principal arguments in favour of the feudal formation in India may better be appreciated in the light of R.S. Sharma's article on the credit system in early medieval times.

The construction of Indian feudalism has not, however, gone unchallenged. There are controversies even among the upholders of the idea of the feudal social formation in India in terms of its chronology, its genesis and its culmination.[181] Many of the standpoints of Marxist historians have been challenged on the grounds of both empirical

[179]B.N.S. Yadava, *op. cit.*

[180]R.S. Sharma, *Urban Decay in India* AD *300–1000*, Delhi, 1987.

[181]D.N. Jha, 'Early Indian Feudalism: A Historiographical Critique', Presidential Address, Section I, *PIHC*, Waltair Session, 1979.

inaccuracies and conceptual lacunae. The debate has immensely enriched Indian historiography. Whether there was an overall crisis in political and socio-economic life is, of course, debatable. But there is little doubt that the situation was changing after AD 600. Here lies the logic of perceiving a new phase in Indian socio-economic, political and cultural life, distinct enough to be labelled as the early medieval period in Indian history.

That the formulation of Indian feudalism has been one of the most important and fruitful debates in Indian historiography has already been touched upon. One of the major premises of arguing against Indian feudalism is found in the study of early medieval trade. It would be difficult to dismiss the reality that evidently all Indian villages certainly did not possess two vital resources: viz., salt and iron. The need to procure these two essentials is hardly compatible with the imagining of a self-sufficient and enclosed village society.[182] A recent study, on the contrary, stresses that early medieval villages were neither undifferentiated nor isolates.[183] This opens up immense possibilities for the evidence of movements among individual villages which were linked with the locality-level centres above them.

Moreover, the critique of Indian feudalism has brought to light considerable evidence of trade, urbanism and the money economy in early medieval India and the distinguishing features of this trade have been discerned by historians.[184] It is true that landgrants which provide us with the bulk of information would be primarily concerned with

[182]M.N. Srinivas and A.M. Shah, 'The Myth of the Self-Sufficiency of Indian Village', *Economic Weekly*, XII, 1960, pp. 1375–78.

[183]B.D. Chattopadhyaya, *Aspects of Rural Settlements and Rural Society in Early Medieval India,* Calcutta, 1990.

[184]The debate concerning Indian feudalism has generated a large number of publications opposed to the image of a slump in trade and urban centres. A more elaborate list is given in the Annotated Bibliography. Here a few works are cited. D.C. Sircar, *The Emperor and His Subordinate Rulers*, Santiniketan, 1982; B.D. Chattopadhyaya, 'State and Economy in North India: Fourth Century to Twelfth Century', in Romila Thapar (ed.), *op. cit.*, pp. 308–46; R. Champakalakshmi, 'State and Economy: South India, circa AD 400–1300', in Romila Thapar (ed.), *op. cit.*, pp. 266–308; a recent statement on the debate is also available in Ranabir Chakravarti, 'Politics and Society in India *c.* AD 300–1000', in K. Satchidananda Murty (ed.), Project on the History of Indian Science, Philosophy and Culture, II (to be published).

the agrarian sector. But painstaking and insightful studies of even the meagre and marginal notices on commercial life in copper plates and other inscriptions have adequately acquainted us with the different types of merchants and the various levels of marketplaces and exchange centres over the greater parts of the subcontinent during the six centuries in question. These certainly speak of the presence of merchants and trade centres. But more fundamentally, their active role is evident in the economic scenario even before *c.* AD 1000, a cut-off timeline which, in the changing perceptions of Indian feudalism, is considered to have brought about some revival of trade. Two other points have to be stressed here. First, the data, however imperfect and limited, highlight the impressive range of commodities at marketplaces, including transactions in daily necessities and agricultural products. This is not surprising as the landgrant economy certainly helped the expansion of agriculture. In fact, even the proponents of Indian feudalism now accept the possibilities of growth in the rural economy.[185] Second, rural and locality-level trade centres of diverse types become conspicuous by their presence during the early middle ages. Their local and regional characters are well pronounced and, in fact, they are rooted to their respective regions. Their rise to prominence can be convincingly explained in the light of the local and regional formations in early medieval India.[186] Many of these trade centres appear to have provided the vital linkage between the rural exchange centres on the one hand and the larger and more complex marketplaces in urban centres on the other. This type of middle category trade centres appears as *maṇḍapikās* in north India, as *peṇṭhās* in the Deccan, and as *nagarams* in the far south. There is a distinct possibility that the genesis of the *maṇḍī* in north India and the *peṭh* in the Deccan can be traced in the early medieval *maṇḍapikā* and *peṇṭhā*.[187] The essays by B.D. Chattopadhyaya and Ranabir

[185] R.N. Nandi, 'Growth of Rural Economy in Early Feudal India', Presidential Address, Section I, *PIHC*, Annamalai Session, 1984.

[186] B.D. Chattopadhyaya, *The Making of Early Medieval India*, Delhi, 1994.

[187] *Maṇḍapikās* and other local-level market centres figure in B.D. Chattopadhyaya's article included in this volume; also see Ranabir Chakravarti, 'Trade at Maṇḍapikās in Early Medieval North India', in D.N Jha (ed.), *Society and Ideology in India, Essays in Honour of Professor R.S. Sharma*, Delhi, 1996, pp. 69–80; 'The Puṭabhedana as a Centre of Trade in Early India', *SAS*, 12, 1996, pp. 33–38 discusses *peṇṭhā*; for

Chakravarti in this volume highlight trade, marketplaces and traders in early medieval society, in arid Rajasthan and coastal Konkan respectively.

One of the principal areas of interest of the historians of trade in early India has been the study of the associations of merchants. The general and common tendency is to label such groups as guilds. Recent scholarship, however, tends to disfavour such a description, as it implies the anticipation of the idea of early modern European commercial guilds during the early middle age in India. Such a loose labelling of the term 'guild' is also largely borrowed from European historiography. This does not deny the existence of the association of merchants in early India. The existence of professional bodies of merchants is hinted at as early as in the Buddhist texts. The references to the representatives of merchants and their official seals are available during the Gupta times. But these 'guild'-like bodies tend to decrease in number in the Ganga valley during the early medieval times.[188] On the other hand, the prominent position of such mercantile bodies is clearly noted in western India (Gujarat) and the far south; in both the areas there are ample evidences of brisk trade during the early medieval times. Early medieval Karnataka, Tamilnadu and Kerala offer profuse information regarding the activities of three such bodies: *nānādeśīs*, *maṇigrāmam* and the 500 *svāmīs* of Ayyavole.[189] Moreover, inscriptions bear out that these bodies were widely distributed in the Deccan and south India; in fact, their presence in Sri Lanka, on the Myanmar coast and even in Sumatra is proved beyond doubt. Their linkages with the Coḷa rulers are particularly important in this context.[190] V.K. Jain and R. Champakalakshmi look at such bodies in early medieval Gujarat and south India respectively. They enlighten us on the role of mercantile bodies in two different areas of the subcontinent, both famous for their widespread trade network in early medieval times.

---

the study of *nagaram* see K.R. Hall, *Trade and Statecraft in the Age of the Coḷas*, Delhi, 1980.

[188]Lallanji Gopal, *op. cit.*, pp. 81–89.

[189]For a general account of these bodies in south India vide, A. Appadurai, *Economic Conditions in Southern India*, in two volumes, Madras, 1936.

[190]K.A. Nilakanta Sastri, *South India and South-East Asia*, Mysore, 1978, pp. 172–78 and 237–48; Meera Abraham, *Two Medieval Merchant Guilds of South India*, Heidelberg, 1988.

It is rather strange that the perceptions of Indian feudalism have taken relatively little notice of the consistent and profuse information on the remarkable expansion of the Indian Ocean trade from around the eighth century, in which India's role and involvement can hardly be minimized. To reconcile the assumed decline in the volume of India's long-distance trade precisely at the time of its obvious growth in the Indian Ocean is a difficult problem to account for. The rise of Islam, with its distinct thrust on commerce and urbanity, undoubtedly provided a very major fillip to long-distance trade, particularly across the Indian Ocean.[191] The sea-borne Asian trade had well-known termini in the west and the east, represented respectively by Siraf and Basra under the Seldjuk and Abbasid rulers and al Fustat (=old Cairo) under the Fatimid Caliphate (since 965) on the one hand and the harbours of China on the other. The round trip between the western and the eastern termini of the Indian Ocean trade was helped by the harbours on both the sea-boards of India which reaped conspicuous advantage as inevitable stopovers, transshipment points, besides themselves participating in the exports and imports to and from the subcontinent. K.N. Chaudhuri locates the beginning of this system of 'segmented voyages' between the eastern and the western termini of the Indian Ocean from *c.* AD1000 onwards. Following his arguments, the segmented voyages would not only lead to the proliferation of ports but also would encourage 'emporia trade'.[192] The impact of segmented voyages and emporia trade must have proved beneficial to India's sea-borne commerce during the early middle ages.

The western littoral with greater indentations than its eastern counterpart was naturally suitable to the growth of estuarine ports. There were a string of ports of outstanding importance on the west coast, starting from Debal in the Indus delta, then to the harbours on the Gujarat littorals like Somnath, Stambhaka (=Khambaya/Kanbaya of the Arab texts) or Cambay and Broach (=Baruch of the Arabic authors); followed by Sthānaka (Thana), Sanjan (Sindjan of the Arabic texts), Śūrpāraka (=Subara in Arabic geographical texts), Cemūlīya, called Saimur by the Arabs (Chaul to the south of Bombay),

[191]G.F. Hourani, *The Arab Seafaring in the Indian Ocean during the Ancient and Early Medieval Times*, Beirut, 1951.

[192]K.N. Chaudhuri, *Trade and Civilisation in the Indian Ocean from the Rise of Islam to 1700*, Cambridge, 1985.

Candrapura or Sindabur near Goa on the Konkan littorals and finally the ports in Malabar, e.g. Maṅgalapura or Manjrur (=Mangalore), Fandarina or Pantalayani and Kulam-mali or Quilon.[193] The ports of course did not remain in static conditions and experienced fluctuating fortunes. The rise and fall of such ports can be explained by a combination of various factors: natural causes, the relation of the port with its hinterland and foreland, the presence or absence of smaller or feeder ports around a premier harbour and the overall political stability or otherwise in a given coastal area. The alternating peaks and valleys in the importance of these harbours can be linked with the periodic shifts in the significance of the Persian Gulf and the Red Sea as the two major sea-lanes in the western Indian Ocean. It is true that the Konkan ports, despite having the best suitable geographical locations, were often overshadowed by the harbours on the Gujarat and Malabar coasts. This prompts us to bring in here the assessment of the geographical factors in the location and development of early Indian ports, a survey made by Jean Deloche. His approach is essentially that of a geographer. The dialogues between history and geography have often been emphasized, perhaps by none more than the Annales school of scholars like Lucien Lefvre, Marc Bloch and Fernand Braudel.

No less striking is the presence of Jewish merchants at Manjrur (Mangalore) from the early eleventh century to the twelfth century. These merchants, labelled as 'India traders', were involved in the brisk trade network mainly between al Fustat (= old Cairo) and Aden, but substantially extending also up to the south-western coast of India. These Jewish merchants, actively participating in the maritime trade of the western Indian Ocean (the Red Sea, the Gulf of Aden and the Arabian Sea), are called 'India traders' by Goitein. The fascinating letters of 'India traders', deposited in and discovered from the Cairo *geniza*, offer us a mine of information on the Indian Ocean trade. According to Jewish belief, no piece of paper containing the name of God could be destroyed. As these business letters usually

[193] A useful overview of these ports with citations from diverse sources is available in S.M.H. Nainar, *Arab Geographers' Knowledge of Southern India*, Madras, 1942; K.A. Nilakanta Sastri, *Foreign Notices of South India from Megasthenes to Ma Huan*, Madras, 1935. The famous port of Calicut seems to have come to prominence not before the first half of the fourteenth century AD. This is evident from the fourteenth-century accounts of Calicut by Ibn Battuta.

began and ended with the customary invocation of God, the letters were left in the *geniza* and hence they survived. The term *geniza* (pronounced gheneeza) is derived from the Persian *ganj*, meaning a storehouse or a treasure. In medieval Hebrew, the term *geniza* means a repository of discarded writings.[194] In the second half of the tenth century, the foundation of the Fatimid Caliphate in Egypt resulted in the emergence of Fustat or Old Cairo as the commercial capital of the 'west'.[195] This further coincides with the gradual receding of Siraf in the Persian Gulf as the premier port of the Arab world. The rise of the Fatimid Caliphate in Egypt was certainly conducive to the rise of the Red Sea as the principal sealane between South Asia and the West. There was a corresponding lessening of the maritime trade in the Persian Gulf after the tenth century. The crucial point here is that the renewed importance of the sea-borne trade through the Red Sea must have proved advantageous for the commercial links between South Asia and the Mediterranean region on the southern shore of which stood the famous Egyptian (Misr) port of Alexandria. Free from ornate court eulogies, fabulous tales, sastric injunctions and the problems of fixing chronologies, these letters expectedly furnish the matter of fact details regarding the commodities transacted, the shipping patterns and the diversities of merchants. The letters are a significant testimony to the exchange of information among merchants in countries at great distances from each other. But the most significant point is the remarkable spirit of cooperation, symapthy and friendly ties among the Indian, the Jewish and the Muslim Arab merchants, irrespective of their diverse ethnic roots and religious

[194]The largest number of *geniza* papers were discovered from a lumber room attached to a synagogue in Fustat. S.D. Goitein, *A Mediterranean Society*, I, Los Angeles and Berkeley, 1967, pp. 1–2. The enormity of the number of Jewish letters is evident in Shaul Shaked, *A Tentative Bibliography of Geniza Documents*, Paris and the Hague, 1964.

[195]For a general account of al Fustat see E.J. Brill's *First Encyclopaedia of Islam*, 1913–36 (rpt. 1987), III. It is particularly significant that excavations at al Fustat have yielded as much as seventeen thousand shards of pottery, out of which twelve thousand pieces were Chinese. These archaeological materials leave little room for doubt about the far-flung network of this port. A summary of different archaeological excavations at Fustat is given by Tsugio Mikami, 'Chinese Ceramics from Medieval Sites in Egypt', in H.I.H. Prince Takahito Mikasa (ed.), *Cultural and Economic Relations between the East and West*, Wiesbaden, 1988, pp. 8–44.

leanings and notwithstanding the obvious elements of commercial rivalries among them.[196]

S.D. Goitein, the most celebrated scholar on the *geniza* documents, started publishing these documents on 'India trade' as early as 1954, it is only very recently that historians of early Indian economy and society have paid attention to these. These are relatively less utilized documents which should be a major stimulant to the study of early Indian trade and the social history of trade.[197] Though the herculean efforts of Goitein and some of his colleagues in studying the *geniza* papers can seldom be matched, there may be some interesting gaps which require to be filled for a better understanding of early Indian trade. Primarily a great authority on the medieval Mediterranean and the Jewish society, Goitein could not but have marginal or peripheral interests in the Indian situation. Further, he seems to have been drawn mainly to the social history of the medieval Jewish community. 'The object of this book', Goitein wrote in the early part of his monumental *Mediterranean Society*, is

> 'society rather than economy, human relations and not technology. So while surveying the main commodities of the Mediterranean area, the routes they travelled and the prices they obtained, we have in mind the people who traded and those who used them rather than the materials themselves.'[198]

This may leave some scope for the historian of early Indian trade of looking into the letters of India traders afresh, with a distinct ori-

[196] S.D. Goitein, *A Mediterranean Society,* in five volumes, Los Angeles and Berkeley, 1967–90; S.D. Goitein, *Studies in Islamic History and Institutions*, Leiden, 1966; S.D. Goitein, *Jews and Arabs: Their Contacts through the Ages*, Leiden, 1964. Goitein also prepared his *India Book* which is his collection of 354 *geniza* documents on the India trade. This invaluable source book is often referred to by him, but remained unpublished during his lifetime. It is expected that it would be published shortly as a posthumous work of this great scholar.

[197] The India trade figured in a prominent way for the first time in the voluminous bibliography of S.D. Goitein in 'Two Eye Witness Reports on the Invasion of Aden by Kais in the Twelfth Century', *BSOAS*, XVI, 1954. Interestingly enough, Amitav Ghosh, a social anthropologist by academic training, has come up with a fascinating account (*In An Antique Land*, 1990) about a Jewish merchant in Mangalore (1032 to 1049) and his Indian slave Bomma, based on the *geniza* records.

[198] *A Mediterranean Society*, I, Los Angeles and Berkeley, 1967, p. 210.

entation to the history of Indian trade in general and India's place in the Indian Ocean commerce in particular.

The eastern littoral was naturally oriented towards the movements of men and traffic in the eastern sector of the Indian Ocean which was further linked up with the Java and the China Seas. The Coromandel coast could boast of Māmallapuram of the Pallava times and Nāgapaṭṭinam during the Coḷa rule as premier ports of international trade.[199] On the Andhra-Kalinga coast was situated Viśākhapaṭṭinam, known at least since AD 1068, which offers the unique example of a Coḷa port being renamed after the reigning king. Kulottuṅga I must have officially enhanced the importance of this Andhra harbour by designating it as Kulottuṅgacoḷapaṭṭinam, though its previous name Viśākhapaṭṭinam was always retained.[200] The sustained Coḷa interests in long-distance seaborne trade will be particularly evident from the three embassies sent by the Coḷas to Sung emperors in China (1014, 1033 and 1079).[201] The close ties between the Coḷa realm and Śrīvijaya (modern Palembang) in South-East Asia are clearly attested to by the cultural patronage of the Śrīvijaya king to a Buddhist monastery at Nāgapaṭṭinam; such cultural interests appear to have been strongly backed by material gains from maritime trade. The likelihood of such an interpretation lies in the well-documented role of Śrīvijaya as an intermediary between south India and China. An inscription of the seventh regnal year of Rājendra records two gifts of Chinese gold (*cīnakkanakam*) made to a temple in Nāgapaṭṭinam by the agent of *Kīḍārattaraiyar* or the king of Kaḍāram (identified with Kedah in the Malaya peninsula). Similarly, the agent (*kanmi*) of the ruler of Śrīvijaya (*Śrīvijaiyattaraiyar*) also made a gift of a jewel to the Karonasvami temple at Nāgapaṭṭinam.[202] The close commercial and diplomatic ties between the Coḷa realm and the kingdom

[199]K.A. Nilakanta Sastri, *The Coḷas*, Madras, 1955, pp. 603–610; K.R. Hall, *op. cit.*

[200]Ranabir Chakravarti, 'Kulottuṅga and the Port of Viśākhapaṭṭinam', *PIHC*, XLI, 1981, Bodhgaya, pp. 142–5.

[201]The annals of the Sung dynasty in China refer to Chu-lien or the Coḷa country. Rājarāja figures therein as Lo-tsa-lo-tsa, and Rājendra as Shi-lo-lo-cha Yin-to-lo-chu-lo, while Kulottuṅga appears as Ti-hua kia-lo. See K.A. Nilakanta Sastri, *The Coḷas*, p. 219.

[202]Ibid. *The Coḷas,* p. 220; also *ARE* 164 of 1956–57 and *ARE* 166 of 1956–57.

of Kadaram in Malaya peninsula are certainly consistent with the image of the Coḷa interests in the affairs of the Bay of Bengal.

Recent researches in the Coḷa attitudes towards economic activities and particularly towards mercantile groups show the awareness that the Coḷas had regarding the importance of commerce.[203] It is true that the Coḷas, unlike most of the major powers of early India, maintained their protracted interests in the political and economic affairs of the Bay of Bengal. The study of the Coḷa naval expeditions[204] has brought about divergent explanations of the Coḷa aggressive designs in Sri Lanka and South-East Asia. The urge for gaining glory by launching daring overseas raids, according to some historians, prompted the Coḷa emperors to undertake maritime campaigns.[205] But the Coḷa policy of launching aggressive maritime raids enduring for over a century and a quarter cannot be convincingly explained by the *digvijaya* model which can, at best, be applied to the reign period of a single charismatic political personality. An alternative to this stance of conventional historiography is found in the imagination of the Coḷa maritime conquests as being mainly motivated by plunder. This implies that the Coḷa maritime campaigns were prompted by the prospects of short-term gains or were conducted due to desperation of exasperated rulers. The graphic account of the systematic looting of the Buddhist monasteries in Sri Lanka by the Coḷas has provided some clues to the plunder motive behind the Coḷa maritime expeditions. This reading of the Coḷa maritime campaigns by Spencer[206] actually takes off from the portrayal of the Coḷa realm as a segmentary state by Burton Stein.[207]

[203]K.R. Hall, *op. cit.*; R. Champakalakshmi, 'State and Economy: South India, *circa* AD 400–1300', in Romila Thapar (ed.), *op. cit.*, pp. 288–90.

[204]For a standard and factual description of the Coḷa maritime conquests of Sri Lanka (by Rājarāja and Rājendra), the Maldive islands (by Rājarāja), twelve places in South-East Asia by Rājendra and the Coḷa expeditions to Sri Lanka during the times of Rājendra's successors, see K.A. Nilakanta Sastri, *The Coḷas*, pp. 183, 199–200, 211–18, 252–53, 271–72 and 317–19.

[205]R.C. Majumdar, 'The Overseas Expeditions of King Rājendra Coḷa', *Artibus Asiae*, XXIV, 1962, pp. 338–42; K.G. Krishnan, 'Coḷa Rājendra's Expedition to South-East Asia', *JIH* (Golden Jubilee Volume), 1973, pp. 109–17.

[206]George W. Spencer, 'The Politics of Plunder: The Coḷas in Eleventh Century Ceylon', *Journal of Asian Studies*, XXVI, 1977, pp. 405–20; George W. Spencer, *The Politics of Expansion—The Coḷa Conquests of Sri Lanka and Srivijaya*, Madras, 1983.

[207]Burton Stein, *Peasant State and Society in Medieval South India*, Delhi, 1980.

Stein negates the possibility of finding in the Coḷa empire a unified and bureaucratic polity, the like of which was strongly advocated by Nilakanta Sastri and T.V. Mahalingam.[208] The segmented polity of the Coḷas, in Stein's formulation, allowed little scope for the imposition and exercise of the effective control of the Coḷa central authority outside the lower Kaveri valley and the Kaveri delta, the core area of the Coḷa empire. The real foci of power are discerned by Stein in the locality-level centres or *nāḍus,* which stood above individual villages. The *nāḍu* was actually an agglomerate of a number of villages.[209] The enormous importance of the local self-governing bodies (*sabhā* in the *brahmadeya* villages and *ur* in the non-*brahmadeya* villages) in the Coḷa polity is explained by Stein from the point of view of the limited central authority and the minimal bureaucratic control of the apex political authority. Among the major functions of the local self-governing bodies was the collection and allocation of resources from villages and locality-level centres. Only a small portion of the resources collected through revenue measures probably reached the Coḷa central coffer. Spencer, subscribing to Stein's formulation of the segmented nature of the Coḷa realm, takes the next step and argues that the constant insufficiency of resources naturally compelled the Coḷas to undertake ambitious and daring raids to distant areas, including the celebrated sea-borne expeditions. This explains why Spencer views the Coḷa overseas expeditions as resource-gathering activities.[210] The formulations of Stein and Spencer have, however, evoked severe criticisms. Marxist historians consider the Coḷa state as feudal and not segmented and, therefore, reject

[208] K.A. Nilakanta Sastri, *The Coḷas*; T.V. Mahalingam, *South Indian Polity*, Madras, 1967. Both the authorities considered that the Coḷa polity had in it a harmonious combination of a highly centralized, almost Byzantine monarchy and the very active role of the local self-governing bodies at the rural level.

[209] Stein's study of the *nāḍu* is largely drawn from Y. Subbarayalu, *The Political Geography of the Coḷa Country*, Madras, 1973 which has highlighted the crucial role of the *nāḍu* in the Coḷa state.

[210] Spencer also thinks that the Coḷas did not command a standing army. The Coḷa army consisted of loose assemblages of diverse forces, including those taken from the organizations of Tamil merchants. Spencer argues that the Coḷas needed to wage constant wars not only for gaining booties from war, but also for keeping their forces under some kind of unity. This led him to describe the Coḷa campaigns as an integrative activity.

Stein's formulation.[211] The application of the feudal model to the understanding of the Coḷa state is frowned upon by Stein for implanting the Pirenne thesis on Indian conditions.[212]

But the feudal and the segmentary models of the Coḷa state, critical of each other, however show a striking consonance in their perception of the early medieval Indian polity. Both the models highlight the processes of disintegration and fragmentation as opposed to a centralized state structure. A third alternative approach criticizes both the feudal and the segmentary concepts and discerns the distinct elements of an 'integrative polity' in the Coḷa realm in which the intervention of the apex political authority into the functions of the locality-level centres and local self-governing bodies has been attested to by epigraphic evidence.[213] The vast corpus of Coḷa inscriptions has been put to rigorous analysis, including statistical analysis.[214] On the basis of these studies it is claimed that the Coḷas did not suffer from shortage of resources and therefore their expeditions to Sri Lanka and South-East Asia cannot be comprehended by the plunder dynamics highlighted by Spencer. The considerable amount of data on the Cola interests in trade, including long-distance trade in the Indian

[211]D.N. Jha, 'Validity of Brāhmaṇa Peasant Alliance and the Segmentary State in Early Medieval South India', *Social Science Probings*, June, 1984, pp. 270–96; R.S. Sharma, 'The Segmentary State and the Indian Experience', *IHR*, XVI, 1989–90. Kesavan Veluthat, *The Political Structure of Early Medieval South India*, New Delhi, 1993.

[212]Burton Stein, 'Politics, Peasants and the Deconstruction of Feudalism in Medieval India', in T.J. Byres and Harbans Mukhia (eds.), *Feudalism and Non-European Societies* (special number of the *Journal of Peasant Studies*), London, 1985.

[213]R. Champakalakshmi, 'Peasant State and Society in Medieval South India: A Review Article', *IESHR*, XVIII, 1981, pp. 411–26; Y. Subbarayalu, 'The Coḷa State', *Studies in History*, IV,1982, pp. 265–306; Hermann Kulke, 'Fragmentation and Segmentation versus Integration? Reflections on the Concepts of Indian Feudalism and Segmentary State in Indian History', *Studies in History*, IV ,1982, pp. 237–63; Hermann Kulke (ed.), *The State in India 1000–1700*, Delhi, 1995: Introduction; B.D. Chattopadhyaya, 'Political Processes and Structures of Polity in Early Medieval India: Problems of Perspectives', Presidential Address, Section I, *PIHC*, Burdwan session, 1983 (also incorporated in B.D. Chattopadhyaya, *The Making of Early Medieval India* and in Hermann Kulke (ed.), *The State in India 1000–1700*.

[214]Noboru Karashima, Y. Subbarayalu and Toro Matsui, *A Concordance of Names in the Coḷa Inscriptions*, Madurai, 1978.

Ocean, cannot be brushed aside. Rājarāja, Rājendra and Kulottuṅga, the three outstanding Coḷas monarchs, appear to have been well aware of the revenue-bearing potential of trade which further supplemented the principal resources of the Coḷa state realized from the agrarian sector.[215] It was this appreciation of the importance of trade on a long-term basis that prompted Kulottuṅga I to abolish tolls and customs (cf. his title *Suṅgandavirttacoḷa*), at a time when he consciously enhanced the status of the port of Viśākhapaṭṭinam.

The Bengal coast during the sixth and the seventh centuries AD was particularly famous for the port of Tāmralipta, which seems to have decayed around the eighth century AD. The adverse economic effects of the decline of Tāmralipta were, however, offset by the rise of a port of considerable importance to the east of the Meghna. This port, generally called Samandar by Arab writers, and Sudkawan by Ibn Battuta, was conveniently located near present-day Chittagong in Bangladesh.[216] The Arab chronicles furnish evidence of the maritime voyages from Samandar to Uranshin (Orissa), Kanja (Kāñcīpuram) and Serendib or Silandib (Sri Lanka). The cultural linkages of eastern and south India with both mainland and maritime South-East Asia could indirectly point to the commercial contacts among these areas.

India seems to have exported textiles of diverse types, aloe wood, teak (for ship building), coconut coir, grains including rice, iron of various types (known especially from the letters of Jewish merchants), spices (both indigenous and those brought from the South-East Asia and trans-shipped from India). The list of items of import is dimly known; silk, wine, tin, precious metals like silver and gold and different spices appear to have been imported into India.[217] The balance of trade may have been favourable to India, which seemingly imported fewer articles compared to her exports. Regarding the import of costly items, attention must be paid to war horses, always a rarity in India and, therefore, invariably imported. The major area for the supply of horses to India up to AD *c.* 600 was the Central Asian steppes wherefrom horses were sent overland to India through

[215] Noboru Karashima and B. Sitaraman, 'Revenue Terms in Coḷa Inscriptions', *Journal of Asian and African Studies*, 5, 1972, pp. 87–117.

[216] B.N. Mukherjee, 'Commerce and Money in the Central and Western Sectors of Eastern India (750–1200)', *IMB*, XVII, 1982, pp. 65–83.

[217] Publications dealing with items of export and import are discussed in the Annotated Bibliography.

the north-western borderlands. Nomadic depredations after AD 600 led to the increasing preference for sea-trade in horses in place of the previous overland transactions. The proliferation of regional powers and their protracted military designs appear to have caused a manifold increase in the demand for the best quality war horses from Arabia, Fers (Persia) and Sham (Syria) which fetched enormous prices and were generally called *bahri* (sea-borne) horses. Victories in war often resulted in the systematic looting of horse stables. Marco Polo, providing insights into the overseas import trade of horses to India, accused the ruler at Tana (=Thana on the Konakan coast)—identifiable with the Yādavas of Devagiri—of connivance with local pirates for illegally procuring war horses from wrecked ships.[218]

IX

The rapid survey of inland and sea-borne trade during the early middle ages clearly conveys an impression contrary to the perception of languishing trade which is viewed as a major ingredient of feudal formation in India. It is hazardous to offer generalizations on the conditions of commerce in the overall background of the subcontinent. One can hardly deny that there would be considerable variations during different periods and places of the subcontinent registering either a decline or a rise in trade. Our preceding arguments, however, may give the general impression that there was neither any major slump of trade within the subcontinent nor any dimunition of India's role in the maritime commerce of the Indian Ocean. But the nature and pattern of trade did develop certain features distinct from what was seen during the early historical times. In fact, many of the tendencies that emerged in the eighth and ninth centuries in the Indian Ocean network reached fruition in the medieval period.[219]

If the above arguments go to show the development as well as a slight shrinkage of commerce during the early middle ages then the

[218]Ranabir Chakravarti, 'Maritime Trade in Horses in Early Medieval India: Shipping and Piracy', in D.C. Bhattacharyya and Devendra Handa (eds.), *Prācīprabhā*, Delhi, 1989, pp. 343–60.

[219]K.N. Chaudhuri, *Asia Before Europe, Economic Civilisation in the Indian Ocean from the Rise of Islam to 1700*, Cambridge, 1990; also J. Abu-Lughod, *Before European Hegemony: The World System AD 1250–1350*, New York, 1989.

related problematic of the medium of exchange has to be addressed at this juncture. The formulation of Indian feudalism has a major underpinning based on the virtual absence of gold (and also silver) coins which, under worsening trade situations, were said to have made the way for cowry shells as the principal medium of exchange, merely suitable for petty trade at the local level. There are grounds to accept the wide use of cowry shells (*kapardaka*) and the less frequent use of coins in precious metals minted by political powers in the period between 600 and 1000. One cannot, however, turn a blind eye to specific information from the early medieval Arab chronicles and the early Portuguese accounts that cowry shells were in fact themselves an item of long-distance maritime trade, being shipped from the Maldives to Bengal. The availability of cowry shells in an area like Bengal cannot straightaway speak of a slump in trade, as Bengal exported rice to the Maldives and imported cowry shells in return. Cowry shells (like trade in grains and rice) have alternatively been perceived as performing the role of ballast and small exchanges in the Indian Ocean maritime trade.[220] On the other hand, the south-eastern-most parts of early medieval Bengal (Harikela and Paṭṭikera for example) are known to have been thoroughly acquainted with high-quality silver currency of 57.6 grains (i.e. struck on the well-known metallic standard of *kārṣāpaṇa*, *purāṇa* and *dramma*). This silver currency was minted and circulated continuously from the seventh to the thirteenth centuries. The same area has yielded Abbasid gold coins too. Numismatic studies have further pointed to the changes in the metrology, shape and execution of the Harikela coinage from the ninth century onwards, showing conformities to the reformed Arabic currency of the same time. The profound importance of this numismatic evidence lies in the fact that it sets at naught the assumed incompatibility between a money-based economy and a land-grant economy, both of which are reported from early medieval Bengal. The minting of coins as a prerogative of state power began in India with the Bactrian Greeks (*c.* second century BC) and went on up to the seventh century AD. The apparent lack of dynastic coinage in India from the seventh to the end of the tenth century has been explained in terms of a changed political attitude to minting, which was not regarded

[220] J. Heiman, 'Small Exchange and Ballast: Cowry Trade and Usage as an Example of Indian Ocean Economic History', *South Asia*, II, 1980, pp. 48–69.

as an expression of sovereignty till the foundation of the Sultanate.[221] To this must be added the in-depth inquiry into the various north Indian coin hoards belonging to the early medieval times.[222] The controversy regarding the nature of trade and the circulation of money during the early medieval period also figures in John S. Deyell's study of the monetary history of early medieval north India. His painstaking study of several coin hoards of early medieval north India points out the fragility of the interpretative models of languishing trade and demonetization.

The historiography of Indian feudalism highlights the close linkages between the slump in trade and urban anaemia in early medieval India. Urban contraction, the logic and evidence of which have been briefly discussed above, was apparently caused by, and associated with rural expansion. The key to this critical situation is located in the practice of granting lands favouring agrarian spread and growth. Thus, agrarian spread is cited as a causative factor in the eclipse of the second urbanization in Indian history. Strangely enough, a number of historians and archaeologists attached the greatest importance to the improved use of iron technology and agricultural development, generating vital agrarian surplus, as the key factor for the rise of cities in early historical times. But the same genre of historical writings portrays agrarian expansion of the early medieval period as the principal villain behind the disappearance of cities on a pan-Indian scale from AD 300–1000.

Such contradictions and inconsistencies in the construction of commerce and urbanism in the early middle ages have made historians re-examine available evidence from literary, epigraphic and field archaeological materials. As the number of early medieval archaeological sites are admittedly few, the field archaeological information is meagre. While several leading urban sites show unmistakable archaeological proof of their downward slide, some other sites provided no signs of desertion. Thus excavations at Chirand, Varanasi, Ahicchatra, Purana Qila in the Ganga valley, and Ahar and Ujjayini in Malwa point to continuous and uninterrupted occupation during AD 700–1200. Intelligent utilization of epigraphic materials establishes

[221]B.N. Mukherjee, *The Media of Exchange in Early Medieval North India*, Delhi, 1992.

[222]Lallanji Gopal, *Early Medieval Coin Types in North India*, Varanasi, 1966. The numismatic situation in south India is dealt with by B.D. Chattopadhyaya, *Coins and Currency System in South India*, Delhi, 1977.

urban features of some new settlements (not known before AD 600) in north India even in the pre-1000 period, e.g. early medieval urban centres at Pṛthūdaka (=Pehoa in Haryana), Tattānandapura (=Bulandshahar), labelled as a *purapattana* in the epigraphic records of AD 867–907, Sīyāḍuni, also labelled as a *pattana*. The early medieval town of Gopādri(=Gwalior) was known as a *koṭṭa*. The said suffix indicates the importance of the urban area as an administrative-cum-military headquarters. That certain areas in an overall rural context could sometimes assume the features of a town is indicated by the presence of a *haṭṭikā* (small rural marketplace) attached to Dhṛtipura (the suffix *pura* is indicative of its urban nature) in early medieval Vaṅga under the Candra kings. That Veṇugrāma (Belgam) in Karnataka too emerged as an eminent point of convergence for merchants of various types who hailed from both neighbouring and distant areas and had an impressive range of products—staples and luxuries—is recorded in an early thirteenth-century inscription. There is clear proof of Veṇugrāma combining features of a commercial and a religious centre.[223] The rise of Kuḍāmukku-Palaiyarai, the twin cities of the Coḷas, to prominence has been attributed to: (i) its access to and linkages with the hinterland for the supply of local agrarian products, (ii) the importation of luxury items for the consumption of the elite groups, and (iii) its role as a religious centre with leading temple establishments.[224]

It may, therefore, be reasonably argued that notwithstanding the decay of a number of prominent towns in India, especially in the Ganga valley, during AD 300–900, a general urban decay did not engulf the subcontinent as a whole. The diagnosis of urban anaemia, leading to ruralization and peasantization, may not serve as an all purpose key to our assessment of the Indian material milieu. Urban developments in the early historical and early medieval times were not primarily conditioned by the highs and lows of external trade. The greater the convergence of economic, political and cultural

[223]B.D. Chattopadhyaya, *The Making of Early Medieval India*, pp. 130–82; B.D. Chattopadhyaya, 'State and Economy in North India: Fourth Century to Twelfth Century', in Romila Thapar (ed.), *op. cit.*, pp. 309–46.

[224]R. Champakalakshmi, 'Growth of Urban Centres in South India: Kuḍāmukku-Palaiyarai, the Twin Cities of the Coḷas', *Studies in History*, I, 1979, pp. 1–30; R. Champakalakshmi, 'State and Eonomy: South India *circa* AD 400–1300', in Romila Thapar (ed.), *op. cit.*, pp. 288–90.

(including religious) activities at an urban centre, the more eminent would be its position than cities with a predominantly single functional role. Urban centres of early medieval times, however, are seen not merely as counterpoints to the feudal social formations, but also as being distinct from cities belonging to the early historical phase. The second urbanization in Indian history (*c.* 600 BC–AD 300) had an epicentre in the Ganga valley (or more precisely in the middle Ganga valley) which acted as a platform for the development of secondary urban areas in other regions of India by the first century AD. An overview of the emergence of urban centres in the early medieval period does not postulate any such epicentre generating urban impulses to disparate regions. Urban centres from AD 600 onwards, on the other hand, appear to have been strongly oriented to their local roots and, therefore, may be judged in terms of their respective local developments and local formations. Such local formations were largely helped by agrarian expansion, generating resources for local or supra-local ruling groups. The mobilization of resources and the urge to procure exotic and luxury items by rulers would encourage the movements of products, both within the region and also beyond it. The growing popularity of sectarian *bhakti* cults was often expressed in the brisk temple-building activities and/or patronage to *maṭha* complexes. Both the temple and the *maṭha* are found to have provided excellent meeting grounds for ruling groups and mercantile communities. The combinations of these formations helped the emergence and development of early medieval cities, which by their distinctiveness are situated in the third phase of urbanization in Indian history.

X

That the subcontinent was a commercial zone of vital importance is evident from the early Indian exchange and trade for nearly three and a half millennia. The new perspectives of and approaches to the study of early Indian trade can by no means deny the predominantly agrarian nature of the economy. The history of early trade and commerce in India has, therefore, to be situated in the over-all agrarian milieu.

One does understand that traders and other peoples involved in exchange networks must have been a minority in early Indian society, like in any pre-industrial and 'traditional' society. The bulk of the population was certainly engaged in agriculture. Agriculture being strongly embedded in the Indian socio-economic milieu, how were trade and traders viewed in early India? The general picture is one of low regard for this profession. But this is perhaps not a static situation. The *Arthaśāstra's* definition of *vārttā* (economics, doubtless derived from *vṛtti* or occupation/profession) includes in it *kṛṣi* (agriculture), *paśupālya* (cattle-keeping/animal husbandry) and *vāṇijya* (trade). All these professions were theoretically to be followed by the vaiśya, the third in the four-fold *varṇa* system. It is true that the vaiśya was looked down upon, from the point of view of the kṣatriya (the ruling power), as one who could be oppressed at will (*yāthākāmapreṣya*) and evicted at will (*yathākāmotthāpya*) in the *Aitareya Brāhmaṇa*.[225] On the other hand, the early Pali canonical texts considered *vanijjā* along with *kasi* and *go-rakkhā* as noble professions (*ukkaṭṭha kamma*), fit to be taken up by members of the noble lineages (*ukkaṭṭha kula*).[226]

Kauṭilya never concealed his suspicion of merchants and Manu also declares trade as a mixture between truth and falsehood (*satyānṛta*, IV.6). It is hardly surprising that the strict sastric code would view the merchant as an open thief (*prakāśyataskara*). The well-known dictum of Manu, banning the brāhmaṇas from undertaking a sea-voyage,[227] later resulted in the branding of a sea-crossing as a *kalivarjya* (an act to be discarded in the Kali age). All these definitely contributed to a negative image of trade as a profession in early India, though we have presented the evidence that it did not act as a deterrent to commerce. In fact, this is not something unique and limited only to the Indian situation and psyche.

Quoting extensively from the *Muqaddimah* of the celebrated historian Ibn Khaldun, K.N. Chaudhuri acquaints us with the generally unfavourable image of merchants. Ibn Khaldun remarked,

> Commerce is a natural way of making profits. But most of its practices and methods, he thought, were composed of tricks and designed to obtain a profit through the difference between the cost price and the selling price. The law permitted cunning in commerce because commerce contained an element of gambling.[228]

[225]R.C. Majumdar (ed.), *The Vedic Age*, pp. 453–56.

[226]N. Wagle, *Society at the Time of the Buddha*, London, 1966; Uma Chakravarti, *op. cit.*

[227]Significantly enough, Manu (III.158) declares a sea-voyager (*samudrayāyin*) unfit to attend a *śrāddha* ceremony, but this does not categorically imply the expulsion of the person from his *varṇa-jāti* status.

[228]K.N. Chaudhuri, 'Reflections on the Organizing Principles of Premodern

On the other hand, there are known historical instances of encouragement to external trade and 'foreign' traders. Embassies from Indian rulers were sent to the Roman court in early historical times and from the Coḷa country to the Chinese court in the eleventh and twelfth centuries.[229] In 1245 the Kākatīya ruler Gaṇapati (of eastern Deccan) issued an edict of security (*abhayaśāsana*) to maritime merchants (*saṁyātrikebhyaḥ*) visiting the port of Motuppalli (not far away from modern Masulipatnam) within his domain, to ensure protection from piracy, because wealth was considered greater than even life (*prāṇebhyoḥ 'api garīyasī*).[230] Such responses can be explained by the rulers' urge to gain from trade and the revenue realized therefrom. One may also offer an alternative explanation, following P. D. Curtin: precisely because trade and traders were given a dubious distinction, external trade and foreign traders were extended a cordial and courteous welcome. The 'dirty job' is best left to an outsider.[231]

In early India the merchant often countered this prejudice by improving his actual status (*vis-à-vis* his ritual status) through making patronage to cultural (including religious) activities. The regular donations of the *seṭṭhi* to the Buddhist *saṁgha* are well attested to

Trade', in James D. Tracy (ed.), *The Rise of Merchant Empires*, Cambridge, 1990, pp. 421–42; quotation is on p. 432.

[229]See E.H. Warmington, *op. cit.* and K.A. Nilakantha Sastri, *The Coḷas*, Madras, 1955 for missions during the Indo-Roman trade and the Coḷa times, respectively.

[230]E. Hultsch, 'The Motupalli Pillar Inscription of Kākatīya Gaṇapati', *EI*, XII, 1912, pp. 188–97; Ranabir Chakravarti, 'Economic Policy of Kākatīya Gaṇapati', *JAIH*, XI, 1977–78, pp. 72–79.

[231]P.D. Curtin, *Cross Cultural Trade in World History*, Cambridge, 1984. Curtin treats the situation of non-indigenous merchants from the point of the 'trade diaspora'. The term diaspora is a Greek word for scattering (as in the broadcasting of seeds). A trade diaspora would consist of interrelated nets of commercial communities forming a trade network. Non-indigenous traders in a trade diaspora are also seen as cross-cultural brokers. They are a minority, specializing in a single kind of economic enterprise in relation to the host society. The latter is, of course, a whole society with diversified occupations, stratifications and political divisions. K.N. Chaudhuri, 'Reflections on the Organizing Principles of Premodern Trade', in James D. Tracy (ed.), *op. cit.*, p. 426, tells us about the astonishment of the fourteenth-century traveller Ibn Battuta at the high status given to visiting Arab merchants in east African trading towns.

and may explain the honourable position accorded to him in the Buddhist texts. In AD 466 two merchants of kṣatriya origin (*kṣatriya-vaṇik*) made a perpetual gift in cash to a Sun temple at Indrapura (= present-day Indore, Bulandshahr district, U.P.).[232] They were making a pious act, but had already transgressed the strict code of occupation related to their specific *jāti/varṇa*. That, however, did not prevent them from making a donation for a religious and charitable cause. Or, precisely because of this transgression the kṣatriya merchants could have tried to make amends by offering their patronage to the temple. At Siyadoni in the Ganga-Yamuna doab region, a salt dealer (*nemakavaṇija*), whose father had also followed the same trade, made several donations to a few shrines at the trade centre (*pattanamaṇḍapikā*) of Siyadoni. At the time of giving the sum total of the donations he made, the inscriptions label him no longer as a *vaṇij*, but as one belonging to the *nemakajāti*.[233] This is a telling instance of how a merchant tried to purchase a respectable *jāti* status through making religious donations. For achieving something intangible like status, patronage through something tangible in the form of monetary donations was a convenient way out.[234] The merchant was certainly capable of spending the required resources for extending such patronage. His patronage to religio-cultural and art activities may come under the categories of *dāna* and *iṣṭa-purta* (construction of works of public utility)[235] which ensured *puṇya* or merit for the merchant and, therefore, could have helped him gain upward mobility in the long run.

Trade as an action at a distance or a cross-cultural activity has immense potential of breaking down the isolation and insularity of a given area or a community. As traders are often purveyors of culture, trade has immense potential for rich cultural exchanges and creative cultural urges. Early India abounds in such examples, like the efflorescence of Gandhara art, the composition of the astronomical treatise, *Yavanajātaka* by Sphujīdhvaja (*c.* AD 150), the spread of Indian religious ideas to East, Central and South-East Asia and so on. There is little difficulty in appreciating that a bilingual inscription (in Sanskrit

[232] *SI*, I, pp. 318–20.

[233] F. Kielhorn, 'Siyadoni Stone Inscription', *EI*, I, pp. 162–79.

[234] Barbara Stoller Miller (ed.), *The Powers of Art, Patronage in Indian Culture*, Delhi, 1992.

[235] For a general account of *iṣṭa-purta* and related textual citations, see P.V. Kane, *History of the Dharmasastra*, V, Poona 1962, pp. 947–49.

and Arabic) would be carved out at Somnath in AD 1264 when the ship-owning merchant, *nakhuda* Nuruddin Firuz of Hormuz, built a mosque (masjid, term Sanskritized as *mijigiti*) there with the help of his local 'Hindu' friend, Chāḍa. The two were referred to as *dharmabāndhava*. The Sanskrit version opened with an invocation to Allah as Viśvānātha (Lord of the World), *Viśvarūpa* (Universal), *Śūnyarūpa* (Formless), *Lakṣyālakṣya* (One who is envisaged and invisible at once).[236] If syncretism and absorption and co-existence of diverse traits within an overarching umbrella of culture are to be considered as the hallmark of Indian traditions, then here is a glowing example.[237] And trade in early India has a significant role to play in such formations. This particularly looms large in the making of the Indian Ocean world in the period from say 900 to 1750 when India's trading importance appears to have encouraged the spirit of co-operation and tolerance.

But trade is associated as much with a peaceful, friendly and tolerant atmosphere as with hostilities, violence and wars. The differential pace of technological progress inevitably results in the inequality of production which in its turn is an important ingredient of trade. The division of labour and the acquisitive urge are dominant factors in trade and war. There are many examples in early Indian history where the prospects of gains from trade prompted ambitious political powers to launch aggressive designs to capture trade centres, ports and routes connecting them. The combination of trade and war, or to put it more appropriately, trade and armed trade, played havoc in India, Asia, Africa and the Americas with the rise of merchant empires and finally colonial powers. But that is a separate story to be told elsewhere and by someone more competent than the present editor.

Yet it is common knowledge how trade, politics, and society in India along with many other nations of the present-day Third World

[236]For a recent study of the Sanskrit text of this record from Veraval near Somnath, see D.C. Sircar, *EI*, XXXIV, 1957–58, pp. 141–50.

[237]The widespread destruction, looting and massacre of human beings during the times of the Ghaznivid and Ghurid invasions are well recorded in the Arabic accounts. But these show only one side of the story; the other side is represented by the Veraval inscriptions and some other documents. It is strange that even at the close of the twentieth century, Jack Goody, *The East in the West*, Cambridge, 1996, could entertain the view that 'while it had its own glories, the advent of Islam proved a great setback to Hindu culture.' p. 117.

underwent a sea change with the arrival of the Europeans in the sixteenth century. The politics of expansion and imperialism associated with the trading of various European East India Companies and especially the English East India Company—ultimately giving birth to colonies under some metropolitan power(s)—is well known. The European mastery has generally been explained in terms of immense technological power and progress (including commercial techniques), the scientific mind and adventurous spirit, the role of individualism, the urge for observing and conquering nature, and above all the Industrial Revolution. Jack Goody has recently challenged the assumptions of the 'European miracle' or the 'uniqueness of the West', on the one hand, and also the much-cherished notion of the backward or static East on the other.[238] In his survey of Indian trade and economy in the medieval and early colonial period (of course, later than our period under review, but certainly relevant to its understanding), he proposes a significant historiographical shift from the dominant view of the contrastive elements in Eastern and Western history and society. Sharply differing from the substantivist portrayal of marketless trading in pre-modern and pre-colonial India, he wonders,

> . . .whether the commercial activities of the Christian Europeans in the Indian Ocean were really so very different, at least in the initial stages, from those of the Muslim Arabs and the Hindu Indians that preceded them. Were they different enough, that is to say, to exclude one from the category of 'trade' and the other from that of 'redistribution'?[239]

The merit of this penetrating observation has to be weighed in our study of 'traditional' Indian trade. Goody, however, argues that the invention of double book-keeping was crucial to the advancement of European commerce. This is unlikely to have existed in ancient and early medieval India.

But on the other hand two collections of essays assert that in the period from the thirteenth to the fifteenth centuries, European powers like Spain and Portugal were poor comparisons to the trading economies

[238] Jack Goody, *op. cit.*

[239] Ibid., p. 97. His bibliography on the trading activities in India prior to AD 1500, however, does not match his overall thought-provoking analysis and requires considerable upgrading. This is particularly relevant to recent advances in the use of archaeological sources for the study of early trade. His appendix on early trade between the East and the West particularly suffers from this weakness.

and aggressive policies of many powers in Asia, Africa and the Americas. They are represented as no less aggressive and ambitious in their expansionist commercial and political designs than their European counterparts. Seen from this angle, the European nations are not considered the inventor of armed trade and colonialism. There was, in the considered opinion of the editor of the volume, a global opportunity for the spread of colonialism. As different non-European powers in various parts of the world wasted or were not equal to these opportunities, then it was the logical and justified turn of the Europeans to exploit them.[240] The opportunities appeared before the Europeans, as it were, by default and were not created by their designs. Trading activities and ventures naturally form a crucial part of such arguments. These projections are attempted at whitewashing colonialism and holding the peoples of many Third World nations themselves (including India) primarily responsible for the development of their underdevelopment. These assertions conveniently relegate to the background the valid thesis of guns and sails holding the trump card to the spread of European mastery.[241] The practitioner of history often wishes to project the past in a way that he or she would like to visualize the future. In a society such as that of recent decades, which champions a market economy and globalization, the perusal of early trade history can be a tricky issue and a powerful implement, if not handled with judiciousness, care and sensibility. The study of the history of trade can be a truly rewarding experience for the understanding of cooperation, sharing and exchange among diverse communities cutting across geographical and cultural distances. But there is also the visible politics of promoting the study of trade history to satisfy expansionist tendencies and its fall-out can very well imperil the historian's craft in the future.

[240]Felipe Fernandez-Armesto (ed.), *An Expanding World, The European Impact on World History 1450–1800*, Vol. I: *The Global Opportunity*, Vol. II: *The European Opportunity*, London, 1995.

[241]Carlo M. Cippola, *European Culture and Overseas Expansion*, Harmondsworth, 1970. Also see the comment of K.N. Chaudhuri made more than a decade ago: 'Before the arrival of the Portuguese in the Indian Ocean in 1498 there had been no organised attempt by any political power to control the sea-lanes and the long-distance trade of Asia... The Indian Ocean as a whole and its different seas were not dominated by any particular nations or empires'. *Trade and Civilisation in the Indian Ocean,* p. 14.

Chapter Two

Harappan Trade in Its 'World' Context*

SHEREEN RATNAGAR

The immediate neighbours of the Mature Harappan cultural zone are several. In the west, in southern Baluchistan, is the Kulli culture; to the north in the Indus plains up to the Potwar Plateau are the sites of the Kot Diji culture; the mountain people of Swat were even further north in less accessible terrain; there were villages at Burzahom and Gufkral in the vale of Kashmir, beyond Manda, a 'Harappan' outpost at the navigation head of the Chenab; other 'neighbours' were hunter-gatherers at Bagor east of the Aravallis and villagers in Malwa further southeast of the Kayatha culture; there were also hunter-gatherer groups at places like Langhnaj in north Gujarat. Much further away in the gold bearing region of Karnataka were other villagers. Archaeological evidence—caches of Harppan beads, or stray metal tool forms, or seals—indicates that different kinds of interaction prevailed between the inhabitants of these places and the Indus plains, if not literally trade in each case.

To my knowledge there is as yet no study which has gone into the details of the artefactual evidence, or asked what kinds of relationships we can expect between an early urban society and its less advanced contemporaries.

Here we will deal only with the long distance overseas trade, and see this phenomenon in the wider framework of complex and multiple-stranded cross-cultural interactions which prevailed in the later third and earlier second millennia BC over an area much wider than that marked by Harappan trade routes.

* *Man and Environment XIX* (1–2): 1994, pp. 115–27.

The intercultural trade embraced contrasting places and cultures, even though all regions are characterized as arid and semi-arid, and the rainfall in all cases except Kachchh and Kathiawad and the relevant tracts of northern Afghanistan being below 300 mm per annum. Sumer and Seistan had relatively high agricultural potential in contrast to the environs of Tepe Yahya in southeast Iran or to northern Baharain. The upper Gulf could offer only dates and pearls for trade whereas in the lower Gulf (the Peninsula of Oman) occur rich veins of copper and hard dark stones like gabbers and dolerites. Perhaps the Harappans were the only participants who had easy access to fine timbers. The largest of the culture areas, the Harappans incorporated areas with marine resources, others with forestry, and yet others known to be agriculturally rich zones.

If we view the third millennium 'world' from another angle, we see that Mesopotamia and South Asia represent literate and urbanized societies, the 'Bronze Age' in every sense of Gordon Childe's usage,[1] but not so the Kulli, or groups at Yahya or in Oman. (Is it only a coincidence that, in spite of the recent evidence from the Gulf, the two urban areas continue to appear as major partners in trade?) In Oman[2] most exotic artefacts occur in graves which were stone structures accommodating large numbers of dead, whereas in Bahrain, Tarut and the Arabian mainland of the upper Gulf (Dilmun), graves contained single burials (Lamberg-Karlovsky 1986: 163–64).

Also of interest is that the various culture areas did not always exhibit the closest ties with those nearest them. It has long been appreciated that Mesopotamia, the agriculturally richest and the most populous area, had huge quantities of grain, oil, and woolen textiles to offer. It was also perhaps the home of the most skilled metallurgists. But it was the largest importer of metals, stones and shells (having none of these locally), most of which came from South Asia, the eastern terminus of the trading circuit. Besides being procurers and suppliers of so many trade items, the Harappans may well have been the most accomplished seafarers, given their privileged access to the best boat-building timbers (these have up to recent times been imported by seafarers of the Gulf from India). It hardly bears repetition that the

[1] Note, however, that the largest Indus centres were less than 150 ha. in size whereas Uruk in Mesopotamia was over 400 ha.

[2] 'Oman' here means the entire Peninsula which closes the Gulf, including the UAE and the Sultanate of Oman.

movement of heavy and bulk items like stone, metal, and timber is immensely cheaper by water (sea or river currents and winds providing the energy for propulsion) than by land (beasts of burden or traction require to be fed, often in desert or sparsely inhabited terrain in many parts of our 'world').

This point about the two urbanized termini of the trade comes across vividly when we consider the trade in silver. Little silver has been found in the intermediate areas of southeast Iran, Seistan, or the Gulf[3]—except for two silver artefacts at Shahr-i Sokhta in Seistan and two silver beads in an Oman grave. It had earlier been argued (Ratnagar 1981: 144–46) that the Harappans, the only people of protohistoric South Asia to have used silver on a substantial scale,[4] imported this metal, most likely from Mesopotamia. A regular movement of silver from the Assyrian merchant colonies of Cappadocia to Mesopotamia is well-documented for the period between 1920 and 1750 BC and texts from Ur which refer to silver being taken overseas by merchants to buy copper in Dilmun (clearly an entrepot) date to the time of Rim Sin of Larsa or 1822 to 1763 BC. It has also been pointed out that silver was found in the two large Harappan settlements, Mohenjo-daro and Harappa, but is almost totally absent at the other sites.

Another argument for Mesopotamia as a source is that, even earlier, around 3500–3000 BC and also later, silver and lead were used on a substantial scale in Mesopotamia and Elam. One example is provided by the Early Dynastic III Royal Cemetery at Ur, with a truly exceptional amount of silver (Moorey 1985: 114 ff,122ff). Second, we now have a run of radiocarbon dates from the silver-lead bearing localities of Dariba, Agucha, and Zawar, near Ajmer in Rajasthan, which testify to mining in the later first millennium BC rather than earlier (Craddock *et al.* 1989). The only earlier mining is attested to at Dariba, but these dates are post-Harappan, viz. later second millennium BC.

Finally it needs to be mentioned that Kosambi (1941/1981) noticed, on a rectangular piece of silver from Mohenjo-daro, traces of cuneiform writing. He expressed his surprise that neither Marshall

[3] However, lead objects aplenty occur at Shahbad on the edge of the Lut desert of eastern Iran. There are deposits of silver-bearing lead in southeast Iran. A mesopotamian royal inscription mentions a military campaign across the Gulf and 'up to the silver mines'. Also, in periods II and III of Tepe Hissar occur appreciable quantities of silver and lead.

[4] An exception is provided by graves in the high mountain region of Swat, where several silver artefacts are reported.

nor Mackay had paid attention to it. But as copied by Kosambi the cuneiform signs are not complete; in fact if the copying is accurate then the sign on the obverse, with one wedge in the wrong position *vis-à-vis* the long stroke, is a fake.

What about the zones adjacent to the two riverain cultures? To date Kulli culture sites have produced fewer Harappan artefacts than have the towns of Mesopotamia. In fact it has been suggested (Ratnagar 1992: 15–19) that the Harappan items at Kulli sites are not so much the result of 'trade' as of the emergence of client cheifdoms in southern Baluchistan, astride land routes linking the Harappan heartland with all-weather ports in Makran. Besenval's (1992) survey confirms the exclusively Harappan nature of Sutkagen-dor and Sotka-koh, in spite of the existence of 'Dasht' and 'Shahi Tump' type sites in their vicinity in Makran. (Dales' brief excavation at Sutkagen-dor, we may recall, unearthed heavy stone fortification.)

Meanwhile the Elamite lowlands can be considered a geographic and cultural adjunct to lower Mesopotamia, sometimes politically annexed to it, even though Elam had its own language and incorporated hill country as well. The same range of Harappan artefacts and materials (ivory, etched beads, shell, seals, and so on) occurs at Mesopotamian sites as at Elamite sites, mainly Susa.

A different situation prevails however in Dilmun (the upper Gulf from Failaka in Kuwait to the Bahrain archipelago), Mesopotamia's other neighbour. Ubaid pottery was found in this region that was actually made in southern Mesopotamia (Oates *et al.* 1977). This means that Mesopotamian sea voyages had begun by 4000 BC. In this entire hyper-arid area, settlement is possible only where sweet water springs occur, and Sumerian and Akkadian literature portrays Dilmun as a region of cosmogonic, ritual, and cultural importance (see Anderson 1986 for a recent interpretation). 'Dilmun' is mentioned several times in the earliest Mesopotamian texts, the 'Uruk Archaic' tablets, sometimes as a generic for particular sorts of axes or textiles.

The archaeological evidence about Dilmun comes from cemeteries, the occasional oyster midden, a temple at Barbar (northern Bahrain), and settlements at Failaka and Qala'at al Bahrain. In the recent literature (Bibby 1986; Zarms 1989; Mortensen 1986; Weisgerber 1986; Cleuziou 1986; Kohl 1986) the view has sometimes (e.g. Hojlund 1989) been expressed that a marked social change characterizes the transition between City I at Qala'at al Bahrain (which began in the later Early Dynastic period, say 2600 BC and City II (say

2100 BC onwards). The settlement was given a fortification only in the second period, when also carnelian beads are in use, together with Harappan weights (although three of the latter did come from City I levels) and 'Dilmun seals' and the temple at Barbar was built. It has been suggested that Mesopotamian and Omani (Umma an Nar) influence/ exchange was more important in the earlier period and Harappan in the later. It is suggested (Bibby 1986: 114–15); but not so Kjaerum (1986), are stylistically and iconographically closer to Harappan glyptic than Mesopotamian. On the other hand it has also been suggested (Cleuziou 1986: 154–55) that in the second phase Dilmun had become the 'sole middleman' controlling all the Gulf trade, and that there were no Harappan merchants now in Mesopotamia—that they remained in Oman.

One wonders if the contrasts (however, they are perceived) have not been exaggerated. In the foundations of the Barbar temple occur hundreds of conical goblets paralled in Early Dynastic I temples in Summer. An Akkadian tablet fragment of about 2000 BC is probably stratigraphically associated with lower City II levels (Bibby 1986:114), and Dilmun seal impressions occur on two tablets. Mesopotamian and Elamite, of the Isin-Larsa period (*c*. 2000–1763 BC), with a reference in a text of the same period to the weight standard of Dilmun (see Roaf 1982). So we cannot deny contact with Sumer in the later period. Moreover, Harappan weights come from Qala'at al Bahrain levels 23 to 19 and thus span periods I and II (Bibby 1986: 110). We may also recall mention in diverse genres of cuneiform literature to Dilmun as a source of timber, copper, ivory and stones like lapis lazuli. Especially relevant are Ur III (2100–2000 BC) tablets from a temple at Ur concerning trading trips to Dilmun, as also temple accounts of the later Isin-Larsa period about tithes paid on the Dilmun trade.

All this evidence together prompts the adoption of a long chronology for the Barbar/Dilmun culture. The major argument for a short chronology has been the absence in the temple and settlement of Bahrain of carved chlorite containers of the early series (see Kohl 1986: 368), which date to Early Dynastic II–III. Such vessels do, however, occur on Tarut Island not far away, and as grave goods. Carved as they are with intricate 'mythological' elements, these containers in some cultures may well have been of exclusively funerary use.[5]

[5] Incised chlorite/steatite/serpentine/talc containers (Kohl 1986; Amiet 1986; Kohn *et al.* 1979; T.F. Potts 1989; Zarins, 1989) were widely dispersed between the Indus and the Euphrates. They have been divided into three chronological groups. Earliest are those carved with a basketry pattern or

It is in the lower Gulf that recent excavations have created the most excitement. A few oases and fairly verdant spine of mountains are flanked by large barren tracts at the mouth of the Gulf. The copper and hard stones of Oman reached Mesopotamia in the third millennium, which is what gives the region its early importance. The archaeological evidence comes from collective burials, metallurgical loci, and settlements which can have round, tower-like structures. These sites are located at the oases, along the mountain slopes, on the west coast near Abu Dhabi and Ras al Khaimah, and on the east coast near Muscat.

Here as in the case of Dilmun, the first known external links are with southern Mesopotamia, in the form of biconical polychrome Jamdat Nasr pottery at a few sites. A Mesopotamian 'colony' collecting and shipping out copper from Oman has been one interpretation, not unlikely considering that the pots in this case too were actual imports (Cleuziou and Tosi 1989: 30), but an interpretation, which does not explain why only one kind of Mesopotamian pottery was present here, and in graves (H.T. Wright on D.T. Potts 1986).

'hut' motifs, animals or snakes, dating to Early Dynastic II–IIIa (Kohl 1986; Zairns 1989) i.e. 2750 to 2500 BC, perhaps continuing later into the Akkad period, 2370 –2230 BC (Amiet 1986). They were made at Yahya IVB and on Tarut island near Bahrain. For Kohl (1986: 374) these vases with their intricate iconography and symbols were luxury goods par excellence. Many occur in temple contexts in Mesopotamia, one in Oman, a fragment also in early levels at Mohenjo-daro. The second group mainly comprises hemispherical pots with a row of concentric circles below the rim, also concave-cylindrical vases and internally compartmented ones bearing multiple incised lines and a corrugated appearance. Dating from the Akkad to the Ur III/Isin Larsa period, these have an equally wide distribution (Elam, Mesopotamia, Tarut, Yahya) but are fewer in Mesopotamia and were made in Oman where they occur in greatest number. They are not highly crafted pieces according to Kohl, although for Cleuziou and Vogt (1985: 254) they were a funerary item. Aside from the two pieces known previously at Mohenjo-daro (Ratnagar 1981: 122), Cleuziou and Tosi (1989: 41, fig. 12) have also found a bowl with a row of concentric circles in the DK-B area of this site. An even later third group of stone containers, large, sloping-sided, with lugs and incised diagonals/circles, come from Wadi Suq-Sunaysl sites in Oman, and also Tarut and Isin-Larsa and Old Babylonian Mesopotamia (Ratnagar 1981: 119), but not, to my knowledge, from Harappan sites. T.F. Potts (1989) offers probably the best study of this 'international' artefact to date.

So again it is Mesopotamian initiative—initiative from a land of neither islanders nor coastal dwellers, a land lacking good wood for ships—which opens the story of external trade around the end of the fourth millennium, although in the later periods, it would be Harappans who ventured into Oman and their seals which would be found in the Gulf and Mesopotamia, rather than the cylinder seals of the latter country. The early Mesopotamian ventures down the Gulf remind us of Childe's characterization (1964:147–52) of Bronze Age economies as inherently externally expanding systems.

More interesting, on the Ras alHamra promontory near Muscat was found a non-local burnished grey pot, squat with a low carination, which on examination was found to have been used to heat a bituminous substance, 'some kind of caulking material'. And it has been inferred (Cleuziou and Tosi 1989: 28–30) that around 3000 BC there sailed to this copper-rich area boats which were (not multiple log dugouts, rafts, or tied reed frond vessels, but made of planks of) wood, thus requiring caulking.[6]

We could argue that materials other than pitch or bitumen, such as rags, rope, moss or wooden wedges, can be used for caulking. Conversely, bitumen caulking is not exclusive to plank boats, as we know from the nineteenth century descriptions of boat building at Hit on the Euphrates (see Hornell 1970: 57–58), where a boat made of rough branches and poles, reeds and straw, is entirely coated with molten bitumen.

Yet, if the connection between the contents of the pot at Ras al Hamra and the plank constructed boat is correct, it is of great significance. It means that this technology is considerably early [the first actually surviving plank boat known to us being the funerary boat of Cheops near the Great Pyramid of Egypt and dating to about 2575 BC. More important, the true potential of the boat as a cargo vessel was realized only when it was plank built. It was this structure that gave boats much larger and deeper bodies which were stronger than the multiple dugout or reed boat. It was the plank boat which could carry a single post mast (in place of the sheer mast of the reed boat)

[6] Caulking material occurs in Mesopotamia and according to Edens (1993, p. 352) on the south Iran coast, Qishm island near this coast and the tip of the Oman peninsula, and near Kerman. It also occurs in eastern Oman itself (Cleuziou and Tozi 1989: 44). Bitumen was used as a bonding material as early as the Ubaid period in Mesopotamia.

which in turn, when rigidly secured, can carry a wide and full sail (Hornell 1970: 49; Johnstone 1988: 45–54).

We may also assume that mariners had begun to recognize and use those timbers which were sea worthy as well as to master the craft of carpentry. In Egypt at least, a range of bronze tools and finely produced pieces of furniture testify to well-developed carpentry around the beginning of the third millennium (Emery 1961: 220–21; Lucas 1948: 508–10). Childe (1944) had suggested that metal tools like the toothed saw could alone have made possible the accurate carpentry necessary for cart and boat construction. Today it is felt (Piggott 1968: 269; 1983: 18ff) that bronze toothed saws of the early Bronze Age were too small for cutting the primary planks, and that it is possible to split a tree trunk down its weak planes with the use of stone adzes and wedges, to get planks. Also, the stone adze can be adequate for a fine finish. There is, nevertheless, the testimony of a relief in the tomb of Ti at Saqqara in Egypt, *c.* 2450 BC, for the use of a large saw for cutting a log standing vertical as tall as a man. More important, for joining the planks of wheels or boats by clamps, lashing, with wooden treenails, or by the use of gouged out mortises fitted with wooden tenons (see Johnstone 1988: 49–51, 70–74, 174–77), the narrow chisel, the hollow gouge, and the rotating drill, necessarily of metal, were indispensable. On the basis of two Dilmun seals which show sailing craft with high stem and stern, Johnstone (1988: 176) infers that plank boats were in use in the Gulf in the third millennium BC. There is also an argument (1988: 172) for the use of plank boats with mortise-and-tenon joints, together with stitched ships, by the Harappans.

We can therefore visualize a mutually reinforcing process in which increasing use of metal enabled more efficient transport mechanism, and vice versa. The approximate chronological coincidence between the beginnings of copper mining in Oman (Weisgerber 1984: 197), the first text references to copper from the Gulf via Dilmun (Nissen 1986), and this evidence for probably caulked planked ships is too striking to ignore. We might also remark that timber and copper are two of the earliest imported items attested to in the cuneiform texts.

While on the subject of copper we may recall that in the cuneiform literature it comes from Dilmun, Magan, and Meluhha (producing places not being distinguished from those with onward trade) But only Gudea refers to tin, which came to him from Meluhha together with gold, copper, lapis, and carnelian. Tin bronze was utilized not only in the two riverain civilizations but also at Mundigak and Shahr-I Sokhta, Tepa Yahya, and the upper and lower Gulf. The baffling problem of the tin of Meluhha is perhaps solved by Berthoud and Cleuziou's report (1982) on an alluvial source and a mine of high grade cassiterite near alluvial source and a mine of high grade cassiterite near Misgaran in western Afghanistan. But an ancient source in Badakhshan is also likely (Stech and Pigott 1986). Moorey (1985: 132), on the authority of Craddock, rules out Bihar and Rajasthan as protohistoric sources of tin (see Hegde 1978). And an important source for Assur and Cappadocia remains unknown (Moorey 1985: 129)—no medieval or modern period tin mining is reported in Iran. For the rest, the multiple sources of tin and copper listed earlier (Ratnagar 1981: 80 ff) stand, but we must now place much greater emphasis on the copper of Oman.

In course of time copper exports to Mesopotamia increased to 'significant quantities' (Cleuziou 1986: 145), even while little Mesopotamian pottery is now evident and instead there are more ceramic connections with southern Iran and Baluchistan. Then, late in the third millennium, Harappan material occurs, from the northwest coast near Sharjah (Tell Abraq) to the mining site of Maysar (Samad 5) and to Ras al Junayz on the eastermost corner of Oman. These Indus connections, which continue into the early second millennium, comprise a few cubical chert weights, a few graffiti on pots with Harappan characters, an ivory comb with dotted-circle motifs, a few etched carnelian beads, Harappan type storage jars with incised 'owners' marks, pedestalled dishes with thumbnail marks in concentric circles, painted motifs like the peacock, and about five stone seals not Harappan in form or material, but in the letters or animal/geometric symbols on the face (Weisgerber 1984, 1986; Cleuziou 1978–79, 1986; Cleuziou and Vogt 1985; Cleuziou and Tosi 1989; Tosi 1986; Edens 1993; T.F. Potts 1993).

At Ras al Junayz where occurred Harappan type jars, two scratched with Harappan signs, as well as pottery painted with motifs resembling Harappan designs, there may well have been a sea port. But can it be categorically 'ascribed to the Harappans' (Weisgerber 1986: 140)? And in what way do the Harappan elements at the site or in Oman in general indicate an 'intensity of trade relationships' (Tosi 1986: 106), not to speak of an 'early Indian thalassocracy' (Tosi 1986: 106; also Cleuziou 1986: 148)? Such inferences are surely premature.

For one thing, they have preceded detailed publication of the finds, their contexts, and co-occurrences. Also, while Cleuziou and Tosi (1989: 40) say that Harappan type sherds are found in almost every site of the second millennium Wadi Suq horizon, it appears from Edens (1993: 336–38) that some sherds are intrusive but others show Harappan influence. Concerning the graffiti at Ras al Junayz we are told (Edens 1993: 341) that the signs are 'not necessarily in the Harappan sign list, but such an identity is likely'. Earlier, Cleuziou (1986: 147) had suggested that actual Harappan artefacts were confined to weights, storage jars, and two or three etched carnelian beads. And then it is hard to believe the suggestion that long axes in Oman are Harappan or exhibit 'a formal similarity' with Harappan axes. This is an extremely elementary tool form; the 'coals to Newcastle' rejoinder would surely apply; and actually in Oman by this time were developed thrust weapons such as socketed spearheads with strengthening midrib of a type superior to Harappan metal weapons.

I would also like to point out that Harappan Sutkagendor, behind the medieval port of Gwadar, lies less than 400 km northeast of Muscat as the crow flies. Seventeenth century Gujarati mariners' itineraries from Muscat followed the coast north to the tip of the Oman Peninsula and then, via Hormuz, turned eastward by the Iranian mainland towards Makran (Information kindly supplied by Dr Kalpana Desai). On this route in fair weather the run from Chahbahar to Gwadar took about fifty-four hours. Yet it will not do to insist on Bronze Age seafaring having been exclusively coastal (Ratnagar 1981: 170, n. 11). And a distance of about 400 km is not excessive: Bahrain is approximately this distance from Failaka island in Kuwait, and both constituted the ancient land of Dilmun. Moreover, in the eighteenth and nineteenth centuries the rulers of Oman held Gwadar as part of their territory. On two occasions Gwadar was the place where ambitious princes took political refuge, later to sail on Muscat/ Mutrah to seize the throne (Philips 1967: 67–69, 141–42). So our archaeological evidence does not necessarily speak for a Harappan thalassocracy: there may have been sailings of Harappans from or via Sutkagendor on some occasions, as also the occasional shipwreck off the Oman coast.

Neither should the Harappan factor overshadow the testimony of Bahrain-Oman contacts. Umm an Nar pottery occurs at Barbar I and Qala't al Bahrain I (Zarins 1989: 79) and an Omani type socketed spearhead at Barbar (Bibby 1986: 111). On Tarut and Bahrain islands occur incised chlorite vessels of Omani manufacture. In turn, in a Wadi Suq context at Tell Abraq occur red ridged Barbar potsherds, and in the contemporary burial site of Mayzad, a seal of the

Dilmun or Late Gulf Type (Cleuziou 1981: 285). It is thus becoming increasingly clear that the peoples of the Gulf could hardly have been inconsequential partners in the circuits of interaction.

Other interpretations may also be controversial. Cleuziou (1986: 153–55) and Weisgerber (1986: 138) place emphasis on the trade initiative of Mesopotamia in the post-Akkad and Ur III periods as a new phenomenon. They suggest that Mesopotamian traders now sailed directly to the resource areas [presumably not including Sind or Gujarat]. But even if we were to rely only on written sources, the picture is not so simple. In 2370 BC. Sargon of Akkad made a general boast about boats of Dilmun, Magan, and Meluhha coming to Akkad; later, Gudea, in his tedious narratives about temple building, details what he procured from Dilmun (timber). Magan (specified timbers), and Meluhha (specified timbers, tin, copper, gold dust of the mountains, carnelian, and lapis lazuli). And then *c.* 2100 BC. Urnammu, founder of the Ur Third Dynasty, claims that for his god he '*re-established* the *former* state of affairs along the coast . . . he rendered safe the boats of Magan' (emphases supplied) (see Ratnagar 1981: 39, n. 20). Here 'boats of Magan' may mean either boats making the Magan run from Ur, or boats of the foreign Magan land. The actual trade documents of Ur III of course refer to merchants of the temple of Ur sailing to Magan to buy copper there, and also to Dilmun, source of ivory and other items in that period. In these texts much of the merchandise reaching Ur (ivory, 'sea wood', timber, carnelian, etc.) is South Asian in origin, and it is hard to believe in an absence of Harappan initiative or that ships of Magan did not sail to Sumer even when Magan is a named trade partner. It has been suggested (Ratnagar 1981: 50–51, 167–68, 222) that 'Magan' could have meant not only Oman, but also Iranian Baluchistan and Pakistani Makran: rough monsoon seas do not plague Harappan Sutkagen-dor and this may have been a major locational factor for this fortified outpost; second, the boats in the Ur III period left Ur mostly in March, which would be convenient for a return trip to Gwadar/Sutkagen-dor. Moreover, in Ur at that time are to be found individuals with names like 'Mr Magan' or 'Man of Magan' (Ratnagar 1981: 42).

It has long been observed (Ratnagar 1981: 226–27) that in the Larsa period Dilmun was playing an active trading role: the only available trade texts concern the Ur-Dilmun run and involve South Asian materials like ivory and lapis, rather than Gulf produce. But I would not go so far as to claim that Dilmun was 'in a position to control all relations throughout the area' (Cleuziou 1986: 154). If we are to judge by texts alone, even when trade began in the Early Dynastic period, Dilmun was the only named overseas partner of the Sumerian cities, providing timber and copper but not local produce. If Meluhhans are not mentioned in Isin-Larsa texts as resident in Sumer, we may recall that even those mentioned in Ur III tablets have no engagement in maritime trade (see Edzard on Parpola *et al.* 1977). Last, there is a typical Harappan seal from a stratified context at Nippur, which dates to the mid-second millennium Kassite context (Gibson 1977).

It has been asked whether there is a significant connection between the stronger role of Dilmun as trader, and the Harappan presence in the Lower Gulf, after 2000 BC. We might add to this chronological coincidence the apparent interest of the Harappans in Chalcolithic Kayatha (2000–1800 BC) where copper technology was relatively advanced (see Ratnagar 1981: 96, note), and also the emergence of the Ganeshwar-Jodhpura 'culture', prolific in copper. For of all paradoxes, the most enigmatic is that by 1900–1800 BC, when Harappan material is visible. Oman suffered a decline in copper production which did not pick up again until after 1000 BC (Weisgerber 1984: 197; During-Caspers 1989: 17).

In truth, our trade networks functioned as part of even wider movements and connections, involving yet other regions. Years ago Tosi had suggested—significantly for this context—a date of about 2000 BC for the copper smelting sites of the Gardan Reg, southeast of Seistan, located by Dales. The evidence is yet more complex. At Mehi (Kulli culture) in southern Baluchistan are known artefacts of Bactrian-Margianan type such as a bronze mirror with anthropomorphic handle, the head appearing only as the reflection of the user; vessels of truncated cone shape; bronze pins with lapis heads and a potsherd with animal figures in the round on its rim (During-Caspers 1992).

Moreover, pedestal goblets with a collar at the junction of cup and stem, dating around 2000 BC in Bactria, have parallels or metal counterparts in late/post-Harappan South Cemetery at Mehrgarh, and at sites of the Wadis Suq-Sunaysl in Oman, and also in Bahrain (During-Caspers 1992). From an unknown site in southwestern Iran comes a stone seal/pendant in the shape of a stepped cross, four eagles holding snakes in their beaks on one face (Brunswig *et al.* 1977: no. 5, pp. 103, 109). The stepped cross is considered a shape typical of Margiana-Bactria in the Namazga VI period, (*c.* 2100 BC onwards). Importantly, one seal at Harappa is of this shape. One Bactrian connection across the Gulf is a bone comb decorated on both faces with a tulip-like flower, from a grave dating before 2000 BC at Tell Abraq in northwest Oman. An almost identical flower is incised on a small steatite vessel from an unknown site in northwestern Afghanistan. The flower may be the Turkmenian tulip, suggests D.T. Potts (1993). Tremendously significant movements or experiments appear to have begun by 2000 BC, perhaps connected with a search for metal, although ritual or cult objects like barrel-shaped stone 'sceptres', grooved stone discs, and grooved miniature stone columns are found variously at sites of the Hissar culture (northeast Iran), Shahdad, Bactrian graves, Mehrgarh and Sibri,[7] the Kulli sites, and in the Gardan Reg (Jarrige and Hassan 1989).

When referring to 'the search for metal' we must take into account the scarcity of tin on the surface of the earth. Tin needs to be added only in small quantities to render copper harder and easier to cast. It has been suggested by a mining geologist (Barnes 1988: 2) that just 'two tonnes [2000 kg] a year was probably enough for the whole ancient world'. It is known that tin bronze was rare in the third millennium at Tepe Hissar in northeastern Iran, and in Turkmenia (Pigott *et al.* 1982: 229–31; Masson 1988: 99), as also somewhat rare in protohistoric India and third millennium Western Asia (Moorey 1985: 33; Cleuziou and Berthoud 1982; T.F. Potts 1993: 391).

But there may have been fluctuations in the use and supply of tin. For it has been calculated that over a fifty-year stretch in the early second millennium, some 100 tonnes of tin were carried between Assur and Anatolia alone, and that the exchange value of tin was a *vis-à-vis* silver (Moorey 1985: 129). Also, we have the intriguing case of bronze mirrors, some of them of Bactrian late-third millennium type, occurring sporadically at Harappan sites, and in the upper Gulf, Kulli region, Mesopotamia, and Elam. For the requisite shine and polish a bronze mirror requires a very high proportion of tin, perhaps even 30 per cent. Whatever future research may show, it is now clear that the end of the trade in the early second millennium cannot be attributed solely to the economic decline of southern Mesopotamia, as had been earlier believed. The picture is far too complicated.

[7] These two neighbouring sites are known for their Central Asian features, reflecting perhaps a small-scale migration down the Bolan pass rather than trade as such.

The reader may have noticed that we have not yet made any mention of scientific work which traces materials to their geological source. Such tests are not producing the kind of clear results that were once expected of them. For example one kind of stone may not exhibit distinct properties between one quarry and another. Thus neutron-activation and X-ray diffraction analyses, emission spectroscopy, and other tests on over 300 vases of carved and incised chlorite from twenty-eight sites (Kohn *et al.* 1979) failed to produce meaningful groups on the basis of the constituent minerals. The chlorite of the quarries near Tepe Yahya was itself far too variable. Similarly one is sceptical about tracing lapis lazuli to its source. Delmas and Casanova (1990) studied the calcium, barium, strontium and other inclusions in excavated and quarry samples and inferred that while some samples from Shahr-i Sokhta are matched in the Pamirs, others are matched at Chagai and yet others in Badakhshan!

It is even more difficult to trace the mine sources of metals. Moorey (1985: 12–14, 74–77, 112) states that the whole assumption about the evidence value of impurities inclusions is questionable even as laboratory procedures are becoming more sophisticated. This is because the properties of metal are significantly altered in the very process of smelting, casting, alloying, and remelting (see also Hughes 1991: 112–14). Lead segregates under heat, arsenic evaporates, a smith may add lead to copper to get a better cast, copper from different mines may be scrapped and remelted together. It is now being suggested that the only reliable 'fingerprinting' is based on lead isotope ratios for ancient lead, copper-lead alloys, or copper with a natural lead content.

Relative chronologies also present complicated problems. This applies even to those chlorite vessels which were inscribed by Mesopotamian kings! One sherd of the earliest group (see note 5) is inscribed by Rimush and mentions his conquest of Iran, but another piece, of the later series, is inscribed by Naram Sin, who ruled only two reigns later, as 'booty from Magan' (T.F. Potts 1989). Also, we find that Kohl (1986: 372) refrains from dating the pots by their inscriptions, arguing that inscription came much later than manufacture of the pots.

We also know that a few radiocarbon dates cannot give us a final relative chronology for our entire region. It was found, for example, (Finkbeiner and Rollig 1986: 224–25) that carbon samples from two strata below a building of Naram Sin (who ruled up to 2230 BC as we know from independent and reliable grounds) at Tell Brak give calibrated dates at 1950 BC! Also, radiocarbon dates from two sites of the same culture in the Habur valley have come out 800 years apart. Thus we ignore the artefactual correlations at our peril.

I prefer to stand by my earlier dates (1981: 201–206) for the Mature Harappan period. It begins by 2600 BC (Early Dynastic III), given that the following come from ED III levels in Mesopotamia: the Harappan seal at Kish; ivory, lapis, gold at the Royal Cemetery; ivory at Ubaid, Mari, Kish; etched carnelian beads at Asmar, Kish, Ur and al Hiba; and texts referring to ivory and timbers from overseas. There is also the early series chlorite fragment at Mohenjo-daro. It would be absurd to date Harappan beginnings later, to the Akkad period, simply because actual text references to trade with Meluhha are available only then and in the post-Akkad period. Similarly, it cannot be argued on the basis of Omani evidence alone that the date is in fact ever later.

The terminal Harappan date may be 1800–1700 BC given Harappan elements in the Wadis Suq-Sunaysl sites in Oman, independently dated to the Isin-Larsa period; the later series incised chlorite pieces identified at Mohenjo-daro (note 5); the Larsa period texts referring to imports of carnelian, ivory items, copper, lapis, gold, coral, and red ochre, albeit in transit from Dilmun; and finally the Namazga VI period Bactrian type cruciform seal at Harappa, mentioned above.

For the rest of this paper we will attempt some interpretation. What was the historical importance of the trade? One possible measure is its scale. We could also ask if engagement in trade was a vehicle for the transmission of ideas and techniques. Another index is the kind of item that moved—this would perhaps indicate the role of foreign trade in the appearance of ruling elites in the earliest Bronze Age states, with their writing, monumental buildings or wealthy burials, skilled craftsmen, and sometimes cities. But before we engage in this kind of discussion we must clarify just what we mean by trade.

As a common sense understanding we can say that 'trade' is an exchange of commodities by parties willing to part with certain things in return for others—transactions which bring advantage in the sense of buy-where-cheap and sell-where-expensive. But all movement of artefacts and materials in the Bronze Age could not have been such trade.

We had mentioned inscriptions which identify chlorite vases as war booty carried away from one land by rulers of another. We know from the anthropological literature (see Ratnagar 1981: 244, n.6) that exchanges of things across islands of the Pacific were made in the course of high status marriages and had nothing to do with gain or the absence of an item on the island to which it was carried. Skilfully crafted items of one society in the Brone Age could have made their way to the elite/ leader/ elders of another society as high level presentations symbolizing recognition of status or respect or peace. We know of instances when rulers of ancient Western Asia sent to other rulers sumptuary gifts which had originated in a third region. Mobile herdsmen requiring access to certain pastures in particular seasons could have presented exotic gifts to local people in return for entry and safe passage, field stubble, or water. There is also the possibility that mobile craftsmen or metal prospectors, or groups of migrants in general, carried with them stone 'discs' or 'sceptres' which were part of their ritual and belief, as we hinted above. Zaccagnini (1983: 257) draws our attention to an episode in a Mesopotamian epic in which an early king carries away from a defeated foreign land not only precious stones and metal, but also moulds for metal casting, plus goldsmiths and lapidaries.

We may now ask if Harappan material at Altyn-depe in Turkmenia speaks for 'trade'. In an elite residence area here with rich burials, and in a ritual complex near the stepped tower, occurred seals, one Harappan in form with two signs of the script (but no symbol), and the other bearing a swastika in double lines (Masson 1981), the latter symbol being known on three artefacts from Harrapan sites. A silver seal shaped as a three-headed composite creature exhibits Harappan features in a 'somewhat weak' way (Gupta 1979: 169). There are also etched carnelian beads at Altyn, and ivory artefacts with no exact Harappan counterpart (Gupta 1979: 165–67). Much more striking are a bronze cosmetic flacon of Turkmenian–Bactrian type at Chanhu-daro (Gupta 1979: 170–74; Sarianidi 1979); and Bactrian type shaft-hole axes, heraldic eagles and bronze pins with animal heads which occur sporadically at Harappa and Mohenjno-daro. Do the latter reflect trade, or the same kind of phenomenon we had observed at late Mehrgarh and Sibri (note 7)?

Thus so far there has been no reference in our discussion to 'internal trade'. This is because of the pattern of the political economy of Bronze Age states in which it was elites who organized goods transfers; as part of tribute collection/surplus mobilization or the organization of craft production (see Ratnagar 1991). Such economic structures would have had little room for commerce in individual hands. For example, Chang (1975) had pointed out mechanisms other than trade for the movement of materials in Shang China: warfare, presentations, the bestowal of gifts by a ruler to a prominent subject, the equipment of craft workshops, and so on.

We do not rule out commodity exchange altogether; it would have prevailed especially at the boundaries of communities or tribes or states. But we have seen that other kinds of mechanisms could also have prevailed. Besides, there is a theoretical argument: commodities and market systems could not have been the organizing principle of Bronze Age economies.

It is a common misconception that before coined money came into use there was 'barter'. Humphrey (1985), amongst others, has shown that there is no known instance of a pure or predominantly barter economy, and none of a money economy emerging from barter; and that 'barter' is not an evolutionary stage but prevails within money-and-market systems, co-existing with monetary exchange and becoming important if money supply falls or the economy disintegrates. In other words, barter is actually a market system phenomenon. And market systems have not existed since the birth of mankind.

To assume or argue otherwise, Meillassoux (1972) observes, is to take one kind of ideological stance. If we argue that ancient economies were only less developed versions of our own, we imply that capitalism is universal, or 'natural', the condition of human existence. (And if something is an unchanging given, one cannot revolt against it.) In this paper the ideological stance, however, is that the demand-supply price-regulated market economy is predicated on the production and exchange of commodities, alienable things with exchange value, which did not dominate the economies of the Bronze Age. (This is argued at length in Ratnagar 1991). Then and in earlier centuries the critical productive resources like land were collectively owned by kin groups, and were inalienable. To treat land as a commodity would flout the very concept of kinship. So such economies could not have worked as *market systems*. As Polanyi (1957: 257) said, 'trade' is as old as mankind. But we cannot assume that because trade existed so did the market system—the two need to be conceptually separated.

If we now ask why we find Harappan type material across the Oman peninsula in the early second millennium, but no Wadis Suq-Sunaysl artefacts in South Asia, our answer may be that Harappan expeditions visited Oman to procure specific quantities of copper. Few discussions of third millennium trade (mine included, I now feel) have given adequate importance to state expeditions as a goods-transfer mechanism. This even though such phenomena are evident in

Egyptian and Mesopotamian texts. The entire epic of Enmerkar, ruler of Uruk, concerns venturing abroad for precious stones and metal; palace texts from Lagash indicate that Lugalanda the king sent merchants to Elam and Dilmun; Naram Sin in one inscription mentions his conquest of Magan and says he quarried stone there to transport home to Akkad (see T.F. Potts 1989: 135–36); Gueda may well be referring to specific expeditions abroad also, in his temple inscriptions. As direct evidence we can cite the Ur III temple texts on merchandise being allotted to merchants for their overseas trips. Then again in Bronze Age Egypt, a Pharaoh who desired amethyst or basalt from the eastern desert would send out a large number of men, fully equipped and provisioned by the treasury, to quarry and transport a specified amount of the stone (see Berlev 1987). We also have autobiographical inscriptions of men like Harkhuf describing journeys to Nubia for ivory, ebony, and other exotica. Thus Gardiner (1966: 89) observed that apart from occasional military forays 'all foreign ventures of the Old Kingdom' were 'journeys to procure to the sovereign the materials wherewith to sate his passion for building [and] to enhance the luxury of his court . . . .'

This is not far removed from Childe's view (1957: 8) that institutions like the Sumerian temple which equipped craftsmen and established demand for their output were aspects of 'totalitarian economies' or indeed from Polanyi's hunch (1957: 260–61) that 'archaic trade' was 'originally specific', organized as trade ventures which were 'a discontinuous affair'.

And so to the problem of assessing the importance of the trade. We have two glimpses of its scale from the cuneiform texts. The first concerns a trade transaction (see Roaf 1982) in which some 18,000 kg of copper were involved. In the second, a consignment of 2380 'gur' (a capacity measure) of barley goes to Magan (see Ratnagar 1981: 80). If, as is commonly accepted, a 'gur' was 240 litres or 180 kg of grain, then 2380 'gur ' is a gigantic amount, and its import requires careful thinking out.

Concerning the spread of ideas and techniques, the main evidence is for the spread of *jowar* as a crop to South Asia (to Pirak at the foot of the Bolan pass from 1700 BC) from northeastern Africa, via Oman where it is in evidence in the third millennium. The importance of this drough-resistant millet for the subsistence economy of many South Asian regions can hardly be over-emphasized. But as regards the two-humped Bactrian camel the picture is not so clear. The people of Shahri Sokhta and Harappan Shortughai knew the beast, but in spite of camel bones at Kalibangan or Harappa, the general impression is that the camel was not of importance in the Harappan economy.

Knowledge about metal ores and techniques and about pyrotechnology appropriate for faience production may have spread wide, as Childe had often said. Yet the socketed spearhead of Oman does not appear to have influenced Harappan tool types which lacked sockets and strengthening central midribs. Most intriguing, in Turkmenia several kinds of alloys—copper-lead, copper-silver, copper-lead-arsenic/tin, and copper-tin-arsenic—were in use (Masson 1988: 99) but in spite of 'contacts' there appears to be no such experimentation with alloying in the Harappan civilization (where tin bronze was the alloy in general use—an alloy which apparently was scarce in Turkmenia!) Do we interpret this as a function of availability of metals, or as resistance to the spread of certain techniques?

Whatever the explanation, we next must consider the importance of metal tools and weapons to the world of the third millennium. We cannot *a priori* assume that metal working revolutionzied agricultural production when neither in the Indus nor the Sumerian sites do we regularly find bronze tools for soil tillage. The famous hoard of second millennium agricultural tools from Tell Sifr, Mesopotamia, includes many tools but no pick or ploughshare (Moore 1971). Further, at Indus sites the amount of metal and the range of tools are certainly an advance on the earlier cultures, but even so the tool forms are elementary and together represent a limited range. We also need to remember that in protohistoric South Asia the regular use of tin bronze is, on present evidence, confined to the Harappan sites. In the subsequent Chalcolithic cultures copper alloys were used only sporadically (see Yule 1985—in spite of its misleading title). Since it was alloys which were superior in terms of strength and casting efficiency to pure copper, this is of considerable significance.

For it tells us that the development of technology must be understood in a social context. Presumably only a well organized and large-scale society could procure for itself tin (always and everywhere a scarce metal). Not only that, if we follow Childe it was the ruling elites who created the demand for crafts and metal tools and ornaments. At Harappan sites we can predict that saws, axes, knives, chisels, points, and punches of metal were part of the newly developed crafts that created faience or utilized ivory, sea shells, steatite, carnelian and metals on a hitherto unprecedented scale—not to speak of the importance of carpentry for carts and ships, discussed above.

But the utilization of bronze in Shang China reminds us that the utilitarian factor was not all. Bronze was used here on a lavish scale for enormous inscribed vessels for the ancestor rituals. Myths connect the Shang Ancestor with the casting of nine such sacrificial vessels. One royal burial at Yin-hsu had a total of 1625 kg of bronze (468 objects) as part of its funerary offerings (Chang 1983: 103).

Shang metal also illustrates the point that it was not the material or nature of an object which made it a luxury or a utilitarian item. What we can call Wealth (Weiner (1985)—in contradistinction to commodity—was something with symbolic meaning and 'cultural value'. Its exchange had nothing to do with profits or loss, but signified social bonds, or cosmological ideas, or was associated with *rites de passages* or changes of social role/status. Perhaps it is this kind of Wealth that we find buried out of circulation in such large quantity also in the Royal Cemetery of Ur: superbly crafted jewellery, musical instruments and weapons, made of metals, shells and stones imported from afar. Land sale contracts of the period, although very few in number (tribal tenure was to continue into later centuries), never list this range of items—etched beads, or lapis jewellery, or electrum vases, or gold—as having been exchanged for land.[8]

An untoward emphasis on the trade in lapis lazuli may justifiably be criticized, and the counter-arguments appreciated. Yet for this writer the conviction remains that this blue stone (to imitate which faience was probably so laboriously made) in a way encapsulates the story of Bronze Age economics. It is the subject of the longest Sumerian epic, as of great importance for the adornment of a temple in Uruk. This epic mentions the beginnings of trade and the invention of writing. Archaeological data have established the importance of Uruk as an urban centre with an early temple cluster, experimentation in architecture, and the earliest monumental art (a stele, a stone head, a magnificent white stone vase carved in relief), and also the earliest written tablets. Thus we cannot dismiss the importance given to lapis and gold in the epic as merely a poetic fancy. Instead, the procurement of precious stone and metal is portrayed in the epic as a royal and heroic feat.

There is an additional argument. If Stech and Pigott's (1986: 47) tin source in Badakhshan can be verified, and if we add to that the

[8] See also Majidzadeh (1982) on exotic stones and gold in a small number of the early tombs at Tepe Gawra.

fact that placer gold was panned in recent times in the beds of the Oxus and the Kokcha Rivers downstream from the lapis mines, then indeed '. . . the coincidence to lapis and tin and perhaps gold in relative proximity is significant..'

Lapis lazuli may initially have been carried afar by nomadic pastoralists. We can study the location of the Chagai and Badakhshan sources on a map of seasonal pastoral migrations to appreciate this (Balland 1989). Later, however, it was Shahr-i Sokhta II–III and Mundigak III.6–IV to which the stone seems to have been moved preferentially, to support lapidary crafts on a substantial scale. But the pattern was to change yet again. The lapis industries at these two centres ceased, the Chagai source may not have continued in use as there is little lapis at Harappan Nausharo on the Bolan route, and Harappan Shortughai was established near the Oxus–Kokcha confluence (see Ratnagar 1992).[9] A reasonable inference is that the Harappans were not content to leave the movement of lapis lazuli to intermediaries or to chance.

To conclude we recall that the Kot Dijian culture is now being interpreted (Shaffer and Lichtenstein 1989; Xu Chaolong 1990) as not only earlier that the Mature Harappan but also continuing as its contemporary and northern neighbour. Even further north at Neolithic Burzahom was found a pot which is Kot Dijian in fabric, shape and decoration, as also another pot containing 950 Harappan type agate and carnelian beads (Thapar 1985: 30–36). In remote upland Swat also there are Kot Dijian elements which Stacul (1985: 363) believes are connected with a search for fine timbers.

Is it then too far fetched to suggest that the emergence of the Harappan Civilization, in curious parallel with the Mesopotamian, coincided with intensification of resource-procurement, manifested by the expansion of the geographic horizons of two contemporary and neighbouring plains societies? Is it too far fetched to suggest that this is tangible evidence for Gordon Childe's externally expanding Bronze Age economy?

[9] Jarrige and Hassan (1989: 152) date the decline of Mundigak and Shahr-i Sokhta to the period of the rise of the Mature Harappan. This supports my argument.

ACKNOWLEDGEMENTS

My sincere thanks to Rollwyn D'Souza and other teachers of the Interscope Institute of Computer Education, Bombay.

REFERENCES

Amiet, P. 1979. Archaeological Discontinuity and Ethnic Duality in Elam, *Antiquity,* LIII, pp. 195–204.

________,1986. Susa and the Dilmun Culture, in *Bahrain Though the Ages* (H. al Khalifa ad M. Rice Eds.), pp. 262–68. London: Kegan Paul International.

Anderson, H.H. 1986. The Barbar Temple: Stratigraphy, Architecture, and Interpretation, in *Bahrain Through the Ages* (H. al Khalifa and M. Rice Eds.), pp. 166–77. London: Kegan Paul International.

Balland, D. 1989. Map 12.7: Afghanistan: Nomadismus and Halbnomadismus, in *Tubinger Atlas des Vorderen Orients*. Wiesbaden: Reichert.

Barnes, J.W. 1988. *Ores and Minerals*. Milton Keynes: Open University.

Berlev, O.D. 1987. A Social Experiment in Nubia, in *Labour in the Ancient Near East* (M. Powell Ed.), pp. 143–58. New Haven: Americal Oriental Society.

Berthoud, T.S. Cleuziou, L.P. Hurtel, M. Menu and C. Volfovsky 1982. Cuivres et Alliages en Iran, Afghanistan, Oman, *Paleorient*, 8, pp. 39–54.

Besenval, R. 1992. Recent Archaeological Surveys in Pakistani Makran, in *South Asian Archaeology 1989* (C. Jerrige Ed.), pp. 25–35. Madison: Prehistory Press.

Bibby, G. 1986. The Origins of the Dilmun Civilization, in *Bahrain Through the Ages* (H. al Khalifa and M. Rice Eds.), pp. 108–15. London: Kegan Paul International.

Brunswig, R.H., A. Parpola and D. Potts 1983. New Indus Type and Related Seals from the Near East, in *Dilmun: New Studies in the Archaeology and Early History of Bahrain* (D. Potts Ed.), pp. 101–16. Berlin: Reimer.

Casanova, M. 1992. The Sources of Lapis lazli Found in Iran, in *South Asian Archaeology 1989* (C. Jarrige Ed.), pp. 49–56. Madison: Prehistory Press.

Chang, K.C. 1975. Ancient Trade as Economics or as Ecology, in *Ancient Civilization and Trade* (J.A. Sabloff and C.C. Lamberg-Karlovsky Eds.), pp. 211–24. Albuquerque: University of New Maxico.

________, 1983. *Art, Myth and Ritual: the Path to Political Authority in Ancient China.* Cambridge: Harvard University.

Childe, V. Gordon 1944. Archaeological Ages as Technological Stages (Huxley Memorial Lecture), *Journal of the Royal Anthropological Institute*, 5, pp. 7–26.

———, 1964. *What Happened in History*. Harmondsworth: Penguin (Revised Edition).

Childe, V. 1957. The Bronze Age. *Pastand Present,* 12, pp. 2–15.

Cleuziou, S. 1978–79. The Second and Third Seasons of Excavation at Hili 8, *Archaeology in the UAE*, 2–3, pp. 30–69.

———, 1981. Oman Peninsula in the Early Second Millennium, in *South Asian Archaeology 1979* (H. Hartel Ed.), pp. 279–93. Berlin: Reimer.

———, 1986. Dilmun and Makkan During the Third and Early Second Millennia B.C., in *Bahrain Through the Ages* (H. al Khalifa and M. Rice Eds.), pp. 143–55. London: Kegan Paul International.

———, and T. Berthoud 1982. Early Tin in the Near East, *Expedition* Fall: 14–20.

———, and M. Tosi 1989. The Southeastern Frontier of the Ancient Near East, in *South Asian Archaeology 1985* (K. Frifelt and P. Sörensen Eds.), pp. 14–48. London: Curzon.

Campagnoni, B. and M. Tosi 1978. The Camel: Finds from Shahr-i Sokhta, in *Approaches to Faunal Analysis in the Middle East* (R. Meadow and M. Zeder Eds.), pp. 91–103. Peabody Museum Bulletin no. 2.

Craddock, P., I.C. Freestone, L.K. Gurjar, A. Middleston and L. Willies 1989. The Production of Lead, Silver, and Zinc in Early India, in *Old World Archaeometry* (A. Hauptamann *et al.* Eds.) pp. 51–69. Bochum: Bergbau Museum.

Delmas, A.B. and M. Casanova 1990. The Lapis lazuli Sources in the Ancient Near East, in *South Asian Archaeology* 1987 (M. Taddei Ed.), pp. 493–505. Rome: IsMEO.

During-Caspers, E.C.L. 1987. In the Footsteps of Gilgamesh, *Persica*, XII, pp. 57–95.

———, E.C.L. 1989. Some Remarks on Oman, *Proceeding of the Seminar on Arbian Studies*, 19, pp. 13–31.

———, 1992. Intercultural/Mercantile Contacts Between the Arabian Gulf and South Aisa, *Proceedings of the Seminar on Arbian Studies*, 22, pp. 3–28.

Edens, C. 1993. Indus-Arabian Interaction During the Bronze Age, in *Harappan Civilization: a Recent Perspective* (G. Possehl Ed.), pp. 335–63. Delhi: Oxford and IBH.

Emery, W. 1961. *Archaic Egypt.* Harmondsworth: Penguin.

Finkbeiner, U. and W. Rolling (Eds.) 1986. *Gamdat Nasr: Period or Regional Style*? Wiesbaden: Reichert.

Francfort, H.P. 1989. *Fouilles de Shortughai.* Paris: Boccard.

Gardiner, A. 1966. *Egypt of the Pharaohs*. Oxford: Clarendon.

Gibson, M. 1977. An Indus Valley Stamp Seal from Nippur, *Man and Environment*, 1, p. 67.

Gupta, S.P. 1979. *Archaeology of Soviet Central Asia and the Indian Borderlands.* Vol. II. Delhi: B.R. Publications.

Hegde, K.T.M. 1978. Sources of Ancient Tin in India, in *The Search for Ancient Tin* (T.A. Wertime and J. Olin Eds.), pp. 39–42. Washington: Smithsonian Institution.

Hojlund, F. 1989. Sources of Ancient of Harappan Influence in the Gulf, in *South Asian Archaeology 1985* (K. Frifelt and P. Sörensen Eds.), pp. 49–53. London: Curzon.

Hornell, J. 1970. *Water Transport: Origins and Early Evolution.* Newton Abbot: David and Charles.

Hughes, M. 1991. Tracing to Source, in *Science and the Past* (S. Bowman Ed.), pp. 99–116. London: British Museum.

Humphery, C. 1985. Barter and Economic Disintegration, *Man*, 20, pp. 48–72.

Jarrige, J.F. and M.U. Hassan 1989. Funerary Complexes in Baluchistan at the End of the Third Millennium, in *South Asian Archaeology 1985* (K. Frifelt and P. Söresen Eds.), pp. 150–66. London: Curzon.

Johnstone, P. 1988. *The Sea-Craft of Prehistory*. London: Routledge.

Kjaerum, P. 1986. The Dilmun Seals as Evidence of Long Distance Relations, in *Bahrain Through the Ages* (H. al Khalifa and M. Rice Eds.), pp. 269–77. London: Kegan Paul International.

Kohl, P. 1986. The Lands of Dilmun, in *Bahrain Through the Ages* (H. al Kalifa and M. Rice Eds.), pp. 367–75. London: Kegan Paul International.

________, G. Hardbottle and E.V. Sayre. 1979. Physical and Chemical Analyses of Soft Stone Vessels from southwest Asia, *Archaeometry*, 21, pp. 131–59.

Kosambi, D.D. 1981. On the Origin and Development of Silver Coinage, in *Indian Numismatics* (Kosambi Papers, B.D. Chattopadhyay Ed.), pp. 85–94, fig. 5.1. Delhi: London. First Publ. 1941.

Lamberg-Karlovsky, C.C. 1986. Death in Dilmun, in *Bahrain Through the Ages* (H. al Kahlifa and M. Rice Eds.), pp. 156–65. London: Kegan Paul International.

Lucas, A. 1948. *Ancient Egyptian Materials and Industries.* London: Edward Arnold.

Majidzadeh, Y. 1982. Lapis Lazuli and the Great Khorasa Road, *Paleorient*, 8.1, pp. 59–69.

Masson, V.M. 1981. Seals of Proto-Indian Type from Altyn-depe, in *The Bronze Age Civilization of Central Asia* (P. Kohl Ed.), pp. 149–62. New York: Sharpe.

________ 1988. *Altyn-depe.* Philadelphia: University Museum.

Meillassoux, C. 1972. From Reproduction to Production, *Economy and Society*, 1, pp. 93–105.

Moorey, P.R.S. 1971. The Loftus Hoard of Old Babylonian Tools, *Iraq*, 33, pp. 61–86.

________, 1985. *Materials and Manufacture in Ancient Mesopotamia.* Oxford: BAR.

Mortensen, P. 1986. The Barbar Temple: Its Chronology and Foreign Relations, in *Bahrain Through the Ages* (H. al Khalifa and M. Rice Eds.) pp. 178–85. London: Kegan Paul International.

Nissen, H.J. 1986. The Occurrence of Dilmun in the Oldest Texts of Mesopotamia, in *Bahrain Through the Ages* (H. al Khalifa and M. Rice Eds.), pp. 335–39. London: Kegan Paul International.

Oates, J., T.E. Davidson, D. Kamilli and H. McKerrell 1977. Seafaring Merchants of Ur?, *Antiquity*, 51, pp. 221–34.

Parpola, S., A. Parpola, and R. Brunswig 1977. The Meluhha Village, *Journal of the Economic and Social History of the Orient*, 20, pp. 129–65.

Phillips, W. 1967. *Oman: a History*. London: Longmans.

Piggott, S. 1968. The Earliest Wheeled Vehicles, *Proceedings of the Prehistoric Society*, 34, pp. 266–318.

——— 1983. *The Earliest Wheeled Transport*. London: Thames and Hudson.

Piggott, V.C., S.M. Howard, and S.M. Epstein 1982. Pyrotechnology and Culture Change at Tepe Hissar in *Early Pyrotechnology* (T.A. and S.F. Wertime Eds.), pp. 215–36. Washington: Smithsonian Institution.

Polanyi, K. 1957. The Economy as Instituted Process, in *Trade and Market in the Early Empires* (K. Polanyi *et al.* Eds.), pp. 243–70. New York: Free press.)

——— 1975. Traders and Trade, in *Ancient Civilization and Trade* (J.A. Sabloff and C.C. Lamberg-Karlovsky Eds.), pp. 133–54. Albuquerque: University of New Mexico.

Potts, D.T. 1986. Eastern Arabia and the Oman Peninsula, in *Gamdat Nasr: Period or Regional Style?* (U. Finkbeiner and W. Rollig Eds.), pp. 121–70. Wiesbaden: Reichert.

——— 1993. A New Bactrian Find from Southeastern Arbia, *Antquity*, 67, pp. 591–96.

Potts, T.F. 1989. Foreign Stone Vessels of the Late Third Millennium from Southern Mesopotamia, *Iraq*, 51, pp. 123–64.

——— 1993. Patterns of Trade in Third Millennium Mesopotamia and Iran, *World Archaeology*, 24, pp. 379–402.

Ratnagar, S. 1981. *Encounters: the Westerly Trade of the Harappa Civilization.* Delhi: Oxford University Press.

——— 1991. *Enquires into the Political Organization of Harappan Society.* Pune: Ravish.

——— 1992. *A Bronze Age Frontier.* Delhi: Indian History Congress Symposia Series 2.

Roaf, M. 1982. Weights on the Dilmun Standard, *Iraq*, 44, pp. 137–41.

Sarianidhi, V. 1979. New Finds in Bactria and Indo-Iranian Connections, in *South Asian Archaeology 1977* (M. Taddei Ed.), pp. 643–59. Naples: IUO.

Shaffer, J. and D. Lichtenstein 1989. Ethnicity and Change in the Indus Valley Cultural Tradition, in *Old Problems and New Perspectives in the Archaeology of South Asia* (J.M. Keynoyer Ed.), pp. 117–26. Madison: University of Wisconsin.

Stacul, G. 1985. A Harappan Post-Urban Outpost in the Swat Valley, in *South Asian Archaeology 1983* (J. Schotsmans and M. Taddei Eds.), pp. 357–67, Naples: IUO.

Stech, T. and V. Pigott 1986. The Metals Trade in South West Asia in The Third Millennium, *Iraq*, 48, pp. 39–64.

Thapar, B.K. 1985. *Recent Archaeological Discoveries in India*. Paris: UNESCO.

Tossi, M. 1986. Early Maritime Cultures of the Arabian Gulf and the Indian Ocean, in *Bahrain Through the Ages* (H. al Khalifa and M. Rice Eds.), pp. 94–107. London: Kegan Paul International.

Voigt, M. and R. Dyson 1992. The Chronology of Iran 8000–2000 BC in *Chronologies in Old World Archaeology* (R.W. Enrich Ed.), pp. 122–53. Chicago: University Press.

Weiner, A. 1985. Inalienable Wealth, *American Ethonologist*, 12, pp. 21–227.

Weisgerber, G. 1986. Dilmun, A Trading Enterpot, in *Bahrain Through the Ages* (H. al Khalifa and M. Rice Eds.), pp. 35–42. London: Kegan Paul International.

Xu Chaolong, 1990. The Kot Dijians and the Harappans: Their Simultaniety, in *South Asian Archaeology 1987* (M. Taddei Ed.), pp. 157–201. Rome: IsMEO.

Yule, P. 1985. *Metalwork of the Bronze Age in India,* Munich: Beck.

Zaccagnini, C. 1985. Patterns of Mobility amongst Ancient Near Eastern Craftsmen, *Journal of Near Eastern Studies*, 42, pp. 245–64.

Zarins, J. 1989. Eastern Saudi Arabia and External Relations 3500–1900 BC in *South Asian Archaeology 1985* (K. Frifelt and P. Sörensen Eds.), 74–103. London: Curzon.

Chapter Three

The Harappan Civilization Beyond the Indian Subcontinent*

MAURIZIO TOSI

In a rare coincidence during the 1920s, Ur and Mohenjodaro were being excavated at the same time, under the leadership of two equally talented British archaeologists, Leonard Woolley and John Marshall, who were to be knighted for their successful enterprises. Also, for the first time the English-speaking public could follow the progress of those ongoing large-scale excavations from a number of lively reports published in a popular weekly magazine, the *Illustrated London News*. These first-hand descriptions conveyed an intriguing image of the Bronze Age civilizations that preceded in southwestern Asia, the age of Biblical prophets of over a millennium. Anyway, the contemporary excavations at Ur (1922–34) and Mohenjodaro (1921–31) should not be remembered just for the excitement they aroused, but much more for having provided the archaeologists with sufficient new material to study the culture of those early urban societies on a much broader cognitive base. In this sense both excavations still overshadow the present research work, commanding aspects of our historical speculations. The publication of both enterprises, promptly undertaken only a few years after the fieldwork had ended (Marshall 1931; Woolley 1934), granted to the archaeology of ancient Near East the dignity of self-standing discipline, breaking the tight bonds with those Biblical studies that had justified the first involvement of European institutions in the nineteenth century.

* *Harappan Civilization: A Recent Perspective*, edited by Gregory L. Possehl second edition, 1991. Oxford and IBH Publishing, Delhi, pp. 365–78.

MORE THAN JUST AN ARCHAEOLOGICAL QUESTION

It was Mohenjodaro that provided the major turning point in the studies of the Asian Bronze Age. By proving the existence of an advanced Bronze Age urban society beyond the Iranian plateau and far to the east of the Fertile Crescent, that vast brick ruin of Sind made the emergence of urbanism a historical problem of much wider implications. At this point it became critical to establish the kind of relation connecting the Indus with the Near East during the third millennium BC.

To what extent the Indus Civilization can be treated as an original phenomenon of pristine urban development is still very much an open controversy. The question is not just a petty academic one, but it is relevant to establish whether the investments in people and resources the Indus Civilization would deserve should compare with those directed in the past to the study of ancient Mesopotamia and, more recently, pre-Columbian Mesoamerica. An archaeological record can tackle complex historical phenomena only when the amount of data collected is large and differentiated enough, to account for the variability present within a complex social system, spreading like the Indus Civilization over greater space and time. Undoubtedly, these dates will only be available if those investments are made, supporting a number of multidisciplinary long-term projects. Like a dog chasing its tail we are trapped in some sort of a dead circle. As long as these new data are not made available to scientific inquiry, most historical speculation will remain subjected to the vagaries of accidental discoveries and preconceived biases.

Earlier explanations for the emergence of the Indus Civilization have ranged between very distant extremes: from the direct colonization of Mesopotamians in the early fourth millennium BC dear to Sumerologist S.N. Kramer to the partonogenetical mode of birth in total seclusion, professed by most scholars in India.

For a vast majority of ancient Near Eastern specialists the Indus Civilization is largely regarded as a late epiphenomenon of the paramount Mesopotamian experience. The emergence of complex state societies across South-West Asia would be in a more or less direct way the consequence of a motion originated in the alluvial lowlands of the Euphrates, Tigris and Karun during the fourth millennium BC. However, conceptually readjusted in more recent years, the Mesopotamo-centric perspective is very much alive today. On the other hand there is at present no good reason to dismiss it, particularly after the spectacular discoveries that from 1969 on have highlighted the great expansion of the Late Uruk-Jemdet Nasr cultural complex outside Mesopotamia. The foundation of entirely new settlements, like Habuba Khabira on the Syrian Euphrates, and the eastward diffusion of Jemdet Nasr ceramics a few generations later into the Oman peninsula have proven in both directions the expansion capacity the lowland early states had reached by the end of the third millennium BC. Assuming that such widespread changes could not have occurred without profound disruptions of preceding socio-political realities, one can expect that the shock waves also reached Baluchistan's eastern fringes, along the Indus Valley western margins. Regrettably one has to conclude that until more direct data becomes available, archaeologists will not be able to use more sophisticated conceptual frames to unfold the relation between cultural contact and social evolution.

For those standing on the opposite end, claiming independent origins for an Indus Civilization viewed as already Indian in the spirit, the issue is further complicated by ideological factors. The British Empire was already a crumbling political entity at the time that Marshall was digging Mohenjodaro, but some of its Victorian ideology of European mastership was still alive. One of its corollaries was that the immense human universe of the Indian subcontinent had to be considered a single historical entity that the morally-superior British civil servants were called to restore to its original splendor. The discovery of Mohenjodaro in the twilight period of the British rule would quite appropriately serve the scope by conveying an image of common ancestry for many of India's historical characters. Those profound internal diversities frozen in the caste system, would then be explained with the disruptions of the mythical Aryan invasions and the impossible amalgam between the victors and the vanquished. This perfect construction would save at once, two necessary political postulates, otherwise radically opposed: the unity of the Subcontinent and the hegemony of a minority. Efforts were made by several leading authorities to emphasize continuity between Bronze Age India and the Hindu traditions, while archaeological explorations were to be focussed on uncovering the local roots of the Indus Civilization in the plains of Sind and Punjab. The best example is a long essay, published by a prominent Indian scholar, Ramaprashad Chanda, Director of the Calcutta Museum, in as early as 1929 in the major official series of the Archaeological Survey of India, with the title *Survival of the Prehistorical Civilisation of the Indus Valley*. This was written while the Mohenjodaro excavations were still open.

Unfortunately for this scheme, the economic depression following the collapse of the American stock market in 1929, was particularly devastating in such marginal areas of the capitalist system as the colonial dependencies throughout the world. Very few funds were available for archaeological activities in India during the thirties. While excavations could still benefit from the cheap manpower, there was no money for specialists and technical support. Although the Archaeological Survey of India became revitalized in the very last years of the British Empire for the efforts of its last director before partition, Sir Mortimer Wheeler, the data made available could only minimally enlarge the original picture. Aimed to equip the Indus Civilization with a more solid chronological skeleton through accurate stratigraphical seriations, Wheeler's strategy remained one of quality, while his basic assumption was that local development of the Indus Civilization had to be assumed until otherwise proven. The quintessential scientist, Wheeler remained throughout his life a man of immense curiosity, loyal to the facts and always ready to accept what new explorations brought to light. The problem was that there were few facts, since the Indus Civilization was for many years in a vacuum. Till the late sixties very little was known of the prehistory of the lands to the east of Mesopotamia, even if they included countries of great importance to the later history of Asia, such as Iran, Turkestan, Baluchistan and Arabia.

One might not have expected that a broader understanding of the Indus Civilization and its role in the history of mankind would emerge from new research in these intermediary regions. The pattern of contacts and exchange that the Harappans established with Mesopotamia and these other countries is a subject that touches the heart of the issue concerning the historical role of their civilization. Spread from the Arabian sea to the Himalaya, the Indus Civilization was the largest continuous cultural system of Bronze Age Asia, aggregating hundreds of thousands of people within its political and social institutions. To assume that its influence was strictly confined to the Subcontinent as a birthplace of the Indian Civilization, is too simplistic and too reductive a perspective. One important target for future research would be to reconstruct the contributions it received from and gave to the countries across the mountains and the ocean

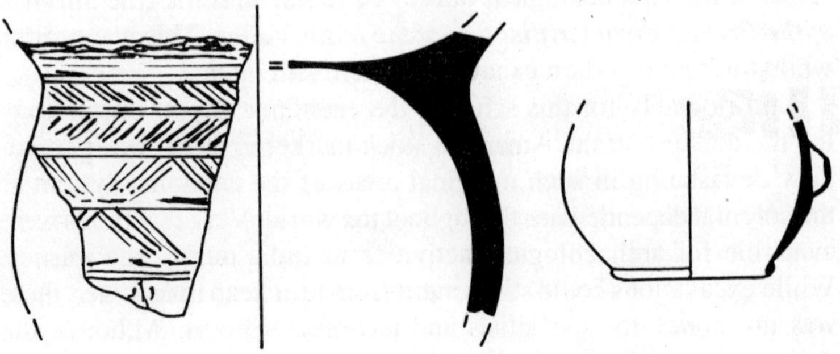

Fig. 3.1: Chlorite vessels from Mehi

bordering India to the west and to the south. Anyway, the available data through the scatter of finds outside the Subcontinent may already convey us an image to widespread involvement, both in Arabia and Central Asia. By reviewing this evidence, this paper attempts to suggest that the relations of the Indus Civilization with these foreign countries might have had a far greater impact than ever expected. (Fig. 3.1).

MESOPOTAMIA: STRAYED SEALS, SCRIPTS AND BEADS

The most characteristic marker of the Indus Civilization is its still undeciphered pictographic script, mostly documented in the elegant epigraphic form it was incised on square stamp seals of glazed steatite. These seals were manufactured in a very standardized square shape with a pierced boss carved on the back. A low-temperature baking of the steatite vitrified their surface to a snow white coating, that increased hardness and polish. They were produced in large quantities for wide circulation. Over two thousand of them have been recovered in Harappan settlements, equally occurring in larger and smaller sites, in houses and specialized compounds, along the mainstream of the great river and in their cultural system's most distant peripheries. That relations between Harappans and Mesopotamians were very much of a reality became evident very soon. While Mohenjodaro was still being excavated, around the same time these seals surfaced also in Mesopotamia. The first one of them was found at Tell Ahaimir, part of ancient Kish, in 1923, a few months before J.

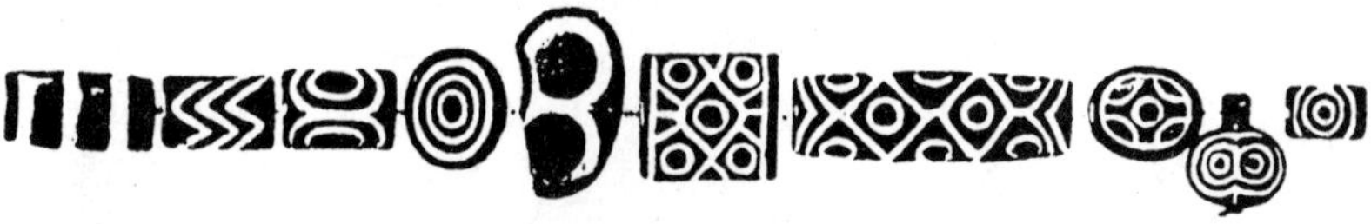

Fig. 3.2: Etched carnelian beads from Ur

Marshall (1924) produced his first report on Mohenjodaro for *Illustrated London News*. It was carved with the most frequent motive of the Indus Civilization: a bull standing in front of a manger with a three sign inscription running on top of it. Also at Kish, and in the same season of exacavations, more evidence for contact was provided by a few etched carnelian beads found in graves. The technique of etching is very common in India: red chalcedony beads are decorated with white bands, produced by the calcination of a sodium carbonate coating in a low-temperature furnace. They represent another tracing element of Harappan connection, as well as an object of Indian trade in historical times, that even better than seals has permitted to reconstruct the extent of the exchange system (Fig. 3.2).

Further evidence for contact was recovered by the French exacavations of Telloh and Susa, major urban centres of the Mesopotamian lowlands, in the perceptible form of other steatite seals. But even more revealing for the expectations of contact and exchange between the two alluvial heartlands, there was recovered from the the Louvre reserves a well-preserved clay impression of an inscribed Indus seal, brought by a dealer to the museum shortly before World War I, before the Indus Civilization had become recognized at all (Scheil 1925). It was said to have come from Jhoka, a site in southern Mesopotamia still unexcavated but identified from the texts collected by looters with the ancient Sumerian city of Umma. The provenance has never been confirmed and never will, but there is no reason to doubt that it came from southern Iraq, where those dealers operated. The impression bears the usual 'bull and manger' motive with a 6-sign inscription running on top (Fig. 3.3a). In 1931 the sealing was donated by the Louvre to the Ashmolean Museum of Oxford on account of its relevance for the British research in the Indus valley. The seal impression had been carefully centered on the front side, while the back bears a clean impression of a cloth tied on a jar mouth by a string run around the neck. A deeper hole on one side marks the knot

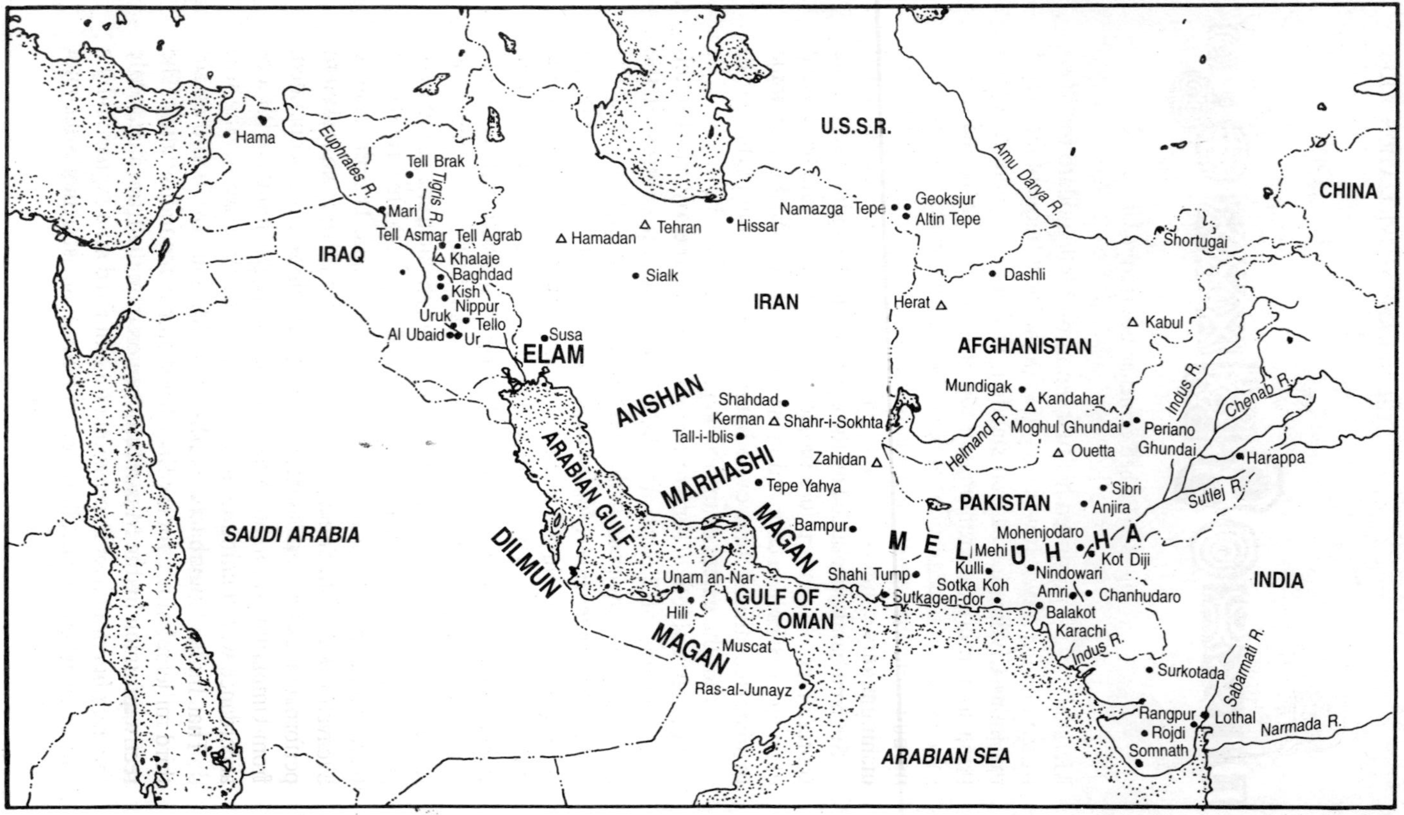

Map 3.1. The Near and Middle East and the Indian Subcontinent

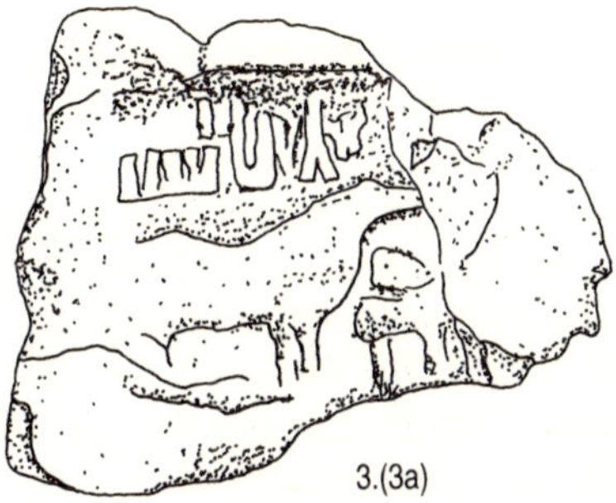

3.(3a)

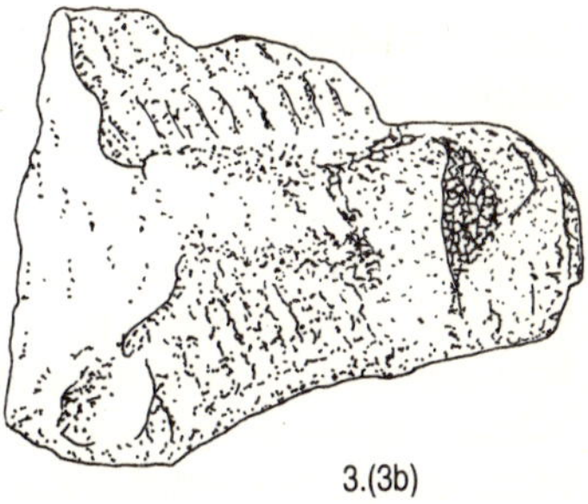

3.(3b)

Fig. 3.3a: Indus seal impression from Tell Umma (?).
Fig. 3.3b: Reverse of Umma (?) seal impression.

the clay lump was covering to seal the jar's content against any illicit manipulation (Fig. 3.3b).

Such clay sealings represent for the archaeologist a uniquely direct source of information on such administrative procedures as the control of storage and shipment of merchandises across the Middle East in the third and second millennium BC. Literally thousands of them have been found across Southwestern Asia, from Nubia to Anatolia and from Syria to Afghanistan. The immediate assumption one could draw from the Umma impression was that it relates to a shipment of expensive goods packed in a sealed container. But a less straightforward explanation might be necessary if we consider that this type of sealing, so common in the Middle East, are unknown from the Indus valley and the countries of the Subcontinent's western borderlands. From Baluchistan, Oman and southern central Asia only a handful of these clay sealings have been recovered. With a ratio between seals and sealings close to 10:1, the Indus Civilization is radically different from all other countries in the Middle East that had adopted seals. Since there is no technical reason left to explain the scarcity of sealings in all excavations, one has to conclude that seals in the Indus valley did not perform the same functions. It might well be that the Harappan sealing from Umma was struck in Mesopotamia for an Indian expatriate, in accordance with local formalities for sealed shipments.

That Indian 'merchants' had settled in Sumer at the end of the third millennium BC, undergoing increasing acculturation we are directly informed by the Mesopotamia texts of the late third and early second millennium BC. Betwen the time of Sargon of Agade and the end of the IIIrd Dynasty of Ur (*c.* 2350–2000 BC), they mention a land of Meluhha, as a country located beyond the Persian Gulf that supplies through maritime trade many exotic goods: ivory objects, inlay works, gold, carnelian and other precious stones, hard woods, rare animals and slaves are most prominent in the lists recorded on the tablets. One could hardly argue that Meluhha provided Mesopotamia some access to resources from tropical lands around the Indian Ocean. In a commemorative inscription, Sargon the Great (2334–2279 BC)claimed among the main achievements of his rule that the ships of Meluhha together with those of other two countries along the shores of Arabia, Dilmun and Magan, moored at the wharfs of his capital, Agade.

A cylinder seal of the same period bears the Cuneiform Akkado-Sumerian inscription *su-i-ḷi-su/*eme-bal me-luh-ha, meaning 'Su-iḷisu Meluhha interpreter' (De Clerca 1888) (Fig. 3.4). Rather symbolically, Su-ilisu is represented on the same seal as a dwarf seated on the lap of a person of a higher rank, possibly the king himself, while addressing two visitors. We may add that about a century later the Meluhhans contributed to the construction of a new temple built at Lagash by the ruler, Gudea, carrying 'wood and other raw materials' from their distant homeland. Finally, towards the end of the third millennium BC, while direct trade with Meluhha is fading from textual evidence a Meluhha village (e-duru me-luh-ha) and Meluhha sons (dumu meluh-ha) are mentioned in a dozen economic texts of the Ur III dynasty, listing persons and debts or dealing with rations and deliveries of cereals. The Assyriologists have interpreted these texts as witnesses of an acculturation process involving one or more enclaves of aliens from the Indian Subcontinent, progressively

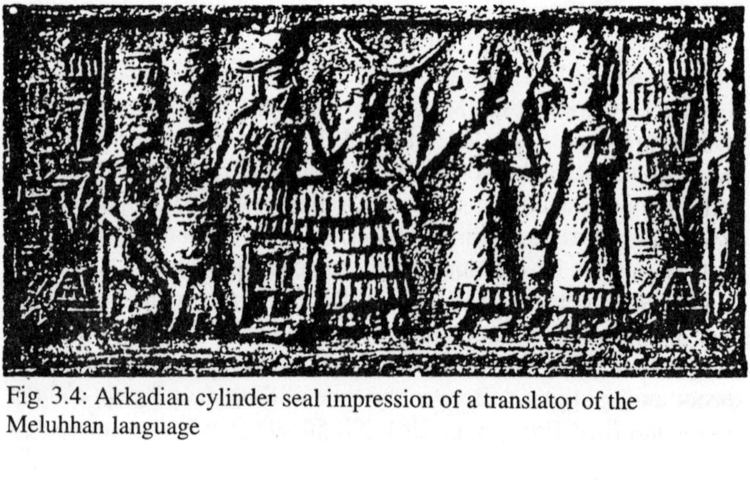

Fig. 3.4: Akkadian cylinder seal impression of a translator of the Meluhhan language

intetgrating into the Sumerian society. Relations might not have been always that peaceful, if one considers an earlier text, probably Sargonid, where a Lu-Sunzida, man of Meluhha, 'has remitted to Urur, son of Amar-LUKU . . . 10 shekels of silver as payment for a broken tooth . . .'.

Although few and dispersed, these texts are telling us that communications were active and involved people as much as goods. For the historian the relevant problem is now to establish how these relations effected their social reality. We know that the two civilizations remained substantially different from each other, but how could one argue that the exchange had no effect on their respective evolutionary trends? Furthermore, one should also consider the possible fallout of the long-distance trade on the lands in between. Here the transformations determined by the trade systems might have been the most conspicuous. Southern Iran, Baluchistan, the Gulf and the Oman peninsula had to be brought on stage as active characters before one could even describe the plot.

Anyway, neither choronological nor historical implications could be derived from any of these imports until some of them were recovered in a stratigraphical context. The Oriental Institute of the University of Chicago excavations in the Diyala Valley of Iraq during the 1930s (Francfort 1933, 1939, Francfort , *et. al.* 1932) made this association possible. At Tell Asmar, the ancient Eshnunna, H. Francfort and his colleagues came across a number of Harappan imports and were finally able to nail down their range of occurrence between the Akkadian dynasty and the end of the Ur III period, between 2350 and 2000 BC. These imports included kidney-shaped ivory inlay pieces, etched carnelian beads and potsherds from small knobbed ware jars, a frequent occurrence at Mohenjodaro. None of the typical square steatite seals was found, but a significant piece of connection to the Subcontinent was added by a cyclinder seal, AS.31:22, made of glazed steatite and deeply carved with a procession of three of the most characteristic animals in India's wildlife: an elephant, a rhinoceros and a garial crocodile (Fig. 3.5). One could have hardly selected a more exotic and intriguing lot to impress a foreign audience. Cylinder seals are not unknown in the Indus Valley Civilization, since four of them are reported so far, but their style and carving technique remained very distinctive from any of the Mesopotamian productions: to say it in Francfort's own words '. . . no Babylonian seal of this quality shows so unbalanced a composition'. Furthermore, he assumed that the rendering of physical details in the animal's body was so vivid to

Fig. 3.5: Cylinder seal from Tell Asmar

leave little doubt on the origin of the artist. While it is conceivable, at least on stylistical grounds, that the seal from Eshnunna had been manufactured by an Indian craftsman, we seem to face here that same combination of formal similarity and functional diversity suggested by the Umma sealing: an object in all effects Indian in character and manufacture, is adjusted to a differing reality. The 'Meluhhans' seem to be part of the Mesopotamian world, while still identified by their particular set of symbols and signs, very much alike the image conveyed by the Ur III texts we previously discussed. AS.31:22 was found in a sloping dump, just outside the outer walls of a large late Akkadian household compound, in period IVa of the site sequence, 2300–2200 BC in date. Although it is not a primary context of deposition, its consistency with the earlier finds from Kish and Ur indicates at 2200 BC a safe quantum limit *post quem non for* the period the Harappan cylinder seal was used at Eshnunna.

Francfort's stratigraphical specification to the Akkadian period of the Harappan material in Mesopotamia provided the archaeologists with the first cross dating relation for the Indus civilization that also agreed with the scanty textual references to Meluhha. Later finds and further studies have largely confirmed this line of reasoning. For example, the distribution of etched carnelian beads across the graves of the Royal Cemetery of Ur recently revised by J. Reade of the British Museum, indicates their earlier introduction to Mesopotamia to the end of the Early Dynastifc III period, around 2350 BC, maybe one generation before Sargon of Akhad, established his dominion over the Babylonian lowlands. This is not to say that previously there was no contact or exchange between the ends of the Gulf, but more simply that none of the diagnostic mature Harappan objects reached Mesopotamia before 2400 BC. To what extent the two aspects are related is still a matter of speculation, that only more exacavations in Iraq and Pakistan could ground on more solid feet.

The last of the inscribed Indus seals to surface in Mesopotamia came to light at Nippur in 1977. It is a perfect glazed steatite specimen of the zebu bull type, but it was unfortunately recovered in a secondary context from a house of late Kassite times, dated around 1250 BC. The steatite is severely worn by prolonged exposure, suggesting a long period of disuse. There is no reason at present to dispute L. Oppenheim's first suggestion that Meluhha, and the Indus Civilization, leave the Mesopotamian world at the time of Hammurabi, in the eighteenth century BC.

In conclusion, the scenario pieced together from the Mesopotamian archaeological record implies that contact between the two great centres of Bronze-Age civilization was a reality, but neither an intense nor a continuous one. Shortly, after 2400 BC, direct traffic in luxury commodities was activated between lower Mesopotamia and the Indus Civilization, along a maritime route of communication. The lack of Mesopotamian imports in the Indus Valley is quite revealing of a lesser significance of these connection for the eastern pole. Very much alike the Roman trade with India and Arabia as described by the *Periplus of the Erythraean Sea* in the first century of our era, the flow of goods towards the head of the Gulf in the late third millennium BC was determined more by the Mesopotamian demand than by degrees of economical integration with the distant lands that supplied those goods from the shores of the Indian Ocean.

WORLDS IN BETWEEN

The Harappan evidence in Mesopotamia was ambiguous from the very beginning. Not only the few true imports exhibited elements that could only be explained in terms of adaptation to local conditions, but some of these early finds related to the Indus Civilization do not match anything known from the Subcontinent. The contemporary excavations of Ur were at the origin of the riddle: sixteen round steatite seals were discovered in different locations of the site, mostly datable to the early centuries of the third millennium BC. Six of them were engraved with Harappan pictograms running above the usual humped bull and manger composition. While their relation to the world of Mohenjodaro was out of the question, the connection was definitely a puzzling one. The critical aspect was not their dissimilarity from the thousands of finely carved square specimens found in the Indus, but their internal morphological consistency as products of a distinctive sphragistic tradition.

Assyriologist C.J. Gadd who published the seals in 1934 was too fine a scholar to take these striking distinctions as irrelevant and he referred to them as *seals of ancient Indian style*, suggesting they were '. . . more probably, a product of some place under the influence both of the Indus and the Sumerian civilization'. Also, he noticed that among the few pictographic signs there were some unreported in the Mohenjodaro inventory. When in recent years an exhaustive listing of all the Indus Civilization signs and concordances was undertaken by Asko Parpola, the distinctive combinatory aggregation in the Gulf inscriptions was further confirmed on a much wider scale. Nevertheless, how close Gadd was to reality by suspecting the existence of an intermediary entity became clear only twenty years later, at the time a Danish expedition initiated the first systematic prehistoric research in the islands of Bahrain and Failaka, along the Arabian coast of the Gulf. Hundreds of steatite stamp seals of the same round type came to light from coastal settlements of the early second millennium BC with the remains of a new Bronze Age culture. It was the land of Dilmun, a recurrent place name in all kinds of Mesopotamian texts during the third millennium BC mentioned as a neighbouring country across the 'southern sea', renowned for its orchards and seafaring suppliers of exotic goods. Woolley's excavations at Ur provided at this point another important connection, through a group of tablets he recovered from houses of the Ur III and Isin-Larsa periods. These were the economic accounts of merchants and investing pools of temple estates and private entrepreneurs involved in the maritime trade with Dilmun, and the further lands of Magan and Meluhha. Copper, ivory, precious stones, ebony are the main commodities listed in the contracts, to be imported against outbound garments, oils and cash payments in silver.

Meluhha is only mentioned in the texts of the Third Dynasty in association with such characteristic Indian imports as ivory or carnelian, while it disappears together with Magan from the Isin-Larsa texts, after 2000 BC. In 1954, Leo Oppenheim, one of the leading post-WW II Assyriologists, proposed that this change reflected the growth of Dilmun as a trading centre. A privileged partnership with

Mesopotamia would have placed the island in a key position to control the flow of goods from the Indian Ocean. Increasingly mediated by this third entity in coastal Arabia, relations between Mesopotamia and the Indus would have decreased, with Dilmun achieving a monopoly in Isin-Larsa times. Between 1954 and 1970 a surprisingly wide body of archaeological evidence could be brought together to support this still very linear proposition of a tripartite mercantile system. The first bit of evidence was implicit in the same Ur excavations, considering that those Isin-Larsa tablets shared the same context of provenance with Gadd's 'Indian style' round seals. On another tablet of the same period, from the Yale University collections, and dated to the tenth year of reign by Gungunum of Larsa (1923 BC) (Buchanan 1967) the cuneiform text was impressed with a Dilmun seal. A few more Harappan inscriptions carved on Gulf seals like the first Ur specimens were found by the Danes at Failaka, together with several other items of 'Indian' origin. Among these, a number of Harappan weights, the characteristic chert cubes were found at Qal'at al-Bahrain, confirmed the sharing of standards, essential to the efficiency of trade performances. Even more impressive was the discovery in 1961–62 of a typical Dilmun seal at Lothal, a mature Harappan settlement at the northern end of the Gulf of Cambay, in Gujarat. Lothal is over 2000 km east of Bahrain, very close to the extreme southern reaches of the Indus Civilization in the Subcontinent (Fig. 3.6) (Rao 1963). This find indicates the extent of the northern seaboard of the Indian Ocean that could have been economically and culturally encompassed by maritime trade around 2000 BC. In archaeological terms evidence for exchange is best based on prod-

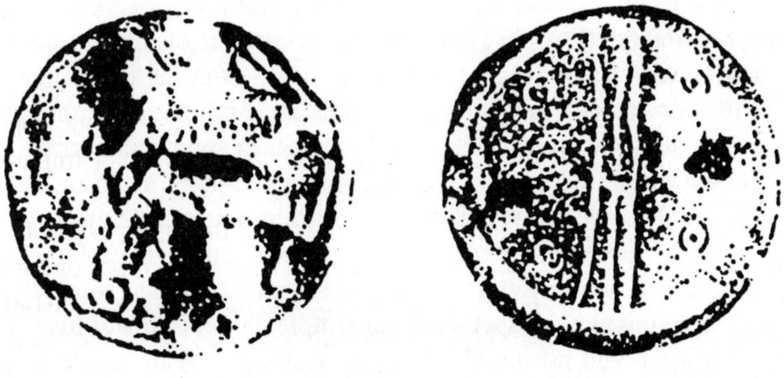

Fig. 3.6: Persian Gulf seal from Lothal

ucts travelling in both directions. The seal found at the other extreme of the Arabian Sea was the first import from the west to surface in a Harappan site. Quite curiously, the excavator of Lothal, S.R. Rao, used the Dilmun seal to argue the importance of the site and the Harappans in general in the Bronze-Age seafaring trade, although in strictly logical terms it should be more simply related to the Gulf merchants' activity in Gujarat. It would now be futile to fashion a controversy from this early proposition. In light of later discoveries in Oman and in eastern Iran, the explanation would be on a different, far more entangled, level of historical interpretation.

The search for the maritime aspect of the Indus Civilization drove G.F. Dales (1962) to survey in 1960 the long arid coastal stretch of Makran. Two strongly fortified Harappan sites were located at Suktagendor near Gwadar and Sokta Koh near Pasni, some 150 km apart. Surrounded by heavy stone walls both sites required a tremendous effort to be built and supplied. Neither of them lies presently on the waterfront, but some 20–25 km from the coast, on seasonal streams guarding important access routes to more densely inhabited riverine oases of the interior. More than seaports they recall strongholds to separate the interior from the coast. Since Neolithic times the population in the highlands of southern Baluchistan was scattered in a mosaic of small oases and wide pasturelands, but by the end of the third millennium BC in spite of the lack of any urban hegemonism, they had reached a higher level of social integration. While incorporating several elements of Harappan technology, the cultural assemblage remains very distinctive from the Sindi lowlands and retains stronger affinities to local Chalcolithic traditions. The name of Kulli culture, generally used by the specialists and derived from the first type-site identified, is still little more than a label for a complex of surprising homogeneity across most of Makran (Possehl 1986b). Political unrest made impossible any further research along the western coasts of Pakistan. As a consequence the relations among the Kulli, Harappans and Arabians have remained an open question, even difficult to formulate in appropriate terms.

In the late sixties most of the intermediary regions, north and south of the Arabian Sea were still for the archaeologists large unexplored territories. Subsequent explorations and excavations in eastern Iran, Afghanistan, Soviet Central Asia and Oman have filled some of the gaps, opening new perspectives our simple model of linear maritime circulation could not tackle. In general, these researches have disclosed that a whole mosaic of early civilizations had developed across the Iranian Plateau and the riverine basins of southern Central Asia, emerging as historically distinctive entities at the end of the fourth millennium BC. The easternmost fringes of these cultural aggregates reached beyond the highlands of Baluchistan and were certainly an important factor in the formation of the Indus Civilization. Around 2500 BC the main centres in each system presented most of the discriminant urban features—monumental architecture, elite houses and burials, craftsmen quarters and forms of administrative organization. For causes still largely unexplained it was an ephemeral accomplishment. All across this vast territory cities came to an end in a few centuries, roughly between 2200 and 2000 BC right at the time when the mature Indus Civilization is most directly connected to Mesopotamia. Very little Harappan material has been found so far, all in contexts shortly preceding or following 2000 BC. An impressed potsherd with a 3 sign inscription comes from Yahya IVA in Southeastern Iran; etched carnelian beads from Hissar IIIc; ivory gamesmen and dice combined with two seals of glazed steatite, one bearing a swastika, the other two pictographic signs, were found at Altyn depe in southern Turkmenia in the locally developed urban context of period NMZ V, datable to the last quarter of the third millennium BC (Fig 3.7). If it was for this handful of imported products we would have concluded by presenting a classical case of lowland–highland cultural discontinuity, with all possible implications for conflict. The picture has been confused by unequivocal as unexpected evidence for deep interdigitation between the two areas.

Already before WW II, explorations in Sind had detected the presence of highland cultures, with distinctive Iranian metal works, intruding Harappan assemblages across the lower Indus valley as at the type-site of Jhukar, only 30 km NW of Mohenjodaro (Piggott 1946). However, the surprising breakthrough came in 1976 with the discovery by a French expedition of Shortugai, a complete Harappan settlement on a tributary of the Amudarya, in Northeastern Afghanistan (Francfort 1989). The site is located on the Kokcha river banks at the foot of the rich Badakshan minerary district. While it is still within an area feasible for farming, Shortugai closely overlooks a bottleneck access to gold, silver, lapis lazuli, copper and lead ores. None of the standard attributes of the Harappan complex is missing, including a canonic stamp seal with a carved rhinoceros below the inscription. If the full package of the lowland culture could be dispatched some 1000 km to the north, across Afghanistan, the most plausible explanation

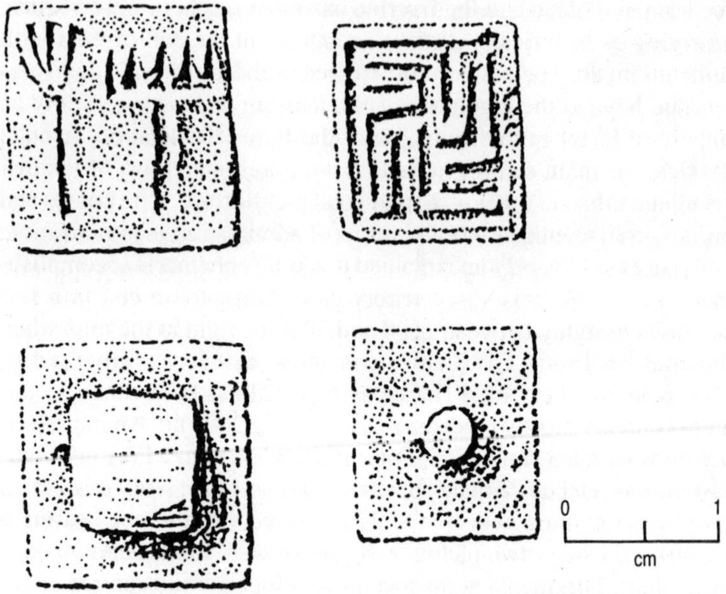

Fig. 3.7: Indus style seals from Altyn Depe

would indicate a form of direct colonization to the north of the Hindu Kush. The discovery of Shortugai does not change the fact that the impact of the Indus Civilization in the Turanian centres of eastern Iran is minimal according to a not-insignificant archaeological evidence.

The overall rarity of Harappan materials all through the highlands and plains of eastern Iran might support the concept of a cultural system locked within the Indian Subcontinent, and largely specific to it. If considered by itself, even Shortugai could fit into the narrow scheme, explained as an episodic intrusion from the south to control resources and trade routes, not unlike several attempts to penetrate Central Asia carried out by the Indian rulers in historical times, from Chandragupta Maurya to Aurangzeb and later, the British. With an imperial Roman frontier in mind scholars could represent Shortugai as a northern or inland outpost counterpart of the fortified strongholds on the Makran coast. Moreover, the series of imposing Harappan settlements at the foot of the Kirthars, like Pathani Damb and Nowshahro, or on the Suleiman plateau, like Dabar kot, may be combined to form a continuous chain running all along Baluchistan's escarpment to seclude the Indian lowlands from the Arabian Sea to the Central Asian steppes. Since the evidence fits so well with a model of distant historical experience, caution should be customary practice.

OMAN DISCLOSES THE INDIAN OCEAN PERSPECTIVE

To the south and across the ocean this schematic image of extreme entrenchment is being totally reversed by the emerging information on the Bronze Age of Oman. Long-delayed by the political isolation of the region, archaeological research has produced in a few years such an overwhelming amount of evidence for cultural contact and economic exchange with the Indus Civilization that one has difficulties explaining the phenomenon in terms of a trade-conquest paradigm. Beginning around 2300 BC Omani sites along the coast as well as in the interior oases, incorporate in their inventory a large number of Harappan artefacts, regardless of size, rank or position. Harappan ceramics are found in affluent oases settlements like Hili (Cleuziou 1984) and in tiny seasonal camp sites like Ghannada, on the western coastlands halfway between Dubai and Abu Dhabi. The local metallurgy and seal cutting crafts are directly influenced by Harappan techniques, collective burials include among the furnishing frit beads and the ubiquituous etched carnelian ones. Even more revealing of the complexities involved is the ceramic industry, once archaeometrical analyses have looked more in details at the composition and manufacture of the Harappan sherds. S. Mery from the French expedition to the Oman peninsula has proven in fact that a good number of the most typical Harappan wares were manufactured locally from the same clays used to make pottery of Omani tradition. Finally, one should point out that the only Bronze-Age inscription so far recovered in Oman is a group of four pictograms incised on a Harappan sherd (Fig. 3.8). It was accidentally found on Christmas Day of 1981, sticking out a site in the sandy embayment of Ra'sal-Junayz, 11 km south of Arabia's south-east counterpoint at Ra'sal-Hadd. The location is important because this area is still the major landmark for the boats crossing from Pakistan to the Gulf and Africa. Between Pasni (Sotka Koh) and Ra'sal-Junayz there are some 450 nautical miles, the largest open stretch of ocean waters to cross on the route from India to Yemen and Africa. South of Ra'sal-Junayz it is coastal navigation all the way, regulated by the ocean surf and the monsoon shifting of the winds, running parallel to the southern Arabian shores. Further inspection of the surface of the site disclosed more Harappan

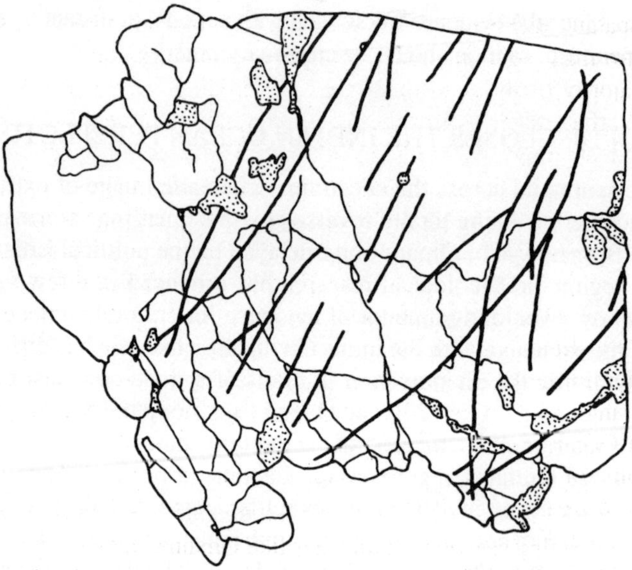

Fig. 3.8: Potsherd from Ra'sal Junayz with Indus script

sherds, amongst local metal and ceramic products with an occupational range between the late third and the early second millennium BC.

Excavations, initiated in 1985 by a joint Franco-Italian expedition (Cleuzion and Tosi 1986) have uncovered structural remains around the sherd's original findspot. A large carefully planned mudbrick building is coming to light, built not earlier than 2300 BC. A wing of seven identical storerooms along the northern side of the complex, each opening on a long corridor room through doors outfitted with stone sills and internal sockets, and connects the building with some specific trading activities. Several stages of occupation are evident, in the last of which the storerooms were used as workshops for the manufacturing of commodities from strictly local resources. Apart from fishes, the direct evidence includes shell rings made from *Conus* and *Pinctata* shells, large conch shells of *Fasciolaria*, turtle carapaces, chert abundant in nearby outcrops and an eye-paint extracted by crushing a magnesium ore, pyrolusite. The associated Harappan imports were collected from a much wider space and represent all kinds of manufactured goods; large pottery jars, copper and steatite seals, alabaster vases, metal objects and, most remarkably, a carved ivory comb with direct parallels in such mainstream centres as

Harappa and Kalibangan. The site was not a foreign entreport, supplied from an Indian mainland; objects of Omani production remain the majority of the consumed goods, including 80 per cent of the pottery, the greater part of the metal or stone instruments, the basic fishing technology. Most interestingly, the site does not seem to have been involved in the shipment of copper, the most important Oman commodity, that certainly ranked first in a trade with the metal-poor Indus Valley. With the closest sources of copper ore at some 150–200 kms to the west of the site, one could hardly be convinced that Ra's al-Junayz was a suitable port-of-trade for Oman's centres in the interor.

Ra's al-Junayz may instead represent one of many such coastal sites, with little or no hinterland, processing a few local resources, but entangled in a wide ranging exchange system along the northern Indian Ocean rim that can supply them with agricultural products and some of the most sophisticated products of the time. Along the desertic coast-lands between Makran and the Horn of Africa resources were scarce. Beyond the wealth of marine life, food and water too scarce for generating enough plant food to integrate a fish diet. A regular cargo circulation would have developed forms of economic integration that were previously impossible. This created an opportunity to integrate commodities and food from outside into economies of value. Integration would have had two main consequences for the later history of this region between East Africa and Pakistan: the growth of economic potential for the specialized coastal populations of fisherman and the expansion of the exchange networks drawing on an increasing number of marginal countries. The Mesopotamian connection from Akkadian times is probably best explained in this wider context, as a marginal contributor to the oceanic circulation system. Egypt and the land of Punt in the third and second millennium BC may present an analogous case of ephemeral interference along the African section of the Ocean rim. The system of coastal circulation was a result of a local adaptation process shared by the coastal populations who were increasing control over the ocean beginning in the early Holocene as demonstrated by the countless number of small sites on the Arabian coastlands from Kuwait to Yemen. The circumnavigation of the Indian Ocean along its northern rim was probably accomplished by 5000 BC and we can hardly believe that such a complex exchange network would have been created by a limited demand for exotic goods in the Mesopotamia, Egypt or the Indus Valley farming economies. The Indus Civilization probably had a major impact and a more active presence, partly as a consequence of its geographical proximity, but to some extent also because it had from its beginning a more intense exchange with the Arabians.

A LONG-LASTING REVOLUTION

In spite of their profound differences, the maritime trade developed between the Indus Valley and Arabia at the end of the third millennium BC might have produced a lasting impact over both countries. There is increasing archaeological evidence that the exchange did not involve only few manufactured articles of prestige and some exotic resources as so directly represented in the Ra's at-Junayz assemblage, but the plants and the animals originally domesticated at the extreme ends of the Indian Ocean. The Indus plain had been colonized quite early in time by farmers with an experience of millennia behind, as witnessed by the discoveries of J.F. Jarrige from the early levels at Mehrgarh. Eastern Arabia on the contrary was a land where farming was very intensive and highly specialized, but limited to a scatter of oases along seasonal watercourses. The main subsistence activities remained forms of food collecting till the late fourth millennium BC. But the very different ecological background ultimately would have made the economies of Arabia and the Indus Valley increasingly complementary to each other, optimizing profit for both the parties. A significant degree of interdependence could have never been achieved with another alluvial plain organiszed around similar sectors of production, such as Mesopotamia. Exchanges would not have been necessarily smaller in the bulk and number of the commodities involved.

Arabia would have supplied the Indus with its unique domesticates, camels and dates, still so important in the traditional agriculture of Sind and Baluchistan, and passed on the cultivars of African ancestry like the millets including sorghum. These crops had been introduced by 4500 BC: a few distinctive charred grains of sorghum have been recovered from fishermen's settlements of this time near Muscat in Oman, associated with domestic ovicaprid and cattle bones also imported from outside the Oman peninsula. By 3000 BC this African cultivar was grown with wheat, barley and dates at Hili as part of the multicropping strategy characteristic of oasis farming in eastern Arabia. Although the palaeobotanical evidence is still incomplete, the picture of a Middle Holocence transfer of tropical African cultivars along the northern Indian Ocean seaboard would confirm the early imaginative theories of the American geographer Carl O. Sauer (1952) on role of seaborne plant dispersal for the development of primitive agriculture. All domesticated plants were first cultivated in the natural habitat of wild growth, often in very circumscribed territories, where they had originated as biological species as the result of adaptation to strictly local environmental conditions. Generation after generation selective pressure by intensified human exploitation will drift genetical variance, with degrees of specific mutation. It was anything but a straightforward process. Several scholars have challenged the gradualistic idea of domestication resulting from a steady intensification of man–plant or man–animal relations, suggesting instead that it would not have happened without a conscious effort and a major energetic investment. *Cultivation* of wild ancestors of today's major staple grains could have gone on forever within the original homelands of natural growth. *Domestication* would result only from radical modifications of those pristine conditions. The same scholars have then suggested that the selective trend towards mutation domestication was set into motion only when the cultivated wild progenitors were planted into new areas, under different environmental conditions. Domestication is then conceptualized as a never-ending process, still active in the present time, as a means to create new resources from nature or adjust old cultivars to an ever-growing demand for food. Whenever two distant regions, independently endeavoured to agriculture have come in contact, the lasting result has been a sensible growth of their farming potentials.

The merging of the Old and New World traditions from the sixteenth to the eighteenth century brought an age of wealth that has made possible the greatest expansion of the human population on earth. A similar revolution was also possible in late prehistoric times, when the African, Indo-Iranian and South-East Asian centres of plant husbandry were connected to the Near East and among themselves by the early maritime trade along the shores of Arabia and India. The Harappan connection with Oman and eastern Arabia would imply that these mechanisms of integration would have been greatly accelerated. Can we claim any factual evidence of agricultural transformation as resulting from this intensified contact across the ocean? If there is any, it would be cast into the palaeobotanical record and some of the available results are very promising. In 1978 plant remains from Pirak, a second millennium agricultural settlement in the upper Kacchi plain of Baluchistan, an environmental transitional zone of piedmont alluvium between the Kirthar highlands and the Indus plain, sampled by J. F. Jarrige and L. Constantini, gave the first insight on the kind of rural landscape that emerged from the 'ashes' of the Indus Civilization (Jarige and Santon: 1979). Far from being the catastrophy scenario historians had fictioned from a literal reading of the Vedic epics, the image was one of economic affluence and diversification. None of the previous crafts were lost, while a lot of new means of production had become customary only a century after the collapse of urban life in Sind. Both rice from tropical South-East Asia and sorghum from the arid plains of Ethiopia, were now abundantly available along with barely and wheat that were locally cultivated since at least 6000 BC. The new cultivars were summer crops, scheduled on a different life cycle: sowing took place in early spring, harvesting in the summer (Possehl 1986a). It became possible to increase subsistence options and productivity by practicing far more efficient fallow strategies, with several crops a year and higher marginal yields. The entire agricultural sector benefited from the expansion. Terracotta figurines and bone remains prove that camels and horses were added to the domestic fauna, probably as a result of an increased availability of plant food. In turn, these new animals expanded the capacity of farmers for packed transport and rapid communications, limited in Harappan times to bull carts. Multicropping and pack animals transformed the whole economical bases of rural economy, setting the structure of traditional Indian agriculture. By 1500 BC Pirak presents us with the image of the Indian village as it will be known to the first Europeans.

That the wide-ranging contacts and the integrative processes activated by the Indus Civilization in the latter part of the third millennium BC were ultimately responsible for a reinvigorated society is more and more evident as our knowledge is enlarged by new archaeological work.

REFERENCES

Buchanan, Biggs, 1967. A dated seal impression connecting Babylona and ancient India. *Archaeology*, 20, pp. 104–07.

Chanda, Rai Bahadur Ramaprasad, 1929. Survival of the Prehistoric Civilization of the Indus Valley, Delhi. *Memoirs of the Archaeological Survey of India*, No. 41, pp. 40.

Cleuziou, Serge, 1984. Oman peninsula and its relations eastwards during third millennium. In *Frontiers of the Indus Civilizaiton*. B.B. Lal and S.P. Gupta, eds. Delhi: Books and Books, pp. 371–93.

Cleuziou, Serge and Maurizio Tosi, editors, 1986. *The Joint Hadd Project: Summary Report on the First Season*. Rome.

Dales, George F., 1962. Harappan outposts on the Makran coast. *Antiquity*, 36, pp. 86–92.

DeClercq, M. 1888. Collection DeClercq: Cataloque Methodique et Raisonne. Antiques Assyriens. Cylinders Orientaux, Cachets, Briques, Bronzes, Bas-reliefs, etc. J.M. Menant, Collaborator. Paris: Ernest Leroux.

Francfort, Henri-Paul, 1989. *Fouilles de Shortughai: Recherches sur l' Asie Centrale Protohistorique.* Two. Vols. Paris: Diffusion de Boccard, 515 pp. + 148 plates and figures.

Francfort, Henri, 1933. Tell Asmar, Khafaje and Khorsabad: Second Preliminary Report of the Iraq Expedition. Chicago: The Oriental Institute of the University of Chicago, Oriental Institute Communication, No. 16.

________, 1939. Sculpture of the Third Millennium BC from Tell Asmar and Khafaje. Chicago: The Oriental Institute of the University of Chicago, Studies in Ancient Oriental Civilization, No. 43.

Francfort. Henri, Thorkild Jacobsen and Conrad Preusser, 1932. Tell Asmar and Khafaje: The first season's work in Eshnunna, 1930–31. Chicago: Oriental Institute Communications. No. 13.

Jarriqe, Jean-Francois and Marielle Santoni, 1979. *Fouilles De Pirak.* Two Vols. Paris: Publications de la Commission des Fouilles Archaeologique. Fouilles du Pakistan. No. 2. Vol. I: 411 and pp. 36.

Marshall, Sir John, 1924. First light on a long forgotten civilization. *Illustrated London News*, 20 November 1924, pp. 528–32, 548.

Marshall, Sir John, editor. *Mohanjodaro and the Indus Civilization*, 3 Vols. London: Arthur Probsthain, pp. 716.

Oppenheim, A.L., 1954. Seafaring Merchants of Ur. *Journal of the American Oriental Society*, 74, pp. 6–17.

Piggott, Stuart, 1946. The chronology of prehistoric north-west India. *Ancient India*, 1, pp. 8–26.

Possehl, L. Greory 1986a. Africa millets in South Asian prehistory. In *Studies in Archaeology of India and Pakistan*. Jerome Jacobson, ed. Delhi: Oxford and IBH and A.I.I.S., pp. 237–56.

________, 1986b. *Kulli.* Durham: Carolina Academic Press.

Rao, S.R., 1963. A 'Persion Gulf' seal from Lothal, 37, pp. 96–99.

Sauer, O. Carl, 1952. *Agricultural Origins and Dispersal.* New York: American Geographical Society.

Scheil, V.E. 1925. Un nouveau sceau Hindon pseudo-Sumerian. *Revue d'Assyriologie et d'Archeologie Orientale*, 22(2), pp. 55–56.

Wooley, C. Leonard, 1934. *The Royal Cemetery, Ur Excavations*, Vol. 2. Two Vols. London/Philadelphia: British Museum/ The University Museum.

Chapter Four

Dāna and Dakṣiṇā as Forms of Exchange*

ROMILA THAPAR

In the study of the society and economy of ancient India information has often to be ferreted out from seemingly unlikely sources. What is often associated with apparently non-economic activity such as religious rituals, can sometimes provide insights into social and economic concerns. It is intended in this paper to examine the custom of *dāna*, the act of giving, in its major forms, from this point of view. The earliest literary sources refer to the giving of *dāna, dakṣiṇā*, etc., to priests and *brāhmaṇs*. The occasions for making these gifts are mentioned and there is generally an itemization of the objects considered appropriate for each occasion. Gradually gift-giving ceased to be something arbitrary and became systemized. This is evident from the discussion in some of the *smṛti* literature on the elements and aspects involved in the concept of *dāna*. Reference is made to six distinct elements and these include the *dātā* (donor), the *pratigrahītā* (recipient), *śraddhā,* the appropriateness of the gift, and the place and the time, for making the gift.[1] Gift-giving gradually evolved its own rules and requirements and can therefore be examined as an important aspect of the social and economic life of the early period.

Gift-giving has been seen largely in the context of its association with religious ritual and symbolism. There are however at least two other aspects which will be explored in this paper. Firstly, there is the obvious one of the changing items included in the listing of *dāna* and

* *Indica*, vol. 13, nos. 1 and 2, 1976, pp. 37–48.

[1] P.V. Kane, *History of Dharmaśāstra,* vol. II, part 2, Poona, 1941, pp. 843 ff.

the correlation of these items with economic change. Secondly, the degree to which the nature of gift-giving reflects the socio-economic structure of the society: this hinges on the question of whether *dāna* and *dakṣiṇā* can be regarded as forms of gift exchange and, if so, at what point do they cease to perform this function. Needless to say, gift-giving in this connection refers to major gifts given on particular and special occasions and not to the daily or routine ritual of small-scale *dāna*.

In the Vedic texts the two more commonly used words for gift-giving are *dāna* and *dakṣiṇā*. The two words are by no means synonymous. The first is the generic word for gift with its etymological root in √*dā, to* give. *Dāna* therefore refers to the act of giving, bestowing, granting, yielding and prestation, irrespective of what is being given and when. *Dakṣiṇā* has a more specific connotation although its meaning remains a little ambiguous. It is a gift by extension of its meaning. The etymon refers to the right side, the side of purity and of respect. It also carries the meaning of invigorating or strengthening the sacrifice for which purpose the gift is made to the performer of the sacrifice.[2] By extension therefore it came to mean either a gift or a donation made to a priest or a sacrificial fee.[3] The *dakṣiṇā* to the gods can be symbolic but that to the priests must consist of actual objects. It has been argued that the *dakṣiṇā* was never a salary or a sacrificial fee, but has to be seen as part of the economic system of Vedic times, that of gift-exchange.[4] It is possible to argue that it was not a sacrificial fee to begin with but came to be regarded as such by the time of the *Manu Dharmaśāstra* when gift-exchange was no longer an important aspect of the economic system.[5]

The concept of gift-exchange (particularly with reference to early Indian texts) was first formulated at length by Marcel Mauss in his now well-known work, *The Gift*. Mauss argued that the earliest forms of exchange were those of total prestation between clan and clan and family and family. Subsequent to this stage comes that of gift-exchange in which certain categories of people are involved in almost ritualized exchanges which are embedded in the larger continuum of social and economic relations.[6] This stage precedes the change to individual contract and the money-market with fixed price and weighed and coined money. Gift-exchange would therefore tend to become less

2 *Śatapatha Brāhmaṇa* II.2.2. 1–2; IV.3.4. 1–2.

3 *Manu* III, 128–37.

4 J.C. Heesterman, *The Ancient Indian Royal Consecration*, p. 164.

5 *Manu* XI. 38–40.

6 M. Mauss, *The Gift*, London, 1954, pp. 45 ff, 53 ff, 71 ff.

embedded in those primarily agricultural societies which experienced the gradual impinging of changing attitudes to land and the ownership of land and where land slowly emerges as the major economic unit. Literary sources which relate both to tribal societies wtih a base in primitive agriculture and to societies with more complex social stratification based on advanced plough agriculture would reflect this change.

Mauss maintains that gift-exchange is not arbitrary but is based on the notion of value. What is exchanged is a token of wealth and this is different from money as it is imbued with a magical power. It is not an impersonal gift as it is linked to an individual or a particular group. Thus utility alone is not the motivating force in this exchange. The accepted token of wealth is significant since wealth is a demonstration of status; it is a means of controlling others by winning followers and by placing those who accept the gift under obligation. The exchange is essentially of consumable items and luxuries—food and clothing for example. The gift is not one-sided and implies a return gift, although the return of the actual gift presented was forbidden. The symbolic motivation in making the gift was the belief that it is reproductive and that the donor would receive the same in larger quantity. More recent studies of the system of gift-exchange in tribal societies have pointed to the functional aspect as well. The system of gift-exchange kept goods and people in circulation in a particular pattern and also acted as a means of maintaining political relationships and ranking.[7]

The earliest references to *dāna* as a distinct function in society come from the *dāna-stuti* hymns of the *Ṛg Veda,* hymns in praise of those who make generous and handsome gifts.[8] The subject of these particular hymns is either the donor or the event which occasioned the gift. Thus in one of the hymns Kaśu, the Cedi king is honoured and in another the victory at Hariyūpīyā.[9] The *dātā* (donor) can be a deity—primarily Indra and occasionally Soma, with Aśvins, Viśvadevas and Sarasvatī also included—but is frequently a king/tribal chief or hero. The *pratigrahītā* (recipients) are the hymnodists, the priests or the bards who have composed the verses in praise of the person or the event. The gift comes from human hands but sometimes

7 J.P.S. Uberoi, *Politics of the Kula Ring,* Manchester, 1962.

8 *Ṛg Veda* VI.63.9; V.27; V.30. 12–14; VI.47; VIII.1.33; VIII.5.37; VIII.6.47.

9 *Ṛg Veda* VIII.5; VI.27.

via the mediation of a god.[10] Thus the god is requested for favours and if these are granted then the kings bestow gifts on the priests who immortalize them in verse.[11] The event is generally a successful battle or cattle raid or victory over the enemy or the destruction of the enemy. In these the role of Indra is pre-eminent: he destroys the forts of the enemy, he attacks the Dāsas jointly and individually.[12] The gift is made therefore not so much in the spirit of charity but as symbolic of success and as an investment towards further success on future occasions. The appropriateness of the gift is exalted but the time and place are rarely mentioned. The association with Soma may imply that it was made on the occasion of the soma-pressing ceremony. Evidently the purpose of *dāna* in the Ṛgvedic age was different from what it was to become in later times.

The *dāna-stutis* have a fairly uniform format. The composer's *gotra* is usually mentioned early on so that his social bona fides are established and this also provides the evidence for the hymns being priestly compositions. The deity is invoked, the exploits of the deity are lauded and an appeal is made to the deity for aid. Frequently, parallel situations are described which in the past had a successful outcome and were followed by generous gift-giving. Reference is made to the giving of gifts by human heroes. The gifts are unambiguously objects of wealth and are recorded in what can only be, on many occasions, exaggerated figures. The most prized gift and object of wealth is cattle with figures ranging from a hundred cows to sixty thousand head of cattle.[13] Horses come next in priority and although smaller numbers are listed they are often described in greater detail than the cows. Ten horses is a common figure although thousands of steed are also mentioned and, in one case, sixty thousand.[14] There is a preference for stallions over mares, whereas in bovine wealth the preference is for cows. Other gifts include wagons, chariots, slave-girls/maidens, camels, treasure-chests, garments and robes, measures of gold and, infrequently, cauldrons of metal.[15] Perhaps the epitome of the *dāna-stutis* is the paean to *dakṣiṇā* itself where the liberal bestowers of *dakṣiṇā,* the *yajamānas* are described as immortals inhabiting the highest heaven, secure from harm, victorious in battle

[10] *Ṛg Veda* VIII.46; X.93.
[11] *Ṛg Veda* VI.47.
[12] *Ṛg Veda* VI.47; VIII.1.
[13] *Ṛg Veda* VI.47; I.126.
[14] *Ṛg Veda* VI.33.1; VI.63.9; VIII.46. 21–4.
[15] *Ṛg Veda* V.30.15; VI.47.

and living with their brides in eternal bliss—the vision of a hero's paradise.[16]

The *dāna-stuti* hymns are expressions of heroic poetry. The givers of *dāna* are the heroes of the tribe, sometimes equated with the tribe, often carrying the tribal name in place of the individual name. The listing of the wealth was an indication of status, for those who gave large gifts such as Kaśu the Cedi king, Divodāsa, Pṛthuśravas or the Yādavas were acknowledged as being more powerful and wealthy than those who made lesser gifts such as Asaṅga or Saṇḍa. The gifts were functional items of wealth and not tokens of wealth. In this case, what was probably the implicit token was not the actual item but the exaggerated quantities in some of the figures.

Among the gifts there is a noticeable absence of the mention of land and, quite evidently, as has been pointed out, it was cattle that was synonymous with wealth.[17] This is also evident from the frequency of words and phrases incorporating cattle as synonymous for other aspects of material life, as for example in the extended meaning of words such as *gaviṣṭi, gopati or gomat.* Even grain is rarely listed as an item of *dāna.* This is indicative of the relative unimportance of land as an economic unit.

It has been argued that the Ṛgvedic evidence suggests that the king was essentially a protector of cattle and not of land; consequently it is cattle which is a source of inter-tribal conflict and not land.[18] This may well indicate that land was owned jointly by the clan and, furthermore, despite the references to agricultural activities scattered throughout the *Ṛg Veda,* land was still seen in essence as territory encompassing both fields and grazing ground. The lifting of cattle was a more serious economic problem than trespassing into fields. The Paṇis are feared for they are both rich in cattle as well as being stealers of cattle. Wealth (*rayi*) was computed primarily in cattle.[19] It is also of some interest that male slaves are rarely mentioned as constituting *dāna,* whereas female slaves were a recognized item of *dāna.* This would suggest that perhaps domestic slavery as a source of luxury among the wealthy was evident but the use of slavery in economic

[16] *Ṛg Veda* X.107.

[17] R.S. Sharma, 'Forms of Property in the Early Portions of the Ṛg Veda', *Proceedings of the Indian History Congress*, 1973.

[18] Ibid.

[19] *Ṛg Veda* I.33.3; IV.28.7; V.34.5; VI.13.3; VIII.64.2.

production was not the prevalent system.[20] That the possible clan ownership of land continued awhile is reflected in the story of the king Viśvakarman Bhauvana who is rebuked by the earth when he tries to gift the earth he has conquered through his *aśvamedha* to Kaśyapa.[21] But this is almost anachronistic since other sections of the same Later Vedic literature include land as part of the recognized *dāna*.

The purpose of extensive gift-making in early societies is three-fold. Ostensibly it serves a magico-religious function where the gift is symbolic of communion with the supernatural. In effect it also has two other less evident functions: one is that the donor and the recipient confer status on each other, although the source of the respective status may be different in each case, and secondly gift-giving acts as a means of exchanging and redistributing economic wealth.

In the *dāna-stutis* of the *Ṛg Veda* the two groups involved in conferring status on each other are the brāhmaṇs and *rājanyas/kṣatriyas*. The former mediate with the gods on behalf of the latter and ensure success in battle and cattle-raids, which success invests the latter with power and political status. The latter bestow wealth on the priests, thus providing them with their major source of income as well as conceding to them charismatic powers inherent in the process of ensuring success. By the time of the composition of these hymns a limited social group was involved in the exchange. However, the existence of a more extensive exchange can be postulated for an earlier phase.[22] A successful battle or cattle-raid resulted in an enforced acquisition of wealth on the part of the victorious tribe.

The process of gift-exchange was however more equitable if it occurred through the performance of the *yajña*, which in turn may be seen as a variant on the potlatch. As far as the redistribution of wealth was concerned, even at the *yajña* it seems by now to have been limited to the same two social groups, the kṣatriya and the brāhmaṇ. Thus, tribal wealth acquired through the labour of the *viś* whether in war or in peace, was channelled via the king of the priests either

[20] R.S. Sharma, *op. cit.*

[21] *Aitareya Brāhmaṇa* VIII.21. *Śatapatha Brāhmaṇa* XIII.8.1. 13–15.

[22] As has been suggested by K.P. Jayaswal, *Hindu Polity*, in arguing that perhaps the *vidatha* was a tribal assembly, pp. 69–70. This has been further discussed by R.S. Sharma, *Political Ideas and Institutions in Ancient India*, Delhi, 1959, pp. 63–80, and J.P. Sharma, *Republics in Ancient India*, Leiden 1968, pp. 70 ff. See also *Ṛg Veda* I.24.3; I.27.6; I.31.6.; I.141.1; II.2.12; VII. 52.21; VII.76. 4–5.

through *dāna* or through the *dakṣiṇā* at the *yajña.* In earlier periods, when it is presumed that the tribe participated in the *yajña,* some of the wealth may have been redistributed among a wider group. But, by the time of the composition of the *Ṛg Veda,* both the redistribution as well as the participation of the tribe in the *yajña* was more limited.

In such a situation there must have been a distinction between those who were the possessors of wealth and the rest of the tribe. Was this distinction expressed in the term *ārya* which Bailey has analysed in considerable detail and which analysis leads him to state that *ārya* referred to the owner or possessor of wealth?[23] This is also suggested in the *Nighaṇṭu* which equates *ārya* with *īśvara* (owner/ master) and in Pāṇini, who explains it by the phrase *āryahsvāmi-vaiśyayoḥ.*[24] The *āryas* as possessors of wealth were distinguished from the *viś,* the rest of the tribe, who by now were no longer equal partners in tribal wealth. As Bailey states, the association of wealth and ownership suggests nobility of class and not an ethnic group. The significance of birth into the *ārya-varṇa* relates an *ārya* to social status and wealth and not to race.

The literature of the Later Vedic period gradually introduces a change in the concept of *dāna.* It is no longer the arbitrary liberality of a generous patron celebrating his success. It is now less a channel of redistribution of wealth and more pointedly a channel of deliberate exchange. The changing concept is expressed in the more frequent use of the word *dakṣiṇā.* The strengthening of the notion of exchange is perhaps best summed up in the statement, *dehi me dadāmi te ni me dehi ni te dadhe.*[25] The donor and the recipient remain the same. The appropriateness of the gift and the faith with which it is given are emphasized and the place and time are made much more precise. This is done by a closer linking of gift-giving with the sacrificial ritual via the *dakṣiṇā.* The justification for *dāna* is also spelled out. We are told that there are two kinds of *devas,* the gods and the brāhmaṇs learned in the Vedas: both have to be propitiated, the former through *yajñas* and the latter through *dāna.*[26] It is also at this point that there is mention of fields and villages as appropriate items of *dāna,* although these references are as yet

[23] H.W. Bailey, 'Iranian Arya and Daha' *Transactions of the Philological Society,* 1959, pp. 71ff.

[24] *Nighaṇtiu* 2.6; *Pāṇini* 3.1.103.

[25] *Taittirīya Saṃhitā* I.8.4.1.

[26] *Śatapatha Brāhmaṇa* II.2.10.6.

infrequent.[27] Although *paśu* or animal wealth is still very significant there are some texts which disapprove of the acceptance of animals as *dāna* and presumably preferred gold and land.[28] This is not surprising since by the mid-first millennium BC animal wealth as an economic asset was gradually giving way to land. An interesting indication of the shift in the items gifted is evident from the study of the Rājasūya sacrifice. The concept of *iṣṭipūrta* becomes more central to the procedure with a distinction being made not only between *iṣṭi* and *pūrta* but between *iṣṭi* and *dakṣiṇā.* This is a ritual distinction but not altogether unrelated to the relative decline of livestock breeding and increase of agriculture. This *iṣṭi* which is the offering made to the gods during the performance of the sacrifice is almost invariably a mixture or a cake of some form of cereal, the most frequently used cereals being varieties of rice. The *dakṣiṇā* on the other hand is in most cases an ox, cow or bull, generally a single animal with specified markings, or else a unit of gold.[29] The number of animals is considerably less than the numbers listed in the Rgvedic dānastutis. Sometimes for the seasonal sacrifices the *dākṣiṇā* may include a chariot and mares or stallions.[30] The more spectacular *dakṣiṇā*, which, for instance, is given during the Soma rituals of the Rājasūya, continues however to be in the form of livestock. The list ranges from one thousand to four thousand cows adding up to a total of ten thousand in some texts—a reasonable figure for a wealthy king, to five thousand to thirty thousand cows with a total of hundred thousand in other texts—an evidently exaggerated figure.[31] Nevertheless the number of cows listed continues to be less than the figures given in the *Ṛg Veda.* Since many of the higher figures in both the earlier and later texts were in any case exaggerated, their significance symbolizes the use of animals rather than the actual numbers involved.

*Dakṣiṇā*s associated with particular royal rituals as part of the major sacrifices often consisted of gifting to the priest the most valuable objects used in the ritual. Thus in one text we are told that the *adhvaryu* receives the chariot of the *yajamāna* and the golden dice used in the symbolic game. The carts are distributed among other priests as are also the one thousand cows used in the mock cattle-raid.[32] The

[27] *Aitareya Brāhmaṇa* VIII.20; *Chāadogya Upaniṣad* IV.2. 4–5.

[28] Kane, *op. cit.*, pp. 837ff.

[29] *Taittirīya Śaṃhitā* I.8.9; I.7.3. Heesterman, *op. cit.*, pp. 49, 174.

[30] *Āpastamba Śrauta Sūtra* 5.23.5; 6.30.7.

[31] Heesterman, *op. cit.*, p. 162.

[32] *Baudhāyana Śrauta Sūtra* 12.7.95.15ff.

adhvaryu and the *hotṛ* who recite the legend of Śunaḥśepa at the Rājasūya are given the golden seats on which they sit for the recitation in addition to a certain number of cows.[33] It is also in connection with this sacrifice that one of the forms of *dakṣiṇā* listed is that of *catuṣpàt kṣetra* (field with four parts) which is given to a priest.[34] It has been suggested that this was the land used in a royal ploughing rite as part of the Rājasūya, being the survival of a rudimentary agrarian fertility rite.

In all these cases the *dakṣiṇā* is specifically linked to a particular ritual or a ceremony. Heesterman has argued at length that the *dakṣiṇā* is not a sacrificial fee or salary; it forms a part of the bigger sphere of gift-exchange.[35] His main point is that the *dakṣiṇā* is given to both the *ṛtvij* or officiating priests and to others such as the brāhmaṇs of the *prasarpaka* category whose role is essentially that of observers sitting in the *sadas*. In one of the texts it is specifically stated that the *dakṣiṇā* to the *sadasyas* is to buy them off from drinking the *soma*.[36] Another text maintains that the *yajamāna* by giving *dakṣiṇā* buys himself loose from obligations to the priest.[37] The ritual link is broken or is at least replaced by a status link. Not all texts however accept that the link is broken. The *dakṣiṇā* is seen as a bond between the donor and the recipient, if not as an act by which the recipient is placed under an obligation to the donor. This implies a danger and the danger can only be averted by careful consideration of the propriety of the gift, the place and the time.[38] It is a moot question as to whether the notion of the implicit danger arose from the ritual connection or whether it was a means of diverting attention from regarding the *dakṣiṇā* as a 'fee'

Heesterman suggests that the *dakṣiṇā* may reflect an earlier stage when the entire clan took part in the ritual and the wealth was shared. This would be more characteristic of the potlatch. In course of time the ritual may have moved into the hands of the sacrificial priests and the others may have become observers. The symbolic nature of the *dakṣiṇā* is evident from the continued gifting of the cattle in a society

[33] *Aitareya Brāhmaṇa* VII.18.

[34] Heesterman, *op. cit.*, p.166.

[35] Heesterman, 'Reflections on the Significance of the Dakṣiṇā', *Indo-Iranian Journal*, 1959, no. 3, pp. 241–58.

[36] *Kātyāyana Śrauta Sūtra* 28.5.

[37] *Āpastamba Śrauta Sūtra* 13.6.4.

[38] *Śatapatha Brāhmaṇa* IX.5.2.16; *Āpastamba Śrauta Sutra* 13.6. 4–6; *Kātyāyana Śrauta Sūtra* 28. 158.4; 159.16.

where land was becoming increasingly more lucrative. Clearly, golden seats and golden dice would have to be converted into more mundane objects for the priests to derive a livelihood from these gifts. The question is whether the *dakṣiṇā* was over and above the normal livelihood of the priest or was it his main source of income. Given the nature of later Vedic society where there are not too many references to brāhmaṇs owning land or large herds of cattle it is likely that the *dakṣiṇā* from the king would often be the basic source of livelihood for those performing the rituals.

The collection of *dakṣiṇā* was not restricted to the large-scale *yajñas,* for the life of the *ārya* was now beset by *saṃskāras*—the rituals of the individual biography, the prescription and practice of which ensured well-being. The definition of donor gradually began to include more than just the king or the tribal chief, for others were also required to perform *saṃskāras.* This widening definition of the donor in terms of social categories reaches a qualitative change in Manu, where logic takes it to the point of stating that it is the duty of the *gṛhastha* (the householder) to be concerned with *dāna.*[39] The relevance of gift-exchange in a tribal context of potlatch activities seemed to be receding.

Marcel Mauss in his discussion of gift-exchange maintains that the *Mahābhārata* is the story of a tremendous potlatch.[40] He has particularly pointed to the *Anuśāsanaparvan* as the section par excellence devoted to gift-giving. Here we find a further elaboration of the categories of *dāna.* The distinction for example between *iṣṭa* and *pūrta* is emphasized. The *iṣṭa* is that which is offered into the *gṛhya* and *śrauta* ritual fires. *Pūrta* is a larger enterprise and consists of the donation of wells, tanks, temples, gardens and lands.[41] The donation of immovable property as a special category is a relatively new concept. Hitherto donations were of animals, gold, slaves, food, clothing, chariots and so on. The listing of what is included in *pūrta* has its own significance since it points clearly to the establishment of an agricultural economy where wells, tanks, gardens and land have a utility which they would not have had in a pre-eminently pastoral economy. Another interesting aspect to this distinction which develops in the legal literature is that the *iṣṭa* can only be handled by the

[39] *Manu* III.78.

[40] M. Mauss, *op. cit.*, pp. 53ff.

[41] Kane, *op. cit.*, p. 844.

ritually pure but the *pūrta-dāna,* which in economic terms was the more effective, can also be made by *śūdras.*[42]

Not only in the items listed but in spirit too the notion of *dāna* had by now undergone further changes. It was no longer given merely in celebration of an event or a heroic personality or in connection with a ceremony. It was now associated with a new idea which in part derived from the concept of *dakṣiṇā,* namely, the ethical aspect of performing an action such as giving a gift. The notion of exchange remains central, but in return for tangible wealth the donor acquires merit. Not that all exchange discussed in the *Anuśāsanaparvan* is motivated by the acquisition of merit. We are told that *dāna* increases one's material wealth; nevertheless, in every act of giving, whether it be the *pañcadakṣiṇā* service of host to guest or offerings at a ritual, there is merit to be acquired as the ultimate aim.[43] Gift-giving almost develops its own ritual in which the six-fold definition of *dāna* as stated in *smṛti* literature is given due emphasis. The definition of the *Pratigrahītā* is further refined and it is stated that the recipient must be deserving of the *dāna.*[44] This has relevance not only to the fact that the acquisition of merit can only accrue if the *dāna* is given to a deserving person but also carries a hint of competition among potential recipients for the acquisition of economic status in a system where, perhaps, more attention was being paid to economic status than in earlier times. *Dāna,* therefore, is not to be given to those brāhmaṇs who are physicians, image-worshippers, dancers, musicians; who perform ceremonies for the *śūdras* and who practise usury. The deserving brāhmaṇs are those who perform the required ceremonies as indicated in the texts, who are of noble birth and who live off alms. Even if any among this category have had to take to professions such as agriculture and soldiery, they still qualify for *dāna.* The emphasis on the time and place for gift-giving is accompanied by threats that untimely gifts are appropriated by the *rākṣasas.* The emphasis on the recipient being a deserving person may also be a reflection of competition for *dāna*-bestowing patrons, a competition extending not only to brahmanical sects but including Buddhist, Jaina and other heterodox sects as well, many of the latter claiming to have wealthy patrons.

The exchange of *dāna* for merit echoes the Buddhist notion of

42 Ibid., p. 845.

43 *Anuśāsanaparvan* II, VII, VIII, IX.

44 Ibid., XXIII.

charity or *dāna.* The idea may therefore have come from Buddhist sources or may have grown independently as a result of changing social forms. For Buddhism the stress on *dāna* was essential; for, even at the mundane level, the Buddhist religious order—the *saṅgha*—was required to subsist on the alms and the charity of the lay followers. All that the bhikṣu or the saṅgha could provide to the donor in exchange for *dāna* was *puṇya* or merit, since exchange was between economically unequal sections of society. In the early stages, when Buddhism was not a powerful religious movement, it could neither provide social status to its lay supporters nor did its doctrinal teaching promise immortality or heavenly abodes. At most it could maintain that a material gift would be reciprocated with preaching the Buddhist ethic which in turn might provide the gift of vision or enlightenment to the donors. Puranic texts are unequivocal in making promises: thus we are told that the acquisition of merit through *dāna* can release one from the chain of rebirth.[45]

The reciprocity of *dāna* with *puṇya* may also have been conditioned by the fact that in the larger towns, where there was a Buddhist following, the gift-exchange economy was on the decline and was being gradually replaced by an approximation to the impersonal market economy of commerce, where the unit of money was the currency of exchange. In such an ethos, gift-exchange made little sense and the *dāna-puṇya* reciprocity held out some compensation for the donor. It is significant that among the non-deserving brāhmaṇs listed in the *Anuśāsanaparvan* are those who practise usury and those whose occupation is trade, both activities closely related to a market system. In contrast to the market system, *dāna* is not an impersonal exchange. It involves two parties in a clearly defined relationship, which relationship is affected by the giving of *dāna.* It is also accompanied by an elaborate etiquette, much more elaborate than the frank appeal for *dāna* in the *Ṛg Veda* or the partially disguised *dakṣiṇā* of the *yajñas* and the *saṃskāras.*[46] It would almost appear that by insisting on the institution of *dāna* and the ensuing nexus there was an attempt to invert the values of the market system and to reincarnate those of the gift-exchange.

It is also at this time that attention is given to the acceptance of food as *dāna.* Manu lists the categories of food chiefly uncooked, which are regarded as legitimate *dāna* for the brāhmaṇ.[47] If a brāhmaṇ

[45] *Agni Purāṇa* 209. 1–2.

[46] *Anuśāsanaparvan* LXXII.

[47] *Manu* IV. 205–25; 235–50.

unwittingly accepts forbidden food he has to fast for three days as expiation. Among the types of uncooked food, it is the produce of agriculture, grain, which is the most acceptable. Manu repeats the dictum that the giver will be rewarded many times but also adds that he who gives and he who receives, both, go to heaven. The eulogizing of the *dāna* of food, especially to brāhmaṇs continues in the later literature of the *Purāṇas* where *annadāna* is sometimes referred to as the highest form of *dāna.*[48] The relative purity of uncooked food is in contrast to the practice of sects of Buddhists and Jainas among whom cooked food is regarded as the most acceptable.[49] In terms of conferring status via exchange, the *dāna* of food has a direct relation to caste status, where the acceptability of particular types of food is dependent on social ranking. The discussion therefore of food as *dāna* is also an indication of the extension of caste society.

The gifting of land and the precedence which this began to take over other items reflects the increased interest in agriculture and the fact that land was more lucrative than herds of cattle. This would certainly conform to the known extension of the agrarian economy during the Mauryan and the post-Mauryan period. The general decline of pastoralism is evident from the fact that cows were still gifted but not as major items of *dāna.* Their gifting was to become almost a symbolic gesture of the process of making a gift. The gifting of land brought its own problems since land was both immovable and indestructible. It could not be transported as could a herd of cattle or other objects, nor did it get consumed or die during the lifetime of the recipient. Land was inheritable and alienable and this brought it under the purview of the legal system relating to the inheritance and the sale of land. A land-gift had therefore to be recorded so that it would remain with the recipient or his family even if he changed his domicile or after his death. A gift of land was even further removed from gift-exchange since it could help establish the family of the recipient for many generations and, to that extent, it was not a momentary episode but an investment for the future.

A discussion on the necessity to record a gift of land suggests that the

[48] *Agni Purāṇa* 211.44–6; *Padma Purāṇa* V.19. 289–307; *Brahmāṇḍa Purāṇa* 218.10.32.

[49] As for example in the *Ācārāṅgasūtra* II.1. 1–10. Manu does however insist that the *saṃnyāsin* must only accept cooked food (VI.38) and the reason for this may well have been that he was outside the norms of social regulations.

record should act as the legal claim of the grantee and his family before kings.[50] Hence the record should be a permanent, signed, sealed edict referring to the lineage of the king, the identity of the recipient, the extent and characteristics of the land gifted, the nature of the gift, the seals of the officials concerned with the grant and, according to some texts, a declaration to the effect that it was not to be resumed at a later date. That these instructions were meticulously observed is evident from the copper-plate and other charters recording such gifts of land from the Gupta period onwards.[51] The granting of land and villages to brāhmaṇs became so institutionalized that it was referred to by the special term of *agrahāra* and later an officer was appointed to look after such grants, the *agrahārika*.

With the granting of land other gifts assumed lesser importance with the exception, of course, of gold which retained its economic value. A special category of gifts was evolved based on gold and referred to as the *mahādānas*.[52] These were made on very special occasions such as can hardly be listed in the normal course of gift-giving. Among the more commonly referred to *mahādānas* were the Tulāpuruṣa (weighing a man against gold) and the Hiraṇyagarbha (the symbolic rebirth through a golden womb often performed during coronations). It is significant that this latter ceremony is particularly associated with those who were claiming *kṣatriya* status. Usually sixteen objects are listed among the *mahādānas* including trees, cows, horses, chariots, vessels, all made of gold, and such objects were gifted to the priests on the conclusion of the ceremony. A golden cow studded with precious stones was a long way away from the ten thousand head of cattle which the Ṛgvedic priests acclaimed as gift. The *mahādānas* are clearly of another category and another time.

Land grants constituted the germ of what was later to develop into a new agrarian structure with its own implications for social and economic formations.[53] For our purposes, suffice it to say that the extensive granting of land as *dāna* changed the comprehension of *dāna* as part of gift-exchange. A new institutionalizing took place, reflecting both a departure from the earlier socio-economic system as well as the evolving of a changed metaphor for both the donor and the recipient.

[50] *Yājñavalkya* I. 318–20.

[51] Inscription of Śivaskandavarman, *EI*, I, p. 7; Maitraka Vyāghrasena, *EI*, XI, p. 221, p. 107, p. 111.

[52] *Agni Purāṇa* 209, 210; *Matsya Purāṇa* 274–89; *Liṅga Purāṇa* II.28.

[53] D.D. Kosambi, *Introduction to the Study of Indian History*, Bombay, 1956: 275ff; R.S. Sharma, *Indian Feudalism*, Calcutta, 1965.

Chapter Five

The Problem of the *Seṭṭhi* in Buddhist Jātakas*

IVO FISER

The clearer explanation of the Sanskrit term *śreṣṭhin* and its Pāli form *seṭṭhi*, and the elucidation of the function and importance of the individual referred to by this term within the structure of ancient Indian society may be of assistance in resolving the some important questions in the history of India. In the following pages I shall try to solve this question with the help of all important passages bearing on it in old Indian, especially Buddhist, literature. The main base of our investigation will be the collection of Buddhist tales called the Jātakas,[1] that immense source of valuable information about social conditions in India at the time of its origin. It is true that the *seṭṭhi* is mentioned in other collections of the Pāli canon as well as in the literature of the Brāhmanas and of the Jainas, but as far as I know these literatures contain no such divergences as would contradict the statements of the Jātakas (though the Vedic term *śreṣṭhin* explicitly differs from that of the other literatures as far as its acceptation is concerned, as we shall see later). That is the reason why most of my conclusions will be drawn from the Jātakas and supplemented by the data of the other sources.

The reconstruction of social conditions in ancient India based on the collection of Jātakas preserved under the title '*Jātakaṭṭhavaṇṇanā*'[2] must be carried through with a certain amount

* In *Archiv Orientalni*, XXII, 1954, pp. 238–66.

[1] Though it will start with a survey of the literature of the Vedas.

[2] *The Jātaka together with its Commentary*, ed. by V. Fausböll, Vols I–VII, London, 1877–97.

of caution. The collection contains material of varying quality and from different times. Some of the Jātakas stories are, of course, of very ancient origin, but it is difficult to distinguish seperate strata within stories of mixed origin and authorship and dating from different periods.

'Not only every large section and every single narrative, but often also every single *Gāthā*, will have to be tested independently as regards its age.'[3] First of all it must be remembered that the 'stories of the present' (*paccuppannavatthus,* nom. pl. *paccuppannavatthūni*), which are in fact a kind of preface, represent a younger element of a Jātaka than the 'stories of the past' (the *atītavatthus*, nom. pl. *atītavatthūni*) which form the substantial part of it (even if not in all cases).[4] This is testified to by the fact that the 'stories of the present' form a frame-work to the stories of the past,' by means of which these can become Jātakas, as also by the themes of these *paccuppannavatthus*, which in many cases either violently disturb the flow of the events contained in the *atītavaṭthus* or only repeat these 'stories of the past'. The scene in which the stories are set also differ in the two parts of the Jātakas.[5] The scene of the majority of the stories of the present is in Sāvatthī[6]—Jāt. I. 84 (366)[7] I.118 (432), I.148 (501), II.232 (224), III. 390 (299), or in Rājagaha—I.12 (145), i.e. in the Eastern part of India (Magadha), whereas the scene of the 'stories of the past' lies in Gandhāraraṭṭna—I. 28 (191), Kāsiraṭṭha—I.137 (478), in the neighbourhood of Benares—II. 254 (287) or in Benares itself as is the case in most of the remaining stories, i.e. in the Western or Central part of India. Fausböll's differentiation of the three components of the Jātaka stories (*paccuppannavatthus, atītavatthu* and *samodhāna*) by means of different types of print, is not always exact.

3 *A History of Indian Literature*, by Maurice Winternitz, Vol. II, Calcutta 1933, p. 122.

4 Cf. e.g. W. Geiger: *Pāli Literatur und Sprache*, in Grundriss, I. B., 7. H. Strasburg 1916, p. 21. 'Atītavatthu is the Jātaka proper,' says B.C. Law in 'Some Observations on the Jātakas', in *JRAS,* 1939: 241. Cf. also B.C. Sen: *Studies in Jātakas, Journal of the Department of Letters*. Vol. XX, Calcutta 1930.

5 W. Geiger, *op. cit.*

6 Cf. B.C. Law: *Geography of Early Buddhism*, London 1932, pp. 5–6.

7 The Roman figures denote the Volume, the next figure is the number of the Jātaka and the last one (in brackets) points out to the page of Fausböll's edition.

Sometime the hand of the Commentator interferes with both parts of the tale,[8] sometimes there is an error on the part of the Editor.[9]

Neither the acceptation of the Pāli term '*seṭṭhi*' nor its Sanskrit equivalent '*śreṣṭhin*' (nom. sg. *śreṣṭhi*) are explained very clearly in the dictionaries. *Śreṣṭhin* (derived from *śreṣṭhaḥ*) is translated by Böhtlingk in his Sanskrit, Wörterbuch as follows: 1. ein Mann von Ansehen, 2. das Haupt einer Innung,—Zunft, Gildemeister.

The Pāli Text Society's Dictionary has got these terms: foreman of a guild, or treasurer, banker, 'City man', wealthy merchant; i.e. two incompatible groups of meanings; 'a wealthy merchant' 'a foreman of a guild', on the one hand and 'a treasurer', a banker on the other, the intermediary term being 'the City man'. The second group of meanings contained in this Pāli '*seṭṭhi*' is not referred to in the meanings given in the Sanskrit dictionary.

The opinions of Pāli and Sanskrit scholars dealing with this question do not differ very much. In fact their conception is based on the statements of Pāli canon, above all on the stories of the Jātakas, and on closer examination it is obvious that they take over their views about *seṭṭhi* to a certain extent from one another. As far as I know, a deeper investigation of this question has not yet been undertaken.[10]

The term '*śreṣṭhin*' does not occur in the Vedic Saṃhitās, i.e. in the dialect of the Mantras, at all.[11] The oldest evidence can be found in the Brāhmaṇas, viz., in the *Aitareya-Brāhmaṇa* and in the *Sāṅkhāyana Brāhmaṇa*. The term *śreṣṭhin* has the same meaning in both places: a man of honour, a man of high rank, a leader. In the *Aitareya-Brāhmaṇa* 3,30 we read: 'Therefore does one of high rank honour at his table him whom he desires.' (*Tasmād u śreṣṭhi pātre rocayaty eva yaṃ kāmayate tam. . .*)[12] The quotation from the

[8] Cf. Geiger, l.c.

[9] I found evidence of this in *Mayhaka-jātaka*—III, 390 (299). The Jātaka contains three tales, the first two of which are considered by Fausböll as paccuppannavatthus and printed in small types. This is incomprehensible to me. The first tale is placed in Sāvatthī and ends thus. . . '*ti vatvā (*sc. Sātthā) *tena yācito atītaṃ āhari.*' The second tale, which is also printed in small types (and whose *gāthās* are not numbered by Fausböll) begins with the words: '*Atīte Bārānasiyaṃ Brahmadatte rajjaṃ kārente . . .*' which is a formula characteristic of the *atītavatthus.*

[10] To the extent I could trace the new literature.

[11] Cf. H. Grassmann, *Wörterbuch zum Rig-Veda*, Neudruck, Leipzig, 1936.

[12] *Aitareya Brāhmaṇa*, ed. by Th. Aufrecht, Bonn, 1879, p. 79.

Sāṅkhāyana-Brāhmaṇa runs as follows: 'In that he sacrifices to Mahendra at the end, (it is because) the leader occupies the end; therefore at the end he sacrificies to him. (. . . *atha yan mahendram antato yajaty antaṃ vai śreṣṭhī bhajate tasmād enam antato yajaty*. . .)[13] The same is the case in the *Sāṅkhāyana-Āraṇyaka* where it is said: 'That self these selves depend on, as his dependents on a rich man. Just as a rich man feeds on his dependents, or his dependents feed on a rich man, so the intelligent self feeds on these selves, or so these selves feed on him.'[14] ('. . . *etam ātmānam eta ātmāno'nvavasyanti yathā śreṣṭhinaṃ svāḥ tad yathā śreṣṭhī svair bhuṅkte yathā vā svāḥ śreṣṭhinaṃ bhunjantyevam evaiṣa prajñātmatair ātmabhir bhuṅkte*).[15]

The word śreṣṭhin is also mentioned twice in the *Jaiminīya-Brāhmaṇa* of the *Sāma-Veda*, i.e. in one of the oldest Brāhmaṇas extant. In both places the term *śreṣṭhin* has the meaning 'a noble man, a leader', in II.152 we read: 'Da erhoben sie (sc. die Götter) einen lauten Jubel, wie man einen lauten Jubel zu erheben pflegt, wenn ein vornehmer Herr ankommt. So soll derjenige, von welchem das Ansehen gewichen ist, dieses (Opfer) verrichten. Es war ja das Ansehen, das von ihnen (d.h. von den Göttern) gewichen war, als ihr mächtiger Herr (Indra) von ihnen wich.'[16] (. . . te [sc. *devā*] *hotkrodaṃ cakrire yathā śreṣṭhinyāgata utkrodaṃ kurvate tathā. . . Tad yasmācchrīr apakrāmet sa etena yajeta; śrīr vai teśāṃ sāpākrāmad yad eśāṃ śreṣṭhy apākrāmat*. . .). This meaning is also testified to in one of the latest examples of Vedic literature, in the *Gopatha-Brāhmaṇa* 2,1,23 and 2,5,9[17] where *śreṣṭhin* occurs in the meaning of 'a leader.' Besides, the first quotation is the same as that of the *Kauṣītaki-Brāhmaṇa* V. 5 mentioned before (see an earlier note).

These quotations from the Vedic literature do not add to help very much in the elucidation of the term. Nothing substantial can be gained from the rare references in the texts. The commentator of the *Kauṣītaki-Upaniṣad* explains the word śreṣṭin by the term kuṭumbin

[13] *Das Kaushītaki Brāishmaṇa*, Vol I., Hersg. von B. Lindner, Jena, 1887, p. 20 (V. 5). The English tr. by Keith in Harvard Oriental Series, No. 25, p. 374.

[14] The *Śāṅkhāyana Ārṇyaka*, ed. by A.B. Keith, London 1908, VI, 20, p. 41.

[15] Ānandāśramasaṃskṛta granthāvaliḥ, Granth. 29, 1925, p. 181–82.

[16] *Jaiminīya-Brāhmaṇa in Auswahl*, v. W.Caland, Amsterdam 1919, p. 172–73.

[17] *Gopathabrāhmaṇam* in *Bibliotheca Indica*, Calcutta, 1872, p. 100.

(*śreṣṭhinaṃ taṃ prādhānyavantaṃ kuṭumbinam ityarthaḥ*).[18] This explanation is, of course, much younger than the text and does not correspond to the original meaning of the word in our text. Even so, it is not very helpful.

As we have seen, the term *śreṣṭhin* is used for the first time in the Brāhmaṇa texts written in prose, i.e. not earlier than at the beginning of the first millennium before our era. In all the relevant passages of the Vedic literature, as far as I could trace them, the word *śreṣṭhin* occurs in the sense 'the best', then 'a leader, a nobleman, a man of honour'. In none of these instances is there any indication of the occupation or way of living of the *śreṣṭhin*. All other references to the *śreṣṭhin* do not go back earlier than the Buddhist period, i.e. the last third of the first millennium before our era. It is thus clear that the Vedic term *śreṣṭhin* cannot be connected with the occupation of a treasurer, banker, or even with the head of a guild. This oldest connotation of the term *śreṣṭhin* is further supported by the etymology of the word. For this period the derivation of '*śreṣṭhin*' from '*śreṣṭha*' is clear.

Now, the time when the word is in its Pāli from (*seṭṭhi*) began to be used in the sense known to us mainly from Buddhist literature, goes back, roughly speaking, to the period of a few centuries before our era, although it is better to take into consideration a rather later period. It was a period of great state formations when agriculture was the main source of livelihood for the majority of the population.[19] The State was ruled by a hereditary monarch (*rājā*) with despotic power over all his subjects without exception. The revenues collected in the form of a yearly tax were the main source of the king's income (besides the spoils of war and the presents which formed an occasional source of profit only).

Several references in the Jātakas make it clear that the *seṭṭhi* originally occupied himself with agriculture, too. But he is always designated by the word '*seṭṭhi*' which is never substituted for any other term, e.g. such as, the term denoting a householder who tilled his fields as did many brahmaṇas.[20] Even in these texts we can already trace the tendency to differentiate those terms denoting two different

[18] Ānandāśramasaṃskṛtagranthāvalih, Granth. 29, 1925, p. 182.

[19] Cf. O. Friš: *Struktura staroindické společnosti* (*The Economic Structure of Ancient Indian Society—in Czech*), Praha, 1953, p. 41.

[20] Jāt. II. 211 (165), III. 354 (162), IV. 495 (363).

categories of occupation. In Jāt. I. 28 (191), which might be considered a very ancient one (among other things the setting of the tale is in Takkasilā in Gandhāra, i.e. in the West of India), the *seṭṭhi* says about himself that he possesses the best bullocks in the whole town: . . . '*sakalanagare pana amhākaṃ goṇehi sadiso n'atthīti' āha'*. At the end of the story he is called a '*seṭṭhi* whose wealth is in cattle' (*govittakaseṭṭhi*). The cattle were probably put to different uses in farming. The connection with agriculture can be see from the fact that the *seṭṭhi* harnesses the bullock to carts loaded with sand, gravel and stones to test his strength and usefulness for hard labour in the fields. This *seṭṭhi* is also denoted as a *seṭṭhi gahapati* in one passage of the above-named story (in the English translation of the Jātakas[21] only as 'merchant' the German translation[22] uses in all cases the term '*Grosskaufmann*'.

The *seṭṭhi* paid taxes from the crops of his fields. So in Jāt. II. 276 (378) the *seṭṭhi*[23] who came to his paddy field laments: 'From this field I have to give a portion to the king' (. . . '*imamhā kedārā mayā rañño bhāgo dātabbo*'). Here the *seṭṭhi's* connection with agriculture is obvious.

Another instance of a *seṭṭhi's* payment to the king can be found in the fourth Volume of the Jātakas:

When the king's officers (*rājakammikā*) came to a village in the province (*paccanta*) to measure the fields (*khettappamāṇagahanatthāya*), the *seṭṭhi* living there requests the brother of the king, who is living with him to send a letter to the king asking him to grant exemption, upon which the king grants him this —Jāt. IV. 467 (169). Let us notice that this *seṭṭhi* was living in the province (*paccante*) which can also be understood as a border district.[24] The *seṭṭhis* living in the province (*paccante*) are mentioned elsewhere, too: Jāt. I. 125 (451), I. 127 (458).

[21] The *Jātaka or Stories of Buddha's Former Births*, tr. from the Pāli by Various Hands. Under the Editorship of Prof. E.B. Cowell. Cambridge 1895–1907, Vol. I–VI. From now on cited under: Cowell.

[22] *Jātakam, Das Buch der Erzählungen aus früheren Existenzen Buddhas*, übersetzt von Dr Julius Dutoit, Band I–VII, Leipzig, 1908–21.

[23] D. Rouse who in this passage translates the term *seṭṭhi* as 'a certain wealthy man,' and farther 'a rich man' (Cowell III, 258), felt probably the difficulty of translating the term whose meaning differed in this place considerably from the common one which the word acquired later.

[24] Cf. *Mahāsīlava-jātaka* I, 51 (262). The minister of the king of Kosala

The above mentioned instances point not only to the conclusion that the *seṭṭhi* engaged in agriculture, but it follows from them that in literary documents the *seṭṭhi* was already distinguished from other men living by agriculture.

Thus we may conclude that the Pāli term *seṭṭhi* appears at a period of the founding of new cities and of the origins and development of commerce and it is inseparably bound up with this period. The *seṭṭhi* living by agriculture usually lived in the province (*paccante*); according to one Jātaka story he is denoted as a country *seṭṭhi* (*janapadaseṭṭhi*)—IV, 445 (37). And here we come to a very important period which gives us an answer to a number of questions still open.

The division of labour resulted in increasing the productivity of the village. Hand in hand with the foundation of new cities and the growth of the old ones, the concentration of people in one spot gradually became denser and the goods and products of the village were more and more in demand. The simple system of barter no longer sufficed. Markets were set up in towns and it was at this time that a metal currency first appeared. The whole of Buddhist literature bears witness to these important changes in the economic structure of ancient Indian society taking place at that time.[25] Commerce first arose when a new group began to separate from the mass of agricultural population—the group of traders (*vāṇijā*). 'Civilization strengthened and increased all the established divisions of labour, particularly by intensifying the antithesis between town and country and added a third division of labour, peculiar to itself and of decisive importance: it created a class that took no part in production, but engaged exclusively in exchanging products—the merchants . . . . . At the stage of development, our young merchant class had no inkling as yet of the big things that were in store for it. But it continued to grow and make itself indispensable, and that was sufficient. With it, however, metal money, minted coins, came

---

wants the king to test the renowned patience and peacefulness of the king of Benaras: '. . . *manusse pesetvā paccantagāmaṃ hanāpethā, te manusse gahetvā attano santikaṃ nīte dhanaṃ datvā vissajjessatīti.*'

Here is clearly meant a border village which very often witnessed an invasion of hostile armies or the plundering raids of many kinds of robbers—III, 348 (147).

Another instance can be found in *Rājaveda-jātaka* II, 151 (2).

[25] It was Mrs Rhys David who pointed out this fact in her 'Notes on Early Economic Conditions in Northern India', *JRAS,* 1901, p. 876.

into use, and with this a new means by which the non-producer could rule the producers and their products. The commodity of commodities, which concealed within itself all other commodities, was discovered; the charm that could be transformed at will into anything desirable and desired. Whoever possessed it ruled the world of production; and who had it above all others? The merchant'.[26]

Here I should like to remind the reader of one important thing: on a closer examination of the literature we see clearly that the term *seṭṭhi* is always used independently from the term *vāṇijā* and that these two terms are never substituted for or confounded with each other. The traders (*vāṇijā*) carried out the exchange of goods, or trade, in the proper sense of the word. Beside the rich horse-dealers (*assavāṇijā*)[27] and dealers in corn (*dhaññavāṇijā*)[28] the Jātakas speak very often about dealers or traders who went from village to village selling various necessaries made by artisans[29] as well as liquors,[30] etc. It is important to realize that they carried on the trade themselves and not through agents: 'And these (traders) went with five hundred wagons of goods to the country, and after disposing their wares they returned with the proceeds again to Benares.' (*Te [vāṇijā] pañcahi sakaṭasatehi bhaṇḍāni ādāya janapadāni gantvā vaṇijjaṃ katvā laddhalabhā puna Bārāṇasim agamiṃsu*—Jāt. I. 99 [404]). They sold the goods themselves and they kept the whole profit to themselves.

Along with the appearance and strengthening of commercial relations the term *seṭṭhi* appears on the stage of ancient Indian history in its new meaning. This occurs at the time when he himself begins to participate in business enterprise.

It is hard to find out exactly when the *seṭṭhi* began to carry on business. There is a gap of several centuries between the occurrence of the Vedic term *śreṣṭhin* and the contents of the Buddhist and later Sanskrit literature. In the course of this period the connotation of the word was changing along with the change in the economic conditions of the life of the society. From the instances adduced earlier we can draw the conclusion that a group of *seṭṭhis* separated itself from the majority of the agricultural population and besides farming began

26 Friedrich Engels: *The Origin of the Family, Private Property and the State*. Foreign Languages Publishing House, Moscow 1948, pp. 235–36.

27 Jāt. I, 5 (124).

28 Jāt. III, 365 (198).

29 Jāt. I, 3 (111), II. 189 (109).

30 Jāt. V, 512 (13).

to engage in commerce. It is natural that the *gāthās*, which from the oldest core of the present collection of the Jātakas, should speak of the *seṭṭhis* living in the country. In some *atītavatthus* they live in small towns, or market towns (*nigamanigamagāma*)—1.137 (478), II, 232 (225), II.254 (287). It may be that some of the *seṭṭhi* began their business career in these small market towns. It seems also probable that they invested in their transaction a certain part of the profits gained in agriculture.[31] At first the *seṭṭhi* occupied himself with business transactions personally. WSe find only one instance of it in the Jātakas—I. 54 (270). The story is about Bodhisatta who was born in a family of a *seṭṭhi*. When he came of age he carried on trade with five hundred carts: '*Bodhisatto seṭṭhikule nibbattitvā vayappatto pañcahi sakaṭasatehi vaṇijjaṃ karonto* . . .'. This allusion was quite involuntarily as the theme of the Jātaka story centres around an accident which happened on a caravan journey. Five hundred is a stereotype figure used for the number of the caravan's wagons. In other stories in the Jātakas the caravan is always led by a pilot (*satthavāha*).[32] By means of such activity the *seṭṭhi* could gain considerable wealth. As the markets concentrated first of all in towns and cities, the enterprising *seṭṭhi* moved to town and began to carry on their business there. As their wealth and influence increased, they gradually limited the sphere of their activities to the capitals of individual kingdoms.

We have instances of *seṭṭhis* living in Takkasilā in Gandhāra—Jāt. I. 28 (191), *Suttavibhaṅga*[33] II. 5; in Sāketa,[34] the capital of Kosala[35]—*Mahāvagga* I.270, Jat. VI. 544 (228); in Sāvatthī, the second capital of Kosala kingdom Jat. I.84 (366), I. 118 (432), I. 148 (501), II. 232 (224), III. 390 (299).[36] *Saṃyutta-nikāya*[37] I.89, 91; in Mithilā in the kingdom of Videha—Jāt. VI. 539 (43), 546 (331, 344,

[31] It is obvious from the evidence of the Jātakas that the *seṭṭhis* living by agriculture were well-to-do although not excessively rich. Their standard was certainly not on the same level with the majority of the agricultural population which, according to the literary tradition, lived in very miserable conditions at that time, earning their bread by ardous toil with the help of only the most primitive tools and equipment.

[32] Jāt. I. 1 (98), I. 2 (107), I. 29 (194), etc.

[33] *The Vinaya Pitakaṃ*, ed. by H. Oldenberg, London, 1879–83.

[34] Ayodhyā, the present-day Oudh.

[35] Cf. B.C. Law: *Geography of Early Buddhism,* pp. 5ff.

[36] All scenes laid in Sāvatthī are found in the *paccuppannavatthus*.

[37] *The Saṃyutta-Nikāya of the Sutta-Piṭaka,* ed. by M. Léon Feer, Part I, Pāli Textbook Society, London, 1884.

364); in Rājagaha in Magadha—Jāt. I. 12 (145), I. 131 (466), IV. 445 (37), *Čulavagga*[33] II. 110, 146, in the kingdom of Kāsi—Jāt. I. 137 (478) and, of course, in most cases in Benares where the majority of the Jātaka stories are set (probably by a final recension); *Mahāvagga*[33] I.15, 18, Jāt I. 4 (120), 40 (231), 42 (242), 47 (252), 53 (269), 63 (295), 78 (349), 83 (365), 84 (366), 90 (377), 93 (388), 103 (412), 125 (451), 127 (458), 131 (466); II. 164 (50), 171 (64), 232 (225), 274 (361); III. 315 (51), 337 (119), 375 (225), 395 (315), 425 (475); IV. 439 (1), 450 (62), 481 (249), 482 (255), 497 (376); V. 535 (382); VI. 542 (135).

As time passed away, two groups of *seṭṭhis* were gradually developing: one in the country and the other in the town. They were combined by a common interest. There was also another bond between the town *seṭṭhis* and those living in the country (or in the provinces): the relationship of both groups. This relationship existed, of course, at the time when the enterprising *seṭṭhis* began to settle down in the towns. Later, both groups were combined by intermarriage. Thus in Jāt. I. 125 (453) the *paccantaseṭṭhi* is delighted to give his daughter to the son of the *seṭṭhi* of Benares. In another story—Jāt II. 232 (225) the *seṭṭhi* living in small market town wants his son to marry the daughter of the *seṭṭhi* of Benares. Jāt. I. 127 (458), IV. 445 (37) contains another example of intermarriage between the two groups. Similar cases are to be found, too, in the Sanskrit work *Vetālapañavimśatikā*.[38]

Both groups were in close contact, especially as regards business matters. From several instances in the Jātakas it is obvious what form this contact assumed. The products of the country (or of the provinces) had a ready sale in the towns and cities. The traders (*vāṇijā*) dealt in various kinds of goods all over the country, it is true, but they carried on their trade individually and directly with the consumer. Their activity could cover the requirements of great cities such as the residences of the kings of Benares, Rājagaha, etc. To meet these needs a man with considerable means and business ability was needed; and such was the *seṭṭhi*. Thus hand in hand with the beginnings of commerce a new kind of occupation arose. The *seṭṭhi* managed the exchange of goods between town and country and thus the *seṭṭhi* of the town had a business friend in the province. With him he exchanged the products of the town artisans for various products from the provinces. There is an instance of this exchange recorded in Jāt. I. 90 (377) and I. 125 (451). In *paccuppannavatthu* of the first story it is said:

[38] Heinrich Uhle: *Die Vetālapañcaviṃśatikā des Śivadāsa*, Vol. 1, Leipzig, 1914, pp. 34, 35.

'There lived a *seṭṭhi* in the country (or in a border district) who was a business friend of Anāthapiṇḍika, but they had never met or seen each other. Once upon a time this *seṭṭhi* loaded five hundred carts with country produce and gave orders to the men in charge to go to Sāvatthī, and barter the wares in the shop of the great *seṭṭhi* Anāthapiṇḍka for their value, and bring the merchandise received in exchange. After they agreed to do this they came to Sāvatthī and met Anāthapiṇḍika. First presenting him a passport they told him their business. 'You are welcome,' said the great *seṭṭhi* and ordered them to be lodged and provided with money for their needs. After kindly enquiries about his friends' well-being he sold the merchandise and gave them the good in exchange.' (*Anāthapiṇḍikassa kir'eko paccantavāsiko seṭṭhi adiṭṭhasahāyo ahosi. So ekadā paccante uṭṭhānakabhaṇḍassa pañca sakaṭasatāni pūretvā kammantikamanusse āha: gacchatha bho. imaṃ bhaṇḍaṃ sāvatthim netvā umhākaṃ sahāyassa Anāthapiṇḍika mahāseṭṭhissa paccakkhena vikkiṇitvā paṭibhaṇḍaṃ āharathā"ti. Te sādhū"ti tassa vacanaṃ sampaṭicchitvā Sāvatthiṃ gantvā mahāseṭṭhiṃ paṇṇākāraṃ datvā taṃ arocesuṃ. Mahāseṭṭhi "svāgataṃ vo"ti tesaṃ āvāsañ ca paribbayañ dāpesi.*)

The *atītavatthu* speaks about a *mahāvibhavo seṭṭhi* of Benares, otherwise the *paccuppannavatthus* of both stories are identical with the *atītavatthus* which are enlarged only by verse. It seems that the story told above was embodied in the frame-work added later when Anāthapiṇḍika became the chief person of the tale.[39]

Several interesting conclusions can be drawn from this Jātaka story. It is stated that the companions did not know each other personally (they were *adiṭṭhasahāyā*). The contact could be established also by means of a written record or through a third person. These business connections could be opened up in certain families of both groups of *seṭṭhis* who did not even know each other in later generations.

The goods made in the province (*paccante uṭṭhānakabhaṇḍaṃ*) were usually conveyed to towns in caravans. The figure 500 denoting the number of carts is again unreliable, but it testifies to the fact that the goods were conveyed in larger quantities by well-equipped caravans, probably because the roads were not very safe at that time and larger quantities of goods diminished the cost of transport.[40]

[39] One must not be misled by seeing the note in the *atītavatthu* that the story continues in the same way as in the *paccupannavatthu*. We cannot confound the present appearance of the Jātaka with its original form.

[40] About Anāthapiṇḍika's caravans, cf. Mr Rhys Davids' 'Notes on Early

From the moment of the caravan's arrival in the city until its departure the *seṭṭhi* took care of the welfare of his friend's people, i.e. provided for their food and lodging. He himself sold the goods and gave his friend's people merchandise in exchange. The amount and value of this merchandise was settled either before hand or in a passport[41] which had been delivered to him. It is the *seṭṭhi* who sells (*vikkiṇitva*)[42] the goods. The difference between the price asked by the sender and the selling price was probably left to the town's *seṭṭhi* as a net profit. The text states clearly that the *seṭṭhi* sold the goods and ordered the merchandise as fixed by previous agreement to be handed over (*dāpesi*) to his partner's people. Such business was sometimes very profitable. Enterprise of this kind required money and connections with the province; the town *seṭṭhis* had both. As far as I know no similar co-operation among traders (*vāṇijā*) has been recorded in Pāli literature.

Everything testifies to the fact that the town *seṭṭhi* acquired considerable wealth much quicker than their opposite numbers in the country. These were dependent either on trade in the provinces which certainly was not very profitable, or on transactions carried out in collaboration with the town *seṭṭhi*. That was the main reason why the country *seṭṭhis* never obtained such a favourable position as their friends in towns, and besides, of course, the country *seṭṭhis* were much more numerous. In some cases they even became poor and in the course of time lost their whole property—Jāt. II. 254 (278), VI. 546 (364).

The story mentioned earlier reveals not only the circumstances under which the business was carried but also who took part in those transactions. The *seṭṭhi* employed business-agents (*kammantikamanussā*), assistants, who carried on business for him and who accomplished all the duties connected with it. They were headed by a *mahākammantika*—the business manager who was their chief and

---

Economic Conditions in Northern India' in *Journal of the Royal Asiatic Soceity of Great Britian and Ireland*, 1901, p. 871–82.

[41] I am convinced that the term '*paṇṇākāro*' must be translated as 'passport' here and not 'a present' as translated by R. Chalmers (in Cowell I, 220).

[42] The verb *vi-kiṇāti* (skt. *krīṇāti*) is very closely connected with the development of commerce and with the origin of money. It would be certainly very interesting to follow the use of this verb which appears only once in *Ṛgveda* (X, 320) in connection with the 'selling' of a cow (if the verb selling can be used, as originally no real 'selling' was probably known to the people of that period; it was only barter.

the *seṭṭhi*'s proxy acting on behalf of his master whenever the need arose and in the *seṭṭhi's* absence. His powers were probably extensive, as we can judge from a note stating that those who wanted some favour of the *seṭṭhi*, applied to him first[43]— Jāt. I. 40 (227). He thus acted as a kind of personal secretary to the *seṭṭhi*.[44]

To complete the picture of a *seṭṭhi* it is necessary to mention another group of people who worked for him. They are called 'slaves and servants' (*dāsakammakarā*)—Jāt. II. 382 (257), who appear only as domestic servants—VI. 540 (69). Their position was very bad; very often they were struck merely because of their master's being out of temper—Jāt. I. 63 (295). They were treated with contempt as chattels—a part of the *seṭṭhi*'s property—III. 340 (129). As food they got the remains of their masters' meals. In *Mahāvagga* I. 272 the wife of the *seṭṭhi* of Sāketa declares the *ghī* used to restore her health to be only fit for 'slaves and servants' (*dāsānaṃ vā kammakarānaṃ vā*). No wonder that under the circumstances the slaves often ran away from their masters' houses—Jāt. I. 125 (451), I. 127 (458), VI. 540 (69) in spite of the possibility of being caught and brought back to their drudgery—I. 127 (459) (. . . *Bārāṇasiṃ eva ānetvā dāsaparibhogena paribhuñji*). Jāt. I. 125 (451) tells us a story about such a slave who was born in the house of the *seṭṭhi* of Benares on the same day as the *seṭṭhi*'s son. Both children were therefore given the same education and when the slave's son grew up, he was given the post of a keeper of stores (*bhaṇḍāgārikakammaṃ karonto*). But even when he was a useful worker, he had no feeling of security as everything depended on his master's mood. So one day he ran away to the province (*paccanta*) fearing lest he should commit some fault for which he would be deprived of his post and beaten like others.

Now let us turn to the *seṭṭhi* again. We know from literature that the *seṭṭhi*'s wealth was immense. But a closer examination of statements of this kind shows that this was not always the case. In stories describing how the *seṭṭhi* engaged in agriculture and paid taxes to the king from the crops of their fields or how they carried on their trade

[43] The goddess (*devatā*) wants to persuade the *seṭṭhi* about the necessity of devoting his life to performance of his duties and so saving his family property. First she goes to the *mahākammantika* who should speak to the *seṭṭhi* in this manner. After she has been refused she goes to the *seṭṭhi's* eldest son who was his father's successor.

[44] The term '*mahākammantika*' is not quoted by the Pāli Textbook Society, Dictionary.

travelling with caravans, no attribute denoting their wealth or the largeness of their property is added. On the other hand the *seṭṭhi* living in towns and cities are often spoken of as men of property. The term, 'a *seṭṭhi* of great wealth' (*mahāvibhavo seṭṭhi*) is often used in speaking of them: Jāt I. 12 (145), I. 84 (366), I. 90 (378), I. 93 (388), I. 103 (413), I. 118 (432), I. 125 (451), I. 137 (478), I. 148 (501), II. 254 (287), III. 317 (56).

The most usual case is that the amount of the *seṭṭhi*'s wealth is expressed by the figure 80 koṭis (i.e. cca 8,000.000 pieces of coins) —'a *seṭṭhi* whose wealth amounts to 80 koṭis' (*asītikoṭivibhavo seṭṭhi*)—Jāt. I. 78 (345) I. 131 (466), III. 317 (56), III. 390 (299), IV. 439 (1), IV. 482 (255), and *asītikoṭidhanavibhavo seṭṭhi* —III. 340 (128), III. 421 (444), V. 527 (210), VI. 544 (228).

Now it is important to realize one significant circumstances: We can see that these terms denoting the immense wealth of the *seṭṭhi* are used specially in Nipātas containing longer Jātakas, i.e. in the third, fourth and fifth volumes of our collection, which we can generally consider as parts that have assumed their present shape in a period posterior to the majority of the simple stories of the first and second Volume. The property of another *seṭṭhi* living in Benares (*Bārāṇāsi-vāsī eko seṭṭhi*) amounts to 40 koṭis (cca 4,000.000)—Jāt. I. 73 (323). The majority of the tales of this kind are set in the East of India and Mrs Rhys Davids says in this connection:[45] 'The millionaires of the Jātakas are, with but few exceptions, notably Anāthapiṇḍika of Sāvatthī, 80 and 40 *koṭi* burglhers (*seṭṭhiyo* and *gahapatiyo*) of Kāsi (especially, of course, of Benaras) and Magadha (e.g. Jāt. I. 466, 478, IV. 1, 382, VI. 68).'

Here, too, evolution can be seen: the *seṭṭhi*'s property gradually increases. In the first volume of the Jātakas a *mahāvibhavo seṭṭhi* is very often spoken of. But more than half of these quotations are to be found in the 'stories of the present' (*paccuppannavatthus*) which do not go so far as the 'stories of the past' (*atītavatthus*), as already stated. References of this kind are contained in Jāt. I. 12 (145), I. 84 (366), I. 103 (412), I. 118 (432) and I. 148 (501).

In some cases caution must be exercised. In the *atītavatthu* of the *Illīsa-jātaka* I. 78 (345), for instance, an *asītikoṭivibhavo seṭṭhi* is introduced, but this story is identical with that of the *paccuppannavatthu*. Thus in my opinion it is possible that at the time

[45] Notes, *JRAS*, 1901, p. 882.

of the compilation of the present collection of the Jātakas the term *asītikoṭivibhavo* has been mechanically transferred from the framework (i.e. the *paccuppannavatthu*) of the story into the story itself (i.e. *atīavatthu*), where originally it did not exist. A similar case would then be the designation '*mahāvibhavo seṭṭhi*' in Jāt. I. 84 (366) and I. 90 (378). If this hypothesis is correct the number of Jātakas in the first Volume describing *seṭṭhi* as men of great wealth would be reduced to a third. Some Jātakas particularly in this volume underwent, of course, considerable changes later, of which an instance is the laborious 'story of the present' of the first Jātaka, where Buddha converts five hundred heretics, friends of Anāthapiṇḍika who appear most frequently in these extensive 'stories of the present' of the first volume.[46]

It is obvious that as time passed the whole interest of the authors of the texts turned to the *seṭṭhis* of the town, whose importance and influence in society had increased. In close connection with these town *seṭṭhis* the meaning of the term '*seṭṭhiṭṭhāna*' has to be determined.

The 'position of a *seṭṭhi*' (*seṭṭhiṭṭhānaṃ*) was very important at that time. We often meet up with this term in Pāli literature. The word *seṭṭhiṭṭhāna* occurs only in connection with towns or cities. This position was held by a *seṭṭhi* until his death. In most cases the position was hereditary, but not before the father died: . . .*so pitu accayena seṭṭhiṭṭhānaṃ labhi*, *pāpuni*, etc.—Jāt. I. 45 (248), II. 171 (64), II. 238 (236), II. 291 (431), IV. 450 (62). When the father died the family property was administered by his eldest son who became also his successor—Jāt. III. 317 (56), III. 390 (299).

But the *seṭṭhiṭṭhāna* was not always necessarily inherited. The *Cullakaseṭṭhi-jātaka* I. 4 (120 and 122) tells a story about a clever youth who after the death of the town *seṭṭhi* gained the position of *seṭṭhi* in that town (*so seṭṭhino accayena tasmiṃ nagare seṭṭhiṭṭhānaṃ labhi*).

[46] The most important data concerning Anāthapiṇḍika can be found in the first volume of the Jātakas. But they seem to be the youngest, too. Anāthapiṇḍika is always presented here as a protector and generous patron of the Buddhist faith and community. No reference to him can be found in the second Nipāta (Volume II) and in the fifth and sixth volume. The rare quotations from the third and fourth volume contain only stereotype phrases with no special meaning (usually he appears together with the king of Kosala and with Visākhā, the great Lay Sister).

The families of *seṭṭhis* had been settled in certain towns for many generations. A *seṭṭhi* who was a newcomer was called '*āgantukaseṭṭhi*'—Jāt. III 390 (299). The king, of course, retained the power to appoint anybody he liked to the position of *seṭṭhi*, nor was this power subject to any limitations. He could give the *seṭṭhiṭṭhāna* to anyone as a gift or as a reward. Jāt. I. 109 (424) tells a story of a poor man who was appointed to the *seṭṭiṭṭhāna* by the king as he honestly handed over to the king the treasure he had found (*rājā tassa seṭṭhiṭṭhānaṃ adāsi*). If the king wanted to choose anyone for this important position, he had to consider carefully all possibilities. The principal criterion was usually the person's wealth. The king was well aware of the fact that without sufficient means the new *seṭṭhi* would not be able to carry on various transactions that were often closely connected with the management of the king's treasury. Therefore, *gahapatis* were chosen for this position, e.g. Jāt. V. 535 (382) (*Atīte Bārāṇasiyaṃ Brahmadatte rajjaṃ kārente eko gahapati aḍḍho ahosi asītikoṭivbhavo. Ath'assa rājā seṭṭhiṭṭhānaṃ adāsi.*) These were the only people who could help the king out of this financial and other difficulties.

The king also appointed some of the *seṭṭhis* to his own services. These services were probably in most cases of a private character, because it was *bhaṇḍāgārika* who was officially appointed to control the king's treasury.

Evidence that the king used to employ a *seṭṭhi* in his service can be found in Jāt. I. 131 (466) (*atīte Magadharaṭṭhe Rājagahe ekasmiṃ Magadharññerajjaṃ kārente Bodhisatto tass'eva seṭṭhi ahosi asītkoṭi vibhavo Saṃkhaseṭṭhiti nāmena*).

The services rendered to the king gave the position of *seṭṭhi* the significance of an office, and this was probably the original sense of the term *seṭṭhiṭṭhāna*. This also explains the question why the *seṭṭhiṭṭhāna* was restricted only to the *seṭṭhis* living in towns, i.e. originally to the *seṭṭhi* living in royal capitals only.

Very often we read that the *seṭṭhi* goes to wait upon the king (*seṭṭhi rājupaṭṭhānaṃ gacchanto*)—Jāt. I. 4 (120), I. 53 (269), II. 171 (64), III. 337 (119), V. 535 (384). The term *upaṭṭhāna* includes not only the meaning 'attendance,' as it is usually translated, but also 'service,' and in this sense the *seṭṭhi*'s waiting upon the king is to be understood. The king was quite often in need of the *seṭṭhi*'s services. In Jāt. III. 425 (475) the *seṭṭhi* goes to the king three times a day (so [sc. *seṭṭhi*] *divasassa tayo vāre rājupaṭṭhānaṃ gacchati*). This corresponds to the *Mahāvagga* VIII. 116 where it is stated, that the *seṭṭhi* of Rājagaha was of much use to the king as well as to the townsmen (*bahūpakāro devassa c'eva negamassa ca*).

The story of Jāt. VI. 542 (135) describes the riot of the citizens of Benares who wanted to keep the king from sacrificing four *seṭṭhis* of that town. The *seṭṭhis* were to be sacrificed along with the king's family to avert the evil consequences of the king's bad dream. In the following lines of the Jātaka one of the most interesting situations is unfolded. When the king's children were being led to execution, no one raised voice to protest. But the text says that the *seṭṭhis* had great connection in the city, and when they were led to the king the whole city rose to protect them (*rañño puttadāre gayhamāne sakalanagaram na kiñci avoča seṭṭhikulāni pana mahāsambandhāni, tasmā tesaṃ gahitakāle sakalanagaraṃ saṃkhubhitvā 'rañño seṭṭhi ñātivaggena saddhiṃ rājakulaṃ agamāsi*). In the following pages of the text these *seṭṭhis* are also denoted by the terms '*negamā*' and '*gahapatayo*'.

Sakalanagaram—'the whole city'—has to be taken here, in my opinion, as meaning well-to-do class of citizens only. They were bound to the *seṭṭhis* by common interests and by business relations and sometimes by ties of relationship as well. Nothing indicates that the *seṭṭhi* acted as a friend towards persons of lower standing as, for instance, towards those who worked for him.[47]

The *seṭṭhi* who often appeared at the king's court is sometimes called '*mahāseṭṭhi*'. But it is rather a respectful form of address than an expression designating the office of Lord High Treasurer, as is the view of Mrs Rhys Davids.[48] So, for instance, the *seṭṭhi* from the province (*paccantaseṭṭhi*) addressed the *seṭṭhi* of Benares as '*mahāseṭṭhi*'—Jāt. I. 125 (453), on the other hand, the *anuseṭṭhi*[49] addressed the *seṭṭhi* in the same way (i.e. '*mahāseṭṭhi* ') while the latter addressed him with the form '*seṭṭhi*'—Jāt. V. 535 (384). The friends of a *seṭṭhi* call him respectfully '*mahāseṭṭhi*', though the text denotes him only as a '*seṭṭhi*'. It is worth noting that the term *mahā-* is very often attached to the simple terms in Pāli only as a polite form and has no special meaning (cf. the PTS Dictionary).

[47] Jāt. III. 415 (406), IV. 445 (38).

[48] *JRAS*, 1901, p. 865. Her views are repeated by T.W. Rhys Davids in his Buddhist India, p. 97.

[49] The position of this '*anuseṭṭhi*' is not very clear, as I could find no other evidence of it in the literature.

In some stories the *seṭṭhi* is designated as *Bārāṇasiseṭṭhi*[50]—Jāt. I. 40 (231), I. 42 (242), I. 63 (295), I. 83. (364), I. 125 (451), II. 274 (361).Other Jātakas state that the Bodhisatta was born in a *seṭṭhi* family (*Bārāṇasiyaṃ seṭṭhikule nibbattitvā*)—I. 4 (120) , I. 47 (252), I. 78 (349), I. 83 (365), I. 84 (366), I. 90 (388), I. 103 (412), II. 171 (64), III. 337 (225), etc. These last-named stories are much more frequent than the previous ones in the Jātakas. In two other tales the *seṭṭhi* is denoted as a '*seṭṭhi* living in Benares' (*Bārāṇasivāsī eko seṭṭhi*)—I. 73 (323), III. 315 (51).I take it as possible that the term '*Bārāṇasiseṭṭhi*' expressed or included in itself a distinct function or privileged position, but there are no proofs at hand to verify this opinion. It may be that the *seṭṭhi* working for the king was meant by this term; he might occupy a privileged position among the other *seṭṭhis*.

It seems to me, in any case, that the *seṭṭhi* who had won the greatest influence in the town or at the king's court, had a decisive word in all matters relating to the other *seṭṭhis*. In Jāt VI. 546 (344) the king rewarding a *seṭṭhi* who showed great wisdom says: 'Let the other *seṭṭhis* be servitors of this' ('. . . *sesaseṭṭhino etass'eva upaṭṭhākā hontu 'ti'*). In another story—Jāt. I. 92 (386)—the purohita (who enjoyed the greatest honour and dignity at the king's court) addressed a *seṭṭhi* by the form '*mahāseṭṭhi*'. And, in Jāt. II. 164 (51) even the king does so. Anāthapiṇḍika is always spoken of as a '*mahāseṭṭhi*'. But we cannot place too much confidence in the story about the king giving the *seṭṭhi* a privileged position among others and show that a certain kind of organisation or perhaps even of a guild of *seṭṭhis* was meant (especially at the time when the commerce began to develop). I see in it rather an endeavour for the suitable reward reserved for the wise *seṭṭhi* who was no other than the Bodhisatta himself. Besides, the king was able to make the other *seṭṭhis* servants of the first one in the period we are discussing. It is obvious that the term 'upaṭṭhākā' cannot be understood in the sense of some relations between the head of a guild and its members.

Attention has already been drawn to the huge figures used in the texts for expressing the amount of a *seṭṭhi*'s wealth. Money was usually hidden in a solitary place—Jāt. I. 40 (227)[51] IV. 482 (256).[52] There were no facilities for depositing the money anywhere. The

[50] Also *Bārāṇasīseṭṭhi*—Jāt. I. 125 (452).

[51] *Añña pan'assa kulasantakā aṭṭhārasakoṭyo nadītīre nidahitvā ṭhapitā.*

[52] *Gaṅgātīre me nihitaṃ kulasantakaṃ dhanam atthi.*

seṭṭhis dwelt in palaces (or mansions) full of gold, grain and many other precious things. Anāthapiṇḍika's house was seven stories high and had seven portals—Jāt. I. 40 (227).

In Jāt. III. 340 (129) we are told what the house of a wealthy *seṭṭhi* comprised: The god Sakka was jealous of a *seṭṭhi's* charity. He was afraid that he would be bereft of his own position in heaven by the *seṭṭhi*'s virtues and so he wants to test the moral strength of his rival. He causes all his property to disapper: '. . . even all his treasure of grain, oil, honey, molasses, and the like . . ., as well as his slaves and work people' (*sabbaṃ dhanadhaññaṃ telamadhuphāṇitādiṇ antamaso dāsakammakaraporisaṃ pi antaradhāpesi*).

Another interesting instance of this kind is preserved in the twenty-fourth story of the Sanskrit work *Siṅhāsanadvātriṃśikā.* The story runs as follows:

When the *seṭṭhi* of the city Purandapurī died, he left four copper vessels to his four sons dividing thus the property in four portions in order to prevent quarrels among them. Of these vessels there was earth in one, coals in one, bones in one, and straw in one. None of them could solve the puzzle until they came to the city of Pratiṣṭhāna and heard the solution from the mouth of the wise Śālivāhana: 'To the oldest he gave earth: that means, he gave (him) all the land which he possessed. To the next he gave straw: that is, he gave (him) all the grain he had. To the third he gave bones: that is, he gave (him) all the cattle that he had. To the fourth he gave coals: that is, he gave (him) all the gold that he had.'[53] The *seṭṭhi* divided his property into four parts, but his eldest son got the most important one, viz., the land which he had cultivated or hired for taxes, as we shall see later. As was pointed out above that the eldest son took care of the family property after his father's death. The second son got the stores of grain that were mentioned also in the previous story. The third son obtained the cattle which was used for various purposes, as draught animals—Jāt. I. 28 (191) or to provide the *seṭṭhi*'s house with food. In Jāt. I. 93 (388) the herdsman looks after the *seṭṭhi*'s cows and regularly sends their products to his master: 'He (sc. the *seṭṭhi*) had a herdsman who, when the harvest time came, drove his cows to the forest and kept them there at a shieling, bringing the produce from time to time to the *seṭṭhi*' (cf. Fausböll: *tass'eko gopālako*

[53] *Vikrama's Adventures or the Thirty-two Tales of the Throne*, Part I, ed. and tr. by Franklin Edgerton, Cambridge, Mass. 1926, pp. 192–93.

kiṭṭhasambādhasamaye gāvo gahetvā araññaṃ pavisitvā tattha gopallikaṃ katvā rakkhanto vasati seṭṭhino ca kālena kālaṃ gorasaṃ āharati). I think that the products mentioned here were intended merely to supply the house of the *seṭṭhi* with everything necessary, and not as an article for the market. Such a case could not be found by me anywhere in the literature. The fourth got a certain amount of money and gold which was usually not very small.

This story is also very important from the point of view of the rights of inheritance. When the *seṭṭhi* had one son only, he inherited all the property left to him by his father and usually succeeded to the position of a *seṭṭhi* (*seṭṭhiṭṭhāna*). But in one instance in the Jātakas it is the mother who takes care of the family property instead of the son who is incapable of doing it himself—Jāt. IV. 439 (1). If there were more sons, they all got their share, as we have seen , of which they were probably free to dispose.

Here we come to an important point. When the texts speak about the sons of *seṭṭhis* (*seṭṭhiputtā*) then these well-to-do private persons are meant as a definite group and not the sons of a definite *seṭṭhi*. Nowhere is it said whether they took part in the activities of their father or eldest brother, who generally succeeded him in the position of *seṭṭhi*. Let us now examine some relevant passages.

In the story of the present (*paccuppannavatthu*) of the Jāt. I. 118 (433) it is stated that at a festival in Sāvatthī besides the son of Uttaraseṭṭhi[54)] also the other sons of *seṭṭhis* with their wives were present (*tassa sahāyakā aññe seṭṭhiputtā sapajāpatikā ahesum . . .*). The presence of their wives and even the fact that they were married is very significant. They could not be their fathers' successors and yet they got married and had their own homes. Nor was their number particularly small. In the 'story of the present' of Jāt. I. 148 (501) five hundred *seṭṭhiputtā* are mentioned as living in Sāvatthī and owning large property (*Sāvaṭṭhiyaṃ kira pañcasatamattā sahāyakā mahāvibhavā seṭṭhiputtā . . .*). Even if we admit that the figure 500 is no reliable pointer to their actual number, I think that we can take it that they were numerous. Of importance is the fact that it is just in the 'stories of the present' (*paccuppannavatthus*) which cannot make much claim to great antiquity, that they are mentioned. The designation

54 Written by Fausböll with capital U. I should take it rather as a chief of or among the *seṭṭhis* and not as a personal name. Nowhere else in the Jātakas does this term occur.

'*mahāvibhavā*' proves that they owned substantial wealth without occupying the position of a *seṭṭhi*. (Afterwards they all go to Jetavana and join the community of monks.)

But let us look more closely at what comprised the wealth of a *seṭṭhiputta*. In *Mahāvagga* I. 15 a story is told about a son born in a rich *seṭṭhi's* family who himself owned three palaces: 'At that time there lived in Benares a *seṭṭhiputta* named Yasa of good birth, beautifully young, who owned three palaces; one destined for the winter, one for the summer and one for the rainy season.' (*tena kho pana samāyena Bārānasiyaṃ Yaso nāma kulaputto seṭṭhiputto sukhumālo hoti, tassa tayo pāsādā honti, eko hemantiko, eko grimhiko, eko vassiko*). The idea of the tale is not original here: In these palaces he passed the time, in each season in turn, amusing himself with music, songs and the dancing of his troupe of dancing-girls. It is explicitly stated there that he himself was the owner of the palaces, not his father. Nor is there the slightest indication anywhere of his being in the position of a *seṭṭhi*. On the contrary: one day, on getting up earlier than usual, he sees his girl-friends lying asleep in disarray without their artificial make-up and begins to feel an aversion towards the world and goes out into the homelessness to seek internal bliss and truth. He asked neither for the consent of his parents nor of the king, which was the practice should the *seṭṭhi* resolve to do so. He simply made up his mind and carried out his intention without asking anybody's permission. It is clear that this could only be done if these three places were his personal property and he could make independent decisions. In other instances it is pointed out that the sons and daughters of *seṭṭhis* had to ask their parents' consent in such a case—cf. Jāt I. 12 (145), VI. 540 (69).

Maṃsa-jātaka—III. 315 bears witness to the independent position of the *seṭṭhiputtā* who formed a particular group. The *atītavatthu* of this Jātaka begins with the words: 'Once upon a time when Brahmadatta reigned in Benares, the Bodhisatta was born as the son of a *seṭṭhi* . . . . At this time four sons of the *seṭṭhis* who were living in Benaras sallied out of the city, and meeting at a convenient place near the road they sat down and conversed with one another about whatever they had seen or heard.' (*Atīte Bārāṇasiyaṃ Brahmadatta rajjaṃ kārente Bodhisatto seṭṭhiputto ahosi. . . Tadā Bārāṇasivāsikā cattāro seṭṭhiputtā nagarā nikkhamitvā ekasmiṃ maggasabhāgaṭṭhāne kiñci diṭṭhasutaṃ samullapantā nisīdiṃsu.*) One of them makes friends with a hunter and takes him with his whole family to his home. Both men live as inseparable friends: 'And he treated the hunter with great hospitality and respect and sending for his wife and son he took him away from his cruel occupation, and settled him on his own estate. And they became inseparable friends, and all their life long lived amicably together.' The property of the *seṭṭhiputta* is mentioned here; it is denoted by the term *kuṭumba*. The introduction of the *atītavatthu* is unique compared with the other one (. . . *seṭṭhikule nibbattitvā* . . . *seṭṭhi ahosi*).[55] Another instance can be found in Jāt II. 261 (322).[56]

The term *seṭṭhiputta* is used in other texts throughout the Pāli canon as well. When the *seṭṭhi* died without children, all his property was taken by the king who had the right to take into his possession everything 'that was without a master'.[57]

When a very rich *seṭṭhi* (*aḍḍho mahaddhano*)died in Sāvatthī, his property was carried into the palace of the king in seven days and nights (*tassāputtakaṃ sāpateyyaṃ rājabalaṃ sattahi rattiṃdivasehi rājakulaṃ pavesesi*)—Jāt. III. 390 (299). A similar case is found in *Saṃyutta Nikāya*—I. 89. From there more details about *seṭṭhis* private life can be learnt. The story runs as follows:

'Reverend Sir, a householder who was treasurer in Sāvatthī has just died leaving no son, and I have come from transferring his property to my royal palace; and, Reverend Sir, he had ten million pieces of gold, and silver beyond all reckoning. But this householder, Reverend Sir, would eat sour gruel and *kaṇājaka*, and the clothes he wore were made of hemp . . ., and the conveyance in which he rode was a broken-down chariot with an umbrella of leaves.'[58] (*Idha bhante Sāvatthiyaṃ seṭṭhi gahapati kālakato. tam aham aputtakaṃ sāpateyyaṃ rājamtepram, atiharitvā āgacchāmi. sataṃ bhante satasahassāni hiraṇṇass'eva. ko pana vādo rūpiyassa. Tassa kho pana bhante seṭṭhissa gahapatissa evarūpto bhattabhogo ahosi. kaṇājakaṃ*

55 The conclusion of the Jātaka (i.e. the *samodhāna*) is forcibly added to the story of the *atītavatthu*. In the *atītavvatthu* only four *seṭṭhiputtā* are mentioned. No connection with the Bodhisatta can be seen there. And yet the Bodhisatta is identified with the fourth *seṭṭhiputta* in the *samodhāna:* . . . *sabbamaṃsalābhiseṭṭhiputto aham evā ti.* It seems, however, that the first lines of the *atītavatthu* were incorporated into the Jātaka later at the time of the Buddhist recension of the story. The same is the case with the end of the *atītavatthu*.

56 Here the story of Bodhisatta is the same as that of the *Maṃsa-Jātaka.*

57 *Assāmikabhaṇḍam nāma raňňo pāpuṇātīti*—Jāt. VI. 546 (345).

58 H.C. Warren: *Buddhism in Translations*, Harvard Oriental Series, Vol. 3, Cambridge, Mass, 1922, p. 226–27.

bhuñjati bilangadutiaṃ. Evarūpo vattabhogo ahosi. sānaṃ dhāreti tipakkhavasanaṃ. Evarūpo yānabhogo ahosi. jajjararathakena yāti paṇṇacchattakena dhāriyamānenā ti.)

We must be aware of the fact that the king wants to point out the contrast between the immeasurable wealth of the *seṭṭhi* and his poor way of living. The contrast is strengthened by the term '*seṭṭhi gahapati*'.

The children of the *seṭṭhis* were brought up in luxury from a tiny age. They did not know worries of daily life and work. Their education was similar to that of the royal princes and the sons born in the families of the brāhmaṇas. In Jāt. I. 40 (231) we read about Bodhisatta who was born in the family of the *seṭṭhi* of Benaras: 'Once in a time when Brahmadata was reigning in Benaras, the Bodhisatta came to life in the family of the *seṭṭhi* of Benaras, and was brought up in all possible luxury like a royal prince. By the time he had reached the years of discretion, being barely sixteen-years-old, he had made himself perfect in all accomplishments.' (*Atīte Bārāṇasiyaṃ Brahmadatte rajjaṃ kārente Bodhisatto Bārāṇasiseṭṭhissa kule nibbatitvā nānappakārehi sukhūpaharaṇehi devakumāro viya saṃvaḍḍhiyamāno anukkamena viññūtaṃ patvā solavassakāle yeva sabbasippesu nipphatiṃ patto*[59]).

In another story—Jāt. IV. 445 (38)—two sons of a *seṭṭhi* and a son of his tailor (*tuṇṇakāra*) in Rājagaha, who were born on the same day, go to Takkasilā to learn the accomplishments (*Takkasilaṃ gantvā sippaṃ uggaṇhiṃsu*). The *seṭṭhi*'s sons paid to the teacher one thousand each; then they taught the tailor's son what they had learnt.

Another tale tells about the son of an *asītikoṭivibhavo seṭṭhi*. This youth is brought up in pleasures and amusements only, but he has got no education, because his father feared his beloved son might be fatigued by his studies. And so the young man knew nothing but amusement. In Jāt. III. 425 (475) a son of the *seṭṭhi* of Benaras gives a beautiful courtesan a thousand pieces a day and is constantly in her society.

The names of the *seṭṭhis*' children are often attributes indicating wealth and power in their bearers. We can find names such as:

[59] In *Mahāvagga* I, 270 a certain youth, who cured the wife of a *seṭṭhi* in Sāketa, was rewarded by sixteen thousands, a man-slave and a girl-slave and a chariot with horses. The story goes on describing how even the most famous physicians were not able to cure her. Nevertheless, they returned to their homes with plenty of gold (*bahuṃ hiraññaṃ ādāya agamaṃsū'ti*).

Mahādhanakumāra—Jāt. III. 425 (475), Mahādhana—Vetālapañč. I. p. 34, Dhanapati—Sinhās. p. 401. Also the name of Anāthapiṇḍika, the well-known millionaire and supporter of the Buddhist community, which literally means 'Feeder of the poor' indicates great wealth transformed into the Buddhist conception of 'dāna' as the greatest virtue of a laymen in Buddhist community.[60]

We have already made it clear that the meaning of the Sanskrit term *śreṣṭhin* and the Pāli form *seṭṭhi* did not remain the same throughout the historical development, but, in the course of time, diverse very considerably in meaning and usage. We have also followed the growth in the *seṭṭhi's* power with the help of Buddhist literature, especially of the Jātakas.[61] Now it is important to verify its importance and how it evolved in the course of historical development.

Great wealth bestowed various honours on the *seṭṭhi*. He enjoyed a high reputation, especially among those people who needed his help, viz. his money. These were, above all, the king and the citizens—Jāt. V. 535 (382), VI. 542 (135). This function is closely connected with his high position in society and the caste hierarchy; he becomes a (noble) 'citizen'[62]

In Jāt. IV. 497 (376) the daughter of the *seṭṭhi* of Benares seeing a caṇḍāla washes her eyes that have been contaminated by a mere glance at that despised person.

It is a point worth noting that the quotations referring to the high position of the *seṭṭhis* in society and in the caste system are to be found in the last Volumes of the Jātakas, in the rambling stories which can lay no great claim to antiquity in their present form; these were much more altered in the final editing than the simple and shorter stories of the first Volumes.

A similar case is preserved in the *paccuppannavatthu* of the Jāt. I. 83 (364). A friend of Anāthapiṇḍika, the famous *seṭṭhi* of Buddhist

[60] The third Volume of the Jātakas contains stories mainly about very rich and very faithful *seṭṭhis* who generously give away part of their immense wealth: III. 337 (119), 340 (129), 382 (257), 390 (299), 421 (444), i.e. half the places mentioning *seṭṭhis* in this Volume. But it is quite possible that the Editor of this Volume added attributes denoting wealth to some *seṭṭhis* at his own discretion thus giving them the possibility to give away from their great wealth and so fulfil their first duty in this way.

[61] The *seṭṭhi* (in its later Sankrit form *śreṣṭhin*) is a popular person in many of the Sanskrit collections of tales and parables of later origin.

[62] Besides *gahapati* he is called also *negama*—Jāt. VI, 542 (137).

literature, becomes poor (*duggato hutvā*) and cannot make his living. He had been an inseparable friend of Anāthapiṇḍika from his childhood and was educated by the same teacher (*sahapaṃsukīḷito ekācariyass'eva santike uggahitasippo*). When Anāthapiṇḍika is told about his friend's poverty, he takes him into his own house and treats him as an equal. But his friends prevail upon him to turn him away, because he cannot be Anāthapiṇḍika's equal because of his poverty (*na c'esa tayā samāno, duggato durupeto, kiṃ te iminā*). Both friends had been comrades from their childhood, they had been brought up and educated together, and yet they cannot live together now, as one of them has become rich and powerful and the other finds himself in poverty and therefore could not be counted to be his friend's social equal in the society of the time. Wealth and property bestowed power upon the men of old India. '*Mayaṃ pi dve issarā*' says the *seṭṭhi* in Jāt. I. 92 (386) in relation to the *purohita* and his own person; and this sentence is very true as regards ancient India.[63]

The instance of Anāthapiṇḍika's poor friend can be contrasted with another story in Jāt. III. 425 (475) which has quite a different conclusion: Once upon a time when Brahmadatta was reigning in Benares, his son, prince Brahmadatta, and young Mahādhana, son of a *seṭṭhi* of Benares, were comrades and playfellows, and were educated in the same teacher's house. The prince became king at his father's death; and the *seṭṭhi*'s son abode near him'. (*Atite Bārānasiyaṃ Brahmadatte rajjaṃ kārente tassa cu putto Brahmadattakumāro Bārāṇasiseṭṭhino ca putto Mahādhana-ugganhiṃsu. Kumāro pitu accayena rajje patiṭṭhāsi, seṭṭhiputto pi'ssa santike yevāhosi*). Here the situation is essentially different. The king makes friends with a wealthy *seṭṭhi* who might be very helpful to him some day in the future.

All the instances of the Jātakas stressing the wealth, power and favour enjoyed by the *seṭṭhis* in towns, cities and royal courts, are found in those parts of the Jātakas which we can with good reason consider a younger element. No doubt the *seṭṭhi's* influence and power developed and became stabilized with his increasing wealth. Finally, the *seṭṭhi* reaches the highest position among the inhabitants of the State, i.e. he occupies first place among the citizens.

Jāt. VI. 539 (43) contains a description of a great festival held in

[63] About 'combined interests' of the princes, brāhmaṇas and *seṭṭhis* and their 'cooperation' cf. *JRAS* 1901, p. 867.

honour of a mighty king. The seating of the guests at this festival is very interesting" '. . . while the crowd of the king's ministers sat on one side, on another a host of brāhmaṇas, on another the *seṭṭhi* and the others, on another the most beautiful dancing-girls.' (. . . *ekato amaccamaṇḍalaṃ nisīdi ekato brāhmaṇagaṇo ekato seṭṭhiādayo ekato uttamarūpadharā nāṭakitthiyo*). At one side sat the ministers of the king, i.e. the officers of the king who formed the king's advisory council and who held various offices in the administration of the State. On the other side were the brāhmaṇas. No wonder they are named separately. Even the Buddhist records do not deny that the brāhmaṇas had an extraordinary position and that they enjoyed a certain amount of general respect, the reason being partly that their priestly office enforced such respect and partly because, in addition to their priestly office they were the real representatives of culture and education which at that time was completely in their hands. The dancing-girls can be left aside, as they took part only in the musical performance accompanied by songs and dance for the entertainment of the king's guests. All the other citizens present at the festival were headed by the *seṭṭhi* as the most prominent personality in the king's court. This fact is also incompatible with the assertion made by some scholars, especially Mrs Rhys Davids,[64] D.R. Bhandarkar[65] and J. Ch. Jain[66] that the *seṭṭhi* was one of the king's ministers (R. Fick was one of those who contested this assertion).[67] The king was, of course an absolute ruler and even the *seṭṭhi* was subject to his authority.[68]

In *Bṛhatsaṃhitā* 29,10[69] of Varāhamihira (who flourished in the first half of the sixth century of our era) this order is maintained:

[64] *JRAS,* 1901, p. 865. It is notable that Mrs. C.F. Rhys Davids translated the term *seṭṭhi* as 'treasurer', whereas T.W. Rhys Davis opposed to the use of this word and translates 'the best, chief'—*Cambridge History of India*, Vol. I, p. 207.

[65] 'Dekkan of the Śatavāhana Period', *Indian Antiquary*, vol. XLVII, 1991, p. 80.

[66] *Life in Ancient India as depicted in the Jain Canons*, Bombay 1947, p. 60.

[67] *The Social Organisation in North-East India in Buddha's Time*, Calcutta, 1920, p. 257.

[68] It was the case particularly when the *seṭṭhi* wanted to undertake some longer journey, etc.,—Jāt. I. 125 (452).

[69] The *Bṛhatsaṃhitā of Varāhamihira*, ed. by H. Kern, in *Bibliotheca Indica*, 1865.

rājā, mantrin, śreṣṭhin, vipra, purohita, balapati. The evidence is thus supported also by another source.

All the facts so far put forward make it clear that the extent of the *seṭṭhi*'s wealth and influence cannot be explained by the factors we have reviewed. The *seṭṭhi* rendered important services to the king, but he was not one of the royal ministers; consequently he was not an officer of the king and was not paid for his services by the king in the form of a regular salary. Did the king reward the services rendered by the *seṭṭhi* and if so, how?

Here we come to one the main sources of the *seṭṭhi*'s wealth, fame and power in the ancient Indian society of the period we take into consideration. The services of the *seṭṭhis* were sufficiently recompensed by the king. He gave the *seṭṭhi* the revenue from the produce of one or more villages in his kingdom. These revenues were probably high enough, as they represented the main and substantial revenues of the king's treasury.[70] In the Jātakas we find several references to occasions when the king gave someone the revenue of one or more villages (this man was called '*gāmabhojaka*'[71] as a reward for an exceptional feat or as a gift to one of his favourites.[72] In Jāt. VI. 546 (344) we read how the king was pleased with the wise reply of a *seṭṭhi*'s son (i.e. Bodhisatta, of course); '. . . and taking the golden vase filled with scented water, poured the water upon the *seṭṭhi's* hand, saying, 'Enjoy the East Market town as gift from the king.—Let the other *seṭṭhis,'* he went on, 'be sevitors of this.' (*Rājā tussitvā gandhodakapuṇṇaṃ suvaṇṇabhiṃkāraṃ ādāya 'pācīna—gāmaṃ rājabhogena bhuñjā' 'ti seṭṭhissa hatthe udakaṃ pātetvā 'sesaseṭṭhino etass'eva upaṭṭhākā hontū'ti. . .*). Here even the ceremony connected with the donating of such revenues has been preserved. Otherwise whenever *bhogagāma* is spoken about, it is in connection with Anāthapiṇḍika and the story mentions how this famous *mahāseṭṭhi*

70 The burden of these taxes lay mainly on the shoulders of the householders (*gahapatikā*)—Jāt. II. 276 (378), IV. 467 (169). The king's collectors very often extorted the revenues by force—Jāt. II. 240 (240), IV. 478 (224), V. 520 (98).

71 The translation of the Pāli Textbook Society Dictionary 'the village headman' is not correct.

72 Jāt. I. 9 (138), II. 239 (237), II. 283 (403), III. 376 (229), V. 514 (44), VI. 545 (261), VI. 546 (344), 546 (363). He could also reduce the taxes or exempt the village from paying it—Jāt. I. 31 (200), IV. 467 (169).

goes to a village whose revenue belonged to him—Jāt. I. 83 (364), I. 103 (413).

Both cases appear in the *paccuppannavatthus*. The second one is very interesting. The *atītavatthu* of the Jātaka runs as follows: *Atīte Bārāṇasiyaṃ Brahmadatte rajjaṃ kārente Bodhisatto mahāvibhavo seṭṭhi hutvā ekaṃ gāmakaṃ nimantanaṃ bhuñjanatthāya gantvā* . . . But it is said in the *paccuppannavatthu*: *Anāthapiṇḍiko kira bhogagāmaṃ gantvā* . . By the word *nimantana* an invitation from a *seṭṭhi* living in that village or from a village community to a certain festival was meant. Then, later on, when the Jātaka assumed its present appearance by the addition of a frame-story, the idea of the *bhogagāma* of the *seṭṭhis* became so familiar that it was taken over into the *paccuppannavatthu* of that Jātaka to replace the meaning of the word *nimantana* which was clearly understood to mean an invitation.[73]

The revenues formed a considerable part of the *seṭṭhi's* income. It was a great opportunity to increase his wealth. And with the help of this wealth the *seṭṭhi* was able to perform other transactions which yielded him even much greater wealth than any other means previously mentioned. Instances of such transactions can be found in two Jātaka stories, i.e. in the frame-stories (*paccupp*) to two Jātakas in the first and last volume.

Jāt. I. 40 (227) describes Anāthapiṇḍika's charity which 'knew no bounds': 'So much did he expend day after day, that his expense knew no bounds. Moreover, many traders borrowed money from him on their bonds, to the amount of eighteen crores; and the great merchant never called the money in. Furthermore, another eighteen crores of the family property were burried in the river-bank. . .' (Cowell I 100). (. . . *evam divase divase pariccajantassa pan'assa pariccāge pamāṇaṃ n'atthi, bahū vohārūpajīvino pi'ssa hatthato paṇṇe āropetvā aṭṭhārasakoṭisaṃkhaṃ dhanaṃ iṇaṃ gaṇhiṃsu. Te mahāseṭṭhi na āhārapeti. Aññā pan'assa kulasantakā aṭṭhārasakoṭiyo nadītīre nidahitvā ṭhapitā.*[74]

It follows that the *seṭṭhi* lent money and, according to the story quoted, they lent considerable sums. They lent the money to people

[73] Cowell's translation (I. 245): 'a rich merchant, who had been to the village to collect his dues', is based on a misunderstanding due to the *paccuppannavatthu*. It is clear that the terms *bhoga* and *bhuñjana* are quite different in their meanings.

[74] For the continuation of the story cf. Jāt. II. 284 (410).

living by trade—and not only to the traders (*vāṇijā*); the word *vāṇijā* was certainly not used here intentionally. This testifies to the fact that trade could be carried on by any member of the three highest *vaṇṇas* if he owned sufficient means for it. For these transactions money was needed—sometimes large sums. The *seṭṭhi* was the man who had sufficient wealth and therefore was a valuable connection for all those people who wished to make their living by trade and who needed some initial capital or, it may be, had run into debt and sought a way out by changing their way of lving.[75] And the *seṭṭhi* willingly lent him money for which he got in return 'promissory notes' or 'debt sheets' (*iṇa-paṇṇāni*).[76] It seems probable that the *seṭṭhis* lent large sums, notwithstanding the fact that the amount of eighteen crores cannot be taken literally. We can also easily have an idea of their immense profits if we realize how high was the rate of interest in ancient India.[77] And, finally, we learn from the story told above that the *seṭṭhis* enforced the payment of debts very rigorously. The compiler of the Jātaka wanted to show that it was a virtue if Anāthapiṇḍika did not enforce the payment of the debts. We can also find a ready explanation for the friendly behaviour of the kings towards the *seṭṭhis* who were such favourites at the kings' courts. The kings very often needed the financial help of the *seṭṭhis* owing to the expensive life of their courts and to the frequent wars they themselves declared or were forced to wage. It is not necessary to remind the reader of it nearer.

Here the *seṭṭhi* appears in a new function, in the role of a real usurer. We can now call him 'treasurer' and with certain reservations a 'banker', because these terms are convenient enough to denote a man of his wealth, position and influence in the society.

[75] Instances of such a kind are quite numerous. So e.g. Jāt. I, 4 (120) tells about a youth from a family that has gone to the realm of misery (*duggatakulaputta*) who, as soon as he gets sufficient capital, outstrips the other traders (*vāṇijā*) and buys up a whole cargo of great value.

[76] I do not understand why the Pāli Textbook Society Dictionary has the phrase '*paṇṇaṃ āropeti*' with the meaning 'to send a letter' and with reference to this passage. here the word paṇṇa has clearly the meaning of 'bonds'. This meaning is indicated still more distinctly in Jātaka IV. (482) (256) where the debtor says: '. . . *tuṃhākaṃ iṇapaṇṇāni gahetvā āgacchatha, Gaṅgātīre me nihitaṃ kulasantakaṃ dhanaṃ atthi, taṃ vo dassāmīti.*'

[77] About loans and interest in ancient India cf. *JRAS*, 1901, pp. 880–81.

But this usurer was not satisfied with the mere lending out of money at interest. He himself was an entrepreneur, he himself hired out the land and employed people who worked for him and carried out various business transactions. He was a sharp and active businessman of the old days, full of enterprise and a keen desire to extend his property and power; he was the man needed for the business which was only in its beginnings in the realm of India.

One of the last Jātakas, Jāt. VI. 540 (69) preserves a very rare and important confirmation of this assertion. The story is found in the *paccuppannavatthu*: The son of a rich *seṭṭhi* of Sāvatthī goes into homelessness and lives like a monk. When he went away, his parents found themselves in misery: 'His parents also, as time went on, became poor, for those who hired their land or carried on merchandise for them, finding out that there was no son or brother in the family to enforce the payment, seized what they could lay their hands upon and ran away as they pleased, and the servants and labourers in the house seized the gold and coin and made off therewith, so that at the end the two were reduced to an evil plight and had not even an ewer for pouring water; and at last they sold their dwelling, and finding themselves homeless, and in extreme misery, they wandered begging for alms, clothed in rags and carrying potsherds in the hands.' (Cowell VI. 38). (*Mātāpitaro pi'ssa gascchante gacchante kāle duggatā ahesuṃ, ye pi nesaṃ khettaṃ va vāṇijjaṃ va payojesuṃ te imasmiṃ kule putto vā bhātā vā iṇaṃ codetvā gaṇhanto nāma n'atthīti attano attano hatthagataṃ gahetvā yathāruciṃ palāyiṃsu, gehe dāsakammakarādayo pi hiraññasuvaṇṇādīni gahetva palāyiṃsu, aparabhāge dve janā kapaṇā hutvā hatthe udakasecanakaṃ pi alabhitvā gehaṃ vikkiṇitvā agharā hutvā kāruññabhāvappattā pilotikanivāsanā kapālahatthā bhikkhāya cariṃsu.*)

Only in connection with this last phase of the development of the *seṭṭhi* can we understand why the term *seṭṭhi* has been translated until now as 'the head of the board of trade',[78] 'ein Gildemeister,[79] der an der Spitze der Gilde der Grosskaufleute steht,' and the most frequently occurring translation 'the foreman, the head of a guild'.[80] Not one of these translations is correct or accurate. No mention of a guild whose head would be the *seṭṭhi*, can be found in literature, except for the

[78] D.R. Bhandarkar in *Indian Antiquary,* 1919, p. 80.

[79] W. Geiger in *Saṃyutta-Nikāya*, I.B. München-Neubiberg, 1930, p. 140 and many other German scholars.

[80] Pāli Textbook Society Dictionary and almost all the English translators.

case of the *uttarasetthi* who could be a chief of the *setthis* in some of the largest cities.[81]

In vain should we search for any connection of the *setthi* with the guilds (*seṇiyo*) in the Jātakas or in the other parts of the Pāli Canon. The idea stated above is based merely on the evidence of one passage in the Jātakas. The sole instance is when a *setthi* appears in connection with an artisan in the Jāt. IV. 445 (38) (*taṃ divasaṃ ṇeva setthiṃ nissaya vasantassa tuṇṇakārassa. . .*). But it is quite intelligible that the *setthi* had his own tailor who lived under the patronage of his employer for whose house he worked. Mrs Rhys Davids, however, draws a surprising conclusion from this place: 'This is the only passage known to me stating explicitly the connection between guild organisation and the minister commonly called 'treasurer' (*setthi*).[82]

I do not see any reasonable connection between the tailor and a guild organisation following from the passage mentioned above, still less any connection between such an organisation and the *setthi*. The head of the guild was the foreman, the chief (*jetthaka, pamukha*). The supervision over all the guilds was in the hands of the *bhaṇḍāgārika*, who was the Royal Treasurer and the king's officer. There is an interesting reference to the appointment to the office of *bhaṇḍāgārika* in the Jāt. IV. 445 (43): 'Then the king gave him the post of Treasurer, and with it went the judgeship of all the merchant guilds. Before that no such office had existed, but there was this office ever after.' (Cowell IV. 27.) (*. . . ath'assa sabbaseṇīnam vicāraṇārahaṃ bhaṇḍāgārikatthānaṃ nāma adāsi. Pubbe kir'etaṃ ṭhānantaraṃ nāhosi, tato patthāya jātaṃ.*)

It follows that the terms 'foreman, head of a guild' are untenable in future, as they are supported by no clear evidence from the scriptures (leaving aside much later commentators)[83] and that it would be

[81] I pass over the case in which other *setthis* were subjected to one of them by the king—Jāt. VI. 546 (344), because I do not consider it as a proof of the existence of a guild of *setthis*. As far as I know no fixed organisation of traders (*vāṇijā*) having the character of a guild is documented anywhere in the Pāli Canon. It is natural that such an organisation could not develop at a time when commerce was just beginning to unfold and when commercial relations had yet been stabilized.

[82] Notes, *JRAS,* 1901, pp. 865ff.

[83] E.G. the scholiasts in Hemačandra's work *Abhidhānačintāmaṇi* explain: *kule baṇigvṛnde śreṣthatvam asya kulaśreṣṭhī.* Of course, that is already the view of the *setthi* presented in this article.

much safer not to translate the term *seṭṭhi* at all, but leave it as it is. However, it has always to be kept in mind that the content of this term underwent considerable changes with the steady development of commercial relations and of society as a whole.

An index of all the instances in which '*seṭṭhi*' occurs in the Jātaka is appended here. It will be a useful supplement to the Index of Jātakas[84] which takes no note of this term. It will also serve as an aid to the study of the materials concerning the *seṭṭhi*.

	No.	Page	No.	Page	No.	Page
I*	4	120	254	287	544	228g.[86]
1.		122	3. 261	322	546	331
	12	145 p.[85]	274	361		344
	28	191	276	367		364
		193		378		
	40	231	291	431	*Anāthapiṇḍika* occurs in:	
42	242		III.			
	45	248	4. 315	49	I	
	47	252	317	56	1.1	95
	53	269	318	60		105
	54	270	337	119	37	217
	63	295	340	128	40	226
	73	323	344	137 p.	45	248
	78	345 p.		138	47	251
		349	5. 363	196 p.	53	268
	83	365	375	225	83	364
	84	366 p.	6. 382	257	90	377
	90	377 p.	390	299 p.	103	412

contd.

[84] *The Jātaka of Stories of the Buddha's Former Births*, Index volume, Cambridge, 1913.

* Roman figures of the first column refer to the volumes, whereas Arabic figures denote the Nipātas.

[85] p. = *pacuppannavatthu.*

[86] g. = *gāthās*

No.	Page	No.	Page	No.	Page
92	384	395	314	121	441
93	388	7.415	406	II.	
103	412 p.	8.421	444	3.254	286
	413	425	475	269	347
109	424	IV.		284	410
118	432 p.	10.439	1	291	431
125	451	445	37	III.	
127	458	450	62	4.337	119
131	466	12.467	169	340	128
137	478	13.481	249	346	141
148	501 p.	482	255	5.363	196
		15.497	376	6.382	257
II.		V.		8.419	435
2.164	50	18.527	210	9.434	520
171	64	21.535	382	IV.	
232	224 p.	VI.		12.465	144
	225	22.539	43	472	188
236	232	540	69 p.	13.479	228
238	236	542	135		229

Chapter Six

Coastal and Overseas Trade in Pre-Gupta Vaṅga and Kalinga*

B.N. MUKHERJEE

I

The country of Vaṅga included in the early centuries of the Christian Era, the areas now in the districts of 24 Parganas (north and south), Hooghly, Howrah and Midnapore and parts of Burdwan (and also of Birbhum, Bankura and Nadia). It also incorporated the coastal region of Bangladesh upto the mouth of the Padma (or rather of the joint streams of the Padma, Brahmaputra, Meghna and Jamuna).[1] This zone was referred to as the kingdom of the Gangaridai or Ganges in Greek and Latin texts[2] and as Hung-chih (Giwang-tsie) and Han-yüeh (Xan-gywat) in Chinese treatises.[3] Rāḍha (Suhma), occupying a part

* *Vinayatoshini*, Benoytosh Centenary Volume, (ed.), Shyamalkanti Chakravarti, Calcutta, 1996, pp. 181–92.

1 B.N. Mukherjee, *Post-Gupta Coinages of Bengal*, Calcutta, 1989, p. 1, B.N. Mukherjee, *Kharoshṭī and Kharoshṭī-Brāhmī Inscriptions in West Bengal (India)*, Calcutta, 1990, Appendix III ('The Earliest Limits of Vaṅga).

2 *Periplus tes Erythras Thalasses*, sec. 63, Pliny, *Naturalis Historia*, VI, 2, 65; Ptolemy, *Geographike Huphegesis*, VII, 1.81.

3 *Ch'ien Han-shu* (T'ung-wen-shu-chu edition), ch. 28 B, pp. 32 a-b; *Wei-Lüeh* (*T'oung Pao,s.* II, vol: VI 1905, p. 519); B. Karlgren, *Analytic Dictionary of Chinese and Sino-Japanese*, Paris, 1923, nos. 164, 389 and 1348; B. Karlgren, *Grammata Serica Recensa*, Goteborg, 1964, no. 864a; B.N. Mukherjee, 'The Territory of the Gangaridae,' *Indian Journal of Landscape Systems and Ecological Studies*, vol. X, no. 2, 1987, pp. 65f; B.N. Mukherjee, 'Chinese Ideas about the Geographical Connotation of the Name Shen-tu,' *East and West*, vol. 38, 1988, p. 302.

of the area to the west of the Bhagirathi, was fully or partly within ancient Vaṅga[4], whose limits were different from Vaṅga of the Pāla-Sena age (from about the middle of the eighth to about the beginning of the thirteenth century) or of still later periods.[5]

Various indigenous and non-indigenous sources, including the recently discovered inscriptions in Kharoshṭī and in a mixed script including Kharoshṭī and Brāhmī letters,[6] furnished valuable data on the trade of Vaṅga in the early centuries of the Christian Era. The inscriptions in Kharoshṭī and Kharoshṭī-Brāhmī (mentioned as *Vimiśrita-lipi* or mixed script in the *Lalitavistara*)[7] have been found mainly in lower West Bengal. So far these have been noticed on plaques, seals, pots and rock.[8]

Agriculture seems to have been the mainstay of economic life of the people of Vaṅga, which had fertile alluvial areas along the Ganges (Bhagirathi) and its branches (Yamuna and Sarasvati), where water (from rain and rivers) was available for cultivation. Paddy and perhaps also cotton were among the chief agricultural produces. Weaving of cotton cloth and production of clay pots, dishes, utensils and objects of art may be mentioned. Among other crafts and industries were fashioning of jewellery (including of lead, stone) sculpting, masonry, manufacture of transports (cart, boat, ships, etc.), structure-building, etc. There must have been trade in surplus agricultural products (rice, etc.) and other saleable commodities including pottery.[9]

4 A. Bhattacharyya, *Historical Geography of Ancient and Early Mediaeval Bengal*, Calcutta, 1977, p. 45f. In the Pāla-Sena age Rādha (North and South) included at least parts of the Birbhum, Burdwan and Hooghly and perhaps of Murshidabad districts (ibid., pp. 50–51). All these districts could have been at least partly in pre-Gupta Vaṅga.

5 Ibid., pp. 56f.

6 B.N. Mukherjee, 'Decipherment of the Kharoshṭī-Brāhmī Script', *Monthly Bulletin, The Asiatic Society*, Calcutta, August, 1989, pp. 1–5. 'Discovery of Kharoshṭī Inscriptions in West Bengal,' *The Quarterly Review of Historical Studies*, vol. XXIX, no. 2, 1989–90, p. 6f, 'Kharoshṭī Inscriptions in Eastern India-New Discoveries', *Journal of Central Asia*, Vol. XIII, no. 1, July, 1990, p. 19f.

7 *Lalitavistara*, 10th Adhyaya, P.L. Vaidya (editor), *Lalitavistara*. Darbhanga, 1958, p. 88.

8 See also the article in the *Bulletin of the School of Historical and Cultural Studies*, vol. II, no. 1.

9 *The Arthaśāstra* refers to *dukūla* (very fine cloth made of the inner bark of

Another important field of industry and trade could have been copper-mining, working in metal and selling of items made of copper. We have evidence of working in the Rakha mines of the Singbhum district (situated close to the limits of ancient Vaṅga) during the period concerned.[10]

Gold of which a mine is located by the author of *Periplous tes Erythras Thalasses* in the Ganges (Vaṅga) country[11] could have been actually imported from outside or procured by washing river sands in or near the territory concerned.

Vaṅga was connected with other parts of India with land and riverine routes.[12] These could have been used for inter-regional trade. For example, we refer to Gangetic nard (spikenard) and malabathrum in the list of items of export of the Ganges (Vaṅga) country as furnished by the *Periplus*.[13] These were products of the Himalayan region and so they were imported in Vaṅga for local use and also for export.

Commercial items could have been exported to other countries through two important ports known as Tamralipti (Tamalites) and Gaṅgā (Ganges).[14] The first was on the Sarasvatī branch of the Ganges (Bhāgīrathī) and in the locality of Tamluk in the Midnapore district.[15] The second was perhaps in the neighbourhood of Deganga in the

---

a plant) and *kārpāsika* (cloth made of cotton) produced in Vaṅga (II, 11). The elephant and its tusk (*Mahābharata,* Sabhāparvan, L II, 20–21) and rhinoceros (*Chien Han-shu*), ch. 28.1.32 b could have been counted among the articles of commerce. For reference to the sources of information see B.N. Mukherjee, *Kharoshtī and Kharoshtī-Brāhmī Inscriptions in West Bengal* (*India*). Calcutta 1990, chaps I and II (or *Indian Museum Bulletin,* vol. XXV, 1990, the first two chapters of our article).

[10] B.N. Mukherjee and P.K. D. Lee, *Technology of Indian Coinage,* Calcutta, 1988, p. 73.

[11] *Periplus tes Erythras Thalasses*, sec. 63.

[12] Strabo, *Geographikon,* XV, I, II: Ptolemy, *Geographike Huphegesis,* VII, 1, 73; *Wei-lüeh* (T'oung Pao, s. II, Vol. VI, 1905, p. 520); *Jātaka* (edited by E.B. Cowell), vol. IV, Cambridge, 1901, no. 442, p. 10; *Mahāvaṁsa,* XIX, 6 and 23; *Journal of the Asiatic Society,* Calcutta, 1974, pp. 92f.

[13] *Periplus,* sec. 63.

[14] Ibid., *Fo-Kuo chi, ch.* XXXVIII, Ptolemy, *op.cit.*, VII, 1, 73.

[15] A. Ray and S. Mukherjee (eds.), *History and Archaeology, A Dialogue between Historians and Archaeologists,* New Delhi, 1990, pp. 245–47.

Chandraketugarh area in the district of 24 Parganas (North) and on the Yamuna branch of the Ganges (Bhagirathi).[16] There is enough data suggesting the territory's maritime trade relations with the peninsular and western India, Srilanka and parts of South-East Asia.[17] There might have been indirect trade with China.[18] Goods of the region were also brought to south India for their onward transmission to the Roman empire, with which Vaṅga had no direct commercial connection.[19]

In the first century AD, the *Periplus* enumerated malabathrum, Gangetic nard (spikenard) and very fine quality muslins, called Gangetic, as items of export of the Ganges (Vaṅga) country.[20] In an earlier age (in *c.* first century BC or very early first century AD) Huang-chih (=Ganges=Vaṅga) country might have exported pearls (after importing them maybe) and opaque glass and imported gold and silk.[21]

The above data are sufficient to prove that there was enough scope for industrialists and traders to conduct a thriving business in Vaṅga during the early centuries of the Christian Era. People of indigenous origin must have naturally participated in the commercial transactions in the region concerned. The participation of outsiders is also suggested in the light of the stories of the outside region connecting wealthy merchants with Tāmralipta[22] and the epigraphic evidence

[16] See above n. 9.

[17] *Milindapañho*, VI, 21, 360, *Mahāniddesa*, 1, 15, 174, (*Etude Asiatique*, vol. II, Paris, 1925, pp. 1–55; *Periplus*, sec. 60; *Ch'ien Han-shu*, ch. 28B, pp. 32 a–b, *Fo-Kuo'chi*, ch. XXXVII; etc.

[18] Ch'ien han-shu, ch. 28 B, pp. 32 a–b, *Journal of the Malayan Branch of the Royal Asiatic Society*, Kualalampur, vol. XXXI, pt. 2, pp. 19–20. See also above n. 3.

[19] *Periplus*, sec. 60. It does not refer to imports (from the Roman empire into the Ganges country) though it enumerates its articles of export. It is interesting to note that Ptolemy noted the names of Tamalites and Gange metropolis (VII, 1, 73 and 79), but did not refer to either of them as a port or emporium. To Ptolemy an 'emporium' was an Oriental market-town in the commerce of which Roman sailors or merchants were interested (B.N. Mukherjee, *Economic Factors in Kushāna History*, Calcutta, 1970, pp. 47–48). The lack of discovery of Roman coins from coastal West Bengal and Bangladesh also indicate absence of any direct contact.

[20] *Periplus*, sec. 63.

[21] *Chien Han-shu*, ch. 28 B, p. 32 a–b. See also above n. 9.

[22] Somadeva, *Kathāsaritsāgara*, Chapters XIII, XVIII, XXXVI, LXXXI, and

about acquistion of vast wealth in that city by three merchants from far-off Ayodhya (in U.P.).[23] No doubt the relevant epigraphic evidence and the stories in their present forms are of a period much later than the pre-Gupta age.[24] But the relevant legends in the *Kathāsaritsāgara* are based on Guṇāḍhya's *Bṛihatkathā* of *c*. second century AD.[25]

The hypothesis about the presence of outside enterprisers in pre-Gupta Vaṅga is further strengthened by the evidence of the newly-discovered inscriptions referred to above.

These inscriptions, noticeable on pots, plaques and seals, bear: (i) Kharoshṭī inscriptions, or (ii) separate legends in Kharoshṭī and Brāhmī, or (iii) inscriptions consisting of Brāhmī and Kharoshṭī letters. The inscriptions in Kharoshṭī and in the Mixed script (Kharoshṭī-Brāhmī) are palaeographically datable to a period from the second half of the first century AD to the first quarter of the fifth century AD. Their language is north-western Prakrit, which had been the vernacular of the Kharoshṭī-using zone in the north-west. Obviously, a community or communities from the north-west settled in lower West Bengal in the early centuries of the Christian Era. Their main settlements were in the areas of Chandraketugarh and Tamluk. While in the second locality was the famous port of Tāmralipti, the first most probably included the emporium of Gaṅgā. The people from the north-west were apparently interested in trade. They were influential and numerically strong enough to retain their script and language. When (surely some time after their initial migration) they learnt Brāhmī, a mixed script was evolved to write the North-western Prakrit which was distinct from local Prakrit, written exclusively in Brāhmī.[26]

The majority of the inscriptions in Kharoshṭī and Kharoshṭī-Brāhmī are on terracotta seals. From the point of view of the purpose of issue

---

XCIII. Chapter (*taraṅga*) 36 refers to a merchant who went from Tāmralipti to the island of Ratnakūta by sea. See in this connection, N.M. Penzar, *The Ocean of Story* (being C.H. Twney's *Translation of Somadeva's Kathāsaritsāgara),* London, vol. I, p. 153; Vol II, p. 71; Vol. VI, p. 209, Vol. VII, p. 78. Somadeva flourished in the eleventh century AD.

[23] *Epigraphia India,* vol. I, p. 345. The relevant inscription, on a rock at Dudhpani Ghat (Bihar), is datable to the eight century AD.

[24] See above ns. 22 and 23.

[25] M. Winternitz, *History of Indian Literature,* vol. III, Pt. 1, tr. by S. Joshi, Delhi, 1963, pp. 37 and 352f.

[26] See above n. 6.

these objects can be taken as: (a) personal badges, (b) royal and/ or administrative seals, (c) traders' identification tickets, (d) religious tokens (issued on the occasions of performance of religious rites), (e) seals of business communities, (f) charms, (g) items of fine arts displaying pictures and descriptive labels, etc.[27]

These documents throw new light on the political, social, economic, religious and cultural history of lower West Bengal from the late first to the early fifth century AD.[28] Thus their evidence is relevant to our study of pre-Gupta Vaṅga.[29]

The documents reveal that people from the north-west came as traders initially. They later became owners of vast agricultural lands, large-scale traders in corn and horses, and even rulers of the land, at least in the territory now included in the district of 24 Parganas (north).[30] One of the inscriptions in the Mixed script on a seal refers to a person called Karachhugma (or Karaphagma) as *Koḍihālika*, (i.e. 'One who has a crore of plough-men'). Apparently he employed a large number of peasants to cultivate his vast land.[31] Another inscription on a seal, displaying a ship referes to a Trapyaga class of ship owned by a 'powerful' family.[32] Thus a class of people from the north-west became wealthy and powerful in Vaṅga through commercial transactions.

The rich traders exported grain to outside areas and foreign countries. Seals displaying ocean going vessels bear inscriptions referring to journeys in different directions.[33] Among the items of trade were corn and horses. The horses were brought from Central Asia and through the north-west to Vaṅga and exported from there to foreign countries, including South-East Asia.[34]

The contact between Tāmralipti (of the Vaṅga country) and South-East Asia is suggested by the combined evidence of a passage in the

[27] Ibid.

[28] Ibid., See also the article in the *Indian Museum Bulletin,* Calcutta, vol. XXV, 1990.

[29] See above ns. 6.

[30] See above ns. 6 and 28.

[31] Ibid. This seal is now in the Balanda Museum, Hadoa (24 Parganas North).

[32] See above n. 28. This seal is now included in the collection of the Directorate of Archaeology, Government of West Bengal. Its accession no. is CKG 180 (T 687).

[33] See above n. 6.

[34] See above ns. 6 and 28.

Liang-shu and a statement of K'ang T'ai. According to the *Liang-shu*, during the epoch of the Wu dynasty in China (AD 220–280) a king of Fu-nan (Cambodia) sent an envoy called Su-Wu to T'ien-chu (India). He first went from Fu-nan to the port of Chu-li (or T'ou-chu-li),[35] situated probably on the western coast of a portion of the Malay peninsula now controlled by Thailand.[36] From there by a sea-voyage directly to the north-west Su-Wu reached the mouth of the river of T'ien-chu. He returned with four horses of the Yüeh-chih country.[37] A statement by K'ang T'ai in his *Fu-nan-Chuan* (as known from a quotation in the *Shui Ching Chu*) identifies the river of T'ien-chu with the Ganges and locates its mouth in the territory of Tan-mei[38] or Tamra, i.e Tāmralipti).[39] Hence Tāmralipti must have been the port used by Su-Wu in taking the horses of the Yüeh-chih country to South-East Asia.

The horses of the Yüeh-chih country must have been the Central Asian animals of the Ta-yüan or Ferghana region.[40] Such steeds were sold to the merchants of the territory of the Yüeh-chih or Kushāṇas and were brought to the north-western section of the Indian subcontinent through *inter alia* the route from Central Asia and via the Pamirs,

35 *Liang-shu*, ch. 54, f. 22b; Ma Tuan-lin, *Wen hsien t'ung K'ao*, ch. 328; *Kou-hin-tou-chou*, Notice on India; S. Levi, 'Deux peuples méconnus,' *Melanges Charlez des harlez*, pp. 22–23, *Journal of the Asiatic Society of Bengal,* 1837, vol. VI, pt. I, p. 64.

36 It is mentioned as Takkola in the *Milindapañho* (VI, 21, 360) and *Mahāniddesa* and as Takola emporion by Ptolemy (VII, 2, 5)(S. Lévi, 'Ptolémée, le *Niddese* et la *Brihatkathā*', *'Étude Asiatique,* vol. II, Paris, 1925, pp. 3–19). It appears from the Sui-shu that the kingdom of Chü-li bordered on the Gulf of Siam, and the *Liang-shu* indicates that the port of Chü-li (i.e. Takola) was on the Western coast from where a ship could go straight to T'ien-chu (B. Wheatley, *The Golden Khersonese*, Glasgow, etc., 1961, pp. 22–24 and 268–72). Takola may have been modern Takuapa or a site on an island off the mouth of the Tukuapa river (Pelliot, 'Le Fou-nan,' *Bulletin de lÉcole Francaies d'Extreme-Orient*, vol. III, 1903, p. 260, H.C. Q. Wales, *Towards Angkr,* London, 1937, p. 47).

37 See above n. 35.

38 *Shui Ching Chu*, ch. I; L. Petech, *Northern India According to the Shui Ching Chu*, Roma, 1950, p. 53.

39 L. Petech, *op. cit*, pp. 52–55.

40 *Shih-Chi*,(Scu-pu-pei-yao edition), ch. 110, p. 60; ch. 123, B.N. Mukherjee, *Economic Factors in Kushāṇa History*, pp. 28 and 42–43 (in 11).

Hunza Gilgit, Chilas, Dasu, Mansehra and Abottabad to Taxila.[41] Numerous figures of horses do appear on the rocks in the Chilas area.[42] The Yüeh-chih merchants, in their turn, made them trained and available at the markets in India. Four of such animals received by Su-wu were brought to Fu-nan by a sea voyage starting from Tāmralipti.[43]

But Su-wu was not the only person responsible for importing Yüeh-chih horses into South-East Asia. We can refer to some information of K'ang T'ai, apparently collected during his mission as an envoy of a Wu emperor of China to Fu-nan in *c.* AD 245–250 and now known from a statement in the *Tai-P'ing Yu-lan.* It states that 'the Yüeh-chih merchants are continually importing them (horses) to the Ko-ying country by sea (on ship). The king buys them all. If one (of the horses) is dead during the voyage and has to be helped by its mane when it is shown to the king, the latter buys it at half-price'.[44] Ko-ying or Chia-ying has been located by P. Felliot in the littoral Malay peninsula,[45] and by O.W. Wolters on the east of Sumatra.[46] The memory of the activities of the Yüeh-chih horse dealers in South-East Asia is probably perpetuated in the representations of two personages clad in the Yüeh-chih dress (?) along with a horse in an engraving on a drum found in the island of Sangeang off the coast of Sumbawa (of the lesser Sunda islands to the east of Java) and dated to the second or third century AD.[47]

The term Yüeh-chih could have been well applied to the people hailing from the core area of the Kushāṇa (Yüeh-chih or Tokkarian)

[41] A.H. Dani, *Human Records on Karakoram Highway,* Islamabad, 1983, p. 76 and map no. 4.

[42] A.H. Dani, *Chilas—The City of Nanga Parvat (Dyamar),* Islamabad, 1983, illustrations numbered 72, 73, 78, 89, 93, 99, 132, etc.

[43] The kingdom in which Su-Wu received the horses of the Yüeh-chih country was ruled by a king with the title *Muruṇḍa* and was situated probably in the area of North Bihar (B.N. Mukherjee, *The Disintegration of the Kushāṇa Empire,* Banaras, 1976, pp. 32–35).

[44] K'ang Tai's *Wu Shih wai Kuo chuan*, quoted in the *T'ai-ping Yu-lan,* ch. 359: *Étude Asiatiques.* vol. II, pp. 248–50.

[45] *Étude Asiatiques*, vol II, p. 250.

[46] O.W. Wolters, *Early Indonesian Commerce, A Study of the Origin of Śrīvijaya,* New York, 1967, pp. 59–60.

[47] *India Antique* (*A Volume of Oriental Studies, Presented by his Friends and Pupils to Philappe Vogel C.I.E.*), Leiden, 1947, pp. 107, 171–72 and 176; pl. XIV, f.

empire with or without having any ethnic connection with the Yüeh-chih.[48] A settlement of such people in South-East Asia is suggested by evidence of Ptolemy, who locates a place called Thagora on the Great Gulf, identifiable with the Gulf of Thailand, and somewhere above the promontory on the Gulf (present-day Nui Bai-Bung).[49] Thagora, apparently a colony of the Thagorian or Tokharian people,[50] should have been at or near Oc-eo, which has yielded *inter alia* a seal matrix in tin bearing an inscription in Kharoshṭī-Brāhmī. Another Kharoshṭī-Brāhmī inscription on a seal was found in the area of U-Thong in Thailand.[52] All these localities were in ancient Fu-nan, whose contact with Vaṅga through the medium of the Yüeh-chih merchants is proved by the discoveries in the territory of the former country of the above-noted inscriptions written in the mixed script, which had been evolved in the latter territory. It appears that Central Asian horses were brought by the merchants hailing from the north-western section of the Indian subcontinent (known popularly as the Yüeh-chih territory) to their settlements in Vaṅga and thence exported to South-East Asia, including Fu-nan (where they had their own colony).

The above-quoted statement of K'ang-Tai, which humorously sets a price even on a horse which had died while being transported to Ko-ying, underlines the importance of this trade in horses to South-East Asia. This trade also became important to the Kingdom of Wu (*c.* AD 222–280), one of three kingdoms emerging from the ruins of the Later Han empire.[54] The Wu territory, situated on the coast of *San-Kuo Chih* clearly indicated that Wei envoys did not agree to supply horses in exchange of horses by Wu envoys who depended on their willingness to accept in exchange luxury articles offered by the (merchants of) the Wu kingdom.[55] This trade was apparently conducted

[48] B.N. Mukherjee, *The Kushāṇa Genealogy,* Calcutta, 1967, p. 22.

[49] Ptolemy, *op. cit.*, VII, 2, 7; *Monthly Bulletin, The Asiatic Society*, June 1990, pp. 3–4.

[50] *Journal of the Asiatic Society,* 1974, p. 143.

[51] *Monthly Bulletin, The Asiatic Society*, June 1990, pp. 1f.

[52] Ibid., December, 1990, pp. 1–2.

[53] W. Eberhard, *A History of China, from the Earliest Times to the Present Day,* 2nd edition, London, 1947, pp. 107f.

[54] Wang Gangwu, 'The Nan Hai Trade,' *Journal of the Malayan Branch of the Royal Asiatic Society*, vol. XXXI, pt. II, pp. 31f.

[55] *San-kuo-chih* (Wu), 2 f. 19b.

more at a diplomatic than at a regular commercial level. So for horses, which must have been in great demand for communication and warfare, the Wu court turned to Fu-nan (Cambodia),[56] which then controlled also parts of the Malay peninsula and the South-East Asian trade on various items, including horses.[57] Until AD 589 the independent states of South China resorted to maritime trade connected with South-East Asia for getting 'Western products' whose supply through overland routes in Central Asia and parts of China was impeded.[58] Fu-nan's pre-eminence in this trade declined in the fourth century AD.[59] Though the trade continued with the emergence of other commercial areas (like Yeh-p' o-ti or Java-Sumatra and Lin-yi in South Vietnam) by the early fifth century AD[60] and the regaining of importance by Fu-nan,[61] the source of supply of Central Asian horses for maritime trade might have been threatened by the turmoil caused in that area by the Juan-juan tribe from about the middle of the fourth century AD and by the Hepthalite Huns from the first quarter of the next century AD.[62] Gradually, Persian horses became well known in maritime trade.[63]

II

Vaṅga's participation in South-East Asian trade brings in the question of the role of Kalinga in this maritime trade in the pre-Gupta age, since the latter territory on coastal Orissa (from about the border

[56] See above ns. 35 and 44.

[57] See above n. 54.

[58] *Journal of the Malayan Branch of the Royal Asiatic Society,* vol. XXXI, pt. II, p. 86.

[59] Ibid., p. 42.

[60] Ibid., pp. 43–52.

[61] Ibid., p. 52; K.S. Latourrette, *The Chinese—Their History and Culture,* 3rd edition, New York, 1960, p. 159.

[62] W. Samolin, *East Turkestan to the Twelfth Century,* The Hague, 1964, p. 53; P. Sykes, *A History of Persia,* 3rd edition, London, 1963, p. 434f.

[63] Cosmas Indikopleustes noticed sometime in the first half of the sixth century AD that Sielediva (Siṁhaladvīpa or Sri Lanka), which had maritime trade contacts with *inter alia* different parts of India, China and Persia, used to receive horses from the last-noted country, *Topographia Christiana,* book XI; J.W. McCrindle, *Ancient India as Described in Classical Literature,* Westminster, 1901, pp. 162–65.

of West Bengal to the Ganjam area and at times upto the Godavari) was contiguous to the former area.[64] Here is an indication that by about the first century AD Kalinga was already a fairly important zone of commerce. At least a passage in the Hathigumpha inscription of about the second half of the first century BC probably indicates that Khāravela, the king of Kalinga, 'caused the procurement of pearls, precious stones and jewels from the Pāṇḍya king.[65] Since the territory of the Pāṇḍyas was far to the south of Kalinga and never experienced any political or military confrontation with the latter the contact could have been commercial. The *Arthaśāstra* refers to the pearls from Pāṇḍyakavāṭa[66] (i.e. the gateway to the Pāṇḍya country), by which expression either the Palk strait or the Gulf of Manar could have been denoted. The early Pāṇḍya country could have at different times been included as the coast of either or both of them. The author of the *Periplus* actually wrote in the first century AD about pearl-fisheries near the coast of the Pandian kingdom.[67] Hence we cannot deny the feasibility of a hypothesis of coastal trade between Kalinga and the Pāṇḍya country.

Our idea of the commercial products of Kalinga in the early centuries of the Christian Era is very vague. The excavations at Sisupalgarh have yielded items of daily necessities (including pottery and iron objects) and ornaments which could have been produced locally.[68] The Bhadrak inscription of Gana records the donation of three idols and some plots of (agricultural) land and thereby indicates sculpting and tilling as the vocations of some section of

[64] The absence of the R.E. XIII of Aśoka, dealing *inter alia* with his bloody war in Kalinga, from his epigraphs at Dhauli (in the Purī district) and Jaugada (in the Ganjam district), indicated that these localities were in Kalinga, where the king did not naturally want to record his atrocities against the people of the region. The *Mahābhāratā* alludes to the extension of Kaliṅga after, i.e. to the south-east of the Vaitaraṇī (to be placed in the Midnapore district) and up to the Godavari (*Mahābhāratā,* Vanaparvan, 114 and 117). In this connection, see D.N. Das, *The Early History of Kalinga,* Calcutta, 1977, pp. 5–7.

[65] D.C. Sircar, *Select Inscriptions Bearing on Indian History and Civilization,* Vol. I, 2nd edition, Calcutta, 1965, p. 217.

[66] Kauṭilya, *Arthaśāstra,* II, 11.

[67] *Periplus,* sec. 59.

[68] McCrindle, *Ancient India*, no. 5, pp. 78f.

people.[69] The results of the excavations conducted at Sisupalgarh and also the evidence of the Hathigumpha inscription suggest the existence of fairly developed urban settlements and economy which would presuppose the existence of at least inland commerce.[70]

Of the natural articles of commerce we can refer to the elephant[71] and the related item called ivory.[72] In the first century AD the author of the *Periplus* heard of the ivory of Desarene[73] (Daśārna), by which he denoted coastal Orissa, i.e. Kalinga of the period concerned. Kalinga's ivory must have acquired an inter-regional fame. Among other saleable natural products were coconut and betel (leaf of *Piper betle*).[74]

It should, however, be noted that Kalinga does not figure in the list of areas touched by the maritime routes described in the *Mahāniddesa*,[75] which was composed by *c.* second century AD if not in a much earlier age.[76] The same is the case in the record of the sea-voyages of successful sailors to different areas cited in the *Milindapañho*,[77] datable to *c.* first or second century AD.[78] Vaṅga, however, appears in both the lists.[79] It seems that up to this period Kalinga did not acquire importance in overseas trade, though it might have practised coastal trade with other parts of India.

In this connection, we may draw the attention of scholars to the recent excavations conducted by Sri Debraj Pradhan, the registering officer of the Archaeological Department of Orissa at Manikpatna (in the southern-most section of Puri district). Situated on the inner side of the bank of the Chilka, it is a natural site for a harbour. Numerous artificial mounds at the site betray its potentiality as an inhabited site in earlier times.

[69] *Epigraphia India*, vol. XIX, p. 169; *Indian Historical Quarterly,* vol. XXXV, p. 327.

[70] D.C. Sircar, *op. cit.*, p. 214; *Ancient India*, no. 5, pp. 62f.

[71] *Arthaśāstra,* II, 2; *Mahābhāratā*, Sabhāparvan, L (or L II), 18–21.

[72] *Mahābhāratā*, Sabhāparvan, L (or L II), 18–21.

[73] *Periplus,* sec. 62.

[74] Kālidasa, *Raghuvaṁśa*, IV, 42.

[75] *Mahāniddesa*, 1, 15, 174.

[76] M. Winternitz, *A History of Indian Literature*, vol. II (translated by S. Ketkar and H. Kohn), Calcutta, 1933, p. 156.

[77] *Milindapañho*, VI, 21, 360.

[78] M. Winternitz, *op. cit.*, p. 175.

[79] See above ns. 75 and 77.

Archaeological excavation in one of the mounds has yielded pots or potsherds at one of the levels datable to *c.* first–second century AD. Several of these are comparable with similar objects found in the Chandraketugarh and Tamluk areas. The most interesting object is a potsherd of black colour bearing a fragmentary Kharoshṭī inscription of *c.* second century AD.[80] These data indicate contact between a Kharoshṭī-using area in Vaṅga and the port on the Chilka Lake. It is not impossible, as it has already been suggested by Prof. K.S. Behara, that Manikpatna can be considered as the site of the city of Paloura.[81]

Ptolemy located Paloura on the coast of the territory on the Gangetic Gulf, situated somewhere above Maisoka or the Krishna-Guntur region.[82] On the coast of the country on the Gangetic Gulf was *inter alia* the mouth of the river called Manda (identifiable with the Mahānadī)[83] and somewhere above it a place called Minnagara or Minagara.[84] Apparently to its east or north-east were *inter alia* the five mouths of the Ganges and a city called Paloura on or immediately to the east of the first mouth known as Kambouson.[85] In

[80] The inscription is in two lines, which can be read as follows:
L.1... (Da) *saśatra de*(va)
L.2... *Kshida*
I am grateful to Sri Pradhan for allowing me to examine this potsherd and other materials unearthed at Manikpatna. Another potsherd bearing *Kharoshṭī* letters has been unearthed at Palora (Paloura of Ptolemy, VII, 1, 16?).

[81] Ptolemy, *op. cit.*, VII, 1, 15.

[82] Ibid., VII, 1, 15, and 93. The river Maisolas in Maisolia is identified with the Krishna. Maisolia also included Kontakassyla (modern Ghantasal near Masulipatam in the Krishna district), Koddoura (modern Guduru near Masulipatam in the Krishna district) and Alosygni (which was apparently near Koddoura or Guduru and so in or near the locality of Masulipatam). Maisolia was also contiguous to the territory of the Salakenoi with their capital at Benagouron (VII, 1, 79), identified with ancient Veṅgīpura and modern Pedda Vegi near Ellore or Eluru. Thus, Maisolia lay mainly to the north of the Krishna. But since the country of the Arouarnoi (Aruvanāḍu) lay roughly between the two Pennar rivers or the Palar and the southern Pennar river (*Bulletin of the School of Oriental and African Studies,* vol. XIII, 1949–51, p. 152), as least some areas to the south of the Krishna (in the Guntur district) could have been within its limits.

[83] Ptolemy, *op. cit.*, VII, 1, 16.

[84] Ibid. VII, 1, 17.

[85] Ibid.

another section of his treatise, Ptolemy included the mouth of the Ganges in the territory of the Gangaridai which had its capital at Gaṅgā.[86] As we have shown elsewhere, the area of the Gangaridai, which included coastal West Bengal and Bangladesh (up to the mouth of the Padma), was the same as the kingdom of the Ganges (described in the *Periplus*) and the ancient Vaṅga country.[87]

It appears that Ptolemy included coastal Orissa (ancient Kalinga) and coastal Bengal (ancient Vaṅga) in one single zone on the Gangetic Gulf, the name of which is a precursor of that of the Bay of Bengal. Apparently to Ptolemy or rather to his sources of information coastal Orissa and littoral Bengal were close enough to each other to be included in one single zone.[88]

One of the reasons for such a relation could have been economic. We have already suggested the connection of the Kharoshṭī-using traders settled in Vaṅga with the port at Manikpatna, identifiable with Paloura. The existence of another Paloura on or near the western-most mouth of the Ganges may allude to contacts between the localities on coastal West Bengal and lower littoral Orissa.

In this connection we can also discuss the importance of the name of Minnagara (or Minagara) located by Ptolemy on coastal Orissa and somewhere to the north (or north-east) of the mouth of the Mahānadī. The term *mīna* is known to have occurred in the names of a few areas dominated by the Śakas or Scythians. The *Stathmoi Parthikoi* locates Minopolis (or the city of Min) in Sakastana (modern Seistan in Afghanistan) 'of the Scythian Sakas'.[89] The capital of Scythia (in the lower Indus country) is placed at Minnagar in the *Periplus*.[90] The same text refers to the metropolis of the Kingdom of Manbanos (or the Scytho-Parthian ruler Nahapāna) as Minnagara.[91] A locality named Binagara (which may be a misreading for Minagara=Minagara) is located in Ptolemy's treatise as being in Indo-Scythia, which incorporated *inter alia* parts of the Indus Valley, Kutch and Kathiawar.[92]

[86] Ibid., VII, I, 81.
[87] See above ns. 3 and 4.
[88] The territories of the Gangaridai and Calingae were indicated as contiguous by Pliny (*Naturalis Historia,* VI, 21, 65).
[89] Isidore of Charax, (*Stathmoi Parthikoi,* 18).
[90] *Periplus,* sec. 38.
[91] Ibid. sec. 41.
[92] Ptolemy, *op. cit.*, VII, I, 55–61.

These data suggest a Śaka (or Scythic) connection of the city of Minnagara in coastal Orissa. It was indeed not impossible for some people of Śaka affiliation to settle in the locality concerned.[93] In the light of the available evidence we may presume that the group concerned initially migrated from the north-west to Vaṅga and later a section of it came to the place in question.

The territory of Vaṅga to Kaliṅga did not have any direct commercial contact with the Roman empire during the best period of Indo-Roman trade (see also above section I), though their items of trade might have reached the merchants of the Roman empire through intermediaries.[94] As we have noted elsewhere, the imitations of the rouletted ware and amphorae unearthed in the zone concerned might have been inspired at least by the imports from the north-west, which had experienced strong Hellenistic influence and from where a group (or groups) of Kharoshṭī-using people had migrated to Vaṅga.[95]

It is significant that Ptolemy, to whom an 'emporion' (emporium) was an Oriental market-town in the commerce of which Roman sailors or merchants were interested,[96] did not locate any emporium or port on the coast of the territory on the Gangetic Gulf.[97] The logical inference is that up to at least the date of Ptolemy's information (or the last of the pieces of relevant information), which must be placed in or before the composition of his *Geographike Huphegesis* in about the middle of the second century AD,[98] the territory concerned was not a direct participant in Indo-Roman trade.

In fact, on the eastern coast of the subcontinent the last two emporia (counting them from the south to north on a correct map of the subcontinent) were, according to Ptolemy, in Maisolia. These were Kontakossyla (modern Ghantasal near Masulipatam), and Alosygni (at or near Masulipatam or Machilipatnam or at least somewhere below the Godāvarī and Kalinga).[99]

[95] D.N. Dass, *op. cit.*, p. 87.

[94] B.N. Mukherjee, 'Coins in Pre-Gupta Bengal', '*Studies in Archaeology, Papers Presented in Memory of P.C. Dasgupta*,' ed. by A.K. Datta, New Delhi, 1991, p. 307; B.N. Mukherjee, 'Trade, Traders and Media of Exchange in Pre-Gupta Vaṅga', *Coinage, Trade and Economy* ed. by A.K. Jha, Nasik, 1991, p. 46.

[95] See above ns. 6 and 94.

[96] See above n. 19.

[97] Ptolemy, *op. cit.*, VII 1, 16–18.

[98] B.N. Mukherjee, *The Kushāṇa and the Deccan*, Calcutta, 1968, pp. 128–29.

[99] Ptolemy, *op. cit.*, VII, 1, 15. See above n. 82.

Kalinga's contact with Maisolia and nearly coastal area (now in Andhra Pradesh) is suggested by the evidence of a gold medallion of *c.* third century AD unearthed at Sisupalgarh.[100] It bears the name of one Dharma-Damadhara and a Kushāṇa coin type on one side (see below) and a copy of a bust and an inscription from a Roman coin on the other.[101] Such a Roman device could have become known through the contact of the people of Kalinga with *inter alia* coastal Andhra, where such coins were imported and imitated.[102]

It should, however, be admitted that Alosygni was not very far to the south of the coast of Kalinga. It should also be noted that Ptolemy described Alosygni (or a place near it?) as the 'starting point' (*apheterion*) of 'those who sail for Khruse Khersonese'[103] (or the Golden peninsula), identifiable with the Malay peninsula.[104] Their first destination could have been the emporium of Takola, included in Ptolemy's Khruse Khersonese[105] and located probably on the western coast of the Malay peninsula.[106] As noted above, the latter port had maritime contacts with Tāmralipti.[107] These data suggest the feasibility of contacts of the merchants of Kalinga with the emporium of Alosygni and of their voyages from that port to the Malay peninsula.[108]

The *Periplus Maris Exteri* by Marcianus (*c.* AD 400) refers to an 'apheterion' ('starting point') 'from which all those navigating to Chryse leave', as 'followed by the large gulf called Gangetic, into

[100]*Ancient India*, no. 5, pp. 95, 100 and plate 1, XLIX, A.S. Altekar's reading of the legend on the obverse is very doubtful.

[101]The scribling on the reverse was apparently copied from a Roman piece.

[102]Several coins of some Roman emperors like Gordian and Constantine found in a hoard in the Singbhum district, might have reached that place from the Andhra country and via Kalinga. See A. Cunningham, *Report of the Archaeological Survey of India for 1874–75 and 1875–76,* vol. XIII, pp. 72–73; P. Berghaus, 'Roman Coins from India and their Imitation', in A.K. Jha (ed.) *op. cit.* pp. 110–11.

[103]Ptolemy VII, 115.

[104]P. Wheatley, *op. cit.*, pp. 144–47.

[105]Ptolemy, *op. cit.,* VII, 2,5.

[106]P. Wheatley, *op. cit.*, pp. 22–24 and 268–72.

[107]See above n. 36.

[108]E.H. Bunbury, *A History of Ancient Geography,* 2nd edition, New York, 1962, p. 660.

which the Ganges flows by five mouths'.[109] Marcianus apparently located the 'apheterion' on the coast of the Gangetic Gulf, whereas the 'starting point' for sailing to Khryse Khersonese as described by Ptolemy was to the south of its coast.[110] This difference may suggest the establishment on the coast of Kalinga 'a starting point' for voyages to South-East Asia.[111]

Thus by the *c.* fourth century AD Kalinga might have established direct contact with South-East Asia.[111a] The continuity of contacts between different points on the coast of Kalinga and Vaṅga is also suggested by the *Periplus Maris Exteri.*[112] It states that the entire 'periplus' ('sailing round') along that part of the Gangetic Gulf goes from the 'apheterion until up to the fifth mouth of the Ganges, which is called Antibole, is 5660 stadia' (or roughly 566 miles). Thus Vaṅga and Kalinga were closely connected with each other through coastal navigation. Overland routes also served as lines of communication.[113]

III

The industry and trade in Vaṅga of the period concerned was, as demonstrated above, to a large extent controlled by a class of people who had emigrated from the Kushāṇa dominion in the north-western section of the Indian subcontinent. They must have been aware of the use of coins for transacting business in the Kushāṇa empire.[114]

[109]Section 37; C. Muller, *Geographi Graeci Minoris,* vol. I, Paris, 1855, p. 533.

[110]No doubt, the work of Marcianus was mainly based on Ptolemy's *Geography*. But the former also consulted other sources (E.H. Banbury, *op. cit.,* pp. 660–61).

[111]In this connection see also our article 'Dosarene-Daśārṇa-Coastal Orissa', *Journal of Orissan History,* vol. III, no. 1, 1982.

[111a] This inference may be supported by a reference to a ruler of Kaliṅga as the 'lord of the great sea' in the *Raghuvaṁśa* (VI, 54) of Kālidāsa, if he is assigned to the Gupta age (AD 320–570).

[112]*Periplus Maris Exteri,* sec. 39; C. Muller, *op. cit.*, p. 536.

[113]*Mahābhāratā*, Sabhāparvan, XXVII (or XXX), 19f; Kālidāsa, *Raghuvaṁśa*, IV, 38f; *Journal of the Asiatic Society,* 1974, pp. 98–99.

[114]B.N. Mukherjee, *The Rise and Fall of the Kushāṇa Empire*, Calcutta, 1988, pp. 357f.

The use of coins in the territory now in lower West Bengal from an earlier period is well-known. No doubt, no stratigraphic evidence indicates the continuation of punch-marked (silver, copper or billon) coins in this region after *c.* first century BC.[115] But cast copper pieces, introduced here in *c.* second century BC, continued to be in circulation up to *c.* third century AD and even in the Gupta age,[116] and so well after the commencement of settlements of the Kharoshṭī using people from the north-west in Vaṅga. These cast copper coins are round (or nearly round), oval, square and rectangular in shape. R. Sharmadhikary has divided them into ten classes on the basis of combinations of symbols and some other indications.[117] As we have shown elsewhere, these coins followed the weight-standard of silver Kārshāpaṇas of 32 ratis or 57.6 grains.[118] Pieces conforming to the weights of Kārshāpaṇa (c. 57.6 grains) and its fractions (three-fourth, half, quarter and one-eight) and multiples (one and half and double) are known.[119]

Such copper pieces were in circulation in Vaṅga at the time of the advent of the Kharoshṭī-using people from the north-west in about the second half of the first century AD. The indigenous population also could have been aware of Kushāṇa coins. A few gold and numerous copper Kushāṇa pieces have actually been unearthed in lower West Bengal. Kushāṇa coins, which are known to have been in circulation in some areas even outside the empire,[120] probably reached Vaṅga by way of trade and commerce. They could have remained there in circulation.

This hypothesis is supported by the evidence of an appreciable number of imitations of Kushāṇa copper coin-types found in the districts of 24 Parganas (North and South), Burdwan, Midnapore, and Bankura (and also Hooghly?). The devices imitated by these pieces

[115]See our article 'Coins in Pre-Gupta Bengal', in the *Studies in Archaeology, Papers Presented in Memory of P.C. Dasgupta, op. cit.*, pp. 287f.

[116]*Ibid.*

[117]R.K. Sharmadhikari, 'Some Observations on the Coins of Early Bengal', *Indian Museum Bulletin*, 1984, vol. XIX, pp. 40–41 and 45–46.

[118]See above n. 115.

[119]See our article in A.K. Datta (ed.), *op. cit.*, pp. 290f. See also our article, 'Kushāṇa Coins in Bengal—An Appraisal' in the volume to be published shortly in honour of Dr P.L. Gupta.

[120]B.N. Mukherjee, *The Rise and Fall of the Kushāṇa Empire,* p. 358.

are attributable to Kanishka I ('King standing and sacrificing at an altar' on the obverse and 'Oado' for 'four armed Śiva', or 'Mao', etc. on the reverse). Huvishka ('King riding on an elephant' on the obverse and 'Mao' on the reverse) and Vāsudeva I ('King standing and sacrificing at an altar' on the obverse and 'seated Ardokhsho' or 'Śiva with bull' on the reverse).[121]

The weight of these coins (as known from some published specimens and our examination of numerous unpublished ones in different collections) is an interesting subject of study. Metrologically these can be divided into seven goups with their weights generally varying from: (a) c. 12 to 16.1 gms., (b) c. 8 to 11 gms., (c) c. 6.05 to 7.25 gms., (d) c. 5.08 to 5.67 gms., (e) c. 2 to 2.28 gms., (f) c. 1.48 to 1.8 gms., or concentrating on (g) c. 3.68 gms. The coins of the first group can be easily related to be reformed Kushāṇa copper specie initially struck (during the reign of Vima Kadphises) on a theoretical weight of Attic tetradrachm (i.e. 268.8 grains or c. 17.417 gms.).[122] Kanishka I appears to have issued copper pieces of the denominations of Attic tetradrachm, didrachm, drachm and hemidrachm.[123] However, an examination of a large number of Kushāṇa copper coins reveals that while the heaviest copper pieces of Kanishka I are struck at c. 17 gms., those of Huvishka (as subdivided on the basis of their types, symbols and/ or fabric) indicate concentrations at 15 to16 gms., 10 to 12 gms., 11 gms., 8 to 9 gms., 9 to 10 gms., 7 to 9 gms., and 6 to 10 gms.,[124] and the issues of Vāsudeva I allude to a standard of c. 8 to 9 gms.[125] Though metrologically the coins of group I may be related to those of Kanishka I the specimens of group 2 to those of Vāsudeva I and the majority of the pieces of Huvishka and the representatives of group 3 to some of Huvishka's issues, the weights indicated by groups 4 to 7 have no strict relevance to genuine imperial Kushāṇa currency.[126]

[121]*The Journal of the Numismatic Society of India,* vol. XXXIII, pt. 1, pl. III; A.K. Datta (ed.), *op. cit.*, p. 291.

[122]D.W. MacDowall, 'Weight Standards of the Kushāṇa Coinages,' *JNSI,* vol. XXIII, 1960, pp. 70f.

[123]Ibid., p. 71.

[124] Ibid., pp. 71–72. See also below n. 126.

[125]Ibid., p. 72. See also below n. 126.

[126]Some copper pieces, attributed to Huvishka (mainly on the basis of their devices), weigh well below 6 gms. or about 94 grains (V.A. Smith, *Catalogue of the Coins in the Indian Museum,* Calcutta, vol. 1, Oxford, 1906, p. 82, no. 51 and p. 84, no. 76; R.B. Whitehead, *Catalogue of Coins in*

Hence we must conclude that though Kushāṇa coins began to be imitated in the lower regions of West Bengal in the days of Kanishka I or shortly after him, the territory concerned soon developed a currency system of its own incorporating Kushāṇa devices and a different weight system.

Here comes the evidence of the group (no. 5) indicating concentration at c. 3.65 gms. or about 57 grains. A specimen (standing figure (?): Śiva with bull) of this group, found at Mangalkoto and now in the collection of the Museum & Art Gallery of the Burdwan University (accession no. 79.123.5C), weighs 3.6 gms. This is obviously struck on the silver Kārshāpaṇa or purāṇa standard of 32 ratis or c. 57.6 grains, followed in Vaṅga for striking not only silver but also copper punch-marked and cast coins.[127] Coins of all other groups can be related to this standard, if groups 1, 2, 3, 4, 6, and 7 are taken to represent respectively tetra-kārshāpaṇa, tri-kārshāpaṇa, double

---

the Punjab Museum, Lahore, vol. 1, Oxford, 1914, pp. 199–206. Nos. 145, 166, 177, 180, 184, 185, and 205). One of them weighs as low as 31 grains or 2.008 gms. (Whitehead, *op. cit.*, no. 177). Most of these pieces are very crude in execution with blundered legend or no legend at all and are often described in the catalouges as 'barbarous'. These seem to be contemporary and/or later forgeries, done in the Kushāṇa and/or later times and used as media of exchange (sometimes of very low value) in certain areas where the Kushāṇa coins had been popular (see also M. Mitchiner, *Oriental Coins and Their Values, The Ancient and Classical World, 600 BC–AD 630*, London, 1978, p. 432). The coins, which are very low in weight (31, 54 grains, etc.) might have been struck on local standards (using popular Kushāṇa devices). In any case these cannot fit in the series of regular and better executed copper series of Huvishka in which the weight of the so-called 'tetradrachm' (or issues of highest denomination) was apparently as a matter of policy) scaled down gradually (*JNSI*, vol. XXXI, p. 73).

A number of copper pieces attributed to Vāsudeva I weigh much less than c. 8 gms. A few weigh as low as 56, 35 or 29 grains. These pieces generally carry blundered legend or no legend and are often referred to as 'barbarous' in published catalogues (V.A. Smith, *op. cit.*, p. 85, nos., 21 and 25; R.B. Whitehead, *op. cit.*, pp. 209–11, nos. 221–26 and 230). As in cases of the above noted copper coins of bad quality and very low weight (attributed to Huvishka), these pieces may also have been comtemporary or later imitations of Vāsudeva I's coins on some local weight standards.

[127]B.N. Mukherjee, 'Coins of Pre-Gupta Bengal', in A.K. Datta (ed.), *op. cit.*, p. 299.

kārshāpaṇa, one and half Kārshāpaṇa, three-fourth (*tripāda*) kārshāpaṇa and half kārshāpaṇa. The coins concerned, which are intended to be round in shape have variable sizes according to their weight.[128]

It appears that Kushāṇa copper coins coming to lower West Bengal by way of trade gained currency there and began to be imitated sometime in or after the period of Kanishka I (*c.* AD 78–100). Soon under an organized authority (of a state or a mercantile guild?) there developed a system of coinage based on well-known Kushāṇa types and the familiar weight-system then followed by uninscribed cast coins. We may call it Kushāṇa-Vaṅga or Kushāṇa-Rāḍha coinage, Rāḍha having been in the period concerned fully or partly in Vaṅga and also in the territory which has yielded such coins.[129]

This development was quite natural in an area where the copper specie had long been in use and so where there would surely be a tendency to integrate imported copper pieces and their well-known devices into its own currency system. Attempts at such an integration are also indicated by a few known coins of very low weight (assignable to groups 6 and 7) bearing 'standing king sacrificing at an altar' the Kushāṇa device on one side and a symbol noticeable on uniscribed cast coins on the other. One such round piece (now in a private collection), weighing 1.8 gms. and measuring 1.5 cm., bears the above-noted Kushāṇa coin type on one side and a tree within a railing (and traces of letters?) on the other. Two roundish pieces (now in the cabinet of the Tamralipta Museum and Research Centre of Tamluk), measuring 1.8 x 1.6 and 1.1 x 1 cm. and weighing 2.22 gms. and 1.8 gms. respectively, display the same Kushāṇa device on the obverse and three small circles within a triangle on the reverse.

The above-noted pieces of the Kushāṇa-Vaṅga or Kushāṇa-Rāḍha series are intended to be round in shape and are (mostly?) die-struck. There are, however, a large number of cast copper coins representing with different degrees of crudeness, the Kushāṇa coin types 'standing king: standing deity Mao'. These have been found in the districts of 24 Parganas (South), Burdwan, Midnapore, Bankura and Purulia. Known finds are more numerous in the Bankura district than in any other district. It is noteworthy that in 1972–3 three lots of coins, weighing together about 28–29 kilograms were recovered from

[128]Ibid., pp. 292f.

[129]A. Bhattacharyya, *op. cit.*, pp. 45f; A.K. Datta (ed.) *op. cit.*, p. 292.

a pond at Tilavani in the Bankura district.[130] A remarkable hoard of 281 pieces were found at Masubazar, 32 miles south of Purulia. These are now in the Indian Museum, Calcutta (Coin Register No. 6491, *c.* 1358–*c.* 1589).

Metrologically these cast coins can be divided into several groups with their weights varying from (a) c. 6.08 to 6.77 gms., (b) c. 3.95 to 5.312 gms., (c) c. 2.88 to 3.78 gms., (d) c. 2.15 to 2.65 gms., (e) 1.43 to 1.95 gms., (f) c. 880 mgms. to 1.07 gms., and (g) 250 mgms. to 7 grains or 0.433 gm. Groups A to E roughly correspond in weight to groups 3 to 7 of the above noted Kushāṇa-Rāḍha coins. And since their devices are based on those of a Kushāṇa coin type (standing king: Mao) which was also popular with the issuers of the Kushāṇa-Vaṅga or Kushāṇa-Rāḍha coins, the latter may be asociated with the former. The cast coins in question may be considered to have formed the second series of Kushāṇa-Vaṅga or Kushāṇa-Rāḍha coinage. Their highest denomination, represented by group 'a' (corresponding to group 3 of the first series), is double Kārshāpaṇa. The other group (b to g) may refer to one-and-half Kārshāpaṇa, Kārshāpṇa, three fourth Kārshāpaṇa, half Karshāpaṇa, one-fourth Kārshāpaṇa and one-eighth Kārshāpaṇa. The last two denominations, not known so far to have been represented in the first series, remind us of the names *pādapana* and *ashṭabhāgapaṇa* mentioned by Kauṭilya in connection with the silver specie[131] (*Arthaśastra,* II, 12). These names may also be applicable here as the coins of the series concerned undoubtedly follow, like uninscribed cast copper coins of Bengal, the weight standard of silver Kārshāpaṇa (c. 57.6 grains or c. 3.721 gms.). It is really striking that one piece, found in the district of 24 Parganas (South) and now in the Asutosh Museum (accession no. 5999), weighs 3.63 gms, and so has its weight almost exactly corresponding to the theoretical weight of a silver Kārshāpaṇa.[132]

[130]M. Sinha, *Paśchima Rāḍha Tathā Bankurar Sanskriti* (in Bengali), Vishnupur, 1899, S.E., p. 66.

[131]*Arthaśāstra*, II, 12.

[132]See above n. 119. The second series of Kushāṇa-Vaṅga coinage can be compared with the round cast pieces generally labelled as 'Purī Kushāṇa', because one of the earliest recorded hoards of such coins was found in 1893 in the Puri district (J. Allan, *A Catalogue of the Indian Coins in the British Museum, Catalogue of the Coins of Ancient India,* London, 1936, p. CXXI).

Like the die-struck variety, the cast of the Kushāṇa-Vaṅga coinage may be considered to indicate an organized currency system under the auspices of a mercantile guild or a government. Both the alternatives are applicable to the immigrants concerned, among whom there were groups of wealthy traders and also rulers of at least a part of Vaṅga. Moreover, as emigrants from the north-west (a part of the Kushāṇa empire), they must have been habituated to the use of Kushāṇa coins and should have a natural inclination for connecting Kushāṇa copper coinage, already known in the territory concerned, with the local copper specie.

The Kushāṇa-Vaṅga coinage begun in about the second century AD. It ultimately replaced(at least partly) the uninscribed cast series of local origin. It could have remained in use up to sometime of the early Gupta age, since the administration of the rulers concerned continued upto the late fourth or fifth century AD (see section I) and since stratified evidence indicates the feasibility of circulation of cast coins even in that period.[133]

Thus the medium of exhange in pre-Gupta Vaṅga consisted of cast copper coins of local origin which had been in circulation from an earlier age, and a Kushāṇa-Vaṅga copper specie including die-struck and cast pieces (incorporating the Kushāṇa indigenous weight systems). If cowries were used,[134] in addition to copper coins of very low denominations, for small-scale transactions, then these might have been imported from *inter-alia* the Maldive islands.[135]

[133]Period V. (now redesignated as Period IV) (from the AD first to third century) at Mangalkot (Burdwan district) has yielded numerous cast coins. The evidence from period VI (now redesignated as Period V) (from the third to seventh century AD) indicated continuity of the use of cast coins (A. Ray, 'Mangalkot: An Ancient Township—Its History and Archaeology', In D. Mitra and G. Bhattacharya (eds.), *Studies in Art and Archaeology of Bihar and Bengal, Nalinikanta Śatavārshikī, Dr. N.K. Bhattassli Centenary Volume,* Delhi, 1989, pp. 387 and 389; A Ray, 'Archaeology of Mangalkot', A. Ray and S. Mukherjee (ed.) *Historical Archaeology, A Dialogue Between Archaeologists and Historians,* pp. 136–37.

[134]Fa-hsien, *Fo-kuo-chi*, ch. XVI, A.K. Datta (ed.), *op. cit.*, pp. 298–99.

[135]For evidence of import of cowries from the Maldivi islands in later periods, see Ibn Battuta, *Travels in Asia and Africa* (1325–1354), tr. by H.A.R. Gibb, London, 1939, p. 243. See also the *Indian Museum Bulletin*, 1982, vol. XVII, p. 80, n. 86.

The discovery of a large number of the relevant copper coins in lower West Bengal may suggest that the daily transaction in Vaṅga was to a great extent carried on in coins.[136] That coins meant wealth in the period concerned is suggested by a terracotta plaque of this age,[137] discovered at Tamluk, which displays a filled-up vase (*pūrṇa-ghaṭa*) a traditionally auspicious symbol of prosperity,[138] as having coins overflowing in it.[139] At least a few of these simulate the imitations of Kushāṇa coins.[140]

The Kushāṇa coins and/or their imitations in cast, generally labelled as 'Puri Kushāṇa', have been unearthed in numbers in the Balasore, Cuttack, Puri and Ganjam and even Srikakulam districts all of which were totally or partly within ancient Kalinga.[141] Similarly Kushāṇa and Purī-Kushāṇa pieces have been discovered in the Mayurbhanj and Keonjhar districts,[142] situated contiguous to the coastal region of upper Orissa and on areas which could have been within the limits of early Kalinga. The so-called Purī-Kushāṇa coins have been recovered also from different sites now included in the Singhbum and Dhanbad (part of the Old Manbhum)[143] districts. These territories were close to Vaṅga on the one hand and Kalinga on the other. The Rakha hill area in the Singhbum district, where Purī-Kushāṇa pieces of *c.* third–fourth century AD have been found at a site 'surrounded by copper slag heaps and close to copper mines',[144] must have been the source of the supply of the metal used for minting coins in Vaṅga and Kaliṅga.

[136]*The Periplus tes Erythras Thalasses* referred in *c.* first century AD to the use of pieces of gold (ingots of a certain weight) as 'pieces of money' (*nomismata*)(sec. 63) (*JNSI*, vol. XLVII, 1986, pp. 77–78).

[137]See below n. 140.

[138]V.S. Agrawala, *Studies in Indian Art,* Varanasi, 1965, pp. 43f.

[139]*Artibus Asiae,* vol. XIV, Ascona, 1951, p. 232, pl. IV.

[140]This evidence invalidates T.N. Ramchandran's claim describing the vase as of 'Śunga type' (ibid., pp. 232–34).

[141]S. Tripathi, *Early and Mediaeval Coins and Currency System in Orissa, c. 300 BC to AD 1568,* Calcutta, 1986, pp. 40–43. See also above n. 132.

[142]*Ibid.*, pp. 42–43; *JNSI*, vol. II, pp, 124–25; *JNSI*, vol XXXVI, 1974, pp. 36–37.

[143]*JBORS*, 1919, vol. V, p. 73; *Indian Culture*, vol. III, p. 727; S. Tripathi, *op. cit.*, p. 44; *JNSI*, vol. XXXVI, 1974, pp. 35–36.

[144]*JBORS*, vol. V, 1919, p. 73.

It appears that Kushāṇa copper coins used to come to Kalinga and nearby territories by way of trade and remained in circulation in Kalinga. The same may be same said about the Sātavāhana coins claimed to have been unearthed in the East Godavari region in the coastal area (which could have been at times in ancient Kalinga).[145] Only six uninscribed cast copper coins (of non-Puri Kushāṇa varieties) have been yielded at different stratified levels at Sisupalgarh, which are datable to the later phase of period II (AD 50–100) early phase of period II B (100–125) and period III (200–350).[146] Similarly only fourteen lead pieces have been recovered from Periods IIB (AD 100–200) and III (*c.* 200–350 AD) at the same site.[147] Significantly enough, such pieces have not been unearthed in any great number within the regular limits of ancient Kalinga, though both the metals were procurable from not far-off sources.[148] This situation, when judged against the background of our knowledge of a large number of the so-called Purī Kushāṇa coins from the area of ancient Kalinga, may lead us to infer that prior to the introduction of this series, there was no locally made copper specie in that territory.

Available data show that ancient Kalinga, like ancient Vaṅga, knew silver punch-marked coinage.[149] The production of coins simulating punch-marked pieces through the casting technique even in *c.* AD 300 is suggested by two moulds bearing devices of punch-marked pieces from the late level of period III at Sisupalgarh, dated to the same age.[150] In fact, in Kalinga, such silver pieces might have continued to be in use even after the popularity of punch-marked coins waned in Vaṅga, perhaps after first century BC.[151] On the other hand, unlike Vaṅga, Kaliṅga did not use any regular copper currency of completely indigenous origin. It became used to Kushāṇa copper currency, with

[145]S. Tripathi, *op. cit.*, pp. 29–30.

[146]*Ancient India*, no. 5, pp. 72 , 97–98.

[147]Ibid., pp. 97, 99.

[148]Copper ore was available from the Rakha mines in the Singhbum district (see above n. 144) and lead ore in the Sambalpur district (*Ancient India,* no. 5, p. 97).

[149]S. Tripathi, *op.cit.*, pp. 2f; A.K. Datta (ed.), *op. cit.,* pp. 282–86.

[150]*Ancient India,* no. 5, p. 97.

[151]'no stratigraphic evidence' indicates the continuation of the use of punch-marked specie in Vaṅga 'after 1st century BC' (A.K. Datta (ed.), *op. cit.* p. 286–87).

the import of the relevant coins in number.[152] Later the Kushāṇa coin-types began to be limited in copper to satisfy the local demand. Two Kushāṇa and four so-called Purī-Kushāṇa copper pieces have been unearthed at Sisupalgarh at a level (Period III) datable to *c*. AD 200–350.[153] A Purī-Kushāṇa piece was unearthed at first–second century AD level during a recent excavation at Manikpatna.[154] A variety of Purī-Kushāṇa coins bearing a new reverse type and the legend *laṅka* or *teṅka* (=*taṅka*), are palaeographically datable to *c*. fourth–fifth century AD.[155]

These data show that the so-called Purī-Kushāṇa coins were current in Kaliṇga in *c*. third and fourth (and also fifth) centuries AD or perhaps from about the late second to the fourth or fourth–fifth century AD[156] and that their prototypes, Kushāṇa copper coins, began to be imported into Kalinga by sometime in *c*. second century AD.[157] The most common types 'of the Purī-Kushāṇa pieces are King at altar' on the obverse and 'The moon-god Mao' on the reverse. A small number of pieces display the 'King riding an elephant' device,[158] copied obviously from a type of the specie of Huvishka.[159]

[152]S. Tripathi, *op. cit.*, pp. 40f. A copper piece of the Kushāṅa king Kanishka (*c*. AD 78–100/101), found at first–second century AD level during an excavation at Asurgarh in the Sambalpur district (*New Aspects of Orissa History,* vol. II, 1978, pp. 66f.) surely indicates that by sometime of this period such coins had begun to be imported in an area not very far from Kaliṅga.

[153]*Ancient India*, no. 5, pp. 97–98.

[154]We have received the information from Sri D. Pradhan, the excavator.

[155]*Archaeological Survey of India, Annual Report, 1924–25*, p. 130; *JNSI*, vol. XXXVI, p. 35; S. Tripathi, *op. cit*., pp. 42 and 44.

[156]The Kushāṇa and Purī Kushāṇa pieces have been found in fairly large numbers and on different occasions at Sitabhinji (Keonjhar district) and at a site near a rock-shelter displaying a painting and an inscription of *c*. AD fourth century. This evidence tends to date the use or continuity of the use of the coins unearthed here to about the same (*JNSI*, vol. XIII, 1951, pp. 69–72).

[157]The import of the relevant coins should have commenced sometime in or after the reign of Kanishka I (c. AD 78–100/101) and before *c*. AD 200 by which date the imitation series might have commenced.

[158]J. Allan, *op.cit.*, pp. CXXI–CXXIII, 205–209; pl. XXX, nos. 1f. See also *JNSI*, vol. XIII, p. 71 for two examples of 'Sun god' reverse and 'elephant rider' obverse.

[159]*JNSI*, vol. XIII, p. 71; pl. V, nos. 3–4; M. Mitchiner, *op. cit.*, p. 437.

Their recorded weights generally vary from 4.775 gms. to 7.665, though still lighter and heavier pieces are known.[160]

The known Purī-Kushāṇa pieces from Kalinga are cast coins. There is no recorded evidence of imitating Kushāṇa devices by the die striking technique. So unlike Vaṅga, Kalinga might not have experienced the die-striking phase of imitation of die-struck Kushāṇa coin-types, which in normal cases should have preceded the casting phase for imitating die-struck types. On the other hand, as in Vaṅga, the relevant coins in Kaliṅga are known to have weighed not only within the range of the weight-system or Kushāṇa copper pieces, but also sometimes much lighter (3.302 gms., 4.775 gms., etc.)[161] The lighter weight coins can be related to the standard of 32 ratis or 57.6 grains (i.e. 3.731 gms.) (see above section III), which had been in use in Vaṅga from a pre-Kushāṇa age for striking copper as well as silver specie. In Kaliṅga it might have been used for minting silver,[162] but not copper pieces.[163] In fact, as noted above, Kaliṅga probably did not have its own copper coinage before minting the Purī-Kushāṇa series. So the impetus for connecting the Kushāṇa standard with the Kārshāpaṇa standard and for issuing lighter coins may have come from Vaṅga, where such pieces have been found in a significantly large number.

Thus in the early centuries AD Kaliṅga might have experienced regular circulation of silver punch-marked coins (up to *c*. AD 300), the Kushāṇa copper coins (second to fourth century AD?) and cast Purī-Kushāṇa pieces (*c*. second to fourth–fifth century AD). Some impetus for issuing cast Purī-Kushāṇa series or rather for connecting the Kushāṇa standard with the Kārshāpaṇa standard for minting copper specie might have been received by Kalinga from Vaṅga.

[160] S. Tripathi, *op. cit.*, p. 46. Some pieces weigh, 11.520 gms. (ibid.), 9.673 gms (*Ancient India*, no. 5, p. 98), 9.152 gms. 10.93 gms. (*JNSI*, vol. XXXII, pp. 25f.), etc. On the other hand, we examined a piece wieghing 3.302 gms.

[161] See above n. 160.

[162] *Ancient India*, no. 5, p. 98; P.L. Gupta, *Coins*, first edition, New Delhi, 1969, p. 13. But we also cannot deny the feasibility of using *śatamāna* standard of 100 ratis or 180 grains for striking its submultiples in silver (S. Tripathi, *op. cit.*, pp. 4 and 25–27).

[163] The rectangular uninscribed cast copper coins and the lead coin, unearthed at Sisupalgarh, weigh below 3 gms. (excepting one, which weighs 3.121 gms.). But these pieces , numbering twenty-three are to be considered as drifts and not local issues (*Ancient India*, no. 5, pp. 97–99).

IV

In Vaṅga coastal and overseas trade (with South-East Asia) was witnessed in the pre-Gupta age (and perhaps from about first century BC). It was boosted with the advent of Kharoshṭī-using people from the north-west of the Indian subcontinent in late first century AD. The Kharoshṭī using merchants had contacts with coastal Kaliṅga and might have even a settlement in that territory. Kalinga's own interest in trade with South-East Asia might have germinated by sometime in *c.* second century AD when there was a 'departuring point' for ships bound for Khryse in a locality almost immediately to the south of Kaliṅga. However, neither Kalinga nor Vaṅga directly participated in Indo-Roman trade, though commercial articles of these areas could have been taken to ports of other zones and thence exported to the Roman empire.

For supporting a brisk trade Kalinga as well as Vaṅga used coin-money (in addition to cowries?). With the gaining of the popularity by the so-called Purī-Kushāṇa cast copper series Vaṅga and Kaliṅga entered into a phase of some sort of joint economic and monetary system. The common interest in coastal and overseas trade might have prompted such a system. Large hinterlands of the ports in these territories also boosted their export capabilities.

In the Gupta period the Indian influence to the South-East disseminated from *inter alia* Vaṅga and the Andhra country and further south. This is tellingly illustrated by the stone inscription of the great sailor (*mahānāvika*) Buddhagupta unearthed in the Northern District of Wellesley Province in Malay peninsula. The inscription is written in Brāhmī of the southern class of about the fifth century AD,[164] while the sailor himself hailed from Raktamṛittikā, identifiable with Chiruti in Murshidabad district of West Bengal.[165]

The importance of Kalinga's overseas trade rose further in the post-Gupta age.[166] On the other hand, in the same period the commercial importance of ancient Vaṅga or rather its coastal West Bengal

[164] D.C. Sircar, *op. cit.*, p. 497.

[165] Ibid., p. 497 and n. 3. In this connection see also *The Indian Historical Review*, vol. XIV, p. 87.

[166] In seventh century AD, Hsüan-T'sang referred to the coastal city of Che-li ta-lo (placed in coastal Orissa) as 'a resting-place for sea going traders and strangers from distant lands' (*Hsi-yü-chi,* chuan X).

section gradually waned due to various factors.[167] However, the loss in the trade of coastal Bengal (West Bengal and Bangladesh), was made up with the gradual rise in commercial importance of the areas like Samtaṭa and Harikela[168] (which ultimately incorporated the former and both of which were within the present limits of Bangladesh).[169] But that is another story.[170]

[167] *Indian Museum Bulletin,* 1982, vol. XVII, pp. 77f.
[168] Hsi-yü-chi, chuan X; *Indian Museum Bulletin*, 1982, vol. XVII, pp. 71f.
[169] *Bangladesh Lalitkala,* vol. I, no. 2, 1975, pp. 115–19.
[170] *Indian Museum Bulletin,* 1982, vol. XIII, pp. 67f.

Chapter Seven

New Light on Maritime Loans: P. Vindob G 40822*

LIONEL CASSON

I INTRODUCTION[1]

In 1985, H. Harrauer and P. Sijpesteijn published a papyrus that is unique.[2] The recto and verso are more or less contemporary, mid-second century AD, and both deal with a shipment of goods from India. This aspect of Egypt's trade, though well known, has up to now been scantily and only indirectly reflected in the documents from Greco-Roman Egypt.[3]

The recto contains part of an agreement that covers the transport

* *Zeitschrift fur Papyrologie und Epigraphik*, Band 84, 1990.

1 I have had much welcome aid from my friend and colleague N. Lewis, including valuable suggestions concerning the text of the papyrus. I owe many thanks to H. Harrauer for informing me of an important new reading and for most helpful comments on several suggestions I presented to him.

2 'Ein neues Dokument zu Roms Indienhandel, P. Vindob. G 40822,' *Anzeiger der Österreichischen Akademie der Wissenschaften*, phil.-hist. Kl. 122 (1985), pp. 124–55.

3 On the trade with India, see L. Casson, *The Periplus Maris Erythraei: Text with Introduction, Translation, and Commentary* (Princeton 1989) 11–35 (cited hereafter as Casson). On the papyrological evidence, see M. Raschke, 'Papyrological Evidence for Ptolemaic and Roman Trade with India,' *Proceedings of the XIV International Congress of Papyrologists*, London, 1975, pp. 241–46.

of goods from the point on the Red Sea where these had been unloaded, no doubt Myos Hormos or Berenice (cf. Casson [n. 3] 94–7), across the eastern desert to Koptos and thence down the Nile to Alexandria (lines 1–12); it also refers to the provisions of a loan κατὰ Μουζεῖριν (line 12); Muziris was a major port on the south-west coast of India (cf. Casson 22–4, 296), and the loan in question must have been a maritime loan that made possible the acquisition of the goods. The verso contains an account of amounts of nard, ivory, and textiles, all of which figure regularly among India's exports (cf. Casson 16–17), and the calculation of their value for customs duty; the account on the verso, though in a different hand, unquestionably is related to the agreement on the recto, both dealing with the same shipment of goods (cf. Harrauer-Sijpesteijn [n. 2] 124, 150).

The papyrus has already evoked considerable discussion. Its publication was quickly followed by an important article by G. Thür in which he reprinted the text with some emendations, provided an extended commentary on the legal clauses in the agreement on the recto, and explicated in masterly fashion the entries in the account on the verso, many of which were extremely puzzling.[4] There have also appeared two articles on the nature of the agreement on the recto, one by myself and a reply by Thür.[5]

In this present article I republish the text with several emendations, including a crucial one that throws light on the purpose of the agreement, and offer a new view of what that purpose was.

II TEXT

The initial part of the papyrus, with the names of the parties and doubtless much else, is missing. At the point at which the preserved portion begins we are well into an agreement in which the party of the first part—*ego*, to use Thür's convenient term—agrees to take care of the transfer of goods across the eastern desert to Koptos and from there down the Nile to Alexandria, all of which goods are to be

[4] 'Hypotheken-Urkunde eines Seedarlehens für eine Reise nach Muziris und Apographe für die Tetarte in Alexandreia (zu P. Vindob. G. 40822),' *Tyche* 2 (1987), pp. 229–45, cited hereafter as Thür.

[5] L. Casson, 'P. Vindob G 40822 and the Shipping of Goods from India,' *BASP* 23 (1986) 73–9; G. Thür, 'Zum Seedarlehen κατὰ Μουζεῖριν P. Vindob. G. 40822,' *Tyche* 3 (1988), pp. 229–33.

put in the name of the party of the second part—*tu*, to use Thür's term. Furthermore, in the event of non-payment by *ego* of a loan he owes, *tu* is empowered to take over the security specified in the loan contract; *tu*, thus was the creditor by *ego*'s loan, and the security unquestionably of the goods involved in this agreement.

Recto

Column 2

→ ̣ ̣ ̣ ̣ο μένων cου ἐτεοων ἐπ[ι]τρόπων ἢ φροντιcτῶν καὶ cτήcαc
[δώcω τ]ῷ cῷ καμηλείτηι ἄḷḷạ (τάλαντα) ẹ[ἴ]κọcι πρὸc ἐπίθεcιν τῆc εἰc Κόπτον
[ἀνόδο]ṿ καὶ ἀνοίcω διὰ τοῦ ὄρουc μετὰ παραφυλακῆc καὶ ἀc̣φ̣αλεịαc
[εἰc τὰ]c̣ ἐπὶ Κόπτου δημοcίαc παραλημπτικὰc ἀποθήκαc καὶ ποι-
[ήcω ὑ]π̣ὸ τὴν cὴν ἢ τῶν cῶν ἐπιτρόπων ἢ τοῦ παρόντοc αὐτῶν
[ἐξουcία]ν καὶ cφραγεῖδα μέχρι ποταμοῦ ἐμβολῆc καὶ ἐμβαλοῦμαι
[τῶι δέ]οντι καιρῶι εἰc ποταμὸν ἀcφαλὲc πλοῖον καὶ κατοίcω εἰc τὴν
[ἐν Ἀλεξ]ανδρείᾳ τῆc τετάρτηc παραλημπτικὴν ἀποθήκην καὶ ὁ-
[μοίω]c̣ ποιήcω ὑπὸ τὴν cὴν ἢ τῶν cῶν ἐξουcίαν καὶ cφραγεῖδα, ταῖc
[τοῦ λοι]ποῦ ἀπὸ τοῦ νῦν μέχρι τεταρτολογίαc δαπάναιc πάcαιc καὶ φο-
[ρέτρου] ὄρουc καὶ ναύλων ποταμίταιc καὶ τῶν ἄλλων κατὰ μέροc ἀνα-
[λωμά]τ̣ων· πρὸc τὸ ἐνcτάντοc τοῦ ἐν ταῖc κατὰ Μουζεῖριν τοῦ δα-
[νείου c]υγγραφαῖc τῆc ἀποδόcεωc ὡ̣ριcμένου χρόνου ἐὰν μὴ δικαί-
[ωc τότ]ẹ χρεολυτῶ τὸ προκείμενον ἐν ἐμοὶ δάνειον τότε εἶναι
[πρὸc c]ẹ̀ καὶ τοὺc cοὺc ἐπιτρόπουc ἢ φροντιcτὰc τὴν ἐγλογὴν καὶ ὁλο-
[cχερῆ] ἐξουcίαν ὡc ἐὰν αἱρῆcθε ποιήcαcθαι τὰ τῆc πράξεωc χωρὶc
[διαcτ]ολῆc καὶ προcκρίcεωc, κρατεῖν τε καὶ κυριεύειν τὴν προ̣κ̣[ει-]
[μένη]ν ὑποθήκην καὶ τεταρτολογεῖν καὶ τὰ λοιπὰ ἐcόμενα μέρη
[τρία μ]εταφέρειν οὗ ἐὰν αἱρῆcθε καὶ πωλεῖν καὶ μεθυποτίθεcθαι
[καὶ] ἑ̣τ̣[έ]ρωι παραχωρεῖν ὡc ἐὰν αἱρῆcθε καὶ τὰ καθ' ἑαυτὴν διοικονο-
[με]ῖcθαι καθ' ὃν ἐὰν βούληcθε τρόπον καὶ ἑαυτῶι ὠνεῖcθαι τῆc ἐπὶ `τοῦ'
καιροῦ φανηcομένηc τιμῆc καὶ ἐκκρού[ει]ν καὶ ἐνλογεῖν τὰ πεcούμενα
[ὑπὲρ τοῦ προκειμέν]ο̣υ̣ δανείου τῆc πίcτεωc τῶν πεcουμένων
[οὔcηc π]ερὶ cὲ καὶ τοὺc ἐπιτρόπουc ἢ φροντιcτὰc ὄντων ἡμῶν ἀcυκοφαν-
[τήτ]ω̣ν κατὰ πάντα τρόπον. τοῦ δὲ περὶ τ̣ὴ̣ν̣ ἐνθήκην ἐνλείματόc
[τ]ε καὶ πλεονάcματοc πρὸc ἐμὲ τὸν δεδανειcμένον κ̣α̣ὶ ὑποτεθει-

Column 3

→ [μένον ὄντοc

2: on the text of this line, see below under Section IV.

3 [ἀνόδο]ν: The editors restored [εἰcόδο]υ̣ but, as N. Lewis points out, the required word is 'road up' [sc. to Koptos]. On Thür's restoration of [cυνόδο]υ̣ in the sense of 'caravan', see below under Section IV.

7 εἰc ποταμὸν ἀcφαλὲc πλοῖον: L. Koenen conjectures ποτάμ(ι)ον.

10 λοι]π̣οῦ: The editors restored πλο]ίοῦ. λοι]π̣οῦ suits the con-

text perfectly and is not excluded by the traces. Thür has accepted the reading; see *Tyche* 3 (1988) 232. L. Koenen, however, expresses doubts. According to his interpretation of the photography, the top of the vertical before ο suits ι better than π; and [τοῦλοι]ποῦ, coupled with ἀπό τοῦ νῦν μέχρι τεταρτολογίας, is redundant.

11 κατά μέρος: I follow a suggestion by N. Lewis and understand this as a ellipsis for κατ' ἐμόν μερος.

11–12 φο[ρέτρου]: On Thür's restoration of the plural, see below under Section IV.

12 The editors assumed that between πρός and τό there is a considerable lacuna caused by a jump of the scribe's eye as he copied from an exemplar. N. Lewis offers a less drastic solution, namely that πρός τό is to be taken with εἶναι in line 14, the words in between being a clumsy insertion to explicate the condition involved; the scribe, on returning to ειναι, added τότε to refer to this condition, and then continued in the infinitive mood. Asyndeton and, in the following lines, change to infinitive construction seem to result, but due to the fact that the beginning of the document is missing the syntax of the beginning of the extant portion of the document is unclear.

17 [διαστ]ολῆς: thus Thür; [προσβ]ολης edd.—προσκρίσεωχ: since the word is unattested, Thür assumes a miswriting for ποοσκλνήεως, a term that occurs in similar contexts.

κρατεῖν σέ τε καί would have been clearer, but can easily be understood.

23 ὑπέρ τοῦ προκειμέν]ο̣υ̣ Thür; τôυ προγεγραμμέν]ο̣υ̣ edd. L Koenen points out that Thür's supplement is little too short and suggests 22 τά πεσούμενα | [σοι——.

24 ἡμῶν: The plural points to the use of agents by the borrower; cf., Thür 237, n.31.

Verso

Column 1

↑] μν(ῶν) νθ
] μ̣ν(ῶν) ι̣δ𐅵
]. μν(ῶν) νη
] κ
]ο̣υ̣ς ρξζ ὁλ(κῆς) (ταλάντων) ρκ μν(ῶν) ιγ
]. . (ταλάντων) κς μν(ῶν) λ
]ν τω τῆς τετάρτης
ὁμ]οί(ως ὁλ(κῶν) μν(ῶν) ιαε𐅵
]. (ταλάντων) κς μν(ῶν) ιηδ𐅵

] (ταλάντων) ιζ μν(ῶν) λγ
] (ταλάντων) δ μν(ῶν) κς
]...... π.. ικω
](ταλάντων) κδ μν(ῶν) κγδ´
]. ὀλ(κῆς) αL´
].. cα
]η
]. [ ]δ´
]β[
]δ∂´
].. [ ]ξ[
]'Γc.ε μν(ῶν)
]κ ἐξ ὧν [ἀ]ντι-
ε]ται η... υ.
]...... ριων
].. μν(ῶν) (δραχμῶν) ψοα
(ταλάντων)] δ (δραχμῶν) λβ
]. μ δ´
].[.]τον

[This is the closing portion of the account, since the final entry summarizes the shipment involved. Six parcels loaded aboard the vessel *Hermapollon*. The preserved lines deal with three, so another three must have been described in the portion that is missing.[6]]

Column 2

↑ νάρδου Γανγιτικῆc κιcτῶν ξ ὧν ὁμοίωc
τιμὴ λογίζεται ὡc τῆc κίcτηc (δραχμαὶ) 'Δφ ἀργυρί-
ου (τάλαντα) με
ἐλέφαντοc ὑγιοῦc μὲν ὁλκ(ῆc) (τάλαντα) οη μν(αῖ) νδ∂´
ὧν ὁμοίωc τιμὴ λογίζεται ὁλκ(ῆc) μὲν (ταλάντων) οη μν(ῶν) μ[γ]
τῶν γινομένων cταθμίοιc τῆc τετάρτηc τοῦ
ταλάντου λογιζομένου πρὸc λί(τραc) ϙε, (γίνονται) λί(τραι) 'Ζυοη,
ἐξ ὧν αἱρεῖ λογιζομένων εἰc τὸ τάλαντον λι(τρῶν) ο[
ὅcῳ cυνήθωc πρὸc τοὺc ἐμπόρουc λογίζεται ὁλ[κ(ῆc)]
(τάλαντα) οc μν(αῖ) με, ὡc τῆc μν(ᾶc) (δραχμαὶ) ρ, (γίνεται)
(τάλαντα) οc (δραχμαὶ) 'Δφ,
τῶν δὲ λοιπῶν ὑπὸ τῶν 'Αραβαρχῶν πλείω ὑπὲρ
τῆc τεταρτολογίαc ἀρθέντων ἐν ἀριθμῷ ὀδόντων
παρὰ τὸ αἱροῦν καὶ τεταρτολογουμένων ὀδόντων μν(αῖ) ια∂
ὡc τῆc μν(ᾶc) τῶν ἴcων (δραχμῶν) ρ [ἀργ(υρίου)] (δραχμαὶ) 'Αροε,
γίν(εται) ἐπὶ τὸ [αὐτὸ] (τάλαντα) οc (δραχμαὶ) 'Εχοε
cχιδῶν νδ ὁλκ(ῆc) (τάλαντα) ιγ μν(αῖ) θLδ´,
ὧν ὁμοίωc τιμὴ λογίζεται ὁλκῆc μὲν (ταλάντων) ιβ μν(ῶν) μ[ζ]

[6] Thür considers the verso to be a copy of the customs declaration itself

τῶν ὡς πρόκ(ειται) γιν(ομένων) ἐκ τοῦ μέρους σταθμίοις μὲν τετάρτης
λί(τραι) 'Ασιδ, καθὼς ⟦και⟧ δὲ πρὸς τοὺς ἐμπόρους λογίζεται ὁλκ(ῆς) (τάλαντα) ιβ μν(αῖ) κζ ὡς τῆς μν(ᾶς) (δραχμαὶ) ο
ἀργ(υρίου) (τάλαντα) η (δραχμαὶ) 'Δσϟ,
τῶν δὲ λοιπῶν πλείω ὑπὲρ τῆς τεταρτολογίας ἀρθει-
σῶν ὡς πρόκειται μν(αῖ) κβḶδ̣´, ὡς τῆς μνᾶς τῶν
ἴσων (δραχμῶν) ο ἀργ(υρίου) (δραχμαὶ) 'Αφϙβ/
γίνεται σχιδῶν (τάλαντα) η (δραχμαὶ) 'Εωπβ/
γίνεται τιμῆς ἐλέφαντος ἀργ(υρίου) [(τάλαντα) ος (δραχμαὶ) 'Εχοε]
ἐπὶ τὸ αὐτὸ τιμῆς μερῶν ϛ̄ τῶν ἐκπεπλευκότων
ἐν τῷ ⟦εμ⟧ 'Ερμαπόλλωνι πλοίῳ φορτίων ἀργυ-
ρίου (τάλαντα) 'Ανδ (δραχμαὶ) 'Βωνβ

4 ν̇δε| : thus Koenen, or νδḶδ´ Thür, approved by H. Harrauer from the original: for writing 3/4 the scribe indiscriminately used LΔ and the common combination of the two signs ε|(Lδ = ε|; throughout this paper Δ is transcribed as δ). νδL edd.

7 Ζνοη: 78 t.@ 95 = 7410 lbs.; 43 m. at same rate = ca. 68 lbs; 7410 + 68 = 7478 lbs.

8 Thür plausibly suggests restoring the end of the line as | ο(λκῆς) ['Ζσϙα].

10 (τάλαντα) ος (δραχμάι) 'Δφ: This, in other words, is the figure that will be used by the collector of the 25% customs duty at Alexandria, and it reflects a concession customarily made to merchants. The gross weight arriving
there was 78 t. 43 m.
but the weight the customs official would use in
calculating the levy was only 76 t. 45m.
i.e., a reduction of 118 m.
Merchants thus got a concession of 1/40 (78 t. + 43 m. = 4723 m.; 118/4723 = 1/40) or 2.5%

13 μν (αῖ) ιαε|: or ιαḶ[δ´] Thür (see above on line 4), μν (ῶν) ιαḶ edd. These 11¾ m. are the difference

---

(244–45, and cf. the title of his article [above, n. 4]). Thus he takes lines 6 and 8 to refer to the actual weighing of the goods in the customs house. The exact weight of the items listed must have been known to the owner since he had no doubt purchased them by weight; thus lines 6 and 18 need not reflect an actual weighing but simply mathematical calculation, the conversion of the known weights expressed in talents and minas into weights expressed in Roman pounds, using the equivalents required by the customs regulations.

between the gross weight that arrived at the Red Sea port of discharge — 78 t. 54 ¾ m.
and the gross weight arriving at the customs house at Alexandria — 78 t. 45 m.

----

11 ¾ m.

It represents the amount that was levied by the Arabarchs at the Red Sea port of discharge, namely roughly 1/400 (78 t. = 4680 m + 54 ¾ m. = 4734 ¾ m.; 11.75/4734.75 = ca. 1/403) or .25%. But even this was subject to the 25% customs duty and hence had to be reported to the customs office at Alexandria.

19 ’Αϲιδ: The true figure is slightly less than 1214: 12 t. @ 95 lbs. to the t. = 1140; 43 m. at the same rate = 68; 1140 + 68 = 1208.

20 (τάλαντα) ιβ μν(αῖ) κζ: The concession in this instance works out to slightly more than 1/40 (2.5%).
The gross weight arriving at Alexandria was — 12 t. 47 m.
But the weight the customs office would use in calculating the levy was — –12 t. 27 m.

----

i.e., a reduction of — 20 m.

Twelve talents, forty-seven minas = 767 m; 20/767 = 1/38 (2.63%)

23 μν(αῖ) Thür; μν(ῶν) edd. —κβ∟̣δ : These 22 ¾ m. are the difference between the gross weight that arrived at the Red Sea port of discharge — 13t. 9¾ m.
and the gross weight arriving at the customs house at Alexandria — –12t. 47 m.

----

namely — 22 ¾ m.

It represents the amount that was levied by the Arabarchs at the Red Sea port of discharge, a percentage considerably higher than the quarter of one per cent levied on the ivory (13 t. 9 ¾ m. = 789 ¾ m.; 22.75/789.75 = ca 1/35 or 2.88%).

III TRANSLATION

Recto, Column 2

[I have paragraphed the provisions for ease of comprehension.]

. . . of your other agents and managers. And

I will weigh and give to your cameleer another twenty talents for loading up for the road inland to Koptos and

I will convey [sc. the goods] inland through the desert under guard and under security to the public warehouse for receiving revenues at Koptos, and

I will place [them] under your ownership and seal, or of your agents or whoever of them is present, until loading [them] aboard at the river, and

I will load [them] aboard at the required time on the river on a boat that is sound , and

I will convey [them] downstream to the warehouse that receives the duty of one-fourth at Alexandria and I will similarly place [them] under your ownership and seal or of your agents, assuming all expenditures for the future from now to the payment of one-fourth—the charges for the conveyance through the desert and the charges of the boatmen and for my part of the other expenses.

With regard to there being—if, on the occurrence of the date for repayment specified in the loan agreements at Muziris, I do not then rightfully pay off the aforementioned loan in my name—there then being to you to your agents or managers the choice and full power, at your discretion, to carry out an execution without due notification or summons.

You will possess and own the aforementioned security and pay the duty of one-fourth, and the remaining three-fourth you will transfer to where you wish and sell, re-hypothecate, cede to another party, as you may wish.

And you will take measures for the items pledged as security in whatever way you wish, sell them for your own account at the then prevailing market price, and deduct and include in the reckoning whatever expenses occur on account of the aforementioned loan, with complete faith for such expenditures being extended to you and your agents or managers and there being no legal action against us [in this regard] in any way. With respect to [your] investment, any shortfall or overage [sc. as a result of the disposal of the security] is for my account, the debtor and mortgager. . . .

Verso Column 2

[The translation is based on Thür's analysis of the entries (*loc. cit.* [n.

4] 238f. nn. 34–44). The abbreviation d. = drachmas, m. = Minas, and t. = talents (of weight when followed by m., of money when followed by d.)]

1-3 Gangetic nard, 60 containers,
whose value (sc. for the one-fourth customs
duty payable at Alexandria), likewise, is being
reckoned at 4500 silver. drachmas per container.............................. 45t.

4-10 ivory, sound condition, weighing .... 78 t. 54 ¾ m.
whose value (sc. for the one-fourth customs
duty), likewise, is being reckoned on a
weight .... 78 t.43 m.
or, converted on the weight scale used
by the one-fourth (customs duty) of 95 lbs.
to the talent, = 7478 lbs.,[7]
of which the amount subject to duty (of one-fourth
at Alexandria), converting lbs. per talent, is a weight
of [7291 lbs.][8] in accordance with the customary
reckoning for merchants, or .... 76t. 45m.
at 100 d.per m .... 76 t. 4500 d.[9]

11–15 the remainder, representing the number in
tusks removed by the Arabarchs, (which
number is) over and above the number
subject to duty (that will be available)
for collection of the one-fourth (customs
duty), which tusks are also subject to the
collection of the one-fourth (customs
duty)................................ .... 11 ¾ m.[10]
at the same rate of 100 silver d. per m. 1175 d.

----

for total of.... .... 76t.5675 d.

16–21 lengths of fabric, 54
weighing.....................................13 t. 9 ¾ m.
of which, likewise, the value
(for the one-fourth customs duty)

[7] See note to verso col. 2, line 7.
[8] See note to verso col. 2, line 8.
[9] See note to verso col. 2, line 10.
[10] See note to verso col. 2, line 13.

is being reckoned on a weight of .... 12 t. 47 m.
which, as above, yields for the parcel
on the weight scale used by the
one-fourth (custom duty),
(a weight of) 1214 lbs.,[11]
but, in accordance with the customary
reckoning for merchants, a weight
(for customs' purposes) of 12 t. 27 m.[12]
at 70 silver d. per m .... 8 t. 4290 d.
22–25 the remainder that was removed (sc. by the
Arabarchs), which, as above, represents an
amount over and above (what will be
available) for collection of the one-fourth
(customs duty) (to the amount of) 22 ¾ m.[13]
at the same rate of 70 silver d.per m .... 1592 d. 3 ob.
Total for the lengths of fabric .... 8 t. 5882 d. 3 ob.
26 total for the value of the ivory .... 76 t. 5675 d.
27–29 grand total for the 6 parcels of the cargo
exported on the ship *Hermapollon* in silver. 1154 t. 2852 d.
===========

IV THE NATURE OF THE AGREEMENT

In the original publication of the document the editors took the agreement on the recto to be the remains of a maritime loan that had been drawn up in Muziris between a shipowner (*ego*) who borrowed from a merchant (*tu*), pledging his ship as security. Both Thür and I independently pointed out the errors in this view.[14] Such phraseology as 'the date for repayment specified in the loan agreements' (lines 12–13) instead of 'the aforementioned date for repayment' aut sim. makes it clear that this document is not itself the maritime loan, and some of the stipulations concerning the security (18–19) make it equally clear that the security was not a ship but items subject to the 25% customs duty on imports; almost certainly *ego* had secured his loan from *tu* by

[11] See note to verso col. 2, line 19.
[12] See note to verso col. 2, line 20.
[13] See note to verso col. 2, line 23.
[14] Casson (n. 5) 76–78; Thür (n. 4) 239–41.

pledging the goods he would buy with the money,[15] precisely as merchants had done centuries earlier in Demosthenes'day.[16]

But if the agreement in this papyrus is not itself the maritime loan, what is it? According toThür, the contract between *ego* and *tu* was drawn up in Alexandria in two separate documents, one that spelled out the maritime loan and another that spelled out the security involved ('getrennte Darlehens-und Sicherungsurkunde'), and what the papyrus contains is a portion of the latter, the document that dealt with the security.[17] In accord with his view that both were drawn up in Alexandria, he interprets ἄλλα in line 2 as referring to the return journey with its counterpart in the lost lines that precede referring to the outbound journey;[18] and he takes the plural ναύλων in line 11 as indicating both outbound and return journeys; and he restores the plural φο[ρέτρων] in 10–11 to cover both the outbound and return journeys (Thür [n. 4] 235, n. 14).

What of the words ἐν ταῖς κατά Μουζεῖριν τοῦ δα[νείους]υνγραφαῖς in lines 12–13 which certainly seem to refer to "loan agreements at Muziris" and not at Alexandria? Thür explains this by taking κατά Μουζειριν as an elliptical way of referring to 'loan agreements (concerning a voyage) to Muziris'.[19]

The drawing up of a loan contract in more than one document, despite the examples Thür offers,[20] is unparalleled. In this instance he attributes it to special circumstances, namely that the security consisted of goods from India which had to pass through customs. He points out that, if the debtor did not pay off his loan on time, the

15 Casson (n. 5) 76; Thür (n. 4) 241.

16 Of the maritime loans mentioned in Demosthenes' speeches, in four instances out of six the loan was secured by the goods purchased with the proceeds (32.14, 34.6 [two loans], 35.10–13).

17 Thür (n. 5) 230; cf. Thür (n. 4) 241–43.

18 Thür (n. 4) 234, n. 7; Thür (n. 5) 232.

19 Thür (n. 4) 235, last line of n. 18; Thür (n. 5) 233.

20 Cf. Thür (n. 4) 241–42. He mentions *SB* 7169, *Tab. Pomp.* 13, and P. Vindob. G 19792. The first, as he admits, is conjectural; the second, as he points out, may not concern a maritime loan; and the third is simply a notice of payment of the proceeds of a loan issued by a bank to the borrower (on this document, see now L. Casson, 'New Light on Maritime Loans: P. Vindob. G. 19792 (=*SB* VI 9571)', in R. Bagnall and W. Harris, (eds.), *Studies in Roman Law in Memory of A. Arthur Schiller,* Leiden, 1986, pp. 11–17.

goods would remain in the customs house, and the creditor, in order to legitimize his right to the three-fourths that was left after duty has been paid, would need a document issued by the debtor; the special 'Sicherungsurkunde,' as he sees it, served the purpose (Thür [n.4] 243–44). Yet would not a single document that included both the details of the loan and the details of the security have served the purpose just as well? In any event, Thür's explanation does not account for the presence of the stipulations concerning the transport of the goods from the Red Sea port to Alexandria; these certainly have nothing to do with getting goods out of customs. There indeed were special circumstances in this instance that called for a separate document—but, as will be shown in a moment, the separate document was quite different in nature and purpose from Thür's 'Sicherungsurkunde'.

What militates most strongly against Thür's view is the new reading I referred to above. His view rests on the assumption that the agreement we are dealing with was drawn up, along with the loan contract, at Alexandria before the voyage to India ever began; the new reading makes it a virtual certainty that it was drawn up at a port on the Red Sea upon the safe arrival there of the goods from India.

In lines 1–3 the editors originally read cτῆcαc [δώcω τ]ῷ cῷ καμηλείτηι ἄλλα (τάλαντα) ρο (δραχμάc) ν πρόc ἐπίθεcιν τῆc εἰc Κόπτον [εἰcόδο]υ. They took cτῆcαc to mean 'wie vereinbart' and επίθεcιν to mean 'Benützung'. Thür rendered cτῆcαc the same way but rightly pointed out that 170 talents was far too great a sum to be paid out on tolls. His solution was to restore [cυνόδο]υ at the beginning of line 3, giving it the meaning of 'caravan,' although that meaning has hitherto been attested only for cυνοδία and to translate ἐπίθεcιν 'Verladung,' a sense also hitherto been unattested but easily derivable from the use of the verb ἐπιτίθημι to mean 'load' (Thür [n. 4] 234, n. 8). Yet the sum would be too great even for the loading of a whole caravan. The hire of a camel in the second century AD was at most four drachmas a day,[21] and the journey from Berenice, the

[21] *Aegyptische Urkunden aus der Koniglichen Museen zu Berlin*, Greichische Urkunden 921.12. Other entries reveal a rate half that or less, e.g., line 26 shows that on the twenty-third of the month, sixteen camels were hired for a drachma each. The rate must have varied according to the size of the load, the number of hours the beast worked, etc.

Red Sea port furthest from Koptos, took at most twelve days (Pliny, *N.H.* 6.103). This would indicate a maximum cost per camel for the trip of 48 drachmas—at which rate 170 talents would rent over 21,000 camels!

H. Harrauer has since reexamined the lines on the papyrus, and he kindly informs me that the proper reading in line 2 is ἄλ̣λ̣α̣ (τάλαντα) ε̣[ἴ]κ̣ο̣c̣ι κτλ. The reading of the actual number may not convince everybody,[22] but it is clear that there is no basis for the reading of a drachma sign. Its elimination provides the key to a solution of the difficulty. It permits us to take the talents here as units of weight, not money. By doing so, and by giving to cτῆcαc here its well-attested sense of 'weigh,'[23] we arrive at a meaning that suits the context perfectly: *ego*, along with all the other services he engages to perform to ensure the safe arrival of the goods at Alexandria, will take care of the assignment of the loads to the cameleers. In the lost lines just before the preserved portion opens, he had obviously agreed to assign at least one parcel to *tu*'s cameleer; in lines 1–3, he agrees to weigh out and assign another, this one, accepting Harrauer's reading, with a weight of 20 talents, a weight that would require no more than three to four camels.[24] The essential point is that arrangements such as these could hardly have been planned and set down in writing at

[22] The word εἴκοcι 'would have been written narrowly and the traces which seems to appear on the photograph do not quite coincide with the expected pattern. The talent sign may be followed by a number filling the entire space, as L. Koenen has pointed out to me.

[23] LSJ S.V. 'ἵcτημι A IV; for examples in the papyri, see *P. Cair. Zen.* 59484 (3rd BC) and *P. Yadin* 21.15, 22.14 (both AD 130).

[24] There is naturally a great variation in the size of the loads reported since these varied with terrain, length of haul, size of beasts, etc. Although the papyri attest camel loads of wheat that run as high as 10 artabs (P. Sijpesteijn, *Customs Duties in Graeco-Roman Egypt,* Zutphen, 1987, p. 53) they usually were 6 artabs, double the standard donkey-load of 3 (Sijpesteijn *op. cit.,* p. 52: cf. B. Boyaval in *Chroniqued'Egypte* 53, 1978 p. 354). Assuming an artab of 40 choenices, the size ordinarily used in private transaction in the Roman period (cf. R. Duncan-Jones in *Chiron* 6, 1976, pp. 242, 258: A. Bowman, *Egypt after the Pharaohs,* London, 1986, p. 237, and assuming a choenix was more or less the equivalent of a liter (Wilcken, Gdz, lxviii), an artab of wheat would be somewhat heavier than a U.S. bushel (35.239 liters), which weighs 60 lbs. Thus 6 artabs would be in the neighborhood of 400 lbs. This agrees nicely with *Ed. Diocl.* 17.4 where a camel load is given as 600 Roman lbs = 430

Alexandria over half a year before *ego* had made a single purchase. They are the sort of arrangements that are made when the actual goods are at hand and are being readied for caravan transport. It follows that the agreement we have is one that was drawn up at Myos Harmos or Berenice right after the ship bearing the goods involved had arrived there from India.

What kind of agreement, then, is this which was made at such a time and place? A clue is to be found in the only complete text of a maritime loan to have survived, that in Demosthenes' *Against Lacritus*.[25] Both Thür and I have remarked on the fact that in a key respect the maritime loan involved in the papyrus and the loan cited by Demosthenes are alike:[26] in both, merchants take out loans pledging as security the goods they will purchase with the money they have borrowed. There is, I believe, another key respect in which they are alike.

The loan cited in Demosthenes' speech was made to a pair of borrowers for a voyage from Athens to the Pontus and back. Among the stipulations is one to the effect that, within twenty days after the safe arrival of the cargo—undoubtedly grain—taken on at the Pontus, the borrowers are to pay off their debt. Moreover, 'they will furnish to the lenders the security intact to hold title thereto until such times as they pay back the money due in accordance with the agreement' παρέξουcι τοῖc δανεῖcαcι τὴν ὑποθήκην ἀνέπαφον κρατεῖν ἕωc ἂν ἀποδῶcι τὸ γιγνόμενον ἀργύριον κατὰ τὴν cυγγραφήν, 35.11). In other words, the borrowers had twenty days in which to sell the cargo and pay back their creditors; during those twenty days, the creditors held legal title to the cargo.

In the agreement between *ego* and *tu* on the recto there are phrases that point unmistakenly to the existence in their original loan contract of a similar stipulation. Just as the debtors in Demosthenes' speech agree that the creditors will 'hold title to' the security until the loan is paid off, so *ego* agrees to put the goods that serve as the

averdupois. S. Goitein, *A. Mediterranean Society* I, Berkeley, 1967, pp. 220, 335 given figures for the twelfth century that indicate loads of ca. 500 lbs. Thus, 20 talents (1200 lbs.) would require three, at most four camels.

[25] Demosthenes 35.10–13. The text is probably a later insertion, but this does not detract from its value as evidence; cf. W. Ashburner, *The Rhodian Sea-Law,* Oxford, 1909, p. ccxii.

[26] Casson (n. 5) 76, n. 10 ; Thür [n. 4] 229.

security 'under the name and seal' of *tu* or his agents (lines 5–6, 9) until the goods reach the customs house; after clearing them through customs, *ego* will be free to sell them and pay off his debt.

In shipments from the Pontus to Athens in the fourth century BC the cargeos of grain were unloaded at the Peiraeus and sold right there;[27] twenty days no doubt was ample time for carrying this out, and, what is more, one of the creditors was an Athenian ('Androcles of Sphettus,' 35,10) and thus able to keep an eye on what was going on. But, in a shipment from India to Egypt in the second century AD, much more was required, both in effort and time. The goods could not be sold, thereby enabling the debtors to satisfy his creditor, until they had been brought from the point of unloading all the way to Alexandria and had gone through customs there. So much, indeed, was involved that, I suggest, at the moment the ship arrived safely at its Red Sea port, a supplementary agreement was drawn up to spell out precisely what the responsibilities of the borrower were from this point on—and it is this supplementary agreement that is preserved on the papyrus.[28] The borrower was to form up a caravan and assign various parcels to cameleers for transport across the desert; he was to assure protection of the caravan against brigands during the crossing; he was to check the parcels in at the public warehouses at Koptos; he was to arrange for safe water transport to Alexandria and check them in at the customs house there. These responsibilities were no doubt set out in such detail because of the costly nature of the shipment: the creditors wanted assurance that the precious goods would not travel on overloaded camels or in leaky Nile craft.[29] Wherever he registered the parcels, he was to place them not under his own name but under that of his creditor; they would remain that way until he made them his own by paying off his debt.

[27] See R. Garland, *The Piraeus,* Ithaca, N.Y., 1987, pp. 85–86.

[28] In an earlier article (see above), n. 5, I had offered an explanation of the agreement which, like the present explanation, assumed that the document was drawn up shortly after the arrival of the shipment at the Red Sea port. However, I took it then to be a revised loan contract that replaced the original, but there are no parallels for such a procedure.

[29] One of the great contributions of the papyrus is the concrete evidence it furnishes of the huge amounts of money that the trade with India required. The six parcels of the shipment recorded on the verso had a value of just short of 1155 talents (col. 2, line 29)–almost as much as it cost to build the aqueduct at Alexandria Troas (7,000,000 drachmas, of which Herodes

The supplementary agreement then spells out what happens if the borrower does not pay off his loan 'on the date for repayment specified in the loan agreements at Muziris'—specified, no doubt, the way it had been in the contract cited by Demosthenes, as a given number of days after safe arrival at Egypt. In that eventuality the creditor takes over the goods that had been pledged as security, and lines 15–27 tell exactly what he may do with them. In the original loan contract the terms concerning the security may well have been set forth only in a general way, since, if the ship went down, the security ceased to have any relevance. But it became very relevant indeed once the ship arrived safely, and this would explain why a detailed presentation of the terms regarding it was included in the supplementary agreement.

If we take the words κατά Μυζειριν to mean '(for a voyage) to Muziris' as Thür suggests, that original contract may have been drawn up at Alexandria. If we take them in their normal sense, as I prefer to do, the original contract was drawn up at Muziris. Either *ego* or *tu* or both may well have been members of the foreign colony resident there.[30]

Atticus contributed 4,000,000 and Hadrian 3,000,000; see Philostratus, V.S. ii.1 [548] and cf. P. Graindor, *Un milliardair antique: Herode Atticus et sa famillie* [Cairo 1930] 32, n. 2). The parcel of ivory and the parcel of fabric together weighed 92 talents and where worth 528,775 drachmas. A Roman merchantman of just ordinary size had a capacity of 340 tons (L. Casson, *Ships and Seamanship in the Ancient World,* Princeton, second edition, 1986, p. 172); it was capable of carrying over 11,000 talents of such merchandise. And the weather conditions on the route to India were such as to require the use of vessels of at least this size (Casson [above, n. 3] 284–85, 289–91). Loaded with cargo of the likes of that recorded in this papyrus, they were veritable treasure ships.

[30] On the foreign colonies at Muziris and elsewhere in India, see Casson (above, n. 3) 24–25.

Chapter Eight

Indian Feudal Trade Charters*

D.D. KOSAMBI

This[1] note comments upon two copper-plate grants of which the older[2] is dated about AD 592 and later[3] approximately AD 710. Had they not been sadly mangled in translation, they might have cast considerable light upon the role of the trader in the development of feudal society. Hitherto, it has been customary to merge two millennia of Indian history together as 'ancient India', which amounts to denial of any basic development.

I. An inscription at Kārle[4] shows that traders' unions of some sort existed even before the Christian Era under the title *vāniya-gāma,* quite apart from the rich Greek and Indian traders who made individual contributions to the magnificent Caitya cave. The ancient meaning[5] of *grāma* as a united mobile kinship (*sajāta*) group rather

* *JESHO*, II, 1959, pp. 281–93.

[1] *EI= Epigraphia Indica*; *JBBRAS = Journal of the (former Bombay Branch of the Royal) Asiatic Society of Bombay*; F= J.F. Fleet: *Inscriptions of the early Gupta Kings* (Calcutta 1888, *Corpus Inscriptionum Indicarum III*), cited by number of the inscription; *S* as in n. 2, below and *M* as in 3, both cited by page.

[2] D.C. Sircar in *EI,* 30, 1957, pp. 163–81; earlier, in the proceedings of the Bombay session (1949) of the All-India Oriental Congress (translation).

[3] V.V. Mirashi's edition of the *Inscriptions of the Kalachuri-Chedi Era* (New Delhi 1955, *Corpus Inscriptionum Indicarum IV*), particularly p. 150ff.

[4] On the right 13th pillar; cf. *JBBRAS* 30, 1956, p. 66 (*Dhenukākaṭa*).

[5] W. Rau, *Staat u. Gesellschaft im alten Indien* (Wiesbaden 1957), pp. 51–54.

than 'village' was carried over in this usage. The collective wealth and power of the merchants' *grāma* does not seem to have been dominant at this stage. Princes of that period such as Usavadāta made donations[6] in perpetuity to the monastic order at Nasik, in the form of interest upon capital deposited with various producers' guilds (oil-men, weavers, &c.)

The word for guild is *śreṇī* or its Prakrit equivalent. This term is common in the *Arthaśāstra* of Kauṭilya for associations of people who had just left the tribal stage but carried their unity—presumably originating in blood relationship—into more than one productive activity. The members of the older *śreṇī* would cultivate grain, herd cattle and colonize waste land. At the same time, they might engage collectively in other production such as that of cloth, or indulge in trade, and take to arms at need. That this flexibility survived to the Gupta period is proved by the famous Mandasor inscription (*F* 8) composed by Vatsabhaṭṭi in AD 473.

The *Arthaśāstra* state was itself the major producer of its day, virtually a monopolist. Merchants were encouraged only to carry on import and export trade between *janapada* territories separated by waste land and forest, but had virtually no control over local production and trade, dominated entirely by salaried royal officials. This system changed during the reign of Aśoka, with the vast new country opened up for the merchants and for village settlement. The older state management could no longer function efficiently enough to collect and to distribute the village surplus, let alone to supply the villages over long distances through difficult terrain with such necessities as salt and metals. The traders took over the two latter functions; corresponding to them there had to be a class of surplus gatherers, the barons, who could collect the surplus as taxes, dues and rent from the villagers.

The essential difference, which developed gradually, was the predominance of merchant guilds controlled by rich families over the older type of workers' *śreṇī*. This implies not only the progressive deterioration of producer's guilds due to greater internal disparities in wealth, but also a denser settlement in villages. Thus, the *vaṇig-grāma*, which spread into the south as *maṇi-grāmam*, was an association of traders related by common interest in trade that had to pass through a paritcular centre, but not necessarily

[6] *EI*, 8. pp. 82–84 & c.

related by kinship nor themselves producers. These traders were given royal charters of the type which form the main basis of this note. They enjoyed speical immunities, but were restrained from excesses against their hired workers.

The change could not have been sudden, nor simultaneous over the whole country. The main contention of this paper is that there *was* a major change in the second half of the sixth century. Āmrakārddava, grandee of Candragupta II, gave (*F*) in the year 412–13 a village and 25 *dīnāras* to the monastery at Sanchi (*Kākanāda-boṭa*). He salutes a 'Council of Five,' which takes no part in the transaction and must have been—as we shall see later—a senate of merchants who acted as witnesses and guarantors for the donation. Ten monks were to be fed daily and two lamps lighted in perpetuity from the total income. The lady Harisvāminī, a lay follower, donated 12 *dīnāras* to the same monastery in 450 (F 62) as a permanent fund (*akṣaya-nīvī*) to feed one monk daily, with four *dīnāras* more for four lamps to be lighted in perpetuity. Assuming no change of local prices or interest-rates in the thirty-eight intervening years, it follows that the state's sixth portion of the grain harvested at Iśvara-vāsaka village which had been transferered by donation to the monastery would be equivalent to the annual interest on about 97 *dīnāras*. It is also clear that Buddhist monasteries still ranked as leading financial houses in the fifth century. The great monasteries along the Deccan trade routes had certainly functioned from about the second century BC as banking houses and major customers for the trade in valuable commodities then transported over long distances by traders' caravans. However, the wealth accumulated in the monastery and temple tended to be frozen in jewels, precious metals, and bronze. This progressive withdrawal from circulation naturally became a hindrance to production and exchange, particularly at the stage when village settlement began to expand at a rate which gave new importance to trade in necessities. A change was certainly due. The producers' guilds were still good investment brokers in the fifth century. For example, the oilmen's guild at Indor (Bulandshahr district, UP) headed by one Jīvanta accepted money in AD 465 from a brahmin Devaviṣṇu (*F*16); the interest was to be used in perpetuity for the annual supply of a specified quantity of oil for the temple lamp. This trust was to continue even if the guild changed residence, provided it functioned as one unit. The prominence of the headman is a new feature which was to be accentuated with time.

It seems to me that the same profound structural change is best reflected in the use of the word *sāmanta.* In the *Arthaśāstra,* it means uniformly neighbour or independent neighbouring king. The *Amarakośa* (2.8.2) defines 'supreme monarch' (*adhīśvara*) as a king who has subjugated all neighbouring rulers (*sāmanta*) without exception : *praṇata-aśeṣa-sāmantaḥ.* On the other hand, *sāmanta* in seventh century and later epigraphs has to be translated as 'feudal baron'. That the change was completed rather late in the sixth century is proved by the fact that Dhruvasena I of Valabhī, on friendly terms with the Guptas but virtually independent and certainly not their vassal, bore the titles *mahārāja-mahāsāmanta,* in AD 526. The latter designation, corresponding perhaps to the earlier *mahā-kṣatrapa,* was soon dropped by his successors. At about the same time, however, Yaśodharman of Malwa (famous for his repulse of the Hun raider Mihiragula in AD 532) boasts (*F*33) of having struck down the pride of *sāmantas* (= surrounding kings) by the power of his arm. This exemplifies the process described elsewhere[7] as 'feudalism from above'. It follows that the *Amarakośa* is earlier than historians of Sanskrit literature like Keith would like to admit; placing its author at the Gupta court in the fifth century would be reasonable. This would also push the date[8] of the poet Bhartṛhari down to a period not earlier than late sixth century.

Administrative decentralization through *sāmantas* accelerated the conversion of communal property into feudal property. Local chieftains were transformed into barons responsible to the king retaining their former rights, but as few as possible of the obligations to their own followers. High officials and legates who would have received a regular stipend under the Mauryans also became such barons or were assigned the state's revenues of some land for stipend. The army was broken up into small police garrisons; the king maintained just enough under his direct command to be able to dominate all the rest. Actual use of currency per head of population was unquestionably

[7] D.D. Kosambi, *An Introduction to the Study of Indian History* Bombay 1956, chaps 7, 8, 9.

[8] By the stanza beginning *bhrātaḥ Kaṣṭam aho* in the northern and *sā ramyānagarī* in the southern version (no. 169 in the critical edition, *Epigrams Attributed to Bhartṛhari,* Singhi Jain Series 23, Bombay, 1948). Here, *sāmanta-cakra* can only mean—in the context—the highest nobles of the great king's court.

far less than under the Mauryans, as indeed we learn from Chinese pilgrims' accounts. The agriculturist paid his tribute of one sixth in kind to the king. The trader converted enough of it in cash to enable the state to meet its obligations. Such a system cannot work unless the density of village settlement rises to a sufficient but not too high level. The village by itself is a poor foundation for such trade; its surplus has to be securely concentrated in relatively few hands. Thus the trader and lord supplemented each other, whether or not they were conscious of the fact. All this would give a special position to the new *vaṇig-grāma* which alone had the accumulated capital necessary to finance the petty trader and the caravans. They would thus take over the surplus from the peasant as well as the feudal lord, supplying household goods to the former and luxuries to the latter, at the period when growth of new village settlements was rapid.

II. Here, the greatest of the published charters is re-translated. The numbered clauses have been grouped subject-wise in paragraphs. Each paragraph is followed by special comment wherever necessary. It must be noted that every clause of the charter relates in some way to the merchants. Thus it is clear that, even in no. 24, the peasants who come to town for seeds would go to the merchant, and not to some landlord.

Points to be specially noted are: First, the considerable incidence of commodity production centred in the town, under the merchants' patronage: wine, sugar, indigo, ginger, oil, woven cloth and clothes, pots and vessels, articles in wood, iron and leather, etc. But the merchants themselves are no longer guild producers, only people who finance and thus control the production. Second, the state regulated prices (as in *Manusmṛti* 8. 402), and checked weights and measures (as in the *Arthaśāstra*), and collected taxes or corvée labour (*Manusmṛti* 7.[1] 38). However, dues and fines are asessed in cash, not produce or penal labour. The standard coin is a *rūpaka* (R) divided into twentieths, an old ancestor of the rupee. The *dhārmika* is interpreted by Sircar as a specially low rate of tax when the goods are for religious purposes; this would be ridiculous when applied to wine-vats (42) and fines (33) for tampering with seals. The *dhārmika* is the equivalent of the *zakāt* (alms) tax under the Muslims. In practice, it was merely a surcharge levied as for charity, though never specifically applied nor accounted for as such. It is surprising to discover this to be a pre-Muslim institution in India.

Charter of Viṣṇuṣeṇa (the Maitraka Viṣṇubhaṭa) dated AD 592, to a merchants' settlement in Gujarat (*EI.* 30.I163–8I):

1) The property of one (who has died) sonless is not to be attached (by the crown, but disposed of according to guild rules). 2) The king's men are not to break into a house (*ummura-bhedo*). 3) A lawsuit without proper attestation is void. 4) No arrest upon (mere) suspicion. 5) A woman is not be apprehended for (her) man's transgression. 6) No prosecution (*chalo*) to be held for the accidental spread of a fire lighted for (normal) beneficial purposes. 7) No prosecution to be held for the self-mutilation of a ear. 8) No process is valid without a party of the first part and respondent of the second part. 9) No prosecution to be held of one seated in the shop (*āpaṇa*, busy with his sales; *cf.* no. 21). 10) A bullock cart is not to be attached.

Mirashi translates *umura-bheda* first as 'distinction of wharfs', and then (in the index) as 'forcible breaking of a house'. Sircar seems to connect *ummura* with *unmudra*, apparently in reference to a house sealed in the owner's absence. The simplest modern equivalent seems to be *umbarā* or *umbaraṭhā,* threshold. Clause 2 thus guarantees the merchant's house against unwarranted trespass by royal officials. *Āpaṇa* in 9 is not a shop in the modern sense, but any place, even a temporary enclosure, where the merchant bought, sold (and may have stored) his specialized merchandise. Otherwise the modern word *dukkān* for shop need not have been borrowed from the Persian.

11) If a baron (*sāmanta*), king's legate (*amātya),* or royal envoy (*dūta*) should turn up, they have not the right to billets, quarters, or cooked food (as prerogatives, from members of the guild, who are thus exempted from ordinary feudal dues and perquisites).

12) All guilds (*śreṇī*) are not to pay the single-market-tax (*ekāpaṇakaḥ*). 13) All guilds are exempt from the *khovā (?)* gift. 14) Royal perquisites (generally in kind) are to be given to members of the royal household, or to authorized officials, not to others. 15) Deposits (*nyāsaka,* of royal dues?) are not to be made with the guild-alderman (*vārika*). 16) A merchant come upon legitimate business from a foreign district is not to be apprehended, merely because he is suspect as a foreigner (of encroaching upon local privilege; *cf.* no. 52).

The term *vārika* implies holding the office in rotation, perhaps from day to day, presumably so that all the leading families might share the prestige and the responsibility by turns.

17) No complaint is acceptable without a personally afflicted complainant. I8) The *sārī* (? bondswoman) is not an admissible witness in case of injury by words or by violence.

Sicar takes *sārī* as *sārikā,* a (female) talking-bird. Having one as witness in the courts would be fantastic even for the Arabian Nights. Unless some debt-slave like the *hārī* is meant, emendation to *bhārikā* (*cf. M,* p.158) is called for. The rejection is then of a poor drudge whose testimony would be subject to bias or pressure.

19) Workers at (brown) sugar boiling pans (*ḍheṅku-kaḍḍhaka*) and at indigo vats (*nīla-ḍumphaka*) are exempted from corvée labour (for the king, in lieu of taxes, because the establishments are taxed as in 49, 48).

20) Attendants for filling (charitable) drinking-water cisterns (*prapā*), and herdsmen (working for the merchants) are not to be apprehended for the king's (forced and free) labour.

21) Those engaged (in their business) at home or at the shop are not be summoned (to court) whether by a sealed document or messenger (*cf.* no.9). 22) Those engaged in a sacrifice (*yajña*), *sattra,* marriage ceremony and the like are not to be summoned to answer in a civil suit on behalf of others. 23) In a debtor's suit, one not fettered by wooden or iron fetters (i.e. not under restraint as a criminal) is to be allowed bail on furnishing a surety. 24) Peasants come (to the market town) from their own district at the (beginning of the) rains for (purchase of) seeds are not to be seized by the lord (for labour on his own estate).

25) Weights and measures are to be shown for checking in the months of *Āṣāḍha* (June-July) and *Pauṣa* (December-January). The (certificate) fee is Rs 1¼ inclusive of tithe surcharge (*dhārmika*). 26) For financial transactions in undeclared goods, acceptance or clearance of (untaxed) grain and the like, a fine of eight times the value of the goods (smuggled) is to be imposed. 27) The shopping-quarter (*peṭavika*) guild-alderman (*vārika*) is to publish the roll of (fixed) prices every five days; for failure to publish, a (fine of) R.6 plus a tithe surcharge of R. ¼. 28) The guild-aldermen (*vārika*) from leading families (uttara-kulika) are not allowed to go forth (from the district) if the authorised stocklist should be lost. 29) If the guild-alderman from the leading familes do not turn up before the registrar after the (registrar's) attendant has called out their names thrice, the default is punishable by a fine of R. 2¼ inclusive of tithe. 30) The recorders of processes and registrar's servants (apparently to be furnished by the guild-merchants) are liable to a fine of R. 6¼ inclusive of tithe for not remaining present (at the registrar's court) till noon and after. 31) (However), the guild-aldermen from the leading families are not (liable to) prosecution (for absence from the registrar's

court) beyond noon. 32) For charging prices beyond (those on the roll of no. 27, the fine is) R. 3¼ inclusive of tithe. 33) For tampering with a seal (i.e. sealed document, presumably licence or roll), the fine is R. 6¼ inclusive of tithe.

34) For a dispute regarding real estate resolved by the neighbours (without appeal to royal courts), the fine is R. 108. 35) If, however, due information be given (to royal officers), R. 54. 36) To the winner of the suit (thus settled out of court), a certificate is to be issued against a fee or R. 3¼

37) For knocking (another person) down and dragging (him or her) along, or for cutting a ear, the fine is R. 27. 38) For verbal injury or injury by violence (beating), R. 6¼ as fine. 39). If (permanent) scars are visible (as a result of the beating), R. 48. 40) For damage by cattle mouthing (*tauṇḍika*: the mouthing of market-goods), a fine of R. 5/20. 41) For buffalos, twice the above (as the buffalo has not the cow's sanctity!).

42) For the inspection of wine-barrels (or vats, a fee of) R. 5. 43). For the first (use of a) wine-vat, the official's fee with tithe is R. 2½. 44). But if one brews a second day without declaration, twice the above is to be imposed. 45) For inspection of a wine-distillery (a fee of) R. 3 (an additional), tithe of R. 1¼ and, as royal perquisite, two quarter-measures of wine.

46) The (royal share of) bell-metal utensils is accepted at the (royal) warehouse after mass inspection and weight-checking, on *Āṣāḍha* full-moon. No (other) fee at the (royal) warehouse. 47) At the royal storehouse, the distillery-*vārika* has no obligation to do any work beyond measuring out and delivery of the measure (due to the king) by ¼ *śoṭī* pots.

48) Indigo-vat dues payable by the dipper (*ḍumphaka*) are R.3. 49) For a sugar-cane depot (the dues are) R. 32; tithe (an additional) R. 2¼ . 50) For a wet-ginger depot, half the above. 51) For an oil-mill, R. 3; tithe (an additional) R. 1¼ .

52) Merchants who have come (from a foreign region) only for shelter through the rainy season are not to be charged import duty (and immigration tax); but export duty (and emigration tax, are to be charged on leaving; *cf.* no 16). 53) The frontier customs duty on a carrier-load (*vahitra* = boat-load or large car-load) of trade-goods (*bhāṇḍa,* which means pots and vessels also) is R. 12; (in addition) a tithe of R. 1¼ . 54) For a buffalo-load (of trade-goods) or a camel-load, R. 5¼ inclusive of tithes. 55) (Frontier) dues on a bullock-load

(of trade-goods) R. 2½ ; tithe (in addition) R. ¼. 56) (Frontier) dues on an ass-load (of trade goods) R. 1¼ inclusive of tithes. 57) Half the above for bundle-packs (such as headloads); for loads suspended (from a pole across the shoulders), R. 5/20. 58) For (a light load of) 100 *palas* (about 8 pounds) R. 2/20 inclusive of tithes. 59) (The frontier duty) for grain is at half the above schedule for trade-goods. 60) The frontier duty for a crate of ginger is R. 1¼ inclusive of tithes. 61) For a boat-load of bamboos, R. 6¼ inclusive of tithes. 62) No duty is to be levied on grain carried on the shoulders (presumably as for the bearer's personal food-supply). 63) From (consignments of) cummin-seeds, black mustard seeds, and coriander seeds, merely a sample of a double handful may be taken (as frontier duty). 64) There is no (frontier) tax to be charged on (people crossing to attend) a marriage, *yajña* sacrifice, pilgrimage festival, or a lying-in ceremony. 65) For a bridegroom's procession, the frontier tax is R. 12; in addition, a registry-tithe (*paṭṭa-dhārmika*) of R. 1¼ .

66) The duty on a (large) load of wine (*i.e.* boatload or cartload) is R. 5; tithes R. 1¼. 67) For a skin of wine, R. 1¼. 68) For (wine) loaded in a jar, half the above. 69) For a quarter-sized jug, R. 5/20 inclusive of tithes. 70) For vinegar (or bitter wine, the royal dues are) 3 quarter-measures of rum (*sīdhu).*

71) The tailor, weaver, shoemaker are (in lieu of taxes or corvée) to supply the royal household, each according to the nature of his work, at half the rates prevalent over the countryside. 72) The blacksmith, sawyer, barber, potter, and the like are to be put to corvée labour by the (respective) *vārika* (in lieu of taxes).

The royal privilege of paying a lower price for craftsmen's work is characteristically feudal, and was later claimed by the barons as well. Clause 24 shows that the peasants of the hinterland were beginning to be held arbitrarily by the feudal lords for corvée labour. The artisans in 72 were no longer the unattached, free, wage-workers or guildsmen of earlier days, nor yet the privileged members of a self-sufficing village community; they must have rendered agreed services to all residents of the corporation area, but not against regular taxable cash payment for each performance.

III. A rise in merchant prestige is visible in the second set of plates of the Cālukya king Bhojaśakti found at Anjaneri near Trimbak in the Nasik district. The date is about AD 710.

(M. 159) Be it known to you (all) that the previously deserted (*utsāditam*)Samagiripaṭṭana with the triplet (of smaller villages)—

Ambbeyapallikā—Savāṇeyapallikā—Maureyapallikā has been resettled by me. It has been bestowed upon the entire Corporation (*nagara*)led by the *śreṣṭhī,* Ela and the *śreṣṭhī,* Karapuṭa. The merchants resident at Samagiri have no tolls throughout the realm as long as the sun and moon shall endure. Furthermore, there is (to be) no confiscation (by the crown) of property (of one dying) sonless. No house-trespass (*umura-bheda*) by, nor rations allowance for, royal officials. For violation of a virgin (a fine of) R. 108. For seduction, R. 32. For cutting off an ear, R. 16. For cracking a head R. 4. For any merchant's son assaulting (sexually) a porter-woman (*bhārikā*), R. 108 (fine). The verdict reached after due deliberation by eight or sixteen senior men of the Corporation will be final. This has been posted by Srī-Tejavarma-rāja.

This compares with the charter in the preceding section. The *rūpaka* is now explicitly defined as the silver coin of Kṛṣṇarāja. The whole town consisted of the merchants and their dependents. Hence the word *nagara* is used in the double sense of a traders' and a civic corporation. The merchants were given the right to trial by a jury of their own seniors. The *śreṣṭhin* had now a special position, and indeed such an association would inevitably be dominated by the richest among them, subject to the need for inner solidarity. The first set of Anjaneri plates (dated 710) confirms this position of the merchants. The word *nagara* there must also refer to another such corporation, at Jayapura. Otherwise, the plates make no sense. For, money and village revenues had been donated by the king for a temple, but not in charge of any priest. Instead, the *nagara* merchants are asked to select five or ten of their number, according to the usage of the *nagara,* to supervise the great annual festival of the god, which would be attended by many pilgrims from afar and last a whole fortnight in the month of Mārgaśīrṣa (December). The administration of the temple estate, including disposal and investment of the revenues, was left in trust with the entire *nagara.* Tejavarman adds a colophon to the plate where he 'releases a meadow in Palittapāṭaka to the south of the (merchant corporation-town of) Jayapura. In compensation (*niṣkraya*) of the god Bhogeśvara's land, to the Jayapura merchant-corporation R. 100 have been given. The interest of that hundred is the price of incense (*guggula* = bdellium) to be given annually in perpetuity (to the god) by the Corporation.' The pasture land was not in Jayapura. Just what did Duke Tejavarman mean by relinquishing the land and then paying R. 100 compensation, whereof the merchants should devote the interest to supplying the temple? The only explanation is that this land would have to be used by some tenant and pay royal dues, which Tejavarman had not the right to excuse or transfer; so passing on the nominal ownership to a distant *nagara* would profit nothing. On the other hand, if the money were given to the state (as in most feudal grants) in commutation of taxes, there would be no incentive for the merchants and the profits might be uncertain from year to year, so that the donor's merit could not be guaranteed.

The sixth *ucchvāsa* of Daṇḍin's *Ten Princes*[9] bears testimony to this higher position of the merchants in independent settlements. We need not discuss the authorship of the *Avanti-sundarī-kathā* and the *Kāvyādarśa.* Both the *Pūrvapīṭhikā* and the *Uttarapīṭhikā* are to be discarded. What remains is still a masterpiece of Sanskrit literature. Its sparkle, verve, gusto, controlled flamboyance, penetrating but subtle humour, gentle irony, command of expression, and acquaintance with a broad cross-section of life would qualify it in any language as an outstanding work. The period familiar to the author could not be far from the seventh century, and should undoubtedly be placed before the influence of Bāṇa withered high Sanskrit prose. The word *sāmanta* is used throughout the work in the feudal sense. The stories are not told as of the long-vanished unfamiliar past. The localities where the merchants were supposed to reside namely Bhāvnagar, Sūrat, Mathurā and Ujjain might be chosen as handy names. But it is clear that merchants travelled over long-distances, not only for trade but to choose a bride. In the story within Mitragupta's narrative, the merchant Balabhadra, accompanied by his wife and a slave-woman of all work (*paṇya-dāsī*) bought on the way, settle in a hamlet (*kheṭaka-pura*). This must have been a trade centre, for 'Even in that small place, Balabhadra, a shrewd business man, multiplied his modest capital into a great forune. He was accounted the leading citizen (*paura-agraṇī*), and had a household of dependents suited to his wealth.' When the servant-woman lodged information upon a supposed criminal charge against him, the king's sheriff (*daṇḍa-vāha*), who hoped to gain from the confiscation of Balabhadra's property, had him brought before the merchant *śreṇī* for trial. That is, the royal officer had not normal jurisdiction over a merchant, even over one suspected of the abduction of some girl. Similarly in the next story of

[9] The current Nirṇaysāgar edition and Ryder's elegant translation (modified as necessary) of the *Daśa-kumāra-caritam* have been followed.

the same *ucchvāsa,* where the picaresque hero agrees to confess only before the *vaṇig-grāma* as to how he came in possession of an anklet lost by the epicene merchant's wife. That is, the *grāma* here is merely the older term for our *nagara,* which was its logical extension with the merchant's rise in status.

The question that remains is why this trend did not continue (as in Europe) to the full course of bourgeois development, though individual merchants became rich. Various reasons spring to the mind. In particular, caste,which prevented the merchant class from having relatives in the administration and the army; foreign conquest by Muslims who valued trade, but were not allowed usury by their canon law, and could never come to satisfactory terms with idolaters. The Hong merchant guilds of China wielded far more power than their counterparts in India. But then, the Chinese merchant normally had landlord relatives, a cousin or two in the imperial service as Mandarin, and could belong to the same *wei kuan* provincial union as they. That is, the merchant's class basis was broader in China than in India. In fact, the merchants in China played a leading part in the creation of the first unified state under Chin Shih Huang-ti in 221 BC; one of them was its first chief minister. The corresponding Mauryan state under the brahmin minister Cānakya showed draconic measures against the merchants. The basic answer, naturally, is that village production had conquered in India. Where most of the produce was consumed in the village and where the artisans were also the special village craftsmen, i.e. village potter, village carpenter, blacksmith, leather-worker, etc., *commodity* production and village purchasing power were both at a minimum. Thus, the merchants tended to congregate at port towns—which always trembled in the shadow of the great inland kingdoms—or at the major emporia. It is notable that none of the charters nor the extant Sanskrit literature gives *nagara* privileges to merchants at or near the capital of any kingdom. The workers' guilds disappeared, so that the merchant could hire enough workers for his goods to be turned into a commodity with greater sales value. But when artisan guilds no longer existed as a power with which even princes had to reckon, merchants were at the mercy of feudal lords who controlled the surplus and who were the major purchases of the costliest merchandise. The very success of a virtually closed village economy struck at the roots of proper bourgeois development.

The ease with which the country fell to successive invaders is explained by the helplessness of carefully disarmed villages with their consequent indifference to change of masters. The extreme rigidity of caste was just one more manifestation of the general 'idiocy of village life'.

The merchant's influence shows in certain new departures. In *M* 369–74, dated AD 1212, the sons of king's priest surrendered the entire annual income from the village Alaura in Rewa to one Dhareka who had risen to the rank of Rāṇaka from a lower (*Ṭhakkura*) feudal landlord family. That the original title derived from a royal grant, presumably to the dead father, seems obvious from the royal seal affixed to the copper-plate deed, which was executed in the presence of high officials (cited) of the ruling king Trailokyamalla Candella. The king's assent to the transaction is thus implied. The original royal grant could not bestow more upon the family than the state's rights to taxes and perquisites (including fees for any future settlement of uncultivated land) in the village. These rights were transferred from a priestly family to a feudal lord who was not a brahmin, though brahmins could be *ṭhakkuras*. Not only is this unique, but the reason for the transfer is even more striking: default on a mortgage, *vittabandha*. The 'Council of Five' whereby 'merchants adjudicated such financial affairs according to their custom' is explicitly mentioned in the deed, so that the pledge was forefeited in accordance with mercantile law, and not feudal usage.

Chapter Nine

Monarchs, Merchants and a Maṭha in Northern Konkan (*c.* AD 900–1053)*

RANABIR CHAKRAVARTI

I

One of the noticeable features of the study of Indian history over the last three decades has been a growing interest in its early medieval phase, stretching roughly from AD 600 to AD 1200. Prior to 1950 scholars chiefly paid attention to the dynastic history of this period which witnessed proliferation of regional powers. In recent researches one sees a definite shift in scholarly interest from dynastic chronicling to the changing socio-economic and cultural scene.[1] One of the salient

* *Indian Economic and Social History Review*, 27, 2 (1990).
Author's note: The author wishes to offer his grateful thanks to Professor K.N. Chaudhuri and Professor Burton Stein who made valuable comments on this paper when it was first presented at a seminar in SOAS, London, in February 1989.

[1] One of the most thorough and pioneering attempts at dynastic chronicling of the early medieval period was made by H.C. Ray, *Dynastic History of Northern India*, 2 vols., Delhi, 1973 (rpt). An insightful and incisive analysis of the process of proliferation of regional powers during this period has been provided from the point of view of 'integrative polity' by B.D. Chattopadhyaya, 'Political Processes and Structures of Polity in Early Medival India: Problems of Perspectives', *Proceedings of the Indian History Congress (PIHC)*, XLIV, 1983, Presidential address, Section 1, See R.S. Sharma, *Perspectives in the Social and Economic History of Early India*, Delhi, 1983, for an analytical treatment of early Indian socio-economic and cultural history. The hallmark of Sharma's writings is his

aspects of the cultural life of early medieval times is the growth of sectarian Brahmanical cults mainly as an outcome of the increasing popularity of *Bhakti* ideology. These cults are often found to have been centred in large monastic complexes which consisted of temples, residential structures for priestly peoples and their disciples and provisions of settlements for diverse professional groups catering to the material needs of the *religieux*. Such monastic complexes were called *maṭhas*, if they housed Brahmanical divinities and *vihāra* if they had Buddhist affiliation. Such monastic organisations which grew in number from the fifth-sixth centuries, have attracted the attention of present day historians who not only study them from the point of view of religious history, but also try to examine the political and material milieu in which these organisations flourished.[2]

In other words, scholars often try to focus their attention on the nature and implications of the patronage which these monastic establishments regularly received. There may be little difficulty in appreciating the fact that a complex society can be broken down into several 'ensembles': the economy, politics, culture and the social hierarchy. As these ensembles act and interact, they cannot be studied in isolation and particularly, the economic situation can only be understood in terms of other 'ensembles'.[3]

Religious organisations prior to the fifth century and especially during the first three centuries of the Christian era, received the major share of their patronage from individual donors like artisans, merchants, various professional groups, important administrative officers and even rulers.[4] Buddhist *vihāras* are known to have received both mov-

---

conspicuous emphasis on the elements of change in the socio-economic and cultural history of early India, presenting thereby a sharp contrast to the much cherished idea of the changelessness of Indian society over millenia. Also see R.S. Sharma and D.N. Jha, 'The Economic History of India up to AD 1200: Trends and Prospects', *JESHO*, XVII, 1974, pp. 48–80.

2 R.S. Sharma, *Indian Feudalism*, Delhi, 1980; R.N. Nandi, 'Client, Ritual and Conflict in Early Brahmanical Order', *Indian Historical Review (IHR)*, VI, 1979–80, pp. 103ff.

3 This has been effectively brought out by Fernand Braudel, *Afterthoughts on Material Civilization and Capitalism*, Baltimore and London, 1977, p. 64.

4 These donors are known from a large number of donative records which contain valuable information regarding their occupations, residences, family organizations and patronage. Interestingly enough, these donors—mostly

able and immovable objects as gifts. A significant change occurred in subsequent times with regard to the nature of donation/patronage to such establishments. This change is best illustrated by the widespread practice of creating *agrahāra*, *brahmadeya* and *devadāna* holdings by which a plot (or plots) of land or a village was permanently donated to an individual priest (or a group of priests) or to a religious institution mainly by or with the consent of a political power through the issuance of a copper-plate charter. The basic difference between the grant of plot(s) of land and that of a village should be clarified here: in the case of the gift of a plot of land, it led to the actual transfer of ownership rights through sale, gift or mortgage; the grant of a village, however, resulted in the enjoyment of revenues appropriated from a village by the donee without having any proprietary rights over the village in question.[5]

The Brahmanical *maṭha* at Sanjan, Thane district, Maharashtra, seems to have flourished for about one hundred and fifty years. Five epigraphic records—all found from Chinchani near Sanjan—help us reconstruct a connected and more or less continuous history of this religious organisation:

1. Of the time of Rāṣṭrakūṭa Indra III, Ś.E. 848 = AD 926.
2. An undated record of the time of Rāṣṭrakūṭa Kṛṣna III (AD 939–65).

consisting of artisans, professional groups and merchants—used their occupational credentials, rather than their *Jāti-varṇa* affiliations at the time of recording their gift. This probably indicates their preference for showing their actual status rather than ritual status. See in this context Romila Thapar, *Ancient Indian Social History*, Delhi, 1978. These donative records are discovered over a widespread area, e.g., Mathura in the Gaṅgetic valley, Sanchi and Bharhut in Central Asia and the eastern and the western Deccan. These records are available in H. Lüders, 'A List of Brāhmī Inscriptions from the Earliest Times to about AD 400 (with the exception of those of Aśoka)', being an appendix to *EI*, X, pp. 1–162. J. Burgess and Bhagawanlal Indraji, *Inscriptions from the Cave Temples of Western India*, 1881; D.C. Sircar, *Select Inscriptions Bearing on Indian History and Civilization*, Vol. I, Calcutta, 1965; K.L. Janert ed., *Mathurā Inscription*, Gottingen, 1961; R.P. Chanda, 'Some Unpublished Amaravati Inscriptions', *EI*, XV, pp. 258–78; H. Sarkar, 'Some Early Inscriptions in the Amaravati Museum', *JIH*, IX, 1–2, 1970–71, pp. 1–13.

[5] Though the practice of donating land and/or grant of villages makes its presence felt in the socio-economic and political scenes from the fourth-fifth centuries onwards, its earliest occurrence can be seen in the epigraphic records from the western Deccan assignable to the early centuries of the Christian era.

3. Of the time of Cāmuṇḍarāja, subordinate of Śilāhāra Chinturāja, Ś.E. 956 = AD 1034.
4. Of Moḍha Vijala, Ś.E. 969 = AD 1048.
5. Of Moḍha Vijala, Ś.E. 975 = AD 1053[6]

Sanjan, known in ancient and early medieval times as Saṁjana or Saṁyāna,[7] is situated on the western seaboard of India. Though both the seaboards have played significant roles in their own ways in the history of India,[8] the west coast—stretching from the mouth of the Indus in the north to Kerala in the South—has apparently drawn greater attention from merchants and scholars alike than the east coast. This is partly because of the fairly long continuum of maritime activities in the west coast since the Harappan civilisation (*c.* 2300–1750 BC). The other possible reason of its greater prominence is its broken nature which facilitated the rise of a number of safe and convenient harbours. The third factor was the combination of available shipping technology and the sailors' dependence on the monsoon

[6] These records are edited by D.C. Sircar, 'Rāshṭrakūṭa Charters from Chinchani', *EI*, XXXII, pp. 45–76; Sircar, 'Three grants from Chichani'. The grant of AD 956 belonging to the period of Śilāhāra Chinturāja has also been edited by V.V. Mirashi, *Corpus Inscriptionum Indicarum*, VI (Inscriptions of the Śilāhāras), Delhi, 1977, no. 12, pp. 71–75.

[7] The earliest reference to this place is in the *Geographike Huphegesis* of Claudius Ptolemy (*c.* AD 150) who calls it Sazantion (VII. 63); see E.L. Stevenson trn., *Geograhike Huphegesis*, New York, 1932. A Yonarāja (i.e., Yavanarāja or a Yavana king) of Sañjayata (i.e., Sanjan) was invited by the Ābhīra ruler Vasuṣeṇa of Nagarjunakonda (*c.* 332–45) on the ocassion of the installation of a wooden image of Aṣṭabhūjasvāmin (= Viṣṇu), D.C. Sircar, 'Nagarjunakond Inscription of the time of Ābhīra Vasuṣeṇa, Year 30', *EI*, XXXIV, pp. 197–203. This Sañjaya is undoubtedly the same as Sanjan or Saṁyāna of early medieval epigraphic records. It is generally called Sindan by early Arab writers. The reference to a Yavanarāja may speak of the presence of a ruler of foreign origin at Sanjan. Non-Indians, therefore, appear to have been present at Sanjan at least as early as the fourth century AD. This evidence of the presence of a Yavana ruler at Sanjan has however not been taken into consideration by Himanshu P. Ray, 'The Yavana Presence in Ancient India', *JESHO*, XXXI, pp. 311–25.

[8] Three outstanding recent studies on the Indian Ocean are K.N. Chaudhuri, *Trade and Civilisation in the Indian Ocean from the Rise of Islam to the Seventeenth Century*, Cambridge, 1985; Ashin Das Gupta and M.N. Pearson, (eds.), *India and the Indian Ocean, 1500–1800*, Calcutta, 1987

winds; it was not possible for a vessel to sail between the ports of western and those of the eastern Indian Ocean without having to stop at some harbour or the other on the west coast of India.

Sanjan is situated in the northern part of the Konkan coast which is a narrow strip of land between the Arabian Sea and the Sahyadri (the Western Ghat) range of mountains, stretching from Daman in the north to Goa in the south (21° N–14° N).[9] The settlement pattern in Konkan is intimately connected with both littoral and estuary ports.

> 'Together with the towns in the estuaries at points where the tides carry in the boats, are formed two, sometimes three lines of settlements corresponding to two or three degrees of marine penetration. At no other parts of the western coast is the parallelism so obvious.'[10]

The better agararian resources of this area and its regular communication with an extensive hinterland through three mountainous passages (*ghats*) made it more prosperous than the southern part of the Konkan

and Satish Chandra (ed.), *The Indian Ocean: Explorations in History, Commerce and Politics*, New Delhi, 1987. The maritime historian working on India and the Indian Ocean seems to have been largely inspired by Fernand Braudel who brought into sharp focus the Mediterranean region and emphasized its unity and coherence. Braudel showed that 'the whole sea shared a common destiny, a heavy one indeed with identical problems and general trends, if not identical consequences.' *The Mediterranean and the Mediterranean World in the Age of Philip II*, tr. by S. Reynolds, Vol. I, London, 1972, p. 14. The influence of Braudel on the studies in the Indian Ocean is evident when M.N. Pearson tries to 'see to what extent we can talk of the unity of the Indian Ocean'. M.N. Pearson, 'The State of the Subject', in Ashin Das Gupta and M.N. Pearson (eds.), *op. cit.*, p. 6. But while Braudel's ideas were largely formulated from his studies on a landlocked sea, the Indian Ocean presents a much more complex and challenging task for the historian in the sense that it offers considerably greater diversities than the Mediterranean from the points of view of population, climate, socio-economic and political organizations, religious beliefs and practices. The term Indian Ocean has its origin in Arabic *al-bahr al-Hindi*; the corresponding Persian term for the same is *darya'i akhzar*; see M.N. Pearson, *op. cit.*, pp. 9–10.

[9] R.L. Singh, *India: A Regional Grography*, Benares, 1977; O.H.K. Spate and A.T.A. Learmonth, *India and Pakistan: A General and Regional Geography*, London, 1967.

[10] J. Deloche, 'Geographical Consideration in the Localization of Ancient Sea-ports of India', *JESHR*, 20, 4, Oct.–Dec. 1983, pp. 439–48.

coast.[11] Konkan, in general, and north Konkan in particular, came to the limelight for the first time during the age of Indo-Roman commerce (*c.* late first century BC–third century AD).[12] The gradual decline of the Indo-Roman trade seems to have adversely affected its long-distance trade, though the possibility of continuous coastal contacts with other parts on the western coast cannot be ruled out.

Overseas long-distance network in the western Indian Ocean seems to have been promoted by the Byzantine empire and the Sasanids in Iran, both the powers being interested in commerce with India. While Indo-Roman maritime trade was mainly carried through the Red Sea, Byzantine and Sasanian power focused their attention principally on the Persian Gulf. As a result of this the Sasanids of Iran assumed an intermediate position between the Byzantine territories and the western littorals of India. The Sasanids had a strong motive to control the maritime trade in the Persian Gulf from the very inception of their power and by the sixth century they became a major force in the western Indian Ocean.[13] All these seem to have favoured overseas commerce in the Konkan coast, though not of the scale one witnessed in the first three centuries of the Christian Era. Towards the close of the sixth century Cosmas Indicopleustes reported on the prosperity of three north Konkan ports, viz., Kalliena (Kalyan), Souppara (Sopara) and Semylla (Chaul).[14] Archaeological excavations ar various Iranian sites have yielded, among other items, Red Polished Ware which are unmistakably of Indian origin and abundant in Gujarat and Maharashtra. 'The examples from Iran occur exclusively on their

[11] R.L. Singh, *op. cit.*, pp. 910–11. The difference in the physical features and resources of north Konkan from those of the south has been highlighted by Himanshu P. Ray, *Monastery and Guild: Commerce under the Sātavāhanas*, Delhi, 1986.

[12] E.H. Warmington, *Commerce between the Roman Empire and India*, Delhi, 1974, (rpt.); R.E.M. Wheeler, *Rome beyond the Imperial Fronteir*, London, 1954; U.N. Ghoshal, 'Economic Conditions', in K.A. Nilakantha Sastri (ed.), *The Comprehensive History of India*, Calcutta, 1957. An exhaustive bibliography on this subject is available in M.G. Raschke, 'New Studies in Roman Commerce with the East', *Aufstieg und Niedergang der Romischer Welt*, Berlin, 1978.

[13] David Whitehouse and Andrew Williamson, 'Sasanian Maritime Trade', *Iran*, XI, 1973, pp. 29–49.

[14] Cosmas Indicopleustes, *Christian Topography*, tr. J.W. McCrindle, London, 1898, pp. 398ff.

coast and without doubt were imported as a by-product of maritime trade.'[15] Ports in the northern Konkan coast seem to have been involved in the overseas trade with the Persian Gulf harbours. It is known from Al Tabari's accounts that the Cālukya ruler Pulakeśin II (610–42) who controlled considerable parts of western Deccan, including the Konkan Coast, sent diplomatic missions to the Persian ruler Khasru I.[16] Such diplomatic contact between a power of the western Deccan and his counterpart in Iran could have been prompted by the prospects of overseas trade between the Konkan and Persian Gulf ports. All these overseas commercial contacts in the western Indian Ocean were overshadowed by the trememdous growth of maritime commerce in the Indian Ocean and particularly its western segments—from the seventh/eighth centuries AD onwards. One of the most important factors in the vigorous oceanic trade in the Indian Ocean was the birth and spread of Islam which had a definite orientation towards trade and urbanism.[17]

Like many areas of north Konkan, Sanjan appears to have been agriculturally prosperous. The grant of AD 926 speaks of the production of śāli rice (*śālyannam*) here.[18] The area seems to have been acquainted with cultivation of oilseeds, obviously for producing edible oil.[19] Konkan was also known for the plantation of coconut, the economic importance of which can hardly be overemphasised, since the first century AD.[20] Sanjan grew both staple (rice) and cash (oilseeds and coconut) crops. The agricultural prosperity of this region was to a considerable extent due to profuse orographic rainfall and the existence of fertile river valleys.[21]

[15] David Whitehouse and Andrew Williamson, *op. cit.*, p. 39.

[16] R.C. Majumdar (ed.), *The Classical Age*, Bombay, 1970. Whitehouse and Williamson have however wrongly placed Pulakeśin II in AD 528 (*op. cit.*, p. 44) who actually ruled from 610 to 642.

[17] K.N. Chaudhuri, *op. cit.*

[18] *EI*, XXXII, p. 52, co. 22.

[19] This will be evident from the reference to an oil-mill (*ghānaka*) in the grant of AD 1034; *EI*, XXXII, p. 67, 11.19–20.

[20] The earliest evidence of largescale coconut plantation in this area is furnished by the Nasik inscription of Nahapāna, years 41, 42, 45, *SI*, pp. 164–67. Also see D.D. Kosambi, *An Introduction to the Study of Indian History*, Bombay, 1956.

[21] O.H.K. Spate and A.T.A. Learmonth., *op. cit.*, pp. 606–608.

These rivers appear to have been navigable at least in their downstream. This will be evident from the reference to the ferry service of a river of Sanjan which must have facilitated riverine communication for an outlet to the sea.[22] The most notable feature of Ṣanjan was that it was a port town, lying in close proximity to the area. Our records call it both a harbour (*velākula*) and a town (*paṭṭaa*) .[23] This is also corroborated by early medieval Arab accounts which not only mention Sindan (or Sanjan) as a port, but also speak of regular voyages between Sanjan and Kanbaya (Cambay), Subara (Sopara) and Saimur (Chaul).[24] It is, therefore, hardly surprising that the epigraphic records under review also contain names and organisations of merchants and artisans at Sanjan.

Sanjan appears to have been a notable commercial centre at the coast having a secure agrarian base and inhabited by diverse types of craftsmen. That the town in question also served as the headquarters of the local administrative unit (*maṇḍala*) extending up to Ākāśikā or modern Agashe is mentioned in one of our records.[25] This particular inscription also refers to the existence of four thousand watch-stations (*draṅgas*) in Sanjan, a figure which seems inflated. Such watch-stations could have been utilised for keeping vigilance over movements of traffic—both by sea and land. One thus finds in this littoral port-town a combination of diverse economic and politico-administrative functions. To this should be added its importance as a religious centre with a Brahmanical *maṭha*.[26]

II

The deity in the *matha* at Sanjan is variously called Devī, Daśamī and Bhagavagtī in our records. The grant of 926 which gives us the

[22] *EI*, XXXII, p. 52, 11.22.

[23] *Velākula* figures in *EI*, XXXII, p. 52, 1.20 and *pattana* in ibid., p. 74, 1.9.

[24] For Arab geographers' accounts see Eliot and Dawson, *History of India as Told by Its Own Historians* (*HIOH*) I, II, and II; also S.M. Nainar, *The Arab Geographers' Knowledge of Southern India*, Madras, 1942.

[25] *EI*, XXXII, p. 74, 1.9.

[26] Such a multi-functional centre like Sanjan must have been placed fairly high in the hierarchy of settlements in the Deccan. Such a hierarchy is proposed on the basis of the concept of 'functional lattice'. Carol S. Crumley, 'Towards a Locational Definition of State System of Settlements', *American Anthropologist*, 78, 1976, pp. 59–73.

earliest information about the *maṭha* begins with an invocation to goddess Mahiṣāsuramardinī Durgā.[27] The *maṭha* was built by a Brāhmaṇa named Annamaiya whose two brothers are also mentioned in the grant of 926. One of the brothers was named Kautuka and the monastic complex is variously called Kautuka and Kavatika *maṭhikā*. The impression one gets is that though Annamaiya was chiefly instrumental in establishing the *maṭha*, it was named after another brother who was probably the eledest of the three.[28]

The record of 926 belongs to the time of the Rāṣṭrakūṭa King, Indra III, but it says that the complex was built during the reign of his father Kṛṣṇa II (875–915).[29] As the local subordinate chief ruling at Sanjan under the overlordship of Indra III was the same as the one serving his father, it may be safely surmised that the *maṭha*, which received patronage from the local ruler of Sanjan, came to be established some time before 926, if not prior to the reign of Indra III. We would like to assign the foundation of the *maṭha* roughly about 900.

Interestingly enough the administration of Saṁyāna *maṇḍala* was entrusted by Kṛṣṇa II and Indra III to a governor of Arab origin (*tājikānvaya*) named Sugatipa Madhumati, son of Sahiyārahāra.[30] D.C. Sircar rightly suggested that Madhumati was the Sanskritised version of the name Muhammad.[31] The name of Madhumati's father, Sahiyarahara, in all probability corresponds to Shahriyar. However, the name Sahiyārahāra can also be read, according to Sircar, as

[27] *EI*, XXXII, p. 51, 11.2–3.

[28] The Raṣṭrakūṭas from the very beginning of their independent political existence contolled both north and south Konkan and had some definite interest in the littoral area in question. Ranabir Chakravarti, 'The Rāṣṭrakūṭa Attitude towards the Konkan Coast' (forthcoming) discusses the topic in details.

[29] *EI*, XXXII, p. 49.

[30] *EI*, XXXII, p. 52, 11.19–21. The inscription actually states that Madhumati conquered on behalf of his overlord all the kings of the harbour (*vijitya karadaṇḍena sarvva-velākulādhipān)*.

[31] *EI*, XXXII, p. 47. This is an interesting but not unusual situation. The same name is Sankritized as Mahumata and Madhumata in two other early medieval records. *EI*, XXXII, p. 66.1.11 and p. 47, fn. 3. The tendency to Sanskritize Muslim names is also demonstrated by the use of the epithet *Sūratrāṇa* in the place of Sultan as title of Alauddin Khalji. Cf. the Cambay Stambhana Pārśvanātha Temple inscription of 1308, *EI*, Appendix to XIX–XXIII, no. 664.

Hiyārahāra or Yārahāra.[32] This is an unusual situation and calls for a closer study.

Early medieval Arab writers like Sulaiman (851), Abu Zayd (916), Ibn Khordadbeh (912), Al Maŝudi (915), Al Ishtakhri (951), Ibn Haukal (943–68), etc., and the *Huḍuḍ-al-Alam* (982) on the other hand regularly refer to the presence of Arabs as merchants in the country called Kamkam/Kamkar/Makamkam which clearly stands for Konkan or Mahākonkan.[33] These authors also speak very highly of the Balhara rulers of Kamkam who are identified with the Rāṣṭrakūṭas, the name Balhara being derived from the customary title of the Rāṣṭrakūṭas, Vallabharāja. One can hardly miss the fact that though the Arab authors invariably described the Rāṣṭrakūṭas or the Balharas as the ruler of Kamkam or Konkan, the Rāṣṭrakūtas were never a power of the coast and were essentially a power of the interior or mainland. This indicates that the Konkan coast was intimately known and held as significant by the Arabs as this coast provided the major meeting point between the Arabs and the Rāṣṭrakūṭas.

We have already pointed to the emergence of the Persian Gulf in the overseas trade of the western Indian Ocean. The importance of the Gulf was further enhanced since the foundation of the Abbasid Caliphate in Siraf and later in Basra. Literary and archaeological data effectively demonstrate that a brisk trade between the Persian Gulf and China developed by the eighth century, if not earlier.[34] Arab vessels

32 If the name is Sahiyārahāra then it may have been originally Shariyar. Cf. the name Bujurg ibn Shahriyar, the author of the famous *Kitab Ajaib al-Hind.* Sircar however did not suggest any Arabic name which could be Sankritized as Sahiyārahāra/Hiyārahāra/Yārahāra.

33 *HIOH*, I, II and III and S.M.H. Nainar, *op. cit.*

34 K.N. Chaudhuri, *op. cit.*; G.F. Hourani, *The Arab Sea-faring in the Indian Ocean in Ancient and Medieval Times*, Beirut, 1963, Archaeological corroboration of Sino-Persian trade comes largely in the form of pottery sherds found in excavated sites of western Asia. See for example, David Whitehouse, 'Excavation at Siraf: Third Interim Report', *Iran*, 1970, pp. 1–18; also see relevant articles in Takahito Mikasa (ed.), *Cultural and Economic Relations between East and West: Sea Routes*, Wiesbaden, 1988, Tabari, Baladhuri and Dinwari spoke of the presence of *sufun min al-sin* and *sufun siniyah* at the Gulf port of al-Uballah at the time of the Muslim conquest. The two terms are generally taken to denote Chinese ships, but some scholars translate these as 'ships that sail to China' and as 'ships carrying Chinese merchandise'. Chinese chronicles on the other hand refer to *Possu* people who are often identified with the Persians.

bound for China and starting from a Persian Gulf port would have found it convenient, following the south-western monsoon wind, to call at some harbours in the Gujarat, Konkan or Malabar littorals. Initially around the eighth century direct voyages between the Persian Gulf and Khan-fu (Canton) were undertaken by Persian ships.[35] But this fell out of practice during subsequent periods, because a single voyage from Persia to China would have required considerable transactional cost and that is why 'shorter, segmented voyages between a number of leading port-cities' came to be preferred.[36] This would probably further underline the importance of harbours on the western sea-board of India—including those in Konkan—in the east-west overseas trade network of the Indian Ocean.

Al Mas'udi's *Kitab Muruj adh-Dhahab wa Ma'adin al-Jauhar* emphasizes the importance of these ports on the Konkan coast. Al Mas'udi's account is particularly important because, (a) he personally visited India and the Konkan coast in 915–16, i.e. contemporary to the reign of Rāṣṭrakūṭa Indra III, and (b) he depended considerably on Arab merchants' and sailors' first hand experiences for his information.[37] He mentions the ten thousand *bayasira* (the significance of the term is explained below) Muslims at the Konkanese port-city of Saimur (= Chaul, near Bombay) where many merchants from Siraf, Uman, Basra and Baghdad also resided. He also mentions a prominent merchant Musa b. Ishaq al Sandaluni and Abu Said Maru'f b. Zakariya, the head (*al-hazmat*) of the Muslims.[38] It is not at all unlikely that a similar situation prevailed at Sanjan, epigraphic records wherefrom strikingly confirm the literary account of close cooperations between the Arabs and the Rāṣṭrakūṭas. The Arab governor at Sanjan (or his predecessors) must have come to Konkan originally as a merchant. Madhumati was allowed to rule over the area mentioned probably as reward for his successful military design. It is difficult to ascertain against which coastal power the Arab governor earned his victory, but the likely adversary could have been the Śilāhāra of north Konkan who had served the Rāṣṭrakūṭas as their

[35] G.F. Hourani, *op. cit.*

[36] K.N. Chaudhuri, *op. cit.*, p. 39; see also accompanying maps.

[37] S. Maqbul Ahmad, 'Travels of Abu'l Hasan Ali B. Al-Husain Al Maśudi, *Islamic Culture*, XXVIII, 1954, pp. 509–24.

[38] S. Maqbul Ahmad, 'Al Mas'udi on the Kings of India', in S. Maqbul Ahmad and A. Rahman (eds.), *Al Mas'udi Millenary Commemoration Volume*, Aligarh, 1960, pp. 97–112.

vassals. The involvement of the Arabs in commerce and local politics of north Konkan must have been designed to further the mutual interests of both the Arabs and the Rāṣṭrakūṭas.

The Arabs of the Konkan coast and Sanjan, in particular, must have been anxious to integrate themselves with the local society. This is especially significant if we bear in mind that many of the Muslim resident merchants in the north Konkan were, according to Al Mas'udi, *bayasirah. Bayasirah* (singular *bayasari*) denote a particular ethnic element that have been excluded from the membership of the Arab tribal groups. They are equated with the weak (*da'if*) people of southern Arabia and described as riff-raff (*ra 'a'al- nas*) and people without any proper origin (*aṣl*). Even today they often earn their living by being servants (*khuddam*) to leading Arab families. Their very name meant impure breed and they were looked down upon by those who were *aṣl*, e.g., Arabs. Persians and the like.[39] It is, therefore, quite likely that a large number of Muslim merchants in the north Konkan coast may not have initially enjoyed social pre-eminence, at least, in the eyes of the othodox Islamic community. Foreign merchants residing abroad do often feel the urge to cultivate amiable relations with the local political authority and the locally important people, as they are usually a minority community in an alien situation. The so-called low or impure origin of many of the Muslim merchants residing in north Konkan (including Sanjan) may have further compelled them to form close linkages with powerful 'interest groups'—politically and socially—of the area. Al Mas'udi also informs us that they married into the local community;[40] such matrimonial connections not only point at the considerable flexible social condition in north Konkan, but also could have paved the way for the acceptance of the Muslims in the coastal society of north Konkan. Another important way of integration into an alien society was to seek affiliations with local religio-cultural institutions/establishments. These points are to be taken into consideration when one tries to examine the association of an Arab governor and Muslim merchants with a Brahmanical *maṭha*.

[39] J.C. Wilkinson, 'Bayasirah and Bayadir', *Arabian Studies*, I, 1974, pp. 75–84. This article has been of particular help for our present discussion, as S. Maqbul Ahmad earlier informed us that 'I have not been able to trace the origin of the word *baysar* (singular of *Bayasirah*)', 'Al Mas'udi on the Kings of India'. *op. cit.*, p. 108, fn. 2.

[40] Al Mas'udi, *Muruj al Dhahab wa-Ma'adin al-Jauhar*, tr. C. Berbier de Meynard and Pavet de Courteille Les Prairies d'Or, 9 vols, Paris, 1861–77, Vol. II, pp. 85–86.

Like any other contemporary ruler in India, Madhumati, the Arab governor of Sanjan, granted land to the *maṭha*; he was requested to do so by Annamaiya. Annamaiya approached Madhumati through his friend Puvvaiya, a Brāhmaṇa minister serving the Arab governor.[41] This indicates the intimate connections between the ruler and the priestly community. Madhumati granted to the monastery a plot of land (½ *dhura* = $^1/_{20}$th of a *bigha*) in the village of Devīhāra and also the following revenues available from the village Kānāduka situated in the district (*viṣaya*) of Kolimahara: major (*udraṅga*) and minor (*uparikara*) taxes, royal share of the produce (*sa-bhoga-bhāga*), fines from ten customary offences (*sa-daṇḍa daśāparādha*), taxes in grain (*dhānya*) and cash (*hiraṇya*), tax payable in lieu of forced labour (*sotpadyamāna viṣṭipratyāya*) and other exemptions.[42] The income accrued from the above heads would be spent for the maintenance and repair of the *maṭha*, offerings to the goddess and for the daily feeding of nine persons belonging to an assembly of Brāhmaṇas,[43] called Pañcagauḍīya Mahāparṣad and/or Āryadeśīya Mahāparṣad. This assembly is known to have consisted of: (i) Sārasvata, (ii) Kānyakubja, (iii) Gauḍa, (iv) Maithila, and (v) Utkala Brāhmaṇas.[44] The *maṭha* had, therefore, already assumed the character of a religious complex, having not only a temple but also a residential area for various types of north Indian Brāhmaṇas who must have managed the affairs of the *maṭha*. The importance of the *maṭha* is futher highlighted by the presence of the following notable people at the time of the grant: revenue officer in charge of the collection of royal share of agricultural produce (*dhruva*), district level officers (*viṣayādhikārikas*) and members of the Hamyāmāna group. The last-mentioned group is often taken by scholars to denote Parsi communities, but D.C. Sircar effectively demonstrated that their term actually stood for a professional body, consisting of representatives of goldsmiths, braziers, blacksmiths, carpenters and stone masons.[45] The religious organization thus appears to have been able to manage patronage and support from various

[41] *EI*, XXXII, p. 52, 11.24–25. *Śrī Puvvayi' obhavadyasya mantrī mantravidamvaraḥ.*

[42] *EI*, XXXII, p. 53, 11.36–37.

[43] *EI*, XXXII, p. 53, 11.29–31.

[44] Chitrarekha Gupta, *Brāhmaṇas in Ancient India,* Delhi, 1979.

[45] *EI*, XXXV, 291–92. The widely accepted and general view is that either Haṁyamāna was nothing but the same as Saṁyāna or it denoted the Parsis in the west coast.

sections of the coastal society ranging from merchants and artisans to administrators and rulers.

III

The Arabs seem to have continued to reside in and manage the local administration of Sanjan during the subsequent period, as will be evident from the undated grant of Kṛṣṇa III (939–67), the last of great Rāṣṭrakūṭa rulers.[46] This record enlists the *Tajiks* or Arabs among people subjugated by and/or paying allegiance to Rāṣṭrakūṭas.[47] The name of the Arab governor, ruling in and around Sanjan, is however not mentioned.

This record speaks of another religious establishment in Sanjan, besides Kautuka *maṭha*. The second temple, said to have been situated adjacent to the Devī temple, belonged to Viṣṇu who is called Bhillamāla Madhusūdanadeva, so called because the temple was founded by merchants from Bhillamāla,[48] modern Bhinmal near Jodhpur in Rajasthan. Bhillamāla was originally known as Śrīmāla, according to the *Niśīthacūrṇi* (X. 225, the text is dated to *c*. AD 675) and the *Kuvalayamālā* of AD 778. The name Śrīmālā may indicate the prosperous condition of the area (*śri* = wealth). Apart from having a regular settlement of merchants, Śrimāla or Bhillamāla was known for its specialist craftsmen/artisans, as is evident from the reference to a family of architects (*sūtradharas*) in a seventh century inscription from Nagar.[49] One can immediately see that Sanjan was able to attract merchants from an already established exchange centre

[46] Between the reign of Indra III and that of Kṛṣṇa III can be assigned Amoghavarṣa II (928–9), Govinda IV (929–34), and Amoghavarṣa III (934–39).

[47] *EI*, XXXII, 59, 11.20–22.

[48] *EI*, XXXII, 59. *Śrī Bhillamādevo vandyairabhinanditānindyaḥ. . . Madhusūdanākhyāyaḥ . . . yodhiṣṭhita . . . śrī Bhillamāla-vaṇijaṁ kulajairamayaiḥ,* 11.23–26.

[49] For Bhinmal see K.C. Jain, *Ancient Cities and Towns of Rajasthan*, Delhi, 1972, p.156ff. That Bhinmal continued as an exchange centre in later days is attested by a grant of 1276. It informs us about a chief Karmasiṁha who was in charge of the export and import department of Bhinmal during the reign of Cauhan Cācigadeva.

situated far into the interior. The spatial mobility of the Bhinmal merchants should be taken into consideration.[50] It is also plainly visible that like the Devī temple the second religious organization at Sanjan also had close linkages with a mercantile community.

The two neighbouring temples are found to have been involved in a bitter dispute over a plot of land. According to Kṛṣṇa III's record, a plot of land, enclosed within the northern boundary wall of Kautuka *maṭha*, actually belonged to the temple of Bhillamāladeva but was the possession of the Devi temple.[51] Rapproachment was reached between the two religious organisations by a *vyavasthā* (meaning a legal decision in a dispute) based on a decree or *sthiti* which is described as being permanent.[52] According to the decision, the disputed plot of land would remain in possession of Kautuka *maṭha* which would, in its turn, pay the Vaiṣṇava organisation an annual rent (*srotaka*) of 40 *drammas* or silver coins.[53] 'The inscription seems to specify the payment in coins minted by a trader named *śreṣṭhin* Gambuvaka' (*Vyavahāruka-śreṣṭha Gambhuvaka dramma*) .[54] The term *vyavahāraka/vyavahārika* stands for a dealer or merchant, and *śreṣṭhi* means a rich merchant. Since the amount of 40 *drammas* is mentioned in close association with the merchant in question, Gambhuvaka may be considered a merchant minting coins (probably under official approval), distinct from a simple moneylender (*kusīdin/kusīidajīvin*) .[55] The amount was to be paid on the day after the Dipāvalī festival (*dīpotsava-bhange*).[56]The *vyavasthā* also

50 Cf. the spatial mobility of *sūtradharas* who moved from Bhinmal to Nagar where they built a step well, see n. 49.

51 *Yathā maṭhikottara-digbhāge sthita-prākārābhyantare, smadīya kiyanmātra bhūmiḥ, EI*, XXXII, p. 60, 11. 36–37.

52 '*Sthityā vyavastheyamācandrārkka-kālam*', EI, XXXII, p. 60, 1.44.

53 . . . *asmadīya kiyanmātrabhūmiriya praviṣṭa tatsambandhe maṭhiikāya'smākam . . . deyaḥcatvāriṁsādaṅkato'pi dra* 40, *EI*, XXXII, p. 60, 11.37–38.

54 *EI*, XXXII, p. 57.

55 Ranabir Chakravarti, 'Merchants of Konkan', *IESHR,* 23, 2, 1986, pp. 207–15.

56 This is probably the earliest epigraphic evidence of the festival of Diwali. The *Yasástilakacampu* of Somadevasūrī, contemporary to Rāṣṭrakūta Kṛṣṇa III, contains a graphic description of Dīpavalī festival. Drinking, merry-making, revelry and a game of dice were inseparable aspects of this festival which was observed on the new moon night of the first fortnight of

expressly states that the conditions of the rapproachment must be strictly followed by both parties (*ubhaya-vargeṇāpi pālanīya*), i.e., by persons who managed the affairs of their respective organizations. These persons are called *vārikas*. It anyone tried to grab land or raise the amount of rent on various pretexts (*srotaka-samvarddhana-vyājenā-nyāyena vā prakārena prākāra bhañjanāya*), including pressurizing other by attempting suicide (*ātmahanana*) or by breaking the compound wall, will incur severe reprobation.[57] The property of an offending merchant-devotee of Madhusūdana would be confiscated (*vaṇijastu rājakulena sarvvasyāpaharaṇam karaṇīyam*), while a Brāhmaṇa devotee would be degraded as low as a dog, donkey and Caṇḍāla.[58] The tone of the settlement leaves little room for doubt that there was considerable tussle and tension between the Devī and Viṣṇu temples.

the month of Kārttika (November) by illuminating the darkness of the night with thousands of lamps. Though Dipāvalī is a festival favourite with all sections of Indian people, it had special association with the mercantile community which worshipped Lakṣmi or the goddess of fortune during Diwali. Besides, the Indian mercantile community often considered the first day after the Diwali festival as the beginning of the new financial/accounting year. The eighteenth century Persian dictionary *Bahar-i-Azam* written by Tekchanḍ Bahar gives interesting information about Diwali. If a merchant pulled down the shutter of his shop and lighted a candle in front of his shop in broad daylight on the day following the Diwali festival, he declared himself thereby a *diwalia* or bankrupt person. (I am grateful to Professor Irfan Habib for drawing my attention to this information in the *Bahar-i-Azam*). The text also indicates the possibility of the Diwali having a special significance for the mercantile community for marking the beginning of the new financial year. Judged in this light, the payment of 40 *drammas* as rent on the day after the Dīpotsava assumes a special significance. The sum was to be specifically paid on that day because it marked the beginning of a new accounting year. We may hence logically infer that the custom of considering Dīpavalī as marking the beginning of a new financial year may be pushed back at least to the tenth century. Ranabir Chakravarti, 'The Earliest Epigraphic Evidence of Dīpavalī' (forthcoming) discusses relevant issues in details.

[57] *EI*, XXXII, p. 60, 11.39–40.

[58] Ibid., p. 60, 11.41–42 and 1.44. H.D. Sankalia, 'Sanjan—A Miniature Bombay in 980', in B.N. Mukherjee *et al.* (eds.), *Dīneśacandrika*, Delhi, 1983, pp. 209–13, attempts to locate structural remains of these two temples at Sanjan. But explorations have only yielded remains of large bricks which may indicate the existence of substantial structures; but no

Two striking features should be highlighted here. The first is the clear evidence of the close cooperation and linkage between religious establishments and their respective merchant patrons. The second is the fact that the dispute was brought to an end by mutual agreement between the authorities of two organisations and not by any direct administrative intervention. But since the terms and conditions of the *vyavasthā* are laid down in an official document of the Rāṣṭrakūṭa monarch, it is likely that he and his local governor were aware and tacitly approved of the arrangements between the temple organizations.

IV

Kṛṣṇa III was the last powerful ruler of the Rāṣṭrakūṭa dynasty. In the ensuing political changes in the Deccan, the Konkan coast once again came under the Śilāhāras, the erstwhile vassals of the Rāṣṭrakūṭas. The rise of the independent rulers of north Konkan brought an end to the rule of the Arab governors at Sanjan.[59] The grant of 1034 shows that Śilāhāra Chinturāja entrusted the administration of Sanjan and the area around it to his subordinate chief Cāmuṇḍarāja.[60] The political change, however, did not spell any harm to Kautuka *maṭha*. On the other hand, the *maṭha* received from Cāmuṇḍarāja, with the approval of his overlord, an oil-mill (*ghānaka*) and oil cakes (*kholikā*) produced in the mill.[61] The importance of the oil-mill is to be appreciated in the light of the cultivation of oilseeds in the neighbouring countryside of Sanjan. The record contains an imprecatory verse admonishing that a destroyer of *ghānaka* could not purify himself from the sin even by the gift of a billion of cows.[62] Similar imprecatory verses were also used with the intention of protecting an irrigation project. This may logically imply the growing importance of oil-mills in the agrarian economy of north Konkan.

---

definite identification of either of the temples was possible. The exploration also yielded some small (1.7–1.9 cm. in diameter) coins of silver weighing 4.16 gms.

[59] For the political history of the Śilāhāras see V.V. Mirashi, *op.cit.*

[60] *EI*, XXXII, p. 66, 11.5–6.

[61] *EI*, XXXII, p.67, 11.19–20.

[62] Ibid., p. 68, 1.28.

The main purpose of the donation of the oil-mill was to ensure the supply of oil with which a holy lamp would be burnt before goddess Bhagavatī and feet of scholars and guests would be massaged.[63] This suggests a considerable enlargement in the scope of activities of the Kautuka *maṭha*. Beginning with a temple and an assembly of Brāhmaṇas in *c*. AD 900, the *maṭha* must have assumed greater complexities by accommodating scholars (*svādhyāyikas*) and guests. The *mahāparṣad* also seems to have been active and its several members (e.g. Agasti, Gāvi, Sindura, Ādityavardhana, etc.) are important enough to be categorically mentioned as being present at the time of the grant.[64] The gift of the oil-mill was received on behalf of the *maṭha* by Cihaḍa, who as a representative of the assembly must have enjoyed a distinguished position in the management of the affairs of the religious complex.[65] Another person named Yājnikara is designated as *śālāsthānamukhya*[66] which may indicate that he was in charge of the assembly hall in the *maṭha*. From the details on the roles of various persons attached to the *maṭha*, one can logically infer the growing complexities in the affairs of this organization.

The fact that the Devī *maṭha* was making its presence felt in the social and cultural life of the coastal town can be well appreciated by the attendance of leading citizens—both government officers and non-official people—at the occasion of the donation of the oil-mill. Among officials we come across the chief exective officer (*mahāmātya*), the minister in charge of war and peace (*sāndhivigrāhika*), the city commissioner (*puramukhya*) and a large number of district officials (*viṣayin/viṣāyadhikārī*).[67] This list of officers when compared with that found in the grant 926 certainly looks more numerous, a fact which leads us to conclude that there was stronger official awareness of and association with the *maṭha* than in the previous period. This is however neither surprising nor unexpected. The Śilāhāras were a power of the coast (unlike the Rāṣṭrakūṭas who were essentially a power of the interior) and consequently showed greater involvement in the littoral areas under its occupation.[68]

[63] Ibid., p. 66, 1.12.
[64] Ibid., p. 67, 1.13.
[65] Ibid., 1.18.
[66] Ibid., 1.12.
[67] *EI*, XXXII, p. 67, 11.4–6 and 1.12.
[68] Inscriptions of the Śilāhāra rulers often bear the royal eipthet 'lord of the western sea' (*paścimasamudrādhipati*). This title is however absent in the

The list of leading citizens is no less impressive than that of the officials mentioned above. These include the names of goldsmith (*suvarṇṇa*), representatives of the craftsmen's guilds (*haṁyamāna*), an ordinary merchant (*vaṇik*) Uva, three wealthier merchants (*śreṣthīs*), viz., Keśari, Suvarṇṇa, and Kokkala, and lastly three Arab merchants, viz., Alliya, Mahara and Mahumata.[69] Though the Śilāhāras reoccupied north Konkan at the expense of Arab governors at Sanjan, they however, appear to have continued the previous policy of encouraging settlements of Arab merchants at Sanjan. One cannot but be impressed by the longdrawn linkages between a religious establishment and the local mercantile communities.

V

The Śilāhāra rule in north Konkan was replaced by that of the local Moḍhas. A Moḍha ruler named Vijala (variously called Vija, Vīja and Vijja) is known to have ruled over this area. He too granted fiscal immunities to the Devī *maṭha*. In 1047 and 1053 the Devī *maṭha* was twice endowed with a tax named *siridirkā*, the specific nature of which is unknown. In 1047 *siridirkā* tax was collected from Kannadda village already under the *maṭha* (*srimat-Kavatika-maṭhikā-prabhujyamāna-Kanāḍḍagrāmma siridirkā*).[70] If such a cess was levied from an already *agrahāra* village, its importance as a source of revenue has to be taken into consideration. The transfer of *siridirkā* tax on two separate occasions was meant respectively for the maintenance of two householders (Bahudhara and Kankua) and a scholar, Lakṣmīdhara, and for the daily feeding of twenty-five Brāhmaṇas at the *maṭha* (*bhojanāksayanīvi*).[71] The presence of householders at the *maṭha* implies that the monastic complex also accommodated ordinary people. As usual important officers like the chief executive (*mahāpradhāna*), and the tax-collector (*dhruva*) and representatives of the craftsmen's guilds (*haṁyamāna*) were present on both the occasions of the transfer of the cess to the *maṭha*.[72]

---

records of the Śilāhāras of Kolhapur who were a power of the interior. See V.V. Mirashi, *op. cit.*

[69] *EI*, XXXII, p. 66, ll.10–11. Also see Ranabir Chakravarti, *IESHR*, 23, 2, 1986, pp. 207–15.

[70] *EI*, XXXII, 70, 11.13–14 and 75, 11.30–31.

[71] Ibid., 70, 1.14–15, and 75, 11.30–31.

[72] Ibid., 69–70, 11.7–8 and 74, 11.10–11.

VI

Let us now take a stock of the accumulated property of the *maṭha* over a century and a half. It had some plots of land under its ownership, enjoyed fiscal transfers from at least three villages and possessed an oil-mill along with the produce of the oil-mill. These landed possessions provided the major source of the sustenance to the *maṭha* and helped it grow over the years. It has been argued by the protagonists of the theory of Indian feudalism, particularly by R.S. Sharma, that such transfer of landed properties and/or revenues to religious bodies and priestly peoples resulted in the rise of landed intermediaries and corrosion of the political and economic prerogatives of the ruler.[73] B.N.S. Yadava also has provided with literary accounts of the decline of trade and a degrading position of the Vaiśyas who were mainly engaged in trade. Yadava strongly supports Sharma's theory of languishing trade, lesser use of minted currency and the rise of a self-sufficient 'closed' economy.[74] Though it is true that no definite

[73] R.S. Sharma firmly believes that the transition in the economic life from the early historical to the early medieval was largely instrumental through the process of widespread land grants, initially made in favour of priestly and religious organisations and then secular benificiaries. The broad developments in the early medieval economy, according to Sharma, are: (i) growth of individual ownership of land at the cost of royal and communal ownership; (ii) subjection of peasantry through subinfeudation, eviction and imposition on non-customary taxes and forced labour; (iii) conversion of income from trade and crafts into benefices, and finally (iv) the existence of a self-sufficient economy buttressed by lesser use of coins and comparative absence of trade.' *Indian Feudalism*, p. 109. Sharma has further elaborated on de-urbanisation in his *Urban Decay in India,* AD *300–1000*, Delhi, 1988, which fits in well with his overall formulation of feudal social formation in early India. Though he upholds that urban decay did not bring about major economic crisis and in fact paved the way for agararian expansion during the early medieval period, he still maintains that there was a slump in trade, urbanism and the money-economy in AD 300–1000.

[74] Yadava has referred to a passage in the *Skanda Purāṇa* that the Vaiśyas in the Kali age would give up their traditional profession of trade and instead become oilmen (*tailakārāḥ*) and rice huskers (*tanḍulakārihnaḥ*). B.N.S. Yadava, 'The Accounts of the Kali Age and the Social Transition from Antiquity to the Middle Ages', in D.N. Jha (ed.), *Feudal Social Formation in Early India*, Delhi, 1987, pp. 65ff and particularly p. 67.

coin of the Rāṣṭrakūṭas has so far been found, our discussion on trade and merchants in Konkan in early medieval times does not fit in with the theory of a slump in trade (including foreign trade) and urban decay in the period from AD 300 to AD 1000.[75] The *maṭha* could have hardly prospered but for its linkages with and support from the

[75] B.N.S. Yadava, *op.cit.*, p. 79 cites a passage in the late Jaina text *Vividhārthakalpa* (AD 1332) which speaks of the gradual ruralization of towns (*nayarāṇi gāmabhuāni hohinti*). There are of course considerable archaeological and literary data on the declining state of several north Indian cities; but still it would be difficult to assume that a general pattern of urban decay set in all over the subcontinent in the period from AD 300–1000. B.D. Chattopadhyaya, 'Trade and Urban Centres in Early Medieval North India', *IHR*, I, 1974, pp. 202–19, has undoubtedly proved that there was an on-going process of urbanization in early medieval times, even prior to 1000. Cities of early medieval India belonged, according to him, to the third phase of urbanization of early India. See B.D. Chattopadhyaya, 'Urban Centres in Early Medieval India: An Overview', in Sabyasachi Bhattacharya and Romila Thapar (eds.), *Situating Indian History for S. Gopal*, Delhi, 1986, pp. 8–33. Sharma's and Yadava's ideas of the lesser use of coins and the consequent decline of trade may also require rethinking in view of the evidence of the continuous use of high quality silver currency in south-eastern Bengal (the territories of Samataṭa–Harikela–Paṭṭikera of past) in AD 600–1300. This has been particularly highlighted by B.N. Mukherjee, 'Commerce and Money in the Central and Western Sectors of Eastern India, 700–1200', *Indian Museum Bulletin*, XVII, 1982, pp. 65–83. This is especially significant as Sharma found in early medieval Bengal symptoms typical of the feudal economy. The presence of cowry shells in Bengal and other areas in north India and the relative lack of minted metallic pieces as mediums of exchange do not necessarily signify a slump in trade, including long-distance trade. The Chinese account of Ma-huan in the early fourteenth century leaves little room for doubt that cowry shells themselves were part and parcel of long-distance commerce, being brought from Maldives in exchange for the rice of Bengal. It is also often argued that the relative absence of gold coins in India in the early medieval period implies lack of foreign trade. Significantly enough, the East African port of Kilwa which played a major role in the Indian Ocean trade in pre-1500 days is known to have used both copper currency and cowry shells. Vide M.D.D. Newitt, 'East Africa and the Indian Ocean Trade: 1500–1800' in Ashin Dasgupta and M.N. Pearson eds., *India and the Indian Ocean, 1500–1800*, pp. 201–23, particularly pp. 201–202, fn. 1 and p. 205. This may indicate the hollowness of a much-cherished notion that long-distance trade could only be carried on with the help of a gold

mercantile community which, in its turn, could provide the required support to the monastic complex only if they enjoyed enough financial success. Mercantile support to a religious complex does not always imply conversion of the commercial wealth into sacred immobile asset.[76] One may also consider an alternative observation. Robert S. Lopez, in the context of medieval Europe, found religious buildings to be reliable economic indicators. Braudel uses this theory with approval and sees in the interruption of building of churches in exchange of Bologna (1223), Sienna (1265) and Santa Maria del Fiore (1301–2) 'a sure sign of economic crisis'.[77] Viewed in this light the continuous growth of the *maṭha* in north Konkan would strongly suggest flourishing economic conditions. And Sanjan being primarily a port-town, its trade and commerce must have contributed considerably to its prosperity. The extensive maritime contacts of Sanjan—both in the coast and overseas—hardly offers a picture of a 'closed' economy. This is further highlighted by the presence of diverse categories of merchants at that port.

Dynastic changes and diversities in religious beliefs among merchants did not prove to be a deterrent to the growth and development of the Kautuka monastery. But what happened to the temple of Viṣṇu which figured in only one of the five epigraphic records? We are not sure of the course of events that took place after the Vaisnava temple had come to some kind of an arrangement with Kautuka *maṭha*. Whatever little we could gather about the Viṣṇu temple sufficiently tells us that it did not receive any substantial support or patronage from local people and local political power(s). All its patronage came from the mercantile group which migrated to Sanjan from Bhinmal.

---

and/or silver currency and that the presence of copper currency and cowry shells is symptomatic of a shrinkage in trade. Attention may also be focussed in this context on the pre-modern trade in the west African kingdom of Dahomey. Dahomey was a unified kingdom embracing a sizable territory, had an extensive bureaucratic organization and thrived on long-distance trade. The regular participation of Dahomey in trade was largely possible due to a '*sophisticated means of exchange before the entry of modern currency*'. This was provided through the use of cowry shells which circulated widely through West Africa. Cyril Belshaw, *Traditional Exchange and Modern Markets*, London, 1965, p. 70 (emphasis added).

[76] R.N. Nandi, *op. cit.*

[77] Fernand Braudel, *The Wheels of Commerce*, London, 1985, p. 35, Fontana paperback edition.

This would reasonably suggest that the Bhinmal merchants probably enjoyed enough material success at Sanjan to build up and support a Viṣṇu temple on their own. It is difficult to explain the reasons of the tension between two religious establishments.[78] Sectarian differences are unlikely to have triggered off such bitterness between the two *maṭhas* at a cosmopolitan exchange centre like Sanjan where religious barriers were often lowered down for material reasons and where religious toleration was unmistakable. Some other explanations may be forwarded, but only as guesswork.

The patrons of Bhillamāla Madhusūdanadeva temple were outsiders to Sanjan while the local political authorities, local merchants—both Arabs and Indians—and local craftsmen appear to have been in close touch with the Devī temple. It may be borne in mind that the name Bhillamāla is clearly associated with the Bhils, a tribal people who are often looked down upon in early medieval sources. A record of 861—not far removed in time from the dispute between two religious establishments—speaks of royal persecution against the Bhillas and other tribal groups.[79] The Rajasthani merchants hailed from an area which was associated with the name of a tribe that hardly evoked a sense of prestige. Could this possibly have acted against the smooth and easy social acceptance of the Bhinmal merchants in the Konkan coast? It may not be altogether impossible that the economic prosperity and the consequent elevation in social standing of the Bhinmal traders became a matter of concern to the local mercantile community. It is a well known fact that patronage to cultural-cum-religious life often leads to the enhancement of the prestige of the benefactor.[80] The local merchants of Sanjan might have become circumspect

[78] This may be compared with a near contemporary and near similar event in Sylhet, Bangladesh. In what is known to be the largest Brāhmaṇa settlement in early Bengal, inhabitants propitiated four identical deities but in two different *maṭhas*, earmarked respectively for *deśāntarīyas* (outsiders) and *Vaṅgāladeśīyas* (local or indigenous people of Vaṅgāla region). Though the reasons of such a development has not been much favoured by local people who preferred to maintain their cultural and social exclusiveness. See the Paschimbahag C.P. of Śrīcandra, AD 930; D.C. Sircar, *Epigraphic Discoveries in East Pakistan*, Calcutta, 1973.

[79] Ghatiyal Inscription of Kakkuka, AD 861, *EI*, I, p. 337, verse 22.

[80] A clear example of this is furnished by the Siyadoni inscription of AD 907, *EI*, pp. 162–79. The most important figure in this record is a salt merchant (*nemakavaṇīija*) who followed his profession hereditarily and resided at

about the economic activities and cultural patronage of a group of merchants who were outsiders to the coastal society. It may be reminded that many of the local merchants of Sanjan could have intimately participated in long-distance maritime trade. Long distance trade, the *Fernhandel* of German historians, was often a preserve of a handful of individuals who closely guarded their exclusivity and did not encourage outsiders to join their group. There can be seen a common tendency on the part of big merchants to keep themselves at a distance from ordinary dealers; such small groups of important merchants were mostly connected with long-distance trade.[81] Seen in this light, the arrival of the Bhinmal merchants and their fast rise to economic well-being and social prominence could have been interpreted by local big merchants as an intrusion into their exclusiveness. Any possibility in the enhancement of the social prestige and status of the Bhinmal traders could have been resisted by the local merchants of Sanjan by measures not necessarily economic. Some tensions having their roots in the material milieu might have surfaced in the religious sphere. One may remember that the Devī *maṭha* had to willy-nilly accept that it illegally possessed a plot of land that had originally belonged to the Viṣṇu temple. But neither the local administration nor the central government appears to have taken any cognizance of or action against such a gross violation of property rights. On the other hand the rent (*srotaka*) payable to the Viṣṇu temple, amounting to 40 *drammas* per annum, was quite high. In a period when 3 *drammas* were considered sufficient for feeding twenty-five Brāhmaṇas, the annual payment of 40 *drammas* to the Viṣṇu temple can be considered a financial strain on the Devī temple. One may then logically surmise that local political authorities and local elite groups, consisting, among others, of leading merchants and craftsmen, probably made

the exchange centre of Siyadoni. He is generally mentioned as a salt-dealer, but at least once he is also described as belonging to the caste of salt-dealer (*nemaka-jāti*). Though the ritual status of salt merchants could hardly have been high in orthodox *sastric* injunctions, his actual status must have been higher than that prescribed in the lawbooks. Hereditary profession, economic well-being and regular patronage of religious-cum-cultural activities may have contributed to the exclusiveness and social compactness of salt merchants to such an extent that they claimed the status of a separe *jāti.*

[81] Fernand Braudel, *Afterthoughts on Material Civilization*, pp. 53–57.

a concerted effort to improve upon the material condition of Kautuka *maṭha*.[82] This served the mutual interest of all the parties involved. In the early Indian situation the political authority often found it advantageous to cultivate amiable relations with the priestly community, obviously for deriving moral and spiritual support to strengthen his temporal power. The religious organization too, in its turn, would be ensured of the vital protection and sustenance it needed so much from the ruler. The merchant could profitably utilize his close ties with a religious complex as a meeting ground between the ruler and himself—a position which was essential for the merchant to prosper.

Our foregoing discussions not only throw some light on the gradual growth of a monastic complex over a fairly long stretch of time, it also demonstrates the linkages and interdependence among rulers, merchants and religious establishments. The evidence presented here effectively shows that religious differences could be tolerated, if not lowered down, in the prospect of material success. We can also form some idea about the attitude of the coastal society in north Konkan to outsiders: it witnessed integration between rulers, local elites and religious organizations, made a common cause with the Arabs, but did not equally favour the activities and aspirations of a community of merchants who chose to migrate to the littoral area from the mainland.

[82] Another point which may be considered here is the fact that Vaiṣṇavism, at this stage did not encourage monasticism. This might have placed the Viṣṇu temple in a less advantageous position than the Devī *maṭha* to participate in the secular economic life of the region. Continued patronage to the Devi *maṭha* at Sanjan is to be seen in the context of the larger religious and trade networks of the Deccan.

Chapter Ten

Markets* and Merchants in Early Medieval Rajasthan**

BRAJADULAL CHATTOPADHYAYA

'All enduring social relations,' as Cyril Belshaw puts it, 'involve transactions which have an exchange aspect,'[1] but since the 'exchange aspect' of trade has specificities which cannot be identical at all times and places, the objective of a study on trade ought finally to locate it in the context of the society in which it takes place as an economic activity. The preliminary areas of investigation in such a study would be: (i) an assessment of the nature of goods that appear as regular items of exchange; (ii) an analysis of the process of mobilization of goods; and (iii) the nature of exchange centres and the nature of authority at such centres. The range of goods that figure as exchangeable items may be large, but it is the regularity or the irregularity with which the items appear at various centres in a region that ought to be taken as a crucial pointer to the nature of commerce in that region. An analysis of the process of the

* The term 'market' is used here in the limited sense of a space where buying and selling of goods take place as a somewhat regular activity. This sense would be conveyed by the expression *kraya-vikraya* (i.e. buying and selling) which occurs in an inscription of the tenth century found at Bijapur, on the route from Udaipur to Sirohi, but traced to the Pali district of the former Godawad region in southeast Marwar, *EI,* 10, p. 24, 1.27. This essay is reprinted from *Social Science Probings,* vol. 2, no. 4 (1985).

** Extracts from *The Making of Early Medieval India*, OUP Delhi, 1994, pp. 89–119.

[1] Cyril S. Belshaw, *Traditional Exchange and Modern Markets,* New Delhi, 1969, p. 4.

mobilization of goods will involve not only differentiation between the various categories of sources of goods and of the agents of exchange but also an understanding of the destinations to which the goods are required to be mobilized. One of the important points that ought to be considered here, depending on the availability of the data for the purpose, is the physical distance which the goods cover to arrive at the place of exchange. In so far as an examination of the nature of exchange centres and of the nature of authority at such centres is concerned, detailed studies of individual centres, to the maximum extent possible, are necessary because the pattern of regional economy can become understandable in a large measure by analysing how the centres integrate various economic activities through the process of exchange.

The theme of this essay is the pattern of local commerce in early medieval Rajasthan. I may as well begin with the confession that the statement of objectives outlined above is rather ambitious, considering that the material available for the theme is both sporadic and sketchy. The material, derived mostly from the epigraphs of Rajasthan, is of a nature which is not commercial but religious. The inscriptions are concerned with specifying levies imposed by authorities on various heads, including items manufactured or exchanged at a locality. The levies which ought to be called 'prestations' were often of an *ad hoc* nature and were acts of patronage. The attempt to analyse the nature of commerce on the basis of such one-dimensional evidence may lead to very questionable generalizations. Secondly, epigraphic evidence, while it may not always exactly contradict the evidence of literary texts, often used for reconstructing the activities of traders in early medieval Rajasthan, does not happily blend with the evidence of such texts either. This point may be illustrated by presenting the major features of trade as they appear in two much-used texts, the *Samarāicca-Kahā* of Haribhadra Sūri[2] and the *Kuvalayamālā* of Udyotana Sūri.[3] The kind of trade they seem to portray had two major features: (i) long-distance trade, involving the organization of caravans as also of maritime voyages. Initiatives for this kind of trade

[2] The text has been dated to the middle of the eight century or later by H. Jacobi, *Samarāicca Kahā: A Jaina Prākṛita Work*, vol. I, Calcutta, 1926.

[3] This text was written in the last quarter of the eighth century, See A.N. Upadhaye, *Kuvalayamālā*, pt. 2, Bombay, 1970 and particularly the section titled 'A Cultural Note on the Kuvalayamālā' by V.S. Agrawala, pp. 113–29.

possibly came from individual merchants of high standing and immense wealth. The distance covered not only extended to different traditional trading regions and centres such as Konkan, Ujjayinī, Tāmralipta and Tagara but also to such trans-oceanic centres of Kaṭāha, Ratnadvīpa, and so on; (ii) the trade was essentially in high-value goods. In one case, for example, reference is made to goods worth five lakhs of *dīnāras*[4] (a term which incidently does not occur in contemporary inscriptions of Rajasthan but is found in Gupta period inscriptions from other parts of India).[5]

High-value goods converged at princely courts which, as centres of exchange, were limited in number as was the circulation of goods traded. Big merchants and long-distance trade are phenomena not absent from western India since the tenth century, more particularly since the eleventh-twelfth centuries, but considering the period of the texts that we have cited, they seem to carry over a stereotype from the past[6] or to project an ideal for the leaders of merchant communities in the initial phase of the early medieval period. In the choice of sources, the verdict will thus be in favour of epigraphy which, because of the chronological and spatial specifications of its evidence, makes it possible to work out the stages of change.

I

In the context of early medieval Rajasthan, the first stage may be taken to correspond to the pre-Pratīhāra as well as the major part of the Pratīhāra period. The period witnessed what may be imperfectly labelled as the emergence of a new thrust which, intermingled with the existing pattern, gradually led to the crystallization of the early medieval pattern of commerce in Rajasthan. Merchant groups, with *praśastis* written for them, are found at several centres and their

[4] Jacobi, *Samarāicca Kahā, op. cit.*

[5] See *EI*, 15, pp. 130ff. Also, Haribhadra Sūri uses the term *kārṣāpaṇa* in the sense of a coin, which is frequent in early historical records but not in early medieval India. See D. Sharma, (ed.) *Rajasthan through the Ages*, I, Bikaner, 1966, p. 497.

[6] This impression is further conveyed by repeated references to such old place names as Hastināpura, Kusumapura and Kauśāmbī and the importance attached to them in the texts cited above.

association with such centres may be derived from the brief genealogies which the records provide. For example, several records from the Sekhavati area, dating back to the early ninth century, refer to *goṣṭhikas* constituted by the *vaṇiks* and *śreṣṭhīs* of the Dhūsara and Dharkaṭa familes; the distribution of the early records of these families at Khandela, Sakrai, Mandikila Tal[7]—all in the former Jaipur state—points to an area of concentration which may have been an operational base of local but important merchant groups. (Such merchant groups and the proliferation of their bases will be discussed in detail later.) *Vaṇiks* also figure in the list of addressees which include officials and brāhmaṇas in the records of the Guhilas of Kiṣkindhā (Kalyanpur in the Udaipur district).[8] At the same time, one significant set of evidence relates to the movement of merchants, sometimes of well-established families, not only to old settled areas, but also to areas which were perhaps being effectively colonized for the first time. A Chitorgarh inscription of the early sixth century, assignable to the period of the Aulikaras of Mandasor, refers to the family of Viṣṇudatta who is described in the record as *Vaṇijāṃ ṣreṣṭho*, 'best among the merchants'.[9] Genealogically he appears to have been connected with the *naigama* or merchant family of Mandasor, referred to in a Mandasor record of 532.[10] A comparison of the two records may thus suggest the movement of a family of merchants, earlier settled in Mandasor, to a not too distant old settled area of Madhyamikā-Chitor in the early part of the sixth century. The Samoli record of 646, on the other hand, suggests movement away from a settled area, Vaṭanagara,[11] identified with Vasantgarh in Sirohi district, by a community of *mahājanas*, headed (two terms in the record, *pramukha* and *mahattaka*, imply this) by a person called Jentaka. The community started an *āgara*, possibly the operation of a mine, at a place called *Araṇyakūpagiri*. That the terrain implied by

[7] See Sakrai stone inscription of AD 822, *EI*, 27, pp. 27ff; Khandela stone inscription of AD 807, ibid., vol. 34, pp. 159–63; Mandkila Tal inscription of AD 986, ibid., 34, pp. 77ff.

[8] See Dungarpur plates of Bābhaṭa, Harṣa era 83, in D.C. Sircar, *The Guhilas of Kiṣkindhā*, Calcutta, 1965, p. 74, 1. ii, also *EI*, 34, p. 175.

[9] Ibid., pp. 53–58.

[10] Ibid., pp. 54–55.

[11] Ibid., vol. 20, pp. 97–99. The record, incidentally, also refers to *nānādideśamāgatā aṣṭādaśavaitālika,* i.e. 'eighteen' bards coming from various countries.

the expression is significant is suggested also by the construction of a *devakula* for the deity Araṇyāvāsinī by the community. The place name mentioned in the record which belongs to an early stage in the history of one of the Rajput lineages, the Guhilas, consists of three parts: *araṇya, kūpa, and giri.* While *araṇya* (forest) and *giri* (hills) are self-explanatory, *kūpa* is not so, but it is significant that many early medieval records of western India contain place names with the suffix *kūpa* or *kūpaka* and sometimes end with *viṣaya*.[12] The significance of the Samoli record lies in the fact that it points to a movement leading to the exploration of a new area and its colonization, most probably providing a supply base for local manufacture.

The evidence of some early Pratīhāra records from the Jodhpur area will have to be seen in the light of this process. These records too imply extension into areas which were previously under the control of such communities as the Ābhīras, of the creation of bases of agriculture and settlements and of the establishment of exchange centres (*haṭṭa*) and of communities of merchants.[13] The village mentioned in one case is incidentally called Rohinsakūpaka. The emergence of exchange centres in different pockets appears to have been a continuous process. This is suggested by an earlier record from Dabok (located eight miles to the east of Udaipur), of AD 644, of the time of the Guhilas of Dhavagartā (Dhod in Bhilwara district), which, apart from containing a curious expression, *vaṇiksāmānyadevadāyatva*, refers to *haṭṭa* and *haṭṭamārga* within the spatial limits of Dhavagartā, close to which lay the fields donated to a religious establishment mentioned in the record.[14]

Several points seem to emerge from the meagre evidence presented so far. There indeed existed old settlement areas and centres of merchant activites in which the merchants as a significant social group are seen as undertaking works of religious benefactions and having *praśastis* composed in honour of their family and caste. But if one takes an overview of a long chronological span, it may be possible to note a new trend with which are associated, at least initially, movements

[12] Examples of such place names are Rohinsakūpa, Khaṭṭakūpa, Tṛṇakūpa, Īśānakūpa, Kolikūpaka, etc. See *EI,* 9, p. 280; ibid., 2, pp. 129–30. It has been suggested to me by several scholars of Rajasthan history that place names with the suffix *kūpa* or *kūpaka* would indicate the presence of a well (literally *kūpa*) in the area; I am still not satisfied with this explanation.

[13] Ibid., 9, pp. 277–80.

[14] Ibid., 20, pp. 122–25; also ibid., 35, pp. 100–102.

of individual merchants and merchant groups and establishments of new exchange centres. This process will have to be seen in the broader context of the history of Rajasthan in this period which was marked by a gradual agrarian expansion[15] and the proliferation of ruling lineages with their various centres of power.[16] The linkage between the proliferation of such centres and of centres of exchange is a possibility which may be kept in mind at this point. Finally, the records from roughly the tenth century present, in one very important respect, a contrast with those preceding it; the pre-tenth records generally lack in information regarding items of exchange. This contrast too may be taken to suggest certain possibilities which will have to be explored by taking into consideration, along with other factors, the spatial contexts of the exchange centres.

II

Although it may be facilely assumed that the power centres of the various ruling lineages of early medieval Rajasthan were all in some way nodes in the local network of exchange, it seems safer to start with references which are specific. The use of two terms—*haṭṭa* and *maṇḍapikā*[17]—was widespred in early medieval times as signifying centres of exhange; *maṇḍapikā* is especially understood to have denoted a centre where commercial cess was imposed and collected. Both terms occur in the records of Rajasthan, and a compilation of references to them in chronological order may help us understand the distribution pattern of the exchange centres in the region. There were, however, centres which are not clearly designated in the records as *haṭṭas* or *maṇḍapikās* but the fact that cesses were collected at these points may perhaps suggest that they too represented some types of exhange centres. Two separate lists of exchange centres, compiled from a variety of early medieval epigraphs from different parts of Rajasthan but by no means comprehensive, follow:

[15] See, ' Irrigation in Early Medieval Rajasthan,' in *The Making of Early Medieval India*, pp. 38–56.

[16] See, 'The Origin of the Rajputs: Political, Economic and Social Processes in Early Medieval Rajasthan,' in *Early Medieval India*, pp. 57–88.

[17] For the significance of these terms, see my paper, 'Urban Centres in Early Medieval India: An Overview' in *Early Medieval India*, pp. 155–82.

TABLE 10.1: List of Exchange Centres

Date	*Location of the Centre of Exchange*	*Ruling Lineage*	*Term Used in the Record with Reference to the Centre of Exchange*
644	Dhod, Bhilwara district[18]	Guhila	*haṭṭa*
861	Ghatiyala, near Jodhpur[19]	Pratīhāra	*haṭṭa* at Rohinsakupaka *grāma*
905	Kaman, Bayana[20]	Pratīhāra	Kambali-*haṭṭa* at Kāmyakīya *Koṭṭa*
916 939 997	Hastikuṇḍikā[21] Godwar area in south-east Marwar, (Pali district)	Rāṣṭrakūṭa	*rājadhānī*
953	Āhāḍa, part of Udaipur[22]	Guhila	*haṭṭa*
1278	Āhāḍa[23]		*maṇḍapikā at* Āghāṭapura
955	Bayana, Bharatpur[24]	Pratīhāra, the feudatory local lineage being Śūrasena	i) *maṇḍapikā* at Vusāvāṭa ii) *maṇḍapikā* at Śrīpatha
961	Rajor, Alwar[25]	Pratīhāra	*haṭṭa* at Rājyapura
1017–18	Shergarh, Kota[26]	Paramāra	*maṇḍapikā*
1080	Arthuna, Banswara[27]	Paramāra	*haṭṭa*

Contd.

[18] *EI*, 20, pp. 122–25.
[19] Ibid., 9, pp. 277–80.
[20] Ibid., 24, pp. 329–36.
[21] Ibid., 10, pp. 17–24.
[22] *The Indian Antiquary*, 58, pp. 161ff.
[23] G.H. Ojha, *Udaipur Rajya Ka Itihasa* (in Hindi), pt. I, Ajmer, 1928, p. 176.
[24] *EI*, 22, pp. 120–27.
[25] Ibid., 3, pp. 263–67.
[26] *The India Antiquary*, 40, pp. 175–76; *EI*, 23, pp. 137–41.
[27] *EI*, 14, pp. 295–310; also H.V. Trivedi, *Inscriptions of the Paramāras, Chandellas, Kachchapaghātas and Two Minor Dynasties* (*Corpus Inscriptionum Indicarum*, vol. 7, pt. 2), New Delhi, n.d., pp. 286–96.

1109	Talabad, 12 miles south of Banswara[28]	Paramāra	*pattanavara*
1115 } 1278	Sevadi[29], Pali district	Cāhamāna	i) Śamīpāṭī-*pattana* ii) *Maṇḍapikā*
1156	Badari, near Nadol[30], Pali district	Cāhamāna	Naḍḍūla-talapada-*śulka-maṇḍapikā*
1161	Nadol[31]	Cāhamāna	Naḍḍūla-talapada-*śulka-Maṇḍapikā*
1178	Kirātakūpa (Kiradu)[32]	Caulukya, local lineage being Cāhamāna	*śulka-*(*maṇḍapikā*)
1184	Mandor, near Jodhpur[33], Jodhpur district	Cāhamāna	*māṇḍavya-purīya maṇḍapikā*
1250	Khamnor, near Udaipur[34]	—	*māṇḍavi*
1276	Ratanpur, near	Cāhamāna	*haṭṭa*
1291	Jodhpur[35], Jodhpur district		
1278	Chitor[36], Chitorgarh district	—	*haṭṭa*
1288	Chandravati, Sirohi[37] district	Paramāra	Candrāvatī-*maṇḍapikā*
1296	Jalor[38], Jalor district	Cāhamāna	*niśrānikṣepa-haṭṭa*

[28] *EI*, 21, p. 52.

[29] Ibid., 11, pp. 30–32; *PRASWC*, 1907–1908, p. 52.

[30] *The Indian Antiquary,* 41, pp. 202–203.

[31] *EI*, 9, pp. 62–66.

[32] *The Indian Antiquary*, 62, p. 42.

[33] *JPASB*, 10 (1914), pp. 405–407.

[34] *Annual Report on the Working of the Rajputana Museum*, Ajmer, 1932, p. 3.

[35] P.C. Nahar, *Jaina Inscriptions*, vol. I, pp. 248–49. The ruler mentioned in the records is Sāmantasiṃha who can be identified with Cāhamāna Sāmantasiṃha of Jalor. See D. Sharma, *Early Chauhan Dynasties,* Delhi, 1959, pp. 159ff.

[36] G.H. Ojha, *op. cit.*

[37] H.V. Trivedi, *op. cit.*, p. 277.

[38] *EI*, 11, pp. 60–61. *Niśrānikṣepahaṭṭa* is taken to signify a part of a *haṭṭa* used for storing merchandise which was to be subsequently moved out for the purpose of exchange, *EI*, p. 60. The term *nikṣepa* which occurs in the *Arthaśāstra* and the *Amarakośa* is taken also to refer to depositing some goods with an artisan or craftsman so that they could be manufactured

TABLE 10.2: Centres not specially so designated but perhaps serving as centres of exchange

Date	Location of the Centre of Exchange	Ruling Lineage	Nature of the Evidence
1138 } 1145	Nāḍulaḍāgika (Narlai)[39], Pali district	Cāhamāna	i) Presence of the *deśī* of Vanajārakas ii) Reference to levies on loaded bulls on transit
1141	Dhalopasthāna, near Nadol[40]	Cāhamāna	The document relates to interception of goods from various categories of people, including traders; *samastamahājana,* including those from Aṇahilavāḍa, among witnesses mentioned in the document
1295	Vāhaḍameru, Juna-Vadmer, near Barmer[41]	Cāhamāna	Presence of a caravan (*sārtha*) of camels and bulls

The distribution pattern of the exchange centres may now be related to their individual spatial contexts. Without making a detailed survey of the areas in which they were located, reference to a few selected centres will serve the purpose of providing a general idea. To repeat the evidence already cited, Rohinsakūpaka where Pratīhāra Kakkuka installed, around 861, a *haṭṭa* with its various shops and established *mahājanas* was a *grāma* (village); his inscription also possibly suggests the introduction of a few agricultural innovations in the area.[42] In 961, Pratīhāra Mathanadeva of Rājyapura (Rajor,

---

into finished items, S.C. Mishra, 'An Inscriptional Approach to the Study of the Arthaśāstra of Kauṭilya', Ph.D. dissertation submitted to Delhi University, 1984, p. 142.

39 *EI*, 11, pp. 36–37, 42–43.

40 Ibid., pp. 37–41.

41 Ibid., pp. 59–60.

42 Ibid., 9, p. 280; for reference to mango-groves and sugarcane plantations in this area, see *Journal of the Royal Asiatic Society of Great Britain and Ireland*, 1895, pp. 513–21.

Alwar) made several provisions for a temple, and the categories of people he addressed were headed by, among others, the *vaṇik* and *pravaṇi*, suggesting their substantial presence at the exchange centre at Rājyapura. Among the varieties of donations mentioned, the following may be underlined: (i) Cultivated fields loacted in the *bhoga* of the donor and neighbouring fields cultivated by the Gurjaras (*samastaśrīgurjaravāhitasamastakṣetra*). The imposts on all crops are mentioned, including those termed in the record as *skandhaka* and *mārgaṇaka* (*samastaśasyānāṃbhāga-khalabhikṣā-prasthaka-skandhaka-mārgaṇaka*).[43] For the spatial context of the Rājyapura exchange centre the expressions are significant for they suggest a range of activities extending to movement of agricultural produce, *skandhaka* and *mārgaṇaka* being imposts on such movement; (ii) Imposts, in cash, on loads of agricultural produce brought at the exchange centre for sale. The exchange centres were thus located in the context of the bases of agrarian production, and a close look at the records will yield the same spatial pattern for most exchange centres in other areas where clusters of rural settlements occur. An excellent example of this is further provided by two records of the second half of the twelfth century from Nadol, the seat of a Cāhamāna ruling lineage. One record of 1160 speaks of twelve villages with Naḍḍūlagrāma apparently as their centre, which were assessed in cash for the purpose of making a donation to the local shrine of Mahāvīra Jina.[44] The second record, of 1161, also mentions religious donations but out of the income accruing from *Naḍḍūlatalapada-śulka-maṇḍapikā*.[45]

Naḍḍūla, even though mentioned as a *grāma* in the earlier record (it is of course elsewhere designated as a *pura*),[46] was a node in a cluster of rural settlements and its emergence as a node and an exchange centre at which commercial levies were collected was obviously related to its being a centre of Cāhamāna power. The integration of rural units of production and of commercial traffic through centres which in the early medieval period were, in many cases, also seats of ruling lineages, is the primary point from which we can start exploring two further aspects of the exchange centres. First, in

[43] *EI*, 3, pp. 263–67.
[44] Ibid., 9, pp. 66–70.
[45] Ibid., pp. 62–66.
[46] Nadlai inscripion of 1171, ibid., 11, pp. 47ff.

a number of cases, the exchange centres, which could not all have been identical in structure, combined inflow of goods from outside with local manufacture. The second aspect concerns the reconstruction of a hierarchy of exchange centres. At Kāmyakīya or Kaman in Bharatpur a record of 905 refers to *Kambalī-haṭṭa* which has been taken to mean a cattle-market. It was, however, not a periodical market although it may have been so originally; *āvārikas* or enclosures with *vīthis* or shops are mentioned in the overall complex of the *haṭṭa*. Other records from the centre speak of *śaṅkhikas* or conch-shell workers, guild of artisans, guild of gardeners, guild of potters (mentioned separately)—all indicating the range of economic activities of the centre.[47] Similarly, the Arthuna (Banswara) record of 1080 lists, apart from the items sold at the *haṭṭa* in which shops were located, at least two categories of manufacturers: *kāṃsyakāras* or braziers and *kalyapālas* or distillers of liquor.[48] It can of course be assumed that each exchange centre may have been a manufacturing centre of some kind as well, but the actual dimensions of the centres are likely to have varied, depending on the range of economic and other activities taking place in the spatial contexts of such centres. No satisfactory finding in this regard is possible without detailed work in the historical geography of the period which also deals with such problems, but the question of hierarchy may, for the present, be approached from several angles. One approach would be to examine, as far as possible, the overall structure of a settlement to ascertain if it accommodates one or more points at which exchange transactions take place. Evidence of this kind is available from various regions of early medieval India,[49] and it may be worthwhile looking for such evidence in early medieval Rajasthan. The second approach would be to try and locate clusters of exchange centres; a series or succession of such centres in given areas is likely to yield, if not a hierarchical ordering of such centres, at least an idea of the areas of concentration. Thirdly, a dependable index for the purpose would be provided by an analysis of the range of goods which were regular items of exchange at a

[47] Ibid., 24, pp. 329–36.

[48] H.V. Trivedi, *Inscriptions of the Paramāras* . . .

[49] Siyadoni inscriptions, ranging in date from 903 to 968, list a number of such points of exchange, *EI*, I, pp. 162–79; for other examples from early medieval India, see ibid., 19, pp. 52–54; ibid., vol. 13, pp. 15–36, No. A.

centre and the variety and number of social groups and institutions which were drawn into the network of exchange. This exercise may be considered relevant for a study of local commerce since no region as a whole represents equal potential for identical economic activities at any period of history, and a reconstruction of hierarchy may indicate the directions along which the flow of commercial traffic was important.

Although it would be impossible to work out the details of this pattern in this essay, particularly in view of the uneven exploration of the historical sites of Rajasthan, attempts may nevertheless be made in relation to a few areas. Clusters of exchange centres seem to have been located along a line from the Jodhpur area down to Banswara in the south. Around Jodhpur, exchange centres at Ghatiyala, Mandor and Ratanpur suggest some kind of cluster. References in twelfth century records suggest more than one exchange point at Ratnapura[50] or Ratanpur. Another cluster can be located about half way between Jodhpur and Udaipur in an area under the control of Cāhamāna lineages; here, the exchange centres at Nadol, Nāḍūlaḍāgikā or Narlai, Dhalopa, Sevadi and Badarī are located close to one another. Arthuna, Talabad and Panahera, all in Banswara, together seem to constitute another cluster in south Rajasthan. Towards the east, the exchange centre of Kāmyakīya-*koṭṭa*, taken along with the *maṇḍapikās* at Śrīpatha and Vūsavāṭa, may be taken to form another cluster. It is perhaps superfluous to add that considering the vastness of Rajasthan as a region, other such clusters may well have existed in this period, but even the kind of limited exercise done above may suggest a pattern of unequal intensity of commercial exchange (see map on page 294).

In so far as the hierarchical order of exchange centres is concerned, two centres appear to stand out as exceedingly important, at least from the manner in which they have been presented in the records. One is Āghāṭapura or Ahar, a part of Udaipur; the other is Arthuna near Banswara. Ahar seems to stand out alone but if the Arthuna evidence is any indication, it would seem that in both the cases there were minor exchange centres located around them. The importance of both lay in the fact that they were points at which varieties of resources converged; this impression is derived from the items which were listed for the purpose of religious levies and from the groups

[50] P.C. Nahar, *op. cit.*, pp. 248–49.

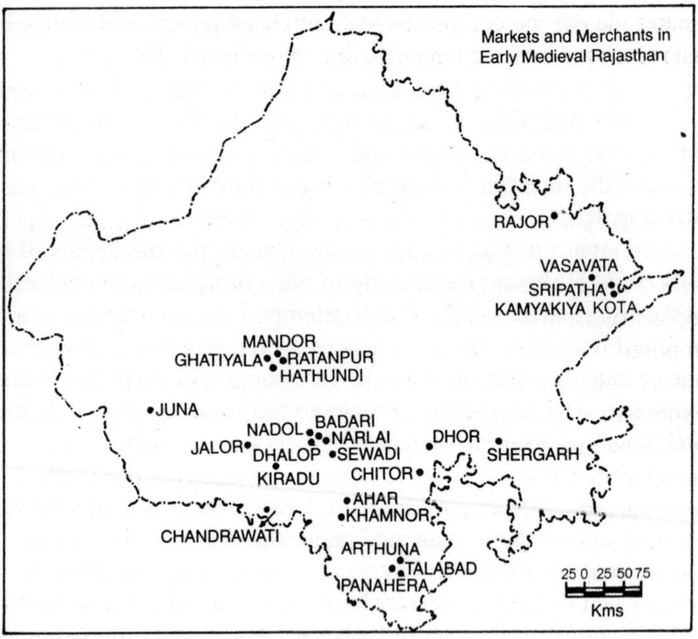

Map 10.1: Markets and Merchants in Early Medieval Rajasthan

which were drawn into such transactions. At Āghāṭapura or Ahar, the merchant groups represented different origins and organizations. Apart from the resident *vaṇiks*, there was an organization of the *deśīs*, members of which are mentioned separately. The third category was constituted of merchants from Karṇāṭa, Madhya-viṣaya, Lāṭa and Ṭakka. The range of the merchandise probably started with agricultural produce but extended, in keeping with the convergence of different categories of traders at the centre, to such high-value items as horses and elephants. The record suggests the existence of more than one exchange point within the settlement complex of Āghāṭapura.[51] Arthuna, to reiterate a point made earlier, cetainly combined trade with manufacture; here too agricultural produce, including several commercial crops and products from them, formed an important component of exchange. Apart from items produced by local manufacturers, there were those used as raw materials for manufacture, such as cotton and *mañjiṣṭhā* both used for textile production. The manner in which the merchants are mentioned suggests the presence of different groups. Of course, we could have formed a

[51] *The Indian Antiquary*, 58, pp. 161ff.

clearer idea of the composition of merchant groups at Arthuna, had the record not been so unintelligible in most parts.[52]

III

The significant trend which can be seen in the increase in specific references to exchange centres coincides with references to items which were available at the centres. It is of course impossible to reconstruct the total range of goods since the levies or prestation imposed upon them were often specified in terms of total dues and not as dues from separate items; this would be suggested by such expressions as *mārgādāya*[53] (collection from *mārga*) or *maṇḍapikādaya*[54] (collection from *maṇḍapikā*) out of which a part would be set aside for the purpose of donation. It is only in cases where the levies are specified as collected from separate items that it is possible to form an idea of the range of goods which were exchanged. Comparisons between exchange centres in this respect would thus be imperfect, but for an understanding of the general trend it needs to be reiterated that clusters of exchange centres seem to occur in areas which were essentially agrarian settlements and that agricultural items entered the centres perhaps with as much regularity as did other items. Few records offer any details but those that do may be used to prepare a table which will provide, for generally fixed points of time represented by the available records, lists of items constituting the nexus of exchange at the exchange centres (see Table 10.3).

Even though the material collected in Table 10.3 is decidedly inadequate for generalizations, it is nevertheless an indicator, at least in two respects, of the nature of commerce in all the major exchange centres: (i) The first point concerns the structure of contemporary demand which generated exchange as a major economic activity. In understanding this structure the crucial fact is the juxtaposition of agricultural goods with high-value items and manufactured items at

[52] H.V. Trivedi, *op. cit.*

[53] *EI*, 23, pp. 137–41. Some inscriptions also have such expressions as *Svīyādāna-madhyāt mārge* (i.e. 'from our collections from the road'); see Nadlai record of Rāyapāladeva of 1138, *EI*, 11, pp. 36–37.

[54] See for example, Shergarh inscription of 1018, *EI*, 23, pp. 137–41. In fact both the terms—*mārgādāya* and *maṇḍapikādāya*—occur in this record.

TABLE 10.3: List of Goods Exchanged

Date	*Centre*	*Agricultural Items Including Items of Commercial Agriculture, Processed Items and Dairy Products*	*Manufactured Items or Items used for Manufacturing*	*Other Items*	*High Value Items*
916, 939, 997	Hastikuṇḍikā Godwar,[55] Pali district	1. wheat 2. barley	1. cotton 2. *mañjiṣṭhā*	1. salt 2. *collika* of leaves	—
		3. pulses	3. products of braziers	3. *kuṃkuma* (saffron)	
		4. product of oil-press	4. *rālaka* (stuff made from animal hair?)[56]	4. gum-resin (*guggula*)	
		5. *dhānya* (rice?)			
953	Ahar, Udaipur[57]	i) unspecified agricultural produce for which two measures, *tulā* and *āḍhaka*, are mentioned ii) produce of *ghāṇaka* or oil mill iii) produce of confectioners			1. elephants 2. horses 3. horned animals (*śṛṅgī*)
960	Rajor, Alwar[58]	i) reference to sacks of agricultural produce? (*goṇi*) ii) butter and oil		*collikā* of leaves (*parṇa*)	
1080	Arthuna, Banswara[59]	i) barley (*yava*)	i) *tumbaka* of liquor	i) salt	

	ii) referecne to *bhāṇḍa-dhānya,* possibly meaning 'loads of grain' iii) *ikṣu* (sugar-cane); separate reference to *khaṇḍa-guḍa*, i.e. candy-sugar and jaggery iv) cotton (*kārpāsa*) v) thread (*sūtra*) vi) clothing fabric (*karppaṭa-koṭika*) vii) sesame oil (*ajyataila*) viii) oil (*taila*) ix) areca-nut x) coconut xi) citron	ii) products of braziers iii) *mañjiṣṭhā* or madder	ii) *parṇa* or leaves iii) cattle fodder?

cont.

[55] Ibid., 10, pp. 17–24.

[56] Angali Bagai, on the strength of the seventh century account of Hiüen Tsang and other sources, suggests that *rālaka* probably denoted some variety of stuff made from animal hair, 'Merchandise and Merchantile community in post-Gupta times in northern India', Ph.D. dissertation submitted at the University of Delhi, 1985, p. 111, fn. 1. Dasarath Sharma, on the strength of the Jaina Prākṛta text, *Kuvalayamālā*, takes *rālaka* to mean winter cover prepared from goats' hair, Presidential Address, Ancient India Section, Indian History Congress, 29th session (Patiala, 1967).

[57] *The Indian Antiquary,* 58, pp. 161ff.

[58] *EI*, 3, pp. 263–67.

[59] Ibid., 14, pp. 295–310; H.V. Trivedi, *op. cit.*

Date	*Centre*	*Agricultural Items Including Items of Commercial Agriculture, Processed Items and Dairy Products*	*Manufactured Items or Items used for Manufacturing*	*Other Items*	*High Value Items*
1143 and 1145	Nadlai,[60] Pali district	i) *dhāna*? ii) *kirāḍauā*, covering such items as gum, black pepper, dry ginger and so on iii) oil iv) ghee v) cotton vi) *puga-haritakī* (myrobalan)	i) iron implements? ii) *mañjiṣṭhā*	i) salt	i) jewels

[60] P.C. Nahar, *op. cit.*, pp. 213ff; *EI*, 11, pp. 42–43.

several points where exchange took place; (ii) second, exchange took place at points where various social groups interacted—not periodically but on a regular basis, and in this sense the major exchange centres were different from periodical markets or fairs, reference to which are available in early medieval records from different parts of India.[61] Movements of specific goods into the exchage centres could be periodical, but major exchange centres had resident populations, including resident *vaṇiks* and manufacturers, and one could thus suppose that exchange relations between these two groups and other sections of the population were not determined by periodical cycles in the movement of goods, even if such movements are taken as an essential component of the mobilization process. Both points, however, require further empirical substantiation. Two records of early medieval Rajasthan may be cited to reveal, at least partially, the pattern of contemporary requirements which would correlate with activities at the exchange centres. The Harsha record of AD 973 from the Shikar area speaks of Vigraharāja of the Cāhamāna lineage in the following terms:

> He has been served with many presents—with strings of pearls, gay steeds, fine garments and weapons; with camphor, quantities of betel, first rate sandal wood, and endless quantities of gold and with spirited rutting elephants, huge like mountains, together with their mates.[62]

The description of 'presents' is, in one sense, a conventional one, similar descriptions being found in other records of the period; in another sense, however, it represents the range of requirements among the ruling elites, which can be used for the purpose of correlation with contemporary commerce. Although the record chooses to list the items as 'presents,' one is entitled to read beyond this label and,

[61] One piece of rather well-known evidence regarding the horse fair in north India is provided by the Pehoa (Karnal district, Haryana) record of the time of the Pratīhāras, *EI*, I, pp. 184–90; the Bali record of 1143 from Rajasthan, referring to the sale of horses, may be another such piece of evidence, ibid., 11, pp. 32–33. For reference to fairs held in different parts of Karnataka and Andhra, see G.S. Dikshit, *Local Self-Government in Medieval Karnataka* (Dharwar, 1964), ch. 8; T. Venkateswara Rao, 'Local Bodies in Pre-Vijayanagara Andhra (AD 1000 to AD 1336)', Ph.D. thesis (Dharwar University, 1975), ch. 5.

[62] *EI*, 2, p. 127. The term *puga* in the record (verse 24) seems to refer to betelnut and not betel.

on the basis of other records of the period, broadly consider them as items which entered into the exchange activities of various merchant groups. Indeed, the same Harsha record mentions that a levy of one *dramma* on every horse was imposed by the rulers on the Heḍāvika group of horse-dealers who visited the Shikar area from Uttarāpatha.[63]

The second record, of 1249, from Bhinmal[64] mentions an amount of several *drammas* deposited at the *bhāṇḍāgāra* of the Jagatsvāmī temple at Bhinmal, the deposit being intended to procure certain resources for the performance of a ritual at the temple. The items required for the ritual were: wheat, rice, pulses, ghee, betel-leaves and nuts, *aguru* and *kuṃkuma*.

Despite their distance in space and chronology, the juxtaposition of the two records cited above would surely reveal the complex pattern of early medieval trade involving a wide range of goods and of exchange relations, necessitating the use of coined money combined with other means of exchange. This will, in turn, reflect on the structure of the centres of exchange as points of convergence of movements of goods and acts of exchange. It may be worthwhile to attempt to examine, from a study, over a wide span of time, of movements of goods and of operations of trading groups, whether any particular form of operation can be seen to emerge as more significant than others. The movement of goods suggest differential distances covered. While the term *skandhaka*[65] (literally, imposts on items car-

[63] Ibid. The Heḍāvika horse-merchants are mentioned not only in the Harsha record of 973. The Heḍāvikas, the different variants of the name being Heṭāvuka and Heḍāvuka, are known from other epigraphic and literary sources as well. Balambhaṭṭa, commentator of *Mitākṣarā*, associates them with Gurjjara-deśa, and it would appear that they constitued a sub-caste of the brāhmaṇas. See Chitrarekha Gupta, 'Horse Trade in North India: Some Reflections on Socio-Economic Life', *Journal of Ancient Indian Histroy*, 14, pts. 1–2 (1983–84), pp. 186–206.
The other point to note is that the horse, as an item of trade, was in demand throughout the country, and was a prized item amongh the royalty, which would explain its extensive itinerary. Apart from the Harsha record, see the evidence of the Kiradu inscription (1161) of Caulukya Kumārapala and his feudatory Paramāra Someśvara. Someśvara claims to have exacted 1700 horses, including one 'five-nailed' and eight 'peacock-breasted' from one prince Jajjāka, *The Indian Antiquary,* 61, pp. 135–36.

[64] Ibid., 11, pp. 55–57.

[65] Rajorgarh inscription of 961, *EI*, 3, pp. 263–67. For a brief discussion of

ried on shoulders) may refer to movement over a very short distance, intercentre movements, by the *vanajāraka* community of traders, for example, were undertaken by loading pack animals and carts.[66] Long-distance movements of exchangeable items were organized in the form of *sārthas*.[67] It can be assumed that traders from outside Rajasthan, to whom the Ahar record of 953 refers,[68] moved from one centre to another in periodic cycles in well-organized caravans.

The nature of the organization which cut across trading groups coming in over long distances as well as certain, though not necessarily all, groups which may be considered to have operated locally is mostly reflected in the use of the term *deśī*. *Deśī* can only loosely be taken in the sense of a guild of traders, and in the records of Rajasthan the term has been used in such expressions as *Bhammaha deśī*[69] and also in relation to the *Vanajārakas*.[70] The reference to the Heḍāvikas, the horse-dealers, in the plural perhaps suggests an organization similar to that of the *deśī*.[71] In the Ahar record of 953,

---

the term, see U.N. Ghoshal, *Contributions to the History of the Hindu Revenue System*, 2nd edition, Calcutta, 1972, pp. 317–18, 420. The term resembles in its import *aṃsa-bhāra* (shoulder-load) occurring in the *Arthaśāstra*, 2.21.24, which specifies one *māṣaka* as the impost on a shoulder-load of goods.

66. For example, the expression *märgge gacchatānāmāgatānāṃ vṛṣabhānāṃ sekeṣu* (Nadlai record of 1138, *EI*, 11, pp. 36–37) refers to incoming and outgoing loads on bullocks which passed through the road at Nadlai. The load of merchandise transported by the trading organization (*deśī*) of the *Vanajārakas* on bullocks (*vṛṣabha-bharita*) are mentioned in another Nadlai record of 1145, ibid., pp. 42–43. A fascinatingly visual idea of how goods were transported comes from the Mangrol inscription of 1144 from the Kathiawar area under the Caulukyas. Referring to the varieties of merchandise arriving at *Śrīmān Maṅgalapura-śulkamaṇḍapikā*, the record includes items transported by *balīvardda* (oxen), *rāsabha* (donkey) and *uṭa* (camel). For the text of the record, see G.V. Acharyya, *Historical Inscriptions of Gujarat* (in Gujarati), Sri Forbes Gujarati Sabha Series, No. 15, pt. 2 (Bombay, 1935), No. 145.

67 For occurrence of term *sārtha,* consisting of oxen and camels, see the Juna record of 1295 from Mallani district, *EI*, 11, pp. 59–60.

68 *The Indian Antiquary*, 58, pp. 161ff.

69 *EI*, 2, p. 124, 1.38.

70 Reference to the *deśī* of the Vanajārakas is available in the Nadlai inscription of 1145 of Rāyapala, ibid., 11, pp. 42–43.

71 Ibid., 2, p. 124, line 38.

seven members of a *deśī* are mentioned by name. It may be significant that the list of *deśī* names is juxtaposed with the name of an individual who is designated as a *vaṇik*,[72] perhaps indicating conscious differentiation between them by the community which was the immediate context of exchange.

The groups participating in commerce in early medieval Rajasthan may thus be considered to have ranged from non-resident merchants from other—sometimes distant—regions, locally mobile groups originating in different centres and coming together for the mobilization of goods, to resident merchant-families. In trying to understand the overall pattern of commerce which the activities of these disparate groups reflected, it is necessary to reiterate two points already made: (i) such activities converged at sedentary points[73] where exchange took place; and (ii) such points were centres of ruling lineages of varying importance. Although the epigraphs do not directly relate to the mechanisms of commerce, the nature of transactions with which they are concerned throws up two impressions from which the commercial trend of the period may be sought to be reconstructed.

IV

The first impression is that of the ascendancy of several local merchant lineages and of the expansion of their network. Mention has previously been made of the Dhūsara and Dharkaṭa families of the ninth century from the Sekhavati area of the old Jaipur state.[74] Although reference to the Dhūsara *vaṃśa* of merchants does not seem to continue, the continuity of the Dharkaṭa lineage is attested by later records. A Rajorgarh record of 922 and another record of the tenth century, preserved in the Mandor museum, contain references to the

[72] *The Indian Antiquary,* 58, pp. 161ff.

[73] The use of the term 'sedentary' should however relate more to the organization of trade than to nodes of exchange; the point which emerges from this essay is that by the close of the period under review 'sedentary' merchants perhaps tended to become more important than itinerant and other categories of merchants in the region concerned. For conceptual clarification, see J. Bernard, 'Trade and Finance in the Middle Ages: 900–1500', in C.M. Cipolla, (ed.), *The Fontana Economic History of Europe: The Middle Ages,* London-Glasgow, 1973, pp. 308–309.

[74] See note 7.

Dharkaṭas.[75] A *vaṇigvara* of the Dharkaṭa family is mentioned in 986 in the Mandkila Tal records from Nagar.[76] The Dharkaṭa *Jāti* further appears in the records of the eleventh century[77] and early thirteenth century.[78] It is believed that the Dharkaṭas or the Dhākaḍas represented a section of the later day Oswals.[79] The Sonis, taken to be another subdivision of the Oswal and deriving their name from Suvarṇagiri or Jalor,[80] are mentioned in a record of 1296 from Jalor.[81] In fact, the emergence of the Oswals as a major merchant group before the middle of the thirteenth century can be considered a certainty. A Mt. Abu record of 1230, while providing details of the composition of various *goṣṭhikas*, refers, at one place, to the merchants of Uesavāla-*jñātīya* from Kāsahradagrāma[82] and, at another, to merchants of Oisavāla-*jñātīya*, probably a more correct form of the name, of Sāhilavāḍā.[83]

Another merchant lineage, that of the Śrīmālas, was also on the ascent from around this period. A Mt. Abu (Sirohi) record of 1144 mentions it as Śrīmāla-*kula*[84] and a Jalor record of 1183[85] has a eulogistic reference to an individual merchant of the lineage, who is described as *Śrī Śrī Mālavaṃśavibhūṣaṇa Śreṣṭhī* Yaśodeva. The ascendancy of the merchant families of the period, some of whom,

[75] R.V. Somani, *Jain Inscriptions of Rajasthan* (Jaipur, 1982), p. 209.

[76] *EI*, 34, pp. 77ff.

[77] A stone inscription, reported to have been discovered in Jodhpur district and dated V.S. 1165 (AD 1198), records the death of a merchant of Dharkaṭa lineage and of Khandaṣa *gotra*. This information is derived from the descriptive label of the record preserved in the Mandor Museum.

[78] P.C. Nahar, *op. cit.*, p. 220. See also *Journal and Proceedings of the Asiatic Society of Bengal*, 12 (1916), pp. 104–106.

[79] According to D.R. Bhandarkar, the name Dharkaṭa survives as Dhākaḍa, which he takes to represent a sub-section of the Oswals, *EI*, 27, p. 29. The Dharkaṭas figure very prominently in the inscriptions at Osian, the temple site located 66 kms to the north-northwest of Jodhpur; the site is considered 'a cradle of the Oswals'. See Devendra Handa, *Osian: History, Archaeology, Art and Architecture,* Delhi, 1984, chs 1 and 6.

[80] *EI*, 11, pp. 60–62.

[81] Ibid.

[82] G.V. Acharyya, Inscription No. 168.

[83] Ibid.

[84] *EI*, 9, p. 151. Curiously, the person mentioned in the record is spoken of as belonging to *Śrīmālakula* and as being an ornament of the Prāgvaṭa *vaṃśa*.

[85] *EI*, 11, pp. 52–54.

like the Sonis or the Śrīmālas, derived their caste or lineage names (the epigraphs use such terms as *kula, vaṃśa, jāti, jñāti,* etc.) from the centres of their origin and of the consolidation of their intraregional as well as interregional network, is perhaps best illustrated by the case of the Prāgvaṭas. The Prāgvaṭas are known from inscriptons at Sirohi (1031),[86] Kiradu (1132),[87] Nadol (1161)[88] and other places such as Candrāvatī[89] but their network extended to Gujarat, and in fact the merchants of the Prāgvaṭa family developed a close association with the Caulukya court of Gujarat.[90] According to early medieval Jaina texts, Ninnaya of the Prāgvaṭa family, originally belonging to Śrīmāla or Bhinmal was invited to settle in Aṇahilavāḍa.[91] Individual members of the family were endowed with such official designations as *mahāmātyavara* and *daṇḍapati* or *daṇḍādhipati, mantrī* and *saciva*,[92] and if the evidence of literary texts is to be believed, Vimala of Prāgvaṭa descent was elevated to the rank of *nṛpati*[93] with proper insignias. The movement towards the ranks of the contemporary political elites is reflected further in the saying attributed to Vastupāla who won a military victory over a Muslim merchant, supported by the ruler of Lāṭa from Cambay: 'It is delusion to think that kṣatriyas alone can fight and not a *vaṇik*. . . I am a *vaṇik* in the shop of battlefield'.[94]

Major merchant lineages such as those of the Prāgvaṭas had understandable links with important centres like Aṇahilapura or Candrāvatī and with royalty, but what is more significant for understanding the growth of their intraregional and interregional network is that they are found associated with various other, possibly rural,

[86] Ibid., 9, p. 149. The association of the Prāgvaṭas with Arbudagiri in Sirohi continued for centuries, ibid. Also G.V. Acharyya.

[87] Ibid., 11, pp. 43–46.

[88] *EI*, 9, pp. 62–63. For reference to *Śrī Nadrala* (Nadol)—*pura vāsī-Prāgvaṭa-vaṃśa*, see also G.V. Acharyya, Inscription No. 148.

[89] *EI*, vol. 9, pp. 149–50; also G.V. Acharyya, Inscription No. 168.

[90] G.V. Acharyya, Inscription Nos. 167, 168.

[91] V.K. Jain, *Trade and Traders in Western India* (AD *1000–1300*), Delhi, 1990, chs. 9, 10. The epigraphic records of the Aṇahilapura family, however, trace the genealogy of the family from the time of Chaṇḍapa, *EI*, 8, pp. 200ff.

[92] See, V.K. Jain, *op. cit.*, pp. 208–13; *EI*, vol. 9, pp. 62–66; V.K. Jain, *op.cit.*

[93] V.K. Jain, *op. cit.*

[94] Ibid.

bases as well. The details of this phenomenon for different parts of Gujarat and Rajasthan are not available, but an idea of the network of the merchant lineages is nevertheless provided by the Mt. Abu record of 1230 which enumerates some of their bases. The Prāgvaṭas are thus found, apart from Aṇahilapura and Candrāvatī, at Uṃbaraṇīkīsaraulagrāma, Brahmaṇā, Ghauligrāma and Dāhaḍagrāma.[95] The merchants of the Śrimāla lineage can be located, on the strength of the same record, at Phīliṇigrāma, Haṃdāudrāgrāma and Dāvāṇīgrāma.[96] The Oswals are found to be associated with Kāsahradagrāma and Sāhilavāḍā.[97]

The expansion of the network of lineages of local merchants, the history of some of which may be traced back at least to the ninth century, appears to have been the mechanism through which resource bases, arteries for the flow of resources and the centres of exchange came to be gradually integrated. The stages of this integration are still far from having been worked out; one may perhaps envisage a change from a situation in which itinerant merchants and the *vanajārakas* were an important component in commercial operations to a situation which was dominated by groups that were being crystallized into trading castes. Certainly by the close of the early medieval period the ascendancy of such merchant lineages as Dharkaṭa, Oisavāla, Śrīmāla and Prāgvaṭa was a phenomenon which patterned commercial as well as non-commercial activities at various centres in Rajasthan. To this may perhaps be added another dimension. The major merchant lineages had by now been considerably stratified. The segment of the Prāgvaṭas, resident at Aṇahilapura (*Aṇahilapuravāstavya* or *Śrīpattanavāstavya*)[98] and high up even in political hierarchy,[99] would be a case in point. It is likely that such merchant families were

[95] G.V. Acharyya, Inscription No. 168. See also *EI*, 8, pp. 219–22.

[96] G.V. Acharyya, Inscription No 168.

[97] Ibid.

[98] Ibid.

[99] Stratification was not necessarily confined within individual merchant lineages, although one could suppose that the difference between the Aṇahilapura Prāgvaṭas and those located in rural bases extended to other merchant lineages as well. Stratification related to different categories of merchants, of which there must have been a wide range. V.K. Jain cites contemporary literary references to Śūdra pedlars, to needy traders and farmers receiving liquid capital from merchants on interest and to the appointment of different types of traders by big individual merchants. The

involved in trans-regional trades during the period through their agents[100] and mediated between them and local resource bases because of their expansive network.

The second impression to which only a perfunctory reference will be made in this essay (since a fuller statement would require far more sustained and detailed work) relates to the manner in which money has been mentioned in the records. References to varieties of coins start appearing in the epigraphs of Rajasthan from about the tenth century. This phenomenon corresponds closely to the proliferation of epigraphic reference to centres and items of exchange. Two points regarding the use of coins in contemporary economic relations may be noted at this stage. First, religious levies at centres of exchange were expressed both in terms of cash and kind;[101] thus monetization, even in the spatial context of exchange centres, was partial. In fact the contributions by ruling elites to the religious institutions were often made in the form of shares which they drew in kind from agricultural and related products—a practice suggested by such expressions as *ātmapāilāmadhyāt,*[102] *ātmaghāṇaka-madhyāt,*[103] etc.

---

complementarity between big merchants and petty traders in the fifteenth and sixteenth centuries in which the terms *sāhu* and *banjārā* or *bāpāri* were used is brought out by Irfan Habib; in this relationship the great *sāhu* is spoken of as God 'served by his millions of *banjārās*, and one whose confidence it is not easy for new *bāpāris* to gain', Usury in Medieval India', *Comparative Studies in Society and History*, vol. 6, No. 4 (1964), p. 400.

[100]See A.K. Majumdar, *Chaulukyas of Gujarat—A Survey of the History and Culture of Gujarat from the Middle of the Tenth to the End of the Thirteenth Century,* Bombay, 1956, pp. 266ff and V.K. Jain, *op. cit.*, ch. 9. It should, however, be made clear that no clear relationship between the major merchant lineages or individual merchants mentioned in this essay and the agents occasionally referred to in other types of sources can be established as yet. All that can be suggested is that it is not beyond the range of possibility.

[101]On this numerous examples can be cited from different parts of India; for early medieval Rajasthan, reference may be made to a select number of records already discussed above in some detail: Ahar record of 953 (*Indian Antiquary*, 58, pp. 161ff); Arthuna record of 1080 (H.V. Trivedi, *op. cit.*); The Rajorgarh record of 961 (*EI*, 3, pp. 263–67).

[102]Nadlai stone inscription of Rāyapāla of 1143, *EI*, 11, pp. 41–42.

[103]Ibid.

By contrast, religious levies are found to have been imposed in cash on communities in areas not necessarily commercial.[104]

Secondly, the situation of partial monetization may be assumed to have emerged because of certain needs for the circulation of money—needs which may be explained in terms of the range of relations from the primary producers to the itinerant merchants and of the varieties of demands, including preparations for the endemic wars of the period,[105] of the ruling elites. At other levels, in situations of direct appropriation of agrarian surplus, for example, the need for cash may not have been great, and with a few and rather unspectacular exceptions,[106] the evidence of local production of coins in this period is decidedly inadequate. And yet, varieties of coins such as *dramma*, *rūpaka* and *viṃśopaka*, along with such extensively used media of exchange as cowries, are found to have been in simultaneous circulation at single exchange centres.[107] As underlined earlier, this coexisted with the system of imposition of religious levies in kind as well, but its general implications for the mechanism of commerce at the exchange centres and more generally in the network of commerce cannot be overlooked.[108]

[104]For example, 2 *drammas* were imposed as annual levy on each village attached to Naḍḍūlai, to be paid on a specified date to Śri Mahāvīra Jina, *EI*, 9, pp. 66–70.

[105]The support expected by the royalty from the merchants in this regard is a common feature of royalty–big merchant collaboration. V.K. Jain refers to the Caulukya king Siddharāja calculating the amount of cash he could expect a merchant to pay for raising an army against Malwa.

[106]Although no inventory of coin hoards relating to the early medieval period is available, references to finds of coins from this region would add up to a substantial quantity. However, coin series which can be definitely attributed to local ruling lineages are not many. Those that can be attributed with any certainty were based on the Indo-Sassanian and 'Bull and Horseman' types. See D. Sharma, *Rajasthan through the Ages*, pp. 499–507. For a recent, detailed investigation, see John S. Deyell, *Living without Silver: The Monetary History of Early Medieval North India,* New Delhi, 1990, part 2.

[107]See, for example, the Shergarh inscription of 1018, *EI*, 23, pp. 137–41; and the Arthuna inscription of 1080, Trivedi. For varieties of coin names in early medieval epigraphic and literary sources from Rajasthan and western India in general, see D. Sharma, *Rajasthan through the Ages*, pp. 497–505.

[108]Maurice Aymard suggests that the role of money could be 'infinitely greater

As a hypothesis, the situation of partial monetization in which the local supply of money was uncertain—an uncertainty perhaps confirmed by the emergence of myths concerning the minting of money[109]—would suggest that the supply of money itself was an important component of contemporary commercial enterprise. For the moment, attention may be drawn to certain contemporary practices which, located in the context of what has been outlined regarding the monetary situation, may be examined to generate further discussion on the relationship between money and commerce in general. The hypothesis presented here cannot be developed further without bringing in comparable and contemporary material from other regions. One can, however, underline the possibility of interconnections in areas of basically commercial import, which may be assumed to be related to the mechanism of money accumulation and circulation, and to provide an explanation of stratification within the community of merchants and perhaps also among manufacturers.

It would appear from the social composition of those who regulated *mārgādāya* and *maṇḍapikādāya* that some form of commercial revenue farming was gradually coming into existence.[110] This was true not only of early medieval Rajasthan but of other regions as well. The autonomous character of such bodies is suggested by the phenomenon that local merchant associations or other corporate bodies could impose levies on local communities and on the items of

---

than the actual circulation of coins might suggest; even when physically absent, money dominated the core economic activity and social relations'. See 'Money and Peasant Economy', *Studies in History*, vol. 2, no. 2 (1980), p. 15.

[109]This impression is derived from the way minting of coins by the Cāhamāna king Ajayarāja (twelfth century) and his queen Somalladevī is eulogized by Jayānaka in *Pṛthvīrāja-vijaya* and by his commentator Jonarāja. See D. Handa, 'Coins of Somalladevi', *Numismatic Digest*, vol. 2, pt. 2 (1978), pp. 42–57; also D. Sharma, *Early Chauhan Dynasties*, p. 41, fn. 55.

[110]This, we understand, is a statement likely to be vehemently challenged, but if followed up, it may lead to a new line of inquiry and explain why the ruling elites themselves are not directly involved in the collection of commercial revenue. For Rajasthan, one relevant record to analyse would be the Shergarh inscription of 1018 which refers to contributions made to Bhaṭṭāraka Śrī Nagnaka from *maṇḍapikādāya* by a body consisting mostly of *Śreṣṭhīs*, *EI*, 23, pp. 137–41.

exchange.[111] To an extent this may have been so, but the phenomenon surely needs a more satisfactory explanation, and in a political situation where 'bureaucracy' lacked a distinctly identifiable character, one way of looking at it would be to consider it a mechanism of control over the acquisition of cash and kind and over their redistribution, assuring at the same time the concerned political powers of a regular return in the form of a share. Of course, this would not apply to *ad hoc* levies intended as contributions to religious institutions, but then terms such as *mārgādāya* or *maṇḍapikādāya* cannot be conceived in terms of *ad hoc* levies alone.

In early medieval Rajasthan, as in some other regions, a trend was developing towards the acquisition, among other things, of immovable assets such as *āvāsanikās* or residential buildings, *āvāris* and *vīthis* or shops.[112] The acquired assets are consistently found to have yielded a rent return in cash. This practice is of course found in our records of religious grants but perhaps a comparison may be made between the functions of cash deposits made with religious establishments in the early historical period[113] with at least one facet of the pattern emerging in the early medieval period. As the Bhinmal record of 1249 cited above shows, cash deposits could bring in resources[114] for keeping the ritual cycle of a temple in operation, but in trying to understand the relationship between cash and the mechanism of trade

[111]For evidence of this kind, see G.S. Dikshit, *op cit.*, ch. 7; T. Venkateswara Rao, pp. 134ff. For Tamilnadu, the functions in this regard of the merchant groups constituting the *nagaram* have been discussed in detail by K.R. Hall, *Trade and Statecraft in the Age of the Coḷas,* Delhi, 1980, chs. 3 and 5. The details given by Hall in ch. 3 seem strongly to suggest that the *nagaram* could well have served as an agency for the collection and redistribution of royal revenues at one level.

[112]For Rajasthan, the practice of assigning or acquiring such assets for religious purposes, sometimes made by the merchants or manufacturers themselves, is to be found in the Kaman inscriptions (*EI*, 24, pp. 329–36) and the Shergarh inscription (Ibid., 23, pp. 137–41). Outside Rajasthan the details from the Ahar record of the Gurjara-Pratīhāra period are quite revealing , ibid., vol. 19, pp. 52–54. For relevant analysis of the record, see R.S. Sharma, *Perspective in Social and Economic History of Early India,* Delhi, 1983, pp. 212–13; also the essay, 'Trade and Urban Centres in Early Medieval North India' in *The Making of Early Medieval India*, OUP, 1994.

[113]For early historical evidence, see *EI*, 8, pp. 82–83.

[114]*EI*, 11, pp. 55–57.

outside the ritual sphere of temples, the particular dimension of cash rent accruing from investments in immovable assets even for temple establishments cannot be lost sight of. Unlike immovable assets, money was more a part of a system of circulation, but its uncertain flow, in a situation of demand created for it by the existence of stages in the exchange process, may have assured it a high return in the form of non-cash resources. This could then be put in the exchange-circuit[115] or could further be used to augment capital for the purpose of ensuring high rent in cash. The premium put on the acquistion of cash by the merchants of western India may be illustrated by citing two cases. D. Sharma cites the *Kharataragacchapaṭṭāvalī* to show that Sādhāraṇa, 'perhaps the richest of the merchants of Chitor fixed 1,00,000 *drammas* as the limit of the property that he would amass'.[116] A document in the *Lekhapaddhati* records that in 1230[117] a resident of a village issued a receipt to his father, in the presence of witnesses, for a sum of 500 *drammas* of his share which he had borrowed for a purpose of operating business transactions on his own. The document has interesting implications pointing to the existence and use of common capital which could be drawn upon before partition, but what is relevant in the *Kharataragacchapaṭṭāvalī* evidence as well as in the *Lekhapaddhati* is the control which could be exercised

[115]This point can be substantiated by citing once again the evidence of the Bhinmal record of 1249 (*EI*, 11, pp. 56–58) which lists the items which two separate cash deposits were expected to yield. These items were a part of the total range of goods which entered the centres of exchange.

1. Annual Interest on 40 *drammas*.

Wheat	2 *seis*
Ghee	8½ *kalasas* or jars
Muṅga pulse	1 *mana*
Chokhā (rice)	2 *pāilis*
Various articles for worship	7 *drammas* in value

2. Interest on a deposit of 15 *drammas*.

Wheat	25 *pāilis*
Muṅga	4 *pāilis*
Chokhā	2 *pāilis*
Other articles of worship	2 *drammas* in value

See also D. Sharma, *Rajasthan through the Ages*, p. 506.

[116]D. Sharma, *Rajasthan through the Ages*, p. 498.

[117]Cited in G.D. Sontheimer, *The Joint Hindu Family—Its Evolution as a Legal Institution,* Delhi, 1977, p. xix.

through access to such substantial amounts of cash over the exchange network.

This brings us finally to the question of the rate of return. The return in the form of resources in kind could, as suggested before, be considered high, but data for calculating actual rates of interest are rather meagre. Even so, barring a few curious exceptions, the rate of interest per annum may be put between 25 per cent and 30 per cent.[118] Despite the absence of evidence on how interest rates related to the general processes of commerce, it is certain that outside their known religious contexts they were also interwoven in the different tiers of secular exchange transactions. The three final sections of this essay relating to the accumulation and circulation of money can therefore be taken as pointers to go beyond the constraints implicit in the evidence and examine more thoroughly a process which evidence emanating from religious establishments partly reflects.

To sum up, the broad survey of the commerce of early medieval Rajasthan offered in this essay seems to establish distinct stages in its history, with overlapping between them in certain respects. The first phase is essentially characterized by the proliferation of local centres of exchange which were situated within the domains of emergent Rajput lineages and the spatial contexts of which were agrarian. Despite being local centres of exchange, they were nevertheless points of intersection for traffic of varying origins, and it is perhaps the nature of the interaction with traffic from the outside that gave rise to a certain measure of hierarchy among exchange centres. The second phase, dating roughly from the eleventh and twelfth centuries, witnessed the resurgence of local merchant lineages already in operation and the emergence of hitherto unfamiliar lineages which established wide intraregional and interregional networks. What this essay cannot claim to offer at this stage is a satisfactory exposition of the structure of commerce which these merchant lineages represented or what changes the structure underwent beyond the thirteenth century.

[118]This estimate is based on D. Sharma, *Rajasthan through the Ages*, pp. 505–507.

Chapter Eleven

Geographical Considerations in the Localization of Ancient Sea-Ports of India*

JEAN DELOCHE

The Indian peninsula, that enormous triangle of land projecting into the Indian Ocean, has from earliest times supported the manifestation of an impressive array of sea-port development. On the great maritime facades there are different regions, connected to rich hinterlands, which are favourable to sea traffic. In the East, for example, there is the opulent Ganges delta and its dense fluvial network opening out into the sea at many outlets; there is Orissa, a large and fertile plain which arches towards the Bay of Bengal; the flourishing deltas of Andhra, natural outlets of the vast valleys of the Krishna and the Godavari; lastly, there is the Coromandel plain with the properous Tanjavur lands.

In the west lies a more disparate and compartmentalized strip of land. Here the backwaters of Kerala have served to bring to points near the river mouth the traffic and trade of the hinterland; further, the Konkan, with its narrow and broken coastal land, has short but much-used rivers to carry all the regional trade towards the Arabian Sea. Next may be mentioned Gujarat with the peninsula of Kathiyavad and Kutch, open to all the influences of the sea, and finally, the fertile Indus delta, which lies at the end of the natural corridor leading to Punjab and Afghanistan.

And yet, in spite of this wealth of geographical variety, if we take

* *The Indian Economic and Social History Review,* XX, (1983), pp. 439–48.

at face value what is constantly repeated in text-books written in English—namely that Indian coasts are inhospitable because of their lack of natural protection, the shallowness of their waters and the violence of their swells—we would imagine that, in the past, India had not developed much maritime activity. It is true that the long coastal fringe offers only a few sites which simultaneously provide deep water and shelter for modern ships as well as for the eighteenth century sailing ships, but we know that ships drawing very little water were formerly used in coastal navigation and accommodated themselves extremely well to these particular conditions. Since voyages were made only in good weather, a rudimentary 'shelter' sufficed as a harbour, or else the hulls were simply dragged ashore.

It must be kept in mind that, in Akbar's time, the sailing vessels and even the ships belonging to the European companies, were of low capacity, that the biggest of them was not more than 200 or 300 tons[1] and that they could, therefore, penetrate some of the shallower estuaries. It may astonish us to learn that even the unwelcoming mouth of the Ponnani River, blocked by a sand bank, sheltered a squadron of sea craft at the beginning of the sixteenth century.[2] Machilipatnam, situated on a small branch of the Krishna River, was considered by Bowrey[3] as 'having a reasonable harbour'; in the eighteenth century, Mahfuz Bandar, the port of Srikakulam, on the Vamsadhara River (no longer usable) was 'continually frequented by boats which came from the coast',[4] and, in 1711, in the Ganjam River, which is now inaccessible, there were '98 three-masted vessels grounded on the beach'.[5] At the beginning of the next century, only ships of low tonnage were still to be seen in the most active zones of the coast. In 1818, the sailors of Kutch, who shuttled up and down the length of

[1] W.H. Moreland, *India at the Death of Akbar: An Economic Study*, Delhi, 1962, pp. 215–18.

[2] L. Varthema, *The Itinerary of Ludovico di Varthema of Bologna from 1502 to 1508,* (1928 edn.), London, 1928, p. 101. The squadron may have left the river on 12 March 1506. Also see Gray's note in *Voyage of Francois Pyrard de Laval to the East Indies,* Vol. 1, London,'1887, p. 398, note 2.

[3] T. Bowrey, *A Geographical Account of the Countries Round the Bay of Bengal,* London, 1905, p. 72.

[4] *Table Geographique et Historique des Indes*, ms, Museum d'histoire Naturelle, Paris, No. 1765, p. 32.

[5] *Lettres éditifiantes et curieuses*, Paris, 1810–11, t. 12, p. 27.

the western coast, pulling close up to the Arabian shores, used 800 boats whose tonnage varied between 14 and 180 tons, and in 1835, the port of Mandvi had no less than than 250 craft carrying 25–200 tons.[6]

We can thus understand why, from time immemorial, a string of little maritime establishments stretched out along the long garland of the coast. Most of them were small trading posts, serving local traffic, but there were also important settlements at places which enjoyed well-developed mercantile activities, as well as the big ports which served the fertile areas engaged in overseas trade.

These establishments were found either on the sea-front or on its immediate approaches, in small bays or coves, behind promontories, at the outlets of rivers and lagoons, or below the tidal estuaries. They can be classified under the following heads.

LITTORAL PORTS

Almost all littoral ports are exposed to the surf and the sea breeze. On the eastern coast of India, there is no natural shelter. European navigators of the eighteenth century discovered nothing more than the city of Coringa which was protected against the sea by a large underwater sand bank. Conditions were better in the west, on the Konkan ria coast, with its rocks, islets and narrow gulfs that penetrate far inland: Goa, Bombay and many other harbours are well protected, but outside these sectors, only a few ports sheltered from the sea can be found. This is why most of the old ports were at the mouths of rivers and, in the case of lagoons, sprang up where vessels could find refuge at the mouth of the outlet to the sea.

Along with the disadvantage of insufficent shelter must be added that of shallow water. The material that littoral currents shift along the coast stops wherever the movement of the water decreases and, as Degrandpré[7] says,

> . . . every day the ocean endeavours to raise the level of the shore that it abandons imperceptibly: along the whole stretch of this coast it increasingly

[6] According to the surveys made by Burnes and Mac Murdo, summarized in *Gazetteer of the Bombay Presidency,* Vol. 5, Cutch, Bombay, p. 117.

[7] Degrandpre, *Voyage dans l'Inde et au Bengale fait dans les années 1789 et 1790,* Paris, 1801, t. 1, pp. 90–91.

heaps up sands and sediments from which it slowly constructs a bank which will one day become the coast against which it will deposit new banks. These sands form what is called the longshore bar on which the waves break furiously all the time.

Access to the littoral, particularly in the Eastern sector,[8] is therefore difficult and ships with a deep draught are obliged to anchor far out at sea.

After the floods, a submerged bar forms at the mouths of rivers; this slowly rises until, in certain places, it emerges above the water level by the dry season. Rivers and lagoons are thus closed for many months in the year. On the Coromandel coast, for example, between the Svarnamukhi River and Marakkanam (north of Pondicherry), all water courses, except the Palar and the Pulicat Lake, are cut off from the sea from March to October.[9] Only the rivers affected by strong tides (tributaries of the Gulf of Cambay, and Ganges delta) are benefited in this respect since the ebb and flow, sweeping through their channels, clears their mouths.

Thus, on the sea-front, only rocky coasts with their crags can offer both shelter and deep water at the same time to form natural harbours. However, a number of minor ports accessible to small vessels were scattered all over. This is possible at any beach over which boats could be dragged, or at the mouth of a river where boats, hauled over the sandbar, could find water-spaces that were closed off from the strong swells and surf; even on the Coromandel coast, boats found protection in the small Cuddalore and Karikal rivers[10] or in shallow

[8] 'From the southern point of the Coromandel coast till Palmyras Point which closes the Bay of Balassor, it is impossible to disembark in European boats' (ibid., p. 90).

[9] A.S. Russell, *History of the Buckingham Canal Project,* Madras, 1898, pp. 42, 52–58. The eastern coast,

> . . . is so flat that the rivers have practically no course and are so slow, even at their mouths, that the sea heaps up a sandbar like it does everywhere else, in such a way that the rivers are closed and filter through the sand. In rainy weather, they swell above the bank that closes them, and the watercourse frays a bed which the sea fills up again as soon as the greater part of the water has flowed in. It must be understood that I talk only of small rivers and not those of which are deep enough to admit vessels (Degrandpré, *op. cit.*, pp. 96–97).

[10] See Cordier, *Historique et Statistique de Karikal,* Vol. 1, Pondicherry, 1971, p. 196.

lagoons like Pulicat. These once innumerable ports are now inactive, but in times past played a role in local transport side by side with better located ports where maritime activities were concentrated.

ESTUARY PORTS

The most important estuary ports were established in river estuaries, even though navigation was difficult due to the lack of depth and because of the danger posed by shifting sand banks which obstructed their channels. Using moorings within the zone where the alternating tides fetch and carry boats, these estuaries offer perfect shelter, and facilitate the linking of the waterway with land routes or with inland navigation. Such were the big ports of the western coast between the Narmada and Goa, as well as the ports on the branches of the Ganges.

TIDES

It is clear, then, that the possibilities of developing ports on the seafront or in the estuaries depended principally upon the range of the tides. The magnitude of the ebb and flow at the highest tide on the coast of Baluchistan and Sindh is about 2 to 2.5 metres; it rises to 2 to 6 metres in the Gulf of Kutch, then comes down to 2.5 metres at Porbandar, only to rise again in the Gulf of Cambay and reach 8.5 metres at Bhavnagar. Along the western coast it diminishes progressively—4metres at Bombay, 1.50 metres at Mangalore, 1 metre at Cochin and 0.70 metre at Colombo. It rises, from south to north on the east coast—0.70 metre at Tuticorin, 1 metre at Madras, 1.30 metres at Kakinada, from 2 to 2.80 metres in Orissa, and finally from 4 to 5 metres between Sagar and Chittagong.[11] It seems obvious that settlements where strong tides acted were more fortunate.

On the Konkan coast there are bays, peninsulas, estuaries and capes, where the influences of land and sea combine. The strength of the tides is still great, for the incoming tide flows into the valleys and penetrates deep into the country. Also, the topography favours settlements along the coast. Together with the towns in the estuaries at

[11] Figures taken from the *Tide-Tables of the Indian Ocean for the Year 1957*, Dehra Dun, p. 298.

points where the tides carry in the boats, are formed two, sometimes even three, lines of settlements corresponding to two or three degrees of marine penetration. At no other part on the western coast is this parallelism so obvious. Today, the towns on the sea-front, with their promontories crowned by fortresses are, with the exception of Ratnagiri, diminutive and decadent ports where commercial life is dormant. In such places, the estuarine agglomerations have lost contact with the sea and have a tendency to go back to their land activities. All of them, however, used to enjoy considerable maritime prominence.

THE MUDBANKS OF THE KERALA COAST

I should also mention a curious phenomenon, well-known to old sailors. At certain places on the Kerala coast (during the South West monsoon) it is possible to find moorings in areas of calm water which depend upon the formation of mudbanks. It has been observed that marine deposits of fine sized particles of green and black mud have been found near certain ports between Pantalayini (25 kilometres north of Calicut) and Quilon (which are 300 kilometres distant from each other). During the monsoon these sediments spread themselves over the entire thickness of the water layer, forming a colloidal suspension that may be 7 kilometres long and 5 kilometres wide, and having the property of reducing the movement of waves. Studies on this subject show that certain mudbanks are permanent (or at least that they have been in existence for a long time), and that others are temporary—four of the first type have been mentioned (two at Calicut, one at Narakal and one at Alleppey) and seven of the second type; it has also been noted that these banks are mobile and that they move from place to place for long distances along the coast.[12]

[12] F. Day, 'Narrikal or Cochin Mudbanks,' *Madras Journal of Literature and Science*, vol. 22, 1861, pp. 260–63; R. Damodaran and C. Hridaynathan, 'Studies on the Mudbanks of the Kerala Coasts', *Bulletin of the Department of Marine Biology and Oceanography*, Vol. 2, Ernakulam, 1966, pp. 61–68 (two maps); also W. Logan, *Malabar Manual*, Vol. 1, Madras, 1951, pp. 35–37; C.A. Menon, *Cochin State Manual*, Ernakulam, 1911, pp. 12–13; V.N. Ayya, *Travancore State Manual*, Vol. 1, Trivandrum, 1939, pp. 89–92; K.P. Narayan, 'Sea Erosion on the Kerala Coast: Steps for Protection', in the *Hindu*, 12 September 1971.

Many of the ancient settlements owe their prominence partly to this phenomenon which allows vessels to throw their anchors safely and of discharging cargo even at the height of the monsoon. It is mainly for this reason that Pantalayini, now an obscure fishing village, is mentioned by all the great travellers of the Muslim period. According to Ibn Battutah, in the fourteenth century, 'it was in this town that Chinese ships passed the winter,'[13] and it is thought that Vasco da Gama's fleet came to take refuge here in the monsoon of 1498.[14] In 1775–76, Stavorinus, talking of the mudbanks at the mouth of the river at Cranganore, north of Cochin, and at Porcad, stated that vessels could moor there in 20 feet of water, without anchor or cables, perfectly secure, during the South West monsoon.[15]

ADVANTAGES OF POSITION AND SITE

If we consider the factors of position and site which once enabled certain maritime settlements to flourish, we notice that they did not have the same distinctive features as they do today. For example, it is astonishing that for centuries preference should have been given to a port on the Indus delta that was constantly threatened by the wanderings of the river, when a relatively protected harbour existed on the sea-front at Karachi. One could also ask why it was necessary to wait for the East India Company to start making use of the exceptional facilities furnished by Bombay, and for what reason, even at the end of the eighteenth century, ships crowded at the entry to Surat which was situated on a river burdened with alluvial deposits. Evidently the explanation is that, in the old days, ports developed mainly in relation to the commercial potential of their hinterland. All the traffic of the Indus valley led necessarily, through the navigable network of the Indus River, to the settlements of lower Sindh; Karachi had to wait till the project of improving the river was given up, and until the town itself became the terminus of the railway coming from the

[13] Ibn Battutah, *Voyages* (trs., C. Defremery and Sanguinetti), Paris, 1853–56, t. 4, p. 88.

[14] *Hobson-Jobson*, pp. 666–67; the remarks of R.H. Sankey on the mudbanks can be found here; C.A. Innes, *Malabar Gazetteer*, Vol. 1, Madras, 1951, p. 465.

[15] J.S. Stavorinus, *Voyage to the East Indies*, vol. 3, London, 1789, p. 215.

Punjab, in order to establish its port. Likewise, the rocky Konkan coast was ideal for a maritime settlement; unfortunately, the barrier of the Ghats shut off the horizon from the land and its ports could not compete with the estuary towns of the prosperous Gujarat, which have been, in spite of their inadequate waterways, the gates of Hindustan.

As for the distribution of the numerous small ports scattered along the coast, it must be mentioned that their existence was not solely a consequence of advantageous position and site, but they also grew due to the deficiency of overland transport. Thus it was not possible to concentrate maritime activity in a few big settlements since the roads on the coastal plains did not facilitate the distribution of commodities; further, traffic existed from creek to creek, shore to shore and village to village, therefore, there were maritime settlements which acted as overland stopping places, spaced every 20 or 30 kilometers.[16] These rural markets, which stayed more or less active according to the seasonal pattern, have not been able to survive in the face of modern changes, and have now been diverted to the fishing industry.[17]

HARBOUR INSTALLATIONS

It can now be asked whether there was much concern about sea works for improving shelter and facilitating access to ports by deepening channels, passes and moorings, constructing embankments, breakwaters and jetties on the sea-front.

On the basis of recent excavation, certain Indian archaeologists claim that artifical harbours have existed ever since prehistoric times. S.R. Rao,[18] for example, postulates that there existed wharfs, jetties,

[16] See Harris A. Norman, 'Factors Controlling Port-Sites, with Special Reference to Western India', *Geography,* vol. 18, pp. 118–25.

[17] This evolution can be followed on the Kathiayavad coast. At the beginning of the nineteenth century, sixty-two active ports could be enumerated. In 1842, twelve of them which were silted up or not adaptable to modern conditions were closed and at the end of the nineteenth century only a dozen played any role at all in maritme life (*Gazetteer of the Bombay Presidency,* Vol. 8: *Kathiawar*, Bombay, 1883, p. 236).

[18] S.R. Rao, 'Shipping in Ancient India', in *Vivekananda Commemoration Volume*, Madras, 1970, pp. 83–107. It is a statement on the discoveries made in this area in different places along the coast.

docks and warehouses, ranging in date from 2300 BC to AD 300. A brick-built structure was discovered at Lothal, 80 kilometres south of Ahmadabad.[19] Said to be a dock, it is trapezoidal in form, and measures 214 metres in length and 36 metres in width. It would have had 2 metres of water at low tide and 3.15 metres at high tide, and was provided with an outlet passage that allowed access to ships coming from the Gulf of Cambay. On the Kathiyavad coast at Hathab, near Ghogha, large country craft now often take refuge in a depression which might have been a dock at the beginning of the Christian era.[20] On the Coromandel coast, at Kaveripattinam, a brick platform was found dated 300 BC[21]. It is 18.28 metres long and 7.62 metres wide and might have been a wharf provided for ships approaching to cast anchor. Some brick structures discovered at Nagapattinam, in the course of pile-driving operations, might have been part of a wharf, and date to the fifth century of our era. At Arikamedu (near Pondicherry), on the river Ariyankuppam, brick walls which are remnants of a warehouse appear to have served as a dock.[22] Finally, at Dhanyakataka, near Amaravati, in Guntur district, near an ancient watercourse was found what might have been a wharf built in the second century AD. S.R. Rao concludes from this that 'on almost all the seaports mentioned by the author of the *Periplus* and by Ptolemy, some kind of a dockyard for anchoring ships and wharfs for haulage of goods must have existed'.[23]

This interpretation, however, seems rather hasty. The vestiges discovered could have belonged to other constructions. As a case in point, it has not been proved that the depression at Hathab is actually the remnant of a dock dating back to the first few centuries of our era; further, there is no positive evidence that the bricks at Nagapattinam or Arikamedu are parts of a wharf. Nor can we be sure that the area of water at Lothal was indeed a dock—in all likelihood the latter was probably a fresh-water reservoir or an irrigation tank.[24]

[19] Ibid., pls. 2 and 3. The site would have been swept by a flood in 1900 BC.
[20] Ibid., pl. 9.
[21] Ibid., pl. 17.
[22] Ibid., pl. 12.
[23] Ibid., pl. 95.
[24] See U.P. Shah, 'Lothal, A Port?', *Journal of the Oriental Institute*, Baroda, vol. 9, 1959–60, pp. 301–20; L. Leshnik, 'The Harappan Port at Lothal', *American Anthropologist,* vol. 70, no. 5, 1968, pp. 911–22; H.D. Sankalia, in *The Prehistory and Protohistory of India and Pakistan*, Poona, 1974,

Finally, and this is most significant, even if the archaeologists have identified them correctly, we are aware that the only important remnants (at Lothal, Kaveripattinam and Dhanyakataka) are not situated on the coast, but inland, on rivers, that is in calm waters (bricks are fragile and cannot withstand the swell for long; consequently, they cannot be used on the sea-front). In other words, these structures are not extraordinary at all; they are reminiscent of the *ghats* (landing places) found in almost all the river towns situated on the great Indian waterways.[25]

Further, we only hear of the periodical digging of sand banks at river mouths, and of the deepening of passes.[26] The reports of the French East India Company show that, at Karikal, from 1760 periodic attempts were made to improve the river by constructing permanent structures to narrow the channel in such a way that the strength of the current was inhibited, resulting in a greater depth to the water on the bar.[27] At Pondicherry, a project to create an artificial port was repeatedly envisaged in the eighteenth century. Bourcet, when he came in 1774, conceived of a large dock on the banks of the Ariyankuppam River which would communicate with the sea through a channel closed by a lock. This idea of a port dug in the river often recurs in the plans made by the engineers of the French settlement;[28] conversely, it is not stated that a jetty should be built on the waterfront.

---

pp. 372–75; Suman Pandya, 'Lothal Dockyard Hypothesis and Sea Level Changes', in D.P. Agrawal and B.M. Pande (eds.), *Ecology and Archaeology of Western India,* Delhi, 1977, pp. 99–103. The last, basing himself on geomorphological, archaeological and ethnographic arguments, has proved almost irrefutably that the piece of water at Lothal could not have been a dock, and has shown that it corresponded to rain water tanks found in that region.

[25] Stavorinus (*op. cit.*, Vol. 3, pp. 158–59) has described a landing stage built by the English at Surat on the Tapti at the end of the eighteenth century.

[26] This fact is stated by the author of the *Nellore Manual,* Madras, 1873, p. 17 and Russell, *op. cit.*, p. 42. Every year, at the beginning of the North East monsoon, fishermen can be seen at the mouth of the Adyar River, south of Madras, excavating the sand bank, so that the waters of the river can flow into the sea.

[27] Cordier, *Historique et Statistique de Karikal,* Vol. 1, Pondicherry, 1971, pp. 24, 28, 30, 32–33, 44, 80, 107, 177.

[28] M.V. Labernadie, *Le Vieux Pondichery, 1673–1815*, Pondicherry, 1936, p. 342.

In any case, if we go by descriptions furnished by foreign observers, harbour installations seem to have been very elementary during the whole of the Mughal period. If there was no need of dockyards and sluice gates in the seventeenth century, why should such an elaborate system have been necessary in, for example, the Harappan period?

EVOLUTION OF THE COAST FROM PREHISTORIC TIME: INDIAN 'BRUGES'

It would have been interesting to write a full history of these maritime settlements. Unfortunately, detailed studies of the different sites are lacking. Historians, because of its influence on human settlements, seem to have been more concerned with the part played by land-building caused by the accumulated discharge of sediments. They discovered that the rapid encroachment of land into the water, in regions where the great rivers bring in enormous quantities of sediment, resulted in the actual displacement of urban centres. In this respect, the Indus delta is comparatively well known as the abundance of literary and archaeological sources allow us to follow its progress from the time of Alexander.[29] That of the Ganges is less documented.[30] As for the others, in the absence of landmarks, it is difficult to trace their history.

[29] A. Burns, 'Substance of Memoirs of the Indus,' *JRGSL*, vol. 3, 1834, pp. 113–56; T.G. Carless, 'Memoir to Accompany the Survey of the Delta of the Indus in 1837', *JRGSL*, vol. 8, 1838, pp. 328–66; J.F. Heddle, T.G. Charles and J. Wood, 'Memoirs of the River Indus, in *Selections from the Records of the Bombay Government,* No. 17, New Series, Part 2, 1855, pp. 401–588; J. Abbot, *Sind: A Reinterpretation of the Unhappy Valley,* Oxford, 1924, pp. 14–15, 366–67; R. Sivewright, 'Cutch and the Ran', *Geographical Journal,* vol. 29, 1907, pp. 518–39; anon., 'Notes on the Lost River of the Indian Desert,' *Calcutta Review,* vol. 59, no. 117, pp. 1–27; Anon., 'The Lost River of the Indian Desert: A Comment by "Nearchus"', *Calcutta Review*, vol. 60, no. 120, pp. 325–51; M.R. Haig, *The Indus Delta Country*, 1894; H.G. Raverty, 'The Mihran of Sind and its Tributaries', *JASB*, vol. 61, 1892, pp. 155–508.

[30] See C.R. Wilson, 'Note on the Topography of the River in the 16th Century from Hugli to the Sea as Represented in "Da Asia" of the Barros,' *JASBB*, vol. 61, pt. I, 1892, pp. 109–17; W.A. Inglis, 'Some Problems Set UP by the Rivers of Bengal', *JPASB*, New Series, vol. 5, 1909, pp. 393–

Today, geographers who study processes of littoral evolution emphasize the importace of earth movements and of eustatic changes in sea levels, but the observation available along the Indian coast are too meagre to enable them to draw firm conclusions.

Evidence for sea level changes has been noted at many places all along the coast of India. A few attempts have also been made to explain changes in some areas. Little is know about when these changes took place or how these features are related to each other or to the worldwide eustatic changes of sea level since Pleistocene times.[31]

When a sufficient number of surveys have been taken along the coast, it might be possible to answer some of the questions that arise. A.V.N. Sarma[32] takes note of the relationship between the successive phases of the Harappa civilization and the variations in sea level. Thus the flowering of this civilization could well have corresponded to the rise in sea level and its decline to the lowering. From this example, we see how systematic observations made on different sectors of the coast would be most rewarding.

To sum up, we know very little about the factors responsible for the evolution of Indian littoral forms, or the varied causes which explain the movement of shores, when the sea encroaches on or when it

---

405; F.D. Ascoli. 'The Rivers of Delta', *JPASB*, New Series, vol. 6, 1910, pp. 543–56. See also the maps of Gastaldi (1561), Barros (1553–1616), Blaeu (1650), van den Broeck (1660), Bowrey (1687), English Pilot (1703), Rennell's *Bengal Atlas* (1779–83).

[31] See S.P. Chatterjee, 'Fluctuations of Sea-Level Around the Coasts of India during the Quaternary Period', *Zeitschrift für Geomorphologie,* N.R. Suppl., Bd. 3, 1962, pp. 48–56 (with map showing the variations in sea level); S.N. Rajaguru and S.J. Guzder, 'A Review of Research on Quaternary Sea Level Changes and Archaeological Sites in India', *Bulletin of the Deccan College Research Institute,* vol. 33, 1973, nos 1–4, pp. 183–207; V. Kalyanasundaram, 'Changes in Level in the Southern Coast of Madras', *Indian Geographical Journal*, vol. 18, 1943; S. Krishnaswamy, 'The Coasts of India', *Indian Geographical Journal*, vol. 29, 1954; E. Ahmad, *Coastal Geomorphology of India,* New Delhi, 1972, especially pp. 180–94 (*bibliography for each chapter*).

[32] A.V.N. Sarma, 'Decline of Harappan Cultures: A Re-look', in *K.A. Nilakanta Sastri Felicitation Volume,* Madras, 1971, pp. 280–94.

recedes from the land.[33] Consequently, we lack knowledge of a significant portion of the history of the coast concerned with the transport and accumulation of sediments, with the threat of mud deposits in the estuaries or with the development of a delta or a coastal sand spit in the bays. The question remains, how many ports have thus been cut off from access to the sea or abandoned?[34]

CONCLUSION

To locate and identify the remains of these ancient ports and settlements, which are probably fossilized under several metres of alluvions (sand or mud) or submerged, more extensive and comprehensive researches are needed. Systematic stratigraphical and geomorphological studies, showing the historical evolution of the landscapes, would enable us to delimit a zone of topographical probability in which the sites could be detected with the help of geophysical, mechanical and geochemical techniques.[35]

[33] According to B.M. Thirunaranan, the peninsular block appears to have tilted at intervals, along a north–south axis, and the coastal features need to be examined in the light of this idea.

[34] Much data has been collected in the *Andhra University Memoirs in Oceanography*, vol. 2, Waltair, 1958, pp. 33–47 (evolution of Visakhapatam beach), pp. 48–60 (study of the deposition of heavy mineral sands at the confluence of some rivers along the east coast of India), pp. 69–74 (causes of the growth of sand spit north of the Godavari confluence).

[35] However, often archeological discoveries, far from throwing any light on the actual state of affairs, pose problems that cannot be solved with the facts available. S.R. Rao (*op. cit.*, pp. 89–90) gives us a significant example. We generally think that Bhṛgutirtha or Bhṛgu-Kaccha, an important port mentioned in the *Mahābhārata*, is identified with modern Broach (known to the Greeks as Barygaza). Yet, the excavations made at this place gave no evidence of very old elements—according to ceramics found there the oldest date of occupation does not go further than 600 BC. Perhaps the port of the Mahabharata is buried elsewhere beneath alluvial layers. Mahegam, which is closer to the sea and whose vestiges go back to 1900–1600 BC would answer better to the description of this town. One could conclude that Bhṛgutirtha was situated at the site of Mahegam, that it was destroyed by a flood in the Narmada and abandoned by its inhabitants who constructed a new town near modern Broach.

In the case of submerged cities, underwater exploration with sophisticated equipment should be conducted methodically. In India S.R. Rao has initiated this new field of investigation, in collaboration with the National Institute of Oceanography. A preliminarly off-shore survey of Kaveripattinam, Dwarka and Gharapuri, has, it seems, yielded encouraging results.

Chapter Twelve

The Medieval South Indian Guilds: Their Role in Trade and Urbanization*

R. CHAMPAKALAKSHMI

One of the more important but less understood areas of economic activity in medieval south India is that of the corporate trading communities often called 'guilds'. The term 'guild' immediately conjures up the image of an association of professionals with a well-defined structure, a carefully framed code of conduct or rules and membership governed by certain regulations and qualifications. It is hard to get indisputable evidence of such an organization from the south Indian records, although the term *Baṇanju dharma* is the nearest to a code of rules that existed and was adhered to by the itinerant merchant bodies. Hence, it is rather a matter of convenience that the term guild has been used to denote these merchant bodies; for there is hardly any similarity between them and the European merchant guilds or the *Hang* of China in Sung and Yuan times or the *Karimi* of Egypt.[1] It would perhaps be more appropriate to use the term organization which is the nearest equivalent to the term *Samaya (m)* used in the inscriptions.

* From D.N. Jha (ed.), *Society and Ideology in India, Essays in Honour of Professor R.S. Sharma.*

1 M. Abraham, 'A Medieval Merchant Guild of South India', *Studies in History*, IV, no. 1, 1982, p. 1. A curious and untenable derivation has been made of the term *Karimi* from *kāryam*, on the wrong assumption that *kāryam,* (affairs or work) is a Tamil word, whereas, in fact, it is of Sanskrit origin and adopted in all the regional languages of India, including Tamil. See Philip D. Curtin, *Cross-Cultural Trade in World History*, Cambridge, 1984, p. 115.

A second important aspect of the problem is the nature of the organization and its membership. Names of several groups occur in the epigraphic records all over south India and it is not always easy to identify them and determine their relationship to one another. To illustrate the point, one notices conspicuous references to the *Ayyāvoḷe* or *Aiññuṟṟuvar, Valañjiyar, Nānādesī* and *Nagarattār* apart from various other groups like the *Maṇigrāmam*, and *Añjuvaṇṇam* in the records ranging from the eighth to the seventeenth centuries AD more specially from the eighth to the fourteenth centuries, both in south India and Sri Lanka. With the exception of *Nagarattār*, all these terms refer to itinerant merchant bodies. While the *Aiññuṟṟuvar* or the Five Hundred figure prominently in most of the records, some forty-six different groups are noticed in association with them at various centres and in different contexts. Listing all these groups K. Indrapala expresses the difficulties in determining the nature of their relationship with the Five Hundred and dismisses as untenable the view that the Five Hundred was a federation of all these bodies or that the latter were sub-divisions of the Five Hundred.[2] Some of these groups were non-mercantile in character as they refer to occupational groups like the *Pañcālas, Kumbhalikas*, etc.[3] and to groups of fighters taken to be mercenaries accompanying the Five Hundred.[4]

From the twelfth to the fourteenth centuries, there is yet another major organization called the *Cittirameḷi Periya Nāḍu*[5] or the *Padineṇbhūmi* or *Viṣaya* of the Seventy-nine *Nāḍus* appearing jointly with the Five Hundred in a position of prime importance in the *praśastis* of the inscriptions recording joint donations of tolls and cesses on merchandise. The pride of place is here given to the *Cittirameḷi* and the Five Hundred is assigned a secondary position, with their respective emblems, namely the *sengol* and *meḷi* (the staff and the plough) of the first and the *paśumpai* (money bag or pouch) of the second.[6] There can hardly be any doubt as to the commercial and urban context in which these joint donations occur. This is to be seen as a result of the revival of long-distance trade in south India in

[2] K. Indrapala, 'Some Medieval Mercantile Communities of South India and Ceylon,' *Journal of Tamil Studies*, II, no. 2, October 1970, p. 31.

[3] Ibid., p. 32.

[4] Ibid., pp. 37–38.

[5] *Cittirameḷi* means 'the beautiful plough', which was the emblem of this organization.

[6] *SII*, VIII, no. 442 (Pirānmalai).

the AD tenth century, which was itself a part of the increase in south Asian trade involving such distant regions as Egypt, West Asia, South-East Asia and China.

The whole corpus of information on south Indian trade at this time centres mainly round the Five Hundred and to a lesser extent on the *Maṇigrāmam* and *Añjuvaṇṇam* and other such organizations. It would therefore be appropriate to start from the Five Hundred and proceed to enquire into the nature of its organization and relationship with other bodies. Only then can the complexity of inscriptional data be converted into useful categories of evidence. For reasons, which would become apparent in the course of this paper, it could also be useful to distinguish between the Five Hundred on the one hand and the *Maṇigrāmam, Añjuvaṇṇam* and the *Nagaram* on the other. The Five Hundred was a large organization of itinerant merchants, of a supra-regional character,[7] and the *Maṇigrāmam* was a localized merchant body operating within specific regions as the designations like *Uṛaiyur Maṇigrāmam* and *Koḍumbālūr Maṇigrāmam*[8] would show, though it had inter-regional and long distance trade links and interacted with the Five Hundred which carried on trade in the regions. The *Añjuvaṇṇam* refers to an organization of foreign merchants who seem to have begun their commercial activities on the west coast, particularly Kerala, in the eighth-ninth centuries[9] and spread out to the other coastal areas of south India from the eleventh century AD interacting with both the local merchants and the Five Hundred.[10] Initially the term *Añjuvaṇṇam* seems to have referred to Jewish traders who came to the west coast and acquired settlements. Later, however, it also came to denote Arab Muslim traders.[11]

[7] Tirumalai Inscription no. 10 of 1924 (*Annual Report of Indian Epigraphy*, 1923–24).

[8] *SII*, XIII, no. 28 (Tiruveḷḷaṛai); 283 of *ARE*, 1964–65 (Kovilpaṭṭi); *SII*, IV, no. 147 (Salem).

[9] M.G.S. Narayanan, *Cultural Symbiosis in Kerala*, pp. 4, 29. Here the *Añjuvaṇṇam* is taken to be an organization of Jewish traders.

[10] Viśākhappaṭṭinam Inscription, *SII*, X, no. 651. See also K. Sundaram, *Economic and Social Conditions in Medieval Andhra,* Madras, 1968, p. 94; Tittandatānapuram (Toṇḍi) inscription, 598 of 1926, *ARE*, 1926–27.

[11] In the Kanara districts a merchant body called the *Hanjamāna* or *Hanjumanna* was active from about the AD fourteenth century. Was it the same as *Añjuvaṇṇam*? Could *Añjuvaṇṇam* and *Hanjumanna* be derived from *Anjuman*?: Kaikini inscription (South Kanara), *Annual Report on*

The designations of these merchant bodies remain the same throughout the period of their activity. The *Nagaram* is a much more specific organization of merchants found in every market centre and collection and distribution centre where local and itinerant traders met and exchanged items of trade.[12] *Nagaram* being a mercantile organization evolving from local groups organizing and controlling local trade, *Nagarattār* became a generic term for all the traders and the trading community, particularly in Tamil Nadu, and hence is used even today by the Nāṭṭukkoṭṭai Cheṭṭiars.[13] The Five Hundred, as an organization of merchants, originated in the seventh century AD in Aihole in the Hungund taluk of the Bijapur district of Karnataka.[14] It has been suggested that the founding of the Ayyāvoḷe Five Hundred may be seen as the result of a decision of a group of *Mahājanas* or brāhmaṇas (*caturvedīs*), also called the 500 *Svāmīs* of the *Mahāgrahāra* of Aihole, to institutionalize control of the existing commerce of that region.[15] Hence, it would be erroneous to trace the origin of the itinerant merchant organization, as Kenneth R. Hall has done, to small groups of expeditionary merchants who serviced less wealthy or isolated communities of the hinterland and found it profitable to band together for mutual protection. It would be equally wrong to assume that the itinerant merchant organizations of the Coḷa age developed from such bands of expeditionary traders into powerful commercial associations.[16] Aihole, also known as Aryapura and Ahicchatra in the inscriptions, was thus both the progenitor and birthplace of the corporation. However, the organization did not remain a single unified body throughout its history; nor was Aihole its permanent headquarters. The number Five Hundred was a conventional one and remained so for the rest of the history of the itinerant traders,

---

Kannda Research in Bombay Province, 1939–40, no. 38. See also K.V. Ramesh, *History of South Kanara*, Dharwar, 1970, p. 253, where the author suggests that *Hanjamāna* represented Arab-Persian merchants.

[12] See Kenneth R. Hall, *Trade and Statecraft in the Age of the Coḷas*, New Delhi, 1980, ch. 5.

[13] *Nagarattār* is the designation of the Tamil trading community now also known as the Nāṭṭukkoṭṭai Ceṭṭiars in the Ramanathapuram and Pudukkottai districts.

[14] Aihole Inscriptions, *IA*, VIII, 1879, pp. 237 ff.; *IA*, VI, 1877, p. 138 n., B.K. 289 of *ARE*, 1927–28.

[15] M. Abraham, 'A Medieval Merchant Guild of South India,' *op. cit.*, p. 6.

[16] Kenneth R. Hall, *op. cit.*, p. 151.

who derived their name from the parent organization, despite the fact that the organization became a much larger one drawing its members from various regions and communities.

Other terms like *Nānādeśi, Ubhaya-nānādeśi, Valañjīyar,* or *Vīra Valañjīyar, Baṇajiga,* etc. were of a descriptive or adjectival nature, and were used to denote the itinerant merchants following the trading profession or the *Bananju dharma*. Hence, these terms are found sometimes used interchangeably in many of the records. Among the other groups, who are mentioned along with the Five Hundred, were mercenary fighters who protected their merchandise, probably in lieu of a share in the profit. The militant character of their mercantile organization derives mainly from these groups whose valour and ferocity are indicated by such epithets such as Ilancingam, Cittiravāḷi, Eṟivīra, Munaivīra, Kongavālar, etc.[17] Some of them became traders through long association with the organization. Craft groups are also sometimes mentioned with the Five Hundred,[18] probably due to the links established between the two for the marketing of the commodities, particularly textile, metalware and pottery. Being the largest itinerant merchant organization covering distant regions and divergent commercial areas, the Five Hundred was the only organization to have mercenaries to protect its goods and to set up protected mercantile towns (with warehouses) called *Eṟivīrap-paṭṭaṇas.*[19] The name *Ayyāvoḷe* became, in Tamil, *Aiyapoḻil* and *Danmapoḻil*, and was often used as a descriptive epithet of its towns and the deities, for example *Aiyapoḻil*[20] Parameśvaī. But the terms Five Hundred is more commonly

[17] In the guild inscriptions of Sri Lanka, the guild members are closely associated with the *Veḷaikkārar*, a mercenary body and the *Valañjīyar* are often referred to as the elders (*mūtātaiyar*) of the *Veḷaikkārar,* who must have moved into Sri Lanka along with the mercantile community. See K. Indrapala, *op. cit.*, p. 33.

[18] K.R. Venkatarama Aiyar, 'Medieval Trade, Craft and Merchant Guilds in South India', *Journal of Indian History*, XXV, pt. 1, 1947, pp. 268–80; K. Indrapala, *op. cit.*, pp. 31–32.

[19] R. Champakalakshmi, 'Urbanization in Medieval Tamil Nadu', in S. Bhattacharya and Romila Thapar (eds.), *Situating Indian History*, 1986, Table VI.

[20] In Karnataka from the eleventh century onwards, the Ayyāvoḷe acquired new bases and established several towns (e.g. 'Southern Ayyāvoḷe') both under the patronage of the Western Cālukyas of Kalyāṇi and the Hoysalas of Dvārasamudra. Interestingly in an inscription of AD 1267 form Dodballapur,

used to denote the group and is sometimes stretched into *Nānādeśiya Tiśai Ayirattu Aiññuṟṟuvar.*

It has been pointed out earlier that the Five Hundred cannot be treated as a single unified body of merchants throughout its history, and that its functioning may not have had a uniform pattern throughout the area of its operation. Although there seems to have been some unity and common purpose in the early years of its activities, it has also been pointed out that with the growth of regional kingdoms and regional interests, there appeared a bifurcation between the guild as it operated in the Kannada speaking areas and as it functioned in the Tamil region.[21]

In Tamil Nadu it acquired the character of a composite body of itinerant traders who came from different parts of the Tamil speaking areas. One of the most remarkable inscriptions from the point of view of its composition comes from Tirumalai in the Sivaganga taluk of Ramanathapuram district. After the usual *praśasti*, it provides a list of the people who belonged to the organization and who met at Tirumalai in the Aiññuṟṟuvar Tirukkāvaṇam of the local Śiva temple. The members hailed from different places and are named after their respective regions like the Tiśai Āyirattu Aiññuṟṟuva of Vaḍakaḷavali Nāḍu, of Tirukoṭṭiyūr Maṇiyambalam of Vembaṟṟūr, of Malaimaṇḍalam, of Alagaimānagaram and many other places.[22] Terms like Aiññuṟṟuva Bhaṭṭan and names like Aiññuṟṟuvan Inban Devan Cetti would also indicate the heterogeneous caste composition of this body. The Five Hundred was thus a group of people of 'disparate origins associating together for a common purpose' that is, trade. In other words, this group consisted of members belonging to several castes, religions and regions.[23]

---

the Ayyāvoḷe merchants claim descent from the Coḷas and Cālukyas (*Coḷa Kulānvitarum Cālukyānvayarum*, *Epigraphia Carnatica*, IX, Dodballapur 31). The 'Southern Ayyāvoḷe' towns are believd to be named after the Ayyāvoḷe in northern Karnataka (See K. Indrapala, *op. cit.*, p. 26). However, most of these towns came up in south Karnataka only after regular interaction between Karnataka and Tamil Nadu was established following Coḷa inroads and the movement of the Tamil merchant organizations into the link areas and Karnataka could be possible. It would hence be tempting to argue that these towns represent an expansion of the Tamil Five Hundred into Karnataka.

[21] M. Abraham, 'A Medieval Merchant Guild of South India,' *op. cit.*, p. 4.

[22] No. 10 of 1924 (Tirumalai inscription dated AD 1233). The other groups mentioned are Pāṇḍimaṇḍala, Perunirāvi, Tiśai, Āyirattu, Aiññuṟṟuvar, Deśivallabha, Tiśai, Āyirattu, Aiññuṟṟuvar, Koḷikkuṟicci, Kaḍittāvula, Tiśai Ayirattu, Aiññuṟṟuvar, etc.

[23] That the members came from different castes, religions and regions is

The earliest reference to the Five Hundred in Tamil Nadu comes from the Pudukkottai region towards the close of the ninth century, and its presence here and in the Ramanathapuram district is almost continuously attested down to the fourteenth century AD. This region is a crucial link area on the route between the Kaveri and Vaigai valleys and the important trading emporium of Toṇḍi on the eastern coast.[24] There is indeed a concentration of the Five Hundred inscriptions in the Pudukkottai and Ramanathapuram districts throughout the period under consideration. In this region the Five Hundred appears to have interacted with the Koḍumbālūr *Maṇigrāmam* and the local *Nagarattār*, some of whom may well have become local representative of the itinerant merchant organization.

The route that the Five Hundred used to reach Tamil Nadu so early(ninth century—Muniśandai) after its foundation in Aihole in Karnataka is not clearly attested. It has, however, been suggested[25] that they moved into Tamil Nadu through the Chittoor region and Palar valley southwards, a route that was probably used by the Kuṛumbar tribes, who are still to be seen in the Pudukkottai area. This was the route followed by the invading Rāṣṭrakūṭa armies under Kṛṣṇa III in the tenth century AD. Equal claims to have been the regular route of migration or movement between Karnataka and Tamil Nadu may be made for the Kongu region, that is, from the Ganga country north of the Kaveri through Kongu into the Kaveri valley and further south. The existence of this route from very early times is attested by the provenance of Tamil Brāhmī inscriptions (Pugaḷiyūr, Aracalūr Tiricirāpalli and Śittannavāsal), the discovery of hoards of Roman coins and by the traditions of the Digambara Jaina migration.[26] However, in both the Palar valley and the Kongu

---

indicated not only by the Tamil inscriptions but also by the Kannada and Telugu inscriptions of Karnataka and Andhra. See M. Abraham, 'The Ayyavoḷe Guild of Medieval South India', unpublished M. Phil. dissertation, Jawaharlal Nehru University, 1978, ch. 5.

[24] The early Brāhmi inscriptions in Śittaṇṇavāsal and the hoard of Roman coins datable to the early centuries before and after the beginning of the Christian era indicate an early trade route through this region. See R. Champakalakshmi, 'South India', in A. Ghosh (ed.), *Jaina Art and Architecture*, 1974, I, ch. 9; Mortimer Wheeler, 'Arikamedu: An Indo-Roman Trading Station on the East Coast of India', *Ancient India*, no. 2. July 1946, pp. 118–21.

[25] M. Abraham, 'A Medieval Merchant Guild of South India', *op. cit.*, pp. 7–9.

[26] P.B. Desai, *Jainism in South India*, Sholapur, 1957, pp. 25–27.

region, the inscriptions of the *Aiññurruvar* appear only from the eleventh century AD. A second wave of Jaina influence in the eighth-ninth centuries, under Rāṣṭrakūṭa patronage, is also indicated by a series of Jaina epigraphs, marking a line of sites in the North Arcot, South Arcot, Tiruchirapalli, Pudukkottai, Ramanathapuram, Madurai and Tirunelveli districts leading on to south Kerala.[27] These migrations may well have followed ancient and early medieval trade routes linking the different cultural regions of south India.

The spatial and chronological distribution of the Aiññurruvar inscriptions also makes an interesting study. In the Pudukkottai region, their activities in the AD ninth-eleventh centuries,[28] were encouraged by the early and middle Colas and their feudatories, and the Irukkuveḷs of Koḍumbālūr. The close matrimonial ties between Coḷas and Irukkuveḷs may well have been inspired by the strategic location of the region linking areas of commercial importance. A rather close identity of interests between this commercial organization and the Coḷas may be recognized not only in the fostering of trade in this region but also in other regions conquered by the Coḷas in eleventh and twelfth centuries AD.

The Five Hundred moved in wherever the Coḷas stepped in as conquerors. Into the region south and north of the upper Kaveri valley, that is, the Kongu and Ganga countries, the *Aiññurruvar* moved in the wake of the Coḷa conquests under Rājarāja I and Rājendra I (AD 985–1044). Talakkad, north of the Kaveri and, Muḍikoṇḍan (Muḍikoṇḍacoḷapuram) south of the Kaveri, marked the two major centres of merchant activity.[29] In Muḍikoṇḍan, the merchants of the 18 *paṭṭaṇas* north of the Kaveri and of the 18 *paṭṭaṇas* south of the Kaveri made huge endowments to the local Viṣṇu temple and exercised control over the temple management.[30] In the eleventh century, Aiyapoḷil Kāttūr and Basinikoṇḍa (Śirāvalli) in the Chingleput and Chittoor districts respectively became Erivīrappaṭṭanas or protected mercantile towns under special charters from the Coḷa rulers for the Toṇḍaimaṇḍalam region, also called Jayankoṇḍcoḷamaṇḍalam.[31] In

27 R. Champakalakshmi, 'Kuruṇḍi Tirukkāṭṭāmpaḷḷi, An Ancient Jaina Monastery of Tamil Nadu', *Studies in Indian Epigraphy*, II, 1975, p. 89.

28 Muniśandai Inscription, *Pudukkottai State Inscriptions,* no. 61; Cettippaṭṭi inscription, ibid., no. 1083.

29 R. Champakalakshmi in *Situating Indian History*, *op. cit.*, pp. 48–49.

30 Muḍikoṇḍān Inscription, 2, of 1910, *ARE*, 1909–10.

31 Kāttūr Inscription, 256 of 1912, *ARE*, 1912–13 and Basinikoṇḍa, 342 of

northern Sri Lanka (Rājaraṭṭha), following the Coḷa conquests of the eleventh century AD, the Five Hundred became active in the organized commerce and movement of commodities with Polonnaruwa as an important centre.[32] After the political unifiction of Veṅgi with the Coḷa kingdom under Kulottuṅga I (AD 1070) the Five Hundred is seen as far north as Viśākhappaṭṭiṇam (Kulottuṅgacoḷan Paṭṭinam) and other coastal towns upto Drākṣārāma in the Ganjam district of Orissa.[33] Under the Coḷa royal patronage Tamil traders moved more frequently into the Andhra region and *Coḷamaṇḍalamuna Vyāpāri* are referred to in a few interior trade centres while Ghaṇṭaśālā or Coḷapāṇḍiyan Paṭṭinam on the coast became an important emporium under the middle Coḷas, Rājarājaj I to Kulottuṅga I, whose interest in developing the Coḷa port of Nāgappaṭṭiṇam is well known.[34] Their trade missions to China, maritime expeditions to Śrīvijaya (AD 1025) and abolition of tolls by Kulottuṅga I[35] undoubtedly encouraged the movement of itinerant traders and helped in establishing trade links with China. The Canton inscription of Kulottunga I is indicative of his trading interests at that port.[36]

In the heart of the Coḷa kingdom, that is, the Kaveri delta, the Five Hundred began its activity in the tenth century in Tiruppuṛambiyam, Tiruviḍaimarudūr and various other centres such as Tiruveḷvikkuḍi, Tirunaḷḷāru, Tiruccengodu, Koyil Tevarāyanpeṭṭai and Tiruchoṟṟu-tturai. It is seen as far south as Ukkirankoṭṭai (Karavandapuram), a fortified town in the Tirunelveli district, in the same period. In the middle Coḷa period the Five Hundred spread out into Toṇḍaimaṇḍalam, Kongu Nāḍu an Pāṇḍi Nāḍu, the most notable example in the Pāṇḍya region being the *Eṟīvīrappaṭṭaṇa* at Tiruvālīśvaram in the Ambasa-mudram taluk (the newly developed Muḷḷi Nāḍu) of the Tirunelveli district with direct access to south Kerala through the Aramboli pass and control over the southern Pāṇḍya region of the Tāmraparṇi.[37]

112, *ARE*, 1912–13.

[32] K. Indrapala, *op. cit.*, pp. 32–33; M. Abraham, 'A Medieval Merchant Guild of South India', *op. cit.*, pp. 12–14.

[33] K. Sundaram, *op. cit.*, pp. 93–96.

[34] Ibid., pp. 92 and 95.

[35] K.A. Nilakanta Sastri, *The Coḷas,* Madras, 1975, (rpt.), p. 331.

[36] M. Abraham, 'A Medieval Merchant Guild of South India,' *op. cit.*, p. 14.

[37] R. Champakalakshmi, *Situating Indian History*, *op. cit.,* Tables IV–22 and Table VI.

The *Eṟivīrappaṭṭaṇa* of this period are seen coming up mainly on the trade routes and even in the region of settled agriculture like the wet zone of the Tāmraparṇi.[38] The participation of local traders and *Nagaram* members in itinerant trade increased to an uprecedented degree and hence a series of settlements named after the *Aiññuṟṟuvar* or *Valāñjīyar* were established as semi-permanent or permanent residential quarters in various centres.[39] It must, however, be pointed out that in the capitals of Tanjavur and Gangaikoṇḍacoḷapuram and the imperial port city of Nāgappaṭṭiṇam and even in the Kancipuram and Mamallapuram, the *mānagarams* or local *nagarams* wielded greater influence and the Five Hundred and other merchant groups were more or less confined to the routes linking all other outlying regions (peripheral areas) with the Coḷa heartland and to the commercially important areas like Pudukkottai and Ramanathapuram districts and Kongu Nāḍu, that is, Salem, Enode (Periyar) and Coimbatore districts.

In the period of the later Coḷas, that is, twelfth and thirteenth centuries, and of the Pāṇḍyas of the thirteenth-fourteenth centuries, we notice a phenomenal increase in the activities of the Five Hundred, with a clear tendency to expand its sphere of influence and to show less reliance on royal support and patronage, although many of the guild inscriptions are still dated in the reign periods of the late Coḷa and Pāṇḍya rulers. We have rather impressive evidence that in most centres of distribution and emporia, the Five Hundred acted jointly with other organized groups like the *Cittirameḷi* or *Padineṇviṣaya* organization in the levy of *maganmai* and *paṭṭaṇappagudi* (tolls and shares or cesses of towns). In the elaborate *praśastis* of these inscriptions mentioning the two organizations, the *Cittirameḷi* is given precedence over the Five Hundred. Notable among these are the records from Tirumalai and Pirānmalai in Ramanathapuram district and Anbil, Koṟṟamangalam, Tuvarankuṟichi and Kovilpaṭṭi in Tiruchirappalli district.[40] Here they exercised their joint authority to levy and grant cesses and tolls to the local temples on merchandise passing through the region.The institutionalization of the coming together of several organizations and their exercising joint authority is a conspicuous feature of the thirteenth and early AD fourteenth centuries. However,

[38] Ibid., pp. 52–53.

[39] Ibid., Table VI, no. 25; 150 of *ARE*, 1935–36.

[40] Tirumalai 10 of 1924; Pirānmalai, *SII,* VII, no. 442; Koṟṟamangalam 650 of 1962–63; Tuvarankurichi 296 of 1964–65; Kovilpatti 286 of 1964–65.

it would appear that merchant bodies, particularly the Five Hundred, had on no occasion the authority to levy and grant such tolls, except in conjunction with the *Cittirameḷi* or the the *Pāṇineṇviṣaya*[41] which refer to the organizations of agriculturists and local elite groups controlling production of agricultural and other goods. Presumably, in the assignment of brokerage and monopoly to individuals or groups of traders on certain items of trade, the Five Hundred exercised its authority jointly with the local *Nāḍu*, *Nagaram* members and the larger agricultural organization of the 18 *viṣaya* or *Cittirameḷi*.[42]

The *Cittirameḷi Periya Nāḍu* was an organization of agriculturists, whose inscriptions appear in important trade and urban centres. It has been described as an agricultural guild by K.G. Krishnan, who has analysed the evidence of inscription not only from Tamil Nadu but also from Karnataka and Andhra,[43] where the *Cittirameḷi* appears from about the twelfth century AD. Although the Okkalu of Karnataka is taken to be a similar organization,[44] there is no clear evidence of the Okkalu being a supra-local organization like the *Cittirameḷi*. Like the Five Hundred, the *Cittirameḷi* also moved into south Karnataka and Andhra regions by the twelfth century AD following the Coḷa conquests. It is referred to as *Meḷi Sāsiravāru* in Karnataka and *Meḍikūru* in Andhra.[45]

Dominant agricultural organizations jointly mentioned in the 'guild' inscriptions probably had commercial transactions with the Five Hundred exchanging agricultural products for exotic and non-agricultural items. The growth in the power of landowning classes is a marked development of the twelfth century AD both in south India and Sri Lanka. The links that developed between the merchant guilds and associations of agriculturists were mainly due to the increase in the importance of agricultural commodities in trade from the twelfth century AD onwards. The urban settlements enchanced the influence of the agricultural classes, for such needs could be satisfied only by

[41] R. Champakalakshmi, *Situating Indian History*, *op. cit.*, Table VI.

[42] *Pudukkotai State Inscriptions*, no. 125; 103 of *ARE*, 1932–33.

[43] K.G. Krishnan, 'Chittirameḷi-Periyanāḍu—An Agricultural Guild of Medieval Tamil Nadu', *Journal of the Madras University,* LIV, no. 1 (January 1982).

[44] M. Abraham, 'A Medieval Merchant Guild of South India', *op. cit.*, p. 21.

[45] T. Venkateswara Rao, 'Local Bodies in Pre-Vijayanagar Andhra', unpublished Ph.D. thesis, Dharwar, 1975, pp. 76–78.

powerful peasant groups, who could mobilize grain and other products for supply to itinerant traders through local markets.

In the late thirteenth and early fourteenth centuries, particularly under the Pāṇḍyas, the joint presence of the weavers with trading communities like the Five Hundred also suggests that there was a closer link between textile production and trade and that a certain legitimacy was derived from the presence of the craft groups. It would appear that weavers gradually took to trading in textiles or worked for the itinerant merchant body by organizing production for a wider market. At this point reference to Cīlai Ceṭṭis in the northern Tamil region (Kancipuram) and in Kongu (Dharampuri) may be noticed in the thirteenth–fourteenth-century inscriptions.[46] The largest craft organization which came to be set up by the fourteenth century AD was that of the weavers, whose *Mahānāḍu* organization had its headquarters in Kancipuram, the most ancient textile centre of south India.[47] The *Kailkkoḷas* and *Sāliyas*, two weaver communities of south India, came to be classified among the Right and Left hand caste divisions,[48] which arose in Tamil Nadu in the twelfth century AD as a paṛadigmatic division to determine the social and caste status of the artisans and craftsmen, among others. Other craft groups also came to be organized largely under this division. With the increase in organized commerce and itinerant trade and the demand for textiles and other products, the artisan communities also obtained special privileges either from local chiefs or temple authorities and sometimes also through the good offices of the merchant organizations.

In a slightly different context the dependence of the craftsmen on the merchant organizations is underlined as seen in the role of the merchants providing asylum to the craftsmen in Erode as early as the eleventh century AD.[49] The merchant body sometimes framed rules for the *Valangai* and *Iḍangai* or granted them privileges emphasizing the interdependence of these two sections of the commercial world, especially in areas where the merchants assumed control and management of temples and acted as protectors and patrons of artisanal

[46] 165 of *ARE*, 1968–69; *SII*, VII, no. 588.

[47] Vijaya Ramaswamy, *Textiles and Weavers in Medieval South India*, New Delhi, 1985, pp. 38–39.

[48] Ibid., pp. 55, 58–59, 107–108.

[49] Erode Inscription, 215 of *ARE*, 1976–77.

groups, as in the Kongu region. The artisan community is seen to be coming into its own after the twelfth century AD that is, in the late Coḷa and Pāṇḍya periods. In the predominantly agrarian set-up of Tamil Nadu, the artisans were more often attached to the locality, that is, to the temple, the land-owning brāhmaṇas and *veḷāḷas* through interdependent land tenures. However, changes in the agrarian organization (especially in the pattern of land ownership) and the introduction of an economy based on inter-regional trade, the demand for their services both by local landed groups and by the itinerant merchant organizations, acquired for them certain concessions and privileges meant to improve their social position. In the late twelfth century the *anuloma rathakāras* in Punjai were conferred special privileges.[50] The artisan community became participants in the gift-making processes as seen in the thirteenth century inscriptions from Noḍiyūr (Tanjavur district) where the Kaṇmāḷas of several places met and agreed to assign a tithe collected from among themselves to the local temple and to get differences settled jointly with the temple trustees and local chief.[51]

Craft production was perhaps more intensive in the Kongu region, where inscriptions from the twelfth to fourteenth centuries refer to large-scale artisanal activity and the participation of artisans in important civic duties for which they were conferred special privileges. Privileges were collectively granted to the Kaṇmāḷar communities in Kāñcikkūval nāḍu (thirteenth century), Vengāḷa nāḍu (thirteenth century), and Kāngeya nāḍu and Pūnduṛai nāḍu (fourteenth century) under the Kongu Coḷas and Kongu Pāṇḍyas.[52] Agreements among artisan communities for various purposes also became common during this period.

Thus organized commerce by *Nagarams, Maṇigrāmam* and long-distance trade through itinerant merchant bodies accelerated the process of urban development, craft organization, a tripartite social stratification in an urban context in multi-temple centres, single large temple centres, some of which became pilgrimage centres and administrative centres. Many of these newly emerging soicio-economic groups were accommodated in the *tirumaḍai viḷāgam* of the temple centres.[53]

[50] Puñjai Inscription, 198 of 1925 (*ĀRE*, 1925–26).
[51] Noḍiyur Inscription, 201 of *ARE*, 1932–33.
[52] 186 of 1911 (*ARE*, 1911–12); 25 of *ARE*, 1967–68.
[53] *SII*, VI, no. 258 (Manimangalam); *SII* , XII, no. 154 (Chidambaram).

The dominant role of the Five Hundred in inter-regional trade and commerce in south India is established beyond doubt by the continuous occurrence of guild records in the three major regions, that is, Tamil Nadu, Karnataka and Andhra Pradesh. Furthermore, their participation in overseas trade is also attested by the presence of guild inscriptions in northern Sri Lanka, Siam (south Thailand), Sumatra and Burma.[54] Notable amongh these records are the Shikarpur inscription in the Shimoga district of Karnataka[55] and the Pirānmalai inscription in the Ramanathapuram district of Tamil Nadu.[56] The Shikarpur inscription refers to these merchants as travelling by land routes, water routes, penetrating into the regions of six continents, with superior elephants, well-bred horses, large sapphires, moonstones, bdellium, sandal, camphor, musk, saffron, etc. and spices and drugs, selling wholesale or hawking about on their shoulders. Through this trade the royal treasury was filled with gold and the royal family encouraged this trade by being the greatest consumers of luxury items. The imported items mentioned in the famous Pirānmalai inscription are of a different kind, like aloeswood, sandalwood, silk, rosewater, camphor oil and perfume, apart from elephants and horses, which are common in most inscriptions of south India. Aloeswood, camphor, sandalwood and horses are mentioned in the Kovilpatti inscription of about AD 1305.[57] Most of these items came from South-East Asia except horses. Significantly, the Barus inscription referring to the Five Hundredand dated in AD 1088 comes from the heart of the camphor growing areas of Sumatra.[58]

Silk from China, elephants from Burma and horses from Arabia came both into the ports of the western coast and perhaps also into Kāyalpaṭṭiṇam on the Pāṇḍya coast. Rosewater came from West Asia. South India was both on the transit trade and terminal trade from West Asia to China, through Sri Lanka and South-East Asia. Toṇḍi and

[54] See K. Indrapala, 'South Indian Mercantile Communities in Ceylon, 950–1250', *The Ceylon Journal of Historical and Social Studies,* New Series, 1, no. 2, July–December 1971; K.A. Nilakanta Sastri, 'Takua Pa and its Tamil Inscription', *Journal of the Malaya Branch of the Royal Asiatic Society,* XXII, pt. 1, 1949, pp. 25–30; *EI*, VII, no. 27, pp. 197ff.

[55] Shikarpur Inscription, *EC*, VII, no. 118, p. 86.

[56] *SII*, VIII, no. 442.

[57] 286 of *ARE*, 1964–65.

[58] M. Abraham, 'A Medieval Mercantile Guild of South India', *op. cit.*, pp. 4, 6.

Kulaśekharapaṭṭinam were the ports at which many of the items were unloaded and distributed. An interesting record from Toṇḍi dated in AD 1269 registers an agreement by the *Añjuvaṇṇam Maṇigrāmam, Sāmanta-Paṇḍaśālis* (probably stockists of commodities at the port) and others residing there, to levy certain taxes on commodities sold and purchased at the port, in order to meet the rebuilding expenses of the *maṇḍapa* of the local Śiva temple.[59] Spices, pepper in particular, and incenses were some of the other important items meant both for local consumption and for long distance trade. The temples and *maṭhas* or monasteries of the Tamil region were, next to the royal family, the greatest consumers of most of the articles mentioned above.

Many other commodities mentioned in the Pirānmalai and other Tamil inscriptions as well as the Chintapalle inscription of about AD 1240 from Andhra[60] refer to agricultural products like paddy, sesame, pulses, betel-nuts and leaves, salt and raw materials like cotton. Metals like copper, zinc, lead and iron also figure among the items of trade. In fact, the only manufactured goods requiring technological skill and organized production was textile (local cloth) and it is for south Indian textiles that there was an ever-growing demand. Hence the weaver community gradually acquired a position of great social and economic importance. This is attested by the references to *Kaikkoḷas* and *Sāliya Nagarattār*, who not only controlled production and marketing of cloth but also participated in temple services, (e.g., donations, conduct of festivals, administration and management).[61] There is also a noticeable change in the pattern of landownership, both weavers and merchants becoming landowning communities and wielding considerable influence in their localities.

If the presence of the guild inscription with their *praśastis* and lists of items of trade may be taken as a direct indication of distribution centres, most of them may be located in the Pudukkottai and Ramanathapuram district and along the trade routes where *Eṛivīrappaṭṭanas* were established. The guild inscriptions often refer to the 18 *paṭṭanas*, 32 *Veḷa* (or *Veḷar*) *purams*, 64 *Kaḍigai-t-tāvaḷams* from where the traders came.[62] Though it would be difficult to iden-

[59] Tittandatānapuram (Toṇḍi)Inscription, 598 of 1926, *ARE*, 1926–27.

[60] 277 of *ARE*, 1934–35.

[61] 196 of *ARE*, 1912; *SII*, VI, nos. 252 and 257; see also Vijaya Ramaswamy, *op. cit.*, pp. 41–46, and 54–55.

[62] 154 of 1903; *SII*, VIII, no. 442.

tify and locate all of them, it is quite likely that some of the major centres with guild inscriptions and the ports constantly used by traders are included among them, such as Vañjimānagaram (Karūr), Koḍumbālūr, Kulaśekharapaṭṭiṇam, Alagaimānagaram, Nārttāmalai, Toṇḍi and Pirānmalai. There also emerged a series of coastal towns starting from Tiruppūlaivanam (Pulicat), the northernmost point in Tamil Nadu, down to Koṛkai and Kāyal on the mouth of the Tāmraparṇi, marking a coastal route with halting stations and distribution points used by the itinerant traders. Kovaḷam, Sadras, and Tranquebar were some of these towns which became prominent in the thirteenth-fourteenth centuries AD.[63]

Organized commerce in this period followed exchange by barter and also the use of money, although monetization in medieval south India at least down to the AD fourteenth century was mostly on a low key, particularly in Tamil Nadu. The Vijayanagar period saw many important changes including greater monetization and emergence of individual traders and master craftsmen, which indirectly affected itinerant trading communities and their *samayam* or organization.

The towns of Tamil Nadu including the ones with guild activities differed in their administrative organization from those of Karnataka. The latter had their *paṭṭanasvāmīs* who were heads of towns and who presided over or participated in the meetings of the merchant bodies and other local groups,[64] as in Shikarpur. No such 'lords' of towns are known to have presided over either the *Nagaramas* or market centres or towns with guilds inscriptions in Tamil Nadu. There are, however, references to *paṭṭaṇasvāmī,* who along with members of the *Pādineṇviṣaya*, levied cesses on merchandise as in Pirānmalai.[65] The *Nagarams* of Tamil Nadu were administered by their members with the help of accountants (*nagarakkaṇakku*)and other employees, and the market was governed by a specific set of rules and regulations and maintained through cesses and levies like *aṅgāḍippaṭṭam*.[66] The merchant bodies were subject to the common rules framed by the *Nāḍu, Nagaram, Pādineṇbhumi, Cittirameḷi* organizations acting

[63] R. Champakalakshmi, *Situating Indian History*, *op. cit.*, Table VII.

[64] K. Indrapala 'Some Medieval Mercantile Communities of South India and Ceylon', *op. cit.*, pp. 29–30; G.R. Kuppuswami, *Economic Conditions in Karnataka* (AD 973–1336), Dharwar, 1975, pp. 101, 113; *EC*, VIII, no. 94.

[65] *SII*, VIII, no. 442.

[66] Kenneth R. Hall, *op. cit.*, pp. 58–60.

jointly in the form of an institutionalized forum, exercising authority through levying cesses and tolls and controlling the distribution of goods.

Localized groups like *Maṇigrāmam* and *Nagaram* were powerful bodies which diversified their activities by marketing special items by forming sub-*nagarams* like the *Vāṇiyanagaram, Śaṅkarappāḍinagaram* and *Sāliyanagaram* and *Śāttumpparisaṭṭanagaram* dealing in oil and cloth respectively at various centres like Vālikaṇḍapuram, Śeṅgālipuram, Tirukkoyilūr and other places.[67] The *Pāraganagaram* or sea-faring merchants were active in the region of Salem (Puḷḷur) even as early as the early Coḷa period.[68] Kudirai Ceṭṭis from Malaimaṇḍalam or Kerala were horse dealers, who catered to the needs of the Coḷa kingdom from the ninth to the thirteenth centuries.[69]

The *Vāṇiya nagaram* organized itself into a supra-local body of several regions or *padineṇviṣaya*,[70] somewhat like the Telikis of Andhra. Individual traders sometimes used the title of *Cakravartī,* indicating the emergence of merchant princes as seen in the thrirteenth-fourteenth century inscriptions of Muṭṭam (in Perūr, Coimbatore) and Śivāyam or Ratnagiri (ancient Tiruvāṭpokki) in the Tiruchirappalli district. Among the signatories to the Pirānmalai guild inscription, mention is made of a *Samaya Cakravarti.*[71] Political stability disappeared with the decline of the Coḷa power in the beginning of the thirteenth century AD. References to *Vīradaḷam* and *Sūradaḷam* in the guild inscriptions of this period[72] probably indicate the usurpation of authority by powerful merchant and local cheifs,

[67] *Vālikaṇḍapuram*, 309 of *ARE*, 1964–65 (Śaṅkarappāḍi); Tiruppangili, 163 of *ARE*, 1938–39 (*Vāṇiyanagaram*); Śeṅgālipuram, 23 and 30 of *ARE*, 1916–17 (*Śāttumpparisaṭṭanagram*); Tirukkoyilūr, *SII*, VII, 901 (*Sālikanagaram).*

[68] Pullur Inscription, 325 and 372 of 1939–40.

[69] R. Champakalakshmi, 'Growth of Urban Centres in South India: Kudamukku-Palaiyārai, the twin-city of the Colas', *Studies in History*, I, no. 1, 1979, p. 12.

[70] Vālikaṇḍapuram Inscription, 264 of *ARE*, 1943–44; Vengalam Inscription, 141 of *ARE*, 1974–75.

[71] Ikkarai-Boluvāmpaṭṭi Inscription, 415 and 418 of 1958–59; Sivayam Inscription, 48 of 1913, *ARE*, 1912–13; Pirānmalai Inscription, *SII*, VIII, 442.

[72] For *Sūradalam* see Vālkaṇḍapuram Inscription, 264 of *ARE*, 1943–44.

who took advantage of the decline of the Coḷa power and the relatively weaker Pāṇḍya power of the thirteenth and fourteenth centuries in order to protect themselves and their newly gained wealth and status from other rivals for power and position. However, after the fourteenth century, it is not easy to follow the history of the mercantile organizations, as their countinous presence is not attested in inscriptions of south India, especially Tamil Nadu. Ther rise of individual merchant families and a change in the nature and organization of craft production may well have led to the gradual disintegration of powerful merchant organization.

Chapter Thirteen

Trading Community and Merchant Corporations*

V.K. JAIN

The brisk commercial activity in western India during the post-tenth centuries led to the emergence of a prosperous and powerful class of merchants which, on account of its opulence, tended to dominate the political, social and economic fabric of the region. These merchants attained a status as high as that of brāhmaṇas in learning and politics, and as that of kṣatriyas in war, and figured as the main subjects of the tales, dramas and romances written during this period.[1]

The traditional concept of regular and lawful means of livelihood (*vārttā*) for vaiśyas, consisting of trade (*vāṇijya*), agriculture (*kṛṣi*) and cattle-rearing (*paśupālyam*) continued to linger on during the early medieval period.[2] There was, however, a gradual tendency of

* From V.K. Jain's book *Trade and Traders in Western India, 1000–1300*, pp. 209–32.

[1] The *Jagaḍucarita* of Sarvananda, which deals with the life and activities of a merchant called Jagaḍu, and the *Vastupālacarita* and other texts, which have merchant-minister Vastupāla as their hero, indicate the growing importance of merchant princes *vis-à-vis* the warlords in society.

[2] *Āpastamba Dharmasūtra* (hereinafter *Āpastamba*), II.5.10.7., trn. G. Bühler in *Sacred Book of the East Series* (hereinafter *SBE*), II, pt I, Delhi, 1965 (rpt.); *Baudhāyana Dharmasūtra* (Baudhāyana); *Nāradasmṛti* (*Nārada*) tr. by J. Jolly, *SBE*, XXIII (rpt.), Delhi 1965; *Gautama Dharmasūtra* (*Gautama*) tr. G. Bühler, *SBE*, II, pt. 1 (rpt.), Delhi 1965; *Manusmṛti* or *Laws of Manu* (*Manu*) tr. by G. Bühler, *SBE*, XXX (rpt.), Delhi, 1967; *Yājñavalkyasmṛti* (*Yāj*).

identifying vaiśyas with trade (*vāṇijya*). In the seventh century, Hiuen Tsang distinctly mentions vaiśyas as a class of traders and śūdras as cultivators.[3]

This tendency became more marked in western India where the Jainas, who formed the bulk of the merchant community, tended to avoid agricultural and artisanal activities because of their belief in the principle of *ahiṃsā* and the fear of causing injury to sentient beings. Jinasena, a Jaina author of the ninth century, tries to distinguish vaiśyas from the rest, and uses the term *vaṇijaḥ* (*traders*) for them.[4] In the *Kathākośaprakaraṇa* of Jineśvara Sūri (AD 1051), vaiśyas are noted as *vaṇiks,* and described as the 'exploiters of farmers'.[5] The same text classifies householders (*kuṭumbins*) into six groups on the basis of their socio-economic status, and place big merchants on a pedestal higher than peasants and artisans.[6] According to it, the first two classes comprised *cakravartins* and small kings followed by the intermediary class (*majjhimā*) of *śerṣṭhins, sārthavāhas,* etc., who derived their livelihood from trade, usury, farming, rearing of cows, buffaloes, camels and horses. In the next group (*vimajjhimā or vimadhyaṁ*) are placed those people who personally tilled the land, made water channels for the irrigation of fields, grew sugarcane and other crops, and used counterfeit weight and measures in business. Below them were the degraded ones (*ahama*) which included goldsmiths, potters, blacksmiths, washermen, and other craftsmen and artisans and their guilds (*śilpa-karmakāra-samudāya*).

The *Kathākośaprakaraṇa* , thus, suggests that big merchants such as *śreṣṭhi* and *sārthavāha,* though engaged in farming, were well-to-do peasant proprietors, and were distinctly superior, socially as well as economically, to small peasant-cum-traders who possessed insufficient holdings or lived on a dependent tenure. The big merchants, in fact,

[3] T. Watters, (tr.), *On Yuan Chwang's Travels in India*, in two volumes, New Delhi 1973 (rpt.).

[4] *Ādi Purāṇa*, XVI. 244. According to Jinasena, the chief means of livelihood for vaiśyas was to carry on trade by making land and water journeys. Though *Manu* (X. 79–80) assigns the occupation of trade, cattle-rearing and agriculture to vaiśyas, he adds that the most commendable profession for them is of trade. See also *SBE*, XXV, fn. 80.

[5] *Kathākośaprakarana* of Jinasena Suri, ed. by Jinavijaya Muni (*KKP*) Bombay, 1949, *Triṣaṣṭhīsalākapuruṣcarita* (*TSP*) of Hemacandra, tr. by Helene M. Johnson in six volumes, Baroda, 1921–62.

[6] *KKP*, pp. 116–17; text, p. 115.

lived on the exploitation of both peasants and artisans. They had the capital to invest and the means to sell goods far and wide, and thus acted as the chief agents of exchange between producers and consumers. The enormous profit which they earned in the process enhanced their social and economic status.[7] They became the leaders of society and managed to make their way into the fold of the ruling aristocracy.[8]

It may be pointed out that artisans and craftsmen occupied a low status even in earlier ages,[9] but during the eleventh and twelfth centuries we notice an increased scorn for the people associated with arts and crafts. Hemādri, a lawgiver of the thirteenth century, includes carpenter, goldsmith, tailor, oilman, ironsmith, etc., in the list of *antyajas* who were considered inferior to śūdras.[10] Alberuni too describes weavers, shoemakers and basket-makers as low castes (*antyajas*).[11] Hemacandra believes that occupations of weavers, tailors, potters, etc. are of little blame, but adds that 'artisans and the low castes, living as a result of their own work' are unscrupulous persons 'who defraud the good man by false oaths'.[12] Jineśvara Sūri, as noted above, puts artisans, craftsmen and their guilds in the category of degraded ones (*ahama*). Medhātithi too betrays a feeling of contempt for all craftsmen, and labels them as persons of 'mean nature' who are prone to stray from the path of honesty.[13]

Thus, even when the situation of production seems to have improved with the growth of trade since the eleventh century, the old stigma continued to be attached to the artisans and craftsmen. Many of them, particularly those in the countryside, remained in subjection, and practised arts and crafts for the ones on whom they were dependent. For instance, in the Khārepāṭan plates of the Śilāhāra chieftain

[7] Hemacandra gives an exaggerated account of some householders (*kuṭumbins*) who had crores of gold 'in deposit, in loans, and in business', and possessed numerous herds of cattle. *TSP*, VI, pp. 206, 208 and 209.

[8] V.K. Jain, *Trade and Traders in Western India 1000–1300,* Delhi, 1989, pp. 233ff.

[9] R.S. Sharma, *Śūdras in Ancient India*, Delhi, 1980 (rpt). R. Fick, *The Social Organization in North-East India in the age of Lucknow*, 1953, Calcutta, 1920 (tr.), V.S. Agrawala, *India as Known to Panīni.*

[10] P.V. Kane, *History of the Dharmaśāstra*, in five vols., Poona, 1941–62 (HDS).

[11] *Alberuni's India*, I, p. 101

[12] *TSP,* II, p. 118; III, p. 156.

[13] *On Manu*, VIII.65

Raṭṭarāja (AD 1008), one family each of washermen potters, gardeners and oilmen are assigned to the service of some Śaiva *ācāryas*.[14] It may, however, be noted that all artisans or craftsmen were not dependent; many of them worked independently also.[15] It were these independent ones who derived benefit of the developing trade and commerce and went up the ladder of social prestige. They made donations to temples, and also occupied high posts in the service of kings in western India. A potter called Āliga who had helped the king Kumārapāla during latter's adversity, was granted the region of Citrakūṭa (Chittor) containing seven hundred villages.[16] Some chariot-makers (*rathakāras*) living at Sanderaka in Jodhpur state are known to have given a piece of land measuring one *hāela* of *yugaṁdharī* for the Kalyāṇaka festival.[17] The oilmen and their chiefs too made contributions of oil for temple lamps. Some of them like Jāna were rich enough to erect a temple of Śambhū in Rajasthan.[18] In short, the mercantile development in western India provided a new base for class stratification, and the position of certain sections of artisans did improve. But, in general, the big merchants, who were identified with city and city-culture, continued to be considered superior to both peasants and artisans.

HETEROGENEOUS CHARACTER OF THE MERCANTILE COMMUNITY

Trade was the chief vocation of vaiśyas, but it was certainly not their monopoly. The pressure of economic circumstances and the urge for economic gains had compelled people from all sections and strata of society to take to trade from earlier times.[19] In fact, the concept of *āpaddharma,* which allowed the people of higher as well as lower *varṇas* to take up trade in times of distress,[20] made mercantile

[14] *EI*, III, p. 296.

[15] Lakṣmīdhara (Gṛhasthakāṇḍa, p. 380) refers to two types of craftsmen, viz. dependent (*āśrita*) and independent (*anāśrita*).

[16] *Prabandhacintāmani*, tr. by M.A. Tawney, Calcutta, 1901 (PCT), *Prabandhacintamani*, ed. by Jinavijaya Muni, Santiniketan, 1933 (PCJ).

[17] Sāṇḍerāv stone inscription of AD 1164, *EI*, XI, p. 47.

[18] H.C. Ray, *Dynastic History of North India*, II, New Delhi, 1973 (rpt.).

[19] B.C. Law, *India as Described in Early Texts of Buddhism and Jainism*, Delhi, 1980 (rpt.).

[20] *Manu*, X. 81–100; *Āpastamba*, I.7.20; *Gautama,* VII. 1–26; *Vasiṣṭha,* II.

community a class in which the cult of wealth cut across the concept of caste.[21] The statement of Mādhavācārya (AD 1300–80), the commentator of the *Parāśara Smṛti,* that the duties in distress became regular duties in the *kali* age,[22] reflects the trend in the post-tenth centuries when trade was being pursued by all and sundry, not as *āpaddharma* but as a regular means of livelihood.

The legal injunctions against the sale and purchase of certain articles by higher *varṇas*[23] also came to be disregarded. In the Pehoa inscription (ninth century) a brāhmaṇa called Vāmuka is mentioned as dealing in horses,[24] though Manu prohibits the sale of animals by brāhmaṇas.[25] Alberuni refers to brāhmaṇas as trading in clothes and betel-nuts.[26] In the Sīyaḍoṇī inscription (tenth century) we come across a brāhmaṇa named Dhamāka who was a betel-seller.[27] Kṣemendra (eleventh century) observes that some brāhmaṇas sold wine, clarified butter, milk, salt, etc.[28] The *Kathākośaprakaraṇa* indicates that there were many brāhmaṇas who worked as petty cultivators.[29] A grant of the time of king Kumārapāla informs us that Rājadeva, Sūradeva and possibly Nagada were brāhmaṇa agriculturists.[30] Thus we notice an increasing number of brāhmaṇas taking up the occupation of vaiśyas. In keeping with these circumstances, the *Mitākṣarā* makes a tenfold gradation of brāhmaṇas, and refers to a category of vaiśya-brāhmaṇas who were devoted to trade, cattle-rearing and cultivation.[31] Medhātithi commenting on Manu indicates that the brāhmaṇas, who indulged in trade not in distress but in ordinary times, assumed the character of a vaiśya after seven nights.[32]

The kṣatriyas, or the *rājaputras* with whom they came to be

22–39; *Yāj,* III. 35–40. Yājñavalkya (I. 120) states that if a śūdra cannot maintain himself by the service of a twice-born, he can become a trader.

[21] V.K. Jain, *op. cit.*, pp. 179–80.

[22] B.N.S. Yadava, *Society and Culture in North India in the Twelfth Century,* Allahabad, 1973 (*SCNI*).

[23] Cf. *Manu,* X. 81–100; *Gautama,* VII. 8ff; *Āpastamba,* I.720. 11ff; *Vasiṣṭha,* II.24ff; *Nārada* (*ṛṇadāna*), 61–63; *Yāj,* III. 40–42.

[24] *EI,* I, p. 184.

[25] *Manu,* X. 89.

[26] *Alberuni's India,* II, p. 132. Manu (X. 87) forbids a brāhmaṇa to sell cloth.

[27] *EI,* I, pp. 173 ff.

[28] *Daśāvatāracarita* (Kāvyamala Series, no. 26), p. 160. These goods are not supposed to be traded in by a brāhmaṇa. See *Manu,* X. 88, 92.

[29] *KKP,* intro., p. 120.

[30] G.V. Acharya (ed.), *Historical Inscriptions of Gujarat,* III, Bombay, p. 38.

[31] *Mitākṣarā* of Vijñāneśvara, p. 210.

[32] *On Manu,* X. 93.

identified from the seventh-eighth centuries are rarely referred to in contemporary inscriptions as taking part in mercantile activities.[33] But, as they constituted the landed aristocracy,[34] they must have been trading in the surplus which their land yielded or in the commodities which they collected as tax from peasants. One of the reasons for the silence of our sources on their mercantile activities may be that kṣatriyas, who involved themselves with trade, soon got merged with vaiśyas. For instance, the bulk of the Osvāla merchants were Solanki Rajputs before they adopted Jainism according to the Jain *prabandhas* and *paṭṭāvalīs,* took place in about AD 743.[35] H.D. Sankalia suggests that most of the families belonging to the regional subcastes of merchants in western India, such as Porvāḍ, Dharkaṭṭa, Osvāla, Śrīmāla, etc. were originally kṣatriyas who later adopted the profession of *vaṇiks.*[36] Dasaratha Sharma points out that the Osvālas, the Jayaswālas, the Khaṇḍelwālas, the Agrawālas and the Maheśvarīs, the five main divisions of vaiśyas in Rajasthan claim a kṣatriya origin.[37] They ascribe their present position as vaiśyas to their conversion to the cult of *ahiṁsā* and vegetarianism preached by Jainism. In the *Purātanaprabandhasaṁgraha,* the sons of Lakṣmaṇa the founder of the kingdom of Nāḍol, from a vaiśya wife are termed as *vaṇik.*[38] They intermarried with other vaiśyas and, as they were in charge of the royal treasury, came to be known as *bhāṇḍāgārikas,* i.e. Bhandaris.[39] The Jalor stone inscription of Sāmantasiṁha (AD 1296) refers to a donor Narapati as *sonī* but mentions his grandfather and great-grandfather as *ṭhākura.*[40] Again,the ministers Vastupāla and

[33] An inscription (AD 1239) from the Kangara region (*EI*, I, pp. 118f.) mentions two merchants belonging to the *brahmakṣatra* stock and, as B.N.S. Yadava points but (*SCNI*, p. 29, also pp. 91–92, fn. 327), the term *brahmakṣatra*) was 'mainly applied to those who were first brāhmaṇas and then became kṣatriyas'.

[34] The *Aparājitapṛcchā*, which appears to have been composed in western India in the twelfth century, clearly reveals that the *rājaputras* constituted a fairly large section of petty chiefs holding estates, each consisting of one or more villages. *AP*, p. 196.

[35] *The Gazetteer of the Bombay Presidency*, 1882–96 (*Bom. Gaz.*).

[36] H.D. Sankalia, *Studies in the Historical and Cultural Geography and Ethnography of Gujarat*, Poona, 1949 (*HGEG*).

[37] D. Sharma, *Rajasthan through the Ages*, Bikaner, 1966 (*RTA*).

[38] *Purātanaprabandhasaṁgraha*, (ed.), Jinavijaya Muni, Ahmedabad and Calcutta, 1936 (*PPS*).

[39] *RTA*, p. 439.

[40] *EI*, XI, p. 61. The term *sonī*, noted in the Ānāvāḍa inscription of AD 1291

Tejaḥpāla are regarded as vaiśyas, probably because they were *vaṇiks* by profession, but in the inscriptions their ancestors are called *ṭha* or *ṭhakkura*[41] which is believed to be a feudal title borne chiefly by the kṣatriyas.[42]

Śūdras, during the early medieval period were largely peasants, though some of them were also engaged in industrial arts and crafts and other vocations.[43] Since they were the producers, some commercial transaction or exchange, at least at the local level, formed an inherent feature of their profession. Generally śūdra traders served as petty shopkeepers or pedlars.[44] It may be pointed out that Kauṭilya permits śūdras to take up trade.[45] Bṛhaspati (*c.* AD 500) too allows them to trade in all articles as one of their normal occupations.[46] Vijñāneśvara, commenting on Yājñavalkya, quotes Devala to show that a śūdra could engage himself in sale and purchase of commodities.[47] Jineśvara Sūri, who seems to include śūdras in the *vimajjhimā* category, suggests that they were petty peasants and cultivators who used false weights and measures in business.[48] Parāśara at one place recommends trade *vāṇijya* for vaiśyas as well as śūdras.[49]

The involvement of śūdras in trade should not necessarily mean a

---

(*IA*, XLI, p. 21) suggests that it was used for dealers in gold.

41 Abu inscriptions, nos 24 and 26–30, *EI*, VIII, pp. 223ff.

42 R.S. Sharma, *Indian Feudalism*, Delhi, 1980; D.C. Sircar, *Indian Epigraphical Glossary*, Delhi, 1966; H.M. Elliot and J.M. Dowson, *The History of India as Told by Its own Historians*, incorporating revisions by S.H. Hodivala and preface by Md. Habib, Vols I–III, Aligarh, 1951 (hereinafter Elliot and Dowson); P. Peterson, *A Collection of Prakrit and Sanskrit Inscriptions*, Bhavnagar, 1905 (by *CPSI*).

43 *Abhidhānacintāmani*, ed. by Nemichandra Sastri and Haragovinda Sastri Varanasi, 1964 (*AC*); *Desināṇamamālā*, ed. with English translation by Muralydhar Banerjee, Calcutta, 1931 (*DN*); *Vaijayanatī* of Yādavaprakāsa, ed. by Gustav Oppert, Madras, 1893, pp. 136–47.

44 In the *Vaijayantī* (p. 136), śūdras are called pedlars and hawkers (*vaivaddhika* and *vārtāhāra*). In the *Abhidhānacintāmaṇi* (II. 28), however, they are mentioned as porters. Some of the śūdras might have become rich enough to undertake long trade journeys, for a śūdra caravan leader (*sārthavāha*) is referred to in the *Kuvalayamālā* (p. 65).

45 Kautilya, *Arthaśāstra,* I.3.

46 Quoted in R.S. Sharma, *Śūdras in Ancient India*, p. 240.

47 Ācāra-adhyāya, v. 120.

48 *KKP*, intro., pp. 116–17; text, p. 115.

49 *Parāśara Smṛti*, Acārakāṇḍa, 2.13.

decline in the status of vaiśyas. It, in fact, suggests that, with the growth of trade and commerce, the socio-economic condition of the śūdras became much better.[50] As more and more vaiśyas confined themselves to trade, other vocations such as agriculture, cattle-rearing and handicrafts became the virtual monopoly of śūdras.[51] They were, however, considered different from vaiśyas who continued to exist as a distinctly separate and a higher class. Lakṣmīdhara allows a śūdra to sell all kinds of goods but forbids a vaiśya to trade in certain articles such as salt, wine, curd, hides, poison, arms, etc.[52] He, thus, appears to suggest that vaiśyas, in keeping up with the characteristics of their higher *varṇa,* should leave the trade of certain inferior things to śūdras. The details of town-planning in the texts on architecture, such as the *Samarāṅgaṇasūtradhāra* and the *Mānasāra,* also indicate that the position of a vaiśya was distinctly above that of a śūdra. However, as vaiśyas and śūdras were the two classes which were associated with almost all the modes and agencies of production and distribution, some sort of economic contact and assimilation between them was natural. In this context we may note the statement of Alberuni who says, 'Between the latter two classes (vaiśyas and śūdras) there is no very distance. Much, however, as these classes differ from each other, they live together in the same towns and villages, mixed together in the same house and lodgings'.[53] It seems that what Alberuni had in mind was the economic rather than social contact between these classes, and his statment may not necessarily reflect the degrading position of vaiśyas *vis-à-vis* śūdras.

In the literature and inscriptions of the Caulukya period, merchants are generally identified by their professions or regions rather than by caste. The *Jaina-pustaka-praśasti saṁgraha* refers to Śrīmāla, Prāgvāṭa, Upakeśa, Pallīvāla, Moḍha, Dharkkaṭa, Nāgara, etc., as merchants.[54] These terms refer to the regions to which merchants belonged, and give no indication of their *varṇa.* In some literary records, the merchant-ministers Vastupāla and Tejaḥpāla are called *vaṇiks*, but in epigraphs neither they nor the members of Oisavāla

[50] Medhātithi recognizes the right of a śūdra to private property and to freedom from waiting on higher *varṇas. On Manu*, VIII. 415; X. 129.

[51] (*SSD*) *Samàrāṅganasūtradhāra* of Bhoja.

[52] Gṛhasthakāṇḍa, p. 258.

[53] *Alberuni's India*, I, p. 101. Brackets are mine.

[54] *Jainapustakapraśatisaṁgraha*, (ed.), Jinavijaya Muni, Bombay, 1943 (hereafter *JPPS*); V.K. Jain, *op. cit.*, pp. 218ff.

(Osvāla),[55] and Śrīmāla castes are described as vaiśyas or *vaṇiks*. It, thus, suggests that trade in western India was not the preserve of any particular caste, and anybody who had the will, skill and enterprise could follow it, though slowly and gradually those who were engaged in it came to be identified with the *vaṇik* caste.

In short, trade in western India, during the post-tenth centuries, was a very important activity and, in spite of the traditional theory relating to the professions to be adopted by each of the four *varṇas*, it was followed by all the segments of society, whether high or low. The orthodox view that the occupation of other *varṇa* was to be given up as soon as the economic distress was tided over was also not adhered to. In fact mercantile developlment provided a new base for class differentiation and stratification. Although land continued to play an important role in determining one's social status, it was no more the sole means of subsistence. Those who had no land could turn to trade or other activities connected with it and, by dint of wealth earned through personal efforts, they, irrespective of their caste or class, could command respect in society.

CATEGORIES OF TRADERS

Commercial activity required the procurement and disbursement of a large number of commodities, and necessitated the involvement of different types of traders, small as well as big.[56] It has rightly been pointed out that, though the craftsman frequently sold his wares directly to the consumer, the peasants' surplus products were largely in the hands of middlemen, and a class of big merchants, as distinct from small traders and pedlars, existed as long back as the time of the Buddha.[57] The big merchants lived in towns and were assisted by ordinary village merchants in collecting local surplus. In fact, every village or a group of villages, which produced a surplus of any kind, had a village merchant who collected the surplus in exchange for the supply of other necessary articles of local consumption, such as metals, cloth, salt, etc. This surplus was carried to the nearest town by

[55] *Oiśa* or *osa* is derived from the original Sanskrit word, *upakeśa*. *EI*, II, p. 40.

[56] There is a reference to *pradhāna-vyāpārinaḥ* in the *Kumārasambhava* of Kālidāsa, VII. 55.

[57] A.L. Basham, *The Wonder That Was India*, London, 1967, p. 242.

pedlars or roving merchants, and from there it was dispatched to other towns in different parts of the country by caravan merchants, or exported to foreign countries by sea-traders. The imported merchandise was distributed by the same machinery working in the reverse order.

The *Kathākośaprakaraṇa* (AD 1051) informs us of various types of traders such as the sellers of ghee and oil, vegetables, fruits, curd, cereals, scents and perfumes, jewellery, etc.[58] The *Kīrtikaumudī* refers to curd sellers and their shops in the town of Canbay.[59] Merutuṅga speaks of an ordinary trader who sold gram (*caṇaka-vikraya-kāra*).[60] Hemacandra refers to grain dealers (*kaṇ-ādi-vikretā-vaṇik*)as *peḍaio*.[61] He also refers to jewellers who were called *veḍio*.[62] The wine-sellers, according to the *Abhidhānacintāmaṇi*, were known by nine names, including *pānavaṇik*.[63] The sea traders were called *sāṁyātrikaḥ* and potavaṇik.[64] The gold dealers (*sonī* or *suvarṇavaṇiks*) and the dealers in medicinal herbs (*oṣadhiya* or *auṣadhika*)[65] are also noted in the texts of the period. The *Śiśupālavadha* of Māgha[66] and the *Tilakamañjarī*[67] indicate that private merchants used to accompany the army on march. They were probably the *banjārās* whose job was to arrange civil supplies for the soldiers. The Sīyaḍoṇi inscription (tenth century) suggests that in western India during the regime of the Pratihāras, salt merchants (*nemika-vaṇik*) and oilmen (*tailikas*) formed important sections of the mercantile community.[68] We also find repeated mention of betel-sellers (*tāmbūlikas*) and horse-dealers in the inscriptions of the period. The Veraval image inscription (AD 1246) refers to *śreṣṭhi* Mūlajoga whose son Jojā was a seller of perfumes.[69] An inscription from Abu (thireeenth century) mentions the term *mudī*[70]

[58] *KKP*, p. 165.

[59] *Kīrtikaumudī*, of Someśvara, ed., Punyavijaya Suri, Bombay, 1961 (*KK*), p. 165.

[60] *PCT*, p. 106; *PCJ*, p. 70.

[61] DN, VI. 59. [62] Ibid., VII. 57. [63] *AC*, III. 564.

[64] Ibid., 539. See also *PCJ*, p. 70. In the *DN* (VII. 78) the term *veḍaio* is used for *vaṇijakaḥ*. Since *beḍa* (DN, VI. 95) means a ship (*ṇauḥ*), *veḍaio* may have been a merchant engaged in shipping.

[65] *Kumārapālacarita*, II. 50.

[66] Hindi Sahitya Academy edn., vs 2009, XII. 26.

[67] *Tilakamañjarīkatha* of Dhanapala, Bombay, 1903 (*TM*).

[68] *EI*, I, no. 21, ll. 27–28, 30–31.

[69] Ibid., III, no. 41, p. 304, 1.3. [70] Ibid., VIII, p. 212.

which, according to H.D. Sankalia, is none other than the Gujarati word *modī* meaning a grocer.[71]

In the sources of the period, we come across a large number of professional and functional designations of merchants, the most common being *śreṣṭhi*, *sādhu* and *sārtha* or *sārthavāha*. The *Lekhapaddhati*[72] refers to such terms as *sāhu, sādhu, pāri* (*pārikh* ?),[73]*va* (*vāṇijyaka* or *vāṇijyāraka*), *śre* (*śreṣṭhi*), *vya* (*vyavahārika*), *mahājana*, etc., which were used for merchants and magnates. It also speaks of two other items, viz., *vahamānaviṇajārā* and *vacchivittaśrā*.[74] According to the editor of the text, the former means a travelling merchant who move with a caravan to sell his goods and the latter implies a foreign merchant or his agent. Most of the terms noted above also appear in various Caulukya inscriptions.[75] The Ānāvāḍa inscription (AD 1291), for example, tells us that gifts to a temple of Kṛṣṇa were made, among others, by *vaṇijyārakas* (*vanjārās* or roving merchants), *nau-vittakas* (ship-owners), and *mahājanas* which, according to the inscription, included *sādhu, śreṣṭhi, sonī, ṭhakkura, kaṁsāras* (braziers), etc.[76] It also refers to a term *pugī*.[77] Since *pugī* in Sanskrit means betel-nut, we venture to suggest that the term may have been used in the sense of betel-nut sellers or their group.

The term *sādhu* is found prefixed in its abbreviated form *sā* in the names of merchants.[78] But in some cases the full word *sādhu* is found, the earliest epigraphical evidence being in the Surat plates of Trilocanapāla (AD 1050). It leaves no doubt that *sā* stands for *sādhu*. This record also makes a distinction between *sārtha* and *sadhu*,[79] and suggests that the former was a caravan leader, while the latter had a fixed habitation. *Sādhu* was also different from *śreṣṭhi*[80] in the sense

[71] *HGEG*, p. 141.

[72] *Lekhapaddhati*, ed. by C.D. Dalal and G.K. Shrigondekar, Bombay, 1925 (*LP*).

[73] *Pārikh* might have been derived from the Sanskrit *parīkṣaka*, and used in the sense of examiner of coins or, as Bühler suggests (*EI*, I, p. 279, fn. 24), a money-changer.

[74] *LP*, pp. 53, 55.

[75] Cf. *HGEG*, Appendix IV, pp. 205–45.

[76] *IA*, XLI, p. 21, 11. 12–19. [77] Ibid., 1. 18.

[78] Literally, the term *sādhu* means pure and virtuous. It became one of the titles of those merchants who joined the reforming sects led by the *sādhus*, particularly the Jainas.

[79] *IA*, XII, p. 203, 11. 12–13.

[80] The Ānāvāḍa inscription (*IA*, XLI, p. 21) mentions both *sādhu* as well as

that he (*sādhu*) was merely a merchant, while *śreṣṭhi* was more of a money-lender or financier, though gradually both came to acquire the same denotation.

Śre or *śreṣṭhi* is the most widely used term in the Caulukya records.[81] Fiser, who discussed the problem of *seṭṭhis* in the *Jātakas*, is of the opinion that they were rich businessmen who managed the exchange of goods between town and country, and apart from this business they sometimes lent money to others.[82] In other words, the *śreṣṭhis* were probably the wholesale dealers, i.e. a class of middlemen between the producers and the retailers, who also supplied liquid capital on interest to needy merchants and farmers. Their influence was, thus, not confined to the four walls of the cities, and was felt even in the rural world. The big and rich merchants who, according to Al Idrisi[83] and Ibn Battuta,[84] purchased the entire cargo of a ship in a single deal, probably belonged to this class of traders.

To carry on commercial transactions, they appointed a number of retailers or agents,[85] probably on a commission basis, and collected a huge profit on the total sale proceeds.[86] The *Upamitibhavaprapañcakathā* refers to a merchant Dhanaśekhara who appointed different types of traders,[87] obviously with a view to sell

---

śreṣṭhi, and distinguishes them from the *vaṇijyārakas*. In this inscription, there are more than twenty references to *sādhu* or *sāhu.*

[81] Most of the names in Jaina inscriptions from Abu bear this title. *EI*, VIII, pp. 220–21. The Ānāvāḍa inscription refers roughly to ten *śreṣṭhis*. *IA*, XLI, p. 21, 11. 12–19.

[82] Ivo Fiser, see his article included in the present volume.

[83] S. Maqbul Ahmed, tr. *India and Its Neighbouring Territories in the Kitab Nuzhat Al-Mushatq of Al-Idrisi,* Leiden, 1961 (*Al-Idrisi*); *Rehala, of Ibn Battuata*, tr. by M. Hussain, Baroda, 1953, 1976 (*RIB*).

[84] *RIB*, p. 193.

[85] The *Cullaka-Seṭṭhi Jātaka* shows that the *seṭṭis* used to make wholesale purchases only to sell them off in part to various small traders. Cf. *The Jātakas,* tr. by R. Chalmer and ed. by E.B. Cowell), I, pp. 19–20.

[86] Kauṭilya (*KA*, III, XII. 179) referring to laws and regulations of the retail trade says, 'Retail dealers, selling the merchandise of others. . . should handover to the wholesale dealers as much of the sale proceeds and profits as is realised by them. . . .' This law seems to have continued to be observed during the eleventh-thirteenth centuries.

[87] *Upamitibhāvaprapañcakathā*, of Siddhasji, ed. by P. Peterson and H. Jacobi, Calcutta, 1899 (*Upamiti*).

his goods in retail. The merchant prince Jagaḍu is known to have carried on trade with Persia with the help of an Indian agent at Hormuz.[88] Similarly, Wasa Abhira, a rich Hindu merchant of Nahrwāla (Aṇahilavāḍa), carried on flourishing trade through his agents at Ghazni.[89] The *Deśīnāmamālā* suggests that big merchants appointed a number of assistants or agents, such as *ṇeṣatthi or vaṇiksaciva, meḍho or vaṇiksahāya, vāḍhi* or a helper.[90]

The *sārthavāha* was a general name for a merchant (*vaṇik*),[91] but in the specifiic sense it referred to a caravan leader under whose leadership and guidance the merchants of a town gathered and carried their goods to distant centres of trade. He was supposed to be a highly capable person knowing not only the routes but also the rules and regulations of sale and purchase in different states. Kṣīrasvāmin, commenting on *Amarakośa*, points out that *sārthvāha* was 'the leader of the travelling merchants who invested their own capital'.[92] In this sense, *sārthavāha* was more of a guide or pilot to inland traders than a trader himself. Sometimes a rich and courageous merchant with sufficient resources came forward to lead a caravan, and attracted other traders to join him by promising them protection and facilities of food, vehicles, etc. on the way.[93] It may be pointed out that there is no reference to a caravan journey from a village. It, thus, indicates that all caravans started generally from the cities where goods had already been brought from the country side by local merchants.

The *sārthavāhas*, who courted miseries and misfortunes during the course of their journeys, were moved not by the spirit of adventure but by the love of gain. They sold their merchandise at a high rate of profit and, thus, earned enormous riches to occupy an influential position in society. The *Pariśiṣṭaparvan* refers to a *sārthavāha*,

[88] A.K. Majumdar, *Chaulukyas of Gujarat*, Bombay, 1956 (*CG*).

[89] *HIED*, II, p. 200.

[90] Motichandra, *Trade and Trade Routes in Ancient India*, New Delhi, 1977 (hereinafter *ATTR*).

[91] *AC*, III, 531.

[92] *Amarakośa*, III. 9.78 ('*sārthān sadhanān pānthān vahati sārthavāhaḥ*). *Sārthavāha* is used in a similar sense in the *Yaśastilakacampū* (Uttarakhaṇḍa, NSP, p. 345). Technically speaking, *sārtha* meant a mobile corporation or association formed by travelling merchants to meet the hazards of the highways. This association was of a temporary nature , and ended at the end of each venture.

[93] See the story of caravan leader Dhana, *TSP*, I, pp. 7ff.

Rāmasamṛddha, who became wealthy by a sudden influx of riches.[94] In the *Triṣaṣṭhiśalākāpuruṣacarita*, there is a reference to a very rich Anaṅgadeva, the son of a caravan leader, Samudrapāla, who used to give alms to beggars and was praised by the bards.[95] Again, the same text refers to a wealthy caravan leader, Vasanta, who pleased a king with presents, and the king, as a token of gratitude, bestowed upon him the kingdom of Tāpasapura(?) and placed him in the rank of a vassal.[96]

The aboriginal tribes such as the Kirātas, the Bhīllas, the Pulindas, the Ābhīras, etc., too formed an integral part of the commercial network. The commentary on the *Dharmabindu* of Haribhadra Sūri as well as some other Jaina texts such as the *Āvaśyakacūrṇī* (seventh century) indicate that merchants used to advance money to the Pulindas for bringing ivory (*danta-vāṇijya*).[97] Referring to Sānudāsa's desire to earn money, the *Bṛhadkathāślokasaṁgraha* tells us about his travels through a narrow track with deep ravines on both sides where merchants lit a fire. Seeing the smoke, the Kirātas assembled from all sides and exchanged their goods including saffron, sugar, rice, oil, etc., with those of the merchants.[98] These references belong to earlier periods, but the involvement of aborigines in trade during the post-tenth centuries cannot be doubted. This is because a large number of commodities which had a wide market, such as honey, lac, saffron, camphor, sandalwood, bamboos, medicinal herbs, etc., were generally found in forests accessible to the aborigines.

In short, commercial activity in western India during the eleventh-thirteenth centuries involved a variety of traders at various stages. The two most important pillars of this activity, however, were the *śreṣṭhi* and the *sārthavāha*. The former collected local goods and also supplied liquid capital on interest to needy merchants, while the latter maintained commercial exchange with different and distant centres of trade by carrying goods to and fro. On account of the wealth acquired through trade and commerce, they gained prominence in society, and played an important role in local administration. The Ānāvāḍa inscription (AD 1291), for example, reveals that *śreṣṭhis* and

94 *Pariśiṣṭaparvan of Hemacandra*, (ed.), H. Jacobi, Calcutta, 1883, 1932. There is also a reference to a *Śarthapati* of Tamralipti. Ibid., II. VV. 314–15.

95 *TSP*, V, p. 30. 96 Ibid., p. 131.

97 *Āvaśyakacūrṇi*, p. 829; see also *RTA*, p. 493.

98 *Brhatkatkhāślokasaṁgraha*, (eds.), P.K. Agrawala and V.S. Agrawala, Varanasi, 1974, pp. 450–61; see also *ATTR*, pp. 136–37.

vaṇijyārakas (travelling merchants) along with *purohitas* and *ṭhakuras* took part in the deliberations of a town council (*panca-mukha-nagara*).[99] In the *Nirvāṇa Lilāvatī Kathā,* Jineśvara Sūri (eleventh century) weaves a plot around five friends, viz., king Vijayasena, his minister, a *purohita, śreṣṭhi* Purandara and *sārtha* Dhana.[100] It indicates the high position which rich merchants occupied in contemporary social life.

PROFESSIONAL EDUCATION AND ETHICS

The success of a trader depended largely upon his commercial acumen and education. Medhātithi advises that a vaiśya should know not only the time and the place where a certain thing fetches a profit higher than elsewhere, but also the variations in the price of metals, weights and measures prevalent in different regions, the excellence and defects of commodities with regard to their storing capacity and the manner of storing them, the nature of the people of different countries and the advantages as well as the disadvantages of trading with them, the rate of wages for slaves and attendants, and the languages of Mālava, Magadha, Drāviḍa and other countries.[101] The term *bhāṣājña-sañjñaḳaḥ* used for a vaiśya in the *Kathāsaritsāgara*[102] indicates that the wandering merchants learnt various languages in the interest of their activities. The Venetian traveller Marco Polo, talking about the training of merchants' sons in south-west India, points out that male children, after having attained the age of thirteen were

[99] *IA*, XLI, pp. 20–21. A number of documents of the Gupta age refer to *śreṣthis* and *sārthavāhas* as important members of the boards which assisted provincial governors and district officers in administration. Cf. D.C. Sircar, *Select Inscriptions*, I, pp. 283ff, 324ff, 328ff, 355, 357. See also *Bhāratīya Vidyā*, X, 1949, pp. 280ff.

[100] Cf. *KKP*, intro., pp. 71f.

[101] *On Manu*, IX, 329–32. The *Varṇaratnākara* of Kavi Śekharācārya (eds.), S.K. Chatterji and B. Misra, Asiatic Society of Bengal, 1940, intro., pp. xxxi, xxxiv, quoted in *SCNI*, p. 402) also reveals that a merchant was expected to acquire the knowledge of various kinds of metals, gems, cloths, spices, perfumes, etc. He was also supposed to be well versed in different techniques of commercial transactions.

[102] *Kathāsaritsāgara*, of Somadeva, ed. by Durgaprasad and K.P. Parab, Bombay, 1930 (hereinafter *KKS*).

dismissed from their home with a small sum of money with which they carried on buying and selling, and gradually became 'trained to be very dexterous and keen traders'.[103] The *Prabandhacintāmaṇi* tells us of one Ābhaḍa, a poor son of a merchant, who lived in Paṭṭana and possessed a keen knowledge of jewels. He once noticed a gem threaded along with ordinary beads round the neck of a goat. He purchased the goat and sold the gem off to a king. With the help of the money received, he bought sacks of madder for sale. He soon became the principal man of the town, and was honoured by the king Siddharāja.[104]

Merchants generally gained commercial knowledge through their association with friends and family members, but sometimes teachers were also appointed to train the young ones in all types of arts and sciences connected with their commercial activities. The *Śṛṅgāramañjarīkathā* of Bhojadeva refers to one Ratnadeva, son of a *vaṇik,* who after having been sent to a teacher by his father, attained distinction in the art of commerce, the methods of handling horses and horse vehicles, the training and care of elephants, the secrets of gambling, the science of harlotry, and the arts of painting, cutting leaves, binding books etc.[105] Jineśvara Sūri talks of a merchant who persuaded his son to give up unproductive and uneconomical activities of dance and drama and got him trained in metallurgy and alchemy.[106] For imparting instructions to the children of a wealthy Moḍha bania family, one Rājakīrtimiśra is known to have copied a manuscript of the *Gaṇitasāra* at Aṇahilavāḍa.[107] The *Prabhāvakacarita* (AD 1277) refers to a rich merchant Lakṣmīpati of Dhārā, who used to write the accounts of his daily sale and purchase on a piece of wall.[108] Kalhaṇa refers to the training of clerks as well as merchants under a teacher.[109] The reference to merchants' assistants such as *ṇeṣatthi, meḍho, vādhī* etc. in the *Deśīnāmamālā*[110] indicates that some rich merchants hired

[103]*MP*, II, pp. 344 f.

[104]*PCT*, pp. 104–105; *PCJ*, pp. 69–70.

[105]*Śṛṅgāramañjarīkathā*, of Bhoja, ed. and tr. by Kalpalata Munshi, Bombay, 1925. (*SMK*), pp. 56ff, intro., p. 83.

[106]*KKP*, pp. 172–73; intro., pp. 123–24.

[107]Cf. *JNSI*, VIII, 1946, pp. 138ff.

[108]*KKP*, intro., pp. 22–23.

[109]*Rājataraṅginī* of Kalhaṇa, tr. by M.A. Stein in two volumes, Delhi, 1961 (hereafter *RT*), II, no. 131, p. 12.

[110]*DN*, IV. 44; VI. 138; VII. 53.

the services of educated persons to assist them in their commercial activities. These assistants must have also helped their masters in writing legal documents concerning sale, purchase, mortgage, bills of exchange, etc., which as it appears from the *Lekhapaddhati,* formed an integral part of trade and commerce during the post-tenth centuries.[111]

The evidence of Hemacandra reveals the existence of *vidyāmaṭhas* in Gujarat.[112] The *Gaṇadharasārdhaśataka* (VS 1295/AD 1238) refers to a Jain *maṭha* where sons of laymen and even orphans received education.[113]

The rich libraries of Paṭṭana, Cambay and Jaisalmer[114] stand as visible monuments of the new spirit of education which was encouraged by the rich merchants such as Vastupāla and Tejaḥpāla.

A large number of traders in western India during the eleventh-thirteenth centuries were Jainas. They were exhorted by their teachers and preachers to follow truthful and peaceful means of earning wealth. Jineśvara Sūri (eleventh century), in his *Ṣaṭsthānakaprakaraṇa,* dilates upon the code of conduct which a merchant was expected to follow.[115] He advises that a merchant should neither weigh less nor charge more.[116] He should deliver the goods of the same quality as seen and approved by the customer, and should never indulge in adulteration. Jineśvara Sūri, suggests that a merchant should not hoard grain as it could be destroyed by worms, but may store such goods as cotton, yarn, cloths, coral, pearls, madder, arecanuts, etc. which could be kept in godowns for a long period without the fear of physical loss.[117] Since a king could be of great service or disservice to merchants, he advises that a merchant should call on the king frequently and flatter him by reciting his good qualities; a merchant should never refute him or keep the company of his opponents.[118] To the money-lenders he advises that a loan should never be advanced for the sake of greed, and that the creditor must not use the pledged items such as carriages, bullocks, etc. for his personal benefit without making a payment.[119] He adds that if a wicked debtor refuses to return the loan

[111]V.K. Jain, *op. cit.*, ch. 8.

[112]R.C. Parikh, intro., to the *Kāvyānuśāsana*, II, pt. 1, pp. ccxl–ccxli.

[113]*Apabhraṁśakāvyatrayī*, intro., p. 15.

[114]Cf. *JPPS*, pp. 3, 4, 5, 13, 15, 19.

[115]*KKP*, intro., pp. 51ff.

[116]Ibid., p. 51. [117] Ibid.

[118]Ibid., p. 53. [119] Ibid., p. 52.

or turns violent, the creditor should be prepared to forego his money rather than fight with him.[120] Hemacandra also advises merchants to remain calm and peaceful in provocative circumstances, and points out that heroism must not be shown by a merchant, even though he is heroic.[121] Since peace is essential for the promotion of commercial activity, merchants at large were advised to avoid all strife, strain and provocation in the interest of their profession.[122]

Since *ahiṁsā* was the cardinal principle of Jainism, agriculture and the trades which resulted in the death of living beings were forbidden for Jain traders. In the *Triṣaṣṭhiśalākāpuruṣacarita,* a ploughman is told, 'What happiness or what good deeds of yours can there be when you live by a cruel means of livelihood? This work of yours, Sir, marked by destruction of life, causes pain not only here (in this life) but leads to pain in other births also. . .' [123] Two edicts belonging to the reign of Kumārapāla[124] enumerate the punishments to be awarded to the *mahājanas, tāmbūlikas,*[125] potters[126] and others for the slaughter of animals on certain days of a month in the Marwar region. These edicts were caused to be promulgated by Pūtiga and Sāliga, the sons of a *śrāvaka* Śubhaṅkara of the Prāgvāṭa *vaṁśa* of Nāḍol. It seems that the promulgators were important merchants of the region, who exerted their influence on the local feudal lords to issue these edicts. The commentary on the *Dharmabindu* of Haribhadra Sūri as well as some other Jaina texts forbid merchants to follow such professions as *lākṣāvāṇijya* (trading in lac), *rasavāṇijya* (trading in liquor), *viṣavāṇijya* (trading in poison), *sphoṭīkarma* (digging and hoeing for cultivation), *vanakarma* (buying forests to cut and sell their wood), *aṅgārakarma* (preparing charcoal), *śakṭīkarma* (plying carts and other vehicles on hire), *nirlāñchanakarma* (castrating bullocks),[127] etc.

However, it is doubtful whether the Jaina merchants really followed the advice of their preceptors. Besides, there were many

[120]Ibid., p. 53.
[121]*TSP*, I, p. 88.
[122]V.K. Jain, *op. cit.*, pp. 234ff.
[123]*TSP*, VI, p. 229.
[124]Kirāḍu stone inscription of Alhaṇadeva of AD 1153, *EI*, XI, no. 12, pp. 43ff; *CPSI*, pp. 172ff; Ratanpur stone inscription, *CPSI*, pp. 205ff.
[125]*EI*, XI, p. 45, 11. 7–8.
[126]*CPSI*, p. 207, vv. 9–10.
[127]Cf. *RTA*, pp. 493–94.

non-Jaina traders who had no inhibitions in carrying on trade in the commodities prohibited by the Jain texts. The *Upamitibhāvapprapañcakathā* reveals that traders resorted to all sorts of fair and foul means to earn wealth.[128] We are told that Dhanaśekhara, a poor merchant of Ānandapura, goaded by materialistic spirit, started his business with a shop where he sold grain, oil cotton, lac, gum, etc. Not satisfied with his earnings, he bought camels and mules, and sent them out with loads of goods. He also obtained from the king a permit (*hastādeśa*) for importing and exporting commodities and appointed a number of traders, probably to look after the retail trade. Still dissatisfied, he resorted to traffic in prostitutes,[129] and traded in *rasa,* (wine, honey, etc.) and ivory.

The character and conduct of traders in western India generally receive high acclaim from foreign travellers. Al Idrisi tells us that a large number of Muslim merchants visited Nahrwāra (Aṇahilavāḍa) because the people of the town were 'noteworthy for the excellence of their justice, for keeping up their contracts, and for the beauty of their character', and adds that the people of the region practised truth and abhorred falsehood.[130] Marco Polo bestows yet more generous praise on the merchants of Lāṭa, whom by a curious mistake he calls Abraiaman or brāhmaṇas. He says, 'you must know that these Abraiaman are the best merchants in the world, and the most truthful, for they would not tell a lie for anything on earth,' and 'if a foreign merchant who does not know the ways of the country applies to them and entrusts his goods to them, they will take charge of these, and sell them in the most loyal manner, seeking zealously the profit of the foreigner and asking no commission except what he pleases to bestow.[131] These observations of the foreign travellers may reflect the general ethos of the mercantile community in western India.

There are, however, many references in the contemporary texts to the dishonest and unscrupulous dealings of merchants.[132] In fact, it

[128] *Upamiti,* pp. 867–68.

[129] *Vihitādhanopārjana gaṇikāḥ*, ibid.

[130] *Al Idrisi*, nos 16–18, p. 60; *HIED*, I, p. 88.

[131] *MP*, II, p. 363. The term Abraiaman seems to refer to the Jainas, for elsewhere (ibid., p. 366) he points out that 'they would not kill an animal on any account, not even a fly, of a flea, or a louse, or anything in fact that has life; for they say these have all souls, and it will be sin to do so'.

[132] *Samayamātṛkā of Kṣemendra,* ed. by Durgaprasad and K.P. Parab, Bombay, 1925.

seems to have been generally believed that 'a merchant does not give up his art of deception even when he is on the verge of death.[133] Hemachandra states that rarely does one find 'a merchant who is not deceitful'.[134] He recounts the story of two greedy merchant-friends who 'wandered through villages, mines, cities, capital villages, et cetera' deceiving 'the people with false weights, false measures, false coins, and false descriptions of articles.'[135] Jineśvara Sūri places petty traders in the *vimajjhimā* category and accuses them of using false weights and measures in business.[136] In strong contrast to the charitable activities of the merchant Jagaḍu of Gujarat, who freely distributed his stored grain to the afflicted people during a famine,[137] the Kashmiri author Kṣemendra refers to a typically avaricious merchant who used to feel overjoyed at the approach of a famine or some other calamity because he could expect good money on his hoarded foodgrains.[138]

MERCHANT CORPORATIONS

Merchants derived power and prestige not only from wealth but also from the guilds or autonomous corporations which they formed to protect their interests. These corporations, organized on a formal basis framed their own rules of membership and professional conduct which even the kings were supposed to accept and respect.[139] The guild-chief performed, *de facto,* the functions of a communal magistrate in deciding the sale, purchase and other economic affairs of the members, and enjoyed considerable influence in royal courts. He dealt directly with the king or the tax-collectors, and settled the market tolls after having agreed to pay, on behalf of his fellow merchants, a fixed sum of money.[140] The guild merchants also acted as custodians

[133] *Yaśastilakacampu* of Somadevasuri, ed. and tr. by S.L. Sastri, Varanasi, 1960, 1971 (hereinafter YTC); also see K.K. Handiqui, *Yaśastilaka and Indian Culture*, Sholapur, 1949, p. 63.
[134] *TSP*, I, p. 67; also *TSP*, III, p. 155.
[135] Ibid., III, pp. 280f. These merchants appear to have been the pedlars.
[136] *KKP*, intro., p. 117; text, p. 115.
[137] *Jaguḍucarita* Sarvāṇanda, ed. by G. Bühler, Wien, 1892.
[138] *Deśopadeśa* of Kṣemendra, ed. by M. Kaul, Poona, 1923.
[139] *Nārada*, X. 2–6; *Bṛh*, XVII, 18; *Kātyāyana*, 49–50.
[140] *Medhā on Manu*, VIII. 41.

of religious interests. They undertook the task of building temples, and made donations by levying a corporate tax on their members. The corporate activity, thus, enabled big merchants to consolidate their power, paralleled only by that of feudatories.

In the digests and commentaries of the period we come across various terms such as *śreṇi, pūga, vrāta, naigama* and *saṁgha* to denote one or the other type of a corporate body. Hemacandra tells us that a group or corporation was known by as many as thirty-five names including *saṁghāta, samūha, samudāya, vrāta, maṇḍalam* and *gaṇa,* and adds that a group of 'human beings' was known as *saṁgha* or *sārtha.*[141] As true nature and character of the corporations noted above may have varied from place to place and also from time to time, they have led to different interpretations by legal authors and commentators. There is however, no doubt that, during the early medieval period, there existed a large number of guilds of both traders and artisans[142] who were united in the interest of their common profession.[143]

The term *śreṇi* is explained by the *Vīramitrodaya* and the *Mitākṣarā* as a corporate body of those 'who follow one occupation but belong to different castes'.[144] The *Mitākṣarā* cites examples of such *śreṇis* as those of horse-dealers, betel-sellers, weavers and leather workers, while the *Vīramitrodya* refers to the organization of merchants

[141] *AC*, VI. 4748.

[142] See Kaman stone inscription (AD 786–905) from Bharatpur state (*EI*, XIV, p. 335, 11. 16, 17, 18); the Vaillabhaṭṭasvāmin temple inscription of AD 876 from Gwalior (*EI*, I, p. 160, 11. 16, 19); the Pehoa inscription of AD 882–83 from Karnal (ibid., pp. 186ff); the Sīyaḍoṇī stone inscription of AD 903–60 (ibid., pp. 173ff, 11. 9, 10, 26, 31). It may be pointed out that artisans acted as merchants too. We must, however, distinguish between dependent and independent artisans, described as *āśrita* and *anāśrita* by Lakṣmīdhara (Gṛahasthakāṇḍa, p. 380). As we have aleady noted, the dependent ones worked for feudal lords or some other agency and had, therefore, no scope for trade; the *anāśrita* ones, however, could indulge in trade and form guilds. D.D. Kosambi seems to be right in pointing out (*JESHO*, II, p. 282) that there was a gradual 'predominance of merchant guilds controlled by rich families over the older type of workers', *śreni'*.

[143] Jaimal Rai vehemently opposes the view of connecting guilds with the system of caste, and feels that 'guilds were, in fact, the most potent factor in destroying the edifice of the caste system'. *The Rural-Urban Economy and Social Changes in Ancient India* 300 BC to AD 600, pp. 268ff.

[144] *On Yāj*, II. 30.

(*vaṇigādisamūha*) as *śreṇi.*[145] Similarly, Medhātithi explains *śreṇi* as a group of 'people following a common profession' such as that of 'tradesmen, artisans, money-lenders, coach-drivers and so forth'.[146] According to Hemacandra, however, *śreṇi* was a group (*gaṇa*) of artisans exclusively.[147] Elsewhere he refers to the traditional view of eighteen types of guilds (*śreṇis*) but does not specify them.[148] However, another Jaina text, *Jambūdvīpa-prajñāpati,* tells us that the eighteen guilds included those of weavers, potters, goldsmiths, betel-sellers, braziers, tailors, oil pressers etc.[149] Jineśvara Sūri too suggests that the persons who formed *śreṇis* (*seṇigayā*) were goldsmiths, blacksmiths, potters, washermen, and other artisans and craftsmen (*śilpakarmakārasamudāya*).[150] Thus, it seems that in western India during the eleventh-thirteenth centuries the term *śreṇi* was used chiefly in the sense of a group of artisans and craftsmen.

The term *pūga* is not mentioned in the *Abhidhānacintāmaṇi,* but is used for an association or a corporation of merchants in the *Vīramitrodaya*[151] and the *Kātyāyana.*[152] According to the *Mitākṣarā*, it was an assembly of persons of different castes and different occupations but dwelling at one place as, for instance, a village or city.[153] The exact nature and composition of the group called *vrāta*[154] is not clear. Jaimal Rai is of the view that it was originally an association of uncivilized persons who lived by violence or physical labour but later 'under the impact of mercantile and industrial economy they turned to trade and industry, retaining nevertheless their old name'.[155] In the *Abidhānacintāmaṇi*, a group of persons who earned their livelihood by physical labour is called *vrātīnaḥ.*[156] Thus, *vrāta* was probably an association of porters and the like.

145Ibid., I. 361.

146*On Manu*, VIII. 41; see also VIII. 2. ('*śreṇayaḥ samāna vyavahāra jivino vaṇik prabhbṛtayaḥ*').

147*AC*, III. 563.

148*TSP*, I, p. 258; III, p. 316. See also *Padmānandamahākāvya*, XVI. 193.

149See *TSP*, I, pp. 258f, fn. 315.

150*KKP*, pp. 116–17; text, p. 115.

151 *On Yāj*, II. 30.

152*Kātyāyana*, 679 (*vaṇijādināma pūgaḥ*). The Ānāvāḍa inscription (*IA*, XLI, p. 21, l. 18) refers to a term *pūgī* which might be related to *pūga.*

153*On Yāj*, II, 30.

154The term *vrāta* is used in the *Ṛgveda* in the sense of a fighting band. *Ṛgveda*, III. 26.2; V. 53.11.

155Jaimal Rai, *op. cit.*, p. 256.

156 *AC*, III. 144.

The term *naigama* is explained by the commentators on legal texts as an association of caravan merchants (*sārthavāhādisamūha*) of different castes who travel together for the purpose of carrying on trade with other countries.[157] In the *Moharājaparājaya*, we are told that the merchant Kubera of Aṇahilavāḍa went out to trade, after having deposited his property with the important *naigamas* of the town (*mahattara naigameṣu nagaram*).[158] It suggests that *naigama* was a corporate body formed by the town merchants engaged in foreign trade. Hemacandra, however, does not mention *naigama* as a group but holds it synonymous with *vaṇik.*[159]

The corporation of merchants was also known as *saṁgha.* Commenting upon the term *deśasaṁgha* in the *Manusmṛti,* Medhātithi points out that it was 'a combination formed by persons professing the same faith or path, even though inhabiting different countries and belonging to different castes', for instance, the confederation of traders (*vaṇijam*), the confederation of mendicants, etc.[160] It seems that the term *deśī,* which is used in some inscriptions of the period for inter-state traders,[161] was the distorted form of *deśasaṁgha.* Another term for an association of merchants was *maṇḍalam*[162] or *maṁḍalika.*[163] The Arthuna inscription reveals that each *maṁḍalika* or traders' association[164] was to pay a monthly tax of one *dramma* in favour of a temple.

In short, the legal commentators by way of explanation disclose the existence of a large number of guilds or corporations. For instance, Medhātithi mentions the guilds of tradesmen (*vaṇiks*), artisans, money-lenders, coach-drivers, etc.,[165] while the *Mitākṣarā* refers to those of horse-dealers, betel-sellers, weavers and leather workers.[166] Their evidence is supported by the epigraphic records which, while referring to pious grants made to religious institutions, indicate the

[157] *Aparārka on Yāj*, p. 796; see also *Viśvarūpa* on *Yāj*, II. 192.

[158] *Moharājaparājaya* of Yasaḥpala ed. by Caturvijaya Muni, Baroda, 1918, p. 61.

[159] *AC*, III. 531; see also ibid., VI. 47–48.

[160] *On Manu*, VIII. 219.

[161] V.K. Jain, *op. cit.*, pp. 41–42.

[162] *AC*, VI. 47.

[163] The Arthuna inscription (AD 1079), *EI*, XIV. p. 302, v. 77.

[164] *vaṇigamaṁḍalikām*, ibid.

[165] *On Manu*, VIII. 41; also VIII. 219.

[166] *On Yāj*, II. 30.

corporate activities of merchants and artisans. For example, the Harṣa stone inscription (AD 977) from Sikar in Rajasthan refers to the corporations of horse-dealers and salt-merchants,[167] the Kirāḍu stone inscription (AD 1153) and the Ratanpura stone inscription from Marwar to those of *mahājanas* (bankers?), betel-sellers and porters,[168] the Ānāvāḍa stone inscription from Patan to those of travelling merchants, ship-owners, and braziers.[169] The Arthuna inscription (AD 1080) from Banswara,[170] the Ṭimbāṇaka grant (AD 1207) from Kathiawar,[171] and the Cambay inscription (AD 1295)[172] too indicate the existence of traders' guilds in those regions. The reference to the *śreṇikaraṇa* in the *Lekhapaddhati*[173] suggests that there was a separate department to look after the *śreṇis* and other corporations during the Caulukya period.

We do not possess adequate information on the exact nature and function of merchants' corporations during the post-tenth centuries, but the legal digests and commentaries of the period[174] indicate that guilds continued to enjoy the privilege of regulating their activities by making their own laws. Medātithi, commenting upon guild laws (*sreṇī-dharma*), points out that certain principal tradesmen (*vaṇiṁmahattara*) used to approach the king, and offer to pay him the royal tax fixed upon verbally. After the king agreed to it, they joined together and laid down among themselves certain rules such as the time and place of the sale of a particular commodity, and the rate of tax to be collected from each for making payment to the king or for arranging religious festivals. If anyone transgressed those rules, he was punished for acting against the guild laws.[175] The king was also expected to honour the commerce conventions of the guilds.[176] He

[167]*EI*, II, no. 8, p. 124, 1.38. The term *samasta bhammaha deśya*, which has been used in connection with the grant of one *viṁsopaka* on every *kūṭaka* of salt, probably refers to a corporation of salt-merchants.

[168]*CPSI*, pp. 172ff, 207ff. See also *EI*, XI, no. 12, p. 45, 11. 7, 8.

[169]*IA*, XLI, no. 21.

[170]*EI*, XIV, no. 21, p. 302, 1. 49.

[171]*IA*, XI, pp. 337ff.

[172]*CPSI*, pp. 227ff.

[173] *LP*, p. 1.

[174]*SC*, III, pp. 520–33. Aparārka and Vijñāneśvara *On Yāj*, II. 185–92.

[175]*On Manu*, VIII. 41, *Kātyāyana* (v. 668) too advises that members belonging to a group (*samūha*) should perform all their acts in accordance with the rules of their groups.

[176]*Kātyāyana*, 49–50.

could intervene only when guild rules were found either contrary to the sacred law of the land or prejudicial to the interests of others. Bṛhaspati provides, 'whatever is done by those (heads of an association), whether harsh or kind towards other people, must be approved of by the king as well, for they are declared to be the appointed managers (of affairs)'.[177] He also suggests that a king should decide a case in accordance with local custom, logic, and 'the opinion of the traders' living in that town.[178] Thus, it sems that conventions of the corporate bodies possessed the sanctity of law. It must have been more so in the region of western India where traders formed an important section of society.[179]

The corporate bodies were also invested with the power to decide law suits amongst their members. Aparārka following Bṛhaspati establishes the power of the head of a guild to reprimand, condemn and even excommunicate wrong doers.[180] The *Smṛticandrikā* lays down that a corporation (*samūha*) should constitute a board of two, three or five superintendents (*kāryacintakas*) to decide cases among themselves.[181] It further states that a king should punish the insolent chiefs (*mukhyas*) of the corporations, but if the *samūha* is at all competent to do so, it alone should exercise this authority to punish the chief.[182] It follows from Medhātithi that the members of traders' guilds and also those of the other guilds generally felt shy of 'any matter relating to themselves going before the king, as that would lend the king's officers an opportunity for interfering' in the work of their guilds; hence they always took from the parties concerned sufficient security

[177] *Bṛh*, XVII. 17–18.

[178] Ibid., II. 26.

[179] The influence which associations of merchants could exert upon the king is vividly reflected in a trade charter of AD 592 from western India. (*EI*, XXX, 1957, pp. 163–81; *JESHO*, II, 1959, pp. 285–89. See also *IF*, pp. 69–71). It refers to a wide range of concessions and immunities which the local community of merchants obtained from the king Viṣṇuṣeṇa free and fearless transaction of their business. Though we do not come across a similar type of charter from the domain of the Caulukyas, there is no reason to disbelieve that guild merchants continued to enjoy well-established rights and privileges during the post-tenth centuries.

[180] p. 794.

[181] *Smṛticandrikā of Devanna Bhaṭṭa*, ed., L Srinivasacharya, in six volumes, Mysore, 1914–21; see vol. III, pp. 526ff.

[182] Ibid., pp. 530ff.

against their deviating from the decision arrived at, before they proceeded to investigate a dispute.[183]

The foregoing discussion is a clear index to the strong position occupied by guilds and guild-chiefs.[184] Kātyāyana suggests that the constituents of a court should include incorruptible assessors (*sabhyas*), wise brāhmaṇas, and those merchants (*vaṇiks*) who form a group.[185] It is significant that apart from respectability of family and good character, wealth came to be regarded as one of the qualifications for being a member of the court. Thus, merchants emerged as a potent factor in local administration. The Ānavāḍa inscription from Patan reveals that the travelling merchants (*vaṇijyārakas*), the ship-owners (*nau-vittakas*) and the *mahājanas* including gold dealers, braziers and a number of merchants with the title *śreṣṭhi* and *sādhu*, formed, along with the *pañcakula* and the *purohita*, a part of the town council (*pañca-mukha-nagara*).[186] The guild merchants also commanded respect at the royal courts. Vijñāneśvara supports Yājñavalkya that a king should bestow gifts, honours and hospitality (*dānamānasatkāra*) on those who visit him in connection with the work of their associations (*samūhakārya*).[187] In the *Moharāja-parājaya*, we are told that, after the supposed death of merchant Kubera of Aṇahilavāḍa, four important merchants of the town (*nagara mahattaro vaṇijo*) came to the king, and asked him to appoint an officer to take an account of the property of Kubera who had left no heir.[188] It suggests that the corporation of merchants (*naigama*) had to be satisfied before the king could take possession of the property of one of its members.

[183]*On Manu*, VIII. 2.

[184]The butchers, who had to give up their trade as a result of anti-slaughter ordinances issued during the time of Kumārapāla, are said to have 're-ceived compensation to the amount of three years income'. Cf. G. Bühler, *The Life of Hemacandrācārya*, p. 39; also *PCT*, introduction, p. xiii. It indicates that the whims and fancies of a king could not come in the way of the commercial activities of the people.

[185]Cf. *Kātyāyana*, vv. 57–59.

[186]*IA*, XLI, p. 21.

[187]*On Yāj*, II. 189.

[188]*MPY*, p. 50.

Chapter Fourteen

Usury in Early Mediaeval Times*

R.S. SHARMA

ATTITUDES TOWARDS USURY

Literally the term usury means the practice of lending money at an exorbitant rate of interest, especially at a higher rate than is allowed by law. This, however, seems to be a later meaning. In many ancient societies the very idea of taking interest was considered to be reprehensible, and the act of charging interest, high or low, was thought to be immoral, so that the term usury has a tinge of something socially and religiously undesirable about it. In early mediaeval Indian society it is not always possible to draw a precise line between usury and interest, and hence the subject can be best studied by examining the data on interest and money-lending.

The present study covers a period of about 800 years, and is mainly based on Smṛti texts. In about the fifth and sixth centuries Bṛhaspati and Kātyāyana present to us fairly developed laws regarding debt. Fragments of law ascribed to their successors add precious little. The subject is also dealt with in the compilations on debt in the digests of the twelfth and fifteenth centuries.

The Dharmaśāstra material can be supplemented by some epigraphic evidence, but even all this stuff does not enable us to treat the whole question in successive stages. Hence we propose to study its important aspects separately but in sequence of time wherever possible.

* *Perspectives in the Social and Economic History of Early India.* Munshiram Manoharlal Publishers Pvt. Ltd., New Delhi, 1983, pp. 193–217.

Ancient and mediaeval Indian Sanskrit texts convey the idea of interest of usury by *kusīda, vārdhuṣa, vṛddhi,* and *vyāja,* of which the last seems to be of a later origin. Since these terms were used indiscriminately by lawgivers, it is difficult to establish whether they used one for usury and the other for interest. Baudhāyana, a lawgiver of about the fifth century BC, prescribes taking interest as a source of livelihood for the vaiśya[1] and condemns a brāhmaṇa who practises. *vārdhuṣa* as a śūdra.[2] On the other hand Gautama permits *kusīda* to a brāhmaṇa who does not do it himself.[3] Manu does not demarcate between *vṛddhi* and *kusīda,* and lays down that the *vārdhuṣika* (one who lends at interest) should take *vṛddhi.*[4] In the opinion of Vasiṣṭha, a *vārdhuṣika* is one who taking cheap lends it on condition of receiving a greater quantity.[5] Whether this applied to grain is not clear from the text. But Nārada defines *vārdhuṣa* (usury) as interest on grain.[6] According to him, interest on grain can rise three times the principle,[7] but it can be regarded as usury only when it is demanded at the rate of 5 per cent on grain given through friendship.[8]

Bṛhaspati's concept of usury was different. According to him, the use of a pledge after twice the principal has been realized from it, compound interest, and the addition of the interest to the principal constitute usury and are to be condemned.[9] Bṛhaspati seems to identify *kusīda* with usury and defines it as that which is taken fourfold or even eightfold without any qualm of conscience from a poor person who is serving or distressed.[10] He gives a fanciful grammatical interpretation of the terms *ku* and *sīda,*[11] which indicates the attitude of derision in which the lawgiver holds usurious rates of interest. The idea is reproduced in the ninth century by Medhātithi, according to whom the term *kusīda* means that which is followed by evil persons, and then the persons themselves.[12] Almost all the legal

[1] *Baudhāyana Dharmasūtra,* Kasi Sanskrit Series, 104, 1934 (hereinafter *Baudh*).

[2] I. 10.25. [3] X. 5–6.

[4] VIII. 140. [5] II. 41–42.

[6] P.V. Kane, History of the Dharmaśāstra, III, Poona, p. 417. (hereinafter *HDS*).

[7] I. 107. [8] 109–10.

[9] XI. 12. [10] XI. 2.

[11] *Sacred Books of the East Series* (hereinafter *SBE*).

[12] *On Manu*, VIII, 152.

texts disapprove of what is not considered *dharmyā vṛddhi,* legal interest, but they do not seem to use any special term of opprobrium for it. Nevertheless, they exhibit a tone of venom against exorbitant interest, which continues into late mediaeval times. The *Vivādacandra,* written by Misaru Mishra of Mithilā in the first half of the fifteenth century, condemns the food of the usurer *(vārdhuṣikasyānna)* who waits for long for the increase of his interest as nightsoil.[13]

The legal texts from ancient to mediaeval times show a changing attiude towards charging interest by members of various social classes (*varṇas*). Lawgivers of the fifth-third centuries BC permit lending at interest only to the vaiśyas. Vasiṣtha lays down that a brāhmaṇa or *śrotriya* shall not act as usurer.[14] In particular a brāhmaṇa usurer(*vārdhuṣika*) is condemend as a śūdra[15] and is not to be treated even as a vaiśya. Vasiṣtha states that if brāhmaṇa murder and usury are weighed in a balance, the murderer of a brāhmaṇa rises to the top while the usurer trembles.[16] Similarly, Baudhāyana declares that if interest (*vṛddhi*) and abortion are weighed, the destroyer of womb rises while the usurer sinks.[17] Usury is therefore considered even worse than the murder of a brāhmaṇa or abortion. Coming as all this does from brāhmaṇa lawgivers, it shows an intense hatred for usurers, who probably did not spare the brāhmaṇas. However, Baudhāyana[18] permits the first two varṇas to charge interest from one who neglects his sacred duties, from a miser, from an atheist, or from a very wicked man, but these cases are exceptional and do not ordinarily allow a brāhmaṇa to practise usury. Gautama[19] permits a brāhmaṇa to lend at interest provided he does not do it himself. But it is doubtful whether this injunction formed part of his original law-book.[20]

[13] Quoted in *HDS*, III, 423, fn. 691.
[14] *Vaśistha* Dharmaśāstra (hereinafter *Vaś*).
[15] *Baudh*, 1. 10.24.
[16] *Vaś*, 11.46.
[17] 1. 10.25.
[18] 1. 10.26. [19] X. 5–6.
[20] Gautama is considered to be one of the earliest lawgivers, if not the earliest. It has been shown by me elsewhere (*Śūdras in Ancient India*, Delhi 1958, pp. 83–84) that he should be dated much later on the basis of his provisions on social matters. His regulations regarding debt confirm my earlier view, and it seems that these were interpolated into Gautama's law-book some time in the Gupta or post-Gupta times. His enumeration of six kinds of interest are not found in any law-book earlier than that of

Manu, the most important lawgiver of post-Maurya times, states in unequivocal terms that the brāhmaṇa or the kṣatriya should not take interest even in times of distress, but should pay some interest to people of mean avocations (*pāpīyase*) out of legal necessity (*dharmārtham*).[21] On the other hand Manu enjoins the king to compel the vaiśya to practise lending at interest and other occupations.[22] Nārada seems to concede this practice in favour of the kṣatriya but lays down that a brāhmaṇa must never resort to usury, not even in a state of extreme distress.[23] Similarly Kātyāyana states that a brāhmaṇa (*dvija*) who is a cowherd, trader, artisan, bard servant, and an interest-taker should be administered the same ordeal by the king as a śūdra.[24] Thus the law-books of the post-Maurya and Gupta period roundly prohibit a brāhmaṇa to live on interest. It is curious that they do not allow even as much latitude to the brāhmaṇa in this respect as Baudhāyana does.

About three centuries later the situation seems to have changed. In the ninth century, commenting of Manu VIII. 140, Medhātithi states that the god Vasiṣṭha, who possessed knowledge of all the three ages and was free from various weaknesses including greed, accepted interest at the rate of $^1/_{80}$ of the principal. He therefore declares that this rate increases wealth, and is not associated with the weakness of greed (*lobha*). From this it follows that if Vasiṣṭha charged interest, the brāhmaṇa were justified in doing so. The position came to be clearly recognized by the twelfth century, when the *Garuḍa Purāṇa* was compiled. This text permits the brāhmaṇa and kṣatriyas to practise *kusīda* in time of distress.[25] It considers *kusīda* to be the most effective of all the modes of livelihood prescribed by sages in abnormal times.[26] Agriculture is hampered by want of rains, royal terror, and the depredations of the mice, etc., but not *kusīda* which keeps on growing at all times and under all circumstances.[27]

Bṛhaspati, whose section on debt is the most developed. Again, his provision that a brāhmaṇa can lend (money?) at interest is not found in this form in any early law-book; on the other hand it is found in post-Gupta texts which allow this to a brāmaṇa only in distress.

[21] X. 117. [22] VIII. 410. [23] I. 111.

[24] *Kātyāyana Smṛti*, ed. and tr. by P.V. Kane, Bombay, 1933 (hereinafter *Kātyā*).

[25] Quoted in *Vācaspatyam* (Chowkhamba Sanskrit Series), III, 2159.

[26] Ibid. [27] Ibid.

Whether brāhmaṇas actually practised money-lending in northern India is difficult to say. Speaking of the eleventh century Alberuni states: 'Usury or taking percentages is forbidden. Only to the śūdra is it allowed to take percentages, as long as his profit is not more than (a) fiftieth of the capital'[28] It is not clear whether 'usury' is the correct word used by Sachau in his translation. But since all the legal texts authorize the vaiśyas to charge interest, there is no reason to believe that this was confined to the śūdras in Alberuni's time. Probably Alberuni's picture is rather idealistic, and projects Islamic ideas which do not permit such percentages.

But in South India temple managements dominated by priests and brāhmaṇas did invest gold with the village assemblies and others, and received interest thereon for the maintenance of worship, perpetual burning of lamps, and similar other purposes. All this was done on religious grounds, and we have yet to find examples of money-lending carried on by the brāhmaṇa for secular purposes.

RATES OF INTEREST

From the fifth century BC onwards metal coins came into use, and loans were given in both cash and kind. Some early lawgivers, such as Baudhāyana[29] and Gautama,[30] clearly mention the percentage in terms of coins, which shows that money-lending was practised. Some later lawgivers do not clarify it, but the rates they laid down apparently refer to loans in cash, for in regard to loans in kind they do not indicate the rate but merely prescribe the maximum to which the interest can rise.

The rates of interest laid down by the legal texts show a tendency towards gradual increase. Baudhāyana prescribes 10 per cent per year,[31] but Gautama, whose law-book was compiled later, raises it to 15 per cent,[32] which is supported by Vasiṣṭha.[33] This rate is endorsed by not only the *Arthaśāstra* of Kauṭilya[34] but also by the law-books of the first six centuries of the Christian era.[35] Medieval lawgivers

[28] *Alberuni's India*, II, ed. and tr. by Edward C. Sachau, London, 1910, 150.

[29] I. 10.22. [30] XII. 29. [31] I. 10.22.

[32] XII. 29. [33] II. 51. [34] III. 11.

[35] *Yājñavalkya Smṛti with Vīramitodaya and Mitākṣarā*, Chowkhamba Sanskrit Series, Banaras, 1930 (Yāj); Nārada Smṛti (*Nar*); Bṛhaspati Smṛti (*Bṛ*).

and commentators held that it applied only to loans for which securities were furnished. Vyāsa, whose code was compiled some time between AD 600 and 900, laid down that the monthly rate of interest was 1/80 of the principal (15 per cent) when a pledge or mortgage was given aginst the loan, 1/60 (20 per cent) when a surety was offered, and 2 per month 24 per cent when the money was lent on personal security.[36] Hārīta, whose law-book belonged to this period, also prescribes 24 per cent in case of absence of security,[37] Vṛddha-Hārīta adds that double the normal interest (30 per cent) may be taken when there is nothing pledged to secure the debt.[38] Thus by about the ninth century there seems to have taken place an appreciable increase in the rate of normal interest, which in general rose from 12 per cent in the fifth century BC to 24 per cent in the ninth century AD. The strikingly lesser use of coin during the four centuries following the Gupta period leads us to think that the supply of cash was limited and consequently the rate of interest higher. Decline in foreign trade may have been an important reason for want of cash.

The rules quoted seem to apply to ordinary transactions in normal times. Money lent for purposes of trade is charged higher interest. Kauṭilya characterizes 15 per cent as legal but lays down 60 per cent for those who are engaged in ordinary trade, 120 per cent for those trader who traverse forests, and 240 per cent for those carry on maritime trade.[39] Exactly the same rates for the three grades of traders are laid down by Yājñavalkya,[40] whose eleventh-century scholiast, Vijñāneśvara, explains the reasons for it. According to him these exorbitant rates are justified by the danger of the loss of even the principal as the debtors may perish on account of shipwreck or the attacks of robbers and wild beasts.[41] Since these rates seem to be too excessive for the Maurya period, it seems that they were introduced into the *Arthaśāstra* at a later stage. The other possibility that Yājñavalkya might have borrowed from Kauṭilya seems to be remote.

[36] *HDS*, III, 421.

[37] Quoted in Caṇḍeśvara Ṭhakkura's *Gṛhastharatnākara* (Bibliotheca Indica, Calcutta, 1918), 447.

[38] *HDS*, III, 420–21.

[39] *Arthaśāstra of Kauṭilya*, (ed.), R. Shamasastri, third edition, Mysore (hereinafter *AS*), III. 11.

[40] II. 38.

[41] *Mitākṣarā* on *Yāj.*, II. 38.

Besides loans for trade, in certain other cases the interest prescribed is high. Katyāyana, a lawgiver of about the sixth century ordains that what is lent through friendship, a deposit, balance of interest, and unpaid purchase money, if not returned on demand, begin to carry interest at 5 per cent per month[42] which works out at the rate of 60 per cent annually. The same rate can be inferred from a provision of Nārada.[43]

The early lawgivers Gautama, Baudhāyana, Āpastamba, and Kauṭilya do not introduce any considerations of *varṇa* in the payment of interest, which is done for the first time by Vasiṣṭha,[44] and followed by the law-givers of the early centuries of the Christian Era.[45] Brāhmaṇas are required to pay 24 per cent per year, kṣatriyas 36 per cent, vaiśyas 48 per cent, and śūdras 60 per cent.[46] According to the mediaeval commentators (the comment of Nanda Paṇḍita to Viṣṇu VI.2) it applies to loans without pledges, but this does not account for *varṇa* discrimination in fixing interest. It might, however, explain a higher rate, i.e. 24 per cent even for the brāhmaṇa which considerably exceeds the normal legal rate of 15 per cent. On the other hand differences in rates according to the *varṇas* might be explained on the ground of the helplessness of the members of the lower orders, whose economic position was generally worse than those of the higher *varṇas*.[47] The practice is followed even now in villages where śūdras are charged higher rates of interest. According to the *Sarasvatīvilāsa,* a work of the sixteenth century, these discriminatory laws do not apply if the debtor and the creditor belong to the same caste; in that case the interest shall be at the flat rate of 24 per cent per year. Thus if a kṣatriya gives loan to a kṣatriya he will charge 24 per cent; if to a vaiśya, 36 per cent; and if to śūdra, 48 per cent.[48] Similarly if a vaiśya gives loan to a vaiśya, he will charge 24 per cent; and is to a śūdra, 36 per cent.[49] The provisions indicate a softening of

[42] Verses 505–506.

[43] I. 109.

[44] II. 48.

[45] *Manu*, VIII. 142; *Viṣṇu*, VI. 2; *Yāj*., II. 37; *Nār.*, 1. 100.

[46] Ibid.

[47] R.S. Sharma, *Some Economic Aspects of the Caste System in Ancient India*, Patna, 1952, pp. 16–21.

[48] *Sarsvatīvilāsa,* quoted in *Dharmakośa*, I, (ed.), Laxman Shastri Joshi in three parts, Wai, 1937–41(hereinafter *DK*).

[49] Ibid.

the *varṇa* distinctions in matters of interest in late mediaeval times though it would be wrong to think they were followed to the letter in early mediaeval times. At least the available epigraphic material does not indicate any social distinctions in the levy of interest.

During post-Maurya times in northern and western India endowments in money were invested with guilds, which undertook to pay a certain amount of interest for carrying on worship and meeting the needs of the monks and other religious people. In a Nasik inscription of the second century AD the rate of interest prescribed for payment is lower than that recommended by Manu.[50] The clearest hint of interest rates is thrown by the south Indian inscriptions of the early mediaeval period. Several tenth-century endowments from the Tamil country under the Coḷas suggest 15 per cent as the usual rate of interest. Two inscriptions of the reign of Parāntaka I, one of AD 936[51] and the other of AD 937[52], can be interpreted in this light. In one case 4½ *kalañju* of gold per year was charged as interest on 30 *kalañju,* which was endowed for burning a perpetual lamp[53] in honour of Mahādeva. In another case gold was invested with the residents of a settlement who agreed to pay interest once in six months at the rate of three *mañjāḍi,* per *kalañju* annually.[54] Since one *kalañju* is equal to 20 *mañjāḍi,* it works out at the rate of 15 per cent per year. Again, an inscription of AD 986 records that in the reign of Uttama Coḷa 200 *kalañju* of gold was deposited with the inhabitants of four settlements on a perpetual interest of 30 *kalañju* per year, which again amounts to 15 per cent.[55] These three instances would show that on gold invested by temples and similar religious institution, which they received as endowment, the village assemblies paid interest of 15 per cent annually, which was the legal rate (*dharmya*) prescribed by the law-books of ancient and mediaeval times.

But we also come across certain variations, which generally exceed 15 per cent and rarely fall below it. Thus an epigraph of AD 979, belonging to the reign of Uttama Coḷa, records that the assembly of a settlement received 24 *kalañju* and agreed to pay an annual interest of one *kalañju* and four *mañjāḍi* of gold, which amounts to 5 per cent per year.[56] However, as early as the eighth century AD gold given for

[50] D.C. Sircar, *Seclect Inscriptions Bearing on Indian History and Civilisation*, I, Calcutta, 1965 (hereinafter *Sel. Inscr.*) I, BK. II, no. 58, LL. 1–3; of *Manu* VIII. 139–42.

[51] *South Indian Inscriptions* (hereinafter *SII*), III, pt. 3, 237.

[52] Ibid., 237. [53] Ibid., 236. [54] Ibid., 237. [55] Ibid., 274. [56] Ibid., 273.

the perpetual burning of lamp in a temple in the Bāṇa kingdom carried an annual interest of 20 per cent, 4 *kalañju* of gold being fixed as interest on 20 *kalañju.*[57] A century later an epigraph of AD 940, belonging to the reign of Parāntaka I, shows that a yearly interest of 40 per cent was charged on a deposit for religious purposes.[58] These examples show the temples as money-lenders and roughly indicate that the rate of interest in south India generally corresponded to the early Dharmaśāstra rate of 15 per cent and not the later rate of 24 per cent.

The epigraphic evidence for the rate of interest in northern India during the some period is slender. An inscription shows that the Mahājanas of Śīvapura paid 25 per cent interest on the deposit of 6 *gadāyanas,*[59] nearly the same as recommended by Vyāsa[60] and Hārita,[61] who prescribe 24 per cent per year. The same rate is mentioned by Alberuni in the eleventh century. He states that only the śūdra is allowed to take percentages as long as his profit is not more than a fiftieth of the capital.[62] Hence in early mediaeval times 24 per cent seems to have been the normal rate of interest on loans in cash in northern India. This was obviously much less than later rates which allowed the principal to double itself in three years. Later lawgivers do not prescribe any such time-limit, and hence the principal can double in six years and eight months at the rate of 15 per cent annually. But in the ninth or the tenth entury, when the normal interest came to be recognized as 24 per cent, it was laid down by Hārita that the principal is doubled after four years and two months at the rate of 8 paṇas per month for 25 purāṇas,[63] one purāṇa being equal to 16 paṇas according to it.

None the less the limit of interest being equal to the principal is generally accepted by all lawgivers. Nārada, however, adds that in some countries a loan grows to twice the principal, in others 3,4, or 8 times.[64] It is not clear whether he thinks here in terms of cash or kind. Bṛhaspati simply sates that the loan and its recovery should be regulated by local custom,[65] which may mean the same thing as Nārada's

[57] *EI*, XI, 228–29.

[58] ¼ *puttakkam* was the interest charged on 1 *ilakkāsu* for one month, and 1 *ilakkāsu* was equal to 7½ *puttakkam*. *SII*, III, part 3, 239.

[59] *EI*, XII, 273.

[60] *Gṛhastharatnākara*, 447.

[61] Ibid.

[62] E. Sachau, *op. cit.*, 150.

[63] *DK*, I, part 2, 608.

[64] *Nar.*, I. 106–107.

[65] XIII. 24.

provision. In the later mediaeval period a passage ascribed to Gautama states that the principal is doubled in sixteen months, which raises the rate of interest to 150 per cent. Thus the tendency to reduce the period in which the interest can reach the maximum seems to be fairly strong in mediaeval times.

As pointed out earlier, the maximum amount of interest that could be claimed by the creditor was equal to the principal—what is known as *dvaiguṇyam* in legal texts. But if double the principal (including principal and interest) was not paid in time, further interest could be charged. Thus Manu seems to suggest that if the interest becomes equal to the principal and is not paid, it should be compounded with the principal.[66] Kātyāyana lays down that if the creditor does not get twice the amount lent by him, to which he is always entitled, this should be compounded with the capital on which further interest shall accrue.[67] Commenting on Manu, VIII. 155, Medhātithi states that the rate of interest on the new principal should be reduced and continued till such time as does not render it oppressive, the idea being that it should be lower than the former rate. The maximum limit of the interest, more than double the principal, is also contemplated by Vijñāneśvara. Commenting on *Yāj.*, II. 39, he stipulates that if the interest is recovered daily, monthly, or yearly and is not claimed in a lump sum at one time, then the total interest received by a creditor may be even more than double the principal lent. This provision is not confined to certain areas or certain articles, as done by Nārada and Bṛhaspati, but made a general rule, which shows that by the eleventh century what ever little prejudice there existed against the maximum accumulation of interest had disappeared, and it could cross the normal limit (double the principal). The law can be better appreciated if we bear in mind the needs of trade which revived in Gujarat and Rajasthan. Since the eleventh century we also find considerable trade in Karnataka and Tamil Nadu.

The idea of compound interest occurs in Gautama,[68] but since none of his contemporaries mentions it may not have occurred in the original law-book. The provision, however, recurs in Manu,[69] Nārada,[70] and Bṛhaspati.[71] Curiously enough it is not referred to by Kātyāyana, whose laws on interest are very elaborate. Asahāya, who flourished

[66] *Manu*, VIII. 155.
[67] Verse 509.
[68] XII. 34–35.
[69] VIII. 156.
[70] *DK,* I, part 2, 625.
[71] XI. 4–9.

some time in the eighth century, defines and illustrates the practice of compound interest at great length. According to him one *dramma* lent as principal can be multiplied by 500 times, and the process of compound interest can continue for 33 years and 4 months.[72]

Considering the nature of the economy in ancient and early mediaeval times it would be reasonable to expect more loans in kind than in cash. The practice of lending grain was as old as the time of Gautama and Vasiṣṭha The ancient lawgivers down to the time of Manu seek to regulate the return of a few articles given on loan, but these provisions became more detailed in the law-books from Gupta times onwards. Vasiṣṭha lays down that the return on grain, roots, fruits, and fluids shall be three times, and that on things that can be weighed shall be eight times.[73] It appears that the articles which can be weighed were meant to be loaned to small traders by big traders or producers. Gautama prescribes a higher rate, although he does not differentiate between various kinds of articles. According to him on loans of grain fruits , wool, and beasts of burden, and products such as ghee and milk from cattle, the total recoverable cannot exceed in any case five times the capital.[74] The provision is literally repeated by Manu.[75] Here again it appears suspicious whether the provision formed a part of the original law-book of Gautama, because his near contemporary Vasiṣṭha mentions a rate of only 3 times on grain. Viṣṇu[76] and Nārada[77] lay down the following schedule more or less on similar lines:

gold	2 times
grain	3 times
cloth	4 times
liquids	8 times
women and cattle	one issue

Bṛhaspati's provision regarding gold is exactly the same as that of the two lawgivers but is somewhat different regarding other articles, as would appear from the following[78].

gold	2 times
cloth and base metals	3 times
grain, edible plants, cattle, and wool	4 times

[72] *DK*, I, part 2, 625.
[73] II. 44–47. [74] XII. 36 [75] VIII. 151.
[76] VI. 11–15. [77] I. 106–107. [78] XI. 13–15.

pot-herbs	5 times
seeds and sugarcane	6 times
salt, oil, and spirit	8 times

Kātyāyana's provision on the point is detailed. According to him precious stones, pearls, corals, gold, silver, fruits, silk, and wool increase by two times; base metals by five times; and oils, liquors, ghee, raw sugar, salt, and land by eight times.[79] That the loan of land increases by eight times is also confirmed by Pitāmaha, who is assigned to AD 600–900.[80] Here the striking thing is the provision for the loan of land, on which eightfold return would mean eight times the produce from one harvest.

Viṣṇu and Bṛhaspati mention certain articles on which increase in interest is unlimited. Viṣṇu states that on wool, cotton, thread, leather, shield, weapon, bricks, coal, etc., there is no limit to interest[81] (*akṣaya*). Bṛhaspati declares that on these articles no interest is ordained.[82] The term *akṣaya,* used by Viṣṇu, is interpreted in another context as 100 times by the *Smṛticandrikā,*[83] which refers to flowers, fruits, roots, etc., in this connection.

It is difficult to account for the difference concerning the maximum accumulation of various articles given on loan. As regards grain, difference in rate ranged from three times prescribed by Vasiṣṭha and Viṣṇu and Nārada to five times prescribed by Gautama and Manu. In between comes Bṛhaspati, who makes it four times. Kātyāyana does not mention it. The difference does not seem to be chronological but regional, for Nārada points out that in certain countries interest grows three, four, or five times.

It is obvious that for day-to-day use the common folk would be more in need of grain, seeds, cattle, etc., than in need of cash. This would be particularly true of the early medieval period which was marked by less of trade, urbanism and coinage. High rates charged for cereals and other articles remind us of similar rates prescribed for vaiśyas, and particularly śūdras, in giving them loans in cash. Apparently in extending loans to the common folk the lawgivers had in mind their inability to pay in time. Another factor that led to the demand for a higher return in the case of some articles was their perishable nature. Since gold and silver were more lasting and valuable, they could increase by two times. On the other hand there was no

[79] Verses 510–12. [80] *DK*, I, part 2, 634.
[81] VI. 16. [82] XI. 16. [83] *DK*, I, part 2, 609.

limit to interest on cheap articles of common use such as ferment (*kiṇva*), cotton, thread, leather, shield, weapons, bricks, charcoal, all enumerated by Nārada and Bṛhaspati, and roots, fruits, flowers, etc., added by the *Smṛticandrikā*. It is remarkable that fruits, on which according to earlier lawgivers the return ranged from two to five times, came to be considered in the mediaeval age as a source of exploiting the people, who, in consequence of their borrowing, could not be free from the eternal obligation of serving their creditors in various ways. What might explain the provision for return on certain marketable commodities such as base metals, salt, raw sugar, liquor, ghee, oil, etc., is the fact that these were borrowed by retail traders who were supposed to earn more profit on them. The provision for borrowing land and giving eightfold return on it, given by Kātyāyana and corroborated by Pitāmaha, seems to be unique in early mediaevel India. It tooks like the practice of temporary subinfeudation for the land so borrowed would have to be returned to the creditor. In effect it would mean adding to the number of temporary tenants. Perhaps such a law refers to a period of economic or political crisis when the distressed and uprooted peasants approached the landowners for some plots of land in search of livelihood.

Very few lawgivers set the time-limit for reaching the maximum in regard to articles given on loan, although it is reasonable to expect such a limit. Commenting on a passage of Hārita,[84] Caṇḍeśvara points out that if payment is made with the gathering of the next harvest within two to three months, grain (taken on loan) becomes double; if it is not given back at that time, it becomes treble but not more than that,[85] an explanation also given in a work of the fifteenth century.[86] According to Hārita this also applies to wool and cotton given on loan.[87] Ghee, salt, and raw sugar increase eightfold in a year according to Hārita and the commentary of Caṇdeśvara in his *Vivādaratnākara* on him[88]. It appears that in mediaeval times this time-limit of one year was prescribed for all articles made over as loan except grain, wool, and cotton for the return of which two or three months were allowed.

[84] *tule tu dvigunaṃ dhānyaṃ triguṇameva vardhate*, *DK*, I, 608.

[85] *Vivādaratnākara* quoted ibid., 608–609.

[86] *Vivādacandra* of Misaru Mishra quoted in ibid. It seems that the principal is to be collected in addition to this.

[87] Ibid. [88] Ibid.

KINDS OF INTEREST

It is curious that the forms of interest seem to be fairly well-developed in the law-book of Gautama, ascribable to the fifth-third centuries BC. It mentions six kinds of interest: compound, periodical, stipulated, corporal(*kāyikā*), daily, and pledge-using.[89] But Manu, who is placed later than Gautama, mentions only four kinds,[90] which raises doubts about the antiquity of this provision inserted in Gautama. Whatever be the precise dating of these provisions, it is definite that the various forms of interest were defined in detail some time between the fifth and seventh centuries AD. Thus Nārada not only[91] enumerates four kinds of interest but also defines each one of them. Bṛhaspati makes it six and describes each one of them in some detail.[92] According to him the *kāyikā* (corporal interest?) means the milk of a pledged cow or animals used by the creditor, which thus excludes the exploitation of the physical labour of the debtor by the creditor. Periodical interest (*kālikā*) means monthly payment. Stipulated interest (*kāritā*) implies the interest promised by the borrower over and above the normal interest in times of distress. Compound interest (*cakravṛddhi*) is interest received everyday; it does not cease growing except on the loss of the head. Interest-bearing pledge (*bhogalābha*) is interest by enjoyment, such as the use of a mortgaged house, the produce of a field, etc.[93] Bṛhaspati adds that hair-interest, corporal interest, and interest by enjoyment shall be taken by the creditor as long as the principal remains unpaid.[94] We do not know why this rule does not apply to periodical (*kālikā*) and stipulated (*kāritā*) forms of interest. Perhaps the first four forms of interest are deducted from capital, but neither of the last two reduces the capital in any way. A later lawgiver, Kātyāyana, does not mention all the six forms of interest, for periodical and compound varieties are left out by him. He, however, devotes seven verses (502-508) to *akṛta vṛddhi*, unagreed interest, not found in other texts. There he contemplates imposition of interest under various conditions. Thus when a person takes a temporary loan and goes to another country before

[89] *cakrakālavṛddhiḥ kāritākāyikāśikhādhibhogaśca*, XII. 31–32 quoted in *DK*, I, part 2, 607.

[90] VIII. 154.

[91] II. 87–89 quoted in *DK*, I, part 2, 624–25.

[92] XI. 4–9. [93] Ibid. [94] XI. II.

repayment, it begins to acquire interest after a year.[95] If a person after taking a loan goes to another country without repaying it even when pressed by the lender, that loan begins to acquire interest within three months.[96] When the borrower of a thing does not return it on demand, the king should make him pay interest since the day of demand, though it was not agreed upon when he was in the country, and though he be unwilling to pay interest.[97] It is apparent that all the cases carry an interest of 5 per cent.

In about the eighth century Asahāya, commenting on the four forms of interest prescribed by Nārada, deals at some length with each one of these. *Kālikā* or periodical interest is that where payment is made every month.[98] *Kāritā* is that which is agreed to by the debtor in times of distress according to the interest laid down by the law-books; here the debtor agrees to pay a higher interest, say 10 per cent more.[99] *Kāyikā* is explained by Asahāya at some length. Herein the capital (*dravyapiṇḍa*) is considered to be *kāya,* and the daily interest that accrues on it in the form of *paṇa* or a *pāda* does not reduce it in any way, and the capital remains as it was. According to Asahāya, this interest is paid by the debtor in the form of daily wages (*divasabhāṭaka-vṛdhyācāreṇa*), which incidentally does not amount to more than a *paṇa* or *pāda.*[100] *Cakravṛddhi,* as shown earlier, is explained in detail by Asahāya. Here the capital can increase 500 times, and the king is instructed to make the debtor pay the interest.[101]

Of the forms of interest prevalent from the beginning of the Christian era onwards there is some confusion about the interpretation of the *kāyikā.* It is not clear from the lawgivers whether the bodily labour of the debtor could be exploited by the creditor in lieu of interest, but the commentators imply this clearly. Asahāya indicates that the interest has to be paid in the form of daily wages, which obviously would accrue to the debtor as his remuneration for working for the creditor.[102]

An early mediaeval lawgiver, Vyāsa, explains *kāyikā* as that which is accompanied by milching and carrying (*dohyavāhya-karmasaṁyutā*).[103] This is explained by Caṇḍeśvara as pledging cows and oxen.[104]

95 Verse 502. 96 Verse 503. 97 Verse 504.

98 *DK*, I, part 2, 625.

99 Ibid. 100 Ibid.

101 Ibid. 102 Ibid.

103 *DK*, I, part 2, 634.

104 *Vivādaratnākara* quoted in ibid.

Medhātithi, commenting on Manu, VIII. 153, made it clear that the *kāyikā* interest has to be cleared through bodily labour.[105] This is roundly supported by Govindarāja (eleventh century),[106] and Haradatta (1100–1300).[107] Sarvajñanārāyaṇa, who belonged to the same period as Haradatta, commenting on Manu, VIII. 153 states that bodily service should be rendered gradually till the principal is not cleared.[108] A verse quoted in the *Smṛticandrikā* of Devaṇṇabhaṭṭa (1150–1225) states that *kāyikā* is based on performance of work.[109] In the ancient period failure to pay debts (which would include both the principal and the interest) was an important source of slavery. The provision to make the debtors work in lieu of interest so long as the capital was not paid implies some kind of bonded labour in early mediaeval times. Such rules leave clear scope for enjoying the manual labour of the debtor in return for interest and remind us of the continuing practice according to which several generations of the same family are reduced to the position of hereditary ploughmen in consideration of a paltry sum advanced to them. Therefore, in view of the general paucity of coins in the four centuries following the fall of the Gupta empire, *kāyikā* should be considered an important and widely prevalent from of interest. However, only the members of a caste lower than that of the creditor could be subjected to bodily labour for recovery of loans, and consequently the incidence of this interest fell more heavily on the members of lower orders.

In the economic context of early mediaeval times the practice of giving pledge for interest deserves as much attention as *kāyikā*. Mentioned in the earlier law-books of Gautama and Manu, pledge became obligatory and prevalent from the Gupta times onwards. Bṛhaspati lays down that a creditor should never lend money without having first secured a pledge of adequate value or a deposit, or some trustworthy security, nor without a bond written by the debtor himself.[110] Along with Nārada[111] he[112] provides for the enjoyment of pledge in lieu of interest. According to him the pledge which was not given in

[105]*kāyakarmaṇā saṃśodhyā*, *DK*, I, part 2, 616.
[106]Ibid., 617.
[107]*Gautama-Mitākṣarā* quoted in ibid., 607.
[108]Ibid., 617.
[109]*kāyikā kāryakarmaṇā*, *DK*, I, part 2, 635.
[110]XI. I.
[111]I. 129.
[112]XI. 7–8.

liew of interest lapses to the creditor a fortnight after the date when the principal is doubled or the stipulated period has expired.[113] On the contrary according to Nārada, the foolish fellow who enjoys the pledge without the authorization of the owner should enjoy only half the interest.[114] Again, the creditor who enjoys pledge (*bandhaka*) without the term (period) of the debt being complete out of greed is not entitled to any profit, for such a pledge should be protected like deposit (*nyāsa*); if it is not, interest is destroyed.[115] The same idea is expressed by Nārada according to whom a pledge should not be used by force; if the creditor does so he should surrender the interest due to him from his debtor. Moreover, he must compensate the owner for the pledge or else he is considered a thief appropriating the pledge.[116]

Early mediaeval law-books represent fields as an important form of pledge; this form is not mentioned by Gautama and Manu or any other early lawgiver. In his provisions regarding pledge Yājñavalkya gives no indication whatsoever that field was given as pledge for enjoyment in lieu of interest, nor does Nārada[117] specify it. The first to include fields as a source of interest is Bṛhaspati. According to him the use of a mortgaged house or the produce of a field is termed *bhogalābha* (interest by enjoyment).[118] Together with Kātyāyana he lays down several provisions regarding the enjoyment of fields. Kātyāyana provides that the boundaries of the house or the land to be pledged and the villages or the countries in which they are situated be defined.[119] The details about the identity of villages made over as religious gifts were given, and the procedure may have appeared in secular transactions.Bṛhaspati ordains that one field mortgaged to two creditors at the same time shall belong to that mortgagee who was the first to obtain possession of it.[120] If both have possessed it for an equal length of time, it shall be held in common (or shared equally) by them.[121] Bṛhaspati ordains that when a field or other immovable property has been enjoyed and the principal and interest actually got out of it by the creditor, the debtor receives back his pledge.[122] This shows that land was given towards the payment of both the principal and the interest. Kātyāyana adds that the debtor can get back his

[113] *Bṛ.*, XI. 27. [114] I. 128.
[115] *Bṛ.* quoted in *DK*, I, part 2, 350.
[116] IV. 127 (quoted in *DK*, I, part 2, 650).
[117] I. 125. [118] XI. 7–8.
[119] Verse 522. [120] XI. 34.
[121] *Bṛ.*, XI. 34. [122] *Bṛ.*, XI. 23.

field, etc., given for enjoyment as interest, from the creditor on paying back the amount he had taken.[123] On the contrary, according to Bṛhaspati, when a house or field is mortgaged for use and period fixed for such use does not expire, the debtor cannot recover his property nor can the creditor recover his loan.[124] But when the stipulated period has elapsed both parties are at liberty to do so. Nevertheless, even before the stipulated period has expired, they may make a special arrangement for recovery by mutual consent.[125]

The practice of mortgaging land for interest, which began towards the end of the Gupta period, continued widely for another three or four centuries. Thus Asahāya (700–750), commenting on two kinds of pledge mentioned by Nārada, cites a house and a field as instances of a pledge for use.[126] Similarly, commenting on Manu VIII. 143, Medhātithi states that a cow is given as *ādhi* for enjoying its produce; hence the creditor is not entitled to any interest (*vṛddhi* or *kusīda*). Vyāsa, who probably belonged to the same period as Medhātithi, explains *ādhi* similarly. When somebody accepts money (*dravya*) having settled interest on it and asks the creditor to enjoy his field in return for interest and to apply the excess towards the payment of principal, it is called *ādhi* or *sapratyaya bhogyādhiḥ;* it is released when twice the amount of the loan is paid.[127] Even where land is not pledged it can be sold to clear off the debts. According to Bharadvāja if the debtor is unable to pay, his property is to be sold for payment, including his land, fields, garden, and house.[128] This again points to the practice of pledging land for the payment of debts. Curiously enough the *Mitākṣarā* does not favour it. But the practice certainly obtained in early mediaeval times, and must have added to the landed property of the creditors on failure of payment of the principal. It is even stated that pledges of land can be enjoyed for one hundred years, like a form of commendation in the feudal context. In mediaeval Europe the poor people surrendered their land to some lord in return for protection. But here it was done in return for a loan. Commendation in Europe entitled the lord to a share of the produce of land surrendered in return for protection afforded by him, but pledge of land in India authorized him to enjoy its whole produce.

[123]Verse 516. [124] XI. 32.
[125] *Bṛ.*, XI. 33.
[126]*SBE,* XXXIII, 73 fn.
[127]*DK*, I, part 2, 658.
[128]Ibid., 731.

Actual instances of mortgage of land are wanting in India, but the provisions of the law-books belonging to AD 600–900 suggest that the practice was widespread. At least two epigraphic records from northern India indicate the mortgage of land. A deed of mortgage (*vittabandha*) of AD 1212 shows the influential head of a Śaivite temple accepting mortgage of a village in consideration of an amount advanced to the mortgagee which might imply pledge in lien of interest. In this case the mortgagee was given all the rights of collecting taxes;[130] he also appears to have been empowered to hold the village in pledge as long as he wished, probably meaning thereby till all the dues were cleared.[131] The other, the Jaunpur brick inscription of AD 1217, shows that a person borrowed 2,250 *drammas* on the security of cultivated lands.[132] There may have have been more inscriptions of this type.

As shown earlier, numerous epigraphic reords refer to the investment of gold by the temples for burning perpetual lamp and performing regular worship, but they do not specify anywhere the mortgage of land by the village assembly or the debtors for the purpose. However, the terms of investment do imply full or partial use of land by the temples in lieu of interest on the principal, mostly made up of a certain measure of gold usually advanced to the village assembly, which set apart a part of the produce of the land as interest for maintaining the offerings on lamps. Thus in AD 877–78 the Pāṇḍya king Varaguṇa-Maharāja granted to a temple 290 *kāśu* of gold, in return for which the members of the temples assembly undertook to measure out 580 *kalam* of paddy per year (as interest, at the rate of two *kalam* for each *kāśu* for meeting the requirements of the offerings 'for a long time.'[133] Significantly enough all the articles meant for offerings and enumerated in a long list given in the Pāṇḍya inscription are priced in terms of paddy, which indicates that the use of coin was very limited at this stage in south India. Thus the interest on the investment of gold was collected in crops, for which it was necessary to set apart certain fields. This can be also inferred from other inscriptions. An epigraph of the reign of Āditya I inform us that a priest of the temple of Āirāvateśvara received from a Pallava queen the

[129]*EI*, XXV, no. 1, lines 10–21.
[130]Ibid.
[131]The meaning of l. 19 is not clear. *EI*, XXV, p. 3.
[132]*JASB*, XIX, 454–56.
[133]*EI*, IX, 91–94.

gold assuring her that, from the interest accruing at the rate of 1/8 of very crop on each *kalañju,* he would maintain the charity; the gift was placed under the protection of the assembly of all Māhaeśvaras.[134] So here also the deposit in gold bears interest in crop. An inscription of AD 910 informs us that the wife of the son of the Coḷa king Parāntaka I gave 60 *kaḷañju* of pure gold as capital to the members of the assembly of a temple who undertook to supply in perpetuity 60 *kalam* of paddy per year, at the rate of 30 *kalam* per harvest[135] as interest. From the Madras Museum plates of Uttama-Coḷa we learn that in AD 992 the assemblies of two places received 250 *kaḷañju* of gold from the temple and agreed to measure every year as interest there on 500 *kāḍi* of paddy.[136] According to a document of the same year 50 *kaḷañju* was received by the assembly of Uḷai-ūr, which agreed to render annually an interest there on of 150 *kāḍi* of paddy.[137] In the eighth year of Pārthivendravarman a village assembly received 15 *kaḷañju* of gold for a temple, and agreed to pay an annual interest of 50 *kāḍi* of paddy on that amount.[138] These examples from the ninth to the eleventh century have been cited to show that in return for gold lent to them on behalf of the temples the assemblies provided certain quantities of produce, probably by earmarking certain fields owned by the assemblies for the service of the gods. An epigraphic record of the second half of the tenth century shows that land was sold to the temples for gold.[139] In several cases in the Coḷa dominions in return for gold the land was made tax-free and its produces transferred to the temples, so that the whole produce of the land was given as compensation for the principal in gold. All these allied practices fit in well with the cutsom of using the produce of fields in return for money loaned to their owners, which must have greatly added to the landed property of the temples in south India.

We have hardly any instance of temples in north India lending gold directly for interest collected in the form of crops or land attached to them. But the Āhār stone inscription shows how the revenues of the temples of the goddess Kanakadevī, situated in the town of Tattānandapura, probably identical with modern Āhāra in Rajasthan,[140] invested its revenues in the purchase of houses which

[134]*SII*, III, part 3, 227.
[135]Ibid., 229. [136] Ibid., 273.
[137]Ibid. [138] Ibid., 363.
[139]*SII*, III, part 3, 263.
[140]R.D.R. Sahni, *EI,* XIX, no. 7.

were let out on rent. The process covers a period of nearly 40 years from AD 864 to 904,[141] and shows that the rent of the houses was estimated in terms of money, to be spent on regular worship in the temple. In all, the inscription contains eight documents, of which four clearly refer to the rent enjoyed by the temple on the *āvārīs*, houses or shops, let out by it.[142] Particularly, Document No. X speaks of the purchase of six *āvārīs,* the rent accruing from which was to be religiously applied to the provision of saffron, incense, flowers, lamps, and flags, and to whitewashing and the repairs of the broken portions of the temples—a condition which is attached to the rent derived from another house acquired by the temple with its own *drammas.*[143] Of these four, two documents clearly refer to surety of house in lieu of 10 *vimśopakas* to be paid to the temple every month.[144] This was to be enjoyed by the descendants of the donor after they had paid every month to the temple.[145] This would imply that the house was owned jointly by the owner and the management of the temple, who enjoyed it as a form of pledge tendered to them. However, in the second case, according to Document no. VIII it appears that probably the descendants of the donor were given some money by the temple in consideration of which they made over the entire rent of the house by a deed of ninety-nine years to the holy Kanakaśrīdevī (so that here the rent would be in the form of interest accruing on the principal invested on the lease of the house). In four other cases, i.e., Document Nos. V, VI, VII, and IX, it is not mentioned whether houses acquired out of the funds of the temple were let out on rent, but the context of the inscription leaves no doubt about it. All these instances show that the temple of Kanakaśrī did not derive any interest on its investments, as did the temples in south India, but received rent from the houses which were purchased with its funds. In form, rent and interest cannot be taken to be the same, but in substance there is hardly any difference between the two. Rent on houses purchased by the temple was obviously the interest accruing on the money with which the houses were purchased.

In the town of Tattānandapura several other temples seem to have lived on rent. This practice could be linked with increasing trade and commerce since the end of the ninth century in western India. What

[141] *EI*, XIX, no. 7.

[142] Ibid., Document nos II, IV, VIII and X.

[143] Ibid., Document no. II.

[144] Ibid., Document nos IV and VIII.

[145] Ibid.

futher distinguishes this town is the fact that rent was to be collected in money, which is not found in the case of south Indian temples which lent the principal in gold but charged interest in paddy or crops. Since many persons from whom houses were purchased by the temple were merchants, Tattānadapura was apparently a great centre of trade and commerce which put considerable amounts of money in circulation.

EXEMPTIONS FROM PAYMENT OF INTEREST, AND DEBT COLLECTION

Exemption from interest on religious grounds is allowed by Kauṭilya, according to whom no interest can be charged where the debtor is engaged in a Vedic sacrifice of long duration, or staying at his teacher's house (*gurukula*) for study, or is a minor, or is a man without substance.[146] We do not know whether this provision, mainly in favour of priests, continued in later times.

Normally, both on money and a commodity, the borrower had to pay interest in early mediaeval times. But under certain conditions exemption was allowed. No interest could be charged on a short-term loan from a friend unless agreed.[147] It could yield interest only if the debtor refused to restore it on demand by the creditor.[148] So here exemption from interest is governed mainly by the nature of personal relations between the debtor and the creditor. According to Nārada no interest can be charged on wages, on a deposit, on a fine, on that which has been idly promised (to bards and the like), and on the stake won in gambling, unless there is an express agreement to pay interest.[149] Kātyāyana also lays down a similar but detailed injunction that hides (or armour), crops, wine, gambling debts incurred as surety do not bear interest at any time.[150] Oddly enough, he recommends at another place eightfold interest on liquor;[151] we do not know how to explain it. Certain abnormal conditions invalidate interest.

[146] *AS*, III. 11.
[147] *Nar.*, I, 108; *Kātyā*, verse 505.
[148] *Nar.*, I, 109; *Kātyā*, verse 505.
[149] *Nar.*, II. 36.
[150] Verse 508.
[151] Verse 511. Here the term used is *madya* and not *āsava* as in verse 508.

Thus Vasiṣṭha declares that interest stops the moment the king dies and begins to run only after the coronation of the successor.[152] Perhaps it is apprehended that in the absence of the king or in a state of anarchy exorbitant interest might be exacted, and hence the basic condition for any normal activity is political order and stability. This provision is elaborated by Prājāpati, a lawgiver assignable to the period AD 600–900. He states that 'in famines, countrywide disturbance (*rāṣṭrasambādhe*), religious work, and distress, only the principal debt is to be given, not the interest; this is definite.'[153] This probably refers to natural calamities, peasant unrest and other types of crisis in early mediaeval times runs counter to the view expressed in the *Garuḍa Purāṇa* that interest grows in all circumstances.

In collecting interest and the principal from the debtors, creditors were backed by the authority of both the state and religion. The Buddhist Order did not admit a person who had not cleared off his debts. The Buddhists dwelt on the virtues of paying off debts. Nārada declares that if the fellow does not pay off his debts, the amount goes on increasing till it reaches one hundred *koṭis* (1,000 million), and the person not paying it is born again and again as a horse, an ass, an ox, and a slave.[154] Kātyāyana adds that such a debtor is born as a slave, a servant, a man, or a beast in the house of the creditor.[155] But these curses are not considered enough to make the debtor pay. The authority of the state is therefore invoked to enforce payment. Nārada states that if the debtor, in spite of being wealthy, does not pay out of bad disposition, he shall be compelled to pay by the king who will be entitled to one-thirtieth of the amount in question.[156] This is less than the fourth payable to the king according to Manu in case of debt collection with royal help.[157] Nārada does not make it clear whether this one-thirtieth of the amount in question payable to the king is over and above the interest and the principal he has to pay. But commenting on Manu, VIII. 176, Medhātithi makes it clear that the creditor shall be paid the whole amount; and the fine, one-fourth of the total debt, shall be paid by the debtor ot the king in addition to what he pays to the creditor.

[152] II. 49.
[153] Quoted in *DK*, I, part 2, 715.
[154] Quoted in *DK*, I, part 2, 695.
[155] Verse 591.
[156] Quoted in *DK*, I, part 2, 724.
[157] VIII. 176.

Even if the debtor had no means to clear off his dues, he could not be let off. Manu enjoins the creditor to compel the member of an equal caste or a lower caste to do sufficient manual labour to repay the principal plus interest, although members of higher castes are made to pay gradually.[158] Thus expolitation of the physical labour of the debtor was considered to be an effective legal way of collecting debts. What is important to note is that this had the backing of the king.[159]

In the case of the death of the debtor his son is placed under the obligation of paying the debt with interest up to the expiry of the term[160] otherwise the property of the deceased person can be put up for sale. Bṛhaspati ordains that if gold (*hiraṇya*) lent is doubled and the debtor is dead or destroyed, his wealth (*dravya*) shall be seized and sold in the presence of witnesses. The price so received shall be kept in safety for ten days in the presence of the people, and the amount on account of the debt (*ṛṇānurūpam*) shall be accepted and the rest returned.[161]

The provisions regarding the recovery of debt enumerated above give the creditor the upper hand. But certain other provisions seem to protect the interests of the debtor. According to Kauṭilya those who exceed prescribed rates shall be punished with an ordinary fine, and each of the witnesses to such usurious transactions shall be punished with half as much.[162] Such a punishment is hardly provided by any Smṛti in early mediaeval times, when rates of interest higher than those prescribed as legal are condemned as usurious and immoral but except for pious denunciations we do not have anything effective aginst the offenders.

On the other hand according to Gautama and Yājñavalkya if the debtor offers to repay the loan and the creditor refuses to accept it, interest stops when the debtor deposits the money in the hands of a third person.[163] Nārada gives a little more protection to the debtor. According to him if the creditor, though pressed by the debtor, does not give an acquittance for the sum paid to him by the debtor, the sum shall yield interest to the debtor henceforth as it had done to the creditor previously.[164] This lawgiver seems to be favourably disposed towards the debtor.

[158] *Manu*, VIII. 177. [159] Ibid. VIII. 178.

[160] *Bṛ.* quoted in *DK*, I, part 2, 707.

[161] *Bṛ.* quoted in *Vivādaratnākara*, quoted in ibid., 726.

[162] III. 11. [163] *Gautama,* XII. 33; *Yāj.*, II. 44.

[164] *Nār.*, I. 115.

CONCLUSION

It is possible to differentiate between the ancient and mediaeval systems of lending. In ancient times the vaiśyas were permitted to live on interest, but in early mediaeval times even brāhmaṇas and kṣatrīyas were allowed to practise lending on interest, which was generally forbidden to them in ancient times. In south India the temples became important money-lenders.

The laws regarding interest generally seems to favour the creditors in early mediaeval times. Kauṭilya, prescribes some punishment for charging usurious interest, but in this he is not followed by later authorities. In spite of their strong disapproval of usury, particularly of lending grain and charging interest on it, by some lawgiver and commentators of the early medieval period, no attempt is made to protect the interests of the debtors in concrete terms.

The ancient normal rate of interest, 15 per cent yearly, was prescribed by the mediaeval legal texts too, but several lawgivers of about the seventh–ninth centuries raised this to 24 per cent, which was more than 50 per cent. Since the list of returns on account of interest on various commodities, including grain, is given separately, it is reasonable to suppose that the increased rate of interest applied to money-lending. In our opinion this increase does not seem to be so much the indication of a stronger tendency of exploitation or of the growing importance of the rentier class as of the comparative absence of metal money and decline of trade in the three centuries following the fall of the Gupta empire.

Varṇa distinctions in the rate of interest are rare in the more ancient texts, but some post-Maurya texts introduce the principle of the lower the *varṇa* the higher is the interest. We do not know how far it was observed, but it certainly reflects the lesser capacity of members of the lower orders to pay in time.

The detailed laws regarding interest on such commodities as grain, cotton, milk products, salt, sugar, fruits, etc., laid down by the lawgivers of Gupta times and their successors show that these were lent to traders as well as ordinary peasant consumers. They create the impression that loans in kind were more frequent than those in cash in early medieval times—a feature in keeping with the largely self-sufficient and predominant agararian economy of the period.

An important form of interest that attracts attention in early medieval times is *kāyikā* or bodily interest. First mentioned in Gautama and Manu, it is explained by Nārada and Bṛhaspati, and by the mediaeval commentators.They generally agree that in this case interest must be paid through services rendered either by the debtor himself or by his cows, oxen, or slaves. The latter alternative could apply only in the case of men of means; debtors of ordinary rank would be reduced to the position of semi-slaves. Thus paying interest through bodily labour could prevail only in an economy where the use of money was limited on account of less of trade and urbanism.

What distinguished the medieval mode of interest was the introduction of land in its mechanism. On the one hand land was mortgaged or its produce earmarked by the debtors in lieu of interest on the principal which they received in money or gold; on the other land was given on loan to the debtors who were required to return eight times the harvest at the maximum. Both cases involve peasant debtors; while the former practice reminds us of commendation, the latter resembles grant of benefices or subinfeudation. The second practice presupposes the presence of such families as possessed large acreage and it seems that one of the methods to get it cultivated was to lease plots of land to needy peasants at exorbitant rates of payment in kind. At any rate the two practices fit in with some kind of feudal economy in which there was less scope for payment in money.

Chapter Fifteen

The Gurjara-Pratiharas*

JOHN S. DEYELL

The upper Ganga basin, known to Indians of the age as *madhyadeśa*[1] or the central country, was centred on Kanyakubja or Kanauj, a formerly grand city with a faded, but lingering, reputation as the scat of imperium. A sharp struggle over possession of this hapless city arose, for with this prize went the symbolic overlordship of the subcontinent. Successive peripheral kingdoms attempted the conquest of the heartland, but their occupations were seldom of long duration. Perhaps the campaigns were *digvijaya:* ceremonial displays of royal ego. Perhaps permanent conquest was never possible to regional powers dependent on overextended lines of communication and supply. Or perhaps successive conquests had rendered the city itself materially unworthy of any long occupation.

The southern empire of the Deccan under the Rashtrakuta dynasty was arguably the richest of the three contenders in material and human resources.[2] The realities of distance, however, prevented the effective long-term extension of the Rashtrakutas' political will into *madhyadeśa*. Their successive northern campaigns took on the character of grand raids without positive permanent effect. This was also true of the efforts of the eastern kingdom of Bengal under the Pala

* John S. Deyell, *Living Without Silver, A Monetary History of Early Medieval North India*, OUP, Delhi, 1990.

[1] Abu al-Raihan Muhammad ibn Ahmad al-Biruni, *Kitāb-ul-Hind,* ed. by E.C. Sachau, London, 1887; (tr.), London, 1910, p. 198.

[2] H.M. Elliot and J.M. Dowson, *The History of India as Told by Its Own Historians,* incorporating revisions by S.H. Hodivala and preface by Md. Habib, Vols I–III, Aligarh, 1951 (hereinafter Elliot and Dowson), p. 3.

dynasty. It was not until the western kings called Gurjara or Pratihara had wielded a stable hierarchy of regional feudatories, that the upper Ganga territories passed under the rule of one line of kings. From the time of Bhoja (*c.* 836–82) to Vinayakapala (*c.* 914–33), the Gurjara-Pratiharas rule over an empire which encompassed at one time or another, parts of present-day Gujarat, Rajasthan, Malwa and the Ganga basin from the Punjab to Bihar. Their feudatories included the Chahamanas or Chauhans[3] and the Guhilas,[4] both in Rajasthan; the Chaulukyas[5] and the Chapas,[6] both in Gujarat-Kathiawad; and the Kalachuris of Gorakhpur.[7] The lines of authority in such a political system were necessarily somewhat diffuse, and the borders would fluctuate with the ebb and flow of military activity of rival kingdoms.

The major source of government revenue at this time was the tax on agricultural production; and the major expenditure of government was on the royal household and the army. The feudal levies due from subordinates to the Gurjara king were supplemented by standing armies garrisoned on the frontiers.[8] The use of money was strongly implied by such a system. Although direct references are elusive, the maintenance of large permanent military forces must have required the regular disbursement of pay or expenses in the form of ready cash. The forms of money would have to satisfy two conditions: sufficiently high value units to be easily transportable from point of collection to point of disbursement; yet sufficiently low value units to meet the modest salary or expenditure levels of individual soldiers.

The commercial enterprises of the Gurjara dominions should also be noted, both as users of money on a regular basis and as a source of revenue through taxes. Some historians have interpreted the period as one in which commerce was moribund, with trade highly localized and dispersed to the village level, where barter relationships

[3] Pratabgarh inscription, *EI*, XIV, pp. 176ff.

[4] Chatsu inscription, *EI*, XII, pp. 13ff.

[5] Una inscription, *EI*, IX, pp. 1ff.

[6] Haddala inscription, *IA*, XII, pp. 191ff.

[7] Kahla inscription, *EI*, VII, pp. 88ff.

[8] The kingdom of the Bodza [=Bhoja: Hodivala (1939), p. 25] . . . has four armies. . . . The army of the North wars against the prince of Multan [Quraishite ruler of Sind] . . . The army of the South fights against the Balhara [Rashtrakuta king] . . . . The other two armies march to meet enemies in every direction.' Abu'l-Hasan 'Abi ibn Husain al-Mas'udi, *Murūj-ul-Zahab*, in Elliot and Dowson, Vol. I, p. 23.

replaced monetary exchanges.[9] Indeed, the dialectic view of history has encouraged use of the term 'feudalism' to describe the political, economic and social process of early medieval India. According to this model, the period was characterized by the decentralization of governmental authority, devolution of economic activity from international to local scale, and de-urbanization.[10] This interpretation is heavily reliant upon the evidence of land-grants, a biased sample which encourages overestimation of the strength or prevalence of a trend.

There are, however, counter-indications to this analysis of decline. Al-Biruni, writing in the early eleventh century (on the basis of Ghaznavid traders' eyewitness reports), detailed a complex of trade routes linking the major cities of the Gurjara realm both internally and with the countries on all frontiers. He left no doubt that these were measured by the caravaneers who frequented them.[11] Arab travellers of the ninth and tenth centuries described a number of trade goods originating in various parts of the subcontinent, which moved to the market by a variety of pack animals.[12] Indeed, one of the most consistently demanded trade item must have been the horse itself: Sulaiman (AD 851) states of the Gurjara king that 'no other Indian prince has so fine a cavalry . . . his camels and horses are numerous.'[13] Ghoshal comments that the Indian authorities of both this period and the later eleventh-twelfth centuries, 'agree in assigning the first rank in their classified list of horses to the foreign breeds . . . and the lowest to the indigenous breeds.'[14] The former indicates well-established trade links.

[9] R.S. Sharma, *Indian Feudalism*, Calcutta, 1965; R.S. Sharma, 'The Problem of Transition from Ancient to Medieval Indian History', *IHR*, I, 1974.

[10] D.D. Kosambi, *An Introduction to the Study of Indian History*, chs 9 and 10.

[11] Al-Biruni, *op. cit.*, ch. XVIII.

[12] There is a survey of other contemporary accounts of the myriad local agricultural and manufactured specialities of different regions, in demand throughout India in the ninth–tenth centuries, by U.N. Ghoshal, ch. XIII in R.C. Majumdar (ed.), *The Age of Imperial Kanauj,* Bombay, 1955. See also P. Niyogi, ch. VI in *Contributions to the Economic History of Northern India*, Calcutta, 1962.

[13] Sulaiman, *op. cit.*, p. 4.

[14] U.N. Ghoshal, ch. XIX in R.C. Majumdar (ed.), *The Struggle for Empire*, Bombay, 1979.

Quite obviously an active exchange of products internal to Indian kingdoms, as well as between these states, and outside, existed during the time of the Gurjara-Pratihara empire. This again implies some degree of monetization of exchange, unless we are to hypothesize a universal barter system. The Arab geographers however frequently mention the types of coins used in the realms which they describe. We may conclude that extensive commercial interest promoted the use of coinage, additional to the needs of the military, described above.

CONTEMPORARY EVIDENCE ABOUT NORTH INDIAN MONEY

The discussion of these factors has emphasized the likelihood that there was a regular and well-used medium of exchange in the Gurjara-Pratihara dominions during the ninth and tenth centuries. Inscriptional evidence confirms this surmise. An epigraph from Bharatpur records the distribution of coins called *drammas* by King Bhoja Deva in AD 905–6 (a successor of his namesake Bhoja, mentioned above).[15] The Siyadoni inscription from Jhansi district recorded a number of donations by individuals to temple deities from AD 902 to 967. Two specific denominations of coins are notable, the *vigrahapāla dramma* and the *ādivarāha dramma*.[16] After careful study, scholars are generally agreed in relating these coin names to specific surviving specimens.[17]

EARLIEST IMPERIAL COINAGE: THE VIGRAHAPĀLA *DRAMMA*

The *vigrahapāla dramma* (and its variants, *vigrahapāla dramma, vigrahapāliya dramma* and *vigrahapāla satka drammal*) is held to be the name of a billion (silver/copper alloy) coin of the class called

[15] *EI*, XXIV, pp. 332ff.

[16] *EI*, I, p. 169.

[17] R.C. Kar, 'Some Observations on the Adivaraha Coins of Bhoja', *JNSI*, XV-II, (1953), pp. 214–19. R.C. Agrawala, 'Dramma in Ancient Indian Epigraphs and Literature', *JNSI*, XVII–II (1955), pp. 64–82. L. Gopal, 'Coins in the Epigraphic and Literary Records of Northern India in the Early Medieval Period', *JNSI*, XXV (1963), pp. 1–16.

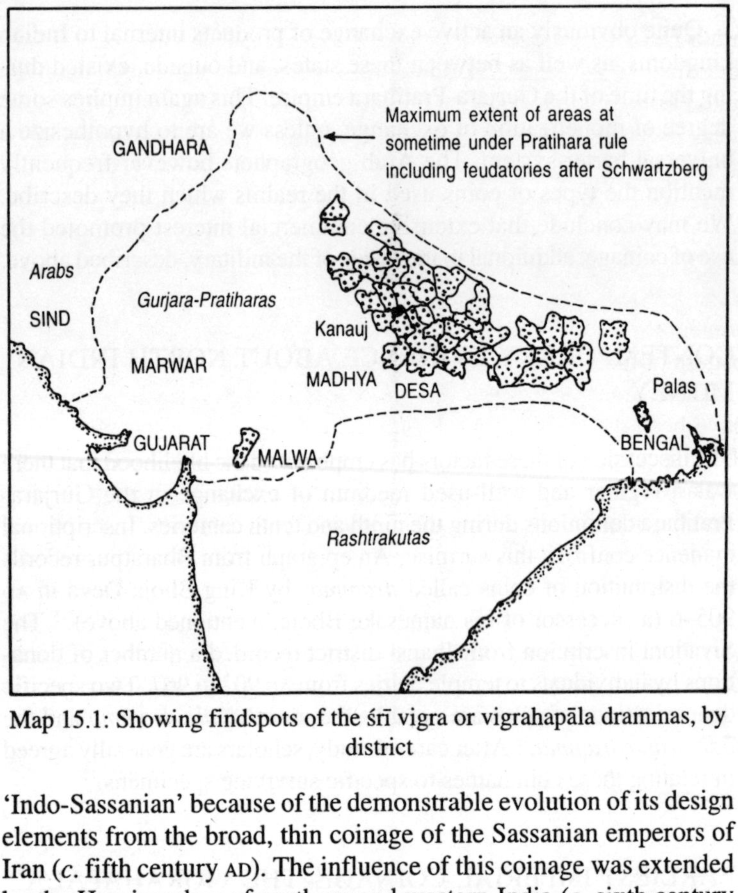

Map 15.1: Showing findspots of the śrī vigra or vigrahapāla drammas, by district

'Indo-Sassanian' because of the demonstrable evolution of its design elements from the broad, thin coinage of the Sassanian emperors of Iran (*c.* fifth century AD). The influence of this coinage was extended by the Hun invaders of northern and western India (*c.* sixth century AD), whose coin types had been adopted by early Gurjara kingdoms in the Sind/Rajasthan border lands (*c.* seventh century AD).[18] The coin has on the obverse, a rude head in right profile, with the late Brāhmī or

[18] This long evolution of coin design with slow degeneration of design elements was possibly first noticed by A. Cunningham and published by J. Prinsep, *JASB,* VI (1836) pl. XIX, 7–14; reprinted in E. Thomas (ed.), *Essays on Indian Antiquities by the Late James Prinsep*, Oxford, 1873, vol. 1, ch. XV, pp. 402–18, pl. XXXIII, 3–14. The best photographic illustration of the stages of change from Sassanian to Gurjara money is given by M. Mitchiner, *Oriental Coins and Their Values: Non-Islamic States and Western Colonies*, Sanderstead, 1979, nos 32–64 (pp. 20–22); nos. 208–18 (p. 40) and nos 325–402 (pp. 57–62).

proto-Devanagari legend *śrī vigra*. The reverse has portions of a fire altar flanked by attendants, sometimes without legend and sometimes with Devanagiri *sa* or *ma*.[19] The mean weight of 145 surviving specimens is 3.81 g. These generally show advanced wear, and the original weight standard of manufacture was likely to be higher. The upper standard deviation of fourteen specimens is 3.92 g, and of another eighteen is 3.94 g; this may approach the coin's weight when new.[20] Analysis by Prakash and Singh reveals that the silver content of the coin was 48.16 per cent (mean assay of 18 coins), which gives an absolute silver content for the *vigrahapāla dramma* of 1.83 g each.[21] The distribution pattern of finds of these coins is shown on Map 15.1.[22]

These areas are not necessarily the only ones where these coins have been discovered, but are the areas indicated in reports where the inspecting authorities have bothered to differentiate these particular types from the general classification 'Indo-Sassanian.' However, the map does prove the concentrated circulation of *vigrahapāla drammas* in the Ganga basin. Their period of circulation, as attested by the Siyadoni inscription, is at least as late as AD 948–9. So they were an accepted money in the Gurjara-Pratihara dominions. The date and agent of manufacture is rather more elusive, in spite of the clear legend. Some observers think them to have been issued by the Pala kings of Bengal.[23] Since the only Vigraphapāla of that dynasty who reigned prior to the Syadoni inscription, ruled in *c*. AD 854–7, and since the area where the coins were mainly circulated was under

[19] V.A. Smith *Catalogue of Coins in the Indian Museum*, Calcutta (hereinafter *IMC*), I, *Coins of Ancient India*, Oxford, 1906.

[20] Mitchiner (1979), *op. cit.*, nos 384–97: quantity=14, mean weight = 3.74 g, standard deviation = 0.18 g, coefficient of variance = 4.8 per cent. S. Prakash and R. Singh, *Coinage in Ancient India*, New Delhi, 1968, Table 22.7, pp. 501–502, nos 1–18: quantity = 18, mean weight = 3.80 g, standard deviation = 0.14 g, coefficient of variance = 3.7 per cent. State Museum, Lucknow, Nos 26720–832; quantity = 113, mean weight 3.82 g.

[21] Prakash and Singh (1968), *op. cit.*, Table 22.8, p. 503. Calculation: 3.80 g @ 48.16 per cent = 1.83 g silver per coin.

[22] Adapted from B.N. Puri, *The History of the Gurjara-Pratiharas*, Bombay, 1957, map facing p. 66, and J.E. Schwartzberg, *A Historical Atlas of South Asia*, Chicago, 1978, plate IV, I-C, p. 31.

[23] E.J. Rapson, *Indian Coins*, Bombay, 1898, pp. 31, 34; *IMC*, Vol. I, *op. cit.*, p. 233; H.C. Ray, *Dynastic History of Northern India*, Vol. I, Calcutta, 1931, p. 330.

the administration of Bhoja I Pratihara during that period, the identification is untenable. This has been pointed out by other writers, who argue convincingly for Gurjara-Pratihara issue of these coins.[24] Kar and Ray argue for a date of manufacture prior to those of Bhoja (*ādivarāha drammas*: see below), on the basis of design evolution. Having closely studied the evolutionary tendencies in the so-called *śrī vigra* coins of the Lucknow Museum, I agree whole-heartedly with this analysis. The progressive stylization of the reverse design indicates convincingly that the *vigrahapāla drammas* were issued prior to the *ādivarāha drammas*; therefore prior to AD 836. As they display several stages of evolution, they must have been issued over a long period, possibly 50 to 100 years. This places their period of manufacture during the reigns of Bhoja's predecessors, but in turn raises difficulties since it is by no means certain that the Pratiharas were in possession of the area indicated by the coin find pattern in Map 15.1, in the second half of the eighth century. It is not my purpose here to go into the subtleties of the chronology of this period; rather to establish the existence of a flourishing currency system at the foundation of the Gurjara-Pratihara dominions. Logic dictates two possibilities: (1) the *śrīvigra* coinage was issued by the successive protagonists for possession of *madhyadeśa* in the eighth century: Indrayudha of Kanauj, Dharmapala of Bengal, Vatsaraja Pratihara of Ujjain, or any of their feudatories and allies, throughout the region of the Ganga basin;[25] or (2) the *śrī vigra* coinage was issued by the Pratiharas in their Malwa/eastern Rajasthan homeland prior to the conquest of North India, and carried into the latter areas with their advancing frontiers.[26] But this latter hypothesis is vitiated by the lack of *śrī vigra* coin finds in Malwa (Map 15.1). So it is

[24] R.C. Kar, 'Vigrahapala Coins—Not a Magadha Type', *Journal of the U.P. Historical Research Scociety* (hereinafter *JUPHS*) II (1954), pp. 72–77; S.C. Ray, 'On Coins Recovered from Nalanda Excavations', *JNSI*, XVIII (1956), p. 105; S. Bandyopadhyay, 'A Note on Sri-Vigraha Coins, *JNSI*, XXXIII (1971), pt. I, pp. 84–89.

[25] R.K. Sethi postulates that a Chauhan ruler of the early eighth century AD issued the prototype of this series. His kingdom would probably have been swallowed by the expanding Pratihara empire. 'The Attribution of Sri Virga Coins', *JNSI*, XXXVII (1975), pp. 161–62.

[26] One other explanation has been advanced by S.P. Singh: that the coins were issued by private bankers throughout the region, 'A Note on Sri Vigraha Coins from Bihar', *JNSI,* XXXIII (1971), pt. II, pp. 73–77.

possible that the Pratiharas found a prototype *vigrahapāla dramma* coinage already in use in *madhyadeśa* at the time of its inclusion in their empire. What is certain is that this coinage, whatever its origin, became a staple coin and passed current with later Pratihara issues. This is attested by the pattern of hoard composition. Of some 52 hoards recovered in the region of the erstwhile *madhyadeśa*, containing *vigrahapāla drammas,* fully 23 hoards included later Pratihara coins (*ādivarāha drammas*; see below).[27]

SECOND IMPERIAL COINAGE: THE ĀDIVARĀHA DRAMMA

The *ādivarāha dramma* of the Siyadoni inscription is believed to be the name of the billon coin, also generally included in the 'Indo-Sassanian' coinage category. Portions of its reverse design are vestigial remnants from the *vigrahapāla drammas* issued earlier. The coin has on the obverse a depiction of the boar incarnation of Vishnu, the *ādivarāha.* On the reverse, in addition to the pictorial elements, is the late Brāhmī, proto-Devanagri legend *śrīmadādivarāha*, 'the fortunate primeval boar'.[28] This is *biruda* or epithet of Bhoja I Pratihara, and there is broad agreement on the attribution of the *ādivarāha* coins of the Siyadoni inscription to that ruler.[29]

The mean weight of 117 surviving specimens is 3.79g. These also show much wear, not to mention considerable evolution of design indicating a long period of issue. The upper standard deviation of 15 finer style (i.e. earlier) coins is 4.02g, and of 12 very worn, cruder style (i.e. later) coins is 3.87 g; this range may represent the coin's weight at time of issue.[30] Analysis by Prakash and Singh detected a

[27] Summarized by Bandyopadhyay (1971), *op. cit.*, p. 87, fn. 4. See also K. Kumar, 'Some Indo-Sassanian Coins from Sarnath', *JNSI*, XXXV (1973), pp. 241–45. The hoard count is derived from A.K. Srivastava, *Coin Hoards of Uttar Pradesh* 1882–1979, Lucknow, 1980.

[28] *IMC*, vol. I, *op. cit.*, pl. XXV, no. 18.

[29] A. Cunningham, *Coins of Medieval India*, London, 1894, p. 49; *IMC*, Vol. I, *op. cit.*, pp. 233–4; Puri (1957), *op. cit.*, p. 235; Kar (1953), *op. cit.*, p. 214; Gopal (1966), *op. cit.*, p. 4.

[30] Mitchiner (1979), *op. cit.*, nos 335–48: quantity = 45, mean weight = 3.86 g, standard deviation = 0.16 g, coefficient of variance = 4.1 per cent. Prakash and Singh (1968), *op. cit.*, Table 22.4, p. 494, nos 1–12: quantity = 12,

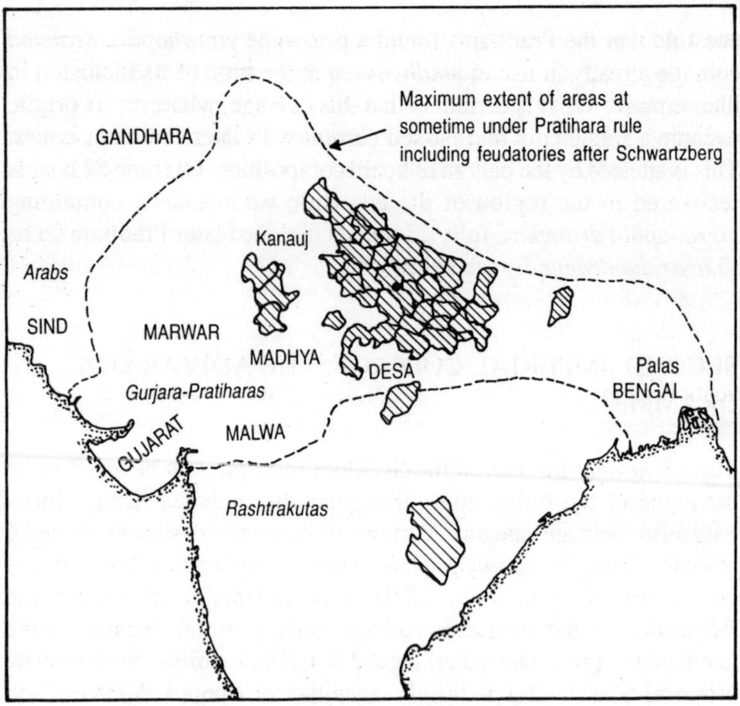

Map 15.2: Showing findspots of ādivarāha drammas, by district

silver content in this coin of 36.38 per cent (mean assay of 12 coins), which gives an absolute silver content for the *ādivarāha dramma* of 1.38 g. This was a lowering of precious metal value by debasement of 24.59 per cent, or roughly a quarter, from the earlier *vigrahapāla dramma*.

As noted, the series shows, signs of considerable change with time, and it is evident that rulers subsequent to Bhoja I continued issuing coins on the same pattern. In AD 1318, the Delhi mint assayed the *ādivarāha* coins then received for melting at an absolute silver content of 1.16 g per coin, still less than the modern assay.[31] It is likely that the

---

mean weight = 3.81 g, standard deviation: 0.66 g, coefficient of variance = 1.6 per cent.

[31] According to the mintmaster Thakkura Pheru, *Dravya Parīkshā*, Gatha 90, Table 17: 100 specimens of *varāha* coins contained 10 *tola*, 7 *masha* of silver = 116.4 g. Therefore the average specimen contained 1.16 g silver.

latest *ādivarāha* issues (of the most debased composition) were the ones most frequently tendered for reminting in the fourteenth century. The distribution pattern of finds of these coins is shown in Map 15.2.

Being of distinctive appearance, it is not likely that the *ādivarāha* coins would be entered in treasure-trove reports under the general title 'Indo-Sassanian'. Hence Map 15.2 shows close correspondence between the area of coin finds and the actual area of circulation of the coins. The coin finds are generally within the bounds of Bhoja's empire, and duplicate the territory where *vigrahapāla drammas* circulated, although there is a tendency towards greater concentration in the Rajasthan borderlands and commensurate lighter representation in the Bihar region. This might be a temporal trend, or might indicate the dispersal of the earlier coins eastward by way of war booty during the Gurjara/Pala wars.[32]

LATEST IMPERIAL COINAGE: THE VINĀYAKAPĀLA DRAMMA

The latest and most degraded in fabric of the *ādivarāha*-type coins have the legend *śrī vināyaka pāla deva*. These coins are attributed to the later Gurjara-Pratihara ruler Vināyakapāla (*c.* AD 913–33) on the basis of continuity of type and hoard association.[33] They are smaller and ruder than the poorest *ādivarāha* coins, and terminate the series. The mean weight of 95 specimens is 3.78 g.[34] The *vināyaka* coins assayed at the Delhi mint before AD 1318 contained 0.88 g of silver per coin.[35] This is lower still than the earlier coins in the series, and indicates an intentional process of debasement or devaluation of the *dramma* billon coinage under the Gurjara-Pratihara

[32] As suggested by Kar (1954), *op. cit.*, pp. 72–77.

[33] V.S. Agrawala, 'Dramma Coins of the Gurjara-Pratihara King Vināyakapaladeva (AD 914–933)', *JNSI*, X (1948), pt. 1, pp. 28–30. The *Vināyakapāla dramma* coins were found in a coin hoard from Hamirpur which contained both *vigrahapāla drammas* and *ādivarāha drammas*, (*JUPHS*, 1954, p. 77).

[34] State Museum, Lucknow, Treasure Trove Lot. no. 77 of 30 Sept. 1970: 86 coins = 325.55 g; B.M.S. Parmar, 'Adivaraha Coins', *JNSI*, XXVI (1964), p. 240: 9 coins = 34.0 g.

[35] *Dravya Parīkshā*, Gatha 90, Table 17: 100 specimens of *vināyaka* coins contained 8 *tola* of silver = 88.024 g. Therefore the average specimen contained 0.88 g silver.

regime governing most of north India. The temporal trend is shown below:

Coin name	*Period of issue*	*Mean weight*	*Pure silver content*
vigrahapāla dramma	c. 750/780? to 836	3.81 g	1.83g (Prakash)
ādivarāha dramma	c. 836 to 913	3.79 g	1.38g (Prakash) 1.16g (Pheru)
vināyakapāla dramma	c. 913 to 933/1000?	3.78 g	0.88g (Pheru)

The secular trend for weight of the Gurjara coinage was stable, fixed at about 3.78–3.81 g from surviving specimens, although we have seen that the original standard could have been as high as 3.9 or 4.0 g. The secular trend for silver content saw a diminution 52 per cent during the approximately two centuries of issue. Had there been quantum drops in silver content with the introduction of new types, then the coins could have been sorted for value by eye, each type being distinctive in appearance. However, Prakash's tables of assays show that initially there was stability in the precious metal content of the *dramma* coinage, with the decline not commencing until the middle period, and a continuing progressive debasement thereafter. The *vigrahapāla dramma* had a relative silver content of 48.16 per cent, with only 1.1 per cent standard deviation in the 18 coins tested. The *ādivarāha dramma* had values ranging from 46.98 to 27.72 per cent silver, with fairly even distribution between these extremes.[36] The eleventh century commentator Al-Biruni observed that the Indians 'want the scales very little, because their dirhams (drammas) are determined by number, not by weight'.[37] If this was true of the Gurjara period, then the phenomenon of coinage debasement must have made the circulation of money a complex process involving testing and haggling over value. This in turn would have created opportunity for a class of professional moneychangers to insinuate themselves into the every day exchange process. That the different types of Gurjara billon coins were not separate denominations in an integrated system of fiduciary or token coinage, is clear from the hoard

[36] Prakash and Singh (1968), *op. cit.*, pp. 495, 503.
[37] Al-Biruni, *op. cit.*, p. 160.

association of all three types of coin. Treasure trove hoards from Uttar Pradesh show in at least twenty-three instances, the coexistence of several fabrics of both *vigraha and ādivarāha dramma* in intact hoards. So all three could not have passed at any one time at the same nominal (as opposed to actual) value: when coins pass at a nominal value above their intrinsic or actual precious metal value, Gresham's Law states that over-valued or 'bad' coinage will drive out the undervalued or 'good' coinage from circulation.

FEUDATORY COINAGES: MARWAR

The distribution of the successive Gurjara *drammas* indicated in Maps 1 and 2 above, shows that these coins did not circulate in the regions of Kathiawad-Malwa-southern Rajasthan. Much of this region was administered by feudatory dynasties acknowledging Gurjara-Pratihara supremacy. The varieties of Indo-Sassanian style *drammas* which are found in these areas are different from the major currency of the Ganga basin discussed above. In Marwar, the coins are broad, thin, and generally closer in fabric to the Sassanian/Hun prototypes. The circulation area of one of these types at least may be localized in the Bhilwara-Mewar region.[38] The coin is distinguished by the total disintegration of the fire altar attendants on the reverse into two

[38] W.W. Webb, *Currencies of the Hindu States of Rajputana,* Hertford, 1893, pl. I, no. 4: 'found in very large numbers in Mewar' (p. 4). R.L. Samar, 'Ancient Coins of Mewar', *JNSI,* XX (1958), pp. 26–37; pl. II, nos. 1, 2, 12, 18; pl. III, nos. 1, 2, 19 and 23 are of this type, attributed by the author to various Guhilot kings of Mewar on the basis of stray letters which the plate photos show poorly and the editor denied in eight footnotes. Still, the coins were of Mewar provenance, brought together during a modern demonetization of obsolete currency and seen by the author in 'vast hoards. . . in the district treasuries at Udaipur, Chittor and Bhilwara . . .' (p. 27). They were found in a hoard of about 3000 pieces in Bhilwara District, Rajasthan; V.C. Bhattacharya, 'Piplaj Hoard of Indo-Sassanian Coins', *JNSI,* VII (1945), pp. 98–100, and J.M. Unvala, 'Note on Indo-Sassanian Coins', *JNSI,* VIII–II (1946), pp. 157–58. This type has been discovered in a hoard as far afield as Jabalpur District of Madhya Pradesh: see B. Jain, 'Indo-Sassanian Coins from Jabalpur District', *JNSI,* XXXIX (1977), p. 169, pl. XIII, 11–13; pl. XIV, 1–3.

symmetrical sets of three vertical chains of diamond beads.[39] The mean weight of 66 specimens is 4.01 g, but the coins have a broad range of weights, the coefficient of variance being as high as 8.9 per cent, with individual coins ranging from 3.7 to 4.5 g.[40] So these feudatory coins were not as carefully manufactured as the main Pratihara series, which at the very worst showed a coefficient of variance (a measure of relative dispersal of weights about the mean) of only 4.8 per cent. Nor were they fashioned with as fine a precious metal content; the assay of two specimens shows a silver fineness of only 16.2 per cent.[41] Thus the coins on an average contained 0.65 g of silver, an amount somewhat lower still than the *vināyakapāla dramma* described above.

These coins enjoyed extraordinary longevity in circulation; Webb relates from oral testimony of the nineteenth century that the most debased of these were called *phadiās*, and were still reputed to have been in circulation in the mid-sixteenth century.[42] Indeed, S.C. Upadhyaya cites inscriptions from districts Sirohi and Jodhpur (Marwar?) in Rajasthan, dated AD 1532 and 1540–1, referring to *phadiyās*.[43] In the early fourteenth century the Delhi mint master quoted the *paḍiyā* as a 'Gurjara coin', reckoning its pure silver content at 0.69 g.[44] This almost exactly matches Prakash's assay of 0.65g

[39] R. Gobl, *Dokumente zur Geschichte der Iranischen Hunnen in Baktrien und Indien*, vol. III, Wiesbaden, 1967, pl. 80, nos 291 e–f. See also Mitchiner (1979), *op. cit.*, p. 59, nos 355–56, 363, 365–76. The full die is illustrated in *Royal Numismatic Society* (hereinafter *RNS*) *Coin Hoards*.

[40] Mitchiner (1979), *op. cit.*, p. 59: quantity = 13; mean weight = 3.94 g; standard deviation = 0.35 g; coefficient of variance = 8.9 per cent. Samar (1958), *op. cit.*: quantity identified from plates = 8; coefficient of variance = 7.1 per cent. *Coin Hoards* (1978), *op. cit.*, note 252: quantity = 53; mean weight = 4.03 g.

[41] Prakash and Singh (1968), *op. cit.*, Table 22.10, nos. 1 and 2, pp. 507–508. Calculation: 4.01 g gross weight @ 16.2 per cent, silver = 0.65 g silver.

[42] Webb (1893), *op. cit.*, pp. 4–5.

[43] S.C. Upadhyaya, 'Phadiyas and Portuguese Foedeas', *JNSI*, XVIII (1956), pp. 114–15. Upadhyaya tried to equate these with Portuguese coins but was effectively rebutted by P.L. Gupta, 'Phadiyas and Portuguese Foedeas', *JNSI*, XIX (1959), pp. 80–81, and C.R. Singhal, 'The Phadiya Coin of Gujarat', *JNSI*, XXI (1959) , pp. 192–95.

[44] *Dravya Parīkshā,* Gatha 88, Table 17: 100 *padiyās* contain 6 *tola*, 3½ *masha* silver = 69.23 g. Therefore the average specimen contained 0.69 g silver.

for the Mewar provenance Indo-Sasanian coin. It is tempting to close the circle of evidence and accept the identity of this coin as a *phadiyā*. The sources however are rather tenuous, and much more research into hoard provenance and metal content must be done to fully establish the attribution. The presence of the same type in central India remains to be explained. It may be said with confidence that there coexisted with the Pratihara main currency, at least one secondary money issued by a tributary kingdom in Marwar, which must have passed at a discount to the former.

FEUDATORY COINAGES: GUJARAT

In Gujarat the feudatory silver coinage was also based on the Indo-Sassanian prototype, although the coins were not as wide and thin as the Marwar coins. Two of the plates are attributable to the Chapa dynasties of Saurashtra and the Sarasvati River valley. In this period, their minimum precious metal content was 3.27 g, which was considerably in excess of the value of coins of Marwar of the Ganga basin. As the Chapa coins show only minor debasement with time, the gap in exchange would have widened as the Pratihara currency lost value. The Gujarat coins would have passed at growing premium over other coins of the realm. Their stable silver content encouraged their use far beyond coastal Gujarat. This coinage survived the passing of the issuing dynasty, as indeed the passing of the imperial money-forms of the Pratiharas. This longevity made it an important currency of the succeeding Rajput period.

OTHER MONEY FORMS

There seems to have been no gold coinage in the Gurjara-Pratihara dominions.[45] The smallest purchases were made not with copper coinage, but with cowrie shells, *cypraea moneta*. This was the major

[45] The unique *ādivarāha* gold medallion in the Lucknow Museum was most likely an art work or presentation piece. See B.N. Mukherjee, 'Gold Coin of Pratihara Bhoja I', *Numismatic Digest*, VII (1983), pp. 60–61. The same is probably true of the unique British Museum specimen of a different ruler.

medium of exchange of contemporary Pala Bengal: 'trade is carried on by means of Kauris, which are the current money of the country' (Sulaiman, p.5). The same was true of the upper Ganga basin, where hoards such as that found at Khajausa (3.75 kg cowries and 638 billon *vigrahapāla* and *ādivarāha drammas*), or at Bhondri (9,834 cowries and 54 billon *vināyakapāla dramma*) demonstrate the use of shells as a fractional currency alongside the metallic coinage.[46] Common use of sea products implies, naturally enough, commercial intercourse with coastal regions.

SUMMARY: MONETARY TRENDS IN THE PRATIHARA EMPIRE

Earlier I speculated on the active requirement of the Gurjara government for a stable currency system in the agricultural revenue system and the military department, matched by the concurrent needs of both local and export traders for a medium of exchange.[47] The physical coinage remains, and inscriptional evidence, support the existence of such a well-regulated currency in the Gurjara state. The monetary system was rational and maintained a standard coinage metrology during the life of the kingdom. Subject states in the periphery were evidently permitted to produce their own coinage, generically related but of a different exchange value to the imperial money.

There is no practical way to estimate the absolute volume of money in the Gurjara dominions. However, by comparing the rates of recapture in modern Uttar Pradesh of hoards of these coins, versus those of earlier and later periods, a sense of scale of the relative volume of money can be achieved.

Table 15.1 permits estimation of two separate measures of the degree of monetization of historical epoch:

1. Given that the number of coin samples (hoards) lost is directly proportional to the volume of exchange transactions conducted, the ratio of surviving hoards to period of issue is one measure of degree

[46] Srivastava (1980), *op. cit.*, hoard 564, p. 100; hoard 970, p. 173. The latter was published by V.S. Agrawala (1948), *op. cit.*, pp. 28–30.

[47] B.N. Mukherjee came to the same conclusion with respect to contemporary Bengal, see his 'Medium of Exchange in Trade of Mid-Eastern India (*c.* AD 750–1200)', *JNSI,* XLV (1983), p. 160.

TABLE 15.1: Coin hoards found in Uttar Pradesh 1882–1979, segregated by coin type and period of issue.

Major coin type or issuing group	*Approx. period of coin issue*	*Approx. length of coin issue (year)*	*No. of hoards recovered*	*No. of coins recovered*	*No of surviving hoards per year of issue*	*No. of surviving coins per year of issue*
Maghada	400–100 BC	300	33	5,314	0.11	77.7
Kusana	AD 50–300	250	42	9,193	0.17	36.8
Gupta	300–500	200	21	159	0.11	0.8
drammas	600–1000	400	110	16,121	0.28	40.3
Rajput	1000–1200	200	61	5,214	0.31	26.1
Sultanate	1200–1550	350	124	45,434	0.35	130.0
Mughal	1550–1800	250	499	48,464	2.00	194.0

Source: Srivastav (1980), *op. cit.* Uttar Pradesh encompasses most of the former Gurjara-Pratihara kingdom. Hoards dating from AD 600–1000 are composed of 'Indo-Sassanian', *vigrahapāla, ādiv arāha* and *vināyakapāla* billon *drammas*, exclusively.

of monetization: the frequency of money usage over time. Plotting the two variables represented by the second and sixth columns of Table 15.1, we get Graph 15.1. This declining trend demonstrates graphically an effect known intuitively: the rate of recovery (or survival) of hoards of a specific period of issue declines over time, since progressively fewer hidden hoards remain to be discovered. The survival rate for coins of the AD 600–1000 period is appropriate for the lapsed time; indeed only Gupta hoards are below the trend line. Hence it is concluded that the volume of exchange transactions *c.* AD 600–1000 was comparable to that of other periods in north Indian history, and probably higher than that of the Gupta era.

2. Given that the number of coins lost is directly proportional to the volume of coinage in circulation, the ratio of surviving coins to the period of issue is a second measure of the degree of monetization: the amount of money used over time. Plotting the two variables represented by the second and seventh columns of Table 15.1, gives Graph 15.2.

This graph demonstrates that the volume of coinage in circulation in North India *c.* AD 600–1000, was comparable to that of the Kuṣana, Sultanate and Mughal period, and clearly superior to that of the preceding Gupta and succeeding Rajput periods.

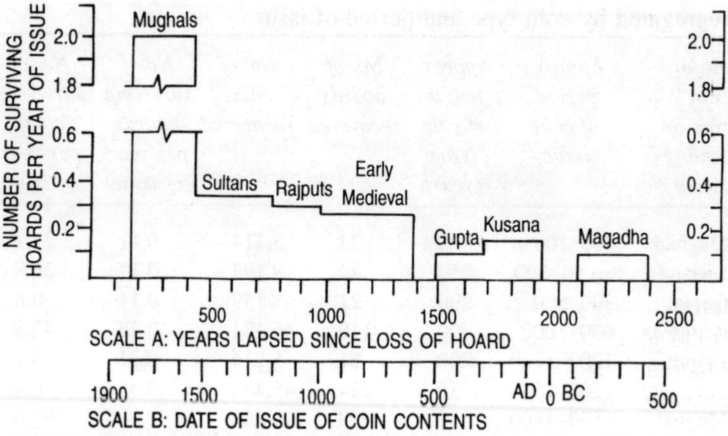

Graph 15.1: Survival rate of coin hoards of various eras

On the basis of this analysis, it can be stated with confidence that there was no shortage of currency in the Gurjara-Pratihara empire of the late eighth to the late tenth century AD, relative to other historical epochs. This fact supports the recent viewpoint that economic activity in early medieval north India was vigorous, although of a different quality to that of the preceding 'classical' age.[48]

The Gurjara currency underwent a long-term decline in intrinsic value because of a steady increase in the base metal alloyed with its

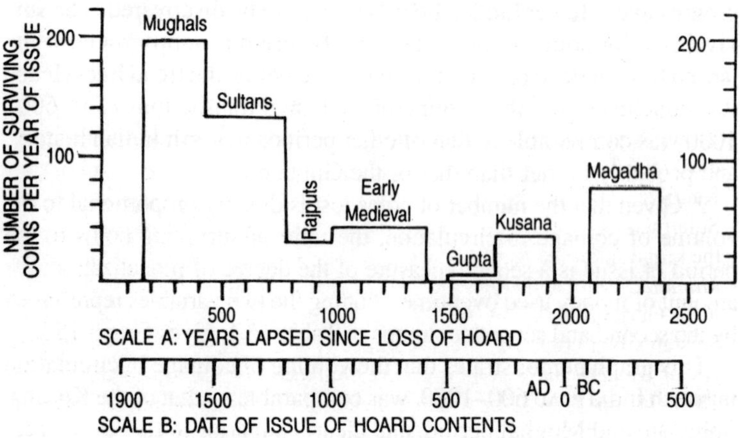

Graph 15.2: Survival rate of individual coins of various eras

constituent precious metal. If the minting operation was contracted to private bankers, this creeping debasement would have represented illicit profit-taking by the contractors. It is difficult to imagine this going undetected or uncorrected for two centuries. If on the other hand, coinage was carefully regulated by government, this debasement was due to an intentional policy of the state.

Several interpretive models are available which seek to identify the motive for such a monetary policy. The first sees debasement as a classic ploy by a revenue-starved administration to generate income by trading on public confidence in the money of the realm, through surreptitious lowering of the precious metal standard. This fiscal tool was delineated as early as the third century BC by the Mauryan minister Kautilya in his manual on statecraft.[49] It was only possible where the coin passed as a denomination by convention, as in a fiduciary coinage, under a government with sufficient power and prestige to regulate the value of money by fiat. Such a currency could not exchange against full-value coinages (money whose value was based on intrinsic metal price) except at a discount; this would explain why the circulation of the Gurjara-Pratihara coinage was restricted to the heartland of the empire, away from the frontiers. Although the Gurjaras controlled the seaports of Gujarat, their *dramma* coinage from the Gangetic plains did not circulate in this area where a high-value feudatory coinage was well established, and where foreign monies were encountered.[50] The Arab travellers in the mid-ninth century specifically state of the king of the Gurjaras, whose 'territories form a tongue of land' (i.e. the Saurashtrian peninsula), that 'exchanges are carried on in his states with silver (and gold) in

[48] B.D. Chattopadhyaya, 'Trade and Urban Centres in Early Medieval India', *IHR*, I, (1974), pp. 203–219.

[49] Kauṭilya, *Arthaśāstra*.

[50] Sulaiman (*op. cit.*, p. 3) refers to the circulation of 'Tatariya dirhams' in the kingdom of the Rashtrakutas; Ibn Khurdaba (*Kitāb-ul-Masālik wa-ul-Mamālik*, Elliot and Dowson, I, p. 13) mentions use of 'Tatariya dirhams' in the Gurjara dominions. Whether these represented specifically Khurasan-Seistan silver coins, as Thomas argued (J. Burgess, *Archaeological Survey of Western India, Report on the Antiquities of Kathiawad and Kuch*, 1874–75, pp. 77–78), or whether the term referred to 'Hunnish' coinage in general, is less important than the fact that foreign coinage did pass into Gujarat in trade.

dust . . .'.[51] This implies that in the coastal regions, the basis of exchange was the intrinsic value of the exchange medium, that is to say its precious metal content.

There are problems in applying this interpretation to the Gurjara-Pratihara money. The Mauryan state was considerably more integrated than the later Gurjara realm, and the Mauryan silver *kārṣāpaṇa* was an universally-accepted currency of normally unvarying composition. Hence a seldom-used emergency measure of debasement was a feasible option to the former government, but it is doubtful that it would have any efficacy as a long-term practice of the latter. Further, we have seen above that the Gurjara coinage was not a unified fiduciary coinage; in this case no windfall profit would accrue to government as a result of debasement activities. It is indeed uncertain whether a government issued the coins; they may have been issued privately under official regulation.

It was noticeable in the inscriptions cited earlier that the various coins of the Gurjara realm, although all struck to a single weight standard, were carefully differentiated by name. Since the purpose of the epigraphs was not to record numismatic details, but to accurately describe financial transactions (normally donations or annuities), the reason for this differentiation must have been the differential value of the various coins mentioned. This reinforces the observation that Gurjara *drammas* were not, in the main, fiduciary, and some other explanation of the temporal debasement must obtain.

The second interpretive model focuses on the secular trend of value of the precious metal contained in the billon coinage. The price of silver was a function of both supply and demand: supply in the Gurjara-Pratihara empire being a question of import quantities, and demand related to the volume of coinage (or its absolute mass) in circulation. Debasement may be seen as a rational efforts, by government or by the marketplace, to control inflationary pressures deriving from the price of silver. If the value of the coin of the realm was to be maintained moderately stable in relation to its purchasing power in terms of goods and services most often exchanged, the silver content of billon coins would have to be adjusted when and if necessary, to allow for either restrictions of silver supply or expansion of the money supply. The latter may well have been the primary cause of the continuing process of debasement, although there is no

[51] Sulaiman, *op. cit.*, p. 4.

strong evidence from other media to support such a viewpoint. There is, however, considerable evidence that not only India, but much of the Asian world experienced severe shortage of silver in the tenth century. The resulting scarcity of silver, expressed as a rise in its value, would be most keenly felt in areas most isolated from the currents of international trade, such as the Ganga basin, the seat of Pratihara power. Downward adjustment of the silver content of the *dramma* had two desirable effects: it put a damper on inflation in the general price structure, and discouraged exportation of the coin, thereby preventing loss of precious metal (since newest coins would be overvalued in relation to older coins, and held in suspicion by foreign traders).

The evidence is somewhat diffuse, and deserves further development. The impression remains, however, of the conscious articulation of a monetary policy which fostered exchange internally in the kingdom, while effectively sealing the frontiers to the emigration of local money. This is the sort of precondition which allowed, for example, the Mughal Empire in the seventeenth century to impose customs duties on all goods passing into the kingdom. It is interesting to speculate if the analogous situation is indicated in the early medieval period.

Chapter Sixteen

From Aden to India: Specimens of the Correspondence of Indian Traders of the Twelfth Century*

S.D. GOITEIN

Since the appearance of my article, 'From the Mediterranean to India: Documents on the Trade to India, South Arabia, and East Africa from the Eleventh and Twelfth Centuries', in *Speculum,* XXIX (1954), 181–97, it was expected that a corpus of such documents would be published soon. Fortunately, the fulfillment of this hope is now in the offing. However, an explanation why a quarter of a century had to pass before this expectation could be realized is in order.

The documents concerned were preserved in the so-called Cairo Genixa, a treasure-trove of Judeo-Arabic manuscripts, mostly fragmentary and completely disconnected with one another. Moreover, they are dispersed today in many libraries, in England, but also in France, USA, Russia, Austria, Hungary, and other countries[1] In order to find out which of them belonged to the topic 'India trade' in the widest sense of the word one had to visit all the libraries concerned and to read all the documentary Geniza material they possessed. By 1958 a very considerable part of the 'India Book,' as the

* S.D. Goitein's paper from *Journal of the Economic and Social History of the Orient*, XXIII, 1980.

[1] For a first orientation on the nature of these manuscripts see the article 'Geniza' in the *Encyclopaedia of Islam*[2], II, 98–89. More in the books quoted in the subsequent notes.

planned corpus was shortly referred to, had been written. By that time, however, it also had become evident that the India trade, as reflected in the Geniza, was only a branch of the great exchange of goods between the Islamic and Christian worlds of the Mediterranean which was in full bloom as from the eleventh century. A study of the society for which the import of Oriental products was only one of many activities, appeared to be imperative.[2] Naturally, my occupation with Mediterranean society delayed the work on the 'India Book.' It had, however, the advantage that about 150 new items were added to the original stock of 250 or so, which were in hand when I sat down to write the first version of the corpus dedicated to the India trade.[3]

In the following, two letters, pieced together from seven Geniza fragments, are presented in translation and in Arabic transcript.[4] All the seven happen to be found in the Taylor-Schechter Collection of the University Library Cambridge, England, but, as the manuscript

[2] S.D. Goitein, *A Mediterranean Society: The Jewish Communities of the Arab World as Portrayed in the Documents of the Cairo Geniza,* Berkeley and Los Angeles, vol. I. *Economic Foundations,* 1967; II. *The Community*, 1971; III. *The Family*, 1978. The fourth and concluding volume, dealing with the individual, his physical environment and spiritual world, is well progressed, but must wait for the completion of the India Book, since the relevant matters found in the latter must be worked into vol. IV, especially its last chapter, 'The Mediterranean Mind'.

[3] Shaul Shaked, *A Tentative Bibliography of Geniza Documents*, Paris-The Hague, 1964, who had, while preparing his volume, the list of Geniza documents included in my 'India Book', as it stood in 1963, notes, if I am not mistaken, 308 items. At the writing of these lines it comprises about 400, see below.

[4] Sixteen other letters from the 'India Book' are translated in S.D. Goitein, *Letters of Medieval Jewish Traders, Translated from the Arabic,* Princeton, 1973, pp. 62–71, 175–229, 299–304, 335–38.

The letters are written in Hebrew characters and contain also a few Hebrew words, especially at the beginning and end, in titles and blessings, and naturally, in references to Jewish matters, such as holidays. As far as necessary, these words are rendered in Arabic translation.

In the English translation, words translated from Hebrew are italicized. They are often written in abbreviated from, which is indicated in the English text by parentheses encompassing parts of the words alluded to in the original only by their initials.

marks indicate, are preserved in six different sections, some between glasses, other in bound volumes, and again other in various series of boxes. Since these two letters emanated from the office of a *wakīl tujjār*, a representative of merchants, who was also superintendent of a port, and are addressed to a merchants stationary in India, they are, despite their shortness, particularly welcome. But experience has taught me that even a small scrap of paper may sometimes contain a valuable bit of information for socio-economic history.[5]

The commentaries accompanying the translations are essentially philological, that is, they are intended to establish the exact meaning of the text and to explain any detail with which the reader might not be expected to be familiar, or of whose significance he might be unaware. The general historical and socio-economic evaluation of the documents translated, naturally, is done in the introductory part of the corpus.

The addressee of these letters was Abraham b. Peraḥyā Ben Yijū,[6] a learned Tunisian Jew, whose mercantile and industrial activities on the Malabar coast of India can be traced during the years 1132 through 1149. He might have visited India before. He operated a brass factory, in which also local Jew and others were employed. As his letter of 11 September 1149, written in Aden on his way home shows, he returned to his native ambience in order to marry his daughter into his own family, as was customary in those days, and probably also to give his little son the opportunity for a better education.[7] He is represented in the Geniza with a great number of items written by, or addressed to, him.

The sender of our letter was Maḍmūn b. Ḥasan b. Bundār, representative of the merchants and superintendent of the port of Aden, and 'Nagid of the Land of Yemen', that is, head of the Jewish communities of that country. He was also a shipowner and, like his

[5] I use this opportunity to express again my appreciation and gratitude to the former and present directors (librarians) and staff of the University Library Cambridge for the unfailing support given to my work throughout the years.

[6] *Ben Yijū* was his family name, derived from that a Berber tribe, probably one under whose protection the family once had lived. Under the form *Benichou* this name is still common among North African Jews. Paul Benichou, the author of *Morales due Grande Siècle* (6th edition, 1948), made the name known in France.

[7] Translated in *Letters* (see n. 4 above), pp. 201–206.

father, the middleman between the Jews of the Mediterranean area and those active in India.[8]

My collection of papers from the Cairo Geniza connected with the trade on the India route comprises about 400 items to date, of which 245 deal with the trade proper, while the balance are letters and documents illustrating the personal, communal, and other activities of the persons involved in that trade.

The two letters translated below give a good idea of the economic concerns of a Mediterranean merchant sojourning in India. He exported iron, a commodity not handled by Jews in Mediterranean, but taking pride of place in the India trade; spices, such as pepper and ginger, and betel nuts, and, of course, the products of his brass factory. Copper and lead were sent to him from the West. India had famous copper mines, and lead was found also east of India, but obviously the supply was not sufficient for a flourishing brass industry. Besides this, the West sent gold coins of various currencies and all those daily commodities which Westerners out in India needed or desired: Spanish and Egyptian textiles, writing paper not to be had in India at all, sugar, raisins, and dates, and household goods of different descriptions.

This article wishes to give the reader an inkling of the problems of research. The type, colour, size, and state of preservation of the paper, as well as the style and quality of the script are not negligible details, but factors which must be taken into account when we go about to piece together the disparate fragments found in the Geniza. The linguistic, technical, financial, and social aspects demand our careful attention. The reader, of course, will linger at those parts which, for one reason or another, will interest him most.

TWO COPIES OF A LETTER BY MAḌMŪN, ADEN, TO ABRAHAM BEN YIJŪ, MALABAR COAST, INDIA

23. TS[9] 6 J 4 fol. 14.
24. TS 18 J 2 fol. 7
25. TS 12.416

[8] About him see *Letters*, pp. 181–85.

[9] TS = Taylor-Schechter Collection in the University Library, Cambridge, England. The numbers 23, 24, etc., are the numbers given to the relevant Geniza texts in my book, *Documents from the Cairo Geniza on the India Trade of the High Middle Ages,* the 'India Book' (in preparation).

Numbers 23 and 24 together from one complete letter. Line 5 of number 23 is identical with the first line of number 24, but the paper was torn in such a way that the first five words of line five are in number 24, while the last word in the line is on the lower left hand corner of number 23. The length of the page is 7.8 + 36 cm. = 43.8 cm., its width 10.3 cm. The paper is light gray and of medium thickness. It is well preserved, except that the ink on the opposite side can be seen through the paper in places.

Number 25 is written on paper of exactly the same type and dimensions. Only the lower half of this copy has been preserved, approximately 22 cm., corresponding to number 24, recto, 11. 18–37, and verso, 11. 1–18 (to the word *kt'by*, 'my letter,' i.e., only two words are missing here).

Number 23 and number 24 recto were written by the clerk who also wrote number 25, i.e., he made at least two copies of this letter. This same scribe also wrote numbers 26, 30, 61 and 199, and wrote the postscripts in the margins of number 32. However, the postscript on the verso of number 24 was written by another hand, the same hand which wrote that to number 199 in a very cursive style. It stands to reason, therefore, that this was the hand of the sender, Maḍmūn, himself. The same handwriting is to be found in numbers 27, 29, 32, and 33–34.

The recto of numbers 23–24 is written in a very ornate style in such a way that the sheet is filled exactly. It is thus clear that it was copied from an original which Maḍmūn himself had written. The question then arises, why Maḍmūn added the postscript on the verso of this scribe's copy, and not on the original itself. The answer is that the calligraphic copy served as the official text of the letter, while the draft was sent in another boat as a replacement in the case that the official text was lost.

It is surprising that the receiver of the letter kept two copies of it during all the years he lived in India and did not dispose of them until he came to Cairo. It is even more strange when we see that number 25 has no more room for further writing. From this we may conclude that he kept the paper, if not for reference, for uses other than writing, for example, 'to wrap over the mouth of a small flask' (*Mishna, Sabbath*, 8, 2, in reference to erased paper'), or 'to stop up the mouth of his flask (*Baba Metzia* 13a, in reference to a cancelled legal document).

CONTENTS OF THE LETTER

A. Acknowledgment of a Ben Yijū's letter and shipment (number 23, 11. 1–5, number 24, 11. 1–10).
B. List of gifts sent to Ben Yijū with 'Abd al-Masīḥ, the deacon (number 24, 11. 10–23).
C. Acknowledgment of a shipment sent by Ben Yijū to the merchant Abu'l-Khair and business dealings of the latter (*ibid.*, 11. 23–29).
D. The market for iron in Aden (*ibid.*, 29–35).
E. Greeting (*ibid.*, 35–37).
Postscript (Arabic text not provided):
F. Request to ask three Indian acquaintances, two Hindus and one Muslim or Jew, to send pepper and iron from Mangalore, and coconuts etc. from Diu (*ibid.*, *verso*, 11. 1–12).
G. Announcement that Maḍmūn was prepared to fit out a ship to sail from Aden in partnership with the aforementioned (*ibid.*, 11. 13–18).

TRANSLATION

A. No. 23. (1) *Your hands (sic) shall be high above your adversaries, and all your enemies shall be cut off.* (2) *To our worthy m(aster) and t(eacher) Abraham, m(ay God remember him) f(avourably), the son of o(ur honored), g(reat) and h(oly) m(aster) and t(eacher)* (3) *Yijū m(ay he rest in the) g(arden of) E(den) (from) your friend Maḍmūn, the son of Ḥasan, m(ay he rest in the) g(arden of) E(den).*

(4) The letter of my lord, the most illustrious elder, arrived; I read (24, 1. i) and understood it, and I was happy to learn that you were well (23,1.5) and your affairs (24, 1.2) in order, for which I thanked God very much, and asked Him to give you more of every good thing. May God unite (4) us under the most joyful circumstances, and in the best of (5) spirits, for he controls this and is able to effect it, if (6) God will.

From what you mentioned, (7) my lord, I learned that you sent the two locks and the two thousand (8) white and red betel nuts. I have already (9) received this and I thank you for attending (10) to it.

B. I have sent you a bundle of (12) Berbera mats, six in number, (11) with 'Abd al-Masīḥ, the deacon. (13) We wrapped them in canvas and your name is written (14) on it in Arabic and Hebrew. With him, I have also sent you (a gift) from me: (16) a new, first-rate, unbleached Dabīqī scarf, (17) which has a pretty band on each side, (18) and is fit to be worn by prominent men. (I) also (sent) with him (19) two sets of fine, large paper—(20) government paper, the like of which (21) no one has. In addition, (I sent) with him two rubā'iyyat of (22) sugar and raisins. See that you receive all this from him.

C. (23) Everything you sent to Abu 'l-Khair arrived, (24) and he has taken delivery of all of it. (25) He bought Egyptian linen and went up into the (26) Highlands. He requested me to ask you to look after his interests (27) and send his remaining (28) iron and cardamon, and the entire balance to his credit. (29) Send him all this on the first boat (30) which sails from India.

D. As for iron, this (31) year it sold (well) in Aden—all (32) kinds of iron—and in the coming year (33) there will also be a good market, because (34) there is none at all left in the city. (35) Please take notice of this.

E. Please accept for yourself the best of (36) wishes, and for your son Surūr, and for Bamah, (37) the most bountiful well-being. *And Peace.*

Verso (in Maḍmūn's hand).

F. (1) Please give Sūs Sītī and Kinbātī [and Isḥā. . .] (2) and Isḥāq the Bānyān my best regards, and tell them (3) of my longing for them. Inform them in my name that as for pepper, in (4) this coming year its value, (that is) the price per bahār, will be (5) thirty dinars, and more, and as for refurbished iron, (6) a bahār will be (worth) not less than twenty dinars, (7) and that the *raqṣ* (shining, glittering iron), which was in the city, is completely exhausted. (8) (Tell them also) to dispatch a ship from Mangalore, if they can, (9) and to send in it any available pepper, iron, (10) cubeb, and ginger; it should set out at the first opportunity for (11) *al-Dyyb* [Diu], taking some coir (coconut fiber), fine aloes wood, (12) mango (?), and coconuts, because all these are selling well.

G. (13) If they are equipping a ship in Aden, and they want me (14) to take part, I will share (in it) with them. If there were (15) a ship sailing from Mangalore this year, I would send them (16) gold, sugar, raisins and (other) goods. Be sure to inform them (17) of all this, and do not be remiss, for you take the place of (18) a letter of mine to them. *And Peace.*

Address in Arabic script, written in the same direction as the postscript below:

(I) The most illustrious elder, His Servant

Ibrāhīm b. Īshū, the Israelite, may God preserve his high position.

Maḍmūn b. al-Ha[san]

Address in Hebrew script, written on number 24 verso on the reverse side, opposite the beginning of the letter:

(1) *To our worthy m(aster) and t(eacher) Abraham, (2) m(ay) God remember him f(avorably), the son of o(ur master) and t(eacher) Yijū, m(ay he rest in the g(arden of) E(den).*

Your friend Maḍmūn, the son of Ḥasan, m(ay) he rest in the) g(arden of) E(den).

COMMENTARY

No. 23

1 *Your hands* shall be high, etc.—*Micah* 5:8; where 'your *hand* (in the singular). . .' This biblical verse and similar ones, are found at the beginning of other letters from that period. This replaces Arabic *wa-kabata a'dāhu*, 'may He crush your enemies,' usually said at the beginning of letters.

2 The abbreviation *z"l* is generally known as a blessing for the dead. In Yemenite usage, however, these letters stand for *z(ākhūr) l(eṭōv[a])* and are used as a blessing for the living.

3 Your friend—spelled *'hbk*, both here and in the Hebrew address, without the *waw*, as often in the Bible, for example, I Kings 5:15, Isaiah 41:8, Proverbs 18:24, Esther 5:10, 14.
Hasan—in the Arabic address with the article.

No. 24

7 Locks—see number 26, verso, 1.28, below.

8 Betel nuts—a common Indian export commodity. See numbers 26, verso, 11. 23–27, below.

11 'Abd al-Masīḥ the deacon—*shammās*. Just as Jewish rabbis and Muslim qadis dabbled in trade, so did ecclesiastical offers of the Christian Church—here probably of the Syrian Church of India. While travelling from Aden to India, he acted as an agent for two Jews.

12 Mats which were brought to Aden from the African port of Berbera. The same gift was also sent in letter 29, 1.46.

14 'In Arabic and Hebrew'—as the two addresses in this letter

demonstrate, the terms 'Arabic' and 'Hebrew' refer not only to the script, but to the language as well.

17 Band—Ar., *silsilah*. This word, which usually means 'chain,' also has the sense of 'collar,' and it seems that it here refers to some kind of decorated fringes.

19 Sets—Ar. *dast,* which designates a number of objects of the same description. The word is once specified in these papers (34, 1.6,) in connection with Chinese cups as a set of six, and once (54, 1.24, referring to paper) as a set of twelve. Paper was also sent in single sheets, as in number 55, 1.15, where fifteen sheets of large Ṭalḥī paper are mentioned. In contemporary Egyptian and Yemenite Arabic *dasta* is ' a dozen,' which in Yemen, when connected to a following word, is shortened to *dast*, e.g. *dast shama'*, 'a dozen candles'. The same word in Modern Egyptian designates 'a quire of paper,' cf. Spiro, *Arabic-English Dictionary of Egypt*, Cairo, 1923, p. 173a, and Dozy, *Supplément* I p. 441a; according to A. Barthélemy Dict. *Ar.-Franc., Dialectes de Syrie,* p. 239, *dast* is 'a set of 400 leaves of paper,' which does not, of course, apply here. The sending of paper as gifts or merchandise to India is mentioned very frequently in our documents.

21 Rubā'iyyāt—According to A. Grohmann, *Südarabien als Wirtschaftsgebiet,* II, 98, who relies on E. Glaser and other 19th century travelers in South Arabia, the rubā'ī has four Tumānī of 2.387 kg. which would make 9.448 kg. In Ṣan'ā', the capital of Yemen, I am informed, the rubā'ī is 1/8 of *Qadaḥ*. The Yemenite *Qadaḥ* (cf. al-Wāsi'ī, *Ta'rīkh al-Yemen*, Cairo, 1346/1927–8, page 200, 1.4) is the equivalent of two modern oil tins. This too would give the rubā'ī a weight of about 10 kg.

24 Abu 'l-Khair—This name occurs frequently in these documents. He is perhaps to be identified with Abu 'l-Khair al-Barqī (199, 1.6; 32, 11.63–4).

26 To the highlands of central Yemen.

32 All kinds of iron—Five different types of iron are mentioned in these documents.

36 Surūr—This Arabic name, which means 'Joy,' corresponds to the Hebrew name Peraḥyā, which means 'Joy in the Lord,' according to the meaning of the Arabic root *frḥ*. Peraḥyā was the name of this Surūr's grandfather. Bamah—the slave and house-steward of Ben Yijū.

Verso

1–2 Sūs Sītī etc.—The first two names are Indian. Isḥāq can be the name of the Jew or a Muslim. Bānyān is the usual designation for an Indian merchant.

11 Diu, an island south of the Saurashtra peninsula of Gujarāt on the northwestern end of the Gulf of Cambay (north of Bombay), was a great emporium of trade in the Late Middle Ages, see *Enc. Isl.*[2], p. 322. The name has the article because it simply means 'island' (*dipa*), a meaning certainly known to the Arabic speaking Middle Easterners.

12 Fine aloeswood, *'krbh*, clearly spelled thus in both copies, has not been found by me elsewhere. I take it as Persian *agar bih*, see F. Steingass, *Persian-English Dictionary*, p. 90, as derived from Sanskrit *aguru* (modern *agar*, information by Professor A.L. Basham).

The item *nw' shk* also has not been traced thus far. Professor Bashman suggested *navāṃśuka*, which might be pronounced something like *nūāshuk*, a compound of *nava*, new, and *aṃśuka*, fine cloth, muslin. I doubt, however, whether textiles would be mentioned between coir and coconuts and wonder whether *nv'shk* could not stand for *nagzak*, mango, see O. Spies, *Ibn Fadlallah al-Omari's Bericht über India*, Leipzig, 1943, p. 33. Mango would be traded as pickles or as a preserve.

13 Equipping—Ar. *jahāz*, cf. 1.8, i.e., buying or building a ship and fitting it out.

16 Gold—the reference, it seems, is to gold coins. Sugar and raisins—generally appear in small quantities sent as gifts for children. Here they are export commodities. (Other) goods—i.e. goods ordered by Indian merchants.

The Arabic Address (the same address, with slight variations, as in 27): 2 Ishū—The name Yijū was also pronounced and written as Yishū, see number 27 in the Hebrew address, and 62, 1. 1, or as Ishū.

FRAGMENTS OF TWO COPIES OF A LETTER FROM MADMŪN TO BEN YIJŪ

26 TS 24.66
27a TS NS J, fol. 5
27b TS 13 J 7, fol. 13

27c TS Box K 25, frgt. 252

No. 26 is a copy, written by the clerk who wrote number 23–24, of the original numbers 27a–c, which is written by Maḍmūn. The fifth line of number 27a matches the first line of number 26. Number 27b begins with the last word in line 5 of number 26. It concludes with the second word of line 35 of number 26. The address has been preserved only in number 27a, since the custom was to write the address on the reverse side of the sheet, opposite the beginning, and the beginning, usually containing only polite phrases, was often torn away as not needed, while paper always was in demand for all kinds of purposes, see above.

The clerk worked with great exactitude. There is no deviation from the original. He did, however, use many more diacritical marks than his master, albeit without any consistency.

The original was written by Maḍmūn carefully and in a more pleasant hand than is usual for him. Deletions, involving the beginning of words, are found in two places only. The writer undoubtedly had accounts before him, from which he copied. We may assume that these accounts were entered in Maḍmūn's ledger, which is mentioned several times in these documents.

No. 26 is written on the same greyish paper as numbers 23–25, but it differs in width (11.3 cm.). This would seem to imply that they cut their paper to different sizes, and that it was not bought already cut in sheets suitable for writing purposes. 52 cm. of the length of the sheet are preserved.

The paper is different in number 27a–c. It appears more brownish, lighter, and smoother than the paper of the other fragments originating from Maḍmūn's office which have been identified up till now. Its width is 10 cm. at the top and 9.5 cm. at the bottom. Its length is 11 cm. plus 25.5 cm. plus 29.5 cm., a total of 66 cm. A space of 12 cm. was left blank on the verso of 27c. Thus Maḍmūn was not forced to cut short, as he sometimes did for lack of space.

On the lower edge of the verso of 26 the receiver of the letter, Abraham b. Yijū, wrote, in his own hand, a calendar for the year 1458 of the Era of the Documents, i.e., AD 1146/7 for the year 1459, i.e., AD 1147/8., and for another year which is difficult to read; most probably it is for the year 1460, i.e., AD 1148/9. The same man wrote a calendar for 1461, i.e., AD 1149/50, on the edge of number 51, and we possess other from his hand.

CONTENTS OF THE LETTER

Aa. Acknowledgment of a letter and a shipment of pepper from Ben Yijū, through the agency of the shipowner Rāmisht, and detailed accounting of what was received for the goods sold, after the deduction of expenses (number 27a, 1. 1–number 26, 1.15).

Ab. Acknowledgment of a shipment of iron through the agency of the shipowner Ibn Abu 'l-Katā'ib, and detailed accounting of what was received for the goods sold, after transfer of part of the shipment to whomever designated, and after the deduction of expenses (number 26, 11, 16–39).

Ac. The balance in favour of Ben Yijū.

Ba. The purchase of copper for Ben Yijū, the price and the freight charges in three different ships (11. 40–50).

Bb. Details of various expenditures on behalf on Ben Yijū, and of purchases of copper, lead, and other commodities (11. 50—verso 17).

Bc. The completion of Ben Yijū's account (verso, 11. 18–19).

C. Acknowledgment of various shipments, and finally, of gifts from Ben Yijū.

D. The shipment of gifts, and best wishes.

In order to lighten the reader's burden, all the accounts contained in this letter have been reduced to a table. The details will be explained in the commentary. It should be kept in mind that a *bahār* contains 300 roṭl, or pounds, and that the dinar, or gold piece, is divisible into 24 *qīrāṭs*, which are combined to an eight, sixth, fourth, third, or half of a dinar, as the circumstances require. The dinars are, naturally, the ones used in trade in Aden in this period, namely, Malikī dinars, which the worth of somewhat more than one third of the Fatimid dinar, as is evident from various references in the India papers, but had here a higher value.

A. THE SALE OF THE GOODS SENT BY BEN YIJŪ AND THE PRICES OBTAINED, AFTER THE DEDUCTION OF EXPENSES

I. Pepper—12 bahār, from which 45 roṭl were removed, leaving 11 bahār, 255 roṭl. The price: per bahār—34 dinars, per roṭl—$^{34}/_{300}$ dinar. Total: 374 dinars + ($34 \times {}^{255}/_{300}$) = 28 $^{9}/_{10}$, rounded out to 28 $^{5}/_{6}$ =

402 5/6 dinar (Malik).

The expenditures on this shipment:

'Tithes' (i.e.) customs	82 1/4 dinars	
Expenses in receiving the goods	4 1/6 dinars	
Baskets and porters	1/6 +	1 1/4 dinars
	87 5/6 dinars	87 5/6

Balance in favour of Ben Yijū from the pepper shipment 315 dinars

II. Iron—20 bahār, 120 roṭl

Amount given to the merchant Joseph	3 bahār,	189 roṭl
Amount given to the merchant Khalaf	2 bahār,	75 roṭl
Total	5 bahār,	255 roṭl

Amount left for sale:	14 bahār, 165 roṭl
Price: per bahār—	17 dinars
per roṭl	17/300 dinars

Total received: 238 + (165 × 17/300= 9.35 rounded out to 9 1/4)

=	247 1/4 dinars
Various expenditures on this shipment	27 1/4 dinars
Balance in favour of Ben Yijū from the iron shipment	220 dinars

Total balance in favour of Ben Yijū =

220 + 315 dinars = 535 dinars

B. SHIPMENT OF GOODS AND REQUESTED ITEMS TO BEN YIJŪ FOR THE AFOREMENTIONED SUM

I. 5 bahār of copper, and expenditures on them 415 dinars (Malik)

Hides for packing them, and the cost of packing	1 1/2 dinars
Exit tolls in Aden	4 1/8 dinars

II. Other purchases and expenses:

Freight charges of the copper 4 1/2 dinars

Registration fee to the captain for the

shipments of iron pepper	2 dinars
Copper bars	8 dinars
Dates	$2^{1}/_{2} + {}^{1}/_{4}$ dinars
An Abyssinian hide	2 dinars
Mats	1 dinars
A carpet	5 dinars
Various items of clothing	6 dinars
Lead	$28\ {}^{1}/_{2} + {}^{1}/_{12}$ dinars
Freight charges for the lead	1 dinar
20 Egyptian Mithqāl, which equal	47 dinars
7 Malikī dinars	7 dinars
${}^{1}/_{4} + {}^{1}/_{8} + {}^{1}/_{12} = {}^{11}/_{24}$,	$535\ {}^{11}/_{24}$, rounded out to $535\ {}^{1}/_{3}$ dinars (Malikī)

However, the ${}^{1}/_{3}$ dinar is not considered by Maḍmūn, who states that with these shipments his account with Ben Yijū for that year is settled.

TRANSLATION

Aa. (27a, 1. 1) The letter of my lord, the most illustrious elder, has arrived; may God make permanent (2) your well-being, may he guard your life and humble those who envy you. It was (3) a most gladdening letter and a most delightful message. I was happy to learn of your well-being (4) and your prosperous circumstances, and I have entreated God (to grant you) more of every good thing, (5) (26, 1.2) in his mercy. I noted from what you mentioned (26, l.z.) in your esteemed letter (6) that you sent (26, 1.3) some pepper in the ship of the Nākhodā (7) Rāmisht (26, 1.4)—twelve bahār of small measure. (8) This has arrived (26.1.5) and your servant went to pick it up.

From this is to be deducted (26, 6)—as you mention in your letter forty (7)-five roṭl leaving you eleven (8) bahār and two hundred and fifty-five roṭl, the price being (8) thirty-three dinars (per bahār). The (full) value is, (thus), four (10) hundred and three dinars, minus one-sixth.

(11) From this (sum) is to be deducted the 'tithe' (i.e. the custom's duty), eighty-two (12) and one quarter dinars, the cost of obtaining the goods, four and one-sixth dinars, (13) the cost of baskets and a porter, one and one-sixth dinars, (14) a total of eighty-eight dinars (in your favour).

Ab. (16) You mentioned that you sent some refurbished iron in the ship of the Nākhodā (17) Abu'l-Hasan b. Abu 'l-Katā'ib (18)—twenty-one bahār—but (19) the Nākhodā Abū 'Abd Allah, his son, only gave me (20) seventeen bahār of large measure; he stated that (21) the Bānyān (the Indian merchant) whom you asked to take charge of the iron (22) delivered no more than this to him, saying that the rest of (23) the iron was in the highlands and had not yet arrived. In reply, I held him to be under obligation (24), if this were not true, (25) to pay the price (of it), according to the sale value in Aden. (26) He is to pay my lord this in India.

(27) The iron I received from you in Aden is about twenty (28) bahār and one hundred and twenty roṭl of small measure. (29) From this is to deducted: for the elder Joseph b. (30) Abraham, three bahār and one hundred and eight (31)roṭl; for Khalaf b. Isḥāq, two bahār (32) and one-quarter—a total of five bahār and two hundred (33) and fifty five roṭl, leaving you four-(34) teen bahār and one hundred and sixty-five roṭl, (35) the price being seventeen dinars (per bahār). Total value: two hundred (36) and forty-seven and one-quarter dinars.

From this is to be deducted (37) the 'tithes,' the expenses, and the (cost of) the porter, twenty-(38)seven dinars, leaving two hundred (39) and twenty dinars.

Ac. Therefore, the sum total coming to you is approximately five hundred (40) and thirty-five dinars.

Ba. Your servant bought you (41) three bags of copper (*ṣufr*), weighing (42) five bahār, at a cost of eighty-three (dinars per bahār). (43) (Total) value: four hundred and fifteen dinars. (44)The number of pieces in each bag is twenty-three. (45) The cost of hides and packing, one and one-half dinars. Exit tolls (46) from the port (of Aden), four and one-eight dinars. I sent you (47) this in the ship of the Nākhodā Rāmisht—(48) one bag—in the ship of al-Muqaddam—one bag—and in the ship of (49) Nambiyar (ani?)—one bag—a total of three bags. Freight charges for (50) this (were) four and one-half dinars.

Bb. (Also) charged to you, the registration fee with the (51) boat's captain for the pepper and the iron, two dinars.

No. 26, Verso

(1) Also, there are charged to you twenty-five roṭl of copper bars, (2) twenty-eight pieces in number, (3) worth eight dinars; a basket of dates, (4) 115 roṭl, worth two and one-half and one-quarter dinars;

(5) two dinars, the cost of an Abyssinian hide; one dinar, the price of ten (6) berbera mats which are in a package (7) which is marked in Hebrew and Arabic; (8) a zodiac carpet, worth five dinars, a *maqṭa*ʿ cloth, (9) and two Manārī kerchiefs, worth six dinars—(10) all this with Abū Ghālib, the ship's captain. (11) He also has with him a piece of lead, weighing (12) two hundred and forty-five roṭl, worth twenty-(13)eight and one-half dinars and two qīrāt, the price (per bahār) being 35 dinars; (14) freight charges for the piece of lead, one dinar. Abū Ghālib, the ship's captain, has with him also a purse in which there are twenty Egyptian Mithqāl (16) worth fourty-seven dinars (Malikī). (17) That purse contains (also) seven Malikī dinars.

Bc. (18) The total sum: five hundred and thirty-five dinars (19) and one third. This settles my lord's account. (20)

C. There also arrived the 'eggs' which you sent in the ship of (21) Ibn Abu 'I-Katā'ib, and this was received by the elders Joseph (22) and Khalaf, along the lines of the division which you indicated (23) in your letter.

The betel nuts also arrived, which (24) you sent to your servant, and this is on the balance of (25) my account with your excellency from last year. (26) But the betel nuts were extremely mediocre, both the white (27) and the red ones. There also arrived what you were kind enough (to send), namely four (28) locks and two bowls.

D. Your servant has sent you (20) with Abū Ghalīb, the ship's captain, two large brazilwood boxes with (30) sugar, and two brazilwood boxes with raisins, and a package with (31) three sets of Egyptian Ṭalḥī paper of the best obtainable quality. Please accept this, my lord, (33) and may you think well of me in your secret thoughts. If you have any (34) need or service (to be done) I would be happy to take care of them. (35) May you have abundant well-being. *And Peace.*

27a

The Hebrew *Address*:

(1) The illustrious elder, my lord Abraham Your Servant Maḍmūn

(2) Ben Yishū—May God preserve your well-being b. al-Ḥasan b.Bundār

The Arabic address, written in the direction of the message, contains exactly the same words with the addition of 'the Israelite,' and in place of 'Yishū' in 1.2: Ishū.

COMMENTARY

No. 26

3 Nākhodā—ship-owner (Persian).

Rāmisht—The ships of this great merchant are frequently mentioned in these papers. Two inscriptions of this Rāmisht have been preserved at Mecca, one, dated 529/1135, relating the foundation of hospice, cf. *Répertoire chronologique d'épigraphie arabe,* Number 3075 (vol. VIII, pp. 196–7), and the second, his epitaph, from Sha'bān, 534/April 1140, cf. *Répertoire,* Number 3099 (vol. VIII, pp. 218–9); see also the Arab historian Ibn al-Athīr, sub anno 532 (ed. Tornberg, vol. XI, p. 43, 11. 5–9). One of his agents brought back from Canton in a single voyage merchandise of the fabulous value of 500,000 dīnārs. In 532/1138, he provided for the covering of the Ka'ba with Chinese silk, Gaston Wiet, 'Les marchands d'épices etc.', *Cahiers d'histoire égyptienne*, Cairo 1955, p. 85; S.M. Stern, 'Rāmisht of Sīrāf, a Merchant Millionaire of the Twelfth Century,' *Journal of the Royal Asiatic Society*, April, 1967, pp. 10–14.

4 Of small measure—the relationship between the small and the large measure is clarified by this document, both here and in 11. 20, 27–28. According to these references, 17 bahār (5,100 roṭl), of large measure = 20 bahār and 120 roṭl (= 6,120 roṭl) of small measure. The ratio is about 1.2:1; also in Number 28, 1. 17, and Number 58, 1.23.

5–7 There is no explanation for the deduction of 45 roṭl from 12 bahār, or any indication as to who received them. It seems, however, that this is a polite way of referring to the fee of the Representative of the Merchants namely, Maḍmūn. This payment, about 1.33%, is not much different from that mentioned in 4, 1. 10, where Maḍmūn's father received one qīrāt out of every two dinars of the price of each pieces, that is $^1/_{48}$.[10]

12 Cost of obtaining the goods—4 $^1/_6$ dinars for goods worth 402 $^5/_6$ dinars, that is, approximately one percent: apparently a government tax.

[10] This refers to the voyage to India of Joseph Lebdi of Tripoli, Libya, in 1095/6, his dealing with Ḥasan b. Bundār, of Aden, and his subsequent lawsits in Fustat, 1097/8, see S.D. Goitein, *Studies in Islamic History and Institutions*, Leiden, 1968, p. 336.

13 The baskets are mentioned elsewhere, for example in 20, verso, 1.17 and 28, 1.18. It seems that pepper and similar commodities were in need of ventilation, and were transferred from the containers in which they had been brought from India to the baskets.

23 The Highlands, of course, of India, and not, as above, 24, 1.26, of Yemem.

29 Joseph B. Abraham, a cousin of Maḍmūn, and prominent merchant.

31 Khalaf b. Isḥqāq, another cousin of Maḍmūn, a philanthropic notable.

46 Port of Aden: al-furḍah, the customs house of Aden, cf. Löfgren, *Aden im Mittelalter*, Uppsala 1950, p. 50.

47 Rāmisht—See 1.3 above. Either the ship which brought merchandise from India took merchandise on the return trip, or in another ship of the same merchant, 11. 17–19, above.

48 Muqaddam—a general term designating a person wielding power; it was the official title of the heads of the Eastern Jewish communities, see S.D. Goitein, *A Mediterranean Society*, II, pp. 68–75. It is not impossible that the reference here is to a Jewish shipowner, but since the owners of the other two boats bear Indian names, the word Muqaddam may refer to the holder of an Indian office. The ships of Ibn al-Muqaddam are mentioned also in 56, 1. 17.

50 Registration charges—*satmī*. All merchandise carried in a ship was registered, and after the arrival of the ship the captain received a set fee for this list. The term designated both the list and the fee. From the fact that the value of the pepper and the iron together, before the various deductions, was approximately 800 dinars, we see that the registration fee was about $^1/_2$% of the value of the merchandise.

26, Verso

3 Basket–*qawṣarah,* a word found in Aden to this day, see E.V. Stace, *English-Arabic Vocabulary* (Aden Colloquial), London, 1893, p. 17 s.v. 'Basket for dates'. Also heard by me.

6 Berbera mats—see 24, 1.12, above.

8 The zodiac, Ar. *burūj*, a common ornament on the floors of churches and synagogues in Byzantine times, decorated this costly carpet.

9 Manārī—Manārah is the name of a locality in south-west Muslim

Spain, near the city of Sidūnah (Yāqūt, *Geographical Dictionary*, p. 648). These woven goods were named after that district or were perhaps brought from there. A city near Saragossa, Spain, also bears this name, Yāqūt, *ibid.* A kerchief of the same type was sent from Aden to India according to 67, 11. 9, 18–19.

10 Abū Ghālib, the ship's captain—v. infra. 1. 15, 29. It is not specified whether this captain commanded one of the three ships mentioned above, recto, 11. 47–49, or another ship.

11 Lead—needed in the manufacture of copper vessels with which Ben Yijū dealt.

15 The Egyptian Mithqāl (or dinar) is here worth only 2.35 Malikī dinars, just as 28, 1. 32, below.

19 One third—Maḍmūn discounts this one third, see recto, 11. 39.40. As was shown, however, in the analysis of the account above, he rounded off small amounts also to the disadvantage of Ben Yijū.

20 'Eggs'—either a type of cardamon, or a form in which iron was shipped, 66, 1.6; 67, 1.29.

Arrived—the merchandise was delivered to the Representative of the Merchants who distributed it to those by whom they had been ordered.

29 Brazilwood boxes, i.e., made from *baqqam*, or sappan wood. This wood was one of the main dyeing stuffs, but, as we see here, served also as material for implements.

31 Ṭalḥī paper—named after Ṭālḥa b. Ṭāhir, ruler of Khūrasān in north-east Persia, who died in 828, see *Enc. Isl.*[2], IV, 419, s.v. 'Kāghad'. It is interesting that the name of a commodity remained constant for over three hundred years.

P.S.

In the final publication of the Geniza material on the India trade it is planned to edit the Arabic texts in a separate volume and to print the comments beneath the translations.

Annotated Bibliography

In the light of the changing perspectives of the study of early Indian trade certain issues are stressed; and these issues and the related debates have enriched our understanding of trade and commerce in early India. A few such issues have already been raised and discussed in the Introduction. This Annotated Bibliography is, therefore, linked with, but not confined to, the Introduction. In a book on history the Bibliography usually begins with references to the primary sources, the very raw material for historians. Then appear the secondary sources, the published studies of these raw materials. This Bibliography departs from this usual format and does not present a list of original or primary sources. Trade documents belonging and related to the early period of Indian history are virtually absent. The kind of trade documents worked upon by Casson, Kosambi and Goitein (included in this volume) are exceptions only to confirm the general nature of available data. Information regarding early exchange-related activities is available from scattered and meagre sources which are not trade documents *per se*. The selection of and preference for source(s) by historians of early Indian trade to drive home their points would be evident from the data cited by them in their respective papers and extracts included in this volume. There will be, nevertheless, citation of those primary sources which have been particularly used by the editor in his Introduction.

The works related to the concepts and theoretical issues regarding early trade— especially the different positions taken up by the formalists and substantivists—have been discussed and commented upon in the Introduction. Their relevance to the study of exchange-related activities in early India have also been examined. So the Bibliography on concepts, models, theories, etc. on early exchange and trade is placed here without further annotations.

GENERAL WORKS

Discussions on exchange and trade in early India are available not only in books and research articles but also in general reference works too. Moreover, trade is primarily related to economic activities in a given society, but economy and trade cannot be studied in isolation or in a compartmentalized manner. As Braudel (1977) showed, a complex society consists of several 'ensembles': economy, politics, culture, social hierarchy, etc. As these ensembles act and interact, economy and trade are best appreciated in terms of other ensembles.

There is strictly speaking no single volume which gives a general and connected account of India's trade from say the Harappan times to AD 1300. Most of the general surveys of early Indian history have a clear emphasis on the narration of dynasties and contain a chapter on economic conditions. Of the general works on early Indian history, the first five volumes of the *History and Culture of the Indian People* (Majumdar ed., 1951–70) present data on trade which forms a section of the chapter on economic history. Though a vast period is covered by these volumes, the chapters on economic conditions are merely descriptive and use dynastic labels for economic situations (e.g. Maurya economy, Gupta economy, etc.). This is more or less the standard approach to the study of economic history in some other compendium volumes (e.g. Majumdar and Dasgupta eds., 1981; Yazdani ed., 1960; Majumdar, 1978). The chapters/sections on trade and economic history are written chiefly on the basis of literary sources, especially the evidence of the normative texts like the Dharmaśāstras. The use of archaeological data is limited to a few pages of discussions on the economic conditions of the 'pre and proto'-historic times which is seen as preceding the age when written materials became available.

It is from about 1950 onwards that general overviews of early Indian history began to highlight the possibilities of changes in socio-economic and cultural life outside dynastic shifts, thanks to the pioneering researches of D.D. Kosambi (1956,1970) who looked askance at 'episodic history'. Taking the cue from Kosambi, R.S. Sharma (1983) discerned a number of distinct stages in the economic history of early India. R.S. Sharma and D.N. Jha (1974) in a bibliographical essay presented a historiography of early Indian economic life and assessed the trends and prospects of the perusal of early Indian material life, including the studies of early Indian trade and urbanism. A more recent attempt in assessing the trends of research in ancient Indian economic history is made by B.D. Chattopadhyaya (1991/1992). A recent collection of essays (B.D. Chattopadhyaya ed., 1987) highlights different economic aspects of life in early India in which some essays are related to trade and commerce. The possibilities of discerning changes and formations in early Indian economic life have been highlighted in a Bengali monograph by Ranabir Chakravarti (1991), who has sought to situate the changing contours of early Indian trade against the overall background of the social, political, economic and cultural developments in early India. The *Journal of the Economic and Social History of the Orient* has been a major scholarly forum for the study of pre-modern South Asian socio-economic history. Hermann Kulke (1993) prepared an extensive bibliographical essay on South Asian society and economy, with a particular thrust on trade in ancient and medieval India. This essay takes into consideration the history of the maritime trade of ancient and medieval India and links it with some vital social and cultural issues. Trade, both within the subcontinent and beyond, figures prominently in the recent collection of essays edited by Romila Thapar (1995b). This volume, containing contributions from leading historians of the Jawaharlal Nehru University, New Delhi, acquaints readers with the new trends and changing perspectives in the social, economic and cultural historiography of early India (up to AD 1300) during the last five decades. Early Indian trade issues are discussed herein not in isolation, but the inter-relatedness of trade with state formation, urbanity and cultural exchanges is emphasized. A major strength of this volume lies in its excellent and updated bibliography relevant to the respective chapters. Adequate attention has been paid to trade in the recent overview of ancient Indian history by D.N. Jha (1998). The importance of trade, including long-distance commerce, is clearly recognized by Jha in the formation of cities, territorial states and growing popularity of Buddhism and Jainism during the early historical times (*c*. 600 BC–AD 300).

The reader will find that the bibliography contains a number of references to books and papers on concepts, theories and models with regard to ancient/pre-modern trade. A considerable number of such works belong to the disciplines of anthropology and/or economic anthropology and ethnoarchaeological studies. The principal concepts and their relevance to and validity for the study of the history of early Indian trade have been discussed in section III of the Introduction.

HARAPPAN TRADE

It is certainly a daunting task to present a bibliography with comments on Harappan trade. The study of the Harappan civilization has itself assumed the character of a distinct sub-discipline within early Indian studies. Pande and Ramachandran (1971) prepared a bibliography of Harappan civilization, soon followed by another (Brunswig, 1974). Five years later the bibliography of the same contained as many as 1607 references to books and research papers (Possehl ed., 1979). The number must have multiplied significantly in the following couple of decades, though the exact number cannot be specified at this moment. The voluminous and ever-enlarging literature on Harappan studies—a sizable number of works being of a highly skilled and sophisticated nature—however, includes a number of excellent overviews. These overviews (Wheeler, 1968; Allchin and Allchin, 1982, 1993, 1997; Possehl ed., 1979, 1982/1993; Sankalia, 1974; Gupta *et al.* eds., 1984; B.K.Thapar and Mughal, 1992) are of immense help in the periodic updating of our knowledge and also in the acquaintance with new perspectives on the Harappan civilization. This is badly required because of the generation of new archaeological data and the emergence of new techniques of probing into this civilization. As the urban character of the Harappan society was established beyond doubt from the very discovery of the two outstanding sites, Mohenjodaro and Harappa, the non-agrarian sector of the economy— crafts and trade—attracted the attention of scholars.

The appreciation of the Harappan civilization—especially its mature phase—now stands on a firmer ground with the discovery of a few pre-Harappan sites in the north-western part of the subcontinent; e.g. Kalibangan (B.K. Thapar, 1985) and Mehrgarh (Jarrige, 1982). Both the sites hold crucial clues to the understanding of the networks of the communication patterns in the extensive zone of the Harappan civilization. The primary raw materials for the study of trade during the Harappan times are available from the principal excavated sites: Mohenjodaro (Marshall, 1931; MacKay, 1938), Harappa (Vats, 1940), Kalibangan (B.K. Thapar, 1975), Lothal (Rao, 1973), Banawali (Bisht, 1982) and Dholavira (Bisht, 1991), to mention only the outstanding sites.

A perusal of the bibliography of the Harappan civilization clearly shows a scholarly interest in the probings into the interactions between the Harappan civilization and its near-contemporary Bronze-Age civilizations in West Asia. Written documentation in this regard is supplied by Mesopotamian cuneiform tablets; availability of artefacts of non-indigenous character, including seals, in northwest India and West Asia also indicates contacts between the Harappan civilization and its West Asian counterparts. A significant step in this direction was taken by Gadd (in Possehl, 1979; originally published in 1932) who discussed 18 seals of the Harappan type discovered from Ur in Mesopotamia. These seals, either Harappan or a close copy of Harappan seals, are indicators of contact between the two civilizations, and even more so of commercial contact between the two and the presence of Harappan merchants in Mesopotamia. The evidence of Harappan/Harappan type seals found from Mesopotamia is admittedly small. But the meagre quantity of data was further supplemented by the readings into Mesopotamian cuneiform documents which speak of brisk commercial contacts between Akkad under Sargon of Agade on the one hand, and Tilmun or Dilmun, Makkan and Meluhha, on the other. The cuneiform tablets also impressed upon the sea-borne trade among these areas. This has resulted in growing literature on maritime commerce in the Arab/Persian Gulf area. The importance of Dilmun in this trade is focused upon by A.L. Oppenheim (1954), who enlisted the items transacted, assessed the importance of the trade in copper and suggested the location of Tilmun/Dilmun close to Mesopotamia. Most scholars tend to identify Tilmun/Dilmun in and around Bahrain on the Persian Gulf, an area which figures in Mesopotamian cuneiform documents as a paradise (Kramer, 1963 and 1964). Up to the end of the 1960s, scholarly opinion tended to favour the location of Makkan/Magan on the Makran coast in Baluchistan, first on the basis of philological affinities between Makkan/Magan and Mak(u)ran, and second because of the discovery of the two westernmost outposts of the Harappan civilization, viz. Sutkagendor and Sotka koh (Wheeler, 1968; Dales, 1962). In recent decades, there is a marked preference for identifying Makkan or Magan with the Oman peninsula, mainly on the basis of the availability of copper in that area, a description repeatedly occurring in the Mesopotamian cuneiform documents (Weisgerber, 1984, 1992; S. Cleuzeo, 1981, 1986, 1992; Tossi, 1986). There is an agreement among archaeologists to identify Meluhha with the Indus valley. The frequent descriptions of Meluhhan (i.e. Harappan) vessels visiting the Mesopotamian harbour during Sargon's reign in the Mesopotamian cuneiform documents have helped historians reconstruct the long-distance maritime Harappan trade with Mesopotamia in the Persian Gulf, with Tilmun/Dilmun playing the role of a commercial intermediary. A general overview of this is provided by Allchin and Allchin (1982), while the most detailed monograph on this subject is by Ratnagar (1981). The last mentioned work is important for an in-depth analysis of the exchangeable products in this trade relation, especially the transaction in diverse metals and minerals. In this connection the importance of Makkan or the Oman peninsula as the principal supplying zone of copper to both Meluhha and Akkad (via Tilmun) has been duly weighed.

The identifications of Tilmun, Makkan and Meluhha became a subject of keen controversy for about a decade from 1975 onwards. Departing from the more or less accepted identifications of the three places stated above, Romila Thapar (1975) suggested 'possible identifications' of Meluhha, Dilmun and Makkan, respectively with southern coastal Gujarat, Saurashtra and Sindh/Baluchistan. She established her hypothesis on the well-known postulate that western and northwestern India during the Harappan times were inhabited by Dravidian speakers. The above ancient toponyms were proposed to be located by her on the basis of Dravidian etymology in coastal Gujarat and Saurashtra (further supported by archaeological findings from Lothal). The most controversial identification was to equate Tilmun with Saurashtra. Her paper sparked off an immediate and sharp rejection of the identifications (Chakrabarti, 1975) on the basis of archaeological arguments. But the most telling critique was launched by During-Caspers and Govindkutty (1978) who strongly backed the well-entrenched idea of identifying Tilmun with Bahrain. During-Caspers' analysis of the cuneiform texts and associated archaeological evidence led her to conclude that 'so far we have found no single scrap of archaeological evidence or any convincing linguistic ground to corroborate Romila Thapar's identifications'. A further rejoinder to During-Caspers was written by Thapar (1983) in support of her Dravidian hypothesis.

E.C.L During-Caspers' sustained output (1979, 1984, 1987, 1991, 1992, 1996) argues very strongly in favour of Harappan maritime trade with Oman, Bahrain and Sumer, obviously through the Arabic/Persian Gulf; she further speaks of the presence of Sumerian merchants in the Harappan civilization. On the other hand, the presence of Harappan merchants in West Asia is demonstrated on the basis of cuneiform documents which speak of the Meluhhan village, an interpreter of the Meluhhan language and the owner of a Meluhhan seagoing vessel (S. Parpola, A. Parpola, and Brunswig, 1977; During-Caspers, 1984; Tossi, 1986 and 1993). Scholarly interest in the maritime trade of the Harappans gained a major impetus with the excavations at Lothal by S.R. Rao, who identified a huge structure as a dockyard and naturally considered Lothal as the premier Harappan port (1973, 1979). Such a claim was challenged by Leshnik (1964). But the importance of Lothal as a major commercial outlet on the Gujarat coast is effectively shown by the discovery of button seals associated with the Persian Gulf zone (Rao, 1964). In her survey of the Harappan trade, Shereen Ratnagar (1981) shows that: (i) Harappan trade was principally oriented to the Persian/Arabic Gulf, and (ii) the urge to procure raw materials (base metals, precious metals and minerals, and semi-precious stones) prompted Harappan merchants to establish trade links with distant areas. In view of the importance of the sea-borne trade of the Harappans with the Oman peninsula, Shahani (1997) urges consideration of ethnological and ethnoarchaeological data on traditional navigation and seafaring in this area to better understand the Bronze Age maritime movements.

Ratnagar's emphasis on Harappan maritime trade has been questioned by Chakrabarti (1990) who, without doubting the external trade contacts of the Harappans, perceives it to be essentially overland in character. Chakrabarti's suggestion that the India-Mesopotamia trade in the Sargonid period was direct does not exactly match his other assertion that the Harappans did not have a thriving external trade. The external overland trade of the Harappans is indicated by archaeological materials from Bactria in north-east Afghanistan which provided a further linkage to the Indo-Iranian borderland (Sarianidhi, 1979). That Iran could have acted as a corridor in the overland contacts between north-western India and Mesopotamia is indicated by the finds from TepeYahya and Shar-i-Sokta in Iran (Lamberg-Karlovsky, 1972). Mason's discoveries (1981) of three seals and a number of ivory pieces of distinct Harappan origin at Altyn depe and of an ithyphallic terracotta figurine (comparable to the one found from Mohenjodaro) from Namagaza are pointers to a northern overland route to southern Turkemenistan via the pre-Harappan site at Mundigak. Asthana (1984) has pointed to the importance of Shahdad in Iran in the history of the Indus-Iranian overland trade. The Harappan contacts with Central Asia, besides the Indo-Iranian borderland, are therefore, brought into the limelight. The Harappan overland trade through Afghanistan seems to have been largely prompted by the prospect of the procurement of precious lapis lazuli from Badakhshan. Close to the lapis mining area in Badakhshan stood the northernmost Harappan site of Shortughai from where it could reach the Indus valley proper and Iran also (Francfort, 1981, 1984; Casanova, 1992). Among the metals traded during the Harappan period, the question of the availability of tin, an indispensable ingredient for making bronze, has generated considerable debate. Hegde (1978) points to Rajasthan and Bihar as the possible sources of tin, but this has been challenged by Moorey (1985). Alternative sources of tin for the Harappans have been suggested as western Afghanistan and Badakhshan (Stech and Piggott, 1986).

A critique of Ratnagar's (1982) perception of Harappa as a 'gateway' city— derived from a recent model for understanding the geographical and economic significance of a certain location—may be seen in Lahiri (1990), who argues that 'the representation of Harappa as a gateway city is significantly dependent on the postulation of an external trade orientation and a lack of local specialised manufacture for it. . . . is clearly untenable'. In this context may also be cited Gupta's study of the internal trade of the Harappans (1984), a subject which has received less scholarly attention than it deserves. A recent assessment of new data and perspectives is presented by Ratnagar (1994), who also suggests a few revisions of previously-held notions about Harappan trade.

c. 1500–600/500 BC

This is the phase which is generally labelled as the Vedic age in Indian history, divided into two broad segments, the Ṛgvedic (*c*. 1500–1000 BC) and later Vedic (*c*.1000-600/500 BC). That there is a major rupture in the material culture from the days of the Harappan civilization to the Vedic period is more or less accepted by historians. General accounts of the economic life of the Vedic times also take into consideration the changes in the settlement pattern and the emergence of a sedentary agricultural society in the Ganga valley from the Ṛgvedic to the later Vedic times (Rapson ed., 1921; Majumdar ed., 1951; Majumdar, 1978). A more in-depth study of the Ṛgvedic economic life leads R.S. Sharma to consider it as a primarily cattle-keeping economy in which there was little urge for surplus production for exchange (1983b). The later Vedic period, according to Sharma, witnessed the consolidation of a sedentary agrarian society and the diversification of crafts (e.g. PGW and iron implements). Naturally, there is not much information on regular trade which, even if in operation, is generally viewed as marginal to the economy. Careful gleanings of data from the Vedic literature about transactions are available in Bandyopadhyaya (1945), who also discusses certain terms like *śatamāna*, *niṣka*, *kṛṣṇala*, etc. in relation to the medium of exchange. Recent historiography, however, does not perceive the emergence of state society with marketplace trade and urban society during the Vedic times (Sharma, 1983a,1983b; Thapar 1984); in fact, the polity of the more complex later Vedic times is viewed at the most as a 'proto-state' (Sharma, 1989). Thapar (1995a) suggests that the immense importance given to numerous rituals and sacrifices, which considerably influenced the way of life of the three upper *varṇas*, resulted in the consumption of the social surplus in sacrificial rituals. This perhaps prevented the mercantile community from utilizing the available resources for regular exchanges. Thapar (1978) highlights the importance of the institution of *dakṣiṇā* or the payment of sacrificial fees to the priest as a form of exchange, distinct from the marketplace transaction of commodities. The redistributive character of *dakṣinā* is situated in the context of the gradual emergence of ruling lineages which replaced the previous clan-based chieftaincies (Roy, 1996).

600/500–200 BC

The material life of India during these four centuries has been more intensively studied by historians than that of the Vedic age. The couple of centuries from the sixth century BC onwards are associated with significant changes in the socio-economic, political and cultural situations in north India, in general, and the Ganga valley, in particular. The emergence of *mahājanapadas*, the beginning of urbanism in the Ganga valley and the rise of Buddhism and Jainism along with some other heterodox religious sects are all pointers to significant changes. That the new religions were more intimate with the urban community than with the rural folk was indicated by Debiprasad Chattopadhyaya (1959) in his seminal study of early Indian materialist philosophy; the point has also been investigated by Ling (1980) and Sarao (1990). The starting point of the study of the Pali canonical texts and the

Jātaka stories for gleaning data on socio-economic life began with the publications of Fick (1897, tr. 1920), T.W. Rhys Davids (1903) and F.C. Rhys Davids (1901, 1921). The greater importance of commerce and urbanism found in the Buddhist and Jaina texts did not go unnoticed in their writings. The *seṭṭhi* or the merchant par excellence figures very prominently in such researches, especially those based on the Buddhist Jātakas. Attention is also directed to the descriptions in the Pali texts of the *sārthavāha* or the caravan merchant. To this genre of narratives of trade and traders in the Buddhist texts—especially the Jātakas—belong the works of Fiser (1954), Sen (1972), Chakraborti (1966), Srivastava (1968) and Motichandra (1972). A more incisive approach taking into account the routes of communication, the diverse types of products and the medium of exchange in the discussion of trade is taken up by Bose (1967). That the overland routes of communication can be studied on the basis of field archaeological materials is shown by Lahiri (1992); she looks at the distribution of certain products and tries to trace the possible findspots/sources of the raw materials on the basis of early modern European notices of the availability of certain metals and minerals. This has been utilized by her to suggest the possible lines of communication for the procurement of raw materials and the distribution of finished products.

A significant historiographical shift in the study of trade during this period is seen in the last three decades. Wagle (1966) and Uma Chakravarti (1987) have made insightful analyses of the social and economic life of merchants on the basis of the Pali canonical texts and not by the indiscriminate use of the Jātaka tales which actually belong to a much later period. Wagle applies the methods of social anthropology in analysing the social data in the Pali texts and clearly brings into the limelight the favourable attitude of Buddhism to trade and traders. Uma Chakravarti enlightens us on the characterization of *vaṇijjā* or trade as an *ukkaṭṭha kamma* (excellent profession) which is related to several *ukkaṭṭha sippas* (excellent crafts) like *muḍḍā* (money matters), *gaṇanā* (accounting) and *lekha* (writing). A key figure in this respect is the *gahapati*, an immensely rich person deriving his wealth primarily from his sizable landed possesions. Thapar (1984, 1995a) shows that the *seṭṭhi-gahapati*, distinct from both the *seṭṭhi* and the *gahapati*, seems to have played the role of a financier of capital to petty merchants and shop-keepers. According to Thapar, a portion of the wealth gained by the *gahapati* from his landed possessions could have been invested in various trades, leading to the emergence of the *seṭṭhi-gahapati*. Another significant development is the growing use of field archaeological materials for the study of trade during the sixth–second centuries BC. In this respect the importance of the distribution of the NBPW from Bihar and eastern UP to different parts of the Ganga valley can hardly be overlooked (Ghosh ed., 1989). That Kośala and Magadha, the two premier *mahājanapadas*, derived considerable advantage out of trade—both overland and riverine—is recognized by Kosambi (1952). The gradual transformation of Pāṭaligāma from a *puṭabhedana* (a trade centre of the nature of a stockade) to Pāṭaliputra, the premier political and urban centre of north India and later of the subcontinent, has attracted historians' attention (Kosambi, 1956; Ranabir Chakravarti, 1996). Of late the studies of trade in this period are integrated and subsumed within the broader issues of the formation of cities and territorial states in the Ganga valley. A preference for the utilization of field archaeological materials for the study of cities and state systems in the Ganga valley is evident nowadays. The interlinkages between urban growth and the formation of monarchical states have been underlined. Enquiries into the non-agrarian sector of the economy are therefore logical, but unlike the conventional approach to economic history, trade and urbanism are sought to be situated in the overall agrarian material milieu in northern India. Some archaeologists and a few historians have emphasized the role of iron technology in the generation of the vital agrarian surplus without which, in their opinion, the crystallization of the monarchical power, the burgeoning of the non-agrarian sector of the economy and the emergence of cities would have been hardly possible (Kosambi, 1956, 1970; Banerjee, 1965; Sharma, 1983a, 1983b, Thakur, 1981). The Marxist approach views technological change (iron technology) as the principal agent of social change (emergence of cities and states), a formulation already seen in the studies of 'first civilizations' by V. Gordon Childe (1950, 1964). An interesting counterpoint is offered by Ghosh (1973), Niharranjan Ray (1976) and Dilip K. Chakrabarti (1973, 1988) who argue against the primacy accorded to technological factors. They consider surplus as a complex social and socio-political product and not merely as a technological product. The ensuing debate has immensely enriched the historiography of city and state formation in the Ganga valley. Recent statements and assessments of this ongoing debate are available in Allchin (1989, 1990, 1995), Dilip K. Chakrabarti (1995), Ranabir Chakravarti (1991), Erdosy (1984, 1987, 1988, 1995) and Thapar

(1984 and 1995a). The linkages among the spread of Buddhism, development of trade and political expansion are underlined by Heitzman (1984).

The tendencies apparent in the economic life in the sixth–fifth centuries BC matured in the Maurya period (*c.* late fourth century to early second century AD). Discussions on the economy of the Maurya period tend to rely rather heavily on the textual prescriptions in the *Kauṭilīya Arthaśāstra.* N.C. Bandyopadhyaya (1944), Kangle (1965), and Ghoshal (1966) regularly utilized the *Arthaśāstra* material to suggest the close surveillance of the Maurya state on commercial activities. Sen (1969) pays particular attention to economic ideas in the *Arthaśāstra* and devotes a chapter on the trade mechanisms. The monolithic and unitary character of the Maurya state, ever vigilant to stamp out the merchant who is always a suspect figure in the *Arthaśāstra*, is blown up in this interpretation. Though the political paramountcy of the Mauryas is not doubted, the altered perception of the Maurya state speaks of a lesser degree of centralization of the economy (Thapar, 1978, 1981, 1987). Recent historiography of the Maurya state and economy has a pronounced thrust on the agrarian economy of the Maurya period, since it provided the most important resource base for the management of the vast Maurya empire, carved out and maintained by a large standing army and an impressive administrative organization. The discussions on trade and communications in the Maurya realm are apparently secondary to those on the agrarian sector (Nilakanta Sastri ed., 1952; Thapar, 1961; Bongard-Levin, 1985). That the Mauryas had a distinct material interest in procuring mineral resources from the Deccan to the advantage of the metropolitan area of the empire, i.e. Magadha, is now well demonstrated (Allchin, 1962; Thapar, 1961, Thapar, 1995). How and to what extent Aśokan edicts provide intelligent clues to the Mauryan interests in providing facilities for communication and contacts has already been discussed in the Introduction. Fussman (1987-88) demonstrates on the basis of the distribution of Aśokan edicts the patterns and problems of communications between the core and the peripheral areas of the empire. Thapar (1987) explores the possible commercial significance of the Dhamma missions sent out by Aśoka to five rulers in West Asia and draws our attention to the importance of Sopara (a well-known port and also the findspot of the set of fourteen Rock Edicts of Aśoka) as the point of maritime contact between the western sea-board and the Persian Gulf. Encouraging results in these types of enquiries are in the offing due to considerable progress in what is called the Gulf archaeology. The Seleucid presence in the Gulf and the commercial role of Failaka Island near Quait are clearly attested to from archaeological materials (Salles, 1987, 1996).

GROWTH OF TRADE AND INDIA'S ROLE IN INTERNATIONAL COMMERCE 200 BC–AD 300

As has been indicated in the Introduction, the collapse of the Maurya empire did not result in any catastrophe in socio-economic, political and cultural life in the subcontinent. In fact, the spread of the Maurya power over vast stretches of the subcontinent helped the intrusion of many traits of the Ganga valley material life in to central India, the Deccan and south India. The impact of this is clearly seen in the advent of sedentary agricultural society, craft organization and brisk trade in peninsular India. The period is marked by the spread of state society and urban centres beyond north India. Kosambi (1956) clearly indicated that the spate of foreign invasions through the north-west did not cause any hindrance to India's contacts with West and Central Asia; in fact, this seems to have paved the way for a brisker and more regular communication with the West than ever before.

The significance of Begram and Taxila in the long-distance overland trade network is unmistakable; the former was categorically described as a clearing house of Indian exports to the West by Wheeler (Wheeler, 1955; Marshall, 1951). The impact of the Hellenistic West on the urbanization at Taxila is clearly betrayed by the grid pattern settlement of the city at the Sirkap mound. It was aptly described by Ghosh as being foreign in conception and layout (1973). The invasions of Central Asian nomadic tribes like the Śakas and the Yüeh-chihs (later Kuṣāṇas) led to intimate commercial and cultural contacts between the north-western part of the subcontinent and Central Asia. An area of crucial importance was Bactria in north-east Afghanistan which was fertile, a major centre of international trade and a seat of power of the Bactrian Greeks, the Śakas and finally, the Kuṣāṇas (Mukherjee, 1969, 1989; Frye, 1996). Dobbins (1971) demonstrates that constant warfare notwithstanding, the Śaka conquest of Gandhāra and Kapiśa was associated with the issuance of coins at a very brisk pace, clearly implying the regularity of overland trade. The discovery of inscriptions and drawings in the

Karakorum highway has immensely enriched our understanding of the importance of Gilgit and Chilas and areas around them for providing a difficult though effective corridor with Central Asia. The presence of the Sogdians and the Chinese in epigraphic records on rocks is a clear pointer to the significance of this route, which in ancient Chinese chronicles figures as the Chi-pin (Kashmir) route (Dani, 1983; Jettmar ed., 1989, 1991).

The growth of overland trade through the northwest was certainly instrumental in the transformation of Mathurā in the Ganga-Yamuna doab from an ordinary city to a vibrant commercial, politico-administrative and cultural centre during its occupation by the Śakas and the Kuṣāṇas. The rise of Mathurā as a leading urban centre in early historical India is not difficult to trace because of the profusion of field archaeological, epigraphic and literary sources and art objects, not only from Mathurā itself, but also from the nearby excavated site of Sonkh (Hartel, 1994; Srinivasan ed., 1988). That Mathurā's pre-eminence was largely due to its position as a nodal point at the convergence of several trade routes is beyond any doubt (Eggermont, 1966; Mukherjee, 1981; Bajpai, 1989). Mercantile activities are seen not only in large urban areas and commercial centres (*nigamas*), but the active presence of merchants and administrative functionaries is also evident in the epigraphic records from a relatively isolated, remote and inhospitable place like Bandhogarh in Rewa, M.P. (Ray, 1990; Chakravarti, 1995). Bandhogarh seems to have been situated on an important trade route linking the Deccan and central India with the middle Ganga valley. The epigraphic evidence of the construction of a gymnasium (*vyāyamaśālā*) there by a merchant cannot but speak of the percolation of Hellenistic culture from the north-west as a result of commercial linkage, direct or indirect (Chakravarti and Dutta, Majumder, 1992). Donative records from two famous Buddhist sites in central India, viz., Sanchi and Bharhut show the convergence of donors at these two places from various places in India; the evidence has led Ray (1987) to consider them as nodal points in the overland trade between the Ganga valley and the Deccan, on the one hand, and between central India and western India, on the other.

The Deccan experienced major historical changes in this period, the most remarkable of which is the formation of secondary states and urban centres (Senaviratne, 1981). Kosambi (1955) clearly established the interrelatedness between the growth of trade, the rise of craftsmen's organizations and the spread of Buddhist *saṁghas* in the western Deccan. It was he who effectively identified the *vaṇiyagāma* in an inscription from Karle as a professional body of merchants, which would attain considerable prominence in early medieval south India as the *maṇigrāmam*. Closely related to this analysis is Palmer's incisive study (1946) of the significance of the passes (Thalghat, Bhorghat and Nanaghat) in the Sahyadri range providing the vital linkages between the ports of Konkan and the mainland. Kosambi's indications have been elaborated by Ray (1986) in her study of the expansion of agriculture, development of commodity production, brisk trade and the increasing prominence of the Buddhist monasteries in the Deccan, often located on or near existing trade routes. In the opinion of Parasher (1996), trade was an agent of social change in the mid-Godavari valley and 'further strengthened economic structures of commodity production'.

A salient feature of the historiography of trade of this period relates to India's role in long-distance commerce with the Graeco-Roman world, the so-called Indo-Roman trade (*c.* late first century BC to AD 250). The most significant aspect of this trade is its increasing orientation to the sea by the better utilization of the more or less predictable alterations of the monsoon wind system in the Indian Ocean. The subject has a very long and equally rich historiography. Thapar (1997) traces the beginning of the study of India's commercial linkages with the Roman empire as early as the eighteenth century on the basis of the Classical accounts. But more sustained enquiries in this direction are seen in the first half of the twentieth century, especially the first three decades. The pioneering efforts came from Rawlinson (1917), Rostovzeff (1926) and Warmington (1928, rpt. 1974). Rostovzeff was one of the few scholars who combined literary and archaeological evidence for the study of the social and economic history of the Roman empire, while Warmington's survey is almost entirely based on the Classical literature. The archaeological corroboration of this long-distance trade comes from the discovery of hoards of Roman coins with a distinct concentration of such evidence from the far south and the excavation at Arikamedu near Pondicherry (Wheeler and Deva, 1948). The main thrust of these works was to highlight the Roman/Western initiative in this trade and to portray India as a mere supplier of luxury items to the West; such a position is taken to represent Roman trade with India as a precursor of the dominance of the European trading companies in India and the Indian Ocean areas. Indian historians soon picked up the cue from their

European counterparts. An excellent statement on the state of the subject up to 1950 is seen in Ghoshal (1957). Chakraborty (1965) and Srivastava (1966) and Adhya (1966) present narrative details of ports, routes, commodities and coinage but without an adequate analytical approach. Margabandhu (1966) discusses Graeco-Roman connections with western India on the basis of archaeological artefacts. In his study of the economic conditions of the Deccan, Das (1969) gleans valuable data on trade from diverse sources, largely literary, but rarely addresses the problem whether trade was a causal factor of urban growth in the Deccan. The most elaborate bibliographical survey of trade between India and the Roman empire was made by Raschke (1978).

How and how much were Indians interested in trade with the West has attracted the attention of scholars. Mukherjee (1970) seeks to establish the distinct economic motive behind the Kuṣāṇa conquest of the lower Indus valley where was located the port of Barbaricum which figured prominently in the *Periplus*. This is a point further probed into by Chakravarti (1986); he tries to demonstrate how the Śaka-Sātavāhana struggle in the Deccan and western India was largely prompted by the prospects of making economic gains out of this trade—especially the maritime trade between India and the western Indian Ocean. Mukherjee (1980–81) further argues that the Kuṣāṇa state was aware of the revenue-yielding potentials of trade, especially long-distance trade and relates this with the Kuṣāṇa monetary policy. Moreover, he considers that India's commercial contacts with Central and West Asia brought about cultural interactions which enriched early Indian culture. Fynes (1996) enlightens us on the religious attitudes and trading communities in western India during the early centuries AD. The rise of a monied community, which included merchants, the increasing instances of donations (*dāna*) made with a view to acquiring merit (*puṇya*) and the social mileage derived from patronage to religious and cultural activities are effectively analysed by Nath (1987).

One can easily note the remarkable spurt of publications during the 1980s and 1990s on the maritime commerce of India with the eastern fringes of the Roman empire. There are two new translations of the *Periplus of the Erythraean Sea* by Huntingford (1980) and Casson (1989). Economic historians have understandably offered stimulating re-readings of the sea-borne commerce by taking up the *Periplus* and other associated Classical authors, like Strabo, Pliny and Ptolemy. Casson's contributions deserve special mention in that he combines the textual evidence with studies of ancient seafaring, navigational and boat-building technologies (1980, 1988a, 1988b, 1991a, 1991b). Casson (1990) has also made a masterly study of a loan contract document between an Indian merchant at the famous Malabar port of Muziris and a merchant at Alexandria, the premier port of Egypt and the eastern Mediterranean. His fresh examination of Pliny's account of the development of maritime routes between India and the West suggests that the most improved stage of voyages brought mariners and merchants from a Red Sea port to Malabar as quickly as in twenty days, which was earlier thought to have taken forty days. Mazzarino (1997) suggests that the commonly known *hipalus* (*hippalus*) wind, mentioned by Pliny, is actually a misreading of the term *hypalum*; his reading would suggest that the wind system was so named not after a Greek sailor called Hipplaus, but the term *hypalum* stood for the seasonal southwest wind. Profound scholarship is writ large in the textual comparison between Classical accounts and the Sangam literature on the commerce between India and the Roman empire by Romanis (1997). Thapar (1992) establishes the signal importance of the pepper of Malabar in the sea-borne trade with the Roman empire; this set the trend for the enormous demand for Malabarese pepper in Europe right up to the early modern times. The immense demand for eastern spices, including pepper, among the Romans has been minutely examined—along with identifications of plant names—by Miller (1969).

The renewed interest in the maritime commerce between the Roman empire and South Asia is immensely helped by the systematic use of field archaeological data. The study of this commercial intercourse was previously based on textual accounts, further supplemented by epigraphic and numismatic evidence. The importance of the Red Sea ports like Myos Hormos and Berenice is now better appreciated in the light of field archaeological researches made there (Sidebotham, 1992). No less interesting is the discovery of the names of Indian merchants in an inscription from Egypt; the names appear to have been those typically of the early historical Deccan (Salomon, 1991). Such evidence clearly shows that the Indian merchant did venture to overseas countries and the commercial initiatives and movements were not necessarily a monopoly of Western traders.

Coming to the situation in South Asia, Begley's fresh excavations and examination of the key site of Arikamedu has considerably changed our perspective (1983, 1986, 1993). The Rouletted Ware, thought by Wheeler to have been a Roman import, is , according to Begley (1991), indicative of pre-Roman Hellenistic contacts with India. The importance of archaeological artefacts like pottery, jewellery, coins, art objects of distant origin for offering material evidence of trade is underlined by archaeologists and historians of early South Asian trade (Begley and de Puma ed., 1991). But this volume edited by Begley and de Puma does not bring the sea in to proper focus though the explicit purpose of the volume was to study ancient sea trade. This is probably because of their excessive thrust on presenting artefactual data on trade. Tchernia (1996) reviewing this volume also cautions that archaeological data should not be projected as the all-purpose key to solve riddles of the past. Casson rightly suggests the growing importance of ports in the Coromandel and Vengi littorals to the Roman/Western traders from the second century AD on the basis of Ptolemy. This is clearly confirmed by recent excavations of many archaeological sites in or near this coastal tract, e.g., Alaganakulam (1991), Vasavasamudram (Raman, 1991), Nagarjunakonda, Salihundam (Sarkar, 1987). The archaeological perspective helps us appreciate the data in the Sangam literature on trade and the growth of urbanism in south India (Champakalakshmi, 1975–76, 1996a). That the entire east coast participated in a network of commerce and communication is clearly seen in the distribution of Rouletted Ware from Mantai in Sri Lanka to Tāmralipta and Chandraketugarh in West Bengal (Begley, 1986, 1991). Minute and complex testing of the clay of the Rouletted Ware has convinced Ghogte (1997) that Tāmralipta and Chandraketugarh in coastal West Bengal were the principal production and distribution centres of the Rouletted Ware along the entire east coast. The discovery of Rouletted Ware in South-East Asia therefore is taken as a pointer of contacts between the east coast and South-East Asia. The early maritime contacts between the eastern littorals of India and maritime and mainland South-East Asia are nowadays better understood by the increasing utilization of archaeological evidence, including pottery, coins, beads and seals and sealings (Glover, 1988, 1996; Ray, 1987–8, 1989a, 1990). Ray (1996a) provides useful overviews of recent advances in archaeological findings in South-East Asia, but the monograph suffers from (a) the lack of a proper methodology for the study of maritime trade, ports and their hinterland, and (b) an overemphasis on Buddhism as the ideology propping up maritime trade and (c) several factual lacunae.

The role of the Bengal coast, having two excellent ports in Tāmralipta and Chandraketugarh, is better illuminated by the reading of inscribed seals and sealings mainly from coastal West Bengal by Mukherjee (1990). According to Mukherjee, these documents were written in a 'mixed Brāhmi-Kharoṣṭī' script. The importance of the spread of Kharoṣṭī from northern to eastern India as a pointer to the growing contacts— cultural and commercial—between northern and eastern India has already been discussed in the Introduction. The spread of Kharoṣṭī to South-East Asia is further indicated by the use of the said script in the coinage of Dvārāvatī (Mukherjee, 1996). Mukherjee's suggestion that the Bengal coast was involved in the maritime trade of north-western horses to South-East Asia seems to have been confirmed by the clear depiction of the figure of a horse aboard a ship on an inscribed terracotta sealing (*c.* third century AD) from Chandraketugarh (Chakravarti, 1992). Chandraketugarh has in fact yielded a few unique inscribed seals showing different types of ships, boats and vessels. These not only highlight the significance of the commercial importance of the riverine port of Chandraketugarh, but also break new ground in the study of ancient navigation on the Bengal coast (Chakravarti, 1992/96).

The period, we have already noted, marks the peak of the second urbanization in Indian history. The subcontinental overview of urban growth is presented by Allchin (1995) and Chakrabarti (1995), though the latter confines himself largely to listing archaeological sites of urban proportion. Urban centres in Andhra Pradesh, though certainly participating in trade and trade with the Hellenistic world (evident from the amphitheatre-like structure at Nagarjunakonda), are viewed as agro-cities by Sarkar (1987), as the commerce there largely revolved around agrarian and animal products and the cities were not essentially manufacturing centres. Champakalakshmi (1996a) attributes the proliferation of urban centres in ancient Tamilakam to trade, including external trade; hence she considers the urban spread in ancient Tamilakam as largely the result of the impact of external stimulus. This is a point also figuring in Gurukkal (1995). It is strange that Ray (1995) does not consider Arikamedu and a few other coastal sites in Tamil Nadu as Indo-Roman trading stations; her assertion does not find support in the essay by Gurukkal (1995) who enlists several such Roman trading stations in coastal Tamil Nadu. The Sri Lankan situation is now studied with the help of Classical notices of the island, the evidence of Tamil-Brāhmī inscriptions and the artefacts found from the Anuradhapura excavations (Boppearachchi, 1998).Trade with the Roman empire was certainly a landmark in early Indian economic history. But it can neither be projected as a forerunner of the European domination of South Asian trade in the early modern times nor as establishing a world system; but that it broke and intruded into some existing trade circuits in South Asia has to be recognized (Thapar 1992, 1997).

AD 300–600

The historiography of trade in India during these three centuries has a rather lacklustre look than that for the first three centuries AD. The principal interests of economic historians are related to the emergence of the *agrahāra* system and its profound impact on the agrarian scene. Maity's (1957) is the single monograph on the economic conditions in north India during the Gupta period and this has factually rich chapters on trade, currency system and credit system. The same conventional approach is seen in Gupta (1977–78) who undertakes a thorough survey of epigraphic, numismatic and literary evidences of commerce during the Gupta times in a chapter on economic conditions.

Marxist historiography argues from an altogether different angle. Gradual decrease in trade, especially long-distance trade with the Roman empire, further buttressed by the land-based *agrahāra* economy, indications of urban decay and a decline in the use of coins are projected as markers of a new socio-economic formation: the formation of Indian feudalism (Kosambi, 1956, 1970, 1972; Sharma, 1958) in which trade is thought to have taken a backseat. Sharma (1983b) further draws our attention to the fact that while the Guptas had, at least during their heyday, excellent gold and silver coinage (pointing to long-distance trade relations), copper coinage associated with transactions at local levels and of daily necessities became less frequent. Combining the accounts of Fa-hsien and Hsuan Tsang on the impoverished condition of many urban centres in the Ganga valley with the field archaeological data on declining civic life, the beginning of urban decay is suggested as a consequence of shrinking trade (Sharma, 1975). The contrast between the monetary situation of north India and the Deccan has been brought under the historian's scrutiny; the absence of any coinage of the Vākāṭakas and a solitary reference to a merchant in the entire range of Vākāṭaka inscriptions have been analysed in the light of the feudal tendencies in the Deccan (Shrimali, 1987). The evidence of lingering trade, particularly in western India, is sought to be situated in the emergent feudal economy (Kosambi, 1958). The presence of a mercantile group called *vaṇiggrāma* is evident from a record of AD 592 (Kosambi, 1958). To this may now be added an even earlier evidence of the same organization in a recently discovered copper plate of the Hūṇa king Toramāna, *c.* AD 500–15 (Mehta and Thakkar, 1978). The image of declining trade and impoverished urban centres is not unanimously accepted. Slump in trade, including maritime trade, is not evident in the two Tamil epics, the *Śilappādikarām* and the *Maṇimekhalai* (Champakalakshmi, 1996a). Bengal also does not appear to have experienced any setback in commerce and urban economy (Sen, 1942; Ray, 1980; Morrison, 1980). Thapar (1997) does not uphold the position that the withdrawal of Roman commercial interests in South Asia after *c.* AD 250 uniformly affected the urban economy in an adverse manner.

THE EARLY MEDIEVAL SITUATION: AD 600–1300

The early medieval period in Indian history has a very impressive bibliography enriched by a major debate on Indian feudalism. The proponents of Indian feudalism portray the crystallization of trends in the economic life, seen in the previous three centuries, during the period from AD 600 to 1000. A major plank of the theoretical formulation of Indian feudalism is the question of trade, or more precisely, the languishing of trade. In the empirically richest study of the feudal social formation in India, Sharma (1980) attaches great importance to the languishing trade—especially external trade—of India, a corresponding decline of coinage and urban decay in three regions of India: Bengal and Bihar under the Pālas, Rajputana and the Ganga-Yamuna doab under the Gurjara Pratihāras and the Deccan under the Rāṣṭrakūṭas. The pan-Indian urban contraction is presented by Sharma (1987) as a contrastive element to rural expansion as a typical feature of a feudal material milieu. The reduction of trade to the margins is further buttressed by the incisive study of varied textual materials by Yadava (1973, also his essays in Jha ed.,1987). The importance of usury in the early medieval situation hence forms a part of the inquiry of Sharma to understand the monetary scenario in the feudal set up. Looking specifically at Bengal under the Pālas and the Senas, Thakur (1993) almost echoes Sharma and offers an image of the dwindling commerce and decaying urban centres. Urban areas, in the eyes of the proponents of Indian feudalism, lost their relevance as centres of manufacture and trade and were reduced to military camps, temporary courts and pilgrim centres. The historiography of Indian feudalism and the perception of a decline in trade has undergone significant transformation in the last two decades. Both Sharma and Yadava (see their papers in Jha ed., 1987) concede to a revival of trade and urbanism after AD 1000; such a situation is explained in terms of the 'climax and cracks' in Indian feudalism (1000–1200). The historiography of Indian feudalism generally upholds an image of crisis and decline in the polity, socio-economic life and cultural conditions, the crisis being explained from the point of view of the Puranic account of the Kali age and the collapse of the centralized political structure after *c*. AD 500 (Sharma, 1982; Sahu, 1997). In a penetrating critique of Indian feudalism such a historiographical stance is labelled as 'epicentric' (B.D. Chattopadhyaya, 1994). While the Marxist historians must be credited for showing the changing character of early Indian society and economy, there is an implicit attempt on their part to relate the decline of trade and urbanism with the end of Roman trade with India and a revival of the same with the onset of Arab seafaring in the Indian Ocean. In other words, the proponents of Indian feudalism look for external stimuli as the agents of change in Indian history. Nandi (1984), however, speaks of the possibility of growth in the rural economy in the early medieval times—largely as an impact of agrarian expansion through landgrants—though the rural growth did not disturb the feudal structure.

The critique of Indian feudalism has already been touched upon in the Introduction. So only the salient points in this critique will be raised here. A major counterpoint is seen in the empirical presentation of thriving trade, contrary to the perception of dwindling commerce. Sircar (1979,1982), celebrated for his customary mastery over epigraphic documentation and effective marshalling of literary data, firmly rejects the notion of any decline whatsoever in commerce and urban economy during the early middle ages. There have been now major advances in the study of the fields of coinage and currency during the early medieval times. The currency situation in Bengal, one of the areas where typical symptoms of declining commerce were found by Sharma, does not appear to have suffered from 'monetary anaemia'; Mukherjee (1982, 1990) leaves little room for doubt about the high quality silver coinage in south-eastern Bengal from *c*. seventh to thirteenth centuries. As Bengal also experienced the landgrant economy, it clearly demonstrates that there was no incompatibility between circulation of coins and the landgrant economy. The north Indian monetary situation has been surveyed by Gopal (1963, 1966). The painstaking examination of various coin-hoards by Deyell (1990) drives home the fragility of the theoretical foundation of the languishing monetary economy. The situation of the currency system in south India has been studied by B.D. Chattopadhyaya (1977).

B.D. Chattopadhyaya (1974) not only provides ample epigraphic data to demonstrate the continuity of trade and urbanism in the early medieval Ganga valley, contrary to the perception of Sharma and his followers, but more significantly suggests that urban development and decay were not necessarily an outcome of external trade. Elsewhere he cogently argues that the practice of issuing landgrants in fact led to the proliferation of agrarian settlements which tapped locally available irrigational and other environmental resources. Thus was paved the way for the formation of the local-level economy which could not be explained, in his opinion, by political decentralization and economic decline (1990). The spread of agrarian society into areas where there was little sedentary settlement before was associated with the emergence of the *jāti-varṇa* society and the formation of local-level monarchical states. This is in keeping with Chattopadhyaya's perception of local formation which experienced the forces of integration, in sharp contrast to the construction of the fragmentation of polity and economy (Sharma, 1980; Yadava, 1973; Jha, 1987) and that of segmented polity (Stein, 1980; Spencer, 1977). The situation was ripe for the emergence of local-level market centres like *haṭṭa* and *maṇḍapikā* in different parts of north India, with a concentration of such trade centres in Rajasthan and Gujarat. The interesting point is that such marketplaces appear in records prior to AD 1000 (Ranabir Chakravarti, 1996a), a date which marks the beginning of brisker trade in the historiography of Indian feudalism. If the *haṭṭas* and *maṇḍapikās* appear as local-level market centres in early medieval north India, the contemporary Deccan witnessed the emergence of a similar type of market centre situated in between the rural-level market centre and the larger urban marketplace. This is variously called the *peṇṭhā/piṇṭha/peṁṭa* in the early medieval Deccan and it corresponds to modern *peths* in the Deccan. The nature of such a *peṇṭhā* has been examined by Ranabir Chakravarti (1996b) on the basis of the *Yaśastilakacampu* of Somadevasuri (AD 959). The situation is not much different either in the far south. An in-depth probe into the large number of Coḷa inscriptions by Hall (1980) shows that the *nagaram* as a locality-level market centre stood above the rural market centres but below the large urban marketplaces or coastal ports. There is, therefore, considerable commonality in the process of the emergence of locality-level marketplaces in north India, the Deccan and the far south. The possibilities of the diversification and specialization of crafts (particularly iron-based industries) and the related improvement in internal trade in the north Indian context is thoroughly studied by Mazumder (1979-80). Mazumder (1982), however, suggests a gradual decline in the importance of the organization of crafts which began to be formed in terms of family line. He also furnishes significant epigraphic evidence of the spatial mobility of the Brahmaṇas (1978–9).

It is rather strange that in the construction of Indian feudalism scholars chose to ignore the substantial evidence of India's maritime trade with the Islamic West, South-East Asia and China available in Arabic and Persian texts, Chinese accounts and medieval European accounts. The rise of Islam certainly provided a boost to Asian trade in general. But even before the rise of Arab trade to great prominence, the distinct interests of both the Sasanid empire in Iran and the Eastern Roman Empire in Byzantium in the maritime trade in the Persian Gulf and the Arabian Sea are now well known (Whitehouse and Williamson, 1973). The importance of Arab maritime trade in Indian economic history was clearly demonstrated by Nainar (1942) and Hourani (1951). Recent advances in the understanding of Indian Ocean trade before AD 1500 have led to a much better appreciation of South Asian maritime commerce (Verlinden, 1987; Varadarajan, 1987; Gunawardana,1987). K.N. Chaudhuri (1985, 1990) has enlightened us on the periodic shifting in the importance of the Persian Gulf and the Red Sea. The beginning of segmented voyages, according to Chaudhuri, around AD 1000 proved to be distinctly advantageous to India's sea-borne commerce. A recent study of the impact of Arab trade as an agent of major change in Indian history (Wink, 1990), however, overemphasizes the role of external trade in Indian history. Wink further bases himself almost entirely on the secondary materials using Arabic and Persian sources. That a more mature understanding of maritime trade and mercantile activities in a coastal area is possible by combining Arabic textual evidence with Indian sources is emphasized by Ranabir Chakravarti (1986, 1990). The impact of Arab trade was best felt in the western sea-board of India, especially in the Gujarat and the Malabar littorals. Gujarat was richly endowed with agricultural prosperity, particularly during the early medieval times, largely due to the spread of irrigation facilities. The area generated excellent cash crops which certainly enhanced its commercial importance. The establishment of the Caulukya house in Gujarat brought about an efficient system of communication between the inland areas and the coastal and estuarine port areas. A study of commerce in early medieval Gujarat, combining excellent empirical research and an analytical framework, is offered by Jain (1989).

The letters of medieval Jewish traders involved in what is called 'India trade' introduce us to the role of Jewish merchants in the south Konkan and Malabar. This is done almost single-handedly by Goitein (1954, 1973, 1980, 1987; also see Shaked, 1964), though the Indian maritime situation was actually not the central academic interests of Goitein. These letters have occasionally been utilized by Chaudhuri (1985, 1990), Abraham (1988), Jain (1989) and Ranabir Chakravarti (1994). Stillman (1971) indicated on the basis of Geniza records that Sindani (possibly Indian) indigo reached Egypt and even as far as Tunisia. The issue has been probed into further by Ranabir Chakravarti (1992/1996a) who seeks to establish that the Gujrati indigo was exported to the West from the Konkan port of Sindan (Sanjan, near Mumbai). In the study of maritime trade, scholarly attention is mostly directed to overseas voyages; the steady and sedate character of the coastal trade has, however, recently been studied in the context of the Konkan littorals (Ranabir Chakravarti, 1998a)

The south Indian scenario as regards maritime trade has been made clearer by a large number of scholars. The works prior to the 1950s are marked by a very strong empirical foundation. This is seen in the overview of the five centuries of economic life (1000–1500) by Appadurai (1936) who furnished rich data on trade and external commerce. The commercial network in the Coḷa realm also figures in Appadurai's work, but the subject is treated with greater specificity by Nilakanta Sastri in his celebrated study of the Coḷas (1955). Nilakanta Sastri (1978) has also enlightened us, in the light of epigraphic evidence, on the spread of the Tamil mercantile bodies to Sri Lanka and mainland and maritime South-East Asia. This is a point which has been elaborately studied in recent times by taking into account both the inland and overseas commercial networks of south India and the Deccan (Abraham, 1988). This commercial network in the Deccan and south India, unlike that during the first three centuries of the Christian era, was firmly rooted in the indigenous development of the agrarian and crafts production. We have already indicated the importance of the *nagaram* as a locality-level market centre of a supra-village nature. Hall (1980) further links it with the emergence of major ports in the Coḷa realm. This in a way counters the notion of Spencer and Stein that the Coḷa attitude to the sea was rooted in the segmentary nature of the Coḷa state and the plunder motive. A more systematic and thorough critique of the concept of the segmented polity is available in Champakalakshmi (1996a; for a critique of the segmentary polity also see D.N. Jha, 1984; Kulke, 1982; Subbarayalu, 1982; Sharma, 1989–90) who stresses the long-term interests of the Coḷas in sea-borne trade, in sharp contrast to a short-term policy of plunder. Champakalakshmi has ably established the complexities of issues related to trade and the interrelatedness among agrarian growth, proliferation of trade centres, politics of integration, urban development and religious and political ideology. The long-term interests of the Coḷas in trade and especially sea-borne trade can be clearly demonstrated by the deliberate enhancement in the importance of the port of Viśākhapaṭṭanam during the time of Kulottuṅga who also abolished tolls and customs to encourage growth of trade (Chakravarti, 1981). In a more elaborate treatment of sea-borne trade in the Andhra coast, Chakravarti (1995) demonstrates how two major ports in early medieval Andhra, viz. Visākhapaṭṭanam and Moṭupalli, had to depend on the political support from the interior for their sustenance.

Another aspect of the close ties between trade and politics in early medieval India is seen in the steady and rising demand for the best-quality war horses among all the regional powers. The overland supply of horses from the north-west and the social position of horse dealers form the subject matter of an essay by Chitrarekha Gupta (1984). Though there is no single monograph on this trade of imported war machines during the pre-medieval times, Digby (1971) presented an incisive survey of the subject in the context of the army under the Delhi Sultanate. Taking the cue from Digby, Ranabir Chakravarti (1989, 1991, 1996d, 1999) takes a close look at the demand for Arabian and Persian horses by early medieval rulers, especially those in the Deccan and south India. Chakravarti argues that the import trade of horses to India became increasingly maritime in character; it explains the emergence of merchants in Malabar specifically dealing in imported horses and the occasional encouragement to piracy on the western seaboard by political powers to ensure the supply of horse by questionable means.

Studies in the maritime trade on the Bengal coast also demonstrate interesting historiographical shifts. The gradual eclipse of Tāmralipta as the premier port of Bengal in the eighth century is often related to the decline of trade in early medieval Bengal, which is thought to have come under the spell of a self-sufficient enclosed village economy (Sharma, 1980; Ray, 1980; Thakur, 1993). The decay of Tamralipta is not doubted, but Mukherjee on the basis of Arabic and Chinese evidence convincingly shows the rise of Samandar (near Chittagong) as the outstanding port of early medieval Bengal, thereby rejecting the assumed decline of maritime trade on the Bengal coast (1982). In fact, the emergence of Harikela (the south-easternmost part of Bengal) to considerable commercial prosperity cannot be dismissed. Al Marvazi's impressions of trade and money in Harikela also point to the same direction (Ghosh Ray, 1995). This explains why the Arabs called the Bay of Bengal the Sea of Harikela (*bahr Harkal)* as early as the middle of the tenth century. Significantly enough, the term *Vaṅgasāgara* is coined almost by the same time, as has been shown by Ranabir Chakravarti (1996c) who further underlines the role of inland riverine ports in the Ganga delta for providing the vital linkages between the port and the interior. Tarafdar (1978) duly recognizes the importance of Samataṭa-Harikela as a commercial zone in the early medieval times, but considers that despite brisk trade the feudal set up remained unaltered. His position has generated two distinctly different responses. Jha (1987) has included this article in the volume to strengthen the argument in favour of the feudal social formation in India; Thakur (1989) in a historiographical essay has launched a severe criticism of Tarafdar for his citing the evidence in favour of the continuity of trade in early medieval Bengal! The gradual participation of Bengal in the maritime trade of the Indian Ocean during the early medieval times reached a period of efflorescence when Cheng Ho's fleets came to Chittagong as many as four times during the first three decades of the fifteenth century (Ray, 1993). It is not surprising that the Portuguese would regard Chittagong as the premier port (*porto grande*); early medieval Bengal marks the foundation and consolidation of this process and not the decline and eclipse of trade. The issues and debates regarding the perceived decline of trade and the onset of feudalism in India still continue and require fresh assessments (B.D. Chattopadhyaya, 1994, 1995; Champakalakshmi, 1995; Ranabir Chakravarti, forthcoming).

The last couple of decades were marked by a growing interest in the maritime situation in India, located in the overall background of the Indian Ocean. A major boost must have been provided in the near simultaneous translations of the navigational manual of Ibn Majid, the most celebrated *muallim* of the fifteenth century (Tibbetts, 1971) and the accounts of Ma Huan on the Chinese voyages in the Indian Ocean by Cheng Ho from 1404 to 1433 (Mills, 1970). Lewis (1973) has made a significant contribution to our understanding of traditional seafaring in the Indian Ocean by his incisive and thorough handling of diverse source materials. The evidence of Indian seafaring and navigational techniques is poor in comparison to the Arabic and Chinese data. But nevertheless Gopal (1970) makes excellent use of the limited textual data from early medieval sources to fill up this gap in our knowledge. In recent times Deloche has made outstanding contributions to this field by analysing geographical factors in the selection of ancient ports (1983) and by utilizing the visual representations of boats and ships in sculptures and painting (1987, 1994). Himanshu Prabha Ray (1996) rightly emphasizes that early Indians did not necessarily require the building of harbours and port structures, a feature seen in the European context; on the other hand, ships stood in deeper water at the roadstead and loading and unloading of passengers and cargo were performed by smaller vessels which could be easily beached. She therefore looks for alternative ethnoarchaeological evidence for the traditional settlements of humble boat builders, salt makers and fishermen which were the spots where the traditional vessels could be beached.

The Reading List

Works marked * indicate articles included in the present volume; those marked + indicate extracts included in the present volume.

Abraham, Meera, 1988, *Two Medieval Merchant Guilds of South India*, Heidelberg.

Abu-Lughod, J., 1989, *Before European Hegemony: The World System* AD *1250–1350*, New York.

Adhya, G.L., 1966, *Early Indian Economics*, Bombay.

Agrawala, R.C., 1955, 'Dramma in Ancient Indian Epigraphs and Literature', *JNSI*, XVII: 64–82.

———, 1958, 'Numismatic Data in the Gaṇitasāra', *JNSI*, XX: 38–41.

Agrawala, V.S., 1953, *India as known to Pāṇini*, Lucknow.

———, 1970, 'A Cultural Note on the Kuvalayamālā', in A.N. Upadhyaye ed., *Kuvalayamālā*, II, Bombay: 113–29.

———, 1987, 'Trade and Commerce from Pāṇini's Aṣṭādhyāyī', in B.D. Chattopadhyaya ed., *Essays in Ancient Indian Economic History*, Delhi: 149–59.

Allchin, Bridget, 1985, 'Ethnoarchaeology in South Asia', in J. Schotsman and M. Taddei eds., *SAA*, 1983, Naples: 21–33.

———, ed., 1994, 'Living Traditions', *Studies in the Ethnoarchaeology of South Asia*, Delhi.

Allchin, Bridget and Allchin, Raymond, 1982, *The Rise of Civilisation in India and Pakistan*, Cambridge.

———, 1993, *The Birth of Indian Civilisation*, second edition, Delhi.

———, 1997, *The Genesis of a Civilisation*, Delhi.

Allchin, F.R., 1962, 'Upon the Antiquity and Methods of Gold Mining in Ancient India', *JESHO*, V: 195–211.

———, 1989, 'City and State Formation in Early Historic South Asia', *SAS*, 5: 1–16.

———, 1990, 'Patterns of City Formation in Early Historic South Asia', *SAS*, 6: 163–73.

———, *et al.*, 1995, *The Archaeology of Early Historic South Asia, The Emergence of Cities and States*, Cambridge.

Allchin, F.R. and Norman, K.R., 1985, 'A Guide to Asokan Inscriptions', *SAS*, 1: 43–50.

Altekar, A.S., 1958, *The Rāshṭrakūṭas and Their Times*, Bombay.

Aṅguttaranikāya, 1885–1900, ed., R. Morris and E. Hardf, London.

Appadurai, A., 1936, *Economic Conditions in South India* AD *1000–1500*, in two volumes, Madras.

Appadurai, Arjun, 1988, *The Social Life of Things: Commodities in the Cultural Perspective*, Cambridge.

Ascher, E.J., 1970, 'Graeco-Roman Nautical Technology and Modern Sailing Information: A Confrontation between Pliny's Account of the Voyage to India and that of the *Periplus Maris Erythraei* in the Light of Modern Knowledge', *Journal of Tropical Geography*, XXXI: 10–26.

Bajpai, Shiva G., 1989, 'Mathurā: Trade Routes, Commerce and Communication Patterns, Post-Maurya to the End of the Kushāṇa Period', in D. M. Srinivasan ed., *Mathurā—The Cultural Heritage*, Delhi: 46–58.

Bandyopadhyay, N.C., 1944, *Kauṭilya*, Calcutta.

________, 1945, *Economic Life and Progress in Ancient India*, Calcutta.

de Bairy, William Theodore ed., 1958, *Sources of Indian Tradition*, New York.

Basak, R.G., 1919, 'The Five Damodarpur Copper Plate Inscriptions of the Gupta Period', *EI*, XV: 113–45.

________, 1929, 'Social Life as Pictured in the Mṛcchakaṭika of Śūdraka', *IHR*, VII: 299–325.

________, 1959, *Asokan Edicts*, Calcutta.

Banerjee, N.R., 1965, *The Iron Age in India*, Delhi.

Basham, A.L., 1949, 'Notes on Seafaring in Ancient India', *Art and Letters*: 60–71.

Basham, A.L., ed., *A Cultural History of India*, Oxford.

Begley, Vimala, 1983, 'Arikamedu Reconsidered', *American Journal of Archaeology*, 87: 461–81.

________, 1986, 'From Iron Age to Early Historical in South Indian Archaeology', in Jerome K. Jacobson ed., *Studies in the Archaeology of India and Pakistan*, Delhi: 297–319.

________, 1992, 'Ceramic Evidence for Pre-Periplus Trade on the Indian Coasts', in Begley, Vimala and de Puma, Richard Daniel eds., *Rome and India: The Ancient Sea Trade*, Delhi (Indian rpt.): 157–203.

________, 1993, 'New Investigations at the Port of Arikamedu', *Journal of Roman Archaeology*, VI: 93–103.

Begley, Vimala and de Puma, Richard Daniel eds.,1992, *Rome and India: The Ancient Sea Trade*, Delhi (Indian rpt.).

Belshaw, Cyril, 1969, *Traditional Exchange and Modern Markets*, Delhi (Indian rpt.)

Berghaus, P., 1991, 'Roman Coins from India and Their Imitations', in A.K. Jha ed., *Coinage, Trade and Economy*, Nashik: 108–21.

Bernard, P., 1967, 'Ai Khanoum on the Oxus: A Hellenistic City in Central Asia', *Proceedings of the British Academy*, LIII: 71–95.

Bernardi, P., 1970, 'The Economic Problems of the Roman Empire at the Time of Its Decline', in Carlo M. Cippola ed., *The Economic Decline of Empires*, London.

Bhattacharyya, G., 1987, 'Dāna-Deyadharma: Donation in Early Buddhist Periods (in Brahmi)', in M. Yaldiz and W. Lobo eds., *Investigating Indian Art*, Berlin: 39–60.

Bisht, R.S., 1982, 'Excavations at Banawali 1974–77', in *HC*: 113–24.

———, 1984, 'Structural Remains and Town Planning at Banawali', *FIC*: 89–98.

———, 1991, 'Dholavira: New Horizons of the Indus Civilization', *Puratattva*, XX: 71–82.

Bongard-Levin, G., 1985, *Mauryan India*, Delhi.

Bongard-Levin, G., and A. Vīsagin, 1984, *The Image of India*, Moscow.

Boppearachchi, Osmund, 1998, 'Archaeological Evidence on Changing Patterns of International Trade Relations of Ancient Sri Lanka', in Osmund Boppearachchi and D.P.M. Weerakkody eds., *Origin, Evolution and Circulation of Foreign Coins in the Indian Ocean*, Delhi: 133–78.

Bose, A.N., 1967, *The Social and Rural Economy of Northern India*, in two volumes, Calcutta.

Boussac, M.F. and Salles, J.F. eds., 1995, *Athens, Aden, Arikamedu: Essays on Interrelation between India, Arabia and the Eastern Mediterranean*, Delhi.

Braudel, Fernand, 1972, *The Mediterranean and the Mediterranean World in the Age of Philip II*, in two volumes, London (trn. by S. Reynolds)

———, 1980, *On History*, London (trn. by Sarah Mills).

———, 1981–84, *Civilization and Capitalism 1400–1800*, in three volumes, London, paperback edition.

———, 1993, *A History of Civilizations*, Harmondsworth, (trn. by Richard Mayne), paperback edition.

Broeze, Frank, ed., 1989, *Brides of the Sea, Port Cities of Asia from the 16th–20th Centuries*, Kensington.

Bronson, B., 1990, 'Glass and Beads at Khuan Lukpad, Southern Thailand', in I.C. Glover ed., *South East Asian Archaeology*, Oxford.

Brown, Norman O., 1969, *Hermes the Thief: The Evolution of a Myth*, New York, second edition.

Brunswig, R.H., Parpola, A. and Potts, D., 1983, 'New Indus Type and Related Seals from the Near East', in D. Potts ed., *Dilmun: New Studies in the Archaeology and Early History of Bahrain*, Berlin: 101–16.

Bulnois, L., 1966, *The Silk Road*, London.

Burgess, James and Indraji Bhagawanlal, 1976, *Inscriptions from the Cave Temples of Western India*, Varanasi (rpt.).

Casanova, M., 1992, 'The Sources of Lapis Lazuli Found in Iran', in C. Jarrige ed., *SAA*, 1989, Washington: 49–56.

de Casparis, J.G., 1983, 'India and Maritime South East Asia: A Lasting Relationship', Third Sri Lanka Endowment Lecture.

Casson, Lionel, 'Rome's Trade with the East: The Sea Voyage to Africa and India', *TAPA*, 110: 21–36.

________, 1983, 'Śakas versus Andhras in the *Periplus Maris Erythraei*', *JESHO*, XXVI: 164–77.

________, 1988a, 'Rome's Maritime Trade with the Far East', *The American Neptune*, XLVIII: 149–53.

Casson, Lionel, 1988b, 'Rome's Trade with the Eastern Coast of India', *Cahiers d'histoire*, Lyon: 303–8.

________, ed. and trn. into English, 1989, *The Periplus Maris Erythraei*, Princeton.

________, 1990, 'New Light on Maritime Loans: P. Vindob G 40822', *Zeitschrift fur Papyrologie und Epigraphik*, 84: 195–206. *

________, 1991a, 'Ancient Naval Technology and the Route to India', in Vimala Begley and Richard Daniel de Puma eds., 1992, 8–11.

________, 1991b, *The Ancient Mariners, Seafarers and Sea Fighters of the Mediterranean in Ancient Times*, Princeton, second edition.

Chakrabarti, Dilip K., 1972, 'Prehistoric Ganges Basin', *JESHO*, XV: 213–19.

________, 1973, 'Concept of Urban Revolution and the Indian Context', *Puratattva*, VI: 27–32.

________, 1975, 'Gujarat Harappan Connection with West Asia: A Reconsideration of the Evidence', *JESHO*, XVIII: 337–42.

________, 1988, *Theoretical Issues in Indian Archaeology*, Delhi.

________, 1990, *The External Trade of the Indus Civilization*, Delhi.

________, 1995, *The Archaeology of Ancient Indian Cities*, Delhi.

Chakrabarti, Dilip K., Goswami, N. and Chattopadhyay, R.K., 1994, 'Archaeology of Coastal West Bengal: Twenty four Parganas and Midnapur Districts', *SAS*, 10: 135–60.

Chakraborti, Haripada, 1966, *Trade and Commerce of Ancient India*, Calcutta.

Chakravarti, Ranabir, 1977–8, 'Economic Policy of Kākatīya Ganapati', *JAIH*, XI: 72–9.

________, 1981, 'Kulottuṅga and the Port of Viśākhapaṭṭinam', *PIHC*, XLII (Bodhgaya session): 142–5.

________, 1986a, *Warfare for Wealth: Early Indian Perspective*, Calcutta.

________, 1986b, 'Merchants of Konkan', *IESHR*, XXIII: 207–15.

________, 1987, 'Rājaśreṣṭhī', in B.M. Pande and B.D. Chattopadhyaya eds., *Archaeology and History, Essays in Memory of Shri A. Ghosh*, II, Delhi: 671–8.

________, 1989, 'Maritime Trade and Piracy in Horses in Early Medieval India: Shipping and Piracy', in D.C. Bhattacharyya and Devendra Handa eds., *Prāci–prabhā (Professor B. N. Mukherjee Felicitation Volume)*, Delhi: 343–60.

________, 1990a, 'Monarchs, Merchants and a Maṭha in Northern Konkan (900–1053)', *IESHR*, XXVII: 189–208. *

Chakravarti, Ranabir, 1990b, 'A Note on Dīpotsava', *Monthly Bulletin of the Asiatic Society*, July: 1–3.

_______, 1991a, 'Early Historical India: A Study in Its Material Milieu', in Debiprasad Chattopadhyaya ed., *A History of Science and Technology in Ancient India*, II, Calcutta: 305–50.

_______, 1991b, 'Horse Trade and Piracy at Tana (= Thana, Maharashtra, India): Gleanings from Marco Polo', *JESHO*, XXXIV: 159–82.

_______, 1991c, *Prachin Bharater Arthanaitik Itihaser Sandhane*, Calcutta (in Bengali).

_______, 1992, 'Maritime Trade in Horses in Early Historical Bengal: A Seal from Chandraketugarh', *Pratnasamiksha*, I:155–60.

_______, 1992/1996a, 'The Export of Sindani Indigo from India to the "West" in the Eleventh Century', *IHR*, XVIII: 18–30.

_______, 1992/1996b, 'Maritime Trade and Voyages in Ancient Bengal', *JAIH*, XIX: 145–71.

_______, 1994, 'Maritime Trade between India and Aden: Gleanings from a Jewish Trade Letter of AD 1139', *PIHC*, LV (Aligarh session).

_______, 1995a, 'Rulers and Ports: Viśākhapaṭṭanam and Motupalli in Early Medieval Andhra', in K.S. Mathew ed., *Mariners, Merchants and Oceans, Studies in Maritime History*, Delhi: 57–78.

_______, 1995b, 'Merchants and Other Donors at Ancient Bandhogarh', *SAS*, 11: 33–42.

_______, 1996a, 'Trade at Maṇḍapikās in Early Medieval North India', in D.N. Jha ed., *Society and Ideology in India, Essays in Honour of Professor R.S. Sharma*, Delhi: 69–80.

_______, 1996b, 'The Puṭabhedana as a Centre of Trade in Early India', *SAS*, 12: 33–9.

_______, 1996c, 'Vaṅgasāgarasaṁbhāṇḍāriyaka: A Riverine Trade Centre of Early Medieval Bengal', in Debala Mitra ed., *Explorations in Art and Archaeology of South Asia, Essays Dedicated to N.G. Majumdar*, Calcutta: 557–72.

_______, 1996d, 'Overseas Transportation and Shipping of Horses in Medieval India', in K.S. Mathew ed., *Indian Ocean and Cultural Interaction AD 1400–1800*, Pondicherry: 149–60.

_______, 1998a, 'Coastal Trade and Voyages in Konkan: The Early Medieval Scenario', *IESHR*, XXXV: 97–124.

_______, 1998b, 'Economy', in N.N. Bhattacharyya ed., *Encyclopaedia of Ancient Indian Culture*, Delhi: 119–26.

_______, forthcoming, 'Politics and Society in India AD 300–1000', in K. Satchidananda Murty ed., *Project on the History of Indian Science, Philosophy and Culture*, II.

Chakravarti, Ranabir and Dutta Majumder, Suchandra, 1992, 'An Ancient Gymnasium at Bandhogarh', *JAS*, XXXIV: 98–104.

Chakravarti, Uma, 1987, *Social Dimensions of Early Buddhism*, Delhi.

Chhabra, B. Ch., 1935, 'Expansion of the Indo-Aryan Culture to South-East Asia during the Pallava Rule, as Evidenced by Inscriptions', *JRASBL*: 1–64.

Champakalakshmi, R., 1975–6, 'Archaeology and Tamil Literary Tradition', *Puratattva*, VIII: 110–22.

Champakalakshmi, R., 1979, 'Growth of Urban Centres in South India: Kuḍāmukku-Palayiarai, the Twin Centres of the Coḷas', *SH*, I: 1–30.

________, 1981, 'Peasant State and Society in Medieval South India: A Review Article', *IESHR*, XVIII: 411–26.

________, 1995, 'State and Economy in South India: AD 400–1300', in Romila Thapar ed., *Recent Perspectives of Early Indian History*, Bombay: 266–308.

________, 1996a, *Trade, Ideology and Urbanization: South India 300* BC *to* AD *1300*, Delhi.

________, 1996b, 'The Medieval South Indian Guilds: Their Role in Trade and Urbanization', in D.N. Jha ed., *Ideology and Society*, Delhi: 81–94. *

________, 1997, 'The Peninsula', in *History of Humanity*, III, UNESCO, Paris: 392–7.

Chandra, Satish ed., 1987, *The Indian Ocean: Explorations in History, Commerce and Politics*, Delhi.

Charles, J.A., 1975, 'Where is the Tin?', *Antiquity*, XLIX: 19–24.

Charlesworth, M.P., 1924, *Routes and Commerce of the Roman Empire*, Cambridge.

________, 1951, 'Roman Trade with India: A Resurvey', in P.R. Coleman-Norton ed., *Studies in Roman Economic and Social History*, Princeton.

Chatterjee, Suniti Kumar, 1951, 'Race Movements and Prehistoric Cultures', in R.C. Majumdar ed., *The Vedic Age*, Bombay: 150–66.

Chattopadhyaya, B.D., 1977a, *Coins and Currency System in South India* AD *225–1300*, Delhi.

________, 1977b, 'Currency in Early Bengal', *JIH*, LV: 41–60.

________, 1983, 'Political Processes and Structures of Polity in Early Medieval India: Problems of Perspectives', Presidential Address, section I, *PIHC*, XLIII (Burdwan session).

________, 1985, 'Markets and Merchants in Early Medieval Rajasthan', *Social Science Probings*, 11: 413–40. *

________, 1988–89/1991, 'Trends of Research in Ancient Indian Economic History', *JAIH*, XVIII: 109–31.

________, 1990, *Aspects of Rural Settlements and Rural Society in Early Medieval India*, Calcutta.

________, 1993–4, 'Urban Centres in Early Bengal', *Pratnasamiksha*, 2–3: 169–92.

________, 1994, *The Making of Early Medieval India*, Delhi.

________, 1995, 'State and Economy in North India: Fourth Century to

Twelfth Century', in Romila Thapar ed., *Recent Perspectives of Early Indian History*, Bombay: 308–46.

Chattopadhyaya, B.D., 1996, 'Dynastic Patterns of the Northern Subcontinent: Commercial and Cultural Links (200 BC to AD 300)', *History of Humanity*, III, Paris, UNESCO: 368–77.

________, 1997, 'The City in Early India: Perspectives from the Texts', *SH*, XIII: 181–208.

Chattopadhyaya, Debiprasad, 1959, *Lokāyata, a Study in Ancient Indian Materialism*, Calcutta.

________, ed., 1986, *A History of Science and Technology in Ancient India*, I, Calcutta.

________, ed., 1991, *A History of Science and Technology in Ancient India*, II, Calcutta.

Chattopadhyaya, Sudhakar, 1958, *Early History of North India*, Calcutta.

Chaudhuri, K.N., 1985, *Trade and Civilisation in the Indian Ocean from the Rise of Islam to 1700*, Cambridge.

________, 1990a, *Asia Before Europe, Economic Civilisation in the Indian Ocean from the Rise of Islam to 1700*, Cambridge.

________, 1990b, 'Reflections on the Organising Principles of Pre-modern Trade', in James D. Tracy ed., *The Rise of Merchant Empires*, Cambridge: 421–42.

Childe, V. Gordon, 1950, 'The Urban Revolution', *Town Planning Review*, XXI, 3–17.

________, 1964, *What Happened in History*, Harmondsworth, revised edition.

Chitalwala, Y.M., 1982, 'Harappan Settlements in the Kutch-Saurashtra Region: Patterns of Distribution and Routes of Communication', *HC*: 197–204.

Cippola, Carlo M., 1970, *European Culture and Overseas Expansion*, Harmondsworth.

Cleuziou, S., 1981, 'Oman Peninsula in the Early Second Millennium BC', in H. Hartel ed., *SAA*, 1979: 279–93.

________, 1984, 'Oman Peninsula and Its Relations Eastwards during Third Millennium', in *FIC*: 371–96.

________, 1986, 'Dilmun and Makkan during the Third and Early Second Millennium BC', in H. al Khalifa and M. Rice eds., *Bahrain through the Ages*, London: 143–55.

________, 1992, 'The Oman Peninsula and the Indus Civilisation: A Reassessment', *ME*, XVII: 94–103.

Coedes, G., 1968, *The Indianized States of South-East Asia*, Honolulu.

Coedre, Helen, 'Exchange and Display', in David L. Sills ed., *International Encyclopaedia of the Social Sciences*, V: 239–45.

Cornwall, P.B., 1946, 'On the Location of Dilmun', *BASOR*, 102: 3–11.

Crone, P., 1987, *Meccan Trade and the Rise of Islam*, Oxford.

Curtin, Philip D., 1984, *Cross Cultural Trade in World History*, Cambridge.
Dales, G.F., 1962, 'Harappan Outposts on the Makran Coast', *Antiquity*, VI: 86–92.
Dalton, George ed.,1968, *Primitive, Archaic and Modern Economics: Essays of Karl Polanyi*, New York.
Dani, A.H., 1983, *Chilas, the City of Nangaparvat*, Islamabad.
________, 1989, *Recent Archaeological Discoveries in Pakistan*, Tokyo, UNESCO.
Darian, Steven G., 1970, 'The Economic History of the Ganges to the End of the Gupta Times', *JESHO*, XIII: 67–87.
Das, D.R., 1969, *Economic History of the Deccan*, Delhi.
Das, S.R., 1968, *Rajbadidanga 1962 Excavation Report*, Calcutta.
Das Gupta, Ashin, 1974, 'Presidential Address', section II, *PIHC*, XXXIV (Jadavpur session): 99–111.
________, 1989, *Vangopasagar*, Calcutta (in Bengali).
Das Gupta, Ashin and Pearson, M.N. eds., 1987, *India and the Indian Ocean 1500–1800*, Delhi.
Delmas, A.B. and Casanova, M., 1990, 'The Lapis Lazuli Sources in the Ancient Near East', in M. Taddei ed., *SAA*, 1987: 493–505.
Deloche, Jean, 1983, 'Geographical Considerations in the Localization of Ancient Seaports of India', *IESHR*, XX: 439–48. *
________, 1987, 'Konkan Warships of the XIth–XVth Centuries as Represented on Memorial Stones', *BEFEO*, LXXVI: 165–84.
________, 1993–94, *Transport and Communication in India Prior to Steam Locomotion*, vol. I: Land Transport, vol. II: Water Transport, Delhi.
Deyell, John S., 1990, *Living Without Silver, Monetary History of Early Medieval North India*, Delhi. +
Dhavalikar, M., 1992, 'Harappans in Saurashtra: The Mercantile Enterprise as Seen from the Recent Excavations at Kuntasi', in *HC*: 555–70.
Dhavalikar, M. and Marathe, A.R., 1978–79, 'Jorwe Pottery— A Statistical Study', *Bulletin of the Deccan College Research Institute*, XXXVIII: 17–22.
Digby, Simon, 1971, *Warhorses and Elephants in the Delhi Sultanate*, Oxford.
Dīghanikāya, 1890–1911, ed., T.W. Rhys Davids and J.E. Carpenter, London.
Dikshit, M.G., 1960, 'Cunningham Collection of Seals in the British Museum', *JNSI*, XXII: 123–30.
Diodorus, *Bibliothekes Historikes*, trn. C.H. Oldfather, London, Cambridge, Mass, 1935–54.
Dobbins, K.Walton, 1971, 'The Commerce of Kapisene and Gandhāra after the Fall of the Indo-Greek Rule', *JESHO*, XIV: 286–302.
During-Caspers, E.C.L., 1979, 'Sumer, Coastal Arabia and the Indus Village in Protoliterate and Early Dynastic Eras', *JESHO*, XXII: 121–35.

———, 1984, 'Sumerian Trading Communities Residing in the Harappan Society', in *FIC*: 363–70.

———, 1986, 'Contacts between India and West during the Early Historical Times', *IMB*, XXI: 22–33.

———, 1987, 'A Copper Bronze Animal in Harappan Style from Bahrain: Evidence of Mercantile Interaction', *JESHO*, XXX: 30–46.

———, 1991, 'The Indus Valley Unicorn: A Near Eastern Connection?', *JESHO*, XXXIV: 312–50.

During-Caspers, E.C.L., 1992, 'Intercultural and Mercantile Contacts between the Arabian Gulf and South Asia', *Proceedings of the Seminar on Arabian Studies*, XXII: 3–28.

———, 1996, 'The Reliability of Archaeological Evidence for Mercantile/Intercultural Contacts between Central and South Asia, the Arabian Gulf and the Near East in the Late Third and Early Second Millennium BC', in Debala Mitra ed., *Explorations in Art and Archaeology of South Asia, Essays Dedicated to N.G. Majumdar*, Calcutta: 123–56.

During-Caspers, E.C.L. and Govindkutty, A., 1983, 'R. Thapar's Dravidian Hypothesis for the Location of Meluhha, Dilmun and Makan: a Critical Reconstruction', *JESHO*, XXI: 113–45.

Edens, C., 1993, 'Indus Arabian Interactions during the Bronze Age, a Review of Evidence', *HC* (second edition): 335–65.

Eggermont, P.H.L., 1966, 'The Muruṇḍas and the Ancient Trade Route from Taxila to Ujjain', *JESHO*, IX: 257–96.

Erdosy, G., 1984, 'The Origin of the Cities in the Ganga Valley', *JESHO*, XXVII: 81–109.

———, 1987, 'Early Historic Cities of Northern India', *SAS*, III: 1–23.

———, 1988, *Urbanisation in Early Historic India*, Oxford.

———, 1995, 'City States of North India and Pakistan at the Time of the Buddha', in *The Archaeology of Early Historic South Asia, The Emergence of Cities and States*, Cambridge: 99–122.

Fernandez-Armesto, Felipe ed., 1995, *An Expanding World, the European Impact on World History 1450–1800*; I: The Global Opportunity; II: The European Opportunity, London.

Fick, Richard, 1920, *Social Organization in North Eastern India during the Buddha's Time* (English trn. by S.K. Mitra), Calcutta; rpt. , Varanasi,1972.

Fiser, Ivo, 1954, 'The Problem of the Seṭṭhi in the Buddhist Jātakas', *Archiv Orientalni*, XXII: 238–65.*

Forbes, J., 1834, *Oriental Memoirs*, in two volumes, London.

Francis, E., 1987, *Bead Emporium: A Guide to the Beads from Arikamedu in the Pondicherry Museum*, Pondicherry.

Francfort, H.P., 1981, 'The Early Periods of Shortughai (Harappan) and the Western Bactrian Culture of Dashly', in B. Allchin ed., *SAA*, 1979, Cambridge: 170–75.

———, 1984, 'The Harappan Settlement of Shortughai', in *FIC*: 301–10

Frank, Andre Gunder, 1992, 'The Centrality of Central Asia', *SH*, VI: 43–98.

Freeman-Grenville, G.P.S. trn., 1980, *Kitab Ajaib ul Hind of Buzurg Ibn Shahriyar* (*The Book of the Wonders of India*), London.

Fried, M., 1965, *The Evolution of the Political Society*, New York.

Frye, R.N., 1996, 'The Rise of the Kushan Empire', in *The History of Humanity*, III, Paris, UNESCO: 456–60.

Frye, R.N. and Litvinsky, Boris A., 1996, 'The Oasis States of Central Asia', in *The History of Humanity*, III, Paris, UNESCO: 461–4.

Fussman, G., 1987–88, 'Central and Provincial Administration in Ancient India: The Problem of the Maurya Empire', *IHR*, XIV: 43–72.

Fynes, R.C.C., 1996, 'Plant Souls in Jainism and Manichaeism, The Case of Cultural Transmission', *EW*, XLVI: 21–44.

Gardin, J.C. and Gentelle, P., 1979, 'L'exploitation du Sol en Bactriane Antique', *BEFEO*, LXVI: 1–29.

Ghosh, A., 1973, *The City in Early Historical India*, Shimla.

________, ed., 1989, *An Encyclopaedia of Indian Archaeology*, in two volumes, Delhi.

Ghosh, Amitav, 1990, 'The Slave of Ms. H. 6', Occasional Paper no. 125, Centre for Studies in Social Sciences, Calcutta: 1–125.

Ghoshal, U.N., 1957, 'Economic Conditions', in K.A. Nilakanta Sastri ed., *A Comprehensive History of India*, II, Calcutta.

________, 1966, *A History of Indian Public Life*, II, London.

________, 1966, 'Economic Conditions', in R.C. Majumdar ed., *The Age of Imperial Kanauj*, Bombay.

________, 1970, 'Economic Conditions', in R.C. Majumdar ed., *The Classical Age*, Bombay.

________, 1972, *Contributions to the History of Hindu Revenue System*, second edition, Calcutta.

________, 1972, 'Economic Conditions', in R.C. Majumdar ed., *The Struggle for Empire*, Bombay.

Glover, I.C., 1989, *Trade between India and South East Asia*, Hull.

________, 1996, 'Recent Archaeological Evidence for Early Maritime Contacts between India and Southeast Asia', in Himanshu Prabha Ray and J.F. Salles eds., *Tradition and Archaeology, Early Maritime Contacts in the Indian Ocean*, Delhi: 293–310.

Göbl, R., 1984, *System und Chronologie der Munzpragung des Kusanreiches*, Vienna.

Goitein, S.D., 1954, 'Two Eye Witness Reports on the Invasion of Aden by Kais in the Twelfth Century', *BSOAS*, XVI:

________, 1964, *Jews and Arabs: Their Contact Through the Ages*, Leiden.

________, 1966, *Studies in the Islamic History and Institutions*, London.

________, 1967–88, *A Mediterranean Society*, in five volumes, Los Angeles and Berkeley.

________, 1973, *Letters of Medieval Jewish Traders*, Princeton.

Goitein, S.D., 1980, 'From Aden to India: Specimens of Correspondence of Indian Traders of the Twelfth Century', *JESHO*, XXI: 43–66.*

________, 1987, 'Portrait of a Medieval India Trader: Three Letters from the Cairo Geniza', *BSOAS*, XLVIII: 448–64.

Ghogte, Viswas D., 1997, 'The Chandraketugarh-Tamluk Region of Bengal: Source of the Early Historic Rouletted Ware from India and South-East Asia', *ME*, XXII: 69–85.

Gokhale, B.G., 1977, 'The Merchant in Ancient India', *JAOS*, 98: 125–30.

Gonda, J., 1968, *Ancient Indian Kingship from a Religious Point of View*, Leiden.

Goody, Jack, 1996, *The East in the West*, Cambridge.

Gopal, Lallanji, 1963, 'Coins in the Epigraphic and Literary Records in Northern India in the Early Medieval Period', *JNSI*, XXV: 1–16.

________, 1965, *The Economic Life of Northern India c.* AD *700–1200*, Varanasi.

________, 1966, *Early Medieval Coin Types in North India*, Varanasi.

________, 1970, 'Indian Shipping in the Medieval Period', in Lokesh Chandra *et al.*, eds., *India's Contribution to World Thought and Culture (Swami Vivekananda Commemoration Volume)*, Madras: 108–22.

Grierson, P.J. Hamilton, 1903, *The Silent Trade: A Contribution to the Early History of Human Intercourse*, Edinburgh.

Groom, N., 1981, *Frankincense and Myrrh: A Study of the Arabian Incense Trade*, London.

Gunawardana, R.A.L.H., 1987, 'Changing Patterns of Navigation in the Indian Ocean and Their Impact on Pre-Colonial Sri Lanka', in Satish Chandra ed., 1987: 54–89.

Gupta, Chitrarekha, 1983–4, 'Horse Trade in North India: Some Reflections on the Socio-Economic Life', *JAIH*, XIV: 186–206.

Gupta, P.L., 1960, *Punch Marked Coins in the Andhra Pradesh Government Museum*, Hyderabad.

________, 1977, *The Imperial Guptas*, in two volumes, Varanasi.

Gurukkal, Rajan, 1995, 'The Beginnings of the Historic Period: The Tamil South', in Romila Thapar ed., *Recent Perspectives of Early Indian History*, Bombay: 237–65.

Habib, Irfan, 1969, 'Potentialities of Capitalistic Development in the Economy of Mughal India', *Journal of Economic History*, XXXII: 32–78.

Hall, K.R., 1975, 'Khmer Commercial Development and Foreign Contacts under Sūryavarman I', *JESHO*, XVIII: 318–36.

________, 1978, 'International Trade and Foreign Diplomacy in Early Medieval South India', *JESHO*, XXI: 75–98.

________, 1980, *Trade and Statecraft in the Age of the Coḷas*, Delhi.

Harte, N. B., 1967, *The Study of Economic History*, London.

Heesterman, J.C., 1977, *The Ancient Indian Royal Consecration*, The Hague.

Hegde, K.T.M., 1978, 'Sources of Ancient Tin in India', in T.A. Wertime and J. Olin eds., *The Search for Ancient Tin*, Washington: 39–42.

Heiman, J., 1980, 'Small Exchange and Ballast: Cowry Trade as an Example of Indian Ocean Economic History', *SA*, II: 48–69.

Heitzman, J., 1984, 'Early Buddhism, Trade and Empire', in K.A.R. Kennedy and G.L. Possehl eds., *Studies in Archaeology and Palaeoanthropology of South Asia*, Delhi: 121–38.

_______, 1991, 'Ritual Polity and Economy: The Transactional Network of an Imperial Temple in Medieval South India', *JESHO*, XXXIV: 23–54.

Herodotus, *Histories*, trn. by Aubrey de Selincourt, revised with an Introduction and Notes by A.R. Burn, Harmondsworth, 1972.

Horner, I.B., 1938–52, trn. *Vinaya Piṭaka*, in five volumes, London.

Hourani, G.F., 1951, *The Arab Seafaring in the Indian Ocean During the Ancient and Early Medieval Times*, Beirut.

Hultzsch, E., 1912, 'The Motupalli Pillar Inscription of Kākatīya Gaṇapati', *EI*, XII: 188–97.

Humphrey, C., 1985, 'Barter and Economic Disintegration', *Man*, XX: 48–72.

Humphreys, S.C., 1969, 'History, Economics and Anthropology', *History and Theory*, VIII: 165–210.

Huntingford, G.W.B. trn., 1980, *The Periplus of the Erythraean Sea*, London.

Jain, J.C., 1980, *Economic Life in Ancient India as Depicted by Jaina Canonical Literature*, Varanasi.

Jain, P.S., 1975, 'An Account of the Trade and Shipping in Prakrit Literature', in R.C. Dwivedi ed., *Contribution of Jainism to Indian Culture*, Varanasi: 270–78.

Jain, V.K., 1987, 'The Role of Arab Traders in Western India during Early Medieval Period', in B.D. Chattopadhayaya ed., *Essays in Ancient Indian Economic History*, Delhi: 164–74.

_______, 1989, *Trade and Traders in Western India*, Delhi. +

Jarrige, J.F., 1982, 'Excavations at Mehrgarh: Their Significance for Understanding the Background of the Harappan Civilization', in *HC*: 79–84.

Jettmar, K. ed., 1989, *Antiquities from Northern Pakistan*, I, Munich.

_______, 1991, 'Sogdians in the Indus Valley', *Histoire et Cultes de l'Asia centrale Preislamique*, LNRS, Paris: 251–3.

Jha, A.K. ed., 1992, *Coinage, Trade and Economy*, Nashik.

Jha, D.N., 1979, 'Early Indian Feudalism: A Historiographical Critique', Presidential Address, section I, *PIHC*, XXXIX (Waltair session): 15–45.

_______, 1984 (June), 'The Validity of Brahmana–Peasant Alliance and the Segmentary State in Early Medieval South India', *Social Science Probings*, 270–96.

_______, ed., 1987, *Feudal Social Formation in Early India*, Delhi.

_______, 1998, *Ancient India in Historical Outline*, second edition, Delhi.

Jones, A.H.M., 1979, *The Roman Economy*, Oxford.
Kane, P.V., 1941–62, *History of Dharmasastra*, in five volumes, Poona.
Karashima, Noboru, 1971, 'Relations between South India and China in Chola Times', in *Professor K.A. Nilakanta Sastri Felicitation Volume*, Madras: 69–71.
Karashima, Noboru and Sitaraman, B., 1972, 'Revenue Terms in the Coḷa Inscriptions', *Journal of Asian and African Studies*, V: 87–117.
Karashima, Noboru, Matsui, Toro and Subbarayalu, Y., 1978, *A Concordance of Names in Coḷa Inscriptions*, Madurai.
________, 1984, *South Indian History and Society*, Delhi.
Kartunen, K., 1989, *India in the Greek Literature*, Helsinki.
Kauṭilya, *Arthaśāstra*, ed. and trn. in three parts by R.P. Kangle, Bombay, 1966–72.
Kielhorn, F., 1891, 'The Siyadoni Stone Inscription of Vikrama Saṁvat 960–1025', *EI*, I: 162–79.
Kipp, R.S. and Schortman, E.M., 1989, 'The Political Impact of Trade in Chiefdoms', *American Anthropologist*, 91: 370–85.
Kosambi, D.D., 1952, 'Ancient Kośala and Magadha', *JBBRAS*, XXVIII (NS): 180–213.
________, 1955, 'Dhenukākaṭa', *JBBRAS*, XXX: 50–71.
________, 1956, 'On the Development of Feudalism in India', *ABORI*, XXVI: 258–69.
________, 1956–57, 'Origins of Feudalism in Kashmir', *JBBRAS*, The Sardhasatabdi Commemoration Volume: 108–20.
________, 1958, ' Indian Feudal Trade Charters', *JESHO*, IV: 281–93.*
________, 1970, *The Culture and Civilization of Ancient India in Historical Outline*, London.
________, 1972, *An Introduction to the Study of Indian History*, Bombay.
Kramer, S.N., 1963, 'Dilmun, Quest for Paradise', *Antiquity*, XXXVII: 111–15.
________, 1964, 'The Indus Civilization and Dilmun, the Sumerian Paradise Land', *Expedition*, VI: 44–52.
Krishnan, K.G., 1973, 'Choḷa Rājendra's Expedition to South-East Asia', *JIH*, Golden Jubilee volume, 109–17.
Kulke, Hermann, 1982, 'Fragmentation and Segmentation versus Integration? Reflections on the Concepts of Indian Feudalism and Segmentary State in Indian History', *SH*, II: 237–63.
________, 1990, 'Indian Colonies, Indianization or Cultural Convergence?' in H.S. Nordholt ed., *Onderzook in Jevdoost Azie*, Leiden: 8–32.
________, 1993, 'A Passage to India: Temples, Merchants and the Ocean', *JESHO*, XXXV: 154–80.
________, 1995, ed., *The State in India 1000–1700*, Delhi.
Lahiri, Nayanjyot, 1990, 'Harappa as a Centre of Trade and Trade Routes', *IESHR*, XXVII: 405–44
________, 1992, *The Archaeology of Indian Trade Routes*, Delhi.

Lamberg-Karlovsky, C.C., 1972, 'Trade Mechanism in Indus-Mesopotamian Interrelations', *JAOS*, 92: 222–9.

Leemans, W.F., 1968, 'Additional Evidence for the Persian Gulf Trade and Meluhha', *JESHO*, XI: 215–26.

Legge, J. trn., 1971, *A Record of the Buddhistic Kingdoms*, Delhi, Indian rpt.

Leshnik, L., 1968, 'The Harappan Port at Lothal: Another View', *American Anthropologist*, LXX: 911–22.

Lewis, A., 1973, 'Maritime Skills in the Indian Ocean 1368–1500', *JESHO*, XVI: 238–64.

Ling, Trevor, 1980, *The Buddha*, London.

Liu, Xinru, 1988, *Ancient India and Ancient China Trade and Religious Exchanges* AD *1 to 600*, Delhi.

________, 1996, *Silk and Religion, An Exploration of Material Life and the Thought of People,* AD *600–1200*, Delhi.

Lopez, Robert S., 1976, *The Commercial Revolution of the Middle Ages 950–1350*, Cambridge.

Mabbett, I.W., 1972, *Truth, Myth and Politics in Ancient India*, Delhi.

________, 1977, 'The Indianization of South-East Asia: Reflections on the Historical Sources', *JSEAS*, VIII.1: 1–14 and VIII.2: 143–61.

Mackay, E., 1938, *Further Excavations at Mohenjodaro*, in two volumes, Delhi.

________, 1948, *Early Indus Civilization*, London.

Mahalingam, T.V., 1967, *South Indian Polity*, Madras.

Maity, S.K., 1957, *Economic Life of Northern India in the Gupta Period (c.* AD *300–550)*, Calcutta.

Majjhimanikāya, 1838–99, ed., V. Treckner and Lord Chalmers, London.

Majumdar, A.K., 1956, *Chaulukyas of Gujarat*, Bombay.

________, 1978, *A Concise History of Ancient India*, II, Delhi.

Majumdar, R.C., 1927–38, *Ancient Indian Colonies in the Far East*, I, Lahore; II, Calcutta.

________, ed., 1941, *History of Bengal*, I, Dacca.

________, 1944, *Hindu Colonies in the Far East*, Calcutta.

________, ed., 1951–72, *History and Culture of the Indian People*, I: *The Vedic Age*, II: *The Age of Imperial Unity*, III: *The Classical Age*, IV: *The Age of Imperial Kanauj*, V: *The Struggle for Empire*.

________, 1960, *The Classical Accounts of India*, Calcutta.

________, 1969, *Corporate Life in Ancient India*, Calcutta.

________, and Dasgupta, K.K., 1978, *A Comprehensive History of India*, III, in two parts, Delhi.

Manusmṛti, ed. by Ganganath Jha, *BI*, 1932–9; trn., G. Buhler, *SBE*, XXV, 1886.

Margbandhu, C., 1965, 'Trade Contacts between Western India and the Graeco-Roman World', *JESHO*, VIII: 316–22.

Marshall, John ed., 1931, *Mohenjodaro and the Indus Civilization*, in three volumes, London.

Marshall, John ed., 1951, *Taxila, an Illustrated Account of Archaeological Excavations*, Cambridge.

Mauss, Marcell, 1967, *The Gift*, New York.

Mazumdar, B.P., 1960, *Socio-Economic History of Northern India (1030–1194)*, Calcutta.

________, 1966, ' Merchants and Landed Aristocracy in the Feudal Economy of Northern India (AD 8th to 12th centuries)', in D.C Sircar ed., *Land System and Feudalism in Ancient India*, Calcutta: 62–71.

________, 1978–79, 'Epigraphic Records on the Migrant Brāhmaṇas in North India (1030–1225), *IHR*, V: 64–86.

________, 1979–80, 'Industries and Internal Trade in Early Medieval North India', *JBRS*, XLV–XLVI: 230–55.

________, 1983, 'Decline of Guilds in Early Medieval India', in J. Chakrabarti and D.C. Bhattacharyya eds., *Aspects of Indian Art and Culture*, Calcutta.

McCrindle, J.W., 1921, *Ancient India as Described by Megasthenes and Arrian*, Calcutta.

McDonell, A.A. and Keith, A.B., 1910, *The Vedic Index of Names and Subjects*, in two volumes, London.

McPherson, K., 1995, *The Indian Ocean, A History of the People and the Sea*, Delhi.

Mehta, R.N. and Thakkar, A.M., 1978, *Baroda M.S. University Copper Plates of Toramāna*, Baroda.

Mill, James, 1817, *History of British India*, London.

Mills, J.V.G., 1970, *The Overall Survey of the Ocean's Shores*, translation of Ma Huan's *Ying-Yai She-lan,* Cambridge.

Mookerji, R.K., 1957, *Indian Shipping, a History of the Sea-borne Trade and Maritime Activity of the Indians from the Earliest Times*, second edition, Bombay.

Morgan, L.H., 1964, *Ancient Society*, ed. by L.A. White, Cambridge.

Morrison, B.M., 1970, *Political Centres and Cultural Regions in Early Bengal*, Tucson.

Motichandra, 1977, *Trade and Trade Routes in Ancient India*, Delhi, 1977.

Mukherjee, B.N., 1969, *An Agrippan Source— Studies in Indo-Parthian History*, Calcutta.

________, 1970, *The Economic Factors in Kushāṇa History*, Calcutta.

________, 1980–81, 'Revenue, Trade and Society in the Kushāṇa Empire', *IHR*, VII: 24–53.

________, 1981, *Mathura and Its Society*, Calcutta.

________, 1982, 'Commerce and Money in the Central and Western Sectors of Eastern India (750–1200)', *IMB*, XVII: 65–83.

________, 1983, *Studies in the Aramaic Edicts of Aśoka*, Calcutta.

________, 1988, *Rise and Fall of the Kushāṇa Empire*, Calcutta.

________, 1990, 'Kharoshṭī and Kharoshṭī-Brāhmī Documents from West Bengal, India', *IMB*, XXV.

Mukherjee, B.N., 1992, *Media of Exchange in Early Medieval North India*, Delhi.

________, 1996, 'Coastal and Overseas Trade in Pre-Gupta Vaṅga and Kaliṅga', in Shyamalkanti Chakrabarti ed., *Vinayatoshini, Benoytosh Centenary Volume*, Calcutta: 181–92. *

________, 1996b, 'Coinage of Dvārāvatī in South-East Asia and the Kharoshṭī-Brāhmī Script', in Debala Mitra ed., *Explorations in the Art and Archaeology of South Asia, Essays Dedicated to N.G. Majumdar*, Calcutta: 527–34.

________, 1997, *The Techniques of Minting Coins in Ancient and Medieval India*, Delhi.

Mukherjee, B.N., 1998, 'The Great Kushāṇa Testament', *IMB*, XXX: 1–105.

Nagaswami, R., 1991, 'Alaganakulam: An Indo-Roman Trading Station', in C. Margabandhu et al, eds., *Indian Archaeological Heritage*, Delhi: 247–54.

________, 1995, *Roman Karur*, Madras.

Nandi, R.N., 1984, 'Growth of Rural Economy in Early Feudal India', Presidential Address, section I, *PIHC* (Annamalainagar Session): 25–91.

Nath, Vijay, 1987, *Dāna, Gift System in Ancient India, a Socio-Economic Perspective*, Delhi, 1987.

Nigam, S.S., 1975, *Economic Organisation in Ancient India*, Delhi.

Nilakanta Sastri, K.A., 1939a, *Foreign Notices of South India from Megasthenes to Ma Huan*, Madras.

________, 1939b, 'Foreign Trade under the Kākatīyas', *Journal of Oriental Research*, VIII: 316–20.

________, 1949, *South Indian Influences in the Far East*, Bombay.

________, ed. 1952, *The Age of the Nandas and Mauryas*, Varanasi.

________, 1955, *The Coḷas*, second edition, Madras.

________, ed. 1957, *A Comprehensive History of India*, II, Calcutta.

________, 1978, *South India and South East Asia*, Mysore.

Niyogi, P., 1962, *Contributions to the Economic History of Northern India*, Calcutta.

Niyogi, R., 1959, *The History of the Gāhaḍhavala Dynasty*, Calcutta.

Oppenheim, A.L., 1954, 'Seafaring Merchants of Ur', *JAOS*, LXXIV: 6–17.

Palmer, J.A.B., 1946, 'The Identification of Ptolemy's Dounga', *JRAS*: 165–73.

Pandeya, Deenabandhu, 1966, 'Cowrie as a Monetary Token in Ancient India', *JNSI*, XXVIII: 127ff.

Parasher, A., 1992, 'Nature of Society and Civilization in Early Deccan', *IESHR*, XXIX: 437–78.

________, 1996, 'Trade and the Nature of Historical Change in the Mid-Godavari Valley 200 BC–200 AD', in D.N. Jha ed., *Society and Ideology*, Delhi: 47–61.

Parpola, S., Parpola, A. and Brunswig, R., 1977, 'The Meluhha Village: Evidence of Acculturation of Harappan Traders in the Late Third Millennium Mesopotamia', *JESHO*, XX: 129–65.

Pelliot, P., 1975, 'Satyānṛta in Suvarṇadvīpa', in J.A. Savlov and C.C. Lamberg-Karlovsky eds., *Ancient Civilization and Trade*, Albuquerque: 227–83.

Pirenne, Henri, 1978, *Economic and Social History of Medieval Europe*, trn. by I.E. Clegg, London (rpt.).

Pliny, *Naturalis Historia*, trn. into English by H. Rackham, London, Cambridge, Mass., 1942.

Polanyi, K., 1957a, *The Great Transformation*, Boston.

Polanyi, K., Arnesberg, C.A. and Pearson, H.W. eds., 1957, *Trade and Markets in the Early Empires*, Chicago.

_______, 1961, 'The Port of Trade as an Ecological and Evolutionary Type', *Proceedings of the Annual Meeting of the American Ethnological Society*.

Pocock, D.S. and Williams, D.F., 1986, *Amphorae and the Roman Economy*, New York.

Possehl, G.L., 1976, 'Lothal: A Gateway Settlement of the Indus Civilization', in K.A.R. Kennedy and G.L. Possehl eds., *Ecological Backgrounds of South Asian Prehistory*, Ithaca: 118–31.

_______, ed., 1979, *Ancient Cities of the Indus*, Delhi.

_______, ed., 1982, *Harappan Civilization, A Recent Perspective*, Delhi; second edition, 1993.

Potts, T.F., 1993, 'Patterns of Trade in the Third Millennium Mesopotamia and Iran', *World Archaeology*, XXIV: 379–402.

Ptolemy, Claudius, *Geographike Huphegesis*, trn. into English by E.L. Stevenson, 1932, New York.

Raman, K.V., 1992, 'Further Evidence of Roman Trade from Coastal Sites in Tamil Nadu', in Vimala Begley and Richard Daniel de Puma eds., *Rome and India: The Ancient Sea Trade*, Delhi (Indian edition): 125–34.

Rao, S.R., 1963, 'A Persian Gulf Seal from Lothal', *Antiquity*, XXXVII: 96–9.

_______, 1965, 'Shipping and Maritime Trade of the Indus People', *Expedition*, VII: 30–37.

_______, 1970, 'Shipping in Ancient India', in Lokesh Chandra et al, eds., *India's Contributions to World Thought and Culture (Swami Vivekananda Commemoration Volume)*, Madras: 83–107.

_______, 1973, *Lothal and the Indus Civilization*, Bombay.

_______, 1979, *Lothal, a Harappan Port Town*, Delhi.

_______, ed. 1988, *Marine Archaeology of the Indian Ocean Countries*, Goa.

_______, 1991, *The Dawn and Devolution of the Indus Civilization*, Delhi.

Raschke, M.G., 1978, 'New Studies in Roman Commerce with the East',

Aufsteig und Niedergang in der Romischer Welt, IX, Berlin: 604–1361.

Ratnagar, Shereen, 1981, *Encounters: The Westerly Trade of the Harappans*, Delhi.

________, 1991, *Enquiries into the Political Organization of the Harappan Society*, Delhi.

________, 1994, 'Harappan Trade in Its World Context', *ME*, XIX:117–27.*

Rawlinson, H.G., 1916, *Intercourse between India and the Western World*, Cambridge.

Ray, Haraprasad, 1987, 'China and the Western Ocean in the Fifteenth Century', in Satish Chandra ed., 1987: 109–24.

Ray, Haraprasad, 1993, *Trade and Diplomacy in India-China Relations*, Delhi.

Ray, Himanshu Prabha, 1986, *Monastery and Guild: Commerce under the Sātvāhanas*, Delhi.

________, 1987a, 'The Yavana Presence in Ancient India', *JESHO*, XXX: 311–25.

________, 1987b, 'Bharhut and Sanchi—Nodal Points in a Commercial Interchange', in B.M. Pande and B.D. Chattopadhyaya eds., *Archaeology and History*, II, Delhi: 621–30.

________, 1987–88, 'Early Trade in the Bay of Bengal', *IHR*, XVI: 79–89.

________, 1989a, 'Early Maritime Contacts between South and South-East Asia', *JSEAS*, XX: 42–54.

________, 1989b, 'Early Historical Trade, an Overview', *IESHR*, XXVI: 437–58.

________, 1990, 'Seafaring in the Bay of Bengal in the Early Centuries AD', *SH*, VII: 1–14.

________, 1995, 'Trade and Contacts', in Romila Thapar ed., *Recent Perspectives of Early Indian History*, Delhi: 142–75.

________, 1996a, *Winds of Change, Buddhism and Early Maritime Links of South Asia*, Delhi.

________, 1996b, 'Maritime Archaeology: the Ethnographic Evidence', *ME*, XXI: 74–85.

Ray, Himanshu Prabha and Salles, J.F. eds., *Tradition and Archaeology, Early Maritime Contacts in the Indian Ocean*, Delhi.

Ray, Niharranjan, 1967, 'The Medieval Factor in Indian History', General President's Address, *PIHC*, Patiala session: 1–30.

________, 1976, 'Technology and Social Change: A Note Posing a Theoretical Question', *Puratattva*, VIII: 132–8.

________, 1980, *Bangalir Itihas* (in Bengali), in two volumes, second edition, Calcutta.

Raychaudhuri, H.C., 1995, *Political History of Ancient India*, eighth edition, with a Commentary by B.N. Mukherjee, Delhi.

Raychaudhuri, Tapan and Habib, Irfan, 1982, *The Cambridge History of India, I (1200–1757)*, Cambridge.

Renfrew, Colin, 1975, 'Trade as Action at Distance', in J.A. Sablov and C.C. Lamberg-Karlovsky eds., *Ancient Civilization and Trade*, Albuquerque: 3–59.

Rhys Davids, C.F., 1901, 'Notes on Early Economic Conditions in North India', *JRAS*: 859–88.

________, 1921, 'Economic Conditions in Early Buddhist Literature', in E.J. Rapson ed., *Cambridge History of India*, I: 176–95 (rpt. 1977).

Rhys Davids, T.W., 1903, *Buddhist India*, London, rpt. Varanasi,1970.

Romanis, Federico de and Tchernia, A. eds., 1997, *Crossings, Early Mediterranean Contacts with India*, Delhi.

Romanis, Federico de, 1997, 'Rome and the Notia of India: Relations between Rome and Southern India from 30 BC to the Flavian Period', in Romanis, Federico de and Tchernia, A. eds. *Crossings, Early Mediterranean Contacts with India*, Delhi: 80–160.

Rostovzeff, M., 1926, *Social and Economic History of the Roman Empire*, Oxford.

Roy, Kumkum, 1994, *The Emergence of Monarchy in North India from the 8th to the 4th Centuries* BC, Delhi.

Roy, T.N., 1983, *The Ganges Civilization*, Delhi.

Ruben, Walter, 1978, 'The Development of the Town in Ancient India', in Debiprasad Chattopadhyaya ed., *History and Society (Niharranjan Ray Festschrift)*, Calcutta.

Sahlins, M., 1965, 'On the Sociology of Primitive Exchange', in M. Bantam ed., *The Relevance of Models for Anthropology*, London.

Sahu, Bhairabi Prasad, 1997, 'Conception of the Kali Age in Early India: A Regional Perspective', *Trends in Social Science Research*, IV: 27–36.

Salisbury, Richard F., 'Trade and Markets', in David L. Sills ed., *International Encyclopaedia of the Social Sciences*, XVI:118–22.

Salles, J.F., 1987, 'The Arabian Persian Gulf under the Seleucids', in A. Kuhrt and S. Sherwin White eds., *Hellenism in the East*: 75–184.

________, 1996, 'Hellenistic Seafaring in the Indian Ocean, a Perspective from Arabia', in Himanshu Prabha Ray and J.F. Salles ed., *Tradition and Archaeology, Early Maritime Contacts in the Indian Ocean*, Delhi: 293–310.

Saloman, R., 1991, 'Epigraphic Remains of Indian Traders in Egypt', *JAOS*, 731–36.

Samhaber, E., 1963, *Merchants Make History*, London.

Sankalia, H.D., 1962a, 'From Food Collection to Urbanisation in India', in T.N. Madan and G. Sarang eds., *Indian Anthropology, Essays in Memory of D.N. Majumdar*, New York: 66–104.

________, 1962b, 'Courses towards Urban Life in India', in R.J. Braidwood and G.R. Wiley eds., *Courses towards Urban Life*, Chicago: 60–82.

________, 1974, *The Pre and Protohistory of India and Pakistan*, second edition, Poona.

Sarao, K.T.S., 1990, *Urban Centres and Urbanisation as Reflected in the Pali Vinaya and Sutta Pitakas*, Delhi.

Sarianidhi, V., 1979, 'New Finds in Bactria and Indo-Iranian Connections', in M. Taddei ed., *SAA*, 1977: 643–59.

Sarkar, H., 1987, 'Emergence of Urban Centres in Early Historic Andhradesa', in B.M. Pande and B.D. Chattopadhyaya eds., *Archaeology and History*, II, Delhi: 631–42.

Schoff, W.W, 1974, trn., *The Periplus of the Erythraean Sea*, Delhi (rpt.).

Sen, B.C., 1969, *Economics in Kauṭilya*, Calcutta.

Sen, B.C., 1972, *Studies in the Buddhist Jātakas*, Calcutta.

Senaviratne, S. 1981, 'Kalinga and Andhra: The Process of Secondary State Formation in Early India', in H.J.M. Claessen and P. Skalnik eds., *The Study of the State*, The Hague: 317–38.

Shaffer, J.G., 1982, 'Harappan Commerce: an Alternative Perspective', in S. Pastener and L. Flam eds., *Anthropology and Recent Socio-Cultural and Archaeological Perspectives*, Cornell: 116–210.

Shahani, Lajwanti, 1997, 'Ethnoarchaeology of Harappan Sea Trade—A Preliminary Study', *ME*, XXII: 9–18.

Shaked, Shaul, 1964, *A Tentative Bibliography of the Geniza Documents*, Paris and The Hague.

Sharma, R.S., 1958, 'The Origins of Feudalism in India', *JESHO*, I: 297–328.

________, 1975, 'Decay of Towns in the Gangetic Valley in the Gupta and Post-Gupta Period', *JIH*, Golden Jubilee Volume.

________, 1980, *Indian Feudalism*, Delhi, second edition.

________, 1983a, *Material Culture and Social Formations in Ancient India*, Delhi.

________, 1983b, *Perspectives on the Social and Economic History of Early India*, Delhi. +

________, 1987, *Urban Decay in India* AD *300–1000*, Delhi.

________, 1989–90, 'The Segmentary State and Indian Experience', *IHR*, XVI: 90–108.

________, 1990, *Origin of the State in India*, Bombay.

Sharma, R.S. and Jha, D.N., 1974a, 'Economic History of India up to AD 1200: Trends and Prospects', *JESHO*, XVII: 41–80.

Sharma, R.S. and Jha, Vivekananda eds., 1974b, *Indian Society: Historical Probings*, Delhi.

Sharma, R.S. and Shrimali, K.M. eds., 1994, *A Comprehensive History of India*, IV, Delhi.

Shrimali, K.M. 1987, *Agrarian Structure in Central India and the Northern Deccan (A Study in the Vākāṭaka Inscriptions)*, Delhi.

________, 1996, 'How Monetized Was the Silahara Economy?', in D.N. Jha ed., *Society and Ideology, Essays in Honour of Professor R.S. Sharma*, Delhi: 95–124.

Sidebotham, Steven G., 1992, 'Ports of the Red Sea and the Arabia-India Trade', in Vimala Begley and Richard Daniel de Puma eds., *Rome and India: The Ancient Sea Trade*, Delhi (Indian edition): 12–38.
Simkin, C.G.F., 1966, *Traditional Trade of Asia*, London.
Sims-Williams, Nicholas and Cribb, Joe, 1995–6, 'A New Bactrian Inscription of Kanishka the Great', *Silk Road Art and Archaeology*, 4: 75–142.
Singh, R.L., 1977, *India: A Regional Geography*, Varanasi.
Sircar, D.C., 1965a, *Select Inscriptions Bearing on Indian History and Civilization*, I, Calcutta.
Sircar, D.C., 1965b, *Indian Epigraphy*, Delhi.
________, 1966, *Indian Epigraphical Glossary*, Delhi.
________, 1969, *Landlordism and Tenancy in Ancient and Medieval India as Revealed by Epigraphical Records*, Lucknow.
________, 1972 ed., *Early Indian Trade and Industries*, Calcutta.
________, 1978–79, 'Synoptical Texts of Minor Rock Edicts I and II of Aśoka', *JAIH*, XII: 1–10.
________, 1979a, 'Aspects of Early Indian Economic Life', *IMB*, XIV: 7–70.
________, 1979b, *Asokan Studies*, Calcutta.
________, 1982, *The Emperor and His Subordinate Rulers*, Santiniketan.
Smith, V.A., 1903, *Early History of India*, Oxford.
Spate, O.H.K. and Learmonth, A.T.A., 1967, *India and Pakistan, A General and Regional Geography*, London.
Spencer, George W., 1969, 'Religious Networks and Royal Influence in Eleventh Century South India', *JESHO*, XII: 42–56.
________, 1977, 'The Politics of Plunder: The Coḷas in Eleventh Century Ceylon', *Journal of Asian Studies*, XXVI: 405–20.
________, 1983, *The Politics of Expansion—The Coḷa Conquests of Sri Lanka and Srivijaya*, Madras.
Srinivas, M.N. and Shah, A.M., 1960, 'The Myth of the Self-Sufficiency of Indian Village', *Economic Weekly*, XII, 1375–8.
Srivastava, B., 1968, *Trade and Commerce in Ancient India*, Varanasi.
Stargardt, Janice, 1971, 'Burma's Economic and Diplomatic Relations with India and China from Early Medieval Sources', *JESHO*, XIV: 38–62.
________, 1984, 'The Isthmus of the Malay Peninsula in Long Distance Navigation—New Archaeological Findings', in *Trade and Shipping in the Southern Seas*, SPAFA, Bangkok.
________, 1990, *The Ancient Pyu of Burma*, I, Cambridge.
Stech, T. and Piggott, V., 1986, 'The Metals Trade in South West Asia in the Third Millennium', *Iraq*, XLVIII: 39–64.
Stein, Burton, 1980, *Peasant State and Society in Medieval South India*, Delhi.
________, 1985, 'Politics, Peasants and the Deconstruction of Feudalism in Medieval India', in T.J. Byres and Harbans Mukhia eds., *Feudalism and Non-European Societies (special number of the Journal of Peasant Studies)*, London: 54–87.

Stillman, Norman A., 1973, 'The Eleventh Century Merchant House of Ibn Awkal (A Geniza Study)', *JESHO*, XVI: 15–88.

Strabo, *Geographicon*, ed. and trn., by H.L. Jones, London and Cambridge, Mass., 1942 (rpt.).

Subbarayalu, Y., 1973, *Political Geography of the Coḷa Country*, Madras,

_______, 1982, 'The Coḷa State', *SH*, IV: 265–306.

Subrahmanyam, Sanjay, ed., 1990, *Merchants, Markets and the State in Early Modern India*, Delhi.

Subrahmanyam, Sanjay, ed., 1994, *Money and the Market in India 1100–1700*, Delhi.

Śūdraka, *Mṛcchakaṭika*, ed., M.R. Kale, Delhi, 1962.

Tarafdar, M.R., 1978, 'Trade and Society in Early Medieval Bengal', *IHR*, IV: 274–86.

Tarn, W.W, 1951, *The Greeks in Bactria and India*, Cambridge.

Tchernia, A., 1995, 'Not by Archaeology Alone', in M.F. Boussac and J.F. Salles, eds., *Athens, Aden, Arikamedu, Essays on Interrelation between India, Arabia and the Eastern Mediterranean*, Delhi.

Thakur, Upendra, 1973, 'Early Indian Mints', *JESHO*, XVI: 265–97.

Thakur, V.K., 1987, 'Trade and Towns in Early Medieval Bengal (*c.* AD 600–1200)', *JESHO*, XXX: 196–220.

_______, 1989, *Historiography of Indian Feudalism: Towards a Model of Early Medieval Indian Economy (c. AD 600–1000)*, Patna.

Thapar, B.K., 1975, 'Kalibangan: A Harappan Metropolis beyond the Indus Valley', *Expedition*, XVII: 19–32.

_______, 1985, *Recent Archaeological Discoveries in India*, Tokyo, UNESCO.

Thapar, B.K. and M. Rafiq Mughal, 'The Indus Valley', in *History of Humanity*, vol. I, Paris, UNESCO, 1992, pp. 245–65.

Thapar, Romila, 1961, *Aśoka and the Decline of the Mauryas*, London.

_______, 1975, 'A Possible Identification of Meluhha, Dilmun and Makan', *JESHO*, XVIII: 1–42.

_______, 1978, *Ancient Indian Social History*, Delhi. +

_______, 1983, 'The Dravidian Hypothesis for the Identification of Meluhha, Dilmun and Makan', *JESHO*, XXVI: 178–92.

_______, 1984, *From Lineage to State*, Delhi.

_______, 1987a, *The Mauryas Revisited*, Calcutta.

_______, 1987b, 'Epigraphic Evidence and Some Indo-Hellenistic Contacts during the Mauryan Period', in S.K. Maity and Upendra Thakur eds., *Indological Studies, Professor D.C. Sircar Commemoration Volume*, Delhi: 15–19.

_______, 1992, 'Black Gold: South Asia and the Roman Maritime Trade', *SA*, XV: 1–28.

_______, 1993, *Interpreting Early India*, Delhi.

Thapar, Romila, 1995a, 'The First Millennium BC in Northern India', in Thapar, R., ed., *Recent Perspectives of Early Indian History*, Bombay: 80–141.

________, 1997a, 'Early Mediterranean Contacts with India: An Overview', in Federico de Romanis and A. Tchernia eds., *Crossings, Early Mediterranean Contacts with India*, Delhi: 12–40.

________, 1997b, 'The Formation of the States and the Mauryan Empire', in *History of Humanity*, III, Paris, UNESCO: 363–67.

Thapar Romila, ed.1995b, *Recent Perspectives of Early Indian History*, Bombay.

Thaplyal, K.K., 1968, 'Nigama and Śreṇī Seals: An Appraisal', *JNSI*, XXX: 133–51.

Tibbetts, G.R., 1971, *Arab Navigation in the Indian Ocean before the Portuguese*, London.

Tossi, M., 1986, 'Early Maritime Cultures of the Arabian Gulf and Trade—A Preliminary Study', *ME*, XXII: 9–18.

________, 1993, 'The Harappan Civilization beyond the Indian Subcontinent', *HC*, second edition: 365–78. *

Touissant, A., 1966, *History of the Indian Ocean*, London.

Udovitch, L., 1970, 'Commercial Techniques in Early Medieval Islamic Trade', in D.S. Richards ed., *Islam and the Trade of Asia*, London: 37–62.

van Leur, J.E., 1955, *Indonesian Trade and Society*, The Hague.

Varadarajan, Lotika, 1987, 'Commodity Structure and Indian Participation in the Trade of the Southern Sea, *circa* Ninth to Thirteenth Centuries', in Satish Chandra ed., *Indian Ocean*, Delhi: 90–108.

Vats, M.S., 1940, *Excavations at Harappa*, Delhi.

Verlinden, Charles, 1987, 'The Indian Ocean: Ancient Period and the Middle Ages,' in Satish Chandra ed., 1987, Delhi: 27–53.

Wagle, N., 1966, *Society at the Time of the Buddha*, Bombay.

Walburg, R., 1991, 'Late Roman Copper Coins from Southern India', in A.K. Jha ed., *Coinage, Trade and Economy*, Nashik: 164–7.

Wallerstein, Immanuel, 1974, *The Modern World System*, New York.

Walker, M.J. and Santoso, S., 1984, 'Romano-Indian Rouletted Pottery in Indonesia', in P. van de Velde ed., *Prehistoric Indonesia, A Reader*, Dordrecht: 376–83.

Warmington, E.H., 1974, *The Commerce between the Roman Empire and India*, London, second edition.

Watson, B., 1961, *Records of the Grand Historians of China*, New York.

Webb, M.C., 1975, 'The Flag Follows Trade', in J.A. Sablov and C.C. Lamberg-Karlovsky eds., *Ancient Civilization and Trade*, Albuquerque: 155–209.

Weisgerber, G., 1981, 'Makan and Meluhha—Third Millennium BC Copper

Production in Oman and the Evidence of Contacts with the Indus Valley', in Bridget Allchin ed., *SAA*, 1979, Cambridge: 196–201.

Weisgerber, G., 1986, 'Dilmun, A Trading Entrepot', in H. al Khalifa and M. Rice eds., *Bahrain Through the Ages*, London: 135–42.

Wheeler, R.E.M. and Deva, Krishna, 1946, 'Arikamedu: An Indo-Roman Trading Station on the East Coast of India', *Ancient India*, II: 17–124.

Wheeler, R.E.M., 1951, 'Roman Contact with India, Pakistan and Afghanistan', in W.F. Grimes ed., *Aspects of Archaeology in Britain and Beyond: Essays Presented to O.G.S. Crawford*, London: 345–81.

________, 1955, *Rome Beyond the Imperial Frontiers*, London.

________, 1968, The *Indus Civilization*, Cambridge, third edition.

________, 1976, *My Archaeological Mission to India and Pakistan*, London.

Whitehouse, David and Williamson, Andrew, 1973, 'Sasanian Maritime Trade', *Iran*, XI: 24–49.

Whitehouse, David, 1990, 'The Periplus Maris Erythrae', *Journal of Roman Archaeology*, III: 489–93.

________, 1992, 'Epilogue: Roman Trade in Perspective', in Vimala Begley and Richard Daniel de Puma eds., *Rome and India: The Ancient Sea Trade*, Delhi (Indian edition): 216–20.

Wink, Andre, 1990, *Al Hind,The Making of the Indo-Islamic World*, I, *Early Medieval India and the Expansion of Islam*, Delhi.

Yadava, B.N.S., 1973, *Society and Culture in Northern India during the Twelfth Century,* Allahabad.

________, 1976, 'Problem of Interaction between Socio-Economic Classes in the Early Medieval Complex', *IHR,* III, 43–58.

________, 1979, 'The Accounts of the Kali Age and the Social Transition from Antiquity to the Middle Ages', *IHR*, V: 31–64.

________, 1980, 'The Problem of the Emergence of Feudal Relations in Early India', Presidential Address, section I, *PIHC*, XLI (Bombay session): 19–78.

Zurcher, E., 1968, 'The Yüeh Chih and Kaniṣka in the Chinese Literature', in A.L. Basham ed., *Papers on the Date of Kaniṣka*, London.

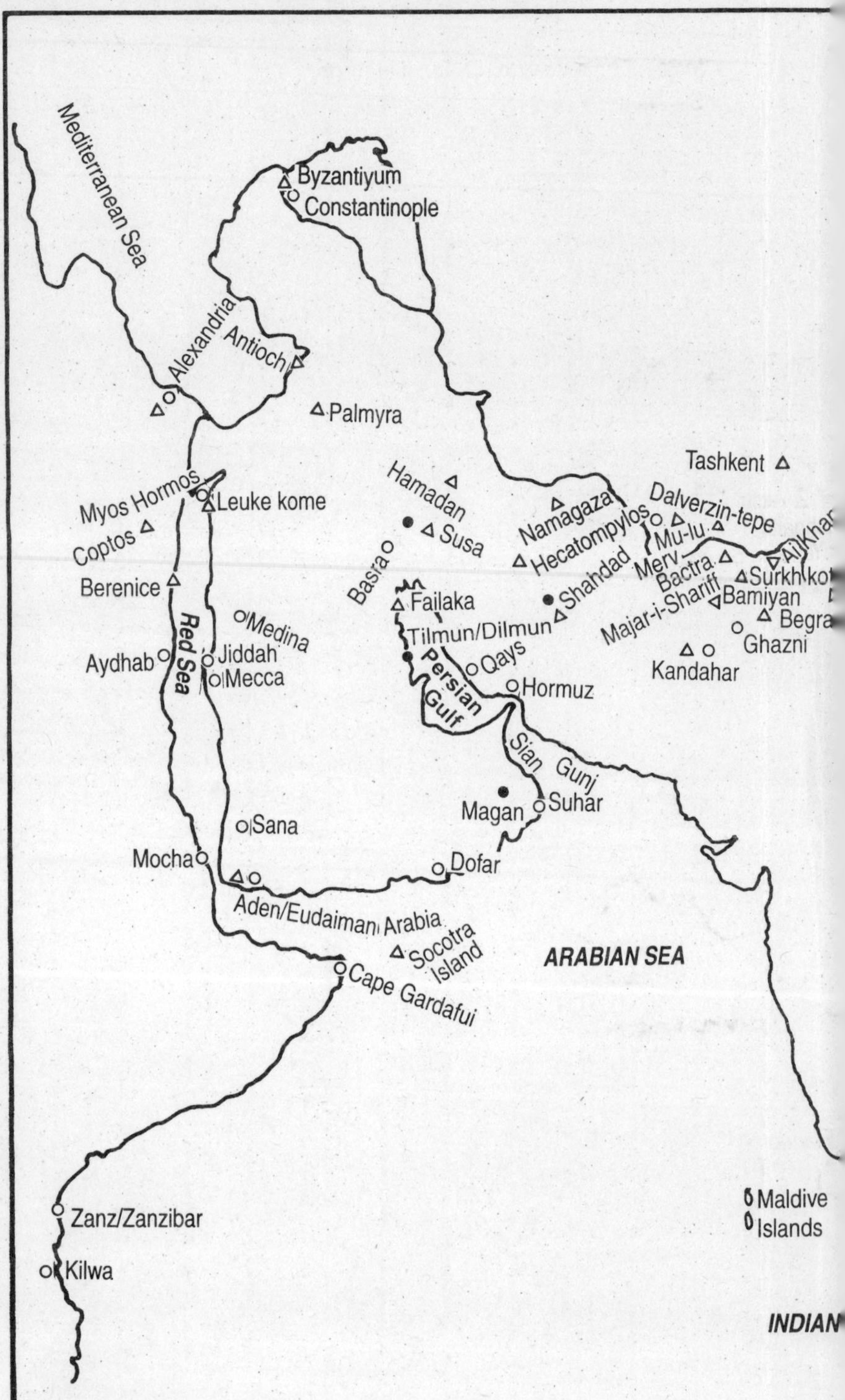
Mediterranean Sea
Byzantiyum
Constantinople
Alexandria
Antioch
Palmyra
Myos Hormos
Leuke kome
Coptos
Berenice
Red Sea
Medina
Aydhab
Jiddah
Mecca
Sana
Mocha
Aden/Eudaiman Arabia
Socotra Island
Cape Gardafui
Dofar
Hamadan
Susa
Basra
Failaka
Tilmun/Dilmun
Persian Gulf
Qays
Hormuz
Sian Gunj
Magan
Suhar
Namagaza
Hecatompylos
Shahdad
Merv
Mu-lu
Dalverzin-tepe
Bactra
Majar-i-Shariff
Surkh kot
Bamiyan
Begra
Ghazni
Kandahar
Tashkent
ARABIAN SEA
Zanz/Zanzibar
Kilwa
Maldive Islands
INDIAN